Matters of Principle

Matters of Principle

Legitimate Legal Argument and Constitutional Interpretation

Richard S. Markovits

NEW YORK UNIVERSITY PRESS

New York and London

NEW YORK UNIVERSITY PRESS
New York and London

Library of Congress Cataloging-in-Publication Data
Markovits, Richard S.
Matters of principle : legitimate legal argument and constitutional
interpretation / Richard S. Markovits.
p.   cm.
Includes index.
ISBN 0-8147-5513-5 (alk. paper)
1. Civil rights—United States—Moral and ethical aspects. 2. Law—
United States—Moral and ethical aspects. 3. United States—Social
policy. 4. Law—Moral and ethical aspects. 5. Social policy—Moral
and ethical aspects. I. Title.
KF4749.M37   1998
342.73'085—dc21   98-19602
                                CIP

New York University Press books are printed on acid-free paper,
and their binding materials are chosen for strength and durability.

Manufactured in the United States of America
10 9 8 7 6 5 4 3 2 1

To Inga,
For never doubting and always sharing.

Contents

Acknowledgments

My greatest debt is to Ronald Dworkin, who showed me why and how moral philosophy and jurisprudence matter. Paul Brest of Stanford University and Philip Bobbitt of the University of Texas taught me to focus on the nature of the legal arguments that courts did make or should have made in particular cases. In essence, all three taught me to take legal argument seriously.

Several colleagues gave me useful comments on Chapter 1: Jeff Powell of Duke University sent me a lengthy, constructive, and supportive critique; Tom Grey of Stanford University mixed support with objections from the perspective of Legal Pragmatism; David Friedman of Santa Clara University raised some useful questions about my treatment of libertarianism; Doug Laycock and Sandy Levinson of the University of Texas raised a variety of objections that the final text articulates and addresses; Scot Powe made numerous legal realist comments that encouraged me to be more concrete; Lawrence Friedman of Stanford University raised various historical and social-science objections to my central jurisprudential claims; and Brian Leiter and Michael Sean Quinn of the University of Texas and Daniel Markovits suggested a substantial number of minor improvements that cumulatively made a considerable difference.

My colleagues Willie Forbath, Scot Powe, and David Rabban checked the accuracy of my account of the "historians of ideology" in Chapter 2. Scot Powe and Sandy Levinson examined Chapters 3 and 4 for any acts of doctrinal malfeasance or non-feasance. John Robertson had several discussions with me about a number of the moral-rights issues that Chapter 4 addresses. The book has also been improved by numerous jurisprudential conversations with Phillip Bobbitt and Bill Powers of the University of Texas over the years. My colleague Alan Rau gave me useful comments on the Introduction and Chapter 1 and was a consistently helpful sounding board for virtually all the arguments in the book.

Thanks, too, to the members of the Law Faculty of the University of Bremen (Germany), Santa Clara University, and the University of Texas, who participated in colloquia on the ideas this book presents.

I am also indebted to the personal assistants who typed the various versions of the manuscript that I produced over the past decade: Irma Santana, then of the University of Texas Law School, and most importantly Pat Floyd of the University of Texas Law School, who labored mightily and with good humor to help me meet my final deadline.

One final word of acknowledgment: The approach of this book is not fashionable. Virtually none of the people who gave me the benefit of their ideas agrees with its central conclusions (though several told me I had made the best arguments they had heard for those conclusions). In addition to supplying useful concrete advice on Chapter 1, Michael Sean Quinn also made several important suggestions for the Introduction. He was able to do so not because he agrees with my conclusions but because he understood why those conclusions and the arguments that support them are important. I am especially grateful for the encouragement provided by his sophisticated grasp of my project.

Introduction

This book presents a coherent, comprehensive account of morally-legitimate legal argument in our culture. In essence, it develops an anthropological, secular version of natural-law jurisprudence. Its approach is anthropological and secular in that it substitutes empirical observation (that, admittedly, is philosophically informed) for purely-abstract theological or philosophical reasoning. The central jurisprudential conclusion of the book is that our society is morally committed to making "arguments of moral principle" the dominant form of legal argument and that such arguments will yield internally-correct answers to all legal-rights questions. I argue that the contrary abstract positions taken by virtually all contemporary legal philosophers, Constitutional-law experts, social critics, and judges reflect their failure to recognize that we engage in two kinds of moral discourse—discourse about moral rights and the moral obligations that are their corollaries, and discourse about what an individual or the State ought to do. (When capitalized, the word "State" signifies government.) Their failure to distinguish between these two types of prescriptive moral discourse has precluded them from seeing that their moral-relativist and subjectivist positions on the status of the norms used in moral-ought discourse (norms I call "personal ultimate values") is perfectly consistent with there being objectively-correct answers to both moral-rights and legal-rights questions in a given rights-based society.

My basic jurisprudential position consists of five central propositions. The first is that ours is a rights-based society. In other words, our society is morally defined by two facts: (1) its members engage in two types of prescriptive moral discourse—discourse about what a private actor or the State is *morally obligated* to do, and discourse about what a private actor or the State *ought* to do[1]—and (2) whenever the two conflict, moral-obligation conclusions and the moral norms they reflect trump moral-ought conclusions and the different moral norms they reflect. To illustrate the difference between moral-obligation and moral-ought discourse, imagine that the football player

Emmitt Smith is visiting a teammate in the hospital. A doctor recognizes him and asks him to visit a boy who is a patient in the same ward. The doctor explains that the boy is in the midst of a medical crisis, that he probably will fully recover if he gets through the night but that "we may lose him tonight," and that a visit from his hero Smith might make all the difference. In this situation, two questions can be asked about Smith's moral position: (1) Is he morally obligated to visit the boy? and (2) Ought he visit the boy? These questions are different. Different moral norms are relevant to answering each, and different answers may be given to each. The answer to the moral-obligation question will turn on such issues as whether Smith has promised the boy or anyone else to pay the requested visit, whether he has a status-relationship with the boy or someone else that places him under an obligation to pay the visit, or whether Smith was a culpable cause of the boy's predicament—considerations whose relevance reflects their connection to the liberal moral norm I specify below. The answer to the moral-ought question will not necessarily be the same as the answer to the moral-obligation question. Even if Smith has no moral obligation to the boy, an evaluator could decide that on the relevant facts Smith ought to visit the boy because that conclusion is implied by the personal ultimate value (e.g., utilitarian or egalitarian) to which the evaluator subscribes. And even if Smith does have an obligation to pay the visit, an evaluator could conclude that Smith ought not fulfill his obligation if the personal ultimate value to which the evaluator subscribes favors this conclusion, taking into account the tendency of a decision by Smith not to visit the boy to undermine the institution of moral obligations. However, in a rights-based culture an individual's failure to fulfill a moral obligation is considered to be highly morally objectionable even if his decision reflects his personal moral convictions—that is, even if it was not made frivolously, carelessly, or to further the actor's narrowly-defined self-interest.

The second proposition is that our moral-rights-related practices are sufficiently rich and dense to enable us to identify both the abstract moral principle on which we are committed to basing our moral-rights practices and its more concrete corollaries with sufficient specificity to yield "internally-right" answers to all or virtually all moral-rights questions. By "internally right," I mean that the answers in question are required by the principles our society is morally committed to using in the relevant context.

The third proposition central to my jurisprudential position is that the moral norm on which our society is committed to basing its moral-obligation discourse (a norm I call the society's "basic moral principle") is the abstract liberal "moral principle" that each creature that has the neurological prerequisites to become and remain an individual of moral integrity is entitled to appropriate, equal respect and appropriate, equal concern for its actualizing its potential to become and remain an individual of moral integrity.[2] It should be emphasized that, although I have characterized this basic moral principle as "liberal," the liberalism it embodies is not utilitarian (as all early liberal philosophies were).

The fourth proposition is that, unlike the personal ultimate values that are relevant to moral-ought discourse, the abstract liberal moral principle and its more concrete corollaries are not only automatically part of the law but provide the basis of the type of legitimate legal argument—arguments of moral principle[3]—that we are committed to making dominant[4] in our legal culture. This proposition is a corollary of the fact that in a rights-based society a legal argument cannot be morally legitimate unless its use is consistent with, if not required by, the State's duty to secure the rights of those for whom it is morally responsible.

The fifth proposition is that arguments of moral principle and the other types of legal argument they reveal to be morally legitimate can yield internally-right answers to all legal-rights questions. I hasten to add, however, that this proposition is consistent with these answers' being contestable or controversial: even assiduous experts who are trying to follow the model of legitimate legal argument I delineate may critically disagree about the formal specification of the concrete corollaries of the basic moral principle that are relevant to a particular case, the "facts of the case," and/or the application of the relevant principles to the relevant facts.

These five propositions describe a jurisprudential position that is simultaneously old-fashioned and revolutionary. For example, they embody the assumption that one can objectively determine the moral norms on which a society such as ours is committed to basing its moral-rights and legal-rights analysis. Moreover, and relatedly, they assert that in our culture there are internally-right answers to all or virtually all moral-rights questions and to all legal-rights questions. And again relatedly, they imply that legal practice is not morally (as opposed to sociologically) self-legitimating.

This book elaborates on and defends this jurisprudential position[5] and compares it with the positions taken by others.[6] It also examines this position's implications for two sets of concrete Constitutional-rights issues and criticizes some of the contrary positions others have taken on these concrete issues.

The first set of concrete Constitutional-rights issues this book explores[7] relates to the obligation of a liberal State to treat all moral-rights holders for which it is morally responsible (hereinafter, all relevant moral-rights holders) with appropriate, equal respect. The specific rights that this obligation implicates are

- the right to have appropriate, equal influence on government decisionmaking;
- the right not to suffer a State-imposed loss for no good reason at all or for a bad reason;
- the right to have government decisions that affect one's welfare made through appropriately-accurate procedures that also show respect by allowing those whose welfare they affect to participate in the relevant decisionmaking process in appropriately-meaningful ways;
- the right not to be the target of State "discrimination" in the pejorative sense of that word; and
- the right to have the State combat the development of prejudices and the commission of prejudiced acts by private parties who do not have a right to indulge their prejudices in the relevant context.

The second set of concrete Constitutional-rights issues on which this book focuses relates to the obligation of a liberal State to show appropriate, equal concern for all its relevant subjects' actualizing their potential to become and remain individuals of moral integrity.[8] This second duty of a liberal State (which is a corollary of the duty of respect) itself has two branches.

One branch requires it to take appropriate steps to enable all its relevant subjects to make meaningful choices about whether to fulfill their obligations, which personal ultimate values to support, and how—given their obligations, rights, values, tastes, talents, and opportunities—to lead their lives. The analysis of this duty will lead us to consider the possible obligation of a liberal State

- to provide its relevant subjects with appropriate educations and an appropriate absolute or relative minimum real income,
- to avoid hindering their participation in the kinds of intimate relationships that can lead to self-discovery,
- to protect their privacy, and

- to prohibit acts or activities that seem likely to preclude some individuals from developing the self-respect that is often a prerequisite to becoming and remaining an individual of moral integrity or from being able to make autonomous choices in the future.

The other branch of the "appropriate, equal concern" duty of a liberal State requires it to allow all relevant moral-rights holders to commit those acts and engage in those activities and relationships that contribute substantially to their self-realization by enabling them to discover what they value and/or to conform their lives to their value-choices. The book will investigate the implications of this second branch of the "appropriate, equal concern" duty for the right of individuals to participate in heterosexual and homosexual relationships, for the right of pregnant women to secure abortions, for the right of individuals to parent their children at all and in various ways, and for the right of individuals to choose to die.

Contemporary legal philosophers, Constitutional-law experts, social critics, and judges have not done a satisfactory job of analyzing either the abstract jurisprudential issues or the concrete Constitutional-rights issues this book addresses. The overwhelming majority believe either that there is no internally-right answer to any moral-rights question or that there is no internally-right answer to any moral-rights question on whose answer there is no overwhelming social consensus. To a considerable extent, these no-right-answer beliefs reflect their subscribers' failure to recognize the difference between moral-rights discourse and moral-ought discourse or the related possibility that there may be objectively-right answers to moral-rights questions in a given culture even if the "ultimate correctness" of those answers cannot be established from an objective external perspective. Convinced that the truth-value of personal ultimate values cannot be established objectively, these moral relativists and moral subjectivists have thrown out the moral-rights baby with the personal-ultimate-value bath water.

The Constitutional-law experts and judges who have accepted this no-right-answer conclusion have split on its jurisprudential implications. By far the larger group of the relevant Constitutional-law experts and a few federal judges have concluded that it implies that there are no internally-right answers either to any moral-rights-related legal-rights questions or to any moral-rights-related legal-rights questions for which there is no overwhelming consensus about what the State ought to do. On one level, this reaction reflects their belief that, since there cannot be any objectively-right answer to such questions, appropriately-right answers can be provided only when there is near-universal agreement on what the State ought to do. On another level, this reaction reflects these experts' and judges' (usually-implicit) conclusion that the various modes of legal argument used in our culture are imbued with moral content and their related realization that if the values one uses in the course of employing textual, historical, structural, precedential and practice, or what Constitutional lawyers call "prudential argument"[9] have not been selected objectively, not only arguments of moral principle but also these other modes of argument cannot yield internal-to-law, objectively-correct conclusions.

A minority of legal philosophers and Constitutional-law experts and a substantial number of federal Supreme Court and Court of Appeals judges have reacted strikingly differently to their conclusion that moral-rights questions cannot be answered objectively.[10] This second group believes that, although there are no internally-right answers to moral-rights questions, this fact does not preclude legitimate legal argument from generating internally-right answers to moral-rights-related legal-rights questions because the modes of legal argument that are legitimate (indeed, to their mind, that must be used if we are to remain true to our democratic commitments) can be employed in a technically-sophisticated way that does not require any reference to moral principles or values. According to these academics and judges, if we are to be true to our democratic commitments, Constitutional text such as the "equal protection" clause must be given a non-moral reading, the historical arguments that bear on the meaning of Constitutional text must be developed without regard to our moral practices, structural arguments must be executed without considering the moral point of our basic governmental structures, doctrine and precedent must be interpreted and applied without taking account of any moral considerations, and prudential arguments must be given weight even when their use might be thought to be inconsistent with the moral obligations of our State.

Not surprisingly, the jurisprudential conclusions of both camps have had a critical impact on their legal consciousness, writing, judicial performance, and teaching. Almost without exception, the scholarship of the law professors and legal philosophers who belong to the first group consists of personal-ultimate-value-oriented policy-analysis rather than legal-rights analysis. Some scholars who execute such non-rights-oriented policy-analyses admit what they are doing. Others try to conceal it. They claim to be doing legal-rights or Constitutional-rights scholarship, make what appear to be traditional legal arguments for their conclusions, and choose not to mention the fact that their selection of which general modes of traditional legal argument and/or which variants of these modes to employ is based on their personal ultimate values. Still others try to conceal the personal-ultimate-value orientation of their "Constitutional-rights" analyses by arguing (unsupportably) that the Constitution should be interpreted to instantiate the (libertarian or communitarian) values these authors happen to support because historical evidence suggests that late-eighteenth-century Americans were committed to these values. Finally, some of these scholars simply ignore the issue of whether the Constitution can legitimately be said to incorporate the values they wish to instantiate—simply assume without argument, for example, that Lockean ideas are part of our Constitution.

This genre of Constitutional-law scholarship is harmful in two ways. First, because the legal-rights conclusions its authors (usually) claim to be reaching are frequently incorrect, it makes it more likely that judges and other government actors will produce wrong answers to the various Constitutional-rights questions they must decide. Second, and more insidiously, because these articles and books manifest their authors' rejection of the possibility of a society's being rights-based in any meaningful way, they tend to undermine our culture's moral identity.

As worrisome as this scholarship is, it is less disturbing than the effect that the belief that there are no internally-right answers to any or any socially-contested moral-rights-related legal-rights questions has had on the teaching of those legal academics who subscribe to it. Most of the academics in question openly teach that there are no internally-right answers to any legal-rights question whose answer is socially contested. In addition, most of these law teachers devote a far smaller percentage of their class-hours to teaching traditional legal argument than did their predecessors.

This second consequence is not a corollary of the first. Professors who do not take legal argument seriously in the sense of believing that it can generate internally-right answers to all moral-rights-related legal-rights questions could decide to teach traditional legal argument because they recognize its professional usefulness. They could recognize that

(1) since many legal-rights questions—namely, those that involve legal rights that are not related to socially-contested moral rights—can be correctly answered through traditional legal argument, lawyers need to be able to make such arguments to help their clients win cases that turn on such issues or structure their activities to keep from violating the relevant laws;

(2) since judges must use legitimate legal arguments to buttress conclusions that they reach for reasons that would not traditionally be considered to be legitimate legal argument, both to satisfy traditional role-expectations and to control the precedential significance of their opinions, lawyers need to be able to supply them with the traditional legal arguments they need to use to "justify" decisions in the lawyers' clients' interests on issues that have no internally-right answers; and

(3) since some of the skills and knowledge that are required to make legal-rights arguments are also important in non-rights-oriented policy-analysis contexts, lawyers need to develop these skills and knowledge to persuade judges who are willing to be persuaded by "external-to-law" arguments as well as other government decisionmakers who are authorized to make law.

I am not suggesting that traditional legal argument is not being taught at all at our law schools. Some such teaching does take place—not just for pragmatic reasons but also because law professors got their jobs because they like and are good at making traditional legal arguments. However, I do think that the proportion of law-school class-hours devoted to traditional (and *a fortiori* legitimate) legal argument as opposed to "external-to-law" policy-analysis has dropped continuously and considerably over the past twenty-five years. Moreover, even when those law professors who believe in the no-internally-right-answer hypothesis teach traditional legal argument, they do not inculcate respect for it or for the law. Since they do not believe that there are internally-right answers to any or any socially-contested moral-rights-related legal-rights questions (right answers that connect the law to our society's moral obligations), they are teaching law students to manipulate like a lawyer, not to discover a law that is worthy of respect. This type of teaching breeds deep moral skepticism and cynicism in law students and the lawyers they become. If the inevitable point of legal argument is to secure favorable answers that are morally disconnected rather than right answers that reflect our society's rights-obligation commitments, why should one be surprised when lawyers construe precedents unreasonably or interpret facts dishonestly (for example, pick their data-sources in result-oriented ways and report favorable statistical correlations without revealing the unfavorable results other regressions produced)?

Unfortunately, the (mistaken) belief of the overwhelming majority of contemporary legal academics that there is no internally-right answer to any or any socially-contested moral-rights-related legal-rights question may turn out to be self-fulfilling. Unless the current trend is reversed, law students will be increasingly taught by people who do not take legal argument seriously in the sense of believing that it can generate internally-right answers because those individuals who become law professors will increasingly be people who like and are good at the kind of (superficial) policy-analysis that now plays such an important role in law-school pedagogy. If this occurs, law students, lawyers, and eventually judges will be unlikely to recognize the difference between legal-rights argument and non-rights-oriented policy-argument, the legal system will become less rights-based (thereby decreasing the pragmatic need to teach legal argument), and the whole culture will cease to be rights-based. This prophecy of doom may be hyperbolic, but it is far more plausible from where I am sitting than may appear to those who are not members of the legal academy. One of my tasks as a professor at the University of Texas Law School is to interview applicants for teaching positions. I am consistently dismayed at the inability of many if not most top graduates of elite law schools to recognize, much less articulate, the difference between legal-rights analysis and non-rights-oriented policy-analysis.[11]

The belief that there are no internally-right answers to moral-rights questions has also affected the performance of its judicial adherents. Judges in this category have reacted to this belief in the same way that their academic counterparts did—by substituting moral-ought policy-analysis for legal-rights or Constitutional-rights analysis. This reaction has reduced their "social product" by causing them to reach conclusions that, although right from their personal-ultimate-value perspective (rights-considerations aside), are wrong because they fail to secure the legal rights of one or more affected parties. Moreover, even when the conclusions they have reached are the internally-right answers to the moral-rights-related legal-rights questions they are supposed to be addressing, these judges' effectiveness has been reduced by their related failure to justify their answers with appropriate, rights-related arguments. Thus, although those Justices in this category who have reviewed the Constitutionality of various affirmative-action programs have correctly concluded that the relevant programs are Constitutional, their arguments for this conclusion have been unpersuasive because they did not focus on the issues that are relevant to the salient rights-issues. More indirectly, these judges' performances have been socially costly because they have tended to undermine our belief that a society can be rights-based.

Many more judges, a minority of law professors, and several well-known social critics who do not believe that objectively-right answers can be given to moral-rights questions in our culture (at least if there is no overwhelming social consensus on the relevant answers) have argued that, despite this fact, internally-right answers can be given to all legal-rights questions. Their position reflects their belief that the various legitimate modes of legal analysis do not have a moral content and (in part for this reason) are capable of generating determinant legal conclusions.

This jurisprudential position has had a considerable impact on the performance of its subscribers. Since I believe that legitimate legal interpretation is not an arcane, technical enterprise that can be undertaken without reference to the moral principles at stake in the relevant cases, or to the moral principles on which our commitment to democracy is based, it should be no surprise that, to my mind, many of the doctrines that the academics and judges in this second category have developed to deal with various Constitutional-rights issues are completely indefensible and that many of the conclusions that they and the relevant social critics have reached about Constitutional-rights issues are simply and simplistically incorrect.

In fact, the attempt of these scholars, social critics, and judges to divorce law from morals—to articulate and use what I take to be a non-moral approach to Constitutional interpretation—produces precisely the same two types of harm that are generated by the non-rights-related policy-analysis of the majority of law professors and the minority of judges who have drawn very different jurisprudential implications from their conclusion that no internally-right answer can be given to any or any socially-contested moral-rights question. In particular, this non-moral approach to legal interpretation is harmful because it leads those judges and other government actors who use it to reach incorrect Constitutional-rights conclusions—to fail to protect some Constitutional rights against State violation and to prohibit the State from making certain choices (e.g., from enacting affirmative-action programs) that may not be directly required by anyone's rights but do reflect the defensible personal-ultimate-value preferences of their supporters. Moreover, this non-moral approach is also harmful because it manifests these judges' belief that no State can be rights-based. (A great deal of social-science research suggests that most people do not pay much attention to what the Supreme Court says. I have always found this fact regrettable, but the performance of these judges tempts me to conclude that their low impact is a blessing in disguise.)

The teaching of the minority of academics who have reacted in this second way to their no-right-answer conclusions has also been deleteriously affected by their beliefs. They do not teach the moral underpinnings of law, and the instruction they give on the modes of traditional legal argument tends to be wooden and misleading.

In short, this book is concerned with two interrelated sets of issues. The first is abstract and jurisprudential: What counts as morally-legitimate legal argument in our culture? The second is concrete and constitutional: What is the right approach to and correct resolution of various currently-debated Constitutional-rights issues relating to equal protection, procedural due process, autonomy, privacy, and liberty? Both sets of issues are tremendously important, and neither is being addressed properly or resolved satisfactorily by contemporary academics, social critics, and judges.

Ours is a liberal rights-based society. The jurisprudential position this book articulates, defends, and applies is a corollary of that fact. I believe that the instantiation of this jurisprudential position would help keep our society true to its moral identity. Indeed, part of my goal in writing this book is to combat the academic forces that are tending to convert us into a goal-based society and the judicial forces that are tending to convert us into an unreflective and unreflected-upon democracy that no longer takes moral and Constitutional rights seriously.

1

Legitimate Legal Argument and Constitutional Interpretation
My Position

This chapter develops a model of legitimate legal argument in the United States and investigates its implications for Constitutional interpretation in this country. Its account of legitimate legal argument is based on the premise that in our culture legitimate argument about "what the law is" is not autonomous. To be legitimate, an argument about the internal-to-law right answer to a legal-rights question must be consistent with our culture's moral commitments. For this reason, the chapter begins by arguing that ours is a liberal, rights-based culture. In particular, it argues that our society is *rights-based* in that moral rights act as a constraint on the pursuit of legitimate social and personal goals. It is *liberal* in that the basic moral norm we use in moral-rights discourse is a requirement that we treat all moral-rights holders as equals in the sense that liberalism would define that egalitarian notion—namely, treat with equal, appropriate respect all creatures who have the neurological prerequisites to become and remain individuals of moral integrity[1] and show equal, appropriate concern for all such creatures' actualizing their potential to be individuals of moral integrity.

My premise that legal practice is legitimate in a rights-based society if and only if it is consistent with the moral commitments of that society has important implications for legitimate legal argument in the American liberal, rights-based society. In particular, this premise implies that "arguments of moral principle"—arguments that explore the direct implications of the basic moral principle described above and its more concrete corollaries by identifying and then balancing the effects of the decision in question on the rights-related interests of all moral-rights holders—not only are generically part of the law but are (with one currently-irrelevant exception) the dominant mode of legal argument. More specifically, in our culture, arguments of moral principle operate not only directly in legal argument when the relevant principles apply but also indirectly (1) to determine whether certain types of arguments lawyers have made and courts have heeded are in fact legitimate; (2) to determine which variant(s) of the various general types of legitimate legal argument is (are) legitimate; and (3) to determine the relationship between the various arguments that are legitimate and evidence that is relevant, on the one hand, and the internally-right answer to any legal-rights question, on the other. I should add that if my account of legitimate legal argument in our culture proves correct, the probability that there are internally-right answers to all legal-rights questions in the United States is far higher than most legal scholars now seem to believe—indeed, if I am correct, there will be internally-right answers to all or virtually all legal-rights questions.

1. The Distinguishing Moral Characteristics of Our Polity

For a society to have moral integrity, its public decisionmakers must behave in a way that is consistent with the moral norms to which the society is committed. For this reason, I reject the view that legal practice in a moral-rights-based society is self-legitimating in favor of the view that any given legal practice is legitimate in such a society only if it is consistent with the society's moral commitments. Hence, before I can analyze legitimate legal argument or legitimate Constitutional interpretation in our culture, I must characterize our polity as a moral entity.

A. The Rights-Based Character of Our Polity

(1) The Positive Evidence

In part, my conclusion that ours is a rights-based society[2] reflects the way in which members and public officials of our society discuss and evaluate proposed and actual State choices. The Declaration of Independence's declamation that government is instituted to secure the inalienable rights of man is not empty rhetoric. It articulates a premise that underlies our discourse about State choices—that a State choice that would otherwise violate someone's rights cannot in general be "justicized" (rendered just and, in this context, Constitutional) by proving that it furthers legitimate social goals whose promotion in the relevant instance is not required by anyone's rights.

However, for the most part, my evidence that ours is a rights-based society relates not to our discussions and evaluations of State choices (either inside or outside legal fora) but to the way in which we analyze the morality of private rather than State choices. Given my basic premise that our non-legal moral commitments control what is legitimate in law, my reliance on such evidence may not be surprising.

My main evidence for the rights-based character of our culture is that

(1) members of our culture distinguish between discussions about what someone (or the State) is *obligated to do* and discussions about what someone (or the State) *ought to do*,

(2) that in such discussions the ability of an actor to demonstrate that from the perspective of values he personally supports he ought not fulfill an obligation does not relieve him of the relevant duty—that is, it does not entitle or enable him to escape a type of moral criticism that members of our culture take very seriously, and

(3) in such discussions the ability of an actor to demonstrate that his proposed or past act would not or did not violate any duty and was motivated by a sincere personal moral conviction does enable him to escape an important type of criticism even by those who disapprove of his choice because they reject the personal ultimate value that led him to make it.

Members of our culture engage in two types of prescriptive moral discourse—discourse about what someone or the State is *obligated to do* and discourse about what someone or the State *ought to do*. These two types of discourse involve different moral norms. Moral-obligation discourse employs moral norms that I call "moral principles." "Moral-ought" discourse employs different moral norms that I designate "personal ultimate values." Further, the two types of prescriptive moral discourse frequently yield different conclusions: in a given situation, a moral agent may have no obligation to do something that from various legitimate personal-ultimate-value perspectives he or she ought to do; or, less often, a moral agent may have an obligation to do something that from some personal-ultimate-value perspective that is legitimate within its appropriate domain he or she ought not to do. Moreover, although most individual or State choices do not implicate rights—that is, they are neither required by nor prohibited by the rights of any rights-bearing entity—virtually all choices do implicate personal ultimate values. Finally, as the conclusion that ours is a rights-based culture implies, when a choice is required or prohibited by the moral rights of one of more of the individuals it affects, a moral-rights conclusion and the moral norms from which that conclusion is derived are lexically prior to (take precedence over) the moral-ought conclusion and the moral norms it reflects. Thus, the fact that an individual of moral integrity sincerely believes that, from his personal-ultimate-value perspective, he ought not fulfill his moral obligation does not relieve him of his moral duty, nor does it exempt him from weighty moral criticism when he fails to fulfill his obligation (though individuals who violate their obligations out of personal moral conviction are clearly regarded differently from those who do so thoughtlessly and carelessly or out of unreflective and crass self-interest).

Assume that I ask someone (call her Jill) to read and comment on a paper I have written before I present it to a Learned Society. We can ask two different prescriptive moral questions about Jill's position: whether Jill has an obligation to help me in this way and whether she ought to do so. Different issues and moral norms are germane to answering these two questions, and different answers may be given to them. In our culture, Jill would not have a moral obligation to provide me with such assistance unless she (1) had promised to do so, (2) had a special status relationship to me (e.g., was a relative, friend, or colleague in the sense of being a fellow-member of a given department), (3) was a culpable cause-in-fact of my requiring assistance (e.g., had carelessly or willfully misinformed me of the date on which I was supposed to give the paper or delayed and handicapped my preparation by failing to return overdue books I had requested at the library), and possibly, though dubiously, (4) was a non-culpable cause-in-fact of my requiring assistance (e.g. had not returned library books she knew I had requested in circumstances in which she had a perfect right to keep them). Therefore, one could not answer the moral-obligation question without investigating these issues. However, these issues (and the liberal moral principle that explains their relevance)[3] might not be nearly so decisive—indeed, they might not be relevant at all—to the determination of what Jill ought to do from one or more legitimate personal-ultimate-value perspectives.

Assume, for example, that Jill clearly does not have an obligation to help me with my work; she had made no relevant promises, had no prior relationship with or connection to me, and was not a cause-in-fact of my need for help. An unconventional utilitarian who accepted my distinction between moral-rights claims and moral-ought claims would still conclude that Jill *ought* to help me if (1) the util-cost to Jill of supplying the relevant help was lower than the util-benefits to me of her doing so, (2) the relevant short-run third-party effects did not cancel out the preceding net util-gain (e.g., that the util-benefits to my listeners were as large as the net util-benefits to others whom Jill's alternative course of action would have affected), (3) Jill's decision to help would not generate net long-run util-costs by encouraging people like me to put ourselves in a position in which we need such help and/or by discouraging people like Jill from developing the capacity to provide such help (the latter cost is unlikely to be generated so long as Jill is not legally required to supply the help in question), and (4) Jill's helping me would not deter alternative decisions that would increase total utility by an even larger amount in comparison with the *status quo ante.*

Similarly, an equal-utility egalitarian would conclude that Jill ought to help if (1) Jill's helping me would equalize our utilities, (2) her helping me would not tend to increase or decrease the disparities in other individuals' utilities in comparison with the *status quo ante* in any other way, and (3) her helping me would not deter behaviors that were even more egalitarian in the equal-utility sense.

The same points can be made by examining the case of a promisor who is considering not keeping her promise. Assume that Jill has promised to read and comment on my paper. The issues that would have to be addressed to determine whether Jill's failure to perform would be excusable (whether a change in circumstances, for example, relieved her of her obligation to render timely performance) might not be nearly so decisive or, from some perspectives, relevant at all to the determination of what Jill and I *ought to do* in these circumstances from various personal-ultimate-value perspectives. Once more, if one were dealing with a case in which nothing relieved Jill of her duty to keep her promise, a utilitarian or equal-utility egalitarian would still conclude that she *ought not* fulfill her obligation or that I *ought not* insist on timely performance if the recommended choices would increase utility or the equality of utility. However, as in the preceding example, the fact that Jill was a person of moral integrity who failed to keep her promise because her personal moral conviction led her to believe that she ought not do so would not entitle or enable her to escape an important kind of social censure. And although an evaluator might criticize me for insisting on performance in such a case—might conclude that I ought not do so, he would still have to grant that I was within my rights in doing so.

These illustrations reveal that different moral norms are relevant to moral-rights-claim discourse and moral-ought-statement discourse. In many situations, the proper answer to the moral-rights question may be "yes" while the right answer to the moral-ought question from some legitimate personal-ultimate-value perspective is "no," or vice versa. People who fail to fulfill their obligations may be subject to weighty criticism even if they act out of sincere personal moral conviction—even if they are individuals of moral integrity—and people who insist on enforcing their rights escape *that type* of criticism even from evaluators who believe that in this case the rights-holders in question ought not enforce their rights.

In my judgment, this bifurcated moral practice clearly manifests the fact that ours is a rights-based society. Although the above examples focus on private individual choices, the general conclusion applies to State choices as well: just as we are committed to the position that an individual's duty to fulfill an obligation is lexically prior to his goal of (interest in) conforming his life to his personal-ultimate-value convictions, we are committed to the proposition that in the public sphere the duty of the State to secure the rights of those for whom it is responsible trumps over its interest in pursuing even legitimate goals.

(2) The Alleged Counter-Evidence: A Critique

Several arguments have been used to counter the claim that our society is rights-based in the sense in which I use that term. Some argue that this claim is defeated by the fact that in our culture rights are not absolute, that (for example) our normal free speech rights do not extend to shouting "Fire!" in a crowded theater. Others cite both the fact that the Constitution authorizes the President to declare martial law and specific historic counter-examples in which prominent Americans advocated and tried to justicize choices that they believed did violate rights (such as Abraham Lincoln's defense of his suspension of habeas corpus in his July 4, 1861, message to Congress). Still others cite the alleged fact that rights often lose out in contest with "compelling interests." In addition, some argue that our practice of giving weight to even incorrect precedents demonstrates that we are not a rights-based society because this practice results in our failing to make legally enforceable some moral rights that would have been legal rights in cases of first impression. And finally, some maintain that the proposition that our culture is rights-based is disproved by the fact that we do not require the State to enforce certain moral rights when the mechanical transaction cost of doing so seems excessive.

The fact that "rights" are not absolute is less telling than some suppose. The non-absoluteness of "rights," in the sense in which the term is used in this context, reflects not the fact that in our culture rights properly so called can be overridden when doing so furthers the achievement of various policy goals or personal ultimate values but rather that such "rights" are not unlimited. Individuals do not have a right (in the strict sense) to speak when and how they wish. They have rights-related interests in speaking, which in particular instances may be outweighed by the net rights-related interests of the other parties affected by the speech in question (and, if we shift our focus to Constitutional rights, its public regulation).

Our "right to free speech" is not violated by an ordinance prohibiting shouting "Fire!" in a crowded theater. As potential speakers, potential listeners, and members of a democratic polity, we do have rights-related interests in free speech, but such an ordinance would not violate our free speech rights because those rights do not include a right to shout "Fire!" in a crowded theater. Indeed, it is not even clear that the ordinance in question would disserve any rights-related interests. To be a rights-related interest, the relevant desire must be appropriately related to the attributes of the rights-holder that give him that status. Individuals may therefore not have a free-speech rights-related interest in shouting "Fire!" in a crowded theater or of listening to such speech or learning its consequences any more than they have a free-movement rights-related interest in swinging their fist to strike a non-threatening other's nose.

Rights conclusions reflect complicated analyses of the effects of a particular choice and its "regulation" on the rights-related interests of both the chooser and others. The fact that the impact of someone's proposed choice on the interests of others affects his right to make that choice is neither surprising nor inconsistent with our culture's being rights-based.

Further, my claim that our society is rights-based cannot be refuted by citing the Constitutional provision authorizing the President as Commander-in-Chief to declare martial law or historical incidents such as Lincoln's suspension of habeas corpus. In part, this conclusion reflects the fact that the claim that a society is rights-based does not imply that it always fulfills its related commitments. But primarily, it reflects the way I would respond to the admittedly-serious and difficult issue that the martial-law clause and the Lincoln example pose for a rights-based society: whether a rights-based State violates someone's rights if it denies him procedural or substantive protections to which he is normally entitled because doing so in the instant case should be predicted to secure rights-related interests on balance by reducing the probability that the existing rights-based State will be replaced by a non-rights-based State (and/or the probable extent to which the replacement State will violate rights). In the relevant emergency situations, the sacrifice of rights-related interests that are normally protected does not violate any-one's "rights" in the non-absolute sense of that word because it enhances rights-related interests on balance. Of course, a rights-based State would be obligated to establish procedural and institutional safeguards to reduce ap-propriately the likelihood that those in control of the State would abuse or mistakenly use any emergency powers they are legitimately granted. My ten-tative conclusion is that in this country these safeguards should include rapid Supreme Court review as a matter of original jurisdiction of all questions of fact and law raised by each exercise of emergency powers.[4]

In our culture, "absolute rights" often lose out in competition with "com-pelling interests" in non-emergency situations as well. In lawyers' talk, I demur to this allegation—that is, although I agree that "absolute rights" are often defeated by "compelling interests," this fact does not seem to me to cut against my claim that our culture is rights-based. At least, it would not cut against this claim if the relevant "compelling interests" were rights-related in-terests that were more weighty than the rights-related interests (misdescribed as "absolute rights") they "defeated"—that is, than the rights-related inter-ests that would have to be the "absolute-right" sacrificed to them in the rel-evant cases.

An example may help clarify this point. Assume that in some divorce cases one party is sufficiently more at fault on balance than the other for the less-culpable or innocent party to have a breach-of-contract-type or tort-type moral-rights claim to compensation. Nevertheless, a rights-based State might be able to justicize failing to make that claim legally enforceable by citing the damage that enforcement would do to privacy-right-related interests (given the legitimacy of the rights-related interests to be served by making this type of trial public) and the rights-related interests of any children of the marriage in question in receiving appropriate nurturing (given the tendency of any "fault" litigation to increase the antagonism the parents feel toward each other and thereby reduce the probability that they will participate in the kind of cooperative parenting after the divorce that will contribute to their chil-dren's actualizing their potential to become and remain individuals of moral integrity). Admittedly, a complete analysis of this situation would have to take account of the tendency of fault-based decisionmaking to deter such promissory breaches and "torts," the probability that judges would incor-rectly resolve the fault issue, and perhaps (though probably not—see below) the mechanical transaction cost of deciding the fault issue. However, even this brief statement may suggest why the fact that a State has chosen not to make certain moral rights legally enforceable (has chosen to sacrifice certain rights-related interests to other so-called "compelling interests") in a non-emergency situation may not cut against the claim that it is a rights-based political entity.

The fact that in our legal system weight is given to erroneous precedents also does not defeat the claim that our society is rights-based, even though this practice may result in the State's not enforcing what would have been moral-rights-related legal rights had the relevant cases arisen as matters of first impression. In part, this conclusion reflects the fact that in practice rights-based societies sometimes fail to live up to their commitments. But, primarily, it reflects the fact that, for "fair-notice" or "reasonable-reliance" reasons that are rights-related (that liberalism would deem legitimate), precedents are supposed to be given weight in both our moral and our legal cultures. Admittedly, however, as is discussed below, the weight assigned to precedent in the United States today may be inappropriate because it reflects various illegitimate prudential considerations.

Finally, some have countered the claim that our culture is rights-based with the fact that we often do not make moral rights legally enforceable when the only possible justification for our failure to do so is mechanical transaction costs. Some cases of non-enforcement that are conventionally explained in transactions cost terms probably actually reflect the belief that the plaintiff has no moral right. For example, some "assumption of risk" cases that have been conventionally rationalized in transaction-cost terms probably reflect the fact that the plaintiff's behavior was actually, though not doctrinally, contributorily negligent—a fact that was (almost certainly incorrectly) perceived to justify his being barred from recovery. However, even if some alleged cases of non-enforcement can be thus explained, others cannot. How can I explain, for example, our failure to enforce the moral right of a donee to a gift promised by a donor who has not subsequently experienced any dramatic change in circumstances or discovered past donee-disloyalty to him when the donee has not been disloyal to the donor after the promise was made but also has not relied on the promise in the way that the law would count as relevant? Or, again, how can I explain our failure to enforce the moral right of an individual not to be bumped into by someone running negligently on a crowded sidewalk?

The popular justification for these negative enforcement decisions is that a liberal State need not make an individual's moral right legally enforceable when the conventional transaction costs of enforcing it seem prohibitive, particularly when the rights-related interests that enforcement would protect are deemed unimportant. Even in its own policy-oriented terms, this justification does not seem persuasive since gift promises can be substantial and since enforcement would protect the rights-related interests not only of the right-holder in this case but also of those others (including prospective gift-givers who want their donees to be able to rely on their promises to execute gift promises in the future) who would be protected by the specific and general deterrence consequences of a positive enforcement decision. However, for my purposes, the crucial fact is that the proximate goal of increasing economic efficiency does not trump rights considerations in a rights-based society. On the contrary, a rights-based society could not justicize refusing to secure a moral-rights-holder's rights-related interests on transaction-cost economic-efficiency grounds unless it could demonstrate that the resource savings such a negative enforcement decision would yield would be necessary for its securing other, weightier rights-related interests that it would then proceed to secure. Given the extent to which our existing State fails to live up to its obligations and the amount of resources it spends in ways that are not rights-securing, I doubt that such a demonstration could be made. I am therefore forced to acknowledge that some of our failures to make moral rights legally enforceable cannot be justicized by the transaction-cost savings those failures permit. However, since the claim that a society is rights-based does not imply that it always fulfills its obligations, this admission does not require me to surrender the claim that our society is rights-based.

In short, for the above reasons, I am not persuaded by the various types of evidence others believe defeat the claim that our culture is rights-based in the strict sense in which I have been defining that phrase.

B. The Liberal Character of Our Rights

The preceding section argued that members of our culture engage in two very different types of prescriptive moral discourse, which can be distinguished, *inter alia*, by the specific moral norms they employ. In my terminology, the moral norms that are employed in moral-ought discourse are designated "personal ultimate values," and the moral norms that are employed in moral-rights discourse are designated "moral principles."[5]

Like Ronald Dworkin, I believe that the basic moral principle we use when asserting and evaluating rights-obligations claims is a liberal principle, though my version of that principle is somewhat different from Dworkin's. In particular, I articulate the basic moral principle to which we are committed in the following way: treat with equal, appropriate respect all creatures who have the neurological prerequisites to become and remain individuals of moral integrity and show equal, appropriate concern for their actualizing their potential to become and remain individuals of moral integrity. In my understanding, an individual has moral integrity when he takes his life morally seriously not only by giving appropriate consideration to his obligations but also by attempting to establish a reflective equilibrium between his personal value-convictions and his life choices. In essence, the basic moral principle just articulated is a liberal egalitarian principle—that is, it is an egalitarian principle that requires moral-rights holders to be treated as equals in a sense that is determined by the liberal conception of the identifying characteristic of a moral-rights holder and that defines the relevant boundary condition (the attribute that makes an entity a moral-rights holder) in a way that links that condition to the substantive rights that attach to its fulfillment (as well as to our culture's relevant boundary-condition practices).

This section first describes generally the empirical evidence that has led me to reach this conclusion about the identity of our basic moral principle and discusses various problems with the protocol I used for this purpose. It then elaborates on the liberal moral norm I have called the "basic moral principle" that members of our culture are committed to using in rights discourse and contrasts this moral norm with several other actual and purported moral norms I label "personal ultimate values," which members of our culture use in moral-ought discourse.

(1) The Liberal Basic Moral Principle: An Outline of the Proof

Glendower: I can call spirits from the vasty deep.
Hotspur: Why, so can I, or so can any man; But will they come when you do call for them?[6]

My claim that members of our society are committed to using the liberal principle I have described and its more concrete corollaries to determine the correctness of moral-rights claims is based on a kind of anthropological study of our moral discourse and conduct. Neither now nor when I discuss legitimate legal argument in our culture do I attempt to stand outside our practices and establish their desirability or moral optimality (though I do assume that a purported moral value must have certain attributes to merit the designation "moral value" and that an individual or society must act in a morally-consistent way to have moral integrity).[7]

This section delineates the appropriate way to identify a rights-based society's basic moral principle. It begins by outlining the protocol that should be followed to identify our society's basic moral principle and then lists various gaps in that protocol and analyzes the feasibility of filling them in nonarbitrarily. In what follows, I refer to the various possible moral norms that could be our society's basic moral principle as "candidates" for the title of "the basic moral principle the society is committed to using when asserting and assessing moral-rights-and-obligations claims."

(A) THE PROTOCOL FOR IDENTIFYING A RIGHTS-BASED SOCIETY'S BASIC MORAL PRINCIPLE: A PRELIMINARY OUTLINE

The first step in identifying the successful candidate for this title is to filter out all those purported "moral norms" that do not in fact deserve that designation—for example, because they make relevant features of the situation that are intrinsically morally irrelevant. Thus, purported moral norms that make relevant attributes of moral-rights holders that these creatures could not control should be filtered out for that reason. The second step is to specify the criteria and overall metric one should use to rank the eligible candidates for the "basic moral principle" title. In my judgment, two criteria are relevant in this context: (1) a "closeness-of-fit" criterion (How well do the various candidates in question "fit" our historical and current moral-rights-and-obligations practices?), and (2) an "explicability-of-(non-fits)" criterion (To what extent are the behaviors each candidate fails to fit explicable in ways that reduce the damage the non-fits of each candidate do to its candidacy?).[8] The third step is to list the various behaviors and phenomenological experiences that the basic moral principle is supposed to fit—that is, to post-dict and predict. The fourth step is to determine the closeness of the fit between the post-dictions and predictions of each candidate for the "basic moral principle" title and the actual facts. The fifth step is to specify the various kinds of non-fit explanations that reduce the damage a candidate's non-fits do to its candidacy. The sixth step is to determine the extent to which the non-fits of each candidate can be explained in the various damage-reducing ways. And the seventh and final step is to evaluate the overall performance of the various candidates in a way that appropriately reflects both the closeness of their fits and the explicability of their non-fits.

(B) THE GAPS IN THE PROTOCOL

The above protocol contains three sets of gaps. Before proceeding to discuss the prospects of filling them in non-arbitrarily, I want to emphasize three facts. First, the following analysis does not represent my best effort to persuade the reader of the feasibility of my proposed anthropological study: I am trying to be as honest as possible about the theoretical difficulties confronting me. Second, the various proposals I will make for filling in the gaps listed are not attempts to resolve such issues in ways that would best serve a utilitarian: to the contrary, although a knowledgeable reader may detect my training as an economist in the analysis that follows, I propose ways to fill in the relevant gaps only when I can derive them from the fact that our society is rights-based—in other words, without specifying the moral norm that underlies our rights practices. Third, the discussion that follows is not intended to be definitive: my hope is to provide a partial analysis that will stimulate readers to take rights seriously—to criticize my description of the relevant gaps and my proposals for filling them in and to offer comments, proposals, and conclusions of their own.

(i) Five Gaps That Relate to the Closeness-of-Fit Criterion

(a) Gaps That Relate to the Facts the Candidates Are Supposed to Fit

The first question is: What facts are the candidate principles supposed to fit? The most important part of the answer to this question is that the overwhelming majority of the relevant facts relate to the assertion, discussion, and assessment of moral-rights claims outside of legal processes. This point needs to be stressed because my concept of "fit" is a highly-elaborated version of the notion of fit Dworkin used when discussing "principles" in *Taking Rights Seriously*,[9] and many Dworkin readers now assume that his concept of fit is concerned solely with various behaviors that relate to the assertion and assessment of legal-rights-and-obligations claims (in the case of "principles" in his terminology) and various "official" behaviors by members of the legislative and executive branches of government (in the case of what he calls "policies").[10]

In any event, the closeness of a basic-moral-principle candidate's fit depends on its fitting

(1) the moral and legal rights-and-obligations claims that were made,
(2) the conclusions that were reached about the moral and legal rights-and-obligations claims that were made,
(3) the degree of confidence various relevant individuals expressed in the correctness of these conclusions,

(4) how close the relevant deciders or observers thought the arguments were (a different notion from its predecessor since one can be sure about a case one thought was close), and/or

(5) the kinds of arguments that were made and accepted when dealing with such claims.

(b) Gaps That Relate to the Connection between the Overall Closeness of Fit and How Closely the Candidate-Principle Fits Each of the Types of Facts It Should Fit

Unfortunately, although I have no doubt that all the above categories of facts are relevant to the assessment of the closeness of a particular candidate's fit, I do not think that one can derive from the fact that our society is rights-based a formula relating its overall closeness of fit to the closeness with which it fits each of the various categories of facts listed above.

(c) Gaps That Relate to the Determinants of the Closeness of Fit between a Candidate and the Conclusions That Were Reached about All Moral-Rights-and-Obligations Claims That Were Made

One dimension of fit relates to the extent to which the candidate in question accurately post-dicts the conclusions that were reached on the moral rights-and-obligations claims that were made. Another gap in my protocol relates to whether a candidate's fit depends solely on the *number* of choices that were inconsistent with the candidate, on the number of inconsistent choices weighted by the *average seriousness* of the inconsistencies, or on some other more complicated set of characteristics of the distribution of the associated seriousness-of-departures distribution—say, one that includes the variance as well as the mean of that seriousness-of-departure distribution. Once more, I see no non-arbitrary way to fill in this gap—that is, I cannot derive any solution from the fact that ours is a rights-based society.

(d) Gaps That Relate to the Various Dimensions along Which the Seriousness of a Non-Fit Should Be Measured

If one concludes that the poorness of a given candidate's fit depends on the seriousness of the departures from principle its advocates must admit the historical record reveals as well as on the number of such departures history contains, one will have to decide whether the seriousness of a given non-fit should be measured by (1) the weakness of the argument for the justness of the non-fit, (2) the net sacrifice of rights–related interests the non-fitting behavior would be deemed to have generated directly if its consequences were evaluated from the perspective of the relevant candidate-principle, and/or (3) some combination of these argumentational and consequentialist error–metrics. Unfortunately, although both the argumentational error and the consequentialist error should affect one's estimate of the seriousness of a non-fit, I see no non-arbitrary way to generate the relevant metric. Unfortunately, this admission is significant: the relative seriousness of the non-fits associated with different principle-candidates may well depend on the dimension by which one measures the extent of any non-fit.

(e) Gaps That Relate to the Metric by Which the Seriousness of a Non-Fit Should Be Measured along Each of Its Relevant Dimensions

The protocol I initially delineated also fails to provide operational definitions of the seriousness of the argumentational error and consequentialist error associated with any given non-fit that transcend the differences between the different candidates for the status of "best-fitting" or "best" candidate for the title of the basic moral principle on which a given rights-based society is committed to basing its rights discourse. However, I think that there is a non-arbitrary way to measure the relevant argumentational and consequentialist errors.

I would measure the argumentational error manifested by a given choice that was inconsistent with a particular candidate for the basic moral principle title by using the principle-candidate in question to measure the relative strengths of the arguments for and against the right that was allegedly violated. In particular, I would use the relevant candidate to assign a total of 100 points to the arguments for and against the existence of the alleged moral (legal) right and measure the seriousness of the relevant argumentational error by the difference between 50 points and the points given the side the principle-candidate implies was incorrectly determined to be the loser. The argumentational error in every situation involving a choice a particular candidate deems violative of rights would therefore be determined by reference to point-assignments derived from that candidate. The fact that the average indicated point-difference for the set of behaviors one candidate implies are non-fits is higher than its counterpart for the set of behaviors a second candidate implies are non-fits would be said to indicate that the average argumentational erroneousness of the non-fits associated with the first candidate is higher than the average argumentational erroneousness of the non-fits associated with the second candidate. The metric I have proposed would therefore transcend differences among the candidates.

I would measure the consequentialist error generated by each choice a particular candidate deemed to be inconsistent with principle by evaluating each such set of consequences on a scale of 1 to 100 where 1 indicates a trivially-bad set of consequences (a small social loss) from the candidate's perspective and 100 indicates a horrifically-bad set of consequences from the relevant candidate's perspective. A von Neumann approach could be used to scale the consequentialist errors associated with any given principle-candidate: the consequential cost of one error will be twice that of another if from the relevant principle's perspective one would be indifferent between a certainty of the latter and a 50 percent chance of the former. Admittedly, this proposal does not solve all the relevant problems. However, if these problems can be solved for each candidate, the resulting measure would transcend differences among the candidates in question.

(ii) Five Sets of Gaps That Relate to the "Explicability-of-(Non-Fits)" Criterion

(a) Gaps That Relate to the Kinds of Non-Fit Explanations That Will Reduce the Damage the Relevant Non-Fits Do to a Principle's Candidacy

The first type of gap can be filled in non-arbitrarily. There are at least four reasons why a principle-candidate might not fit a fact it was supposed to post-dict or predict other than its not being the moral norm on which our society is committed to basing its moral-rights discourse and decisions—four explanations of such non-fits that reduce the damage the non-fits do to the principle's candidacy.

First, candidates will be less damaged by their failure to post-dict the moral-rights-and-obligations claims and legal claims that were made, the resolutions of those claims, and perhaps the arguments that were used to justify these conclusions to the extent that the non-fits can be explained by the greater social or political power of the parties that benefited from the non-fits in question.

Second, the damage that a non-fit does to a principle's candidacy will be reduced if the non-fitting behavior can be shown to be in the interest of the actor who engages in it even if all just moral claims will be recognized and complied with and all unjust moral claims will be rejected. It is easiest to explain this point in relation to moral-rights-related legal-rights claims. Even if the courts always support all valid moral-principle-based legal claims and reject all invalid legal claims that purport to derive from moral principles, many valid legal claims of the relevant type will not be asserted while many invalid legal claims will. More specifically, valid legal claims of the relevant type will sometimes not be asserted because the relevant right-holder finds it stressful to deal with lawyers and court-personnel and/or will have to incur attorney's fees and court costs that reduce his expected net recovery below the sum of the time-opportunity cost and emotional cost he would have to incur to pursue his claim. In the other direction, invalid legal claims will sometimes be asserted because the plaintiff hopes to extract settlements from defendants who wish to avoid the substantial cost of litigation, to build a tough reputation that will improve his position in future disputes, or to obtain publicity for his cause that might help him secure legislative redress. A full account of this type of explanation for these non-fitting behaviors would be far more complicated because it would take into account the reputational status of the claim's targets or defendants as well as the interests of the lawyers on each side, which may conflict with their respective clients' interests and cause the lawyers to make choices that are not in their respective clients' interests. I should add that counterparts to all these possibilities will also be present when the claim is a non-legal moral claim, private advisors stand in the shoes of lawyers, and the claims are assessed not by judges but by one or more private actors or just the "accused."

Third, in some cases, the damage a non-fit does to a particular principle's candidacy will also be reduced if it is possible to offer a plausible account of the conceptual intellectual error that may have caused an actor who was trying to address the claim in question in an intellectually-appropriate way to make the error the principle-candidate implies he made. For example, a basic corollary of the liberal basic moral principle I have articulated is that the State must not treat any individual or the members of any group in a way that is insulting to them—that fails to manifest the equal, appropriate respect that is their due. Laws that discriminate against certain groups (say, Blacks in the United States) in the sense of placing them at a disadvantage when such treatment cannot be justicized by its promoting other legitimate goals to an appropriate extent clearly violate this part of the liberal basic moral principle. By way of contrast, this anti-discrimination principle would not be violated by laws (say, some affirmative-action programs) that place members of a certain group (say, Caucasians) at a disadvantage in circumstances in which the laws in question were necessary to achieve one or more legitimate goals to an appropriate extent. Such laws would not violate the anti-discrimination principle, properly so called, because they would not "discriminate against" Caucasians in the sense of this expression that is appropriate in this context—roughly speaking, to disadvantage some individual or the members of some group when there is no appropriate justification for doing so (when the act in question fails to treat them with the respect that is their due). Now, assume that, contrary to this analysis, some courts held unconstitutional various affirmative-action programs that promote a variety of legitimate social goals on the ground that they insult the Caucasians whom they disadvantage. No doubt, such rulings would in part reflect the political power of the Caucasians they benefit relative to the political power of the various minorities they harm. However, I suspect that in addition they reflect an intellectual error that relates to an ambiguity in the term "discriminate"—namely, the fact that we use the word "discriminate" and its cognates both in a neutral or positive sense to refer to the recognition of distinctions or differences that are present and should be noted (as in the phrase "a wine expert's 'discriminating' palate") and in a pejorative sense to refer to the drawing of distinctions that are illegitimate—for example, that reflect prejudices (as in the phrase "a bigot's 'discrimination'"). To some extent at least, I suspect that the anti-affirmative-action decisions that the liberal basic moral principle I have articulated would have to classify as non-fits reflect a conceptual intellectual error caused by this ambiguity in the world "discriminate"—that is, they reflect the fact that the judges failed to see that although the laws in question distinguished between Blacks and Caucasians, they did not discriminate against Caucasians in the pejorative sense that is relevant in this context. In my opinion, the availability of this explanation of the non-fits in question reduces the damage they do to my liberal basic moral principle's candidacy.

Fourth, the damage a principle's non-fits do to its candidacy may also be reduced if the non-fits can cogently be attributed to other sorts of ignorance or errors the parties to the dispute may make or to the prospective errors of the individuals or institution that will decide the dispute (in the case of a moral-rights-related legal claim, the courts). Disputant-ignorance of different kinds can account for a variety of non-fits. Thus, a moral-right holder may not bring a justified claim for the loss he sustained from an injury or illness because he did not know the origin of his loss or the identity of his injurer, because (when the non-fit involves a failure to file a legal claim) he did not know his legal rights or unjustifiably distrusted the legal system, or because (when the non-fit involves a failure to make a moral-rights claim) he unjustifiably distrusted his injurer's willingness to respond appropriately or his compatriots' willingness to induce his injurer to fulfill his obligations by censuring him or imposing sanctions on him if he fails to do so. Similarly, when the non-fit involves a right-holder's failure to make an appropriate moral-rights argument or moral-rights-related legal-rights argument, the damage the non-fit inflicts on the relevant principle's candidacy may be reduced if the relevant party's omission can be attributed to his mistaken belief that his addressee will not grasp the relevant argument's relevance or force.

Obviously, prospective errors by those who will decide moral-rights disputes or moral-rights-related legal-rights disputes may also account for a variety of non-fits. Thus, parties to such disputes whose observation of the relevant decisionmaker's or institution's past behavior leads them to correctly conclude that the dispute in question will be decided incorrectly or that the relevant decisionmakers will fail to grasp the pertinence or force of certain good arguments may fail for these reasons to bring claims or to make arguments that the basic moral principle implies are respectively justified and relevant. When this is the case, the non-fits that result will not count so strongly against the relevant principle's candidacy.

Admittedly, my original statement of the protocol for identifying the basic moral principle or principle-combination on which a rights-based society is committed to grounding its moral-rights discourse failed to specify the various kinds of explanations of non-fits that will reduce the damage the non-fits do to the relevant principle's candidacy. However, as I hope this section demonstrates, this gap can be filled in non-arbitrarily.

(b) Gaps That Relate to the Social or Political Power of the Non-Fits' Beneficiaries and Victims

The conclusion that the damage that a non-fit will do to the candidacy of the relevant moral principle will be reduced if the non-fits' beneficiaries have greater social or political power than its victims creates two gaps that my previous brief discussion of this issue did not fill. First, it implies that the approach I have outlined cannot be operationalized without operationalizing the concepts of the social and political power of a behavior's beneficiaries relative to that of its victims. Unfortunately, this task is nothing short of daunting. Not only is it extremely difficult to specify the determinants of a given party's or group's general social or political power, it is even more difficult to specify the relevant determinants of such power in relation to a particular claim since a party or group that is generally more powerful may be placed at a disadvantage on that account in relation to a particular issue because that issue's otherwise-appropriate handling may endanger the respect that provided the basis for the relevant party's or group's general power or may bring to light various facts that would reduce the relevant group's power in other ways. The intellectual obstacles to filling in this gap are therefore not morally conceptual so much as empirical. I will not even attempt to deal with the relevant issues here.

Second, the potential relevance of social and political power explanations creates another gap because it necessitates an analysis of the circumstances in which moral-rights-related conduct is likely to be controlled or affected by the relative power of its potential beneficiaries and victims. Since the effect of such power is likely to vary with the issue concerned, various attributes of the forum in which it is to be debated and decided, and the various attributes of the decisionmaker in question, it will clearly be extremely difficult to fill in this gap in practice, though, once more, it should in principle be possible to do so non-arbitrarily.

> (c) Gaps That Relate to Transaction Costs or Other Factors That
>   Make the Pursuit of Valid Claims Disadvantageous as Well as
>   Gaps That Relate to the Possible Advantageousness of
>   Pursuing Some Unjustified Claims

Admittedly, it will be extremely difficult to determine the facts that the above explanation makes relevant to the damage some non-fits do to the relevant principle's candidacy. The monetary transaction cost of bringing a legal suit or making a moral claim, the opportunity cost of the complainant's time, the added emotional cost of making and prosecuting a suit rather than letting matters lie, the value of any reputational advantage that making or defending a claim (in a particular way) may yield, the value of any advantages in legislative fora or other arenas that making or defending a claim (in a particular way) may yield, the possible interests of a complainant's or defendant's advisors or lawyers that may conflict with the interests of the relevant advisees, and the various factors that affect the ability of the advisor to influence the advisee's behavior will also be hard to estimate. Limitations of space, knowledge, and skill deter me from even attempting to work out protocols for the relevant empirical inquiries here. Once more, however, it should be possible to fill in the resulting gaps non-arbitrarily.

(d) Gaps That Relate to a Conceptual Error That May Have Caused Individuals Who Were Trying to Deal with the Relevant Moral Claim in an Intellectually-Justifiable Way to Make the Mistake the Candidate Implies Was Made

The possibility that the damage done to a principle's candidacy by a non-fit may be reduced by an argument that it reflected a comprehensible conceptual error creates a need to specify the way to measure the persuasiveness of the conceptual-error explanation of any given non-fit. I do not know whether a non-arbitrary metric can be generated for this factor.

(e) Gaps That Relate to the Possibility That a Non-Fit May Reflect Other Sorts of Errors Made by Moral-Right Holders or Obligors or Prospective Errors by Moral-Right-Dispute Deciders

Clearly, this possibility makes a large number of facts relevant to the identification of a rights-based society's basic moral principles, some if not all of which will be difficult to ascertain. Once more, however, the relevant problems are empirical rather than morally conceptual and should in principle be resolvable non-arbitrarily.

One corollary of the preceding analysis of damage-reducing explanations of non-fits is worth pointing out at this juncture. When deciding whether the United States' adjudicatory process deserves to be called principled at all, one should give little weight to the fact that arguments of moral principle are articulated in a straightforward way far less often by lawyers and judges than my account of legitimate legal argument implies would be the case. In part, the relative absence of straightforward arguments of moral principle in adjudicatory settings reflects the consensus that such arguments led the Supreme Court to make incorrect decisions when in the first third of this century it held in such cases as *Lochner v. New York*[11] that the Constitution was based on *laissez faire* libertarianism. And in part, it reflects the fact that the lesson that lawyers and law professors drew from this history—that law and "morals" are separate[12]—was distorted by their failure to distinguish moral-rights analysis from moral-ought analysis and therefore even to contemplate the possibility that there may be internally-right answers to moral-rights questions and to moral-rights-related legal-rights questions.[13] This set of historical errors by the Court has deterred contemporary lawyers and judges from making straightforward arguments of moral principle by generating a judicial backlash to such arguments that led both lawyers and judges to conclude that straightforward moral arguments would not be accepted. And the erroneous analysis of these historical errors has deterred contemporary lawyers and judges from making such arguments by leading them to conclude that in adjudicatory contexts they are illegitimate and/or undesirable from a personal-ultimate-value perspective.

It seems to me that this explanation of why contemporary lawyers and judges make straightforward arguments of moral principle far less often in adjudicatory settings than my analysis suggests is warranted reduces the damage this non-fit does to my account of legitimate legal argument. I hasten to add that the preceding statements should not lead one to conclude that arguments of moral principle rarely play a significant role in contemporary adjudication. In addition to their occasional direct roles, arguments of moral principle often operate indirectly or surreptitiously in a wide variety of ways:

(1) by influencing the interpretation of doctrines and texts that appear to be "technical" in the sense of abstruse or non-moral but that are at base moral in content;

(2) by influencing the role assigned to ratifier intent, the breadth of historical inquiries, and the significance attributed to historical findings;

(3) by influencing our conclusions about the structure of our government and its interpretive implications;

(4) by influencing our practice of precedent; and

(5) by influencing decisions which cannot be attributed to their articulated rationales.

In fact, the actual role that considerations of moral principle play in contemporary adjudication fits my account of legitimate legal argument far better than most would claim—indeed, to my mind, far better than it fits the accounts of legal justification others have offered. Still, it is important to note that the damage that the relevant non-fits do to the candidacy of my jurisprudential position is at least somewhat reduced by my ability to account for the non-fits in question.

(iii) One Gap That Relates to the Extent to Which Explanations of Non-Fits of Any Given Degree of Persuasiveness Reduce the Damage the Non-Fits Do to the Relevant Candidate-Principle's Candidacy

Finally, I do not see how one can derive from the fact that our society is rights-based or from any other relevant social practice a non-arbitrary metric for measuring the damage-reduction that non-fit explanations of given persuasiveness accomplish.

Although I have filled in some of the gaps in the protocol this section began by sketching and hope that others may be able to fill in gaps I have been unable to eliminate non-arbitrarily, I fear that many of those gaps cannot be filled in non-arbitrarily. However, for three reasons, this pessimistic conclusion may not defeat my project of providing an account of legal justification that implies that there are internally-right answers to all moral-rights-related legal-rights questions in our culture (answers that can be ascertained *inter alia* by making arguments of moral principle). First, the way in which one fills in the relevant gaps may not affect the identity of the highest-ranked candidate for the basic moral principle title. Second, even if the existence of gaps that cannot be filled in non-arbitrarily prevents the identification of a uniquely-best candidate for basic moral principle, the various candidates that cannot be said to be worse than best may all yield the same answer to any moral-rights question. Third, even if the existence of gaps that cannot be filled in non-arbitrarily does render the internally-right answer to some moral-rights questions indeterminate, the legal system may contain conventions that yield internally-right answers to all legal-rights questions that relate to moral-rights questions whose answers are theoretically indeterminate.

(2) *The Substantive Liberal Basic Moral Principle: Some Elaborations and Comparisons*

This section elaborates on three expressions contained in my formulation of the substantive liberal basic moral principle that I think we are committed to use in rights discourse and then compares this principle with the other moral norms (actual and alleged personal ultimate values) to which many members of our culture individually adhere.

(A) AN ELABORATION OF THE SUBSTANTIVE BASIC MORAL PRINCIPLE

(i) The Boundary Condition

According to the basic moral principle, the set of moral-rights holders contains all creatures and only those creatures who have the neurological prerequisites to become and remain individuals of moral integrity. Negatively, this condition excludes from the class of moral-rights holders non-human animals, foetuses below a certain stage of development (say, thirty weeks),[14] "human beings" in irreversible comas, those severely-retarded human beings who do not have the neurological prerequisites to become and remain individuals of moral integrity, and perhaps humans whose incurable insanity precludes them from becoming or remaining individuals of moral integrity. Positively, this condition implies that the class of moral-rights holders includes foetuses above a certain stage of development (say, thirty weeks) and all other human children and adults who once possessed and have not lost the neurological prerequisites for becoming and remaining individuals of moral integrity (including those who are too young to be able to engage in moral discourse or who are asleep, unconscious, in reversible comas, or debilitated by a mental illness that renders them temporarily incapable of having moral integrity).

As previously indicated, I have used two criteria to evaluate the various possible boundary conditions for identifying moral-rights holders. The first is the "closeness-of-fit" criterion, which focuses on the consistency of the proposed boundary condition both with the conclusion I have reached about the substantive principle we are committed to using in rights discourse and with our consensus conclusions about the rights-bearing status of different sorts of creatures in different sorts of circumstances. The second is the "explicability-of-(non-fits)" criterion.

I believe that the boundary condition I have selected best fits both the basic substantive principle's emphasis on respecting creatures who have the potential to become and remain individuals of moral integrity and our social consensus on the rights-bearing status of different creatures. The strong connection between the boundary condition I have proposed and the substantive moral principle on which all moral-rights holders' rights are based should be obvious. The boundary condition just delineated also fits our social consensus about the rights-bearing status of most creatures in most situations. For example, it fits our conclusions that non-human animals and "humans" in irreversible comas are not moral-rights holders as well as our conclusions that non-adult humans (including newborns and small children) and humans that are asleep, unconscious, or in reversible comas are moral-rights holders. Admittedly, the basic moral principle's boundary condition appears to be inconsistent with the probable consensus that severely-retarded humans who do not have the neurological prerequisites to become and remain individuals of moral integrity are moral-rights holders and provides what would undoubtedly be a hotly-contested conclusion about the rights-bearing status of foetuses and, perhaps, some irreversibly but relevantly insane individuals and some social psychopaths as well. However, these apparent non-fits either can be shown not to deserve that characterization or can be explained in ways that make them less damaging to my boundary-condition conclusion.

In particular, I suspect that the view that the relevantly-handicapped have rights partly reflects

    (1) our conclusion that their parents and other relatives and friends have rights-related interests in their welfare,

    (2) our distrust of the State—our fear that the State may use any power it may otherwise have to treat such entities (and others it incorrectly assigns to their category) harshly in order to punish or discipline political opponents and to chill political opposition,

    (3) the contestable view that treating creatures that look like moral-rights holders in a way that would violate their rights if they were moral-rights holders will undermine our society's members' or the State's general commitment to rights, and

    (4) the personal-ultimate-value convictions of many that for non-instrumental reasons such creatures ought to be treated as if they were moral-rights holders.

Since all these accounts of what underlies the conclusions of many that the relevantly-handicapped should be treated as if they were moral-rights holders are consistent with my boundary-condition conclusion that such beings are not moral-rights holders, their hypothesized empirical importance reduces or eliminates the extent to which the consensus in question counts against my boundary-condition conclusion.

Similarly, I suspect that those who reject the implication of my boundary condition that foetuses under the age of, say, thirty weeks are not moral-rights holders also do so because they would oppose such foetuses' being treated in ways that their status would permit for reasons that do not presuppose our secular practices' implying that they are moral-rights holders. Thus, many of those who believe that foetuses under the age of thirty weeks are or should be treated as if they were moral-rights holders do so (1) out of religious conviction, (2) because they fear that rules that permit abortions of such foetuses in normal-pregnancy situations will undermine our rights-commitments in general, and/or (3) because for non-religious and non-instrumental reasons they think that foetuses under the age of thirty weeks ought to be protected. In the other direction, I suspect that those who reject the implication of my boundary condition that foetuses over the age of thirty weeks are entitled to all the protection that is owed moral-rights holders tend to do so because their personal-ultimate-value-related convictions make it difficult for them to accept a boundary condition that cuts against their conclusion that women have the right to make all choices related to the continuation or termination of their pregnancies. To the extent that the preceding explanations of these conclusions capture the conclusion-holders' views, their doing so reduces or eliminates the damage that the popularity of these views does to my boundary-condition hypothesis.

Finally, the damage done to my boundary-condition conclusion by the fact that many want to treat as moral-rights holders insane or psychopathic individuals who would not be assigned such a status by my boundary condition is reduced by the reasons that led them to their conclusion. More specifically, many if not most of those who disagree with my conclusion about the moral status of such entities do so for one or more of the following five reasons, all of which are consistent with my conclusion that such entities are not moral-rights holders—namely, because they

(1) incorrectly assume that the relevant individuals' incapacity is reversible,

(2) want to protect the rights-related interests of the friends and relatives of the parties in question,

(3) fear that the State will use any power to treat the relevantly insane in a way the State could not treat moral-rights holders to deter and punish political opponents,

(4) believe that the relevant decisions would undermine our commitment to securing the rights of moral-rights holders, and/or

(5) are committed to religious or personal-ultimate-value positions that lead them to conclude that the relevant individuals *ought* to be treated the same as moral-rights holders.

Of course, to make the case for the boundary condition I believe we are committed to implementing, it would be necessary to compare its performance with that of its most promising alternatives: all sentient creatures, all extra-utero members of the genus *Homo sapiens* who are alive and not brain-dead, all creatures that are capable of engaging in rights discourse, all entities that are extra-utero members of the genus *Homo sapiens*, or all creatures that will develop into such humans if "nature takes its course," and so on. I will confine my comments to the last.

An analyst who believes that this last boundary condition is more appropriate than the condition I have proposed might argue that since I am focusing on potentiality rather than actuality there is no justification for my denying rights-bearing status to creatures that clearly have the potential to develop the neurological prerequisites for becoming and remaining individuals of moral integrity—indeed, who will actualize that potential unless something untoward occurs. Although I could try to counter this argument in relation to first-trimester foetuses by pointing out the high percentage of early pregnancies that abort spontaneously, such a response would not be satisfactory: it would not save my position in relation to foetuses that have reached the stage of development at which spontaneous abortion is highly unlikely (say, thirteen weeks), and it might not save it at all since foetuses at earlier stages of development are still far more likely to develop the relevant neurological features than to die in a spontaneous abortion prior to their having done so. Hence, rather than trying to counter this critique with such a fact-dependent argument, I would rather do so in a conceptual way that is practice-related. Just as we recognize that an acorn is not an oak tree even when it has been buried in fertile, moist earth, the fact that a foetus that does not yet possess the neurological prerequisites for becoming and remaining an individual of moral integrity will develop them if nothing untoward happens does not make that foetus the moral equivalent of a creature that already possesses these prerequisites. And just as an individual who has dug up a buried acorn that would have developed into an oak tree if nothing untoward occurred would not be held to have violated an ordinance that prohibits the destruction of any oak tree, a person who has aborted a foetus that does not yet have but will develop the attributes that make a creature a moral-rights holder if nothing untoward occurs should not be held to have committed a homicide.

Supporters of the conclusion that our relevant practices imply that a foetus that does not have but will develop the neurological prerequisites for becoming and remaining an individual of moral integrity if nothing untoward occurs is a moral-rights holder might also try to justify their position by citing the principle of moral symmetry. According to this principle, if it is wrong to convert a creature of type A into a creature of type B, it is equally wrong to refuse to convert a creature of type B into a creature of type A (or to prevent a creature of type B from becoming a creature of type A). In the current context, the type-A creature is the foetus that has the neurological prerequisites to become and remain an individual of moral integrity and the type-B creature is the foetus that does not yet possess but will develop those features if nothing untoward occurs. According to the principle of moral symmetry, since I would agree that it is wrong to convert a type-A moral-rights-bearing foetus into a type-B foetus, I must also agree that it would be wrong to prevent a type-B foetus from becoming a type-A foetus (say, by aborting it). In my judgment, this argument is wrong for the same reason that the principle of moral symmetry is always wrong in this type of case—because it declares morally irrelevant the difference in the moral statuses of the creatures in question. Thus, it violates the rights of a type-A foetus to convert it into a type-B foetus because the type-A foetus is a moral-rights holder, but it does not violate the rights of a type-B foetus to prevent it from becoming a type-A foetus because the type-B foetus is not a moral-rights holder. For these reasons, I reject the argument that the boundary condition to which I think we are committed does not capture our practices as well as one that would accord moral-rights-bearing status to all creatures that will develop the neurological prerequisites for becoming and remaining individuals of moral integrity if nothing untoward occurs.

(ii) The Rights of Moral-Rights Holders

My conclusion is that in our rights-based culture all moral-rights holders must be treated with appropriate, equal respect and that appropriate, equal concern must be shown for their actualizing their potential to become and remain individuals of moral integrity. After analyzing the concept of "becoming and remaining an individual of moral integrity," this section examines in broad terms what the "appropriate, equal respect and concern" obligation entails.

(a) Becoming and Remaining a Person of Moral Integrity

To be a person of integrity, an individual must take her obligations seriously, make a meaningful personal-ultimate-value choice, and make meaningful other choices that make her life conform with her value choices. This statement implies, *inter alia*, that the liberal moral norm that I think our culture is committed to instantiating in its rights-and-obligations conduct reflects a high valuation of an "examined life." Someone who fulfills her obligations and behaves consistently with a conventional set of personal ultimate values without thought—simply out of conformity with authority, tradition, or custom—is not a person of moral integrity. However, I do not mean to imply that to be a person of moral integrity one must think through one's values before making any significant life-choices (any choice whose content will be affected by one's personal-ultimate-value choice). In practice, even the most cerebral of us tend to discover both our personal ultimate values and their connection to different aspects of our lives in the course of living our lives. My assumption is that we begin our responsible lives with more or less vague ideas about our values and how they are implicated by the various activities in which we engage. We then engage in work activities, non-working interpersonal relationships, and pleasure-seeking activities that are independent of the former two types of activities. Throughout our lives, we use our experiences to reconsider the various personal ultimate values we support, the mix of them we think it appropriate to pursue, and the extent to which each can and should be furthered by the various types of activities in which we engage—for example, the extent to which we value our work activities according to the benefits they generate for others, the monetary rewards they give us, the satisfaction they yield us by enabling us to develop or make use of our various talents and skills, the quality and quantity of the interpersonal relationships they involve, the esteem they enable us to enjoy, and so on. I therefore assume that experience and contemplation are interdependent in a well-considered, morally-serious life, not that one first decides what one values and then chooses a life that is consistent with the value-choices one has made.

I do not deny the contestability of the concept of "a person of moral integrity." Some might claim that in our culture an individual who consistently conforms his behavior to a given set of values prescribed by custom, tradition, or authority that he has never really questioned is considered to be a person of moral integrity. Others might claim that in our culture a person who has "meaningfully chosen" to follow custom, tradition, or authority unthinkingly in the future should in that future still be considered to be a person of moral integrity. I disagree.

Of course, I have not yet said much about what I mean by "meaningful choice." The kind of liberalism to which I think our culture is committed rejects both the premise that our choices are fully determined by our genetic endowments, socializations, and options and the premise that we make meaningful choices as unencumbered selves whose values and preferences are either self-generated or come from nowhere. Not only does liberalism recognize the importance of socialization and the empirical reality that many individuals positively value the benefits others receive, it takes full account of what I take to be the substantial extent to which our involvement in intimate relationships contributes to our discovering our personal ultimate values, talents, tastes, and dispositions. The liberal State I am envisaging is not inhabited by atomized creatures.

Still, the type of liberalism to which I think we are committed does assume that individuals can make meaningful choices in appropriate circumstances. For choices to be autonomous, the individual chooser must have significantly-different, potentially-valuable options available to him, must not be coerced by the State or by private parties, must have information about a reasonably-diverse subset of the options available to him and the intellectual ability to assess them reasonably, must have the self-respect and confidence needed to make such choices, and must choose what to do rather than succumbing to coercion or conforming to tradition, custom, or "non-coercive" authority.

I do not deny that this statement of the liberal concept of "meaningful choice" leaves much to be debated. For example, some would claim that the kind of family environment that is conducive to an individual's developing the self-respect that enables her to make meaningful choices inevitably socializes the individual into values that she cannot meaningfully be said to have chosen. What I do deny is that any statement of this length could eliminate or substantially reduce the need for such debate.

(b) Showing Appropriate, Equal Respect and Concern for All Moral-Rights Holders

A rights-based State that is liberal in my sense has a number of duties that derive from its obligation to show all moral-rights holders appropriate, equal respect—respect that is valuable both in itself and because our ability to make meaningful life-choices depends on our self-respect and our self-respect depends on the respect we receive from others.

In particular, a liberal rights-based State's duty to respect its moral-rights holders prohibits it from discriminating against them (in the pejorative sense of that word that Chapter 3 argues is appropriate in this context) and requires it[15] to take positive steps to educate its subjects not to discriminate against each other and to protect its subjects from discrimination in which the discriminators do not have a right to engage.[16] Moreover, a liberal rights-based State's duty to show appropriate, equal respect for its moral-rights holders also requires it to give each citizen who has the appropriate qualifications equal power in selecting government officials and determining general governmental outcomes (in some admittedly-hard-to-define and contestable sense of this expression). For similar reasons, a liberal State must also give its moral-rights holders an appropriate role in any decisional process in which the law is applied to one in a way that significantly affects one's welfare and to adopt decision procedures at both the law-making and the law-applying stages that decrease to an acceptable level the probability that a moral-rights holder's welfare will be reduced pointlessly or mistakenly. In addition, a liberal State's duty to respect moral-rights holders precludes it from adopting an official position on personal ultimate values or on what might be called proximate values (though this does not prohibit it from basing its decisions on some personal-ultimate-value preference since such a prohibition would limit a liberal State to making whimsical, random, or compromise decisions). Thus, a liberal State may not endorse one type of meaningfully-chosen life-choice over another if neither violates anyone's rights. (On the other hand, a State that is committed to valuing meaningful choice may be justified in prohibiting choices that preclude the chooser or someone else from making meaningful choices in the future.)

Further and relatedly, as Chapter 4 explores and illustrates, when liberty interests properly so-called conflict, a liberal State must give appropriate weight to the liberty interests in question and must not endorse one liberty over another in ways that imply the superiority of one conception of the first-order good over another. Finally, a liberal State's duty of respect also requires it to provide all the moral-rights holders for which it is responsible with appropriate, equal opportunities to make meaningful choices about what they value and how they want to lead their lives.

This last statement requires me to come closer to operationalizing a liberal State's duty to show appropriate, equal concern for all its moral-rights holders' actualizing their potential to become and remain individuals of moral integrity. At a minimum, this duty implies that a liberal State is obligated to guarantee that each of its subjects obtains the police protection, nutrition, clothing, shelter, and medical services she requires to survive (so long as the State can provide such resources without sacrificing more weighty rights-related interests of others and perhaps so long as the subject in question has not voluntarily created her need for such assistance). In addition, the principle implies that a liberal State is obligated to guarantee that each of its subjects receives any additional nutrition, shelter, clothing, and medical care that may critically affect whether she can actualize her potential to take her life morally seriously. At least arguably, individuals who are struggling to obtain the resources necessary for them or their loved ones to survive (e.g., who are starving or homeless) or individuals who can survive only by living a life of constant drudgery are not really in a position to make meaningful life-choices.[17] Furthermore, this duty of appropriate, equal concern implies that a liberal State is obligated to take appropriate steps to insure that each moral-rights holder has the kind of parental services, more general psychological support, and (in our materialist society) material resources (perhaps the relevant figure is the higher of some absolute minimum and some specified share of the average material income in our society) that favors a person's developing the kind of self-respect and self-confidence that contributes to his being able to make meaningful life-choices. In addition, this duty obligates a liberal State to provide each moral-rights holder with the formal knowledge, exposure to a variety of life-choices, intellectual skills, understanding of the value of being the author of one's own life, privacy, and opportunities to enter into, develop, and maintain intimate relationships that contribute to their participants' abilities to make meaningful life-choices. Finally, the duty also implies that a liberal State is obligated to combat the efforts of parents, friends, and others to coerce or unacceptably pressure individuals into making particular life-choices.

Admittedly, this still-relatively-abstract account of the more concrete implications of the basic moral principle to which I think our society is committed risks inducing many readers to dismiss as not only wrong but empirically absurd my claim to have derived the liberal basic moral principle just operationalized from social practice. How can one claim that a society in which the word "liberal" is a political epithet, an "L" word analogous to the dreaded "N" word, is in practice a liberal, rights-based society? My response is sixfold:

(1) the liberal principle best fits the horizontal rights claims that members of our society make against each other and the arguments that are made for and against these claims;

(2) the liberal principle lies behind the position of many significant post–Civil War political movements that citizens have positive moral rights to a wide variety of resources and opportunities, as well as the

position of many of these movements that constitutional democracies are obligated to secure these rights and/or that the contemporaneous United States Constitution guarantees these rights;[18]

(3) the liberal principle also lies behind the change in justice-consciousness that has taken place over the last 150 years—the tendency of our people to expect total justice, to assert their right to compensation for losses that they previously would have accepted as their human fate;[19]

(4) the liberal principle also lies behind the steady increase in the range of humans who are seen to be entitled to full rights;

(5) many if not most of those who reject the public-law implications of the liberal principles that underlie their horizontal-rights-claiming behaviors have a material stake in opposing these implications and the political power to make their opposition successful; and

(6) although non-fits clearly count against the candidacy of a moral norm for the "basic moral principle" title, even substantial non-fits are not decisive evidence against it: just as the fact that many American citizens supported slavery in the eighteenth and nineteenth centuries does not disprove the hypothesis that ours was a liberal rights-based society during those periods, the fact that many or even most Americans sometimes fail to grasp some important public-law or vertical-rights-claiming implications of the liberal principles that I claim underlie their horizontal-rights-claiming-and-assessing behaviors does not disprove the hypothesis that ours is a liberal society.

(B) A COMPARISON OF THE LIBERAL PRINCIPLE JUST ARTICULATED WITH A LIBERAL PRINCIPLE FOR WHICH OTHERS HAVE ARGUED

Liberals are committed to placing the same value on the successfulness of each moral-rights holder's life. Because this commitment has substantial implications for the distributions of income and wealth that are legitimate in a liberal State, the way in which liberalism is understood to measure the success of a moral-rights holder's life critically affects the obligations of a liberal State.

The liberal basic moral principle to which I think our society is committed assumes that liberalism measures the success of a moral-rights holder's[20] life by the extent to which he or she becomes and remains a person of moral integrity. To be a person of moral integrity, an individual must (1) take his moral obligations seriously and (2) lead a life that is consonant with (A) the non-obligational distributive norms he endorses and (B) the other values, ideals, and virtues he supports. For an individual's life to have integrity in these terms, he need not subject it to constant examination. Although I would like to think that self-examination promotes integrity, I know that it often does not, that some people "who just get on with living" lead lives of moral integrity, and that even from the perspective of moral integrity the lives of some individuals are ruined "by detailed planning and constant trial-balance assessments of progress."[21] I have already indicated that, *inter alia*, this liberal moral-integrity-oriented metric of a life's success implies, *inter alia*, that a liberal State must secure for each relevant moral-rights holder the minimum real income that is often a prerequisite to an individual's becoming and remaining a person of moral integrity (a minimum that may be the higher of an absolute amount and some specified share of the average income in the relevant society). However, it does not imply that each moral-rights holder be given the same amount of resources.

In this respect, the implications of this metric of a life's success differ from those of the most prominent alternative metric of a life's success supported by any liberal philosopher. In particular, at least some liberal philosophers such as Dworkin *seem* to assume that, for a liberal, a life's success depends on the extent to which the relevant individual has achieved the various diverse types of "goals" he has set for himself,[22] rather than by the extent to which the relevant individual has led a life of moral integrity in my sense of that expression.[23] If, as they suppose, liberals are committed to measuring the success of an individual's life by the extent to which he achieves the various goals he sets for himself, their premise that liberals are also committed to placing the same value on the success of the life of each moral-rights holder might lead them to conclude that liberalism obligates the State to provide each moral-rights holder with the same amount of resources.[24] At least, this conclusion might follow if they believed as well that in most cases it would be illiberal to provide one individual with more resources than another because, given their respective goals and abilities, the former required more resources to achieve the goals she set for herself to some relevant extent than the latter required to achieve the goals he set for himself to the same extent—that providing the former individual with more resources on this account would in most cases be to subjugate the latter to the former impermissibly. (The possible exception would be giving additional resources to relevantly-handicapped individuals.)

Three arguments favor my hypothesis that the basic moral principle we are committed to using in rights discourse adopts the moral-integrity-oriented metric for the successfulness of a life rather than its "individually-selected mixed bag of goals"-oriented alternative. The first and primary argument is that the moral-integrity-oriented metric better fits our relevant practices.

Two sets of practices seem relevant in this context. The first is both more general and more telling. Specifically, the fact that we engage in two kinds of prescriptive moral discourse and generally assume that the domain of rights is limited and leaves much territory open to the operation of personal ultimate values favors the integrity-oriented metric because, unlike its alternative, its implementation would not fully determine the legitimate distribution of income and wealth.

The second set of practices—those related to the income distribution—is more specific. It seems to me that the relevant State programs—welfare programs, Social Security, unemployment-insurance and disability-insurance programs, health-care subsidy and guarantee programs, and negative-income-tax proposals—have more to do with securing a minimum real income for each moral-rights holder than with giving each such creature equal resources. Indeed, even the current income-tax structure has more to do with securing minimum real incomes than with equalizing resources. Thus, our redistributive practices are also more compatible with the moral-integrity-oriented metric for a life's success than with the "achievement of an individually-selected mixed bag of goals"–oriented metric, which is assumed by its advocates to require resources to be equally distributed.

Of course, one could argue that our income-redistribution policies are inconsistent with our commitments. (Indeed, I would agree that they are.) But, at least in conjunction with the general structure of our prescriptive moral practices, the fact that the extant policies and proposals fit the implications of the moral-integrity-oriented metric better than those of the "achievement of an individually-selected mixed bag of goals"–oriented metric does seem to me to favor the conclusion that we are committed to a moral-integrity-oriented metric for the success of a human life.

The other argument that favors my conclusion about liberalism's metric for a life's success is that the metric I ascribe to liberalism is more operational than its "mixed bag of goals"–oriented alternative. You may think that the pot has just called the kettle black, but I do think that the "mixed bag of goals"–oriented principle cannot be operationalized without resolving a series of issues that are either difficult or impossible to settle. Among other issues, the relevant list would include:

(1) whether we are more responsible for our tastes or ambitions than for our talents;

(2) whether we are responsible for the costliness of satisfying our tastes and ambitions to the extent that the cost of doing so depends on the distribution of income and wealth in our society and the tastes of its members for the goods and services that could be produced with the resources we need to satisfy our preferences or fulfill our ambitions;

(3) whether we are responsible for the preferences of others that preclude us from gaining respect for doing what we want to do (or do we have no right to enjoy respect for what we do and hence no right to have our success in securing such respect count in the assessment of the "successfulness" of our lives); and

(4) if economic-efficiency considerations lead one to reject the conclusion that the principle that "an equal value must be assigned to any successful life or to any life well-lived" requires each moral-rights holder to be given the same amount of resources, how does distributive justice relate to the economic inefficiency associated with different distributions (*inter alia*, if one is concerned about the extent to which such inefficiency reduces "the total or average successfulness of the lives of all moral-rights holders," how does one measure variations in the success of any life or compare the changes in the successfulness of different lives that will be caused by economic-efficiency-enhancing, unequal distributions of resources)?

Third, the case for my conception of our basic liberal principle is strengthened by the fact that I can offer a persuasive account of the conceptual intellectual mistake that I think lies behind the error others have made when analyzing liberalism's metric of a life's successfulness. I believe that this mistake relates to the liberal tenet that, although a liberal State is obligated to make substantial efforts to induce those for whom it is responsible to fulfill their moral obligations, beyond the domain of rights it is illegitimate for a liberal State to tell these individuals what to value—what personal ultimate values to adopt and what personal goals to seek. Those who believe that liberalism measures the success of an individual's life by the extent to which he achieved the goals he set seem to think that this metric-conclusion is a corollary of the liberal tenet just articulated. They are wrong. Liberal societies are obligated to leave personal-ultimate-value and goal selection to each individual moral-rights holder for which they are responsible not because such societies value in itself allowing the individual to make her own value-choices but because they are committed to the position that what is most valuable is a creature's becoming and remaining an individual of moral integrity and realize that an individual cannot do so unless she can choose her personal ultimate values and goals for herself (in the only sense in which "choice" may be possible in this context). I believe that the metric-error I have described primarily reflects this mistake (though I admit that to some extent it also reflects some scholars' sloppiness in the usage of such terms as "goals" and "values").

I return to this issue of the appropriate conception of liberalism in section 3 of Chapter 2. There, I argue that an alternative to both my conception of liberalism and Dworkin's that is currently enjoying considerable support among academics also fails to capture our society's commitments. In particular, our society is not committed to "political liberalism" because this ideology fails to recognize our commitment to giving individuals the opportunity to become and remain individuals of moral integrity *inter alia* by making meaningful life-choices. Political liberals mistakenly assume that the fact that our State is committed to not endorsing any conception of the first-order good implies that our State is committed to endorsing no value at all whereas in reality the former commitment is a corollary of our State's commitment to the second-order good of autonomy in choosing one's values and conforming one's life to that choice.

(C) A COMPARISON OF THE LIBERAL BASIC MORAL PRINCIPLE JUST ARTICULATED WITH THE VARIOUS PERSONAL ULTIMATE VALUES TO WHICH MANY AMERICANS SUBSCRIBE

The liberal basic moral principle I have articulated also differs substantially from the various norms that many members of our society use either alone or in combination when making and evaluating moral-ought statements. Thus, the liberal moral norm differs from the classical and modern utilitarian norms, which respectively evaluate any claim (act) according to the effect of its recognition (commission) on (1) the total utility experienced by all entities whose utility counts and (2) the average utility experienced by all entities whose utility counts.[25] Although, like the liberal principle, these utilitarian norms can also be described as being egalitarian in that they treat all entities whose utility counts as equals by giving the same weight to each unit of utility (by not making the value of a unit of utility depend on the identity or history of the entity experiencing it), utilitarian norms differ from liberal norms in that they proceed from a different assumption about the attributes of an entity that cause it to be rights-bearing. In particular, utilitarian norms implicitly assume that the ability to experience utility is the relevant defining characteristic of an entity[26] while, as we saw, the liberal norm assumes that the potential to become and remain an individual of moral integrity is the relevant defining characteristic for this purpose.

The liberal moral norm also differs from both the equal-utility egalitarian norm and various non-liberal equal-opportunity egalitarian norms. According to the equal-utility egalitarian norm, the moral worthiness of a claim (or desirability of a choice) depends on the impact of its recognition on the equality of the utility experienced by each moral-rights holder. According to the various non-liberal equal-opportunity egalitarian norms, the worthiness of a claim (or choice) depends on its impact on the extent of the inequalities in the opportunities that different moral-rights holders have to do things other than become and remain individuals of moral integrity—for example, to develop certain mental or physical skills or to perform certain valued social roles.

Admittedly, both the equal-utility and various non-liberal equality-of-opportunity norms can be described as egalitarian because, as their very names suggest, they do treat individuals as equals in the sense of making the identity and, for that matter, the behavioral history of a recipient irrelevant to the evaluation of his or her experiencing utility or being given various opportunities. However, both these norms differ from the liberal norm in that they proceed on the assumption that the defining characteristics of an entity for these purposes is its potential to have "a successful life" in some sense other than becoming and remaining an individual of moral integrity. Supporters of the equal-utility norm measure a life's success by the utility the relevant entity experiences, while supporters of the non-liberal equal-opportunity norm assume that making good use of the particular type of opportunity they want to be equally available to all is a uniquely-valuable activity and measure the success of a life by the number and importance of the relevant opportunities of which the individual took advantage. I should add that supporters of equal-opportunity norms have not been very forthcoming about their reasons for valuing the opportunities on which they focus. In fact, some may value an individual's making good use of the relevant opportunity for reasons that do not relate in any sense to his or her "welfare"—namely, because they subscribe to an ideal that values an individual's making good use of the relevant opportunities in itself. Relatedly, I should admit that some equal-opportunity norms that strike me as non-liberal may actually be liberal (at least in intent)—that is, they may reflect their supporters' view that an individual's making good use of the opportunities in question plays an important role in his or her becoming an individual of moral integrity.

The liberal principle differs as well from the equality-of-resources norm, according to which a claim would be held valid (an act would be deemed moral) if and only if its recognition (commission) would increase the equality of the resources (measured in allocative-cost terms) available to each moral-rights holder. This equality-of-resources norm resembles the liberal principle not only in that it is egalitarian in the sense of rendering irrelevant the identity and the history of each moral-rights holder but also in the sense that it allows each individual to select his or her metric of success. However, the equality-of-resources norm also differs from the liberal principle in two respects: (1) in its focus on the individual's getting specific things that he values rather than on the individual's becoming and remaining a person of moral integrity (*inter alia*, choosing what he values), and (2) in its particular concern with the resource-constraint[27] (as opposed to the taste-of-the-community constraint)[28] on an individual's being successful in the terms in which the norm defines success.

Finally, the liberal moral norm differs from the various norms that different libertarians endorse. Libertarianism clearly differs from liberalism on distributive-justice issues and may differ from liberalism in other respects as well. In relation to distributive justice, libertarians believe that each moral-rights holder is entitled to keep or ought to be allowed to keep all the resources it obtained through behavior that did not directly violate anyone's rights—by earning them, finding them, getting them through luck in general, or receiving them as a gift or bequest.[29] I will first point out two ambiguities in the libertarian distributive-justice position and then contrast it with the liberal distributive-justice position.

The two ambiguities relate to the concept of what an individual has "earned." The first reflects the fact that although libertarians sometimes talk about the right to keep what one has "earned," their justifications for this supposed right focus on the right to keep what one has "produced" not for his employer but for the society—in economist terms, on the individual's allocative product rather than on his revenue product (his "product" for his employer). The question is: Do libertarians believe that individuals are entitled *inter alia* to their revenue products or their allocative products? The second ambiguity arises regardless of whether the relevant referent is "product for employer" or "allocative product." The libertarian must decide whether each individual is entitled to the dollar-value produced by the last equally-industrious and equally-skilled worker to do his type of work (the marginal product of this class of workers) or to the same proportion of the average product of all equally-industrious and equally-skilled workers to do his type of work.[30]

Regardless of the way in which these two ambiguities are resolved, the libertarian position on distributive justice will differ from its liberal counterpart in that libertarianism will reject the liberal conclusion that each moral-rights holder has a right to the resources it requires to become and remain a creature of moral integrity even if the only way to secure the relevant resources for a moral-rights holder is by transfer from others who obtained them without directly violating anyone's rights. This liberal position clearly has implications for the duties of a liberal State and may have implications for the duties of an individual in such a State when the State fails to fulfill its distributive-justice obligations or cannot secure the relevant resources for a moral-rights holder without sacrificing weightier rights-related interests.

Libertarianism may also differ from liberalism in relation to other choices that individuals may make, given the material resources at their disposal. Thus, I am not sure about the implications of libertarianism for the right of an individual to indulge his prejudices in different contexts or for the right of one individual (say, a parent) to constrain the information available to another individual (say, a child). Does libertarianism entail a duty of respect for all moral-rights holders? If so, does libertarianism imply that this duty of respect is violated by private choices that reduce the ability of a moral-rights holder to become an individual of moral integrity—to make well-informed choices on what he values and how he wants to lead his life? I am not sure, though the libertarians' failure to articulate the attributes of a creature that make it full-rights-bearing or an object of moral concern make me doubtful.

Admittedly, libertarian values resemble the liberal basic moral principle I have articulated in two respects. First, like that liberal principle, the various libertarian values might be described as being egalitarian in that they do make an individual's identity (though not his or any relevant donor's or testator's history) irrelevant to the assessment of the moral desirability of the individual's receiving any given amount of resources. Second, like the liberal moral principle I have articulated but unlike the total-utility, average-utility, equal-utility, and non-liberal equal-opportunity values, libertarian values assign to the rights-bearer the task of choosing what is valuable for her. However, to repeat, libertarianism clearly differs from the liberal principle on which I believe our society is committed to basing its moral-rights discourse in that it is indifferent to whether the creatures it deems moral-rights holders become and remain persons of moral integrity. Moreover, libertarianism may also differ from the liberal basic moral principle in its implications for the duty to respect others as well as in its understanding of what any such duty might entail.

So far, I have implicitly assumed that libertarianism deserves to be called a personal ultimate value. In fact, I do not think this is the case. Libertarianism seems to proceed on the premise that individuals (1) ought to be given or are entitled to receive the value of their own product and (2) ought to be allowed to dispose of or are entitled to dispose of what they receive in any way that does not directly violate anyone's rights. The first part of this premise lies behind the contention that people ought to be paid (or are entitled to be paid) according to what they produce; the second part lies behind the contention that individuals ought to be allowed to (or are entitled to) keep whatever they receive through gift or bequest, a conclusion that allegedly derives from the rights of the donor or testator. (Admittedly, why people are entitled to keep what they obtained though luck remains obscure to me.) However, for this two-part premise to have any moral appeal that is independent of the dubious notion that it is wrong to take something from someone who has obtained it without directly violating anyone's rights, individuals must be responsible for what they produce—that is, each individual's product must entirely or overwhelmingly reflect choices for which he deserves credit. In my admittedly-armchair empirical judgment, this condition is clearly not fulfilled. Interpersonal productivity differences primarily reflect factors over which the individuals in question had no control: their genetic endowments; the nutrition that their mothers obtained when the individuals were in utero; other aspects of their mothers' conduct during pregnancy; the quality of the parenting, nutrition, shelter, clothing, medical services, schooling, more extended family relations, and neighborhood environment they received or experienced during their childhoods; fortuities of accidents and illness; the supply curve of complementary inputs to their own labor efforts; and perhaps the tastes of people in their community and the distribution of income and wealth in the society in which they live, which jointly determine the effective demand for (the monetary value of) their labor. Clearly, if most interpersonal differences in productivity reflect factors over which the relevant individuals have no control, the distributive-justice premise of all variants of libertarianism would have little or no moral appeal (even to people who believe that individuals ought to be given what they are morally responsible for producing).

★

I have devoted so much space to describing and exemplifying the differences between the liberal value I denominate our basic moral principle and the various other values I denominate personal ultimate values because this distinction is critical to my account of legitimate legal argument in our culture. Thus, on my account, the basic moral principle and its more concrete corollaries are generically part of the law—indeed, arguments of moral principle are the dominant mode of legitimate legal argument in our culture—while each personal ultimate value is part of the law only when the legal issue under consideration relates to the interpretation of a statute or Constitutional provision that was designed to effectuate the value in question, only when for this reason ambiguous or open-textured statutory or Constitutional language should be interpreted in the way that effectuates the value that the statute or Constitutional provision in question was designed to promote.

2. Legitimate Legal Argument in Our Liberal Rights-Based Culture

My account of legitimate legal argument in our culture is based on two premises: (1) that ours is a rights-based culture and (2) that in such a culture legal argument can be legitimate only if it is consistent with the relevant society's moral commitments.[31] These premises imply that courts in rights-based cultures are obligated to make arguments of moral principle the dominant mode of legal-interpretation argument. This section explains what I mean by "arguments of moral principle," defines and gives various examples of the six modes of legal argument that lawyers make and judges sometimes heed in our culture,[32] operationalizes and illustrates my claim that arguments of moral principle are the dominant mode of legal argument in our rights-based culture, examines the relationship between the various types of legitimate legal argument in our culture and the internally-right answer to the legal-interpretation questions they are relevant to resolving, and explains why if my account of legitimate legal argument is correct there will probably be internally-right answers to all or virtually all questions about what the law is.

A. The Nature of Arguments of Moral Principle

Arguments of moral principle focus on the rights-related interests of the parties that an individual or State choice will affect—that is, on the effect of the relevant choices on the interest that such creatures have in actualizing their potential to become and remain individuals of moral integrity and, more generally, in being treated with the respect that is due all those who have the neurological prerequisites to become and remain individuals of moral integrity. Because State attempts to enforce moral rights will affect rights-related interests in ways that they would not be affected by the voluntary choices of individuals to fulfill their moral obligations, the moral-principle argument about whether a liberal rights-based State has an obligation to enforce a particular moral right will often be somewhat different from the moral-principle argument about whether the relevant individual has the moral right in question. Finally, moral-principle arguments about both individual rights and the obligations of a rights-based State to enforce the individual's moral rights involve the balancing of rights-related interests.

At this juncture, three additional points need to be made about arguments of moral principle. First, the kind of balancing that such arguments involve—balancing the net effect of the choice under review on the rights-related interests of all moral-rights holders whose rights-related interests that choice affects—is very different from the kinds of utilitarian or other non-rights-related-interest balancing of effects that has been discussed in the Constitutional-law literature.

Second, with one possible recent exception, the "balancing of net effects on rights-related interests" approach is different from the various doctrinal tests of Constitutionality the Supreme Court has promulgated: the ordinary-scrutiny test (Is the State choice rationally related to the achievement of a legitimate State goal?); the intermediate-scrutiny test (Is the State choice substantially related to the achievement of an important State goal?); and the strict-scrutiny test (Is the State choice necessary and narrowly-tailored to the achievement of a compelling State goal?). The recent possible exception is the "undue burden" test that Justice Sandra Day O'Connor used in the joint opinion issued by the Court in *Planned Parenthood of Southeastern Pennsylvania v. Casey*[33] to assess the Constitutionality of a state regulation that made it more difficult for a pregnant woman to obtain an abortion prior to the foetus's viability. On the one hand, O'Connor's verbal formulation favors the conclusion that she has adopted a "balancing of rights-related interest" approach: linguistically, one would expect that under an "undue burden" approach the burden a State regulation is found to impose on a pregnant woman's obtaining an abortion would be said to be "undue" only if the associated rights-related interests of the woman the regulation sacrificed were more weighty than the net rights-related interests it secured for all other moral-rights holders. On the other hand, O'Connor's operationalization of her "undue burden" test in *Casey*—under which any state regulation that creates a "substantial obstacle" to a pregnant woman's obtaining an abortion prior to the foetus's viability would be deemed to create an "undue burden"—disfavors the conclusion that she is proposing a balancing-of-rights-related-interests approach since the conclusions her operationalization generates clearly fail to reflect the balance of the relevant parties' rights-related interests. In part, O'Connor's operationalization reflects the fact that she refuses to face up to the issue of when the foetus becomes a moral-rights holder: rather than considering the foetus's possible rights-related interests, she simply asserts that the State has an interest in the "potential life" of the foetus only after viability and assumes that this State "interest" can legitimate the states' restricting a woman's abortion-choices. However, primarily, it reflects two other facts:

(1) in most cases, prior to the foetus's becoming a moral-rights holder (in my judgment, to its developing, prior to viability, the neurological prerequisites to become an individual of moral integrity), regulations that cannot be said to impose a substantial obstacle to abortion should still be held to create an undue burden on a woman's obtaining an abortion; and

(2) after the foetus becomes a moral-rights holder, the State almost certainly has an obligation to take more steps to prevent the foetus's abortion in most cases than merely creating a substantial obstacle to its mother's securing an abortion.

The third point is that in most instances the arguments of moral principle that courts do or should use to analyze actual cases will not make direct reference to the basic moral principle or the abstract interests to which it refers—the interest of all moral-rights holders in being shown appropriate, equal respect and concern. Instead, the arguments of moral principle that are used in actual cases will tend to focus on interests of intermediate abstraction that can be derived from the basic moral principle and the abstract interests to which it refers. These interests of intermediate abstraction include (somewhat-overlapping) interests in

(1) the various resources and experiences (e.g., traditional educational experiences and other sorts of nurturing experiences) that significantly affect the likelihood that a child will develop the kind of self-

respect, obtain the kinds of information, and develop the intellectual skills and emotional capacity to actualize its potential to become and remain a person of moral integrity,

(2) the various types of resources, employment opportunities, information, and intellectual training that relate to an adult's survival, self-respect, and opportunity and ability to make meaningful moral choices,

(3) privacy,

(4) freedom of conscience, religion, association, and expression,

(5) autonomy in general,

(6) bodily integrity and security,

(7) having your rights against private parties enforced by the State,

(8) not having the State disappoint the reasonable legal-rights expectations it created,

(9) not being discriminated against by the State,

(10) not suffering losses from legislative, administrative, civil-law, or criminal-law decisions made through processes that did not provide sufficient quality-control,

(11) political participation, valued for its own sake, and

(12) participation in administrative and judicial processes that affect one's welfare, valued for its own sake.

These interests of intermediate abstraction and others that are similarly concrete will be the interests that are explicitly considered in deciding actual cases involving liberty issues, abortion issues, issues of privacy properly so-called, equal-protection issues, political-participation issues, and positive-rights issues of all other kinds. I should emphasize, however, that the fact that the relevant analyses focus explicitly on these more concrete interests does not imply that the more abstract interests to which the basic moral principle refers can be ignored: one will have to make reference to the more abstract interests to which the basic moral principle refers and from which these intermediately-abstract interests derive in all cases whose correct resolution turns on the characterization, operationalization, and/or weighting of these intermediately-abstract interests. I should also emphasize that the preceding list reveals the fact that my jurisprudential position is not conservative (does not disfavor change by implying that all State choices or practices are self-legitimating): indeed, our State falls sufficiently short of fulfilling its liberal obligations for my position to imply that it is obligated to change its conduct in many substantial ways.

B. The Six Modes of Legal Argument Actually Employed in Our
Legal Culture

This section defines and exemplifies the six general modes of argument
used to discover the law in our legal culture and the various sub-types of
these modes that seem most notable to me. Because my greatest doctrinal expertise is in Constitutional law, all the examples are drawn from this field.
However, counterparts for all or virtually all the types of arguments listed can
be found in other doctrinal fields.

(1) Arguments of Moral Principle

Arguments of moral principle are arguments that articulate and examine
the implications of the basic moral principle that we are committed to using
in rights discourse and the more concrete corollaries of that principle. As I
have already indicated, and as the next section discusses in some detail, arguments of moral principle operate not only directly but also indirectly to determine the legitimacy and significance of the other types of arguments that
have been made in Constitutional cases.

(2) Textual Arguments

The starting point of any textual analysis is the ordinary meaning of the
words in the text at the time that they were written. In addition, the appropriate interpretation of a text will sometimes be influenced by the nature of
the document that contains the text in question. For example, as Chief Justice John Marshall said in *McCullough v. Maryland,* "we must never forget, that
it is *a constitution* we are expounding."[34] On occasion, the meaning of a text
will also be influenced by certain organizational features of the document—
for example, whether the specific text in question is in a power-granting
section of the Constitution or a section that delineates prohibitions or limitations on powers. Moreover, in some cases, the meaning of the text of one
provision will be influenced by the content of other provisions in the document:

(1) the specificity of the other provisions dealing with the subject-matter
in question;
(2) the substance of analogous provisions of the text that bear on how
broadly an individual provision should be interpreted—as in James

Madison's argument that the fact that the granting of a "power to declare war" did not obviate the explicit granting of a power "to raise and support armies" or "to make rules and regulations for the governmental armies" implies that the granting of powers to "borrow money" and to "lay and collect taxes" does not imply the power to charter a bank whose operation would facilitate their exercise;[35]

(3) the way in which other provisions of the text have struck the balance between various groups or values the text to be interpreted also implicates; and

(4) the presence of other provisions in the document that would be rendered redundant or would be undercut if the provision in question were interpreted in a particular way.[36]

Two other kinds of textual materials will also sometimes be relevant to legal interpretation. In some cases, the appropriate interpretation of a text will be influenced by the substance of textual alternatives that were rejected in its favor. And finally, in some cases, the appropriate interpretation of a text will be influenced by textual arguments that relate to the substance of the texts of the documentary antecedents of or successors to the document that is relevant to the case at issue—for example, the appropriate interpretation of the Constitution's text will be influenced by the text of the Declaration of Independence or the Articles of Confederation.

(3) Historical Arguments

I label historical those arguments that focus on various "historical" facts. Thus, as we have seen, in some cases the appropriate interpretation of a text will depend on the historical meaning of the words it contains at the time they were written. In other cases, historical evidence about the "intent" of a text's framers and ratifiers—their specific expectations about the way in which it would or should be interpreted or applied—will be relevant to its appropriate interpretation. More specifically, interpreters may on this account appropriately consider such "intent evidence" as

(1) the drafters' and ratifiers' contemporaneous or subsequent statements;

(2) the general ways in which courts interpreted texts at the time at which a text was adopted or the way in which it was expected that courts would come to interpret such texts; and/or

(3) related decisions that the drafters, ratifiers, or various relevant governments made before or just after the text in question was adopted—for example, the legislative decisions made by the First Congress or the decisions made by various state legislatures about the legality of homosexuality or abortion at the time at which the Fourteenth Amendment was adopted.

Relatedly, the appropriate interpretation of a Constitutional text may also be influenced by evidence that reveals the "intent" of the Constitution's framers and ratifiers about the weight that would be given to their "intent" in the "specific expectation" sense. As we have already seen, in some cases, textual interpretation may also be properly influenced by historical evidence about either or both the rejected alternatives to the text that was adopted and/or the texts of the documentary antecedents of or successors to a particular text. Moreover, in some cases, the appropriate interpretation of a text may be influenced by evidence about the historical events that led to the provision's inclusion. For example, the fact that the "interstate commerce" clause was included in the Constitution to preclude the problems that decentralized decisionmaking had caused under the Articles of Confederation clearly bears on the proper interpretation of the "interstate commerce" clause. The fact that the "obligation of contracts" clause was a response to the perceived problems that "debtor relief" statutes caused under the Articles of Confederation clearly is relevant to the proper interpretation of the "obligation of contracts" clause. Finally, in cases that require moral language to be interpreted, interpretation will be influenced by all the kinds of evidence that I argued is relevant to the moral characterization of our society and the identification of the moral norms we are committed to effectuating.

(4) Structural Arguments

Structural arguments focus on the ends that our polity is designed to secure and the various institutional and substantive-rights provisions of the Constitution that are designed, *inter alia*, to increase the likelihood that our State will strive to secure those ends. In our society, the government is supposed to help its subjects become and remain individuals of moral integrity. Positively, this claim implies that the State must protect the rights of its subjects. Negatively, it implies *inter alia* that the State may not choose the personal ultimate values its citizens and other subjects should pursue—that is, it may not impose a particular view of the good life on its subjects.

Various Constitutional provisions are designed *inter alia* to increase the likelihood that our State will conform to these injunctions. The first is the fact that the central government has only those powers that the Constitution grants to it —a fact manifest in Article I's enumeration of the powers of Congress and Amendment X. The second is the related fact that the Constitution creates a federal system of government in which all powers not granted to the central government are reserved to the states or to the people. The third is the fact that the central government is divided into three branches that are (*inter alia*) supposed to check each other. The fourth is the fact that the Press Clause of the First Amendment is designed (*inter alia*) to protect a private institution that performs a useful checking function on government. And the fifth is the fact that the Second Amendment (the right to "keep and bear arms") was designed (*inter alia*) to check the development of a tyrannous government. In my terminology, structural arguments are arguments that link the interpretation of these Constitutional provisions to the metric for evaluating our State's performance.[37]

(5) Arguments from Judicial Precedent or Practice

Arguments in this category focus on the conclusions or holdings of previous cases, the doctrines announced in previous cases, and the practices of interpretation courts have employed. In this latter category, I include such practices as the presumption that "ordinary meaning" controls, the practice of not interpreting contracts in a way that renders the agreement clearly *ex ante* disadvantageous to one or more of the contracting parties, and the practice of interpreting in favor of the government ambiguous language in a government contract that might limit the government's power.

(6) Prudential Arguments

Five different types of argument have been or might be labeled "prudentialist"—namely, arguments that focus on

(1) the possible social-goal-related consequences of the government choice under review;

(2) the possibility that what would at least otherwise be the internally-right legal decision might not be obeyed by the population to which it would be addressed;

(3) the possibility that what would at least otherwise be the internally-right legal decision might not be enforced by the relevant enforcement-officials,[38] including lower-court judges;

(4) the possibility that the announcement of what would at least otherwise be the internally-right legal decision might generate a more general set of moral-rights and legal-rights violations (a more general kind of lawlessness) directly because some or many citizens and residents are not ready to accept the internally-right answer to the relevant legal-rights question and would react lawlessly to its announcement; and

(5) the possibility that what would at least otherwise be the internally-right legal decision might generate a political backlash that would endanger or weaken the federal courts—a possibility that might concern the judges because they have a personal stake in the courts' prestige and/or because they fear that any weakening of the courts' position will increase the extent to which moral rights are violated.

C. The Claim That Arguments of Moral Principle Are the Dominant Mode of Legal Argument in Our Culture: The Indirect Roles of Arguments of Moral Principle

In our liberal rights-based culture, arguments of moral principle are dominant[39] in that they are supposed to operate not only directly but also indirectly in three interrelated ways. First, they control the legitimacy of the other kinds of arguments that are sometimes made in adjudicative contexts and heeded by courts; second, they determine the variant(s) of the various legitimate general types of legal argument it is legitimate to use; and, third, they control the force of those variants of the various legitimate types of legal argument that it is legitimate to use to determine what the law is. I will now elaborate on these three indirect roles of arguments of moral principle.

(1) Determining the Legitimacy of Arguments That Lawyers Sometimes Use and Judges Sometimes Heed When Analyzing What the Law Is: The Illegitimacy of Most Types of Prudential Arguments

In a rights-based culture, legal practice is not self-legitimating—that is, the fact that lawyers have made and courts have heeded particular arguments does not *ipso facto* make their use and acceptance legitimate. More positively, in a rights-based culture such as ours, a legal practice is legitimate if and only if it is consistent with the moral principles we are committed to using in rights discourse. For present purposes, the importance of this conclusion is its implication that arguments of moral principle determine the legitimacy of legal practices. Although proper versions of textual, historical, structural, practice and precedential, and prudential arguments are all legitimate—that is, consistent with the basic moral principle we are committed to using in moral-rights discourse, considerations of moral principle imply that most of the various types of prudential argument to which courts have actually given weight are illegitimate.

One kind of prudential argument is legitimate—namely, arguments that focus on the tendency of a choice under review to promote a legitimate social goal. Such arguments are relevant to the Constitutionality of most State choices because (1) the fact that a choice does promote a legitimate social goal (or *a fortiori* is consistent with a legitimate personal ultimate value) is relevant to the chooser's motivation and (2) motivation is relevant to Constitutionality. This second premise reflects the fact that a State choice is unconstitutional if it insults its victims because it manifests its supporters' view that for illegitimate reasons its victims' welfare is inherently of less concern than its beneficiaries', it manifests its supporters' desire to inflict harm on its victims, it is motivated solely by illegitimate goals (whose pursuit fails to show its victims the respect that is their due), or it injures its victims carelessly for no purpose whatsoever.

However, our moral-principle commitments make it illegitimate for any of the other four types of prudential argument listed above to be given weight in arguments about what the law is. These last four types of prudential argument differ from the first in that they purport to be based on the prediction that the decision that would at least otherwise be internal-to-law correct would not secure rights-related interests either at all (because the decision would not be obeyed or enforced) or on balance (because it would lead to independent rights-violating sacrifices of [net] rights-related interests). My conclusion that these types of prudential argument are nevertheless illegitimate reflects an argument of moral principle—namely, that a society that is committed to the liberal basic moral principle is obligated to devote the resources and effort necessary to achieve obedience to law by both its citizens and its enforcement officials, that such a society cannot justicize either making what would otherwise be internally-wrong enforcement decisions or avoiding decisions on the merits by its inability to secure obedience to law.

I realize that my rejection of these types of prudential argument as un-principled appears inconsistent with my conclusion that it is legitimate for a rights-based State to make choices in certain emergency situations that would in normal times violate someone's rights if the choices in question would prevent the greater violation of rights that would otherwise be pre-dicted on the weighted average to result from the possible replacement of the rights-based State in question with either a non-rights-based State or a rights-based State that was likely to be less successful at protecting or secur-ing the rights of those for whom it was responsible. Still, it seems to me that outside the relevant type of civil-war or foreign-war situations, a principled society must devote the resources and effort necessary to secure obedience to law by both its citizens and its judges and enforcement officials and can-not justicize announcing what would otherwise be internally-wrong deci-sions or avoiding decisions on the merits[40] by its inability to secure obedi-ence to law.

Three considerations reconcile my position on the possible legitimacy of exercising emergency powers in ways that would in other circumstances violate rights with my claim that the last four types of prudential argument listed above are illegitimate. First, the emergency arguments I am willing to call legitimate all claim that the choices in question will protect rights-re-lated interests on balance whereas in practice the last four types of pru-dential argument listed above do not involve such a calculation. Second, in the kinds of situation in which the last four types of prudential argument are made, the State is more likely to have (I am tempted to say "almost cer-tainly has") superior ways to prevent the feared disobedience to law (ways to prevent such disobedience that secure more weighty rights-related in-terests on balance than the proposed internal-to-law incorrect legal deci-sions being advocated) whereas no such superior alternatives may be avail-able in the relevant emergency situations. And third and perhaps most im-portantly, in the situations in which the last four types of prudential argument are being made, the judges are assessing the legitimacy of their own behavior (are judging their own case, so to speak) in a situation in which they may have crass personal stakes in the outcome, whereas in the emergency situation the relevant State choices are being made by non-judges and assessed by judges who not only are disposed to protect rights by their professional training but have a career stake in maintaining judicial control over executive and legislative decisions. In any event, in my judg-ment, with the one very partial exception that this analysis initially considered, arguments of moral principle reveal that the practice of giving weight to prudential arguments is illegitimate.[41]

(2) Determining the Variant of a Legitimate General Type of Argument That It Is Legitimate to Use When Analyzing What the Law Is

Arguments of moral principle are also dominant in that they influence or control the variants of the various types of legitimate legal argument that it is legitimate to use to determine what the law is. I will now elaborate on these claims in relation to each of the other five general types of legitimate legal argument.

(A) TEXTUAL ARGUMENT

Arguments of moral principle control legitimate textual argument most obviously when the text in question contains ambiguous, vague, or open-textured moral language. The Constitution of the United States contains many examples of such language. At the extreme, there is the Ninth Amendment's reference to "[un]enumerated" "rights . . . retained by the people," the Tenth Amendment's reference to "powers . . . reserved to the states respectively, or to the people," and the Fourteenth Amendment's reference to "the privileges or immunities of citizens of the United States." However, the Constitution also contains many other provisions that are almost equally open-textured: for example,

(1) the First Amendment's references to laws "respecting an establishment of religion, or prohibiting the free exercise thereof," "the freedom of speech, or of the press," and "the right . . . peaceably to assemble";

(2) the Second Amendment's reference to "the right . . . to keep and bear arms";

(3) the Fourth Amendment's reference to "the right to be secure against unreasonable searches and seizures";

(4) the Eighth Amendment's prohibition of "cruel and unusual punishments"; and

(5) the Fourteenth Amendment's guarantee of "equal protection of the laws."

Arguments of moral principle (or my account of our culture's moral identity) imply that all such language should be interpreted to refer to the basic moral principle I believe we are committed to using in rights-discourse, the more concrete corollaries of that principle, or the Constitutional-rights conclusions to which that principle would lead. This conclusion is not banal or unimportant. It implies, for example, that it is not appropriate to make arguments from such texts that rely exclusively on the dictionary meanings of the words they contain. More ambitiously, it implies that, at least in principle, judges can interpret the vague or open-textured moral language the Constitution contains without imposing their own personal ultimate values—that the Constitutional texts in question point to moral principles that can be objectively inferred from our culture's rights-and-obligations practices.

(B) HISTORICAL ARGUMENT

Our moral practices also control the variants of historical argument that it is legitimate to use when analyzing what the law is. Two points are relevant in this context. First, arguments of moral principle control the content of historical arguments that try to establish what the law is by inference from historical evidence about the events that led to the adoption of a particular Constitutional text. More specifically, the fact that the basic moral principle to which we are committed is an abstract principle that has broad implications implies that the events that led to the passage of a Constitutional or statutory provision should be interpreted broadly when used to illuminate its meaning. For example, arguments of moral principle imply that when using the events that led to the adoption of the Reconstruction Amendments to interpret their texts one should not characterize these events narrowly to be "the enslavement of some individuals of African descent" but should characterize them more broadly to be "State and private acts that failed to manifest appropriate respect and concern for some moral-rights holders by depriving them of their freedom." Similarly, when using the events that led to the adoption of Article I's prohibition of state laws "impairing" the "obligations of contracts" to interpret this provision, one should not define these events narrowly to be state-passed "debtor-relief" statutes but more broadly to be "state decisions that fail to show the respect moral-rights holders are owed by failing to enforce their contractual rights."

Second, arguments of moral principle (or more precisely an understanding of the appropriate way to determine the principles on which we are committed to basing our moral-rights discourse) also determine the kinds of historical evidence one should ideally use to establish the meaning of any moral language the law contains. This point has both positive and negative implications.

Positively, it suggests that to be complete a historical argument of this type should be based on all facts of all the types listed in the protocol for identifying our basic moral principle and its more concrete corollaries. Negatively, the point has two major implications. The first is that although the "intent" of a relevant Constitutional or statutory provision's ratifiers (and framers)—their expectations about the way in which the relevant provision would be interpreted—is relevant to the provision's interpretation (since it indicates these individuals' understanding of the moral concepts in question and their understanding is relevant to an assessment of the society's understanding), it is not decisive (since their understanding may diverge from the interpretation of the concept to which the protocol implies our society is committed—a protocol that reflects a wide range of choices and comments made primarily by non-ratifiers though including those made by ratifiers).

I should perhaps point out that the preceding conclusion is clearly manifest in our analogous social practices. When Polonius instructs Laertes "to thine own self be true," he does not expect Laertes to be bound by Polonius's own understanding of Laertes's essential nature or Polonius's conception of the meaning of "being true to yourself." He is instructing Laertes to decide these issues for himself in a serious, responsible way. Given this fact of general social practice, it would be surprising if the ratifiers of a Constitutional provision or amendment whose implications are highly fact-dependent would expect its interpreters to be bound by the ratifiers' conception of the concepts it contains or the ratifiers' expectations about the way in which it would be applied to particular cases. Historical research has revealed that the specific intent of our Founding Fathers was that the interpreters of the Constitution would not be bound by the Founding Fathers' specific expectations about the way in which any Constitutional text would be interpreted.[42] However, even if we did not possess the relevant historical information, our understanding of the practice of giving open-textured moral instructions that are supposed to apply over an extended period of time would lead us to conclude that our Constitution's ratifiers' "specific intent" should not bind its interpreters.

The second negative implication that my protocol for identifying a rights-based society's basic moral principle has for historical argument relates to the argument that Constitutional or statutory texts should be interpreted in specific cases to be consistent with the decisions that other governmental institutions made in relation to the specific type of conduct those cases involve at the time at which the provisions in question were drafted and passed.

In particular, my protocol implies that this argument is wrong in three respects:

(1) the historical analysis should not be restricted to government decisions but should consider all relevant private choices as well;

(2) the historical analysis should focus on all relevant state and private choices throughout the history of the Republic—should consider prior and subsequent choices and not just those choices that were contemporaneous to the adoption of the provision to be interpreted; and

(3) the historical analysis should focus on all choices that relate to the values the behavior in question implicates and not just on all choices that relate to the specific type of conduct involved in the case in question.

Thus, when deciding whether laws that disadvantage homosexuals violate the Fourteenth Amendment's "equal protection" clause, we should not restrict our historical research to determining the percentage of states that had criminalized homosexuality or disadvantaged homosexuals in 1868. Rather, we should cast our historical net more broadly to include all private and State practices toward sexual conduct in general, toward intimate relationships that lead to self-discovery, toward behaviors or institutions that promote such intimate relationships, and toward the exercise of autonomy in general not just for the time at which the relevant provision was ratified but throughout the history of the Republic. To repeat: this conclusion is a corollary of the positive conclusion that the set of historical arguments that are legitimate to use when interpreting the law includes all the "moral anthropological" research that is relevant to the identification of the basic moral principle we are committed to using in moral-rights discourse.

(c) STRUCTURAL ARGUMENTS

Arguments of moral principle—actually, the defining characteristics of our society as a moral entity that account for the type of arguments that we use in rights discourse—also reveal the various features of our governmental system on which structural arguments focus. In so doing, they reveal when and how such structural arguments should be used. Admittedly, our federal system of government partially reflects the fact that the states preceded the central government—indeed, were the source of the central government's[43] limited powers.[44] However, federalism and all the other structural features previously listed were also designed to increase the probability that our government would conduct its affairs in a way that is consistent with our being a liberal rights-based society. Thus, all the relevant structures were created (1) to emphasize the fact that it is not legitimate for the central government of the United States to tell its subjects how to lead their lives when the relevant individual choices are not required or prohibited by our rights-commitments and/or (2) to reduce the probability that our government (in the last part of the eighteenth century, most importantly, our central government) would violate our rights. The fact that the basic structures of our governmental system (balance of powers, federalism, the Press Clause, the right to bear arms, etc.) were designed *inter alia* to secure our rights affects the way in which various provisions of the Constitution should be interpreted. I will illustrate this point by analyzing the proper way to interpret the "interstate commerce" clause and the Second Amendment (the right to keep and bear arms).

The fact that the Constitution's framers and ratifiers created a federal system of government *inter alia* to reduce the likelihood that the government they created would violate its citizens' rights is relevant today because one-party government is more likely to lead to liberal-rights violations than a viable multi-party system. One-party government is also less likely to develop in a system in which state (and local) governments exercise significant power than in a system in which the central government has all significant governmental power (since parties that are out of power at the national level are more likely to be able to recruit ambitious and capable new leaders if they can offer them the possibility of exercising significant power in state and local governments that the party that is a minority party at the national level still controls).

The moral-rights relevance of federalism has important implications for the appropriate way to interpret the provisions of Article I, Section 8, which enumerate the powers of the Congress, and the Tenth Amendment, which reserves the powers not granted to the central government to the states or to the people. However, I will focus here primarily on the "interstate commerce" clause.

In my judgment, the moral-rights relevance of federalism implies that the "interstate commerce" clause should be interpreted to authorize the central government to preempt the state governments only if the externality-related justification for centralized decisionmaking[45] outweighs not only the "superior access to local information" and "state sovereignty" arguments for authorizing the states to make the relevant decisions but also the moral-rights-related reasons for giving states significant political power. At a minimum, this analysis implies that the "interstate commerce" clause should be interpreted to authorize Congress to act only for certain purposes—for example, it should not be interpreted to authorize the Congress to prevent lotteries it regards as noxious,[46] sexual intercourse it regards as sinful,[47] or private acts of discrimination[48] it regards as immoral[49] (since it limits the central government's interstate commerce power to situations in which the states' exercise of power would damage the collectivity because of the externalities that would critically distort the decisionmaking incentives of the individual states).[50] In addition, in my judgment, the conclusion that the Constitution's allocation of powers was in part designed to protect our rights and the premise that the risk of government tyranny is inversely related to the power that state and local governments exercise also favor interpreting the Constitution to authorize Congress to pre-empt the states in situations in which they may face collective-action problems only if

(1) Congress has built a persuasive factual record that demonstrates that (A) the decisions that the individual states would be likely to make if they were unable to coordinate their decisions would be appropriately likely to be critically distorted by the externalities each state's choice would impose on the others and (B) the states were appropriately unlikely to take collective action in their joint interest and

(2) the Congress has made a reasonable attempt to help the states overcome the collective-action problems that would otherwise preclude them from making collectively-desirable decisions.[51]

The moral-rights-related account of the Constitution's basic structures will also affect the appropriate way to interpret non–power-allocating structural clauses of the Constitution such as the Second Amendment, which prohibits the central government from infringing "the right of the people to keep and bear arms." As my colleague Sanford Levinson has persuasively argued,[52] this amendment was adopted not only to secure the individual's right to protect himself against criminal conduct (at a time when there was no professional police force even within large American cities) but also for structural reasons to provide the citizenry with a last-resort response to political corruption or tyranny. My point is that the moral account of this "checking"[53] function of the right to keep and bear arms suggests that the structural and individualist rationales for this right have a common metric— the securing of individual rights. Obviously, this conclusion does not make it easy to apply the Second Amendment—to determine, for example, whether it prohibits the central government from criminalizing the possession of handguns or assault weapons. One will still have to resolve many difficult empirical issues such as the ability of a citizenry armed with handguns to check a twentieth-century government or the effect of handgun prohibitions on the incidence of violent crimes. But at least the moral-rights account of the structural functions of the Second Amendment eliminates a possible kind of incommensurability that might preclude the existence of an internally-right answer to many Second Amendment interpretation questions.[54]

Examples could be multiplied. However, the preceding analyses should suffice to show how "arguments of moral principle" control the way in which the Constitution's structural provisions should be interpreted as well as the way in which the Constitution's basic structures should affect the interpretation of its various power-allocating provisions.

(D) ARGUMENTS FROM JUDICIAL PRECEDENT AND PRACTICE

Arguments of moral principle also reveal the legitimating point of and control the legitimate use of arguments from judicial precedent and practice. More specifically, arguments of moral principle reveal that our practice of giving judicial precedent and practice weight in themselves is an outgrowth of our duty to show respect to all moral-rights holders by giving them fair notice (by making our conclusions about their legal rights and obligations consistent with their reasonable expectations). I do not think that this obligation to give fair notice can be fulfilled only through giving weight to precedents. For example, although the following alternative may be precluded by the Constitution's limitation of the power of federal judges to cases and controversies, the obligation to provide fair notice could be satisfied by a system that instructed judges or specified others to write frequent reports on the content of the law and instructed judges in future cases to be bound by the conclusions of these reports rather than by prior judicial decisions. However, a practice of giving weight to precedent certainly is consistent with—is one way of fulfilling—the obligation to show respect for all moral-rights holders by giving them fair notice (an obligation that also accounts for the rule that criminal laws that are unacceptably vague are unconstitutional).

Moreover, our conclusion that to be legitimate any legal doctrine or decision must be consistent with our society's rights-commitments also has implications for the appropriate way to interpret legal doctrines and prece-dents—namely, in the way that makes them reflect our rights-commitments and the norms that underlie them.

(E) PRUDENTIAL ARGUMENTS

Finally, as I have already suggested, arguments of moral principle also de-termine the relevance and appropriate use of the only kind of "prudential" argument that is legitimate in our culture. More specifically, arguments of moral principle reveal the constitutional relevance of a demonstration that a government choice would generate or has generated consequences that could result in its being evaluated as desirable from a defensible personal-ultimate-value perspective. In particular, arguments of moral principle show that such a demonstration is relevant to the assessment of the Constitu-tionality of the choice in question because choices that could not conceiv-ably be found desirable from any personal-ultimate-value perspective will almost always violate the rights of those they disadvantage. Specifically, such choices will almost always be morally impermissible on one of three grounds:

(1) because they were motivated by a prejudice toward their victims (a tendency to give less weight to the victims' welfare or, at the extreme, an unjustifiable desire to impose losses on their victims);
(2) because they were designed to achieve impermissible goals (e.g., to impose a view of the good on the State's subjects or to advantage their beneficiaries unjustifiably); or
(3) because they fail to show the respect that is due their victims (appro-priate concern for their victims' welfare) by imposing losses on these individuals for no good reason whatsoever.

The "almost always" qualification to the preceding conclusion relates to the third possibility just listed—namely, to the fact that the State's duty of ap-propriate respect may obligate it not to avoid all pointless decisions that im-pose losses on some of those they affect but to create a quality-control sys-tem for making and reviewing its decisions that reduces to an acceptable level the incidence of pointless, harmful choices the government makes. In other words, the "almost always" qualification reflects the fact that the ap-propriate level of quality control may be compatible with some decisions that are absolute clunkers' being made.

(3) Determining the Relationship between a Legitimate Argument or Relevant Piece of Evidence and the Right Answer to the Legal-Rights Question under Consideration

Arguments of moral principle also control the weight or role of various arguments or pieces of evidence that can be legitimately considered when analyzing what the law is. Thus, as we saw, arguments of moral principle reveal that it is not legitimate to give historical evidence about the intent of a provision's ratifiers and/or about the contemporaneous decisions made by the same or other units of government a decisive role when interpreting the provision in question. Indeed, arguments of moral principle imply that such evidence should be given much less weight than it would be given by most scholars who agree that it should not be given decisive weight.

On the other hand, arguments of moral principle imply that structural arguments deserve more weight than many seem to give them by revealing that *inter alia* such arguments reflect our commitment to protecting the moral rights of all those for whom our State is responsible.

In addition to revealing the moral-rights justification for our practice of precedent, arguments of moral principle also make it clear that it may be illegitimate to follow precedents that were wrong when initially announced. More specifically, arguments of moral principle reveal that judicial precedent and practice should not be followed if they were sufficiently-clearly wrong when they were announced or have been revealed by subsequent events to be sufficiently-clearly wrong for it to be unreasonable for anyone to expect that they would be followed and/or for any rights-related interests that would be sacrificed by disappointing arguably-reasonable expectations to be less weighty than the rights-related interests that would be sacrificed by the repetition of a decision or application of a doctrine that was initially erroneous.

Arguments of moral principle also reveal why judicial precedent and practice need not always be followed—in particular, because some judicial decisions and pronouncements were sufficiently-clearly wrong when they were announced or have been revealed by subsequent events to be sufficiently-clearly wrong for it to be unreasonable for anyone to expect that they would be followed and/or for any rights-related interests that would be sacrificed by disappointing arguably-reasonable expectations to be less weighty than the rights-related interests that would be sacrificed by the repetition of a decision or application of a doctrine that was initially erroneous.

Admittedly, at least if one accepts as accurate the account of the factors that determine the weight given to judicial precedent by judges in our legal culture offered by the various Justices who addressed this issue in *Casey*,[55] the way in which we actually handle judicial precedents is only partly consistent with my account of our society's moral commitments. On the one hand, the following seven or eight parts of our judicial-precedent practices are consistent with my account of our moral commitments:

(1) giving more weight to precedents on which people have relied (though such reliance cannot justify the courts' failing to overrule incorrect precedents prospectively);

(2) giving less weight to precedents that have been undermined by subsequent legal developments (since reliance would be less reasonable in such circumstances);

(3) giving less weight to precedents that were based on factual premises that are no longer correct (since reliance would not be reasonable in such circumstances if the change in facts made the precedent inapplicable to the present situation);

(4) giving less weight to precedents whose factual premises have subsequently been shown to have been incorrect (since reliance would not be reasonable in such circumstances);

(5) giving more weight to precedents when the issue in question was subject to "full-dress argument" prior to the original decision (since it is more reasonable to rely on decisions that were thoroughly considered);

(6) giving less weight to dicta as opposed to pronouncements that were essential to the resolution of the cases in which they were made (both because dicta are likely to have been less well-considered and because our practice has always been to distinguish between dicta and the most-narrowly-defined holding of a case);

(7) giving weights to precedents that vary inversely with their original "wrongness";[56] and perhaps[57]

(8) giving less weight to precedents that have proved "unworkable" in practice (since it is not reasonable to rely on "unworkable" precedents).

However, in the other direction, two parts of our reported precedent-weighing practices strike me as being illegitimately prudentialist because they are inconsistent with our moral commitments:

(1) giving more weight to precedents whose reversal would undermine our belief in the rule of law by creating the impression that judicial decisions are not principled[58] and

(2) giving more weight to precedents whose reversal would destroy social peace in relation to the issues in question (both directly by stirring things up and indirectly by giving parties who oppose the existing consensus an incentive to challenge the established rule).

The claim that you can increase people's commitment to the rule of law by pretending that Constitutional-rights decisions are decisions on which well-informed, highly-skilled individuals cannot disagree in good faith is very dubious. Although I claim no expertise on this social-psychology issue, it seems to me that our citizens are far more likely to develop a commitment to the rule of law if they are given a realistic account of legal reasoning that reveals why the disagreements about legal interpretation they will often observe may be generated by the good-faith efforts of well-informed, highly-skilled legal analysts to determine the internally-right answer to a contestable legal-rights question.

Finally, arguments of moral principle reveal that the type of prudential argument that is legitimate—arguments that demonstrate that the decision under review did promote one or more legitimate social goals—is not decisive, as many appear to suppose. In particular, arguments of moral principle reveal that choices that promote legitimate State goals will still be unconstitutional if they disserve rights-related interests on balance (motivational considerations aside) or if their support was critically affected by illicit motivations. Of course, it will often be more difficult to demonstrate the requisite illicit motivation in cases in which the choice could have been made for legitimate reasons.

D. Right Answers to Legal Rights Questions?

In at least seven different ways, my account of legitimate legal argument in our culture—more particularly, my conclusion that arguments of moral principle are supposed to dominate the other modes of legal argument used in our culture—favors the conclusion that there are internally-right answers to all legal-rights questions in our society:

(1) by declaring illegitimate prudential arguments that may disfavor the conclusions favored by the modes of legal argument that are legitimate;

(2) by showing that even the one type of consequentialist prudential argument that is legitimate is not supposed to be decisive when it favors the Constitutionality of a choice that moral argument implies is unconstitutional;

(3) by coopting precedential argument by making the weight attributed to a precedent vary directly with its original soundness (with its conformity to the conclusion favored by the other modes of legitimate legal argument) and by pointing out that in cases in which initially-wrong precedents should be given a critical weight that procedure is compatible with our moral principles (that in such cases arguments of moral principle will favor a different conclusion from the conclusion they would have favored had the case arisen as a matter of first impression);

(4) by making less problematic the fact that at the time at which a Constitutional or statutory provision was passed government officials treated the rights-related interests it implicated in a way that was inconsistent with the society's basic moral principle;

(5) by making less problematic the fact that the society or the relevant government or governments have treated some particular, narrowly-defined type of conduct in a way that contravenes the moral principles to be inferred from our general moral behavior by revealing that the relevant historical research and arguments should not focus exclusively on the way in which individuals and the State have responded to the particular conduct on which the State choice under review focuses but on the way in which individuals and the State have reacted to all conduct that implicates the broadly-defined rights-related interests involved in the private behavior to which the State choice under review relates;

(6) by making less relevant (at a minimum, rendering non-decisive) evidence about the specific expectations of the framers and ratifiers of a Constitutional provision about the way in which it would or should be interpreted; and

(7) by giving a moral account of our government's basic structural features that reduces the likelihood that structural arguments will conflict with arguments of moral principle or historical arguments.

Admittedly, arguments of moral principle may conflict with textual arguments when the plain meaning of the text at the time at which it was ratified is inconsistent with a moral principle. However, for two reasons, this possibility does not cut against my claim that in our culture there are internally-right answers to all or virtually all legal-rights questions. First, as I have already noted, since the Reconstruction Amendments, the Constitution contains no applicable text that conflicts with our society's basic moral principle. Second, in my judgment, at least when the relevant ratifiers understood the plain meaning of the text they ratified, textual argument dominates arguments of moral principle when legal interpretations are being debated.

I have already argued that a rights-based State may not be obligated to enforce all the moral rights of those for whom it is responsible. There will be occasions on which such a State will not be obligated to enforce moral rights because its attempt to do so will sacrifice rights-related interests on balance for reasons that do not involve the unlawful reactions of its subjects or officials to its efforts. Before proceeding, I want to emphasize that even if this were not the case my account of legitimate legal argument in our culture— my claim that (with the one textual exception just discussed) arguments of moral principle are the dominant mode of legitimate legal argument in our culture—does not imply that members of our culture have all those legal rights and only those legal rights that arguments of moral principle favor. The exception—the fact that textual argument based on a Constitutional text that was ratified by individuals who understood its ordinary meaning trumps arguments of moral principle when the text is inconsistent with the relevant society's rights-commitments—lies behind the fact that a particular Constitutional right's being favored by arguments of moral principle is not a sufficient condition for its existence. Admittedly, however, this possibility is not currently a reality in the United States.

More importantly, members of our culture have a large number of legal rights that are not moral-rights-based. In part, this conclusion reflects the fact that the Constitution clearly creates a large number of rights that, though consistent with our basic moral principle, are not required by it. The Constitutional right that most obviously belongs in this category is the right not to be disadvantaged by governmental acts that are unconstitutional because they violate the power-allocating clauses of the Constitution (the balance of power the Constitution establishes among the branches of the federal government or the principle of federalism). Although these power-allocations are rights-related in that they reduce the probability that a corrupt or tyrannous government will violate the moral rights of those for whom it is responsible, I would not say that these elements of the structure of the government the Constitution created are required by our society's moral commitments.

The Constitution also creates many procedural rights that are consistent with, though they are not corollaries of, our basic moral principle—that is, they can be attributed neither to our obligation to show respect for moral-rights holders by allowing them to participate in certain types of decisionmaking processes that affect their welfare nor to our obligation to establish decisionmaking processes that reduce to an acceptable level the probability that decisions that adversely affect an individual will be made for impermissible reasons or for no good reason at all (out of carelessness). In this category, I would place (perhaps *inter alia*)

(1) the Third Amendment right not to have troops quartered in time of war in a privately-owned house without the consent of the owner "but in a manner to be prescribed by law";

(2) the Fourth Amendment right (in "non-emergency" situations) not to be searched or to have property seized unless warrants based on probable cause are issued "particularly describing the place to be searched, and the persons or things to be seized";

(3) the Fifth Amendment right to an indictment by a Grand Jury and right not to be compelled in a criminal case to be a witness against yourself (more specifically, not to have your refusal to testify count against you);

(4) the Sixth Amendment right in all criminal prosecutions to a trial "by an impartial jury of the State and district wherein the crimes shall have been committed"; and

(5) the Seventh Amendment right in suits at common law to a trial by jury whenever the value in controversy exceeds twenty dollars.

Finally, I would say that the Constitution also creates at least one substantive right that is not required by our moral-rights commitments—the Third Amendment right of a homeowner not to have a soldier quartered in his house without his consent in time of peace (presumably even if just compensation would be paid for any loss such quartering would inflict on the homeowner in question).

Obviously, individuals have many non-Constitutional legal rights that are not required by our moral-principle commitments. Hosts of statutes that were enacted to further personal ultimate values or their supporters' self-interest create such non-moral-rights-related legal rights and, even on my account, some (mistaken) common-law decisions may (given our practice of precedent) generate such legal rights as well.

In short, the claim that (with one exception) arguments of moral principle dominate the other modes of legal argument would not imply that our Constitutional rights or legal rights can be derived solely from such arguments even if (as is currently the case in the United States) the exception made no practical difference.

3. Three Moral Issues That Relate to My "Right Answers" Thesis

A. The Importance of the Existence of Internally-Right Answers to Legal-Rights Questions

If my account of legitimate legal argument is correct, the probability of there being internally-right answers to all legal-rights questions will be far higher than most scholars believe. Why should we care whether internally-right answers to legal-rights questions exist? To begin with, if there is no internally-right answer to the question whether a criminal or civil defendant has violated the law, then any finding that he is guilty or civilly liable subjects him to judicially-promulgated *ex post facto* legislation. Our question is: Would such *ex post facto* legislation violate the moral and Constitutional rights of such defendants or anyone else?

I can think of at least four moral-rights-related objections to such judicial decisions. First, in most criminal-law cases, findings of guilt condemn the defendant for violating the legal and often the moral rights of the criminal-law victim, and in many civil-law cases, findings of liability condemn the defendant for violating the moral rights of the plaintiff. Since this condemnation would not be appropriate in the no-right-answer case, decisions holding defendants guilty or liable in such cases would violate our duty of respect to them.

A second objection to such judicially-promulgated *ex post facto* legislation could be characterized as a variant of the first. In criminal-law cases, basing a finding that a moral-rights holder has committed a criminal-law violation on a judicially-supplied answer to a legal question for which there is no internally-right answer will violate our respect-related duty not to find a moral-rights holder guilty of a criminal act unless we are sure of his culpability beyond a reasonable doubt.

Third, judicially-promulgated *ex post facto* legislation will also often violate the moral and Constitutional right of moral-rights holders to fair notice.

And fourth, allowing judges to promulgate such legislation may also violate the moral rights of the defendants because it creates an unacceptable risk that judges will use their power to punish their or someone else's personal enemy, to punish political opponents, and/or to deter political opposition (both specifically and generally). In fact, a system that granted judges this power would violate not only the rights of the defendants in question but also the First Amendment rights of all citizens to hear the positions of those whose political participation might be deterred.

I concede that not all *ex post facto* legislation can be criticized on these grounds. Retroactive legislation that was passed by a legislature that gave notice of its intention to promulgate the relevant statute once it achieved a quorum might not be objectionable on these or any other moral-rights-related grounds. Similarly, a "judicial" ruling that a defendant violated a law that could not be said to exist unless the "judges" supplied an answer to a question for which there was no internally-right answer might also not be objectionable if the judges issued a declaratory judgment indicating their intention to promulgate such legislation in the future. But that is not our system. In our culture, decisions against defendants in cases that turned on the resolution of issues to which there are no internally-right answers would almost always violate the defendants' rights.

Admittedly, the Founding Fathers' position on *ex post facto* legislation may not be fully consistent with this argument. Although they did prohibit *ex post facto* legislation in Sections 9 and 10 of Article I of the Constitution, the Founding Fathers seem to have believed that this prohibition applied only to criminal laws: that is why they found it necessary to prohibit the states from "impairing the Obligation of Contracts"[59] in addition to prohibiting them from passing *ex post facto* laws.[60] Of course, the Founding Fathers might simply have been wrong in believing that only *ex post facto* criminal laws were generically objectionable: a proper construction of the moral principles to which their society was committed may still lead to the conclusion that in it all such laws violate moral-rights—that *ex post facto* laws of all kinds would violate the unenumerated rights to which the Ninth Amendment refers.

B. The Evidence for and against the Existence of Internally-Right Answers to Legal-Rights Questions

(1) The Evidence for Internally-Right Answers

My case for the conclusion that there are internally-right answers to all or virtually all legal-rights questions rests primarily on

(1) my discussion of the evidence for the conclusion that we are a rights-based society (in which moral-obligation conclusions trump over moral-ought conclusions),

(2) my explanation of why the existence of gaps in the protocol for identifying the basic moral principle we are committed to using in moral-rights discourse (gaps that cannot be filled in non-arbitrarily) are unlikely to leave indeterminate the internally-right answer to many or any moral-rights (or *a fortiori* moral-rights-related legal-rights) questions,

(3) my argument for the proposition that in a rights-based society such as ours a mode of legal argument is legitimate if and only if its use is consistent with the relevant society's moral commitments,

(4) my related analysis of the way in which arguments of moral principle control the variants of the other modes of argument that can legitimately be used to discover the law as well as the relationship between legitimate legal arguments of this sort and the internally-right answer to legal-rights questions,

(5) my explanation of why my analysis of the role of arguments of moral principle in legal-interpretation discourse implies that there are internally-right answers to all legal-rights question, and

(6) my explanation of the moral problems that would be raised by the absence of internally-right answers to legal-rights questions.

However, I may also be able to strengthen my right-answer argument by pointing to some behavioral evidence. In particular, two facts deserve some weight. First, when lawyers argue before judges they argue that their clients are entitled to win their cases because the internally-right answers to the relevant legal-rights questions yield this conclusion (i.e., lawyers do not argue for their clients by arguing that a decision in their client's favor would be good policy unless they can link their policy argument to one of the legitimate modes of legal argument). Second, to an overwhelming extent, judicial opinions purport to analyze the internally-right answers to the relevant legal questions rather than to execute external-to-law policy analyses of the issues in question (the exception is the illegitimate prudential arguments that appear in some judicial opinions).

Of course, these behavioral facts may manifest nothing more than the relevant actors' use of empty rhetoric (which may, as members of the Critical Legal Studies movement might suggest, be designed to conceal or have the effect of concealing from the masses the fact that judicial decisionmaking involves nothing more than the exercise of the kind of power that legislatures are acknowledged to possess). However, given the seriousness of there being no internally-right answers to legal-rights questions and (I hope) the plausibility of my argument for their existence, I think that skeptics should have to bear the burden of demonstrating that those who engage in the behaviors just described are kidding themselves and/or us.

(2) The Evidence against Internally-Right Answers

At least four kinds of evidence have been cited to support the claim that there are no internally-right answers to many (most, or—at the ridiculous extreme—any) legal-rights questions. First, some have argued that the right-answer claim is disproved by the fact that the internally-right answer to many important legal-rights questions is controversial. I am not at all surprised or troubled by the existence of such controversies. On my account, the determination of the basic moral principle, the derivation of its more concrete corollaries, the analysis of text, history, structure, practice and precedent, and the prediction or determination of the interpretively-relevant material consequences of many State choices will all be highly contestable. Good-faith analysts of acceptable skill and industry as well bad-faith analysts who let their judgment be influenced by illegitimate prudential or venal considerations will disagree about the internally-right resolution of these issues and relatedly about the internally-right response to the legal cases to which they are relevant. Moreover, as Dworkin has pointed out,[61] it is significant to note that most analysts who disagree on the proper resolution of contestable legal issues or legal-rights questions believe that they are disagreeing about the internally-right answers to the relevant questions—that is, they themselves seem to believe that there is an internally-right answer (theirs) to the questions about which they are arguing.

Second, some members of the Critical Legal Studies movement such as Roberto Unger believe that the internally-right-answer claim is disproved by the existence of inevitable internal contradictions (so-called antinomies) in liberal legal practice.[62] In fact, however, the evidence provided by these scholars does not support their conclusion that our rights-based legal system does contain and indeed any such system must contain such contradictions. More particularly, each of their examples does no more than establish that a principle that favors the winning conclusion in some cases disfavors the winning conclusion in other cases in circumstances in which neither set of outcomes is regarded as mistaken. Although this "fact" would establish the internally-contradictory character of liberal legalism if the principles in question were rules, it has no such implication given the fact that principles are not rules. Rules are decision-standards that are supposed to be decisive whenever they apply. A system that contains contradictory rules is therefore internally contradictory. By way of contrast, the concrete corollaries of the basic moral principle are decision-standards that are not supposed to be decisive whenever they apply. These principles have a dimension of weight. Such a principle may be weightier in some cases in which it is more implicated than in others in which it is less implicated, and more than one principle of this kind (indeed, principles that favor different outcomes) may be involved in a given case. Hence, the fact that a principle—call it *A*—which favors the actual decision in one case is not decisive in another case to which it is relevant creates no logical crisis for the legal system. Thus, no net-counteracting principles *B–Z* may have been relevant to the resolution of the former case while the latter case may have implicated one or more other principles that were on balance counteracting and more weighty than *A* in the context of the case in question. Alternatively, the net-counteracting principles *B–Z* that were relevant in both cases may have been less weighty than *A* in the former case and more weighty than *A* in the latter case.

The third type of evidence that opponents of the right-answer claim cite in support of their position is that when practicing lawyers advise their clients they focus not on the internal correctness of their client's actual or possible legal position but on the probability that the relevant court will or would decide in their client's favor and the consequences of its doing so. Although from a liberal rights-based perspective our world would be a better place if legal actors were more concerned with obeying valid laws for non-instrumental reasons, I am not surprised that many law clients are primarily interested in predicted legal outcomes and that lawyers' communications reflect this fact. However, except to the extent that this possible "fact" undermines my claim that we are a rights-based as opposed to an amoral society, I do not see how it undermines my claim that there are internally-right answers to legal-rights questions. Even if such answers always existed and judges always gave them, clients would still want and lawyers would still cast their communications as outcome-predictions rather than internally-right legal answers. Obviously, the conclusion that lawyers would behave in this manner would follow *a fortiori* if there always were internally-right legal answers but judges did not always give them.

The fourth type of evidence that opponents of the right-answer claim like to cite is the fact that most legal academics now reject that claim because they believe that significant numbers of cases pose critical legal-rights questions for which there are no internally-right answers. Although neither these opponents of my right-answer claim nor I have researched this empirical proposition, I am inclined to believe that their empirical hypothesis is correct. However, "is" does not equal "ought." In my judgment, the relevant law professors are wrong. They have been misled by their failure to recognize that our society is a rights-based society that engages in two types of moral discourse, that the moral norms that determine moral rights and obligations in our society can be objectively determined, that the legitimacy of using a particular argument when debating a legal interpretation in a moral-rights-based society depends on the consistency of its use with the relevant society's moral commitments, and that the moral principles that control our rights-and-obligations discourse are not only inside the law but dominate legitimate legal argument in our culture. More abstractly, the relevant law professors have been misled by two mistaken beliefs. The first is the belief that our inability to give a definitive propositional account of our moral practices and, indeed, of many other social practices as well—an inability that I will assume *ad arguendo*—precludes us from generating internally-right answers to legal-rights questions. The second is their belief that moral relativism precludes the existence of internally-right answers to legal-rights questions—in other words, their mistaken assumption that the fact that personal ultimate values are primitives (cannot in the end be justified) and that the moral superiority of rights-based societies and *a fortiori* of liberal rights-based societies cannot be objectively established implies that no morality-related question can be given an objectively-right answer of the relevant kind.

The first of these beliefs is mistaken because the posited inability to give a full account of any complex, subtle social practice would not eliminate the point of giving the best account one can of that practice and basing any related decision on that account (any more than our inability to measure the monetary multiplier incontrovertibly accurately [for both empirical and theoretical econometric reasons] defeats the point of making the best estimate we can of this figure and of requiring macroeconomic decisionmakers to make cost-effective estimates of this figure or to explain the basis of the policy-choices they made).

The second belief is mistaken because from the internal perspective of a rights-based society the impossibility of establishing the objective moral superiority of our rights practices or of any personal ultimate value does not defeat the point of making legal-rights-related institutions and decisions consistent with our rights-commitments—does not preclude us from generating right answers *of the relevant kind* (the answers that are consistent with our rights practices).

C. Liberalism and the Counter-Majoritarian Objection to Judicial Review

The standard objection to (non-elected) federal judges' reviewing the Constitutionality of the decisions of other (often elected) officers of government is that this procedure is anti-democratic. Indeed, many defenders of judicial review accept the legitimacy of this type of objection to judicial review. They defend the practice by arguing either (1) that appointed judges are no less "representative" than elected officials, given the frequency with which new judges are appointed through a process that is initiated by Presidential nomination and completed by Senate confirmation and the various imperfections in our electoral processes and power-allocating procedures within Congress,[63] and/or (2) that the anti-democratic nature of judicial review is less harmful than the governmental decisions that judges invalidate when exercising judicial review.

In fact, however, the defense that the "Supreme Court is not as democratic as the Congress or President, and the institution of judicial review is not as majoritarian as the lawmaking process." does not seem to be empirically sound.[64] Indeed, although one may be able to strengthen this defense by arguing that the non-representativeness of the judiciary offsets the non-representativeness of the legislative and executive branches of the central government and of each state government and improves the "representativeness" of the government as a whole, even this more complicated, second-best argument does not seem convincing across all cases in which judicial review is practiced.[65]

Fortunately, in a liberal rights-based society, a very different kind of argument can be used to defend judicial review against the accusation that it is anti-democratic: a conceptual argument that grants that judicial review is non-democratic but disproves the contention that judicial review is anti-democratic by showing that both judicial review and democracy are consistent with the basic moral principle that a liberal rights–based society is committed to following in rights discourse. To establish this point, I will first examine the liberal justification for judicial review and then discuss the liberal justification for democracy.

From the perspective of a liberal rights-based society, judicial review is justified because such a society's basic moral principle commits it to preventing the violation of individual rights even at the cost of sacrificing perfectly-legitimate social goals and judicial review (at least the type of judicial review we have) is a sound institutional method to protect and secure individual rights—it is consistent with, if not required by, this basic liberal commitment.

Similarly, from the perspective of a liberal rights-based society, democracy is justified because such a society's basic moral principle commits it to showing respect for the moral-rights holders for which it is responsible and this duty of respect requires that citizens that have the capacity to do so govern themselves (be the authors of the laws to which they are subject).[66]

Since, therefore, both the practice of judicial review and the commitment to democracy are consistent with the basic moral principle that grounds a liberal rights-based society's rights-practices, judicial review is not anti-democratic in a liberal rights-based society. Hence, supporters of judicial review face no "counter-majoritarian difficulty" in a liberal rights-based society.

Conclusion

A summary may be in order:

(1) Using a particular type of argument to determine the content of existing law is legitimate in a moral-rights-based culture if and only if doing so is consistent with that culture's moral commitments.

(2) Our culture is a rights-based culture—that is, in our culture, an individual cannot excuse or justicize (demonstrate the justness of) a choice that violates someone's rights by demonstrating that it was consistent with the personal ultimate values to which the individual subscribed and the State cannot excuse or justicize a choice that violates someone's rights by demonstrating that it helped the State achieve one or more goals the State is authorized to pursue. The pri-

mary evidence for this conclusion is that members of our culture engage in two kinds of moral discourse—discourse about what an individual or the State *ought to do* and discourse about what an individual or the State *is obligated to do* and that in this discourse moral-obligation conclusions (and the moral norms on which they are based) trump over (are lexically prior to) moral-ought conclusions and the moral norms from which they are derived.

(3) Our culture is a liberal rights-based culture, a rights-based culture whose rights conclusions are derived from a liberal basic moral principle—namely, that individuals in our culture and the State are obligated to show appropriate, equal respect and concern for all creatures that have the neurological prerequisites to become and remain persons of moral integrity (*inter alia*, concern for their actualizing this potential by taking their obligations seriously and striving to establish a reflective equilibrium between their personal value-convictions and their conduct). This principle implicitly measures the successfulness of an individual's life by the extent to which she becomes and remains a person of moral integrity (not, as some seem to suppose, by the extent to which the individual succeeds in achieving a variety of other goals she sets for herself). Although the protocol one should use to identify the basic moral principle to which a rights-based society is committed contains some gaps that cannot be filled in non-arbitrarily, our commitment to a *liberal* basic moral principle can be demonstrated by the use of the relevant protocol. Specifically, the liberal principle just adumbrated is the best candidate for the title "basic moral principle members of our society are committed to using in rights discourse" if we assess all such candidates by applying some combination of two criteria. The first relevant criterion is how closely the respective candidate-principles' post-dictions and predictions fit the following facts—(A) the rights-claims that were made and not made, (B) the arguments that were made and not made in support of the claims in question by both the claimants and those who evaluated their claims, (C) the conclusions that were reached about the claims in question, (D) how close the cases in question were perceived to be, and (E) how certain people were about the proper resolution of the claims in question. The second relevant criterion is how explicable the non-fits associated with each candidate were—to what extent could the non-fits be explained by (A) the greater power of the non-fits' beneficiaries, (B) the presence

of mechanical transaction costs or other types of costs that make it unattractive for parties with justified claims to pursue their claims or attractive for parties to pursue unjustified claims, (C) conceptual intellectual errors that the relevant actors might very well have made, and/or (D) other sorts of errors made by moral-rights holders or obligors or prospective errors by deciders of moral-rights or moral-rights-related legal-rights disputes.

(4) Not only is the basic moral principle that a rights-based society is committed to following in rights discourse part of the law, arguments of moral principle are (with one exception) the dominant mode of legitimate legal argument in a rights-based culture. More specifically, arguments of moral principle dominate legitimate legal interpretation in a rights-based culture in that they determine the legitimacy of using the other general modes of argument that have been used for this purpose, the variant of each legitimate general type of argument that can be legitimately used to discover the law, and the legitimate relationship between each legitimate sub-type of legal argument and the internally-right answer to the relevant legal-rights question. In particular, arguments of moral principle establish (A) the illegitimacy of most types of prudential arguments in the law-interpretation context, (B) the variants of textual, historical, structural, precedential, and prudential argument that it is legitimate to use to discover the law, and (C) the non-decisiveness in law-interpretation contexts of the kind of prudential argument that is legitimate, arguments of "ratifier intent," historical arguments that focus on related State choices made at the time at which a provision was drafted and passed, historical arguments that focus on private and State choices that relate most directly to the conduct or attributes of individuals whose rights are alleged to have been violated by the State decision under review, arguments that focus on the narrowly-characterized historical antecedents of a Constitutional or statutory text, and arguments based on the most-clearly-applicable judicial precedents. The exception to my claim that arguments of moral principle dominate the other forms of legal argument relates to textual argument: the plain meaning of a Constitutional text that was understood by its ratifiers dominates arguments of moral principle when the two conflict.

(5) The preceding analysis implies the existence of internally-right answers to all or virtually all legal-rights questions in the United States—that either the various legitimate legal arguments will not

favor different conclusions or in cases of conflict the set of arguments that is weightier will in theory be identifiable.

(6) The existence of internally-right answers to legal-rights questions is important in a liberal rights-based society or indeed in most other types of societies because decisions to impose liability on defendants (and perhaps on plaintiffs as well) in cases that turn on the answers to legal questions to which no internally-right answers can be given in effect promulgate *ex post facto* legislation.

(7) The evidence that most opponents of my right-answer claim cite to disprove it does no such thing: the existence of internally-right answers to all or virtually all legal-rights questions cannot be disproved by pointing out that the internally-right answer to many legal-rights questions is contestable and controversial, by establishing that principles that favor the actual outcome of some cases which implicate them disfavor the actual outcome in other cases to which they are relevant, by proving that lawyers usually advise clients about the probability of their winning rather than about the internal-to-law correctness of their actual or potential legal positions, and/or by demonstrating that most law professors reject my right-answer claim.

(8) The account I have given of legitimate legal argument in our culture implies that judicial review cannot be opposed on the ground that it is anti-democratic in a liberal rights-based society. This conclusion reflects the fact that in a liberal rights-based society judicial review and democracy are consistent because both derive from the basic moral principle on which such a society is committed to basing its rights discourse. Liberal rights-based societies are committed to democracy because their duty to respect all moral-rights holders requires them to allow all such creatures to play a significant role in their government (to let the people be the author of the laws to which they are subject). Judicial review is consistent with the basic moral principle to which a liberal rights-based society is committed because that principle requires the State to protect individual rights even at the cost of sacrificing desirable State goals and judicial review of the type that the United States has established is a good institutional way to secure the rights of our government's subjects.

My conclusion that there are internally-right answers to all or virtually all legal-rights questions—answers that can be derived by the sophisticated execution of legitimate legal arguments—is old-fashioned and unpopular.

Those Legal Realists who argue that there is no internally-right answer to many or most significant legal-rights questions and their Critical Legal Studies successors have carried the day in the groves of academe. Virtually none of the small number of academics who have opposed the no-right-answer consensus has given an account of legal justification that makes their opposition seem plausible. Basically, my few allies have done little more than point out the dire implications of there being no internally-right answers to legal-rights questions. Even if my account of legal justification does not convince you that there are internally-right answers to all or virtually all legal-rights questions, I hope that it will stimulate you to take this possibility and legal argument more seriously.

2

Alternatives

Chapter 1 set forth my position on legitimate legal argument and legitimate Constitutional interpretation in the United States. This chapter compares my position with the positions others have taken on the moral principles to which we are committed, legitimate legal argument in our culture in general, and the appropriate kinds of arguments for American courts to use when interpreting the United States Constitution. Since the twelve alternatives this chapter discusses differ significantly from each other, it should be no surprise that my reasons for rejecting each of them are somewhat different. Nevertheless, two of my objections apply sufficiently often to be worth listing here.

Many of the interpretive positions this chapter analyzes differ from mine in that they reject my conclusion that members of our culture engage in two kinds of moral discourse—rights discourse and ought discourse. Many of the scholars and judges who reject this conclusion believe that its rejection implies the illegitimacy of my moral interpretation of the Constitution and strive to rely on textual, historical, and doctrinal or precedential arguments that they (incorrectly, to my mind) believe can be made without taking morality into account. Other scholars and judges who ignore the distinction between moral-rights analysis and moral-ought analysis or reject the conclusion that this distinction plays an important role in our culture's moral practice believe that the kind of moral relativism that is a corollary of their understanding of our culture legitimates the use of personal ultimate values to resolve all legal issues.

Several of the interpretive positions this chapter analyzes implicitly accept both my conclusion that our culture distinguishes between moral-rights arguments and moral-ought arguments and my conclusion that the moral norms we use in moral-rights discourse (unlike those we use in moral-ought discourse) are generically inside the law; however, they disagree with my conclusion about the substance of the moral norm that underlies moral-rights discourse. More specifically, these scholars reject my claim that our moral-rights discourse is based on what I have called the liberal moral principle of showing appropriate, equal respect for all moral-rights holders and appropriate, equal concern for their actualizing their potential to become and remain individuals of moral integrity. They argue that our moral-rights discourse is based instead on a principle of appropriate disinterestedness, on libertarian (as opposed to liberal) values, or on communitarian values (which they think are more fundamentally inconsistent with liberalism than I believe).

The other critiques I make of the twelve alternatives to my position considered in this chapter are too disparate to be worth articulating at this juncture. Still, I cannot resist mentioning the fact that at least two of the "alternatives" to be discussed (John Hart Ely's and Douglas Laycock's) are probably no alternatives at all—that is, they require judges to do exactly what I think they are obligated to do but do not face up to that fact.

1. A Comparison between My Positions and Ronald Dworkin's on Various Jurisprudential Issues

In the 1960s and 1970s, Ronald Dworkin wrote a series of articles eventually collected in a book entitled *Taking Rights Seriously*.[1] From my perspective, the four most important points that Dworkin was making were:

(1) our society is a rights-based society (in the sense in which I have defined that term);

(2) in a rights-based society such as ours, moral principles are part of the law so that judges who are taking them into consideration are not going outside the law or employing their own personal values;

(3) a society's moral principles have not been promulgated by a sovereign on a specific date but rather are manifest in and must be inferred from the everyday interactions of a society's members; and

(4) unlike specific policy-goals, which are relevant to legal interpretation only when the issue is the proper interpretation of a statute or regulation that was motivated by the desire to achieve the goal in question, moral principles are relevant to legal interpretation whenever they could apply to the situation in controversy.

I readily acknowledge that Chapter 1 could be regarded as nothing more than an elaboration of these points.

In more recent years, Dworkin seems to have changed his position in significant respects. In such works as *Law's Empire*,[2] he has emphasized the importance of societal "integrity" and argued that, like an individual, a society can have moral integrity only if its official decisions (including legislative and administrative decisions) reflect a consistently-applied personal-ultimate-value position. I do not find this very different position persuasive.

The first part of this section lists the most salient distinctions and conclusions that I have borrowed from the Dworkin of *Taking Rights Seriously*. The second explains the eight respects in which my analysis differs from Dworkin's in *Law's Empire*.

A. Points of Agreement

I have taken over a large part of Dworkin's conceptual apparatus and agree with the vast majority of his controversial conclusions. In particular, I have adopted

(1) Dworkin's general distinctions between and among personal ultimate values, popular morality, and the values that a particular community is committed to using when asserting and assessing rights-and-obligations claims;

(2) Dworkin's distinction between rights-based societies and goal-based or ideal-based societies (societies in which rights do not trump over the pursuit of goals or ideals) (*TRS* 171–72);

(3) Dworkin's conclusion that the meaning of all language that has legal relevance can be discovered only through interpretation, that even when it seems obvious that one should interpret some specimen of legal language mechanically (say, by looking up the word's or words' meaning in a dictionary), that conclusion will reflect (or at least can be justified by) a sophisticated interpretive argument;[3]

(4) Dworkin's distinction between concepts (abstract definitions—for example, of a moral principle) and conceptions (less abstract [operationalized] interpretations or applications of that principle) (*LE* 70–72) and relatedly with his argument that the intent of the framers or supporters of a Constitutional provision that is relevant to its interpretation is the intended concept and not the intended conception;[4]

(5) Dworkin's distinction between the various senses of the word "discretion" and relatedly with his contention that the crucial issue for ju-

risprudential purposes is whether judges must exercise discretion in the strong sense (of being authorized to use personal ultimate values)[5] to resolve particular disputes;

(6) Dworkin's distinction between creating law in the sense of legislating by using one's own personal ultimate values, popular morality, and so on. and interpreting law creatively;

(7) Dworkin's conclusion that jurisprudentially there is no difference between analyzing enumerated rights and unenumerated rights[6] or between resolving hard cases and easy cases[7]—that all such tasks can be executed only by engaging in legal interpretation, whose essential character will be the same in all the instances in question;

(8) Dworkin's conclusion that any attempt to characterize his approach to legal interpretation (or mine for that matter) as being "bottom-up" or "top-down" misses the essential point that our approaches are simultaneously top-down and bottom-up (in that they seek *inter alia* to establish a fit between theoretical concepts and cultural practices);[8]

(9) Dworkin's conclusion that not all purported personal ultimate values qualify for that designation (*TRS* 248–53; *LE* 145) and that not all purported moral principles qualify for that designation;

(10) Dworkin's distinction between conventions (practices in which people follow rules because they expect others to follow the same rule and because they believe that "on balance having some settled rule is more important than having any particular rule") (*TRS* 248–53; *LE* 145) and consensus convictions (which are present when there is "agreement in conviction" so that "everyone follows the same rule ... principally because he thinks it independently the best rule to follow") (*TRS* 248–53; *LE* 145);

(11) two of the three criteria Dworkin claims we should use to identify the basic moral principle to which a rights-based society is committed (as well as to identify the more-concrete principles that are derived from it and the weights that they should be given when they conflict)—the "closeness-of-fit" criterion and the "explicability-of-(non-fit)" criterion;

(12) Dworkin's conclusion that the United States is a rights-based society that is committed to a liberal basic moral principle (though my specification of that principle is somewhat different from his);

(13) Dworkin's claim that moral principles are inside the law while policy-goals are outside the law except when the task is to interpret a statute or regulation passed to achieve the goal in question; and

(14) Dworkin's conclusion in *Taking Rights Seriously* that in the United States there are internally-right answers to all legal-rights questions (*TRS* 279–90). Admittedly, this conclusion is hard to reconcile with his chain-novel-writing analogy to legal interpretation, with his claim that the ideal judge should be guided by a "best light" criterion as well as by a "best fit" criterion, and by his related claim that when language, precedent, and practice do not yield a unique, internally-right answer, "thoughtful judges" must decide which interpretation "does most credit to the nation."

I could delineate a large number of other concepts and conclusions I have borrowed from *Taking Rights Seriously*, but the preceding list should suffice to demonstrate and acknowledge my debt to Dworkin.

B. Points of Disagreement or Difference

This section delineates and comments on the nine important respects in which my analysis does or may differ from Dworkin's analysis in either or both *Taking Rights Seriously* and/or *Law's Empire*.

(1) My Rejection of Dworkin's "Relative Intrinsic Moral Appeal" or "Best Light" Criterion

I agree with Dworkin that not all purported moral principles deserve that classification and that not all purported personal ultimate values merit that title. I also agree with Dworkin that the first step in identifying the moral principle that deserves the basic-moral-principle title (or the relevant more-specific-moral-principle characterization and weighting title) is to filter out all those candidates that are not in fact "moral principles." Dworkin puts the justification for this procedure succinctly: "a successful interpretation must not only fit but also justify the practice it interprets" (*LE* 285). However, at times Dworkin seems to go further, indicating that *ceteris paribus* the case for a particular basic-moral-principle candidate (or more concrete principle or principle-weighting) will depend not only on its being a "moral principle" but on its relative appeal as a moral principle. Thus, at different times and in different contexts, Dworkin states that the strength of the case for a particular candidate for the basic-moral-principle title or for the title "concrete corollary of the basic moral principle" will depend on whether it (1) offers "the best interpretation" (*LE* 94) of a practice; (2) contributes to "the correct or best theory of moral and political rights" (*LE* 97)—a question, he says, that an individual cannot answer without making reference to "his own personal convictions" (*LE* 97); (3) offers the best justification of "past decisions" (*LE* 120); (4) "helps show [the relevant practices] in a better light" (*LE* 215); and (5) "shows the community structure of institutions and decisions— its public standards as a whole—in a better light from the standpoint of political morality," a determination, he once more indicates, that the interpreter cannot make without "directly engag[ing] . . . his own moral and political convictions" (*LE* 256). Although this collection of quotes is in one sense chaotic in that the interpreters to whom they refer are engaged in offering sometimes an account of "justice," sometimes an account of "integrity," and sometimes an account of particular judicial or legislative decisions; and although some of these statements may be thought to be unclear on the relevant point, collectively they and many others Dworkin makes both in *Taking Rights Seriously* and in *Law's Empire* lead me to conclude that he is advocating that the relative strengths of the cases for candidates that clearly are moral principles depend on their relative intuitive moral appeal. If this is so,[9] I reject the use of this criterion—in part because its use obliterates both the distinction I draw between moral principles and personal ultimate values and the case I have made for my conclusion that there are internally-right answers to moral-rights-related legal-rights questions (the only case I can make for that conclusion, given my rejection of Dworkin's claim that our society can be said to have official ultimate values that bind its legislative, executive, and hence judicial decisionmakers).

(2) My Concepts of "Moral Principles" and "Personal Ultimate Values" Versus Dworkin's Concepts of "Principles" and "Policies"

In *Taking Rights Seriously*, Dworkin defines a "principle" to be "a standard that is observed, not because it will advance or secure an economic, political, or social situation deemed desirable, but because it is a requirement of justice of fairness or some other dimension of morality (*TRS* 22)." Dworkin contrasts this concept of "principle" with his concept of a "policy"—"that kind of standard that sets out a goal to be reached, generally some improvement in the economic, political, or social feature of the community (*TRS* 22)." These definitions imply that Dworkin's distinction between "principle" and "policy" will be identical to my distinction between "moral principles" and "personal ultimate values" if and only if two related conditions are fulfilled: (1) Dworkin is defining "justice" and "fairness" in the same way that I do so that they are achieved to the extent that the members of a society and its State fulfill their respective moral obligations—to the extent that the moral rights of those for whom the society is responsible are secured—and (2) Dworkin is defining "policy" to refer to a choice that is oriented to a goal that seems desirable from what I would label a "personal-ultimate-value perspective."

Unfortunately, this issue cannot be resolved by examining Dworkin's formal definitions of these concepts. *Taking Rights Seriously* contains no such definitions,[10] and the formal definitions Dworkin provides in *Law's Empire* do not resolve the issue.[11] It is tempting to try to resolve this ambiguity by examining the kinds of issues to which Dworkin applies his concepts of justice and fairness. It is clear that Dworkin applies his concept of justice to the resolution of many distribution-of-resource issues that I do not think can be resolved directly by reference to our community's basic moral principle. However, for two reasons, this fact may not imply that—unlike my concept of "moral principles"—Dworkin's concept of "justice" and hence of "principles" make relevant their applier's personal ultimate values. The first reason relates to Dworkin's beliefs that (1) to be just, a community must be a community of principle, and (2) to be a community of principle, a community's legislative and executive decisions must be sufficiently consistent to be said to have "integrity." These beliefs imply that, for Dworkin, the resolution of an issue that cannot be resolved directly by inference from what I call the community's basic moral principle may still pose an issue of principle in my sense (because to him the community's basic moral principle and justice will require that the issue be resolved in a way that is consistent with the [political] resolution of similar issues by the community in question because to him a community cannot be just [cannot be a community of principle] unless its legislative and executive decisions manifest integrity in the sense of being consistent).[12] The fact that Dworkin would consider many distributional issues to be matters of principle that I would not classify in this way may therefore reflect my disagreement with his conclusion about "societal integrity" rather than our using the word "principle" in different ways. The second reason relates to the fact that Dworkin finds a "product" rather than a "process" variant of egalitarianism to be most attractive—a "product" variant which, unlike its process alternative, implies that egalitarianism completely dictates the distribution of income—leaves no room for the legitimate play of personal ultimate values. If Dworkin believes that our society is committed to the variant of egalitariansim he concludes is most attractive, the fact that he thinks that distributional issues that I conclude must be resolved through personal ultimate values are matters of principle would reflect our disagreement about the variant of egalitarianism to which our society is committed rather than our divergent definition of the concept "principle."

Although Dworkin's applications of his concept of justice do not reveal whether his distinction between principle and policy parallels my distinction between moral principles and personal ultimate values, his insistence that candidates for the title of "best definition of justice" or "best definition of a community's basic principle" be evaluated in part by their relative intuitive moral appeals[13] does establish that his two key concepts are different from mine. At least in *Law's Empire*, Dworkin's principles are "infected" with the interpreter's personal ultimate values. His distinction between principles and policies is therefore not nearly so stark as my distinction between moral principles and personal ultimate values.

My original view that Dworkin's distinction between principles and policies is the same as my distinction between principles and personal ultimate values may simply have been wrong. The moral notions that Dworkin labeled principles in *Taking Rights Seriously* may have been no more than a series of disconnected "moral-ought conclusions" expressed as aphorisms such as "a man shall not profit from his own wrong," rather than more-or-less-concrete corollaries of a moral norm that is foundational to our moral-rights discourse as opposed to our moral-ought discourse.

(3) The Operationalization of the "Closeness-of-Fit" and "Explicability-of-(Non-Fit)" Criteria

In *Taking Rights Seriously*, Dworkin made virtually no effort to specify the facts that a "basic moral principle" candidate is supposed to fit. And in *Law's Empire*, he restricted his "specific" comments (as opposed to his more general discussion of the nature of "integrity" and the role of that concept in interpretation of different kinds) to two statements: (1) that an interpreter trying to assess "fit" "must take into account not only the numbers of decisions counting for each interpretation, but whether the decisions expressing one principle seem more important or fundamental or wide-ranging than the decisions expressing the other" (*LE* 248); and (2) the statement that "fitting what judges did is more important than fitting what they said" (*LE* 248). Obviously, Chapter 1's thorough delineation of and response to the various gaps in Dworkin's general description of the protocol he believes should be used to identify best candidates for the title of basic moral principle is far more specific than Dworkin's scant comments on these issues. I hasten to add that I would not be surprised if Dworkin had no objections to anything I pointed out or proposed in that section.

(4) My Liberal Basic Moral Principle Versus Dworkin's Liberal-Egalitarian Principle of Equal Concern and Respect

My liberal basic moral principle is closely related to Dworkin's principle of equal concern and respect. However, it differs from it in four inter-related ways:

(1) it makes explicit my admittedly-contestable conclusion that only those creatures who have the neurological equipment necessary to become and remain individuals of moral integrity are moral-rights holders (a conclusion that plays a major role in the resolution of various abortion-issues as well various issues related to the continuation or termination of the lives of creatures that were moral agents but no longer have the neurological equipment to function as moral agents);[14]

(2) it states that the equal respect that is owed is the special respect owed all creatures that have the neurological prerequisites for becoming and remaining individuals of moral integrity;

(3) it makes explicit that the equal concern that is owed primarily relates to the concern that all individuals who have the neurological prerequisites to become individuals of moral integrity be given the wherewithal to actualize that potential; and

(4) it is a "process-oriented" principle, in the sense in which I earlier described that expression, and not a "product" principle.[15]

(5) Differences in Both the Types and Quantity of Uses to Which Dworkin and I Put Our Basic Principles

As just noted, unlike Dworkin's basic principle, my basic moral principle indicates the feature of creatures that my review of the evidence leads me to conclude our society believes entitles them to appropriate, equal respect and concern—namely, their possession of the neurological capacity to become and remain individuals of moral integrity. Relatedly, my basic moral principle also indicates the nature of the equal concern to which such moral-rights holders are entitled—namely, concern for their having the opportunity to take their lives morally seriously as well as for their actually taking their lives morally seriously. These characteristics of my basic moral principle enable it to perform a variety of functions that Dworkin's less-detailed basic principle cannot perform. First, unlike Dworkin's principle, my basic moral principle can generate responses to the boundary issue—can help identify the set of creatures that have Constitutional rights. In many Constitutional-law contexts—most saliently today in the context of abortion and right-to-die cases[16]—this advantage of my approach is substantial.

Second, in contrast with Dworkin's basic principle of equal respect and concern, my basic moral principle provides more information relevant to the generation of its more-concrete corollaries. The additional information that my principle-definition provides yields two benefits. It makes my resolution of particular issues or cases less ad hoc. For example, my statement of the basic moral principle to which our society is committed puts me in a position to explain why our State is obligated to ensure that each moral-rights holder for which it is responsible obtains the wherewithal to take its life morally seriously. And again, my definition of the basic moral principle enables me to give an account of our conclusions about the kinds of choices that we are committed to leaving up to the individual—to explain, for instance, that the moral permissibility and Constitutionality of laws forbidding people to tear down Georgian houses and replace them with "post-modern pastiches"[17] turns on whether such prohibitions can be said to prevent their addressees from choosing their values or living a life that is consistent with their values. In my judgment, this account is less ad hoc and more persuasive than Dworkin's argument that such prohibitions are not impermissible because they do not relate to moral choices, a reason that is imperfectly captured by Dworkin's explanation that they do not relate to beliefs that are analogous to religious beliefs.[18] In addition and relatedly, the greater specificity of my basic moral principle has the intellectual advantage of reducing the number of basic working parts of my analysis (admittedly at the cost of increasing the complexity of its basic working parts).[19]

(6) My Distinction between "Policy Conclusions" on the One Hand and "Moral Principles" and "Personal Ultimate Values" on the Other Versus Dworkin's Tendency to Refer to Both "Policy Conclusions" and the Personal or Official Value-Convictions That Underlie Them as "Policies"

I distinguish clearly between the various types of moral norms relevant to non-rights-oriented and rights-oriented policy evaluation and policy conclusions themselves. As Dworkin recognizes, he uses the term "policy" in several different senses—sometimes to refer to the type of moral norms I call personal ultimate values, sometimes to refer to particular concrete collective goals (whose attractiveness may, in my terms, be attributable to either the basic moral principle or one or more personal ultimate values or a personal-ultimate-value combination), and sometimes to refer to particular concrete policy-options (*LE* 311). I think that Dworkin's use of the term "policy" creates unnecessary confusion, whereas the separate terms I substitute for Dworkin's various senses of the word "policy" facilitate both communication and analysis.

(7) My Rejection of Dworkin's Claim That Not Only "Moral Principles" in My Sense but Also "Official" Ultimate Values Have General Constitutional Legal Force

In most respects, Dworkin's argument in *Law's Empire* is a more systematic, highly sophisticated elaboration of the positions he first set forth in the various articles that he incorporated into *Taking Rights Seriously*. There is one major exception to this generalization. In *Taking Rights Seriously*, Dworkin argued that although "principles" in his sense have general gravitational legal force, "policies" do not have such force. At least implicitly, Dworkin offered two justifications for this second conclusion: (1) in practice, the policy-decisions of the rights-based societies he knew were not sufficiently consistent with any ultimate-value position through time to permit a conclusion that the State had officially adopted a particular ultimate-value perspective (in practice, one could not establish the contrary by combining data on the substance of the State's policies with data on the explanations of that substance by bill sponsors or floor leaders, etc.); and, more fundamentally, (2) a society can be principled even if the overwhelming majority of the decisions that its legislative and executive branches (weighted by their importance) made over time did not consistently implement a give ultimate value. In *Law's Empire*, Dworkin reverses his position on both these premises and the conclusion to which they relate. He claims that

(1) the decisions and decision-explanations of our society's legislative and executive branches are sufficiently consistent with some ultimate-value orientation to justify the conclusion that the unspecified ultimate value in question is our State's "official" ultimate value;

(2) the ultimate values that these branches of government have "officially" adopted do have general gravitational legal force;

(3) (by implication) the ultimate-value conviction that underlies an individual legislative or executive choice does tend to have general gravitational legal force to the extent that it influences the legal interpreter's conclusion about the relevant State's official value-perspective; and

(4) the existence of the relevant "official"-ultimate-value position is morally desirable both (A) because no community can be "a community of principle" unless its legislative and executive branches have an official value-position to which they consistently adhere—that is, manifest "integrity" in the sense in which an individual manifests moral integrity when he makes decisions that consistently flow from a given ultimate-value position;[20] and (B) because communities of principle are more likely to be able to persuade their members to abandon their parochial interests when engaging in political decisionmaking in favor of the pursuit of legitimate ("official") ultimate values and to feel personally responsible for and hence to combat injustices perpetrated by their government officials.[21]

I disagree with the position I have just claimed Dworkin took on these issues in *Law's Empire*. However, before explaining my grounds for disagreeing, I want to admit that this attribution may be unjustified. To be frank, I have had a great deal of difficulty understanding Dworkin's discussion of this issue. At least two major pieces of evidence cut against my interpretation of *Law's Empire* on this point. First, when Dworkin initially (*LE* 178–86) explains his opposition to what he calls "checkerboard"[22] laws—laws that treat similar situations differently to produce a compromise across-the-board outcome or laws that treat all similar situations in a compromise consistent way that does not fully correspond to the norms any given group of evaluators would prefer to apply to the relevant choices—his discussion assumes that "matters of principle are at stake" (*LE* 179), that "people are divided about justice" (*LE* 179), and his illustrations focus on issues (abortion)[23] that involve rights and obligations and "moral principles" in my sense. Second, toward the end of the book, Dworkin argues that "the Constitution cannot sensibly be read as demanding that the nation and every state follow a utilitarian or libertarian or resource-egalitarian or any other particular conception of equality in fixing on strategies for pursuing the general welfare," that "the Constitution leaves each state free in matters of policy, subject only to the constraint ... that each state recognize certain rights" (*LE* 382). If Dworkin had been using the relevant terms—"matters of principle," "justice," "rights"—in my senses or with my denotations, these passages would indicate only that (1) what I call moral principles have general gravitational force and (2) it is morally impermissible for communities of principle to adopt compromise solutions to controversial rights-and-obligations issues when the controversy relates to the appropriate characterization and weighting of the relevant concrete moral principles—that any such response would "compromise" the moral status of such a community. I would agree with both these propositions, and neither would be inconsistent with anything Dworkin wrote in *Taking Rights Seriously.*

However, Dworkin thinks that his principle of integrity requires far more than that—in particular, it requires executive and legislative consistency in the resolution of issues that individually do not involve rights, obligations, and hence moral principles in my sense. This conclusion is implied by the fact that Dworkin refers to utilitarianism, libertarianism, and resource-egalitarianism as "conception[s] of equality" (*LE* 382). The conclusion that the principle of integrity requires all legal outcomes to be consistent is close to explicit in the following sentence, which appears between the two passages quoted in the preceding paragraph: "The Constitution does insist that each jurisdiction accept the abstract egalitarian principle that people must be treated as equals and therefore that each respect *some* plausible conception of equality *in each of its decisions* [emphasis added] about property and other matters of policy."[24] The crucial words in this passage are "in each of its decisions" because they imply the critical predicate of Dworkin's conclusion that a community of principle must have an official, defensible (i.e., consistent with Dworkin's basic moral principle) ultimate-value position (in my usage). More specifically, these words are crucial because they indicate that Dworkin believes that his basic moral principle of equal respect and concern requires *all* policy choices to be governed by his integrity-constraint. This position probably reflects Dworkin's conclusion that the most attractive version of egalitarianism (the one to which our society is committed?) is a product-oriented variant of that concept, which completely controls the distribution of resources, rather than the process-oriented variant to which I think our culture is committed, which does not completely control the legitimate distribution of resources. In any event, in conjunction with Dworkin's preference for a product-oriented variant of egalitarianism, this statement convinces me that Dworkin has changed his position on the gravitational force of "policy" in *Law's Empire.*

Dworkin justifies his claim that each of the individual states and the federal government are obligated to have an official ultimate-value position that has general gravitational legal force by drawing an analogy between individuals and communities. He argues that just as an individual must operate consistently from a coherent moral position to be a person of integrity, a State's choices must be consistent from a defensible value-perspective (in his terms, conception of equality) to be principled. Since Dworkin would not need this analogy if his "principles" dictated the legitimate outcome, I will assume for present purposes that he accepts the general role I have assigned to personal ultimate values.

On this assumption, my objection to Dworkin's analogy is a public-choice objection. Even if one ignores the difficulties posed by the fact that changes in Administration (changes in the identity of the political party in power) are likely to cause the operative convictions of governments to change more frequently than the personal convictions of individuals, there would be a public-choice reason to reject the conclusion that States can be said to be communities of principle only if (in addition to implementing their basic moral principle consistently in all other respects) they adhere consistently to some ultimate-value conviction. Assume that every member of a legislature has a clearly-understood ultimate-value conviction and that each such person consistently casts his vote in the way that that conviction requires. Of course, different legislators with different convictions may reach different conclusions on the various policy issues they must consider. The legislative decision on each policy will be determined by majority vote. Even if each individual legislator consistently implements a defensible ultimate-value conviction, legislative outcomes—determined by majority vote—will often be inconsistent from the perspective of any defensible ultimate value.

Table 1 illustrates this point by examining the relationship between the legislative decisions of a three-person legislature and the various ultimate-value convictions of its members. The first three rows of the table refer to individual legislators identified by their ultimate-value conviction (utilitarian, egalitarian, libertarian), and the fourth row refers to the legislature as a

TABLE 1

*The Relationship between Legislative Decisions and the
Ultimate-Value Convictions of Legislators*

Voter	Policy		
	A	B	C
Utilitarian	Y	Y	Y
Egalitarian	N	Y	N
Libertarian	N	N	Y
Legislature	N	Y	Y

whole. The columns indicate three policies (A, B, and C) that the legislature must either vote for or against. The entries in each cell indicate the way in which the individual or institution indicated by the row in question will vote on the policies concerned. The entries "Y" (for "yes" or "aye") and "N" (for "no" or "nay") indicate how the relevant legislator's convictions will lead him to vote for the policy in question, as well as how the legislature will vote.

As you can see, given my assumptions about the way in which the relevant values would lead the legislators who held them to vote on each policy, the legislature would end up making choices that were inconsistent with the ultimate-value convictions of each of its members. Admittedly, the legislative decisions in question might be consistent with some ultimate value (which happens not to be held by any of its members) but (1) it might not and (2) even if it were it would be perverse to conclude that the legislature subscribed to an "official" ultimate value that none of its members supported. Moreover, although the preceding outcome clearly depends on my assumptions about the implications of the indicated personal ultimate values for the desirability of the policy-options in question, I see no reason to believe that those assumptions or others that will produce the same conclusion will not often be fulfilled. Indeed, even if I make assumptions that will result in the legislature's votes' being consistent with one personal ultimate value, I cannot see the moral significance of this fact, given that it indicates no more than that the votes of the legislature were consistent with the convictions of one-third of the legislators. Admittedly, a more sophisticated analysis of this issue would have to take logrolling, agenda-control, and a number of other complexities into account, but I am certain that doing so would not change my basic point.

I also have empirical objections to Dworkin's position on the general gravitational legal force of our government's "official" ultimate-value convictions: (1) to the extent that Dworkin's position rests on his claim that personal ultimate values are regarded as competing conceptions of the egalitarian norm to which our society is committed, it is undermined by our practice of distinguishing moral-rights claims from moral-ought claims; and (2) Dworkin's position on this issue is also undercut by the fact that the decisions (and relevant comments) of our legislative and executive branches are insufficiently consistent with any legitimate personal ultimate value to permit any such value's being denominated our State's "official ultimate value."

I want to close this discussion with two comments—one substantive and one "stylistic." The substantive point is obvious: I share Dworkin's distaste for legislative and executive decisions that are in effect political payoffs (or pork-barrel legislation) and also find unpleasing most logrolling arrangements. But the non-angelic quality of both government officials and the people over whom they govern and the absence of an official Zeus to tell us how to lead our lives (indeed, the presence of a State-defining constraint on there being any official line on this issue) lead me to conclude that such conduct does not violate our basic moral principles.

The stylistic comment relates to Dworkin's "style." I have already indicated that I have had trouble unpacking Dworkin's position on the relationship between his concepts of "principles," "policies," and "goals" and that this difficulty has made it hard for me to unpack his argument for the propositions (1) that a community cannot be a community of principle unless its legislative and executive behavior manifest "integrity," and (2) that our society's relevant executive and legislative behaviors do manifest the required integrity. I want to emphasize that Dworkin rarely poses such difficulties for me. He virtually always manages to be wonderfully fluent without being glib. His writing is full of illuminating distinctions, carefully drawn—for example, his accounts of the three senses of the word "discretion" (*TRS* 31–33), the three types of strict constructionism (*TRS* 133–37), and the various types of "communities" worth distinguishing (*LE* 195–216) manage to be simultaneously very clear, enormously entertaining, and extraordinarily illuminating. The fact that I have had such problems reconstructing Dworkin's argument for the position on which this section has focused is surprising to me, given the clarity with which he normally manages to convey even the most subtle of arguments.

(8) My Problems with Dworkin's Statements That a Community's Law Is to Be Inferred from Its Officials' Political Decisions

In many passages in *Law's Empire*, Dworkin gives the impression that the primary data that any candidate for the title of "legal principle to which a community of principle is committed" must fit is data that relate to the official decisions of that community's public officials. Thus, in *Law's Empire* Dworkin states: (1) "legal rights are those flowing from past *political* decisions" (*LE* 96, emphasis added); (2) "legal rights" are "rights that follow from past decisions of political institutions" (*LE* 134, emphasis added); (3) "law as integrity supposes that people are entitled to a coherent and principled extension of past *political* decisions" (*LE* 134, emphasis added); and (4) "a person has a legal right, according to our abstract, 'conceptual' account of legal practice, if he has a right flowing from past *political* decisions, to win a lawsuit" (*LE* 152, emphasis added).

For at least three reasons, I disagree with the implication of these statements that the only or even the most important kind of data that legal conclusions must fit are data about "political" decisions. First, such a conclusion ignores the fact that such political decisions may themselves be based on moral principles that have been derived from their fit with moral-right-and-obligation asserting-and-assessing behavior in non-legal fora so that any attempt to characterize the political decisions in question would have to consider the non-political behaviors from which the relevant moral-rights conclusions were derived. Second, Dworkin's statements ignore the fact that even if judges have failed to instantiate a moral principle to which we are committed by our relevant non-legal behaviors, that principle would be part of the law. And, third, Dworkin's statements on this issue ignore the fact that legal precedents or doctrines that are inconsistent with or unrelated to our relevant moral principles will have less weight on that account (though our moral principles do imply that—for reasons of fair notice—the fact that a precedent or doctrine favors a particular outcome should be given some weight in many cases involving behaviors that it influenced even when the precedent or doctrine is wrong).

All these observations imply that legal rights depend on moral-principle-relevant behaviors by non-officials in non-legal fora as well as (indeed, in my view more than) on the government's relevant officials' political decisions. To the extent that Dworkin disagrees with this conclusion, I disagree with him. I hasten to add that *Taking Rights Seriously* argues that legal rights can be based on non-official-choices as well as on official, political decisions. To the extent that Dworkin continues to adhere to this position, my claim would be not that his views on this issue are wrong but that *Law's Empire* gives a misleading impression of his views.

(9) My Uncertainty about Dworkin's Position on Whether There Are Internally-Right Answers to All Legal-Rights Questions

The Dworkin of *Taking Rights Seriously* clearly believed in the existence of internally-right answers to all legal-rights questions. Thus, although he acknowledged that experts sometimes disagreed on those answers, it is indicative that he insisted that when they disagreed they were disagreeing about what those internally-right answers were (*TRS* 279–90). However, I am far less certain about Dworkin's current position on this issue.

Three pieces of evidence suggest that Dworkin may no longer believe in the existence of internally-right answers to all legal-rights questions. The first is Dworkin's famous analogy between legal interpretation and writing a chain novel (*LE* 228–38). This analogy raises doubts because, although later chapters of a chain novel may clearly be unfaithful to what has been written before (may clearly constitute internally-wrong extensions of the earlier text), there are always a large number of significantly-different tacks authors of later chapters can take that will be equally faithful to their predecessors.

I have already discussed the second Dworkin position that seems inconsistent with a belief in internally-right answers to legal-rights questions—his claim that the internally-ideal judge would be guided by a "best light" as well as a "best fit" criterion.

The third piece of evidence suggesting that Dworkin no longer believes in the existence of internally-right answers to all legal-rights questions is related to the second. In *Freedom's Law*, Dworkin states that when different conceptions of a relevant Constitutional principle fit language, precedent, and practice equally well, "thoughtful judges must then decide on their own which conception does most credit to the nation" (*FL* 11). Admittedly, if anything, this claim downgrades the role of his "best light" criterion by suggesting that it is relevant only when text and fit do not settle the issue. However, it still seems to imply that there are no internally-right answers to at least some legal-rights questions.

However, these pieces of evidence may not be decisive. Dworkin's comments suggest that he regards the chain-novel example as an imperfect analogy introduced for the limited purpose of illustrating the fact that the activity of legal interpretation involves neither "total creative freedom" nor "mechanical textual constraint" (*LE* 234). And Dworkin's conclusion that when text and fit are not determinative judges must turn to a "best light" criterion may reflect a view that one conception of a contestable concept can be shown to be objectively most attractive or, more likely, most consistent with all official decisions of our polity (even if it cannot be shown to "best fit" all our relevant moral practices and/or all our relevant judicial decisions). Certainly, Dworkin never thought that his assertion that legal interpretation would sometimes have to be based on a "best light" criterion was inconsistent with a belief in the existence of internally-right answers to all legal-rights questions: the Dworkin of *Taking Rights Seriously* asserted both the legitimacy of the use of the "best light" criterion and the existence of internally-right answers to all legal-rights questions.

Of course, Dworkin may simply be wrong—he may be trying to have it both ways when it is not possible to do so. Many of Dworkin's statements on this issue do not seem to be consistent. Thus, Dworkin's comments on his claim that in the relevant cases "thoughtful judges . . . must decide on their own" do not seem to me to be faithful to the language of the relevant passage or his various discussions of his "best light" criterion. Specifically, Dworkin says: "My claim . . . is not that judges should appoint themselves constitutional tie-breakers instead of leaving that office to legislatures, but that they must exercise the judgment I describe in consequence of their view of what the Constitution *requires* of them."[25] The problem with this exegesis is that, in the relevant cases, *ex hypothesis*, the text of the Constitution, precedent, and the other relevant practices do not produce a unique, internally-right answer (though they may reveal that some answers are internally wrong). Dworkin tries to finesse this fact by claiming that he was assuming no more than that in some cases "different interpreters will undoubtedly think different interpretations the most plausible"[26]—that he was not assuming that an objectively-correct answer cannot be generated from text, precedent, and practice. But if this is the case, why does one need a "best light" criterion? Why must judges ask "which conception does most credit to the nation"? Surely, Dworkin could not be assuming that the metric for "doing credit to the nation" is purely a "fit" metric, for such an assumption would render the "best light"criterion otiose.

I admit to being confused about Dworkin's position on the internally-right-answer issue. The fault is not my own. If Dworkin no longer believes that there are internally-right answers to all legal-rights questions, we disagree on this basic issue. And if Dworkin believes that when text, judicial precedent, and moral-rights "practice" cannot generate a unique, internally-right answer, such an answer can be generated by abstract philosophical analysis or reference to non-judicial official behaviors, his approach to finding the internally-right answer to some legal-rights questions and, presumably, his answers to some such questions will differ from mine.

I have just listed and explained nine different respects in which my approach to legal interpretation and my description of both moral analysis and the relationship between moral analysis of different kinds and legal analysis do or may differ from Dworkin's positions on these issues. The most significant of these differences (both in itself and because it underlies various others) relates to my claim that we engage in two different kinds of moral analysis (moral-rights analysis and moral-ought analysis) that respectively use two different kinds of moral norms (which I respectively call "moral principles" and "personal ultimate values"). Dworkin now seems to think that there is only one universe of moral discourse—the universe of principle—and that the norms that I call "personal ultimate values" are competing conceptions of his basic principle of equality rather than independent moral norms with a different domain of relevance. My disagreement with Dworkin on this issue is fundamental. Our dispute is not semantic but empirical. It can be resolved only by an anthropological analysis of the moral practices of members of our culture.

2. John Rawls's Conception of Justice as Fairness

I have neither the space nor, in all likelihood, the philosophical sophistication to do justice to John Rawls's *A Theory of Justice*.[27] However, my project has a sufficient amount in common with Rawls's to make it useful for me to compare his approach and basic conclusions with mine. My analysis of Rawls is divided into four parts. The first summarizes Rawls's project and conclusions. The second delineates four conceptual similarities and four differences between Rawls' analysis and mine. The third criticizes Rawls's account of what lies behind the substantive-justice principles to which he thinks our culture is committed. And the fourth criticizes his treatment of his substantive-justice conclusions and compares his conclusions with my own.

A. Rawls's Goals, Basic Approach, and Basic Conclusions

In *A Theory of Justice* Rawls attempts to articulate the principles of substantive justice to which members of our society are committed, to reveal what underlies these principles, and to show that these principles will yield a workable, stable society. He gives the impression that the first two of these goals must be achieved separately—that his conclusions about the substantive-justice principles to which members of our society are committed must be derived separately from the account of those principles that he gives (independently of his explanation of what lies behind our commitment to these principles). In part, this conclusion reflects Rawls's claim that what lies behind the substantive-justice principles in question is not a more basic substantive-justice principle but a principle of procedural fairness. Rawls provides an analysis of the way in which one might discover the substantive-justice principles to which we are committed in a way that does not duplicate his account of those principles—namely, an analysis of the process by which an individual should discover the principles of substantive justice or the personal ultimate values to which that individual is committed, the process of achieving a reflective equilibrium (hereinafter "reflective equilibration"). According to Rawls, an individual achieves "reflective equilibrium" by adjusting his initially-perceived principle-commitments and/or his initially-perceived concrete-rights-claim conclusions to make the adjusted principles and conclusions consistent with each other through a deliberative process in which the "equilibrator" is more likely to abandon specific rights-conclusions "if he can find an explanation for the deviations [between his applied rights-conclusions and the principles to which he thinks he is committed] which undermines his confidence in his original [rights-] judgments" (*TJ* 48). However, although Rawls could have used this process to determine the substantive-justice principles to which our society as a whole is committed, he never does so.

In any event, Rawls concludes that the members of our society are committed to the following three principles of substantive justice: the "equal-liberty" principle, the "fair equality of opportunity" principle (hereinafter the "fair-opportunity" principle), and the "difference" principle. According to Rawls's equal-liberty principle, "each person is to have an equal right to the most extensive total system of equal basic liberties compatible with a similar system of liberty for all" (*TJ* 302). According to his fair-opportunity principle, all "offices and positions" are to be "open to all under conditions of fair equality of opportunity" (*TJ* 83). And according to his "difference principle," "[a]ll social primary goods—liberty and opportunity, income and wealth, and the bases of self-respect—are to be distributed equally unless an unequal distribution of any or all of these goods is to the advantage of the least favored" (*TJ* 302).[28] Rawls also concludes that the members of our society are committed to ordering these three principles lexically in the sequence in which they were just given. More specifically, Rawls maintains that society is committed to refusing to sacrifice even the smallest degree of equal liberty to achieve even the largest conceivable improvement in either fairness of opportunity or the position of the worst-off group, and to refusing to sacrifice even the smallest improvement in the fairness of opportunity in order to obtain even the largest conceivable improvement in the position of its worst-off group (*TJ* 302–3).

Rawls claims that these substantive-justice commitments derive from a more basic commitment to procedural fairness. In particular, Rawls argues that our substantive-justice principles derive from procedural principles of disinterestedness or impartiality that we are committed to recognizing as fair (*inter alia*) in what he takes to be the relevant (constitutional-convention) context. Thus, Rawls argues that the best account of the principles of substantive justice to which we are committed (principles that reflective equilibration would enable us to discover) is that they are also the principles of substantive justice that would be unanimously selected at a constitutional convention by Founding Fathers whose appropriate disinterestedness was guaranteed if the Founding Fathers could assume that the society whose constitution they are promulgating "has achieved the minimum degree of material affluence at which the basic material wants of individuals can be fulfilled" (*TJ* 542). Rawls goes on to specify that, to be appropriately disinterested, his Founding Fathers should know nothing about their empirical selves and the society in which their empirical selves will live—in particular, about (1) their physical, intellectual, and emotional attributes either absolutely or relative to those of others; (2) their social or economic position; (3) their personal history; (4) their values, theory of the good, concept of an ideal human being, notion of justice, or beliefs about right and wrong; (5) with some exceptions to be discussed below, their preferences; (6) the natural or geographic situation of the society in which their empirical selves will live; (7) its political, economic, and social structure; (8) its stage of development; and (9) any other of its features that might depend on the time at which their empirical selves will live (*TJ* 121, 137, 187).

Finally, Rawls argues that a society that instantiates the principles of substantive justice to which we are committed and for which he has accounted will be politically stable. His arguments for this conclusion are complicated and subtle. To a considerable extent, they turn on the fact that by instantiating his principles society will manifest its respect for all its subjects, that such a society will thereby foster mutual respect among its subjects and a belief in the justness of the substantive-justice principles it is effectuating, and that such respect and beliefs will promote if not guarantee political stability (*TJ* 105, 499, 500).

The relevance of Rawls's project to mine should be apparent. If Rawls is correct in maintaining that (1) one can discover a societal commitment to his principle of procedural fairness, (2) our commitment to this principle commits us to the principles of substantive justice he claims his Founding Fathers would select if they were governed by this principle of procedural fairness, and (3) people who are disinterested in the sense he thinks our culture is committed to recognizing as appropriate in the constitutional-convention context would all select his principles of substantive justice, judges could decide constitutional disputes without imposing their own values by using Rawls's three lexically-ordered principles of justice to operationalize the Ninth Amendment's concept of "unenumerated rights," the Fourteenth Amendment's concept of "privileges or immunities," and when appropriate other pieces of Constitutional text that refer to vague moral concepts.

B. A Preliminary Comparison between Rawls's Approach and Underlying Assumptions and Mine

(1) Four Similarities

First, Rawls's project is similar to mine in that both of us are trying (*inter alia*) to articulate the basic moral norms that underlie the rights-conclusions of our society.[29] Admittedly, however, his analysis focuses on issues of perfect justice,[30] while mine is equally concerned with issues of corrective justice.

Second, although Rawls never uses this approach to identify (as opposed to account for) our substantive-justice commitments, his discussion of reflective equilibration implies both that it is the approach he thinks one should use to identify a society's substantive-justice commitments and that it involves the use of the same "closeness-of-fit" and "explicability-of-(non-fit)" criteria I use to identify our basic moral principle and its more concrete corollaries.

Third, Rawls's distinction between "the right" and "the good" and his conclusion that "the concept of the right is prior to that of the good"[31] parallels my distinction between "moral-rights talk" and "moral-ought talk" and my claim that moral-rights conclusions trump over moral-ought conclusions in our society.[32]

Fourth, the boundary condition Rawls believes defines the class of moral-rights holders is very similar to mine. Thus, according to Rawls:

> [I]t is precisely the moral persons who are entitled to equal justice. Moral persons are distinguished by two features: first they are capable of having (and are assumed to have) a conception of their good (as expressed by a rational life plan); they are capable of having (and are assumed to acquire) a sense of justice, a normally effective desire to apply and to act upon the principles of justice, at least to a certain minimum degree. . . . One should observe that moral personality is here defined as a potentiality that is ordinarily realized in due course. (*TJ* 505)[33]

Although Rawls has not attempted to operationalize the "potentiality that is ordinarily realized in due course" and might reject my resolution of this difficult issue, his boundary-condition position is clearly highly analogous to mine.

(2) Four Differences

As important as the commonalities just listed are, Rawls's *A Theory of Justice* is at least as different from as it is similar to the position I took in Chapter 1. In particular, *A Theory of Justice* differs from my analysis in at least four ways worth noting.

The first difference may be purely linguistic. In my vocabulary, the statement that an act or decision is "just" implies that it is consistent with our rights-commitments. Rawls says that legislative choices that are not required or precluded by our rights-commitments also involve "justice"—in particular, those that turn on competing conceptions of "justice" (*TJ* 198–99, 357). This difference between us may be important because it calls into question my previous conclusion that in distinguishing between the "right" and the "good" and maintaining the priority of the right over the good, he is agreeing with my finding that we are a rights-based society that engages in two different types of prescriptive moral discourse and that in our society rights-conclusions trump over ought-conclusions.

The second difference relates to the role that self-respect and respect for others play in our analyses. Although Rawls repeatedly stresses the importance of self-respect and mutual respect (*TJ* 62, 179, 180, 234, 336–37, 396, 543) and admits that his principles of justice will be effective only if the members of his society have a sense of justice and therefore respect one another (*TJ* 586), he nonetheless argues that "the notion of respect or of the inherent worth of persons is not a suitable basis for arriving at these principles" (*TJ* 586). For Rawls, any notion of the inherent worth of a person presupposes "principles [of justice] already independently derived" (*TJ* 586). My position is precisely the opposite. I think that the basic notion is the value of creatures' becoming and remaining individuals of moral integrity and that our more-or-less-concrete substantive principles of justice must be derived from the duty to show appropriate, equal respect for all creatures that have the neurological prerequisites to become and remain individuals of moral integrity and the duty to show appropriate, equal concern for their actualizing that potential. In fact, I doubt that Rawls's approach will yield any substantive-justice conclusions unless he assumes that his Founding Fathers carry with them an idea of what makes moral-rights holders worthy of respect.

The third difference between Rawls's position in *A Theory of Justice* and mine is related to the second. Unlike my basic moral principle (which is a principle of *substantive* justice), Rawls's basic principle is one of *procedural* justice. The next part of this section explains why I reject Rawls's claim that his principles of substantive justice are a manifestation of our commitment to a procedural principle of appropriate disinterestedness.

The fourth difference between Rawls's analysis and my own are the conclusions we reach about substantive justice. Although I agree that moral-rights holders have rights-related interests in his basic liberties and that they must be treated as equals in respect to those interests, I believe that moral-rights holders have a wider set of rights-related interests than Rawls's list of basic liberties seems to suggest, do not think that in our society justice requires that equal liberty be given priority over fair opportunity, and conclude that justice in our society imposes a relative and absolute minimum "real-income" constraint on the State, which is quite different from Rawls's difference principle. The last section of this analysis of Rawls explores these disagreements as well as other aspects of Rawls's discussion of substantive justice.

C. Three Objections to Rawls's Approach to Discovering Our Society's Principles of Substantive "Perfect Justice": A Critique of Justice as Fairness

(1) A Critique of Rawls's Principle of Appropriate Disinterestedness

I do not think that members of our culture are committed to the principle of impartiality that Rawls thinks we are committed to using in constitutional-convention and other political contexts.[34] In particular, I think he is wrong in asserting that members of our culture consider it unfair for people to take their own values into consideration.

Clearly, self-serving decisionmaking is often suspect in public contexts. But whether it is improper for a decisionmaker to allow her decision to be influenced by her personal ultimate values is uncertain, even if the choice benefits her materially as well. For example, assume that an individual who personally believes in equal-resource egalitarianism votes for policies that will effectuate that value. Is it impermissible for her to base her vote on her personal support of this value? So long as her value-conviction is sincere, I think not—even if the vote in question serves her narrowly-defined material interests because she originally had fewer resources than the average member of the community. If rights-considerations do not control all government decisions, choices that are not determined by rights-analysis must be made on some basis. Although the social-choice mechanism for making these choices must be procedurally fair, it is not ipso facto unfair for individuals to base their votes on their personal ultimate values when the choices in question are not required or prohibited by our society's substantive-rights commitments. Obviously, if Rawls is wrong in asserting that a Founding Father would be acting in an inappropriately-self-interested way if he allowed his vote to be influenced by his knowledge of the personal ultimate values his empirical self supported or would support, this fact would call into question Rawls's claim that he can justicize his substantive principles of justice by citing the fairness of the procedures he claims would lead his Founding Fathers unanimously to select his principles of substantive justice if they acted behind his veil of ignorance.

(2) A Critique of the Argument from Agreement or Consent

Although Rawls seems to disavow this claim (*TJ* 21, 167), some of his followers believe that his substantive-justice conclusion can be established by citing the significance our culture is committed to attributing to the fact that some individual has agreed to some set of terms—that one can justify holding actual people to the principles he thinks his Founding Fathers would select behind the veil of ignorance by attributing to our society's current members the Founding Fathers' hypothetical agreement both to his principle of procedural fairness and to the principles of substantive justice he claims they would unanimously support behind his veil of ignorance. In fact, however, this argument has two weaknesses.

The first is its apparent assumption that individuals are always bound by any terms to which they actually agreed. That assumption is not consistent with our rights-obligations practices. In particular, in our culture a party may not be bound by his agreement if one or more of the following four conditions, all of which are arguably fulfilled in Rawls's context, is satisfied:

(1) he was incompetent at the time at which he entered into the agreement,

(2) his agreement reflected his unilateral mistake—or better yet his and his contractual partners' mutual mistake—about an essential character of some feature of the agreement,[35]

(3) his agreement was obtained by fraud, misrepresentation, or a failure to disclose,[36] and

(4) conditions have changed dramatically and—a fortiori— unforeseeably for him between the time the agreement was signed and the time at which someone is trying to enforce it.

These rights-obligation practices imply that no empirical self might be bound by Rawls's principles even if Rawls's constitutional convention did take place and the empirical individuals he is seeking to obligate actually did participate in it. Thus, these empirical individuals might not be bound even on these assumptions because Rawls's veil of ignorance

(1) might be said to have rendered them temporarily incompetent at the time of the agreement by depriving them of all information about themselves, their society, or their own or their society's values,

(2) might be said to have resulted in all his Founding Fathers' mistaking the essential character of the agreement they were making (from their respective empirical selves' value-perspectives) by depriving them of all information about their own personal ultimate values and their society's moral principles,

(3) might be said to have misled them into making the agreement (by requiring them to act on the basis of various counterfactual assumptions about their empirical selves' preferences or by telling them that canons of rationality required them to maximin) and by failing to disclose essential information to them (such as information about their empirical selves' personal ultimate values or their society's moral principles), and

(4) might be said to have put the relevant individuals into a position in which the conditions under which the relevant agreement would be enforced would be dramatically and unforeseeably (from the relevant agreement-participants' perspectives) different from the conditions under which it was made.

Perhaps an argument-from-agreement could survive this kind of critique, but even if it could these issues certainly must be addressed.

The second weakness in this argument-from-agreement relates to its implicit assumption that its force is not vitiated by the hypothetical character of the agreement on which it focuses.[37] In reality, of course, Rawls's constitutional convention never took place. Certainly, no empirical individuals ever agreed to his principles of substantive justice and their lexical ordering (no empirical individuals were actually Rawlsian Founding Fathers). Hence, arguments from consent cannot rely on actual acceptance but only on hypothetical, counterfactual acceptance. Unfortunately, hypothetical acceptance or agreement simply cannot bind. Some examples should make this clear. Surely, the fact that I would have sold you my painting for one hundred dollars on Monday when I thought it was a copy (or believed I hated it) would not bind me to sell it to you for that price on Wednesday (at least if I withdrew my offer before you accepted) after discovering that it was an original (or that I loved it). Similarly, the fact that I would have accepted certain rules for playing a game with you on Monday because I really wanted to play and could not find any other playmates would not obligate me to accept such rules on Wednesday when I was less anxious to play or could find alternative playmates: you had your chance and missed it. I need not now accept rules I dislike, find disadvantageous, or find unfair simply because I would have accepted them two days earlier. Since hypothetical consent will not bind even when actual consent would, the argument-from-agreement cannot succeed.

(3) A Critique of Rawls's Claim That His Founding Fathers Would Unanimously Select His Principles of Substantive Justice If They Operated behind His Veil of Ignorance

This section criticizes Rawls's claim that his Founding Fathers would unanimously choose his three principles of justice and place them in the lexical order in which he claims our society is committed to ranking them. Before I can proceed with this task, I must delineate Rawls's assumptions about his Founding Fathers' knowledge and "rationality." I have already listed the various facts about their empirical selves and the society in which they will live that Rawls's veil of ignorance will conceal from his Founding Fathers. However, Rawls does not assume that his Founding Fathers are irrational, faceless ignoramuses. To the contrary, he assumes that they will know all "the general facts about human society." Rawls includes in this category the facts of "political affairs," "the principles of economic theory," "the basis of social organization," and "the laws of human psychology,"[38] which he assumes are not culturally dependent (which he assumes would preclude the possibility that a society that was structured very differently from our own might give rise to a truly "new man").

Rawls also assumes that his Founding Fathers will be "rational" and will have certain preferences that he appears to think the laws of human psychology make inevitable. More specifically, and highly debatably, Rawls seems to think that rationality requires his Founding Fathers to make their choices on the following assumptions:

(1) that their empirical selves will prefer more to less of the primary goods of liberty, opportunity, wealth, and authority;[39]

(2) that "other things equal, human beings enjoy the exercise of their realized capacities (their innate or trained abilities), and this enjoyment increases the more the capacity is realized, or the greater its complexity"[40]—in other words, the Founding Fathers will know that this so-called Aristotelian Principle is true; perhaps relatedly

(3) that "one of the main forms of human good" is "the realization of self that comes from a skillful and devoted exercise of social duties";[41]

(4) admittedly counterfactually, that their empirical selves will feel no envy[42] or, more generally, (A) will place no weight on the resources available to or success or utility experienced by others[43] so long as any difference between their own position and that of others does not manifest injustice as defined by Rawls (*TJ* 530) and (B) will be indifferent to the extent to which our society conforms with their notions of justice or approaches their ideal; and

(5) that it is best ("rational") to choose a maximin strategy (to select that option that will maximize the worst [minimum] outcome their empirical selves could experience) (*TJ* 152–57).

Although Rawls does not put it this way, he also assumes that his Founding Fathers' knowledge of the laws of human psychology will lead them to conclude that once their empirical selves have satisfied their basic wants, they will prefer even the smallest increase in equal liberty or equal and fair opportunity to any possible increase in material welfare. In the case of equal liberty, this assumption probably reflects his belief that the Aristotelian Principle is a psychological law. In the case of the equal-opportunity principle, this assumption reflects Rawls's belief in the universally-high value of "experiencing the realization of self which comes from the skillful and devoted exercise of social duties" (*TJ* 84), a belief that may also be a corollary of his view that the Aristotelian Principle is a law of nature.[44]

I will now examine whether Rawls's Founding Fathers would unanimously choose his three principles of substantive justice and would order them lexically in the way he claims if they operated behind his veil of ignorance. I have two objections to this claim.

First, to the extent that Rawls's conclusions depend on his belief that (1) maximin strategies are "rational," (2) the Aristotelian Principle is a universal law of psychology, (3) it is irrational to feel envy or, more generally, to care about the utility or welfare of others, and/or (4) it is irrational to be concerned about the quality of society from a personal-ultimate-value perspective, the arguments that support Rawls's conclusions will be highly contestable. In fact, Rawls's difference principle does seem to reflect his belief that maximining is rational (as well as his belief in an incorrect argument [see below] that suggests that the instantiation of the difference principle will promote the stability of the society he is imagining). Moreover, Rawls's claim that the Founding Fathers will conclude that once their society has attained some minimum level of material welfare, it would be unjust for it to sacrifice even the smallest amount of any basic liberty or the smallest degree of equality of opportunity for the largest increase in utility it could conceivably obtain from doing so seems to reflect his belief in the Aristotelian Principle as well as his possibly-related belief in the extraordinarily-rewarding character of performing skillfully and devotedly an important social role. In addition, Rawls's conclusion that his Founding Fathers would unanimously vote to protect various basic liberties (e.g., freedom of conscience) partly reflects his assumption that rationality requires each of their empirical selves to ignore the welfare of all other members of their society. Obviously, the facts that (1) maximining is "rational" in the normal sense of that word only for choosers who are extremely risk-averse, (2) the Aristotelian Principle is almost certainly not a law of nature, (3) envy is common and most people include the utility or success of one or more others in their own maximand (the function they are seeking to maximize), and (4) many are concerned about the quality of their society for reasons that do not solely reflect their narrowly-defined interests all undercut Rawls's arguments that his Founding Fathers would vote for the difference principle, would prefer liberty or equal opportunity to utility, and would choose to protect various basic liberties such as freedom of conscience.

Second, even if the four assumptions just discussed were justified, I doubt that Rawls's Founding Fathers would unanimously vote for his principles or order them in the way he claims they would. I will illustrate this objection by examining whether Founding Fathers operating on Rawls's four assumptions behind his veil of ignorance would choose to protect liberty of conscience as a basic liberty.[45]

On Rawls's assumption that it is rational to maximin, his Founding Fathers would choose to protect freedom of conscience only if the experience of being a persecuted heretic is worse than that of being a member of a majority that is unable to satisfy its desire to punish heretics. I think that it is far from obvious that Rawls's Founding Fathers would find it worse to be a persecuted heretic than a member of a majority frustrated by a prohibition against punishing heresy. Thus, in the one direction, one should not overestimate the cost of martyrdom, especially since a decision to allow a majority to punish heresy could be combined with prohibitions of torture or other types of painful or prolonged punishment that would reduce those costs and, at least for some martyrs, the costs that remain would be somewhat offset by various perceived "benefits": "material" benefits such as a paradisal afterlife or spiritual benefits such as the feeling of having done one's duty or of having been true to one's faith or political or moral convictions. And, in the other direction, one should not underestimate the cost of being a member of a frustrated majority, even on Rawls's assumptions—the "costs" some people incur (1) when they witness their own beliefs being rejected, criticized, or derided and (2) when "heretical" speech or acts (a) embarrass them, (b) cause them to have feelings or desires they regard as sinful, (c) tempt them to betray their own convictions—to engage in acts that they consider sinful, immoral, or non-virtuous, (d) prevent them from parenting in the way they deem appropriate, and (e) prevent them from producing children who want to interact with them in a way they deem satisfactory. Moreover, if we relax Rawls's assumptions that his Founding Fathers are indifferent to the fate of others and the quality of their society insofar as it does not affect them "directly," the "freedom of conscience" principle will also impose costs on them by allowing immoral individuals or sinners to escape retribution, corrupting and damaging others (including the frustrated majority's own children), reducing the ability of the frustrated majority to produce children of whom it can be proud, and reducing the pride the frustrated majority can take in its society. Since it is not clear that it would be worse to be a punished heretic than a member of a majority frustrated by its inability to punish (and thereby deter) heresy, it is not clear that even maximining Founding Fathers who did not know their own ultimate values or their society's moral principles would choose to protect freedom of conscience.

I can just hear the Rawls scholars shouting "Ouch!" (Rawls himself is far too much of a gentleman to do so.) Yes, I do realize that Rawls's own argument for equal liberty of conscience is quite different from the one I have just criticized. According to Rawls:

> It suffices that if any principle can be agreed to, it must be that of equal liberty. A person may indeed think that other persons ought to recognize the same beliefs and first principles that he does, and that by not doing so they are grievously in error and miss the way to their salvation. But an understanding of religious obligation and of philosophical and moral first principles shows that we cannot expect others to acquiesce in an inferior liberty. Much less can we ask them to recognize us as the proper interpreter of their religious duties or moral obligations. (*TJ* 208)

Rawls's analysis of the reasons why his Founding Fathers will vote for equal liberty of conscience is consistent with his account of the reasons that they will support equal liberty in general:

> [E]qual liberty of conscience is the only principle that the persons in the original position can acknowledge. They cannot take chances with their liberty by permitting the dominant religious or moral doctrines to persecute or to suppress others if it wishes. Even granting (what may be questioned) that it is more probable than not that one will turn out to belong to the majority (if a majority exists), to gamble in this way would show that one did not take one's religious or moral convictions seriously, or highly value the liberty to examine one's beliefs. (*TJ* 207)

I understand why liberalism as I have defined that term implies what Rawls claims "an understanding of religious obligation and philosophical and moral first principles shows" (*TJ* 208), but I do not understand why the understanding of such obligations and principles as abstract concepts reveals what he claims it reveals. Why cannot a non-liberal who values highly the ability to examine his beliefs vote against freedom of conscience because he also values the ability to act on his beliefs sufficiently highly to justify such a vote, given the fact that the probability of his being a member of a majority is higher than the probability of his being a heretic? I do not think that Rawls could dispose of this argument by citing the Aristotelian Principle, even if it were a law of nature—at least, he could not do so without assuming that the human capacities to which the Principle refers are restricted to those capacities whose exercise is consistent with liberal principles.

In short, I do not think that Rawls's Founding Fathers' understanding of religious obligations and moral and philosophical first principles in the abstract would lead them to support equal liberty of conscience. In this and in many other instances, Rawls's Founding Fathers would not reach the liberal conclusions he says they would reach unless one assumes that they know that they are committed to liberalism—unless one stipulates that religious and moral principles are liberal by their very nature or that the kinds of human capacities to which the Aristotelian Principle refers are ones that can be exercised without violating liberal principles.

Again, Rawls claims that "an understanding of religious obligation and of philosophical and moral first principles shows that we cannot expect others to acquiesce in an inferior liberty. Much less can we ask them to recognize us as the proper interpreter of their religious duties or moral obligations" (*TJ* 208). If the expression "personal-ultimate-value commitments" were substituted for "religious duties or moral obligations," I would agree that the preceding quotation expresses a central tenet of liberalism as I have defined that moral position. I simply do not think that it expresses a defining attribute of moral positions in general. Indeed, if it did, one would not need the rest of Rawls's procedure to generate his conclusions about the principles of justice.

D. Rawls's Conclusions about the Principles of Substantive Justice to Which We Are Committed

This section begins by making some general comments about the specificity of Rawls's substantive-justice conclusions. It then briefly discusses each of Rawls's three principles of substantive justice and their lexical ordering.

Rawls and I both start with an extremely abstract moral principle: I, with a principle of appropriate, equal respect and concern, and he, with a principle of appropriate disinterestedness or impartiality. However, I end up much more concrete than Rawls—with a non-exhaustive list of numerous, moderately-specific, rights-related interests whose contours and relative weights in various contexts are examined in some detail. Rawls ends up with a much more abstract set of interests—in equal basic liberties, in fair and equal opportunity, and in not being disadvantaged solely to improve the position of one or more others who were better off in the first pace. In my judgment, Rawls's discussions of these interests never become appropriately concrete.

Of course, Rawls knows that God is in the details (the applications) as well as in the broad, abstract statements. He also knows both that much of his discussion is "unhappily abstract"[46] and that the boundaries of many of his key concepts are "unsure."[47] However, although he sometimes admits that his analysis "at this stage" (*TJ* 205) is very abstract, he rarely fulfills the implicit promise this statement conveys to become more concrete. Thus, he never follows up on his acknowledgment that his basic liberties may conflict (may "collide with each other" [*TJ* 203]) by describing situations of conflict sufficiently thickly to enable him to define his liberty interests helpfully or to assess the determinants of their relative weights in an illuminating way. For example, although he recognizes that the institution of the family may disfavor equality of opportunity (*TJ* 74), he never adequately discusses how this problem will be solved—indeed, never explicitly refers to the possible "basic" liberty interest in parenting, which I suspect has far more to do with self-realization for most of us than does the political participation or skilled and devoted performance of important social roles that Rawls so highly values. Similarly, although Rawls recognizes that "the larger part of society [may have] abhorrence for certain religious or sexual practices, and [may regard] them as an abomination" (*TJ* 450), he says no more about this fact than that society may not prohibit the practices in question on this account because they do not "injure" (*TJ* 450) the members of the majority whose "intense convictions" they violate. I can understand why the commitment of the members of a liberal society to respecting the life-plans of others may preclude them from prohibiting these practices, but Rawls precludes his Founding Fathers from knowing about this commitment. If Rawls thinks that his Founding Fathers can infer this commitment without knowing their value-orientation, he needs to be far more forthcoming about the non-value-specific source of this knowledge.

In fact, on the few occasions on which Rawls is more specific about individual rights, his comments do not seem to me to be very encouraging. Thus, when discussing political inequality, he states: "Perhaps the most obvious political inequality is the violation of the precept one person one vote" (*TJ* 231). Admittedly, there are at least two interrelated reasons why liberals are committed to giving all competent members of a society equal political influence: the notion that to be free an individual should be the author of the laws that constrain him and perhaps, more importantly, the fact that one way of showing appropriate, equal respect for each relevantly competent moral-rights holder is to give each such person an equally-important role in choosing his governors or the laws that constrain him. Admittedly, Rawls's discussion of equal political liberty does emphasize that in this area true equality requires, *inter alia*, that "all citizens should have the means to be informed about political issues" and that "all citizens should have a fair chance to add alternative proposals to the agenda for political discussion" (*TJ* 225). Moreover, Rawls does recognize that to fulfill these conditions of political equality, "a variety of devices can be used": "property and wealth must be kept widely distributed, ... government monies [must be] provided on a regular basis to encourage free public discussion, ...[and] political parties [must be] made independent from private economic interests by allotting them sufficient tax revenues to play their part in the constitutional scheme" (*TJ* 225–26). Nevertheless, even if the preceding conditions have been fulfilled, "one person one vote" has little to do with the effectuation of "equal political influence," regardless of how that highly-contestable notion is operationalized. In part, this conclusion reflects the fact that persons influence governmental outcomes not only by voting but also by donating money and time, by making use of connections, by convincing others through relevant argument, and by taking advantage of their personal influence. In part, it reflects the fact that a group's political power is not always proportionate to its share of the vote—for example, that a swing group may have more power-per-vote than other groups. And in part, it reflects the fact that the "one person one vote" constraint has virtually no effect on the ability of those who control the voting process to disadvantage some individuals or groups unfairly.

I will now comment briefly on Rawls's three principles of justice and their lexical ordering.

(1) The "Equal Basic Liberty" Principle

According to Rawls, the most basic primary good is self-respect (*TJ* 544). In his judgment, the "equal basic liberty principle" must be instantiated and be given priority over all other principles because "[t]he basis for self-esteem in a just society is not ... one's income share but the publicly affirmed distribution of fundamental rights and liberties" (*TJ* 544).

I have five points to make about Rawls's treatment of his equal-liberty principle. The first relates to his list of basic liberties: political liberties (the right to vote and be eligible for public office, freedom of speech and assembly, liberty of conscience and freedom of thought, freedom of the person), freedom from arbitrary arrest and seizure, and the right to hold personal property.

In my judgment, Rawls's list contains several that are relatively unconnected with self-realization and omits (or at least fails to specify) some that I think are very important in this regard. Thus, as I have already suggested, Rawls seems to me to exaggerate the importance of political liberties and politically-related speech-and-assembly rights for self-respect and self-realization and to ignore the importance of our interest in forming and maintaining parental and other intimate relationships, our interest in privacy, and our interest in receiving the formal education and having the life-experiences that contribute significantly to our ability to make a meaningful life-plan choice.

Second, as I have also already indicated in relation to liberty of conscience, I do not think that Rawls's Founding Fathers would choose to protect his basic liberties unless they knew they were societally or personally committed to valuing these liberties highly.

Third, again as previously stated, Rawls makes little effort to define his basic liberties or to see which of them would be protected when they conflict in a given situation.[48] If Rawls did acknowledge his moral-rights holders' liberty interest in parenting as well as their interest in formal and informal education, how would he resolve the conflict between the interest of a parent in inducing his child to accept a certain way of life and the interest of the child in having the level of education and awareness of alternatives necessary for him to make an adequately-informed life-plan choice (a conflict that comes to the fore when parents try to secure their objective by withdrawing their child from public education in order to limit the child's exposure to alternative life-plans)?[49]

Fourth, I do not find Rawls's handling of the distinction between equal liberty and equal worth of liberty satisfactory. According to Rawls, the equal liberty to which his principle refers can be violated by custom, public opinion, social pressure, or the interference of specific private parties as well as by law (*TJ* 202). However, in Rawls's judgment, except in relation to political-participation rights, equal liberty is not violated by financial constraints or the relevant subject's own ignorance (or [presumably] stupidity, disorganization, shyness, or inarticulateness) (*TJ* 204). In Rawls's view, such financial and other parameters affect the worth of liberty rather than liberty itself, and their treatment is therefore governed by the difference principle rather than by the equal-liberty principle. I do not find this conclusion persuasive. Why, for example, should liberty be violated by social pressures that deter a pregnant woman from having an abortion and not by financial pressures that preclude her from doing so (by preventing her from paying for an abortion)? Since Rawls does not think that individuals are entitled to profit from accidents of birth and natural endowment (*TJ* 100), he would have to admit that these sorts of financial disabilities or personal limitations are substantially within the State's control. What are the State's obligations in relation to (1) the kinds of medical, ethical, or religious ignorance, (2) stupidity, or (3) indecisiveness or disorganization that may result in a pregnant woman's having or not having an abortion? Does the State have no responsibilities in relation to these issues or are its responsibilities defined by the difference principle? I address these difficult issues in Chapter 3. For present purposes, I just want to note Rawls's failure to discuss them in any detail.

The fifth point I wish to make about Rawls's analysis of his equal-liberty principle relates to its lexical ordering. Given Rawls's views about the extraordinarily satisfying character of the experience of performing an important social role skillfully and devotedly, I cannot understand his making the equal-liberty principle lexically prior to the equal-opportunity principle. And given his recognition that in the real world—though"[c]learly this situation is a great misfortune" (*TJ* 545)—"[t]o some extent men's sense of their own worth may hinge upon ... their income share" (*TJ* 546), I am not convinced that within his system his equal-liberty principle should be ranked lexically above his difference principle.

(2) *The Equal and Fair Opportunity Principle*

According to Rawls, his Founding Fathers would vote for his fair opportunity principle because their understanding of human psychology would lead them to conclude that "the skillful and devoted exercise of social duties" yields an especially-meaningful kind of "realization of self"—an experience that constitutes "one of the main forms of human good" (*TJ* 84). I have already indicated my doubts about both this universal claim and the Aristotelian Principle to which it is related. I will confine myself here to two other related issues: Rawls's conclusions about the lexical ranking of his fair and equal opportunity principle and his failure to analyze at an appropriately-operational level the various kinds of steps his Founding Fathers would require their society to take as a matter of justice to secure fair and equal opportunity.

As previously suggested, Rawls's high evaluation of the experience of performing social duties skillfully and devotedly may be inconsistent with his giving his fair-opportunity principle a lower lexical ranking than his equal-liberty principle. In addition, Rawls's conclusion that his fair-opportunity principle is lexically prior to his difference principle may be inconsistent with his admission that an individual's self-respect and ability to take his life seriously may depend on both the absolute amount of material resources available to him and his relative wealth-and-income position in his society (given that the implementation of the fair-opportunity principle will almost certainly reduce the size of the social pie quite considerably).

My first example of Rawls's failure to be appropriately specific connects my comments on priority and specificity in that it involves the possible conflict between parental liberties (which he admittedly does not list as a separate basic liberty) and his fair-opportunity principle. Thus, *A Theory of Justice* does not explicitly address whether a parent has a legitimate interest in giving his or her children an advantage over competitors for important social roles, whether this interest would be violated by government programs designed to offset the advantage the parent's efforts would otherwise give his or her children by providing education, training, or useful life-opportunities to those whose family connections are less fortunate in this respect, whether the fair-opportunity principle might obligate a just State to control who can parent which children—to transfer children whose skills or devotedness to duty would otherwise be disqualifyingly low and/or lower-than-average to more "productivity-enhancing" families or conceivably to transfer children whose "productivity" would otherwise be higher-than-average to less productivity-enhancing families (when the enhancement in question is not caused by financial expenditures that could be controlled without removing the child from the families concerned), whether the fair-opportunity principle might obligate a State to adopt eugenic policies designed to prevent the creation of creatures whose genetic make-up will tend to make them more-than-usually-able or less-than-usually-able to perform significant social tasks skillfully and devotedly.

Rawls also is insufficiently concrete when discussing a number of other issues raised by his fair-opportunity principle. For example, he does not indicate whether the realization of self that he claims individuals experience from the skillful and devoted performance of importance social roles increases continuously with the skillfulness and devotedness of the relevant actor's performance or is dichotomously related to the relevant performance-quality variations.

Rawls also does not indicate whether the actor's experience of self-realization depends on her perception of her performance or on her actual social product in the relevant social role. This latter distinction may critically affect two related obligations of a Rawlsian just State. First, if perception is all, Rawls's principles of justice might require a just State to define "jobs" so as to maximize the number of people who could perceive themselves to be performing important roles skillfully and devotedly rather than the number of people who actually could do so. Second, if perception is all, Rawls's just

State might be obligated not only to train people who would otherwise be insufficiently able to perform the relevant jobs satisfactorily to enable them to execute the relevant tasks skillfully and devotedly but also to train all people to perceive themselves to be performing such tasks skillfully and devotedly (regardless of whether they have done so) when they are given the opportunity to perform such tasks.

Rawls's failure to operationalize the relevant conceptions of skill and devotedness also precludes him from indicating the amount of conventional social pie his fair-opportunity principle will require a just society to sacrifice in various circumstances.

I admit that there may be some way to resolve all of these issues within Rawls's framework. My complaint is that Rawls has not made an appropriate attempt to do so.

(3) The Difference Principle

(A) RAWLS'S ARGUMENTS FOR HIS CONCLUSION THAT HIS FOUNDING
FATHERS WILL ADOPT HIS DIFFERENCE PRINCIPLE BECAUSE
CANONS OF RATIONALITY REQUIRE THEM TO ADOPT A
MAXIMIN STRATEGY

As I have already indicated, although maximining Founding Fathers would choose Rawls's difference principle (if they ignored the problem of stragglers), their adoption of such a strategy is not required by canons of rationality, and most empirical selves would not in fact adopt such a risk-averse approach (and would certainly not do so in the circumstances in which the difference principle is operative—that is, after their "basic wants" have been "fulfilled"). As I will argue in Section (C), people who are committed to liberal values would try to minimize the probability that their material welfare and social status would fall to a level that would prevent them from or militate against their having the kind of self-respect that is a prerequisite for taking one's life morally seriously. However, for two reasons, this "fact" cannot be used to justify Rawls's difference principle: he is assuming that his Founding Fathers do not know their empirical selves' personal ultimate values or the moral principles to which their society is committed and, as we shall see, the liberal minimum real-income constraint is very different from Rawls's difference principle—it will sometimes require the difference principle to be violated and will have no implications for the necessity of adopting some

Constitutional principles or legislative policies the difference principle will require to be adopted.

(B) RAWLS'S ARGUMENT THAT HIS DIFFERENCE PRINCIPLE IS ALSO
JUSTIFIED BY THE FACT THAT ITS SELECTION WILL PROMOTE
POLITICAL STABILITY

Rawls seems to think that his difference principle is justified not only by the "fact" that it would be chosen by his Founding Fathers behind the veil of ignorance but also by the "fact" that its selection would promote political stability (*TJ* 105, 499, 500). I have two objections to this claim: even if the difference principle would guarantee political stability, I do not see why it would be justified or justicized by that fact, and I do not think that the implementation of the difference principle will tend to lead to political stability.

Rawls's primary argument for the stabilizing effect of the difference principle seems to be based on the following three premises:

(1) violations of the difference principle fail to respect the members of the worst-off group because they treat members of the worst-off group not as ends but as means for the improvement of the non-worst-off individuals whose absolute welfare would be enhanced by the difference-principle-violating choice (*TJ* 179);

(2) the respect of others is an important and often critical prerequisite of self-respect—of having a sense of our own worth, a sense that our life-plan is worth carrying out (*TJ* 178); and

(3) individuals who have self-respect are less likely to destabilize a regime.

There are at least two problems with this argument. First, unless one can make an argument to the contrary—one that probably presupposes values of which Rawls's Founding Fathers are supposed to be ignorant, a decision to implement the difference principle seems as likely to destabilize the political regime by undercutting some citizens' self-respect as a decision to violate the difference principle since the implementation of the difference principle always involves using those members of the non-worst-off group whom the choice in question would harm as a means for the betterment of the members of the worst-off group (even if I assume that the composition of the worst-off group is invariant). Second, individuals who have been treated with respect in the sense in which the difference principle secures this result may be more likely rather than less likely to engage in revolution to improve their positions.

The second argument that some appear to believe implies that the difference principle will lead to political stability is a materialist argument. This argument has two premises:

(1) the most likely source of revolution are individuals in the worst-off group in a society whose worst-off group could be made better off and

(2) the implementation of the difference principle guarantees that the least-advantaged or worst-off group cannot be made better off by an alternative regime.

For three reasons, this argument is mistaken. First, even if the most important or only sources of political instability were the members of a worst-off group whose membership would not be affected by any relevant change in social arrangements, the difference principle would not lead to political stability because it would not guarantee that the worst-off group as such could not be made better off by a shift to a different regime. Rawls's difference principle guarantees only that the worst-off group as such could not be made better off in terms of straightforward material welfare or social status without sacrificing equal worth of political liberty, equal formal liberty of other kinds, or fair opportunity, and even if his Founding Fathers would be unwilling to sacrifice these things to obtain additional material welfare or social status behind the veil of ignorance when they did not know what they valued or whether they would be members of the worst-off group, the empirical members of the worst-off group might very well prefer to make that trade-off in the actual, real-world situation they confront.

Second, even if a higher floor for the worst-off group as such could not be achieved even at the cost of some sacrifice of equal worth of political liberty, equal liberty of other sorts, or fair opportunity, the difference principle would not guarantee that the individuals who comprise an existing worst-off group would have no reason to prefer an alternative regime. Even if a change in regime could not prevent society from having a worst-off group that was as badly off as the least-advantaged group under the existing regime, a change in regime could change the identity of the people in the worst-off group: it could provide the existing worst-off group's members with an incentive to revolt (the incentive of escaping the worst-off group). Indeed, the prospect of a change in regime's changing the membership of the worst-off group might also lead the original members to revolt against the kind of political changes the difference principle requires if there were some chance that they would be the stragglers in the new regime—stragglers who would be worse off than they were as members of the worst-off group under the old regime even though the worst-off group as such would be better off under the new regime than under the old.

Third, this materialist argument that the difference principle would promote political stability is wrong in that it mistakenly assumes that members of the worst-off group in a society are the most likely source of political instability. Even if we ignore the possibility that stragglers may foment revolution, the members of the worst-off group are not the most likely source of political turmoil. These individuals are usually too numerically insignificant and too uneducated, unorganized, and down-trodden to generate any significant revolutionary challenges. The real danger is more likely to be posed by members of the lower middle class—especially those who have experienced a rise in expectations—who may want to change to a regime that would improve their position as individuals even if it worsened the position of the worst-off group as such in their society.

In short, the justicizing effect of any tendency of Rawls's difference principle to promote political stability is dubious. And that tendency itself is far more open to question than Rawls seems to have supposed.

(C) THE IMPORTANCE OF RAWLS'S DIFFERENCE PRINCIPLE, GIVEN
THE CONTENT AND PRIORITY OF HIS EQUAL–LIBERTY AND FAIR–
OPPORTUNITY PRINCIPLES

On some definitions, Rawls's equal-liberty and fair-opportunity principles would make his difference principle irrelevant. Thus, Rawls could define his "equal worth of political liberty" and "fair opportunity" principles in a way that required a minimization of material-goods disparities that would come close to guaranteeing the maximization of the absolute (as well as the relative) position of the worst-off group (if it did not require the worst-off group and *a fortiori* everyone else to be made worse off in the service of equality of outcomes). Of course, one could argue that the emphasis Rawls places on his difference principle implies that he is not defining the other principles in question in a way that would eliminate its importance. But this issue need not be resolved in an all-or-nothing way: at a minimum, it is clear that some of Rawls's liberty principles and his fair-opportunity principle would reduce the amount of benefits that would have to be provided to the relevant society's worst-off group in the name of Rawls's difference principle.

(D) THE RELATIONSHIP BETWEEN RAWLS'S DIFFERENCE PRINCIPLE
AND THE MINIMUM-REAL-INCOME CONSTRAINT TO WHICH I
THINK A LIBERAL SOCIETY IS COMMITTED

I have already indicated my belief that our culture is committed to liberal moral principles that obligate our government to show appropriate, equal respect and concern to all creatures that have the neurological prerequisites to become and remain individuals of moral integrity. I also think that in the United States this commitment is Constitutionalized by the Ninth Amendment as well as by the Fourteenth Amendment's "privileges or immunities" clause. To my mind, this general commitment implies a more specific commitment on the part of the State to providing all moral-rights holders for whom it is responsible with whatever they require to be able to take their lives morally seriously. At a minimum, this would require the State to provide each such individual with enough food, clothing, shelter, and medical help for his condition to permit him to focus on moral issues as opposed to survival or minimal comfort; with a certain level of "education" (of intellectual training and knowledge—including knowledge of moral alternatives); with the exposure to alternative life-choices, privacy, and opportunities to enter into and nurture intimate relationships that will help him to decide what he values; and perhaps with the share of the average amount of material resources that the members of our society enjoy that (in our materialistic society) may significantly increase the likelihood that he will have the kind of self-respect that is a prerequisite to becoming and remaining an individual of moral integrity. It is easy to see why liberals would support the Constitutionalization of a liberal individual-real-income constraint—why people who valued becoming and remaining individuals of moral integrity above all might be unwilling to sacrifice even the smallest probability of their being able to take their lives seriously in this sense for any conceivable increase in their straightforward material-welfare utility. However, this fact would not account for Rawls's Founding Fathers' Constitutionalizing his difference principle even if it were the same as the liberal minimum-real-income constraint, for behind the veil of ignorance Rawls's Founding Fathers cannot know that their empirical selves will be liberals.

In any event and more to the current point, Rawls's difference principle is not identical to the liberal minimum-real-income constraint. Thus, Rawls's difference principle will continue to operate even after the liberal minimum-real-income constraint has been satisfied—that is, it will preclude choices that make members of the worst-off group worse off even if their reduced position would still not violate the liberal absolute and relative minimum-real-income constraint.

Moreover, if the liberal State in question is too poor to give all those for whom it is responsible a sufficiently-high absolute and relative real income to be able to take their lives morally seriously, the liberal minimum-real-income constraint may require it to organize its affairs in a way that violates Rawls's difference principle. The actual implication of the liberal minimum-real-income constraint depends *inter alia* on whether the ability to become or remain a person of moral integrity is eliminated or simply reduced by violations of the constraint and, in the latter case, by the extent to which an individual's ability to take his life morally seriously is compromised by his material welfare's falling different amounts below the constraint. This issue is critical because it will affect whether a liberal society is obligated to minimize the number of people whose material welfare falls below the constraint or some more complicated function that reflects not only the number of people below the constraint but the amounts by which they are below the constraint. If a liberal society is obligated to minimize the number of moral-rights holders whose material welfare falls below the constraint, the liberal minimum-real-income constraint clearly will require a liberal State to violate Rawls's difference principle—to sacrifice some individuals' material welfare *ex post* to minimize the number of moral-rights holders that have the material prerequisites to become or remain individuals of moral integrity. Moreover, if on the other hand, a liberal society must minimize some number equal to a weighted sum of the moral-rights holders whose material welfare is below the constraint (weighted by some function of the amount by which their welfare is below the constraint), the liberal minimum-real-income constraint is also highly likely to require a liberal State to violate Rawls's difference principle since the obligations of a liberal State in the circumstances described will only fortuitously be consistent with Rawls's difference principle.

I have learned a great deal from *A Theory of Justice*. However, I do not think that Rawls's approach to discovering our justice (rights-and-obligations) commitments is correct, and I do not think that his commitment-conclusions are correct. This section has explained my reasons for reaching these conclusions.

However, before proceeding, I want to make one last comment. I have spent most of my career as a legal scholar criticizing law professors for being insufficiently theoretical. My complaint is that lawyers and legal academics often focus exclusively on the peculiar facts of the case and fail to see the more general, abstract issue that the case raises. As a result, the classes of cases that lawyers create often include cases that raise very different issues, and cases that raise the same issue are often put into different case-categories. This problem is most likely to arise when the courts have used the same doctrine to treat cases that actually demand different treatment or different doctrines to resolve cases that should be approached in the same way. Unfortunately, the resistance of many academic lawyers to abstract thinking leads them to make these mistakes as well in many situations in which the courts are not at fault.

Nevertheless, this time, I have not come to criticize lawyers for being in-adequately abstract. This time, I have come to praise lawyers (in contrast to many philosophers) for being appropriately "concrete." Lawyers would never write 585 pages on social justice without dealing with lots of hypothetical and actual cases whose analyses would reveal our relevant moral practices in all their subtlety and complexity.

Many philosophers seem to think that philosophers do real moral analy-sis and that lawyers are concerned with theoretically-unimportant details—that lawyers resemble low-level engineers while philosophers resemble high-level theoretical scientists. Nothing could be further from the truth. Legal and moral rights-and-obligations analyses must be built on details, on in-sightful "empirical descriptions" of our complex moral practices. Good law professors have a detailed grasp of the relevant moral practices and also have the moral insight to be able to describe those practices and characterize the principles that underlie them in a convincing and revealing abstract way. They engage in reflective-equilibrium analysis in its full richness. Rawls's analysis of the concept of a reflective equilibrium shows that he realizes that this is the kind of work that needs to be done. That makes me even more sur-prised and disappointed that *A Theory of Justice* does so little of it.

3. *Political Liberalism*

Political Liberalism is not only the title of John Rawls's most recent book,[50] it is also the name given to a political moral position that is critically different from the moral-integrity-oriented version of liberalism on which I think our society is committed to basing its rights-and-obligations discourse and conclusions. Among law-school teachers, the most famous proponents of political liberalism are Bruce Ackerman[51] and Thomas Nagel.[52]

Stephen Gardbaum has succinctly articulated the (to my mind) purported "syllogism that states the basic argument for political liberalism":

(1) *The liberal principle of legitimacy.* Only principles of political association that all citizens may reasonably be expected to endorse are justified.

(2) *The fact of reasonable pluralism.* Our society is permanently characterized by the fact that citizens affirm a diversity of reasonable yet incompatible comprehensive religious, moral, or philosophical doctrines or ideals, which means that no particular core of them satisfies this stated criterion of legitimacy; therefore:

(3) *Political liberalism.* In place of political principles based on such controversial doctrines and ideals, a more limited conception of justice must be constructed on principles that do not privilege any one of them the scope of which encompasses not the whole life but only the basic institutions of society. Only this political not metaphysical conception of justice can command the reasonable consent of all citizens.[53]

I have five observations about this purported syllogism. First, it represents an attempt to *justify* political liberalism—to explain why it is an attractive political position in the situation in which we find ourselves. In this respect, it is a different kind of argument from the one I made to support my claim that we are a rights-based society that is committed to instantiating moral-integrity-oriented liberalism. In crude terms, my argument is an "is" argument while the argument Gardbaum delineates is an "ought" argument. Indeed, my argument for the proposition that our society is a rights-based society that is committed to moral-integrity-oriented liberalism is an "ought" argument only to the extent that the basic moral principle to which a rights-based society is committed must deserve to be called a moral norm.

Second, the ideology this argument is trying to justify is less comprehensive than the moral-integrity-oriented liberalism I have described in that the latter covers the horizontal behaviors of the relevant society's moral-rights holders toward each other as well as the basic political, economic, and social institutions of the society in question.

Third, the first premise of the argument for political liberalism—that justification requires reasonable assent—is both unclear and contestable. It is unclear because the meaning of "reasonable assent" is unclear. It is contestable for four reasons:

(1) because actual rather than hypothetical assent may be necessary,
(2) because political liberalism and perhaps other political ideologies may cause political life to be organized in a way that leads the subjects of the relevant polity to assent to its conception of political justice,
(3) because a political ideology may also be justified by a demonstration that the conception of the good it fosters or presupposes is most valuable for reasons unrelated to human flourishing, and
(4) because a political ideology may also be justified by a demonstration that the conception of the good it presupposes or the political institutions it will instantiate contribute substantially or critically to human flourishing.

Fourth, as Gardbaum himself stresses,[54] the second factual premise of the alleged syllogism he delineates—the fact of diversity of conceptions of the first-order good—ignores what I take to be the consensus in our society for the value of moral integrity and relatedly of individuals' exercising meaningful choice about the good (leading autonomous lives).

Fifth, given the possibility that a society in which there is no consensus on the first-order good may have a consensus supporting the great value of the "second-order" good of exercising meaningful (autonomous) choice, the fact that there is a consensus on the high value of such choosing in our society, and the fact that the liberal principle that embodies this consensus on the second-order good clearly deserves to be called a moral norm (the "fact" that "all citizens may reasonably be expected to endorse" this principle), the conclusion that political liberalism is justified does not follow from what Gardbaum terms "the liberal principle of legitimacy" and the actual fact of pluralism in our culture.

One should not make the mistake of assuming that nothing turns on whether a society is committed to political liberalism or moral-integrity-oriented (autonomous-choice-valuing) liberalism. Political liberalism requires the State to be neutral not only among different conceptions of the first-order good but also between lives (conceptions of the good and behaviors based on those conceptions) that are autonomously chosen and lives that are the product of the unthinking acceptance of custom, tradition, or authority (acceptance that may reflect the ignorance, lack of self-respect, and lack of self-confidence of the moral-rights holder, non-State coercion, or the paucity of the options available to the individual in question).

Societies that are committed to moral-integrity-oriented liberalism do have to remain neutral among all conceptions of the good whose instantiation does not violate the rights of others, manifest their adherents' lack of moral integrity, or deprive their adherents of the ability to review their life choices in the light of experience. But such societies do not have to remain neutral between autonomously chosen lives and lives that were not meaningfully authored by those who led them. To the contrary, as I argue in Chapter 1,[55] rights-based States that value individuals of moral integrity have obligations to free the moral-rights holders for whom they are responsible from all kinds of coercion, to insure that their subjects have meaningful options available to them, to encourage their subjects to make meaningful life-choices, and to give them the self-respect, self-confidence, knowledge, and skills necessary to make meaningful choices of these fundamental types in a satisfactory manner. Chapter 4 explores some of the more concrete implications of this duty, which distinguishes the kind of liberal State I believe we are from the State that political liberalism claims is justified in our pluralistic society.

4. Learned Hand's Position That Judicial Review Should Be Limited to Cases That Turn on the Correct Interpretation of Power-Allocating Clauses as Opposed to "Fundamental-Fairness" Clauses

Learned Hand is almost certainly the most famous American judge never to have been a Justice of the Supreme Court. In the 1950s, Hand published two books[56] that argued that the courts should stand ready to declare unconstitutional government choices that violate the Constitution's power-allocating clauses but should not investigate the Constitutionality of government acts that are alleged to violate the Constitution's various "fundamental fairness" clauses.

Hand made three arguments for this conclusion. First, he argued that judges should interpret the power-allocating clauses but not the "fundamental-fairness" clauses because there are internally-right interpretations of the former clauses while conclusions about fairness are purely a matter of opinion (or perhaps, in my terms, a matter of personal-ultimate-value conviction). Second, and relatedly, Hand argued that lawyers have expertise when it comes to interpreting power-allocating clauses (that they do that kind of thing all the time when interpreting contracts, incorporation agreements, trust agreements, etc.) but have no special expertise when it comes to interpreting fundamental-fairness clauses (since notions of fairness are just matters of opinion). Third, Hand argued for his conclusion by asserting that courts should not act in a way that endangers their political viability and contending that the courts are more likely to get into political trouble by declaring a government decision unconstitutional on the ground that it violates a fundamental-fairness clause than by declaring a government decision unconstitutional on the ground that it violates a "power-allocating" clause. I reject all three of these arguments as well as Hand's conclusion that government power-allocation choices are more appropriately subjected to judicial review than government fundamental-fairness choices.

Thus, since I think that disputes that arise out of the Constitution's fundamental-fairness clauses raise rights-and-obligations questions that have internally-right answers and not "ought" questions whose resolution is a matter of personal-ultimate-value convictions, I disagree with the premise of Hand's first argument that the proper interpretation of the fundamental-fairness clauses either is just a matter of opinion or turns on personal-ultimate-value convictions. Indeed, although I agree with the second premise of Hand's first argument—that there are internally-right answers to the legal questions raised by Constitutional challenges that arise out of the power-allocating clauses—I am less convinced of the truth of this premise than of the existence of internally-right answers to moral-rights questions and hence to moral-rights-related legal-rights questions.

I also reject Hand's claim that lawyers have more expertise in relation to the interpretation of power-allocating clauses than in relation to the interpretation of fundamental-fairness clauses. Thus, in the one direction, on my account, a very high percentage of legal cases can be and are resolved through the kind of applied moral analysis that has to be executed to interpret a fundamental-fairness clause. And, in the other direction, although I agree that lawyers have substantial expertise in interpreting power-allocating clauses in various contexts, interpreting Constitutional power-allocating clauses is not akin to interpreting power-allocating clauses in contracts, incorporation agreements, or trust agreements. Although textual, historical, and moral analysis will no doubt be of some use (the last since the proper resolution of most controversial Constitutional power-allocation disputes will turn on such structural concerns as "which allocation of power is more likely to prevent government tyranny that will endanger our community's liberal commitments"), the analysis of both the relevant history and the applicable, legitimate prudential considerations will involve such "good government" issues as which allocation of power is more likely to produce efficient decisionmaking, given the desirable tendencies of decentralization to place decisions in the hands of officials who have better access to the relevant facts and values and to promote experimentation and the undesirable tendencies of decentralization to generate externalities and to sacrifice relevant economies of scale. Lawyers are not trained or experienced in analyzing these types of political-economy issues.

Moreover, since my whole approach to Constitutional interpretation derives from the premise that our community is a community of principle that is committed to upholding its various rights-commitments, it calls into question the legitimacy of Hand's third (prudential) argument for his conclusion—that is, it implies the illegitimacy of a court's basing its decision in a given case or class of cases on the political consequences for the judicial system of its responding to the cases in question in one way or another. In fact, even if this type of prudential argument were legitimate, I doubt that it would favor reviewing claims that turn on the interpretation of power-allocation clauses over cases that turn on the interpretation of fundamental-fairness clauses. Indeed, both theory and history seem to me to cut against Hand's conclusion. Thus, since holdings that certain power-allocations are unconstitutional will disfavor the politically-organized group to whom the relevant power had been allocated—for example, the federal government or the executive branch of the federal government, theory suggests that rulings of this kind may be more likely to anger a forceful political opposition to the courts than a ruling of unconstitutionality in a fundamental-fairness case, which is likely to disadvantage a dispersed and usually-politically-unorganized majority. Although I have not systematically investigated this issue, my impression is that the facts confirm this tentative hypothesis: for example, although *Brown v. Board of Education*[57] clearly did impose some political costs on the federal courts, their position was far more endangered by their decisions to strike down various parts of the New Deal on unconstitutional-power-allocation grounds.

In any event, if my analysis is correct, "philosophical," skill, and perhaps "prudential" arguments will (if anything) favor judicial review of fundamental-fairness cases over judicial review of power-allocation cases. If anything, then, Hand should be stood on his head, though I think that judicial review of both fundamental-fairness and power-allocation cases would be more legitimate than such a Hand-stand.

5. *John Hart Ely's Proposal That Judicial Review Be Limited to the Protection of Rights to Fair Judicial Procedures, Rights to Fair Representation in the Political Process, and the Substantive Rights of Minorities Systematically Excluded from Successful Participation in the Political Process*

In *Democracy and Distrust*,[58] John Hart Ely makes six basic points:

(1) both the Ninth Amendment[59] and the "privileges or immunities" clause of the Fourteenth Amendment[60] acknowledge and Constitutionally protect unenumerated (substantive and procedural) rights;

(2) any attempt by judges to identify those unenumerated rights protected by the Ninth Amendment and the "privileges or immunities" clause of the Fourteenth Amendment without making reference to the rest of the Constitution's text would inevitably involve the exercise of strong discretion in the sense of the imposition by judges of their own (or someone else's) ultimate values;

(3) such an exercise of discretion by judges would be inconsistent with our commitment to democracy;[61]

(4) it is possible to confine judicial discretion to an acceptable extent by instructing judges to protect under the Ninth Amendment or the "privileges or immunities" clause of the Fourteenth Amendment only those values that the rest of the text of the Constitution reveals to be fundamental;[62]

(5) properly interpreted, the text of the rest of the Constitution reveals the fundamental Constitutional values to be rights to fair judicial process, rights to fair representation, and rights of minorities not to be unfairly disadvantaged because they do not have a fair share of political power; and

(6) restricting judicial review to these values is justifiable (A) because such a restriction is based on a proper reading of the rest of the Constitution, (B) because it confines judicial discretion sufficiently to make judicial review compatible with democracy, and (C) because it limits judges to assessing the desirability of those executive and legislative decisions and only those executive and legislative decisions that courts are better-placed to evaluate than are these coordinate branches.[63]

I will now respond to each of these points in turn.

First, my analysis of rights and obligations obviously is consistent with (indeed, confirms or supports) Ely's conclusion that the Ninth Amendment and "privileges or immunities" clause of the Fourteenth Amendment should be read to protect unenumerated rights.[64] Indeed, my analysis implies that any short-list of specific rights will leave some rights unprotected so that any community of principle that adopts a Bill of Rights will have to include in that document some provisions that are so vague or open-textured that the task of interpreting them will *obviously* be no different from the task of identifying an unenumerated right, a catch-all provision (such as the "privileges or immunities" clause of the Fourteenth Amendment) designed to cover all rights not protected by the more specific provisions, and/or a provision (like the Ninth Amendment) indicating that the list of specific rights is not intended to be exhaustive.

Second, my analysis contradicts Ely's conclusion that judges will not be able to define unenumerated rights without exercising strong discretion in the sense of relying on personal ultimate values.

Third, my analysis implies that although the exercise of such strong discretion would almost[65] certainly violate our democratic principles, the protection of individual rights against violations by majorities is fully consistent with our commitment to democracy. This conclusion reflects two facts: (1) although democracy might be supported for other (e.g., utilitarian) reasons as well, liberal societies such as ours are committed to democracy because the political procedures of democratic systems of government manifest appropriate, equal respect for those moral-rights holders who are relevantly competent, and (2) another implication of our commitment to showing such appropriate, equal respect is our obligation to secure the rights of all moral-rights holders—to establish a government that does not make positive decisions that violate rights, that prevents private parties from violating rights when doing so will protect rights-related interests on balance, and that supplies all moral-rights holders with the positive rights to which they are entitled.

Fourth, my analysis casts doubt on the proposition that various limited categories of rights to which the United States Constitution refers can be said to be more "fundamental" than other enumerated or unenumerated rights, calls into question the proposition that an instruction to judges to protect only those specifically-unenumerated rights that fall into some "fundamental"-right category will limit their discretion sufficiently to make its exercise consistent with our democratic commitments, and (once more) rejects the assumption that such limitations on judicial discretion are necessary—

that judges cannot identify unenumerated rights without exercising strong discretion. I want to elaborate on the first two of these three points since my comments are also relevant to my discussion in the next section of Douglas Laycock's "loose clause-bound" approach to Constitutional interpretation.

My conclusion that our society's basic moral commitment is to show appropriate, equal respect and concern for all moral-rights holders calls into question Ely's claim that the three Constitutional rights he considers to be fundamental (the right to fair judicial process, the right to political representation, and the right not to be unfairly disadvantaged because one does not have a fair share of political power) deserve that characterization. In particular, my analysis implies that the three rights he considers to be fundamental would be so only if they were more connected with the defining characteristics of moral-rights holders (with what our society is committed to valuing) than various other rights that I think we have (some of which have explicit textual references in the Constitution and some of which do not). Although I do think that all three of the rights Ely lists as fundamental are Constitutionally protected, I do not think that they are more fundamental than many other rights—for example, than the right to enter into intimate relationships that are both satisfying in themselves and conducive to self-discovery and self-definition, the right to express ourselves in non-political as well as political ways, the right to privacy and various other "goods" that importantly affect our ability to become and remain individuals of moral integrity.

My analysis also calls into question Ely's implicit assumption that the task of determining which rights are fundamental is critically different from the task of identifying unenumerated rights in that the former but not the latter task can be executed without employing personal ultimate values—without exercising strong discretion. I do not think that Ely's conclusion on this issue is correct. Clearly, my approach implies that one cannot establish that certain rights are *morally* more fundamental than others without executing a basic-moral-principle analysis that is in no relevant way different from the task of identifying the concrete unenumerated rights that our society is committed to securing. Nor do I think that there is a category of fundamental *Constitutional* rights that are distinct from our *moral* rights. At least in part, this conclusion reflects my view that our Constitution is a moral document in the sense that a major objective of even the political structures that it establishes is to create a State that will *inter alia* act in a way that is consistent with our society's moral obligations. Hence, even if I did think that certain rights were more fundamental than others (in some sense other than their being more abstract than others), I would not think that instructing judges to enforce only fundamental rights would obviate their exercising strong discretion or reduce the discretion they had to exercise to an acceptable level (whatever that might mean). After all, judges would have to determine whether Ely's conclusion about which rights were fundamental were correct.

Fifth, as the preceding paragraph indicates, I also disagree with Ely's conclusions about the Constitutional rights that are most fundamental—indeed, about the existence of such a category of rights. As Laycock has discussed, Ely's conclusions about the values the Constitution's text implies are fundamental appear to reflect the fact that "he finds it just as offensive to bind today's political majority by the substantive views of the Framers as to bind that majority by the substantive views of five Supreme Court Justices."[66] This predisposition leads Ely to deal with the Constitution's substantive provisions (which he dislikes as types)[67] in a way that is often not very convincing. Of course, if I am correct, the substantive provisions of the Constitution should be said to reflect the moral commitments of our society and not just the views of its framers and ratifiers—commitments that are consistent with democracy since they derive from the same liberal principle that underlies our commitment to democracy.

Sixth, my preceding comments imply that I reject all three of Ely's arguments for his proposal: (A) I do not think that it is based on a proper reading of the text of the Constitution; (B) I do not think that it can be justified on the basis that it limits judicial discretion both because I do not think judges have to use personal ultimate values to identify unenumerated rights and because I do not think that Ely's proposal would critically change the nature of the task facing a Constitutional adjudicator; and relatedly (C) I do not think that Ely's proposal can be justified by its supposed tendency to restrict judges to tasks that they are better-placed to execute than are legislators or executive-branch members both because judges are more skilled as a class than legislators and executive-branch members at identifying what I call moral principles and (once more) because Ely is not significantly changing the task that confronts them.

6. *Douglas Laycock's "Loose Clause-Bound" Approach to Constitutional Interpretation*

In his review of Ely's *Democracy and Distrust*,[68] Douglas Laycock makes the following argument:

(1) as Ely shows, the Ninth Amendment and the "privileges or immunities" clause of the Fourteenth Amendment do recognize the existence of unenumerated Constitutional rights and authorize the courts to protect them;

(2) any attempt by judges to protect unenumerated rights without grounding their analyses in some more specific provision of the Constitution would involve the exercise of discretion in the strong sense in which that exercise is inconsistent with democratic principles;

(3) one can make the Ninth Amendment and the "privileges or immunities" clause of the Fourteenth Amendment efficacious without putting judges in a position in which they have to exercise strong discretion by requiring judges to adopt a "loose clause-bound" approach to the interpretation of these provisions under which they would be held to protect all concrete rights that belong to any intermediately-abstract family of rights to which any concrete right specifically protected by another piece of Constitutional text belongs; and

(4) in addition to preventing judges from acting in a way that is inconsistent with our democratic principles, this approach would have the further advantage of producing opinions that would be more likely to convince or at least to assuage opponents of a Supreme Court decision holding some State choice unconstitutional.

I want to comment on the last three of these points. Laycock repeatedly claims that judges cannot define unenumerated rights without imposing ultimate values unless they accept the kind of "loose clause-bound" method of interpretation he is advocating. Because the language is so typical, I will begin with some quotations in which Laycock makes this point. Thus, Laycock says: (1) instructing judges to base their decisions directly on the Ninth Amendment or the "privileges or immunities" clause of the Fourteenth Amendment would be to "free [them] from all constitutional constraint in the creation of new rights";[69] (2) an approach that would permit judges to enforce unenumerated rights that cannot be derived if only by implication from specific Constitutional language would give them "unfettered discretion";[70] and (3) although people like David Richards and Ronald Dworkin "claim to start with the Constitution . . . , neither seems willing to be limited by it."[71] I disagree with each of these claims because all fail to recognize the distinction between moral principles (which are generically inside the law) and personal ultimate values (which are not) and the fact that the moral principles to which our society is committed can be detected by an objective moral anthropological analysis of our culture's relevant behaviors.

I also disagree with Laycock's assertion that his "loose clause-bound" method of interpretation will eliminate or at least acceptably limit judicial discretion. In fact, from the perspective of a concern about "discretion," I do not think that the substitution of Laycock's approach for mine will have any effect whatsoever on the nature of the interpretive process.

To facilitate my exposition, I want to develop some vocabulary to describe the different levels of abstraction at which rights can be defined. In particular, in what follows, I will assume that there are three levels of rights, defined in terms of their degree of abstractness: (1) level-one rights, the most basic category—in my case, the right of all creatures with the neurological equipment to become and remain individuals of moral integrity to appropriate, equal respect and concern; (2) level-two rights, a category of intermediately-abstract rights that would include all the families of intermediately-abstract rights to which Laycock refers; and (3) level-three rights, a category of concrete rights that would include concrete enumerated rights as well as the concrete unenumerated rights that judges may be asked to protect and which (according to Laycock) may or may not belong to one of the families of intermediately-abstract rights to which the Constitution's various enumerated rights belong. Laycock's proposal is that judges interpret the Ninth Amendment and the "privileges or immunities" clause of the Fourteenth Amendment to protect those unenumerated, concrete (level-three) rights that belong to the same (level-two) family of intermediately-abstract rights to which other level-three rights enumerated in the text of the Constitution belong. I think that the substitution of this approach for mine would not change the nature of the task that judges have to perform. How would judges decide how to characterize the level-two, intermediately-abstract family of rights to which a level-three right enumerated in the text of the Constitution belongs? How would judges decide whether a given alleged, unenumerated, level-three right belongs to one of the intermediately-abstract level-two rights they associated with the various level-three rights enumerated by the Constitution? Laycock realizes that these upward and downward movements must be controlled by some supervening value. He claims to find those values in the Constitution: "The Constitution protects a pair of substantive values that I would label 'individualism' and 'personal autonomy.'"[72] However, his definitions of these values reveal not only their resemblance to my liberal basic moral principle but also the fact that he did not derive them from any self-declaring meaning of the Constitution's text—

that is, his conclusion that they are Constitutionally fundamental primarily reflects his certainly-armchair and perhaps-not-fully-conscious execution of the "anthropological" procedure I indicated should be followed to identify a rights-based society's basic moral principle. Even if one could not demonstrate the impossibility of discovering the substantive values the Constitution protects simply by attending to the self-declaring meaning of the Constitution's text by pointing out that the relevant provisions of the Constitution have no self-declaring meaning, one could establish the nature of the intellectual process Laycock used by attending to the philosophically-sophisticated way in which Laycock reads the Constitution when he engages in "textual" interpretation.

In fact, Laycock's proposal is that judges identify the intermediately-abstract values to which we are committed by observing our society's relevant moral practices, assign the various level-three concrete rights the Constitution enumerates to intermediately-abstract level-two categories, and determine whether other alleged unenumerated level-three rights belong to one of the level-two categories of more abstract rights to which some enumerated right belongs. My proposal is that judges use the same kind of data Laycock employs to identify the intermediately-abstract (level-two) values the Constitution protects to identify our society's (level-one) basic moral principle, derive level-two principle-characterizations and principle-weightings from my level-one basic moral principle, and derive still more concrete principle-characterizations and principle-weights from my level-two conclusions. At least from the perspective of judicial "discretion," there is no difference between our two proposals.

Admittedly, it may appear that Laycock's protocol may reduce judicial discretion by obviating the judges' identifying our basic moral principle. However, Laycock's protocol achieves no such result. Thus, the procedure Laycock's judges should follow to identify level-two (intermediately-abstract families of) values is not critically different from the procedure my judges would follow to identify our society's basic moral principle. Moreover, Laycock's judges would not actually be able to operate without identifying our basic moral principle. Many cases will turn on the way in which one characterizes the intermediately-abstract family of values, the concrete unenumerated value, and/or the concrete enumerated value Laycock's proposal requires to be defined. Since, in each of these cases, the correct characterization of these values or families of values will depend on the way in which one characterizes our society's basic moral principle, Laycock's approach does not obviate the identification of that level-one value—does not assign to judges a different set of tasks from those that my account of their judicial obligations assigns to them.

I do not think that judges would have to exercise discretion in the strong sense to implement my proposal. But, if they do, they will have to do so to precisely the same extent to engage in the kind of "loose clause-bound" interpretation Laycock advocates.

Finally, although I am certainly not expert in political psychology, I also disagree with Laycock's claim that his proposal would secure more acceptance of judicial decisions protecting unenumerated rights than would mine. Indeed, in my opinion, the avowed use of my procedure would be less likely to evoke hostility than the use of Laycock's approach if the latter were claimed to be "textualist." People who oppose judicial decisions to uphold unenumerated rights usually do so because they have a narrow view of individual rights against the State and/or because they believe that the full meaning of the Constitution is exhausted by the self-declaring meaning of the text and our knowledge of the expectations of its drafters or ratifiers about the way in which it should or would be applied and think that any Constitutional "interpretation" by judges that is not based on such self-declaring meaning or evidence of drafter or ratifier intent is unauthorized and anti-democratic. Obviously, to the extent that judges employing Laycock's procedure reach the same conclusions as judges employing my approach, members of the public whose opposition to the relevant opinions reflects their opposition to the conclusions these opinions reach will be as dissatisfied with courts that use Laycock's approach as with courts that use mine. And, to the extent that the potential judicial critics in question are opposed to judges' basing their decisions on anything but the self-declaring meaning of the text or our knowledge of its drafters' or ratifiers' specific expectations, their opposition will also not be assuaged by the substitution of Laycock's approach for mine: once they see the (to my mind) sophisticated way in which Laycock interprets the Constitution's text, they will realize that he is not confining himself to self-declaring meanings and historical information about framers/ratifiers' "intentions" any more than I am. In fact, I would not be surprised if the relevant potential judicial critics preferred my approach to Laycock's or, at least, my straightforward description of what my approach entails to Laycock's implicit representation that his approach is "textual," when it is anything but "textual" in the sense in which they would understand that term.

In short, although I agree with Laycock that the Ninth Amendment and the "privileges or immunities" clause of the Fourteenth Amendment authorize the courts to protect unenumerated rights, I disagree with his claims that judges cannot do so without exercising strong discretion unless they base their analyses on other, more specific Constitutional provisions, his "loose clause-bound" method of interpretation is critically different from my proposal—that is, it limits discretion in a way that makes the relevant judicial review compatible with our democratic traditions whereas mine does not, and his method of interpretation will be more politically acceptable than mine.

In fact, because I have specified my approach to identifying the basic moral principle we are committed to using when asserting and assessing rights-and-obligations claims in greater detail than Laycock has specified his procedures for identifying level-one, level-two, and level-three values and because my specifications of the liberal basic moral principle to which I think we are committed is more detailed than Laycock's definitions of his level-one values of "individualism" and "personal autonomy,"[73] my proposal would place greater constraints on judges than Laycock's. For example, has Laycock provided judges with any basis for choosing between the liberal conception of "individualism" and "personal autonomy" I think we are committed to implementing and the libertarian conception of these "values" to which members of the Federalist Society believe we are committed? If not, how would Laycock's instructions constrain judges confronted with the various liberty and property-right (redistribution of income) issues that arise under our Constitution? How, for example, would Laycock's approach tell judges to respond to state regulations requiring pregnant women who wish to obtain abortions to delay their decisions until they have been exposed to various types of information they allegedly require to make a well-informed choice? How would Laycock's approach tell judges to respond to state regulations requiring children to attend schools that give secular instruction beyond the age at which their parents wish to withdraw them from such schools? How would Laycock's approach tell judges to respond to state or federal tax-and-spend programs that fail to provide those for whom our society is responsible with the nutrition, housing, health care, and schooling they need to develop into creatures who take their lives morally seriously? The appropriate response to all such cases will depend upon whether we are committed to a libertarian or a liberal conception of "individualism" and "personal autonomy." Admittedly, considerations of space will prevent me (as they did Laycock) from reviewing and assessing the evidence that is relevant to whether we are a liberal or libertarian rights-based society (assuming *ad arguendo* that libertarian "values" cannot be dismissed through the *a priori* argument I believe is decisive). However, I have at least defined the basic moral principle to which I think we are committed and delineated the procedure that led me to reach this conclusion.

7. *Legal Realism*

The term "Legal Realism"[74] refers to a jurisprudential movement that developed in the United States in the 1920s and 1930s and continues to have enormous influence on American legal culture, legal education, and scholarship. Although not all Legal Realists subscribe to both these propositions,[75] all Realists do agree with at least one of them:

(1) legitimate legal argument does not generate unique, internal-to-law correct conclusions in all cases, and, when it does not, legitimate legal argument does not cause judges to make the decisions they make; and

(2) in some cases in which the law is determinate (in which legitimate legal argument does yield a unique, internal-to-law correct conclusion), legitimate legal argument also does not control what judges actually decide.

This section analyzes these propositions and their implications for my approach and conclusions.

A. The "Substantive Indeterminacy" of Legitimate Legal Argument

The Legal Realists did not think that there were no internally-right answers to any legal-rights question. Rather, their most extreme jurisprudential claim was that whenever a plausible legal argument can be made on both sides of a question (whenever both sides have good arguments and reasons to appeal an adverse decision on an issue), there is no internally-right answer to the relevant question.[76] For example, Legal Realists argue that if the implications of precedent depend on whether past decisions are interpreted narrowly or strictly when both narrow and strict construction are regarded as legitimate by a significant percentage of the profession,[77] or if the meaning of a statutory text depends on which of two or more canons of construction is used to interpret it when each of the relevant canons is considered to be legitimate by a significant percentage of the profession,[78] there will be no internally-right answer to the relevant legal question.

I disagree. As I argue in Section 11 of this chapter, which discusses Philip Bobbitt's position on Constitutional interpretation, for me practice is not self-legitimating: the fact that a significant number of lawyers and judges have interpreted precedents in a particular way or used a particular canon of construction to interpret a statute does not legitimate these practices jurisprudentially (though it may make them "socially acceptable"). There will always be an internally-correct method of interpretation in the relevant circumstances in the relevant rights-based legal culture. Chapter 1 outlines the approach that courts in our culture are obligated to take to such admittedly-difficult issues.

Brian Leiter has offered a philosophically-sophisticated explanation for the Legal Realist conclusion that law is indeterminate—namely, that they embraced a type of philosophical naturalism that Quine subsequently made famous. This kind of naturalism argues that foundationalist justification is impossible "in part because evidence always underdetermines the choice among theories, and thus does not *justify* only one of them."[79]

My own account is less intellectually sophisticated. To my mind, some Legal Realists at least gave the appearance that they subscribed to a substantive-indeterminacy conclusion because they were interested not in legal truth per se but in the advice that lawyers give to clients.[80] In the situations in which these Realists claimed there was no internally-right answer, what they really meant was: "A lawyer cannot give a client a reliable prediction of what the courts will decide."

And again, to my mind, some Legal Realists who seemed to be indicating a view that there is no internally-right answer to many legal questions really believed that no such answer could be generated by the kind of wooden, doctrinal analysis they saw lawyers, judges, and their academic colleagues executing. Thus, Neil MacCormick (a professor of jurisprudence) and Zipporah Wiseman (an expert on Karl Llewellyn) recently argued that although Llewellyn's writings contain many statements that suggest or claim the indeterminacy of law, these passages were actually

> simple rhetorical flourishes in first-year lectures aimed at warning students away from too profound a trust in rules that they or textbooks and treatises might formulate as capturing the point of some precedent. . . . In effect, Llewellyn's skepticism about rules is not about rules themselves or their real importance in law. It is a skepticism about a certain doctrinal view of legal rules, one which gives them a simple, absolute and invariant form. . . . This insight does not mean that there is no legal certainty, but that the basis of legal certainty is not the mere fact of the existence of some rule or rules.[81]

In my terms, Llewellyn is emphasizing two conclusions that I agree deserve emphasis:

(1) some propositions of law are principles (which have a dimension of weight) rather than rules (which are supposed to be decisive whenever they apply) and

(2) both principles and rules must be interpreted non-mechanically.

As we shall see, these are lessons of which not only traditional legal analysts but also non-traditionalists such as members of the Critical Legal Studies movement need to be reminded.

B. The Causal Inefficacy of Legitimate Legal Argument

Many Legal Realists believe that legal argument does not cause judges to reach the decisions they reach. This conclusion clearly is plausible in those cases in which the internally-correct resolution of a case is indeterminate, but many Legal Realists believe that legitimate legal argument is inefficacious in reality even when it does yield internal-to-law correct answers.

If judges' decisions were usually or even frequently not controlled by legitimate legal argument, even when such arguments did generate internally-right legal conclusions, that fact would have substantial implications for my analysis. At a minimum, it would imply that our legal system was not a system of principle—that not only our judges but our legal regime as a whole was illegitimate in that it failed to behave consistently with our obligation to secure the rights of the moral-rights holders for which our society is responsible. And, because the legal system is such an important part of our society, it would also call into question my conclusion/premise that ours is a rights-based society.

I therefore want to explain why four pieces of evidence that some Legal Realists believe imply the inefficacy of legitimate legal argument are less persuasive than they have concluded. First, the fact that explicit moral argument plays a relatively minor role in judicial opinions is not nearly so significant as some seem to suppose. It is important to remember in this context that legitimate legal argument may have a greater effect on judicial *decisions* than on judicial *opinions*. Although arguments of moral principle are to my mind the dominant mode of legitimate legal argument in our culture, I am not surprised that they play less of a role in the opinions that judges write to justify their decisions than my account of their importance implies would be appropriate.

Since the *Lochner* era, courts have been wary of explaining their conclusions in value-oriented terms. As I have already indicated, this reaction reflects the judges' failure to distinguish between personal ultimate values (which are generally legally irrelevant) and moral principles (which are inside the law). However, in my judgment, arguments of moral principle influence judicial decisions, both directly and indirectly, far more than the judges acknowledge—by determining the interpretations they give to texts, the scope of the historical inquiries they undertake, the way in which they interpret and use precedents, their use or non-use of illegitimate prudential arguments, and so on. One cannot infer the inefficacy of legitimate legal argument from the fact that the explicit role of important types of such argument is not so great as my analysis of legitimate legal argument suggests is warranted.

Second, the fact that changes in law over time are positively correlated with changes in the political power of different groups that are independent and partially-independent of judicial decisions also does not demonstrate the inefficacy of legitimate legal argument. Many of the relevant changes reflect changes in legislation or administrative regulations that neither violate nor are required by individual rights. It is also not surprising that shifts in the distribution of political power will affect the rights-related decisions that courts make by changing the perception that those who perform judicial roles have of our basic moral principles and/or its more concrete corollaries. Indeed, such shifts will produce this result both by causing different people to become judges and by altering the perceptions of given individuals.

Third, the fact that lawsuits often turn on facts does not belie the importance of legitimate legal argument. I do not doubt the importance of facts, but legitimate legal argument determines which facts are important and why and how they are important.

Fourth, the fact that particular judges' decisions can be predicted from their backgrounds and/or consistently reflect a given value-commitment is also not inconsistent with legitimate legal argument's efficacy. As I have already indicated, the values that I denominate "moral principles" are part of the law. I have no doubt that a judge's background will affect the way she characterizes and weights the interests these principles commit us to considering (characterizations and weightings that are often contestable), and the fact that a judge's resolution of these issues is consistent is neither surprising nor troubling.

In short, none of the pieces of evidence that some Legal Realists and others have cited to demonstrate the causal inefficacy of legitimate legal argument strikes me as convincing. My admittedly-limited practice-experience suggests to me that legitimate legal argument is a major determinant of judicial outcomes.

8. *Critical Legal Studies*

The Critical Legal Studies (CLS) movement began in the late 1960s and reached its zenith in the late 1970s and early 1980s. Its analysis proceeded from the supposed Realist conclusion that law was indeterminate[82]—though CLS adherents argued that there was no right answer to virtually any legal question (in contrast to the Realists, who believed at most that there was no right answer to legitimately-contestable legal questions). The CLS arguments for legal indeterminacy were also different from the more-legally-imbedded arguments that led some Realists to their conclusion on this issue. This section briefly responds to the three arguments that CLS scholars use to justify their conclusion of legal indeterminacy.

A. Meaning Is Created by the Interpreter, Not by the Interpreted

Many CLS members claim that there can be no internally-right interpretation of a legal text because legal texts—like all texts—have no meaning in themselves, since all the meaning of all texts is provided by the interpreter, not by the writer or the words. Although everyone admits that the shapes that constitute most written words do not convey meaning "by themselves" and at least some CLS scholars recognize the existence of binding practices of interpretation that are supposed to limit the discretion of the interpreter, members of the Critical Legal Studies movement maintain that in the end the existing conventions are virtually always insufficiently dense and detailed to eliminate the strong discretion of the interpreter.[83] Obviously, I disagree.

B. The Inevitable Inherent Contradictions in Legal Liberalism

Members of the Critical Legal Studies movement also try to justify their conclusion that there are no internally-right answers to legal-rights questions by arguing that the contribution of the philosophical tradition that many non-Crits suppose can help supply such answers—liberalism—is destroyed by its internal contradictions (antinomies).[84]

In my judgment, this argument turns out to reflect its advocates' misconstrual of two facts: (1) that one or more liberal principles that are decisive in one case are not in another and (2) that a set of liberal principles that outweighs another set of liberal principles in one case may be outweighed by the latter set of liberal principles in another case. Rather than manifesting the inconsistency of liberalism, these facts manifest the following realties:

(1) unlike rules, principles have a dimension of weight;
(2) liberal principles can conflict (favor different outcomes) in particular situations;
(3) not all liberal principles are relevant to all cases; and
(4) the relative importance of two or more moral principles that are implicated in various cases will in general vary from case to case.

C. The Fact That the Proponents of a Given Model of Legitimate Legal Argumentation Sometimes or Often Disagree about the Correct Resolution of a Legal Issue or Case

The assertion that the various approaches to legal interpretation others have recommended cannot bind judges even in theory because those who use each of these individual approaches reach different conclusions on given questions[85] is also unjustifiable. Neither the fact that an approach's users reached different conclusions because some of them clearly misapplied the approach nor the fact that they reached different conclusions on individual issues or cases because they reached different conclusions about contestable theoretical issues related to the proper implementation of the approach or about contestable factual issues the approach deems relevant would be inconsistent with its being the internally-right approach—that is, with there being an internally-right way for judges to interpret the Constitution. Of course, the fact that the proper way to operationalize any such approach is contestable will make it difficult to police a requirement that judges restrict themselves to (properly) adjudicating the Constitutional cases they hear. But the difficulty of enforcing the relevant obligation is irrelevant to its existence (the "predicate" that Critical Legal Studies adherents are trying to disprove).

In short, I reject the Critical Legal Studies movement's claim that Constitutional interpretation is inevitably political for both positive and negative reasons: positively, because I do think that our binding practices of moral argument and legal interpretation are sufficiently dense and detailed to deprive judges who are trying to adjudicate Constitutional cases of discretion in the strong sense and, negatively, because I reject the CLS arguments against the kind of liberal model of legitimate legal argument I have proposed and any other approach that could be developed.

9. The Historians of Ideology and the Libertarian and "Civic-Republican" Legal Academics Who Claim to Gain Support from Them

I would rather not have written this section. Like most legal academics, I "lack the perspective, time, [and] knowledge of sources to pursue historical study well."[86] In addition, I am well aware of the temptation to write (and, relatedly, the risk that I have written) a "law-office history"—that I have "pick[ed] and cho[sen] facts and incidents ripped out of context that serve [my] purposes."[87] Finally, even if I had more confidence in my skills, knowledge, and objectivity, the conclusions I reach about the ideological convictions of Americans between 1776 and the early 1800s about the appropriate role of the State would at best reveal only part of the facts that are relevant to my enterprise. My interest in the work of the historians of ideology reflects my belief that the proper moral reading of the Constitution depends (*inter alia*) on the moral character of our society during the Critical Period (from the Revolution to the Constitutional Convention), the Foundation Period, and the Immediate Post-Foundation Period. The arguments that Americans made during this period and the conclusions they reached about who should govern, how they should govern, and what the State is obligated to do and forbidden from doing clearly are relevant to the moral character of American society in the 1776–1800 period. However, as I argue in Chapter 1, the moral identity of a society has at least as much if not more to do with the moral norms that control its members' conduct in their horizontal relations with each other as with their positions and pronouncements on matters of State (on political vertical relationships). The historians of ideology seem to have little to say on these horizontal issues, and I have not made any attempt to investigate them by reading personal diaries, fictional literature, religious literature, or judicial opinions of the period in question.

What I have done is read (or at least seriously look through) a few of the more salient pieces of primary literature,[88] some of the best-known secondary studies,[89] a number of tertiary studies by historians,[90] several articles in which Constitutional lawyers have made use of the historians' findings,[91] some articles that critique the use that lawyers have made of the relevant history,[92] and two articles in which lawyers defend their own use of this history and/or discuss the appropriate way for academic lawyers to use history.[93]

In short, I claim no expertise as a historian of ideology. And I admit that, despite my efforts to make my report "objective," I have no doubt been influenced by my desire to discover a story that is compatible with my independently-derived conclusions about the moral character of our society and concomitantly about legitimate legal argument in our culture.

Still, this section had to be written. Its argument is set out in four parts. The first explains the relevance to my project of the history of American ideology in the 1776–1800 period. The second explores various problems that would make it difficult for even a well-qualified, properly-assiduous, unbiased historian of ideology to discover the ideological convictions of late-eighteenth-century Americans. The third summarizes the evidence that during the last quarter of the eighteenth century a significant number of Americans based their political conclusions on what I call liberal principles, libertarian principles, and civic-republican notions. The fourth states my admittedly-imperfectly-informed and possibly-biased conclusions about American ideology in the final quarter of the eighteenth century, explores the implications of these "ideological" conclusions (the ambiguity is intentional) for my main jurisprudential claims, and comments briefly on the use to which at least some academic lawyers seem to be putting the history of ideology.

A. The Relevance of America's Moral Identity in the 1776–1800 Period to My Central Thesis

Two groups of contemporary legal academics have made different claims about the State-related ideologies of Americans in the last quarter of the eighteenth century that are relevant to my project. Citing the works of various historians of ideology, republican revivalists such as Cass Sunstein[94] have argued that the Founders and others were at least substantially influenced by the ideology of civic republicanism, which these scholars seem to claim was concerned primarily if not exclusively with ensuring that the rulers be drawn from the virtuous class of the ruled and that government take place through a process of reasoned deliberation in which the decisionmakers' narrowly-defined self-interest played no role. Although these republican revivalists never state this proposition explicitly, an implication of this civic-republican ideology may be that the only rights that individuals have against the State are those that serve the purpose of supporting the rule of the virtuous and government through reasoned deliberation.

The second group of relevant scholars is headed by Richard Epstein.[95] Their claim appears to be that the relevant actors in the last quarter of the eighteenth century strongly believed in the right to have obligations of contract enforced and the right to have property taken only for public use and with just compensation. Although Epstein himself does not make this claim, many appear to believe that his arguments imply that during the relevant period Americans were committed to a version of Lockean liberalism that is closely related to if not identical with the most extreme forms of modern libertarianism. On this account, the Constitution was adopted by, and hence instantiated, the values of a libertarian, rights-based society. This section explains why I have found it necessary to assess and respond to these two claims about our late-eighteenth-century moral cultural heritage.

The premise of my central claim about legitimate legal argument in our culture is that ours is a rights-based society whose rights-and-obligations practices are based on what I call a "liberal" moral principle of appropriate, equal respect and concern. For my purposes, therefore, the best historical "news" would be that from the onset of the Critical Period, ours has been such a liberal, rights-based society. Correlatively, the worst historical "news" would be that during the Critical Period, the Foundation Period, and the Immediate Post-Foundation Period, ours either was not a rights-based culture or was a rights-based culture that was based on a non-liberal moral norm (especially one that deserved to be called a moral norm). Even if I could prove that our contemporary society was a liberal, rights-based society, these conclusions about our historical society would cause me significant problems.

At a minimum, either version of the worst news described above would force me to change my conclusions about legitimate legal argument in the Immediate Post-Foundation Period. A finding that American society was a non-liberal rights-based society in the 1776–1800 period would preserve my argument for the legitimacy of judicial review, my account of legitimate legal argument, and my conclusion that there were internally-right answers to legal-rights questions during the period in question, but it would change the content of arguments of moral principle and, presumably, the right answer to many legal-rights questions during that period. A finding that the American society of the last quarter of the eighteenth century was not a rights-based society would have far more serious implications, at least for that period. It would undermine the legitimacy of judicial review (or, at least, my argument for its legitimacy), require a different account to be given of legitimate legal argument, most likely[96] imply the non-existence of internally-right answers to legal-rights questions, and presumably change the right answer to many legal-rights questions as well.

In fact, both variants of worst news just described would also call into question the conclusions I have reached for our current society about the legitimacy of judicial review, the content of legitimate legal argument, the existence of internally-right answers to legal-rights questions, and the substance of those answers. The reason is that I am not persuaded by Bruce Ackerman's claim that our Constitution can be legitimately amended outside the Article V amendment process[97] and the hypothesized change from a non-rights-based culture or a non-liberal rights-based culture to our (assumed) liberal, rights-based culture clearly did not take place through the Article V amendment process. Of course, I have to admit that the Article V process was not used to effectuate many other important changes that (to my mind) could have been legitimately effectuated only through the formal amendment process. The growth of administrative agencies with rule-making powers whose exercise violates the maxim "power once delegated shall not be redelegated" is but one prominent example of this phenomenon. I suspect that the same consideration that would lead me to acquiesce in the operation of the federal administrative agencies would also lead me to acquiesce in the acceptance of the legal-rights ramifications of the hypothesized change in our moral culture on which this part is focusing: the appropriateness of accepting precedents that were wrong when initially announced in order to avoid disappointing reasonable expectations based on those precedents. But I do feel uncomfortable with this conclusion.

Of course, the actual historical "news" is neither best nor worst. Section B discusses the relevant evidence, and Section C analyzes these facts' implications for my central claims.

B. Some Problems That Increase the Difficulty of Determining the Operative American Ideology (Ideologies) in the 1776–1800 Period

Five problems substantially increase the difficulty of determining "the American position" in the last quarter of the eighteenth century on such "vertical-relationship" issues as who should govern, how the governors should govern, and what rights individuals have against the State. The first is that during the relevant years "Americans drew from a multitude of traditions that may look contradictory today, but did not at the time."[98]

Second, although the same words consistently appeared in key documents throughout the 1760–1800 period, their meaning changed critically. "Whole new concepts . . . [took] shape behind an unvarying set of terms."[99] For example, according to Joyce Appleby,

> In the context of classical republican thought virtue meant civic virtue, the quality that enabled men to rise above private interests in order to act for the good of the whole. By the 1780s this meaning is less clear. Speakers begin to add a modifier to make their point, as when John Adams said "disinterested virtue is disappearing among us." . . . [B]y the end of the century virtue more often referred to a private quality, a man's capacity to look out for himself and his dependents—almost the opposite of classical virtue.[100]

Similarly, the word "liberty" had a very different denotation in different contexts:

> Probably the least familiar concept of liberty . . . was that most common to us—that is, liberty as personal freedom bounded only by such limits as are necessary if others are to enjoy the same extensive personal freedom. Before the Revolution liberty more often referred to a corporate body's right of self-determination. . . . To have liberty [in this sense] was to share in the power of the state. . . . Equally rooted in history was another concept of liberty familiar to Englishmen on both sides of the Atlantic. This was the liberty of secure possession—the enjoyment of the legal title to a piece of property or the privilege of doing a particular thing without fear of arrest or punishment.[101]

Obviously, these ambiguities substantially increase the difficulty of reading documents correctly.

Third, the difficulty of determining which if any of the various extant ideological orientations was dominant or triumphant during the relevant period or any part of it is increased by the uncertainty about the content of Lockean liberalism. Some scholars assume that Lockean liberalism should be identified with modern libertarianism and the political philosophy of possessive individualism[102] (sometimes described as classic economic liberalism). Others argue that Lockean liberalism is far closer to the kind of normative approach that I (in the tradition of Rawls and Dworkin) denominate liberalism.

Fourth, the difficulty of determining the ideological convictions of Americans between 1776 and 1800 is also increased by the fact that the real-world choices they made are consistent or inconsistent with more than one ideological orientation. Thus, on the inconsistency side, the various governmental-organization features that could be said to manifest a commitment to civic republicanism in that they encourage public-spirited deliberation both by (1) putting each organ of government in a position in which it must convince the members of other organs of government of the correctness of its views (e.g., federalism, bicameralism, the separation of powers, the Presidential veto, the electoral college, the election of Senators by state legislatures) and (2) by giving citizens the opportunity to participate in governmental affairs (e.g., trial by jury and free speech) can also be said to manifest a commitment to the non-participatory rights of the individuals for whom the State is responsible. Thus, federalism and separation of powers reduce the likelihood of majority tyranny, trial by local juries offers protection against transportation and conviction by biased strangers,[103] and free speech may be valued because of the non-political importance of self-expression as well as for its political utility. Similarly, on the inconsistency side, the exclusion of women, Blacks, and Indians from political participation is clearly inconsistent with both libertarianism and liberalism in my sense. Admittedly, since some civic republicans believed that the allegedly greater political virtue of the aristocracy or propertied classes reflected their genetic endowments and the empirical reality was that virtually no women, Blacks, or Indians had the upbringing or economic advantages that other civic republicans thought were the basis of the propertied class's superior political virtue, the exclusion of women, Blacks, and Indians from political participation or power was probably not inconsistent with at least the more hide-bound versions of civic republicanism. Still, the fact that the fits and non-fits of the relevant ideological competitors overlap each other considerably reduces our ability to determine the ideological convictions of Americans in the 1776–1800 period from what they did and said, making it unlikely that we can reach any conclusions by using the criterion of behavioral fit.

The fifth and final obstacle to identifying Americans' "political" convictions in the last quarter of the eighteenth century is the fact that their avowed beliefs may have been critically affected by their undue optimism on several issues. Thus, the Americans of 1776 clearly underestimated the likelihood that the rule of the aristocracy would lead to violations of individuals rights (regardless of whether they were viewed as non-Lockean natural rights, Lockean rights, or the customary rights of Englishmen). And the Jeffersonian Republicans of 1800 clearly did not appreciate the risk that their position on private property and equality of opportunity might produce a "class-divided society," in which persons were not (in various senses) equals.[104] Although we have some evidence of the way in which the Americans of that period would respond to the realization that rule by the aristocracy or popular sovereignty might lead to the violation of non-participatory rights, we really are not well-placed to speculate on the way in which the Republicans of 1800 would have reacted to a better prediction of the consequences of the combination of laissez faire capitalism and a non-redistributive State.

Admittedly, there are some difficult issues that I need not address. For example, I need not decide the extent to which actual behavior is caused by ideological convictions that are independent of socio-economic forces or by socio-economic forces (directly or via their impact on ideological convictions). And I probably can avoid studying the relevant parties' conclusions about such vexing issues as the necessity of judicial review and the legitimacy of civil disobedience in various circumstances (though, admittedly, the way in which an individual resolves these issues may have some bearing on his more general ideological convictions). But even if I am allowed to dodge these issues, the non-personal obstacles to assessing the relevant ideological convictions of Americans between 1776 and 1800 clearly are formidable.

C. American Political Ideologies in the Last Quarter of the Eighteenth Century

I will begin with my five basic conclusions, even if they are (I regret to say) almost entirely borrowed from others. First, "different groups approached the Revolution from different perceptions of what America was and should become. . . . [N]o simple ideology could serve them all."[105]

Second, class differences in ideology (which had an economic as well as a social basis) continued—indeed, increased—throughout the post-Revolutionary period and formed the basis of the political dispute between the Federalists and Jeffersonian Republicans in the 1790s and early 1800s.[106]

Third, the ideological convictions of many individuals were rudimentary and contained internal inconsistencies.[107]

Fourth, "[i]f early American constitutional history reveals anything, it reveals that neither those who would base their theories preeminently on rights and autonomy, nor those who would ground their paradigms exclusively on self-government and democracy, can lay easy claim to the tradition that the Constitution itself embodies"[108]

Fifth, "American constitutional thought, taken as a whole, did undergo discernible shifts from the Revolution to the Critical Period to the Framing. . . ,"[109] shifts that involved *inter alia* a change to a far more positive view of both the nature of man[110] and the economic prospects of at least Americans.[111] In essence, two or perhaps three shifts seem to have taken place:

(1) from an emphasis on political liberty (self-government) to an emphasis on individual liberty, (2) from a belief in the virtue of the aristocracy and its fitness to rule to a belief in the equal ability of all to rule *inter alia* because no one would manifest the desired virtue of disinterestedness, and perhaps (3) from a primary concern with economic individual liberty to a more-encompassing view in which economic liberty was valued not only in itself but also because of its connection to personal and family development more broadly conceived.

I will now briefly discuss the extent to which Americans seem to have been committed to (1) liberalism in my sense, (2) libertarianism, and (3) civic republicanism in the 1760–1800 period. Because my claim is that the dominant mode of legal argument in our culture is argument from liberal moral principles, I will devote most of my attention to evidence of liberal ideology in America in the second half of the eighteenth century.

(1) Liberalism

In my judgment, Americans in the latter half of the eighteenth century manifested their commitment to liberalism by making a variety of different kinds of arguments that indicated a belief that their society was a liberal, rights-based society. Some of these arguments explicitly referred to Natural Law. Others referred to a "well-defined set of English rights"[112] not just to political participation (self-rule) but to individual freedom (manifest in various fundamental "contracts," custom, and a variety of binding legal precedents and analogies).[113] Still others were based on the "law of reason" or what was considered to be "reasonable" according to the "special artificial reason" of the common law, "infused with the dictates of custom, experience, and the professional training of lawyers."[114] Many referred to the arguments of Locke, whose philosophy (to my mind) is quite different from Hobbes's political philosophy of possessive individualism in that, unlike Hobbes's, Locke's recognizes the importance of the affective connections between individuals[115]—their need for and possible obligations to one another.[116] Finally, many were influenced by Natural-Law theorists from the European continent such as Samuel von Pufendorf, Jean Jacques Burlamaqui, and Emmerich de Vattel, and by their English counterpart Thomas Rutherford, who argued that "[l]egislative authority was limited to 'the laws of nature and God' as well as by the Constitution."[117]

I will now list some prominent examples of what I (sometimes admittedly-contestably) take to be political manifestations of ideological convictions that are liberal in my sense. The first examples of these kinds are claims or arguments that rely directly on Natural Law. In this category are James Otis's argument in 1761 that writs of assistance (which gave royal customs officials sweeping powers to search for smuggled contraband) violated "natural Equity,"[118] the New York Assembly's argument in 1764 that the Stamp Act violated a right of self-taxation that was a "natural Right of Mankind,"[119] Thomas Hutchinson's claim in 1766 that the Stamp Act was "against our natural rights,"[120] Samuel Johnson's claim in the Circular Letter of 1768 that the Townshend Duties violated the "natural . . . right" of a man to "what [he] has honestly acquired,"[121] the claim of the First Continental Congress in 1774 that Americans had the rights to "life, liberty, and property" *inter alia* "by the immutable laws of nature,"[122] Thomas Paine's argument in *Common Sense* that all men had a natural right to self-government,[123] the Declaration of Independence's references to rights that precede the formation of any polity,[124] Roger Sherman's draft bill of rights' reference to "natural rights,"[125] John Adams's statement in 1797 that the "basic spirit of republics [encompasses] . . . the rule of law, checks and balances, security of property, religious toleration, and *personal liberty*"[126] (emphasis added), and Justice Samuel Chase's Natural-Law opinion in 1798 in *Calder v. Bull*.[127] In addition, numerous tracts and statements cited Blackstone's claim that "the law of nature is of course superior in obligation to all others."[128] Indeed, according to Clinton Rossiter, this statement of the legal supremacy of natural justice was the passage in the Blackstone *Commentaries* most quoted by the American colonists.[129] Of course, I am not claiming that all those who made Natural Law arguments were self-consciously committed to the kind of liberalism to which I believe contemporary American society is committed. However, I do think that the basic liberal moral principle I have articulated and its more concrete corollaries are consistent with (could be described as legitimate elaborations of) the natural rights these writers were citing. It should be remembered that to Locke natural rights encompassed more than just property rights in a narrow sense—extended to "lives, liberties, and estates"—and that what was "startling" to even the mid-seventeenth century readers of Hobbes "was his insistence that men were naturally equal."[130] In this regard, Robert Shalhope's characterization of "the emerging legal structure of late eighteenth-century America" is revealing: "No longer could the legal system be viewed as a means to preserve local power, support a local consensus-building process, or as a mirror of stable, homogeneous moral and ethical values. It had become in large part a mechanism that encouraged individuals to make their own choice of ethical values and to enforce whatever decisions resulted."[131] One can hardly imagine an account of the law that is more compatible with my statement of our society's basic moral principle.

The second set of examples that, to my mind, manifests a commitment to liberal principles contains all the arguments John Reid collected in which Americans supported their conclusions with citations of English custom, legal precedent, and "contracts" between the rulers and the ruled.[132] For my purposes, it does not matter whether the Americans of 1760–1800 cited relevant English customs and law or Locke and/or Natural Law because the English customs, "contracts," and law seem to me to embody the kinds of liberal principles to which I think our contemporary society is committed. Nor, for three reasons, does it matter that during the relevant period English courts refused to void acts of Parliament on the ground that they violated "fundamental law." First, "[w]ell into the period of the American revolution itself, leading English lawyers and statesmen continued to assert that a fixed constitution and fundamental law limited even Parliament."[133] Second, the devaluation of custom, "contracts" such as the Magna Carta, the traditional legal rights of Englishmen, and "the law of reason" in English courts had far less effect on American views than on English views. Third, I am interested not in the legal force of custom but in the character of that custom. For my purposes, it suffices that the relevant customs and "contracts" are consistent with liberalism in my sense. In any event, it is clear that during the period in which I am interested, colonists, patriots, and post-Revolutionaries often based their arguments on such sources as "the common law,"[134] the rights of Englishmen,[135] "the fundamental Principles of the [English] Constitution,"[136] and "the principles of the English constitution, and the several charters or compacts."[137] Again, I admit that much interpolation is required to link the principles of the common law, various "contracts," English customs, and "the law of reason" to the kind of liberalism to which I have argued our society is committed, but I do think that such a connection to at least a nascent form of liberalism can legitimately be made. Certainly, the parts of these materials that deal with non-political-participation rights cannot be said to reflect civic-republican notions even if it is harder to demonstrate their liberal as opposed to libertarian orientation in part because libertarians have not done an acceptable job of examining the concrete common-law-rights implications of libertarian "values."

I also think that late-eighteenth-century Americans were manifesting a commitment to what I call liberalism whenever they explicitly referred to or without citation[138] made use of Locke's natural-rights theories, which recognize the importance of ties between individuals and community membership.

In short, a considerable amount of evidence supports the claim that at least many Americans supported liberal principles during the Critical Period, the Foundation Period, and the Immediate Post-Foundation Period.

(2) Libertarianism

As I argue in Chapter 1,[139] I do not think that the versions of libertarianism that are currently popular can be said to be based on a moral norm. This conclusion reflects the fact that at least those versions of libertarianism that claim that individuals have a right to profit from their genetic endowments and family associations are asserting the moral relevance of factors whose presence is morally arbitrary—of talents, dispositions, and opportunities for which individuals deserve no credit. It should therefore not be surprising that I would be reluctant to conclude that Americans were libertarians in the last quarter of the eighteenth century.

I have no doubt that Americans of this period had a great distrust of central government, believed that their property rights were in some sense fundamental, and (perhaps relatedly) were strongly opposed to any State-imposed barriers to their economic advancement. I also recognize that many Americans during this period thought that at least the first two of these convictions were shared by Locke and Blackstone.[140]

Still, there is a huge gap between these positions and libertarian conclusions. The colonists and post-Revolutionaries did not oppose taxation on principle but taxation without representation. They recognized the legitimacy of taxing *individuals* who did not want to be taxed for purposes other than maintaining a minimalist, watchguard State. The Jeffersonian Republican opposition to State interference with the market was in the service not of the type of possessive individualism associated with Hobbes but of an "affective individualism" that entailed "a concern for one's fellow citizen and the larger community."[141] They thought that "free markets" would lead to true equality. Their optimism precluded them from seeing that, at least in the absence of strong redistributive policies, the kind of equality of opportunity that they thought that laissez faire would guarantee might be associated with class divisions[142] and inequalities in the abilities of individuals to make and conform their lives to meaningful ethical choices, options that they valued highly.[143] One simply does not know how these persons would have reacted to a more realistic assessment of the consequences of the combination of a free-market economy and a non-redistributive State or, more to the point, given my and probably their confusion about their rights-commitments, how those commitments (if any) imply they were obligated to react to such information. I should add that (as I am sure Epstein realizes) a State's redistributive potential would not be much restricted by the "obligation of contracts" and the constraint that it take individual property (either directly or through regulation) only for public use in conjunction with a payment of just compensation. In fact, properly understood, constraints of these kinds would seem desirable from my kind of liberal as well as from a Nozickian libertarian perspective.

For these reasons, I do not think that the undoubted fact that Locke had great influence throughout the Foundation period or the contested fact that Blackstone's *Commentaries* (which clearly had significant influence on the colonists on some issues) support the existence of strong property rights imply that in the 1776–1800 period a substantial percentage of Americans were even partially or inconsistently committed to Nozickian or even a more moderate version of libertarianism.

(3) Civic Republicanism

Clearly, a substantial number of Americans were civic republicans between 1760 and the early 1800s. Scholars such as Bernard Bailyn, Gordon S. Wood, and J. G. A. Pocock have amply demonstrated[144] that in common with the Country set in England (Whigs opposed to the Court party under Walpole) many Americans in the 1776–1800 period embraced a distinctive set of political and social ideas now labeled civic republicanism. However, it appears to be equally clear that the content of civic-republican ideas changed during this period[145] and that the percentage of Americans who were actively committed to or acquiesced in these (changing) ideas diminished as the last quarter of the eighteenth century progressed.

In essence, civic republicans seem to have subscribed to the following eight propositions:

(1) individuals are naturally self-seeking and depraved;
(2) the members of society have a common, social interest in a collective social good that is not a function of the individual goals of a society's members;
(3) the individual pursuit of individual self-interest will produce social catastrophe;

(4) to prosper, a society must inculcate virtue;

(5) government responsibilities can be properly carried out only by the virtuous—only by those prepared to seek the social good as opposed to their narrowly-defined self-interest;

(6) only the able, well-born, and rich will in practice have the ability to become men of civic virtue;

(7) reliably-good governmental decisions can be generated only by reasoned deliberation by individuals of civic virtue (whose lives will, in addition, be immensely enriched by their participation in this process); and

(8) governments should be organized to promote decisionmaking through reasoned deliberation by men of civic virtue.

Although many Americans did subscribe to these views, a substantial percentage—particularly of those who did not belong to the American "aristocracy"—appear never to have supported them.[146] And as the last quarter of the eighteenth century proceeded, the percentage of Americans who rejected and actively opposed these views dramatically increased. Thus, in the 1790s, those who became Jeffersonian Republicans appear to have subscribed to the beliefs that human beings are naturally good and that ugly human qualities are caused by authoritarian political institutions—"the errors and abuses that have at every period existed in political establishments."[147] As I have already indicated, the Jeffersonian Republicans (who carried the election of 1800) seem also to have subscribed to the view that the social good consists of individuals' achieving their goals.[148] Moreover, changes in economic circumstances (the fact that famine was not the risk in 1800 America that it had been in previous times in Europe) and the "invisible hand of the market" argument of Adam Smith led the Jeffersonian Republicans to conclude that at least in the America of 1800 the pursuit of individual interest would lead to social prosperity rather than calamity.[149] Jeffersonian Republicans also rejected the view that for either genetic and/or situational reasons the aristocracy was generally fit to rule.[150] Indeed, even such prominent Federalists as John Adams appear to have grown "skeptical about the idea that anything but self-interest could be the basis for political behavior,"[151] regardless of whether one could instantiate a government of the aristocracy. Finally, although our Constitution did incorporate many features that many republicans believed[152] would promote the kind of deliberation they thought was essential to good government, it did not incorporate many others that had been included in post-Revolution republican state constitutions.[153]

In short, although I certainly do not deny that many Americans subscribed to several civic-republican views during the 1776–1800 period, I do not think that one can claim that civic republicanism was the dominant political ideology in America in the last quarter of the eighteenth century. From my perspective, this conclusion is obviously good news: although the civic republicans were clearly more interested in the question of who should govern and how government should be organized and conducted, they also had views about individual rights that were illiberal in my sense— views about virtue and the importance of communities of shared values that in the modern context would probably favor such illiberal policies as prohibitions of pornography and other "speech" viewed as offensive by the majority of some communities, and might even support various kinds of "community-enhancing" policies of religious and secular-moral intolerance.

D. "The Ideology" of Late-Eighteenth-Century Americans, the Implications of My Conclusions for My Central Claims, and Some Comments on the Use to Which Some Academic Lawyers Have Put the Relevant History

The consensus view now seems to be that by the end of the eighteenth century Americans had combined the various ideologies that had attracted some of them in the preceding years (civic republicanism, nascent liberalism, and elements of what I have called libertarianism) into a "hybrid"[154] "political theory worthy of a prominent place in the history of Western thought."[155] I do not find the coherence or consistency that this consensus seems to attribute to American thought at that time. Indeed, the only consistency I find is that between the belief that (regardless of class) rulers will be motivated by narrowly-defined self-interest and the conclusion that government should be organized to "economize on virtue"—to militate against the ability of the inevitably-self-interested members of any group to deprive members of other groups of their rights.

Americans in the late eighteenth century embraced the French Revolution[156] and the ideals in whose name it was fought without appreciating the extent to which those ideals would be compromised by their simultaneous advocacy of laissez faire capitalism and their opposition to redistributive policies.[157] The revitalization of organized religion and churches in the 1790s (churches that stressed not only the importance of community but also the positive rights of individuals and the obligations of one individual to another) may provide grounds for optimism about the way in which Americans of that era would have changed their conceptions of their governments' obligations if confronted with the actual consequences of the regimes they thought were appropriate. But the implicit hope that they would have opted for a more liberal State had they been better-informed may be at least as unduly optimistic as the Jeffersonian Republicans were about the social consequences of the kind of equality of opportunity that government withdrawal from market regulation would generate.

From the perspective of my central jurisprudential claims, the historical "news" I have just "announced" is somewhat mixed. I would like to be able to tell the following story: Americans in the last quarter of the eighteenth century subscribed to a variety of different ideologies, but as time progressed they increasingly rejected potentially-illiberal civic republicanism in favor of a political philosophy that emphasized the equality of all men and the contribution that free markets would make to individuals' putting themselves into positions in which they could make and live by their own ethical choices. The value-orientation of this latter philosophy is actually liberal in the sense in which I am using this term—it would lead individuals who were aware of the actual consequences of a non-redistributive, laissez faire State to reach conclusions about State and individual obligations that I claim in Chapter 1 our society is committed to instantiating.

There is more than something to this story, but I hesitate to endorse it entirely. Fortunately, I do not think that my basic jurisprudential claims depend on the accuracy of this tale of nascent liberalism. For my purposes, it suffices that late-eighteenth-century Americans believed in rights, were confused about the rights they believed they had, and were increasingly attracted to notions that if not yet liberal were at least nascently liberal.

The neo-republican legal academics who talk about "the idea of a usable past" seem to me not to be taking either history or legal argument seriously. They have sought to provide a historical justification for legal conclusions that they favor for personal-ultimate-value reasons that have nothing to do with legitimate legal argument. In part because they have confused liberalism with the libertarian political philosophy of possessive individualism, they believe that the society they want to create—a society that is affective, communicative, and community-based—cannot be instantiated by legal liberalism (which they mistakenly believe presupposes and values a world of atomized, unencumbered selves). The search of the neo-republicans for a past that is usable for their project has led them to misrepresent our history.[158] I hope that I have not committed a similar sin.

10. *The "Strict Constructionists"*

The phrase "strict constructionist" has typically been used to refer to American Constitutional-law analysts who subscribe to all of the following four positions:

(1) the interpretive and institutional view that judges are not authorized to exercise strong discretion when interpreting the Constitution;

(2) the interpretive position that the United States Constitution has judicially-cognizable meaning only to the extent that its concrete meaning can be derived either mechanically from the text itself or historically from extrinsic evidence revealing the concrete meaning the text's drafters or ratifiers[159] thought it had;

(3) the "substantive outcome" view that in the United States individuals have few Constitutional rights against either the central government or the state governments; and

(4) the pragmatic view that even if (A) the United States Constitution could be said to have judicially-cognizable meanings in addition to the meanings that judges could derive mechanically from the text or historically from information about the way in which the text's framers or ratifiers "specifically expected" it to be applied—meanings that would enable judges to decide cases without imposing personal ultimate values (without exercising strong discretion)—and (B) the first-best efforts of first-best judges in first-best institutions of judicial review to discern such additional meanings would effectuate the principles the Constitution was designed to secure, in practice instructing our actual worse-than-first-best judges in our actual worse-than-first-best judicial system to try to discover these additional Constitutional meanings when performing judicial review will result in their imposing their own values (exercising strong discretion) and thereby undermining the principles the Constitution was supposed to secure.[160]

At the outset, I want to emphasize two points about strict constructionism. First, strict constructionists do not always articulate the above positions as clearly as they might. In particular, strict constructionists often give the impression that their position reflects a conclusion that the text of any document can have meaning only if that meaning is self-declaring or can be ascertained from extrinsic evidence about the "specific meaning" attributed to it by its author or ratifier. In fact, the more sophisticated strict constructionists do not subscribe to this patently-silly position. Strict constructionists do not need to deny that the Constitution's various vague or open-textured provisions (most importantly, the Ninth Amendment and the "privileges or immunities" clause of the Fourteenth Amendment) have no meaning: they need deny only that these provisions have a meaning that is judicially cognizable. Thus, strict constructionists could admit that the Ninth Amendment and the "privileges or immunities" clause of the Fourteenth Amendment "mean" that the parties to whom they refer have unenumerated rights against the central and state governments respectively that cannot be mechanically ascertained or discovered by reference to a ratifier's "specific intent" and still demonstrate that in the American system judges cannot take this meaning into account when reviewing the Constitutionality of government decisions by establishing that the only way for judges to identify unenumerated rights in these circumstances is to impose their own personal ultimate values and such an exercise of strong discretion by judges is inconsistent with our society's moral and Constitutional governmental-process commitments (to "democracy" or "majoritarian rule" or "representative government" in some sense). Although I believe that this argument is wrong, it is certainly not silly.

The second point I want to emphasize at this juncture is that it is logically consistent to subscribe to one or more strict-constructionist positions without subscribing to all of them. For example, I subscribe to the first strict-constructionist position (that judges are not authorized to exercise strong discretion when executing judicial review) but not to the second, third, or fourth positions delineated above.[161] Indeed, one might even argue that the combination of the second and third positions just described is inconsistent with the first. Strict constructionists face a real problem in determining the "meaning" that a Constitutional text's drafters or ratifiers attributed to it. This problem is particularly acute when the relevant text has a moral dimension. Virually no strict constructionist believes that the "meaning" of any Constitutional text is limited to the way in which a text's drafters or ratifiers expected it would be interpreted in relation to the specific cases they had in mind when drafting it, discussing it, or voting on it. However, strict constructionists are also unwilling to adopt the approach to interpreting such texts that I think would enable an interpreter to operate without imposing her own values—interpreting a moral-rights-related Constitutional text in light of the moral principles on which the society is committed to basing its moral-rights discourse. In particular, strict constructionists would reject such a moral reading of this type of Constitutional text because it would generate conclusions that contradict the third strict-constructionist position—the view that in the United States individuals have few Constitutional rights against the central or state governments. Unfortunately from their perspective, if the strict constructionists reject both the type of moral reading of any such text that I think is legitimate and the view that the meaning of any such text is limited to the specific expectations that their drafters and ratifiers had about its implications for cases they specifically had in mind (a category whose content is itself highly contestable), it is hard to see how they can interpret such texts non-arbitrarily—how they can determine how far to generalize the outcomes the drafters and ratifiers specifically had in mind without exercising strong discretion—without violating the first strict-constructionist tenet. In any event, I will now analyze each of the four strict-constructionist positions in turn.

A. The Claim That Judges Are Not Authorized to Exercise Strong Discretion When Engaging in Judicial Review

This conclusion is said to reflect our commitment to democratic procedures or majority rule or representative government—a commitment that is manifest in the procedures the Constitution establishes for the operation of the central government[162] and in the requirement that the states provide a republican form of government[163] and not override what the Tenth Amendment describes as "the powers of the people."[164] Of course, since the Constitution establishes a complicated and hard-to-characterize set of government institutions and governing processes and since the American public has (I believe) accepted for nearly two centuries the notion that judges can legitimately declare unconstitutional decisions made by "representative" government officials, strict constructionists who want to explain why in our polity it is impermissible for judges to exercise strong discretion in the practice of judicial review will not be able to establish either the defining features of our governmental-process commitments or the point of those commitments in a mechanical way. I cannot assess whether the strict constructionists' conclusions about the point of our society or, relatedly, about the defining features and point of the governmental processes to which we are committed as a society imply the illegitimacy of judges' exercising strong discretion when reviewing the Constitutionality of the decisions made by other branches and/or levels of government because the strict constructionists have never even attempted to characterize our society or its governmental-process commitments in a relevant way. Unless the strict constructionists provide such characterizations, I cannot even assess the consistency of the first strict-constructionist position with their other relevant conclusions. For even this limited purpose, I need a place to stand, and they have not provided me with it.

I will therefore restrict myself in what follows to explaining why my conclusion that our society is a liberal, rights-based society implies that it is illegitimate for judges in our society to exercise strong discretion when reviewing the Constitutionality of decisions of other government officials. As already indicated, I believe that this conclusion that ours is a liberal, rights-based society implies a commitment to governmental processes that manifest appropriate, equal respect and concern for all creatures with the neurological prerequisites for becoming and remaining individuals of moral integrity. That commitment implies that our governments may not violate (indeed, must actively secure) the rights of all such creatures—an obligation that need not but certainly may be met *inter alia* by establishing a procedure of judicial review by lifetime appointees of all government choices. It also implies that all decisions that are not required or prohibited by such creatures' rights and obligations be made through governmental decision-processes that give something like equal power (a concept that is at best extraordinarily difficult to operationalize) to all relevantly-competent citizens. This account of our governmental-process commitments simultaneously does two things. First, it legitimates judges' declaring unconstitutional State decisions that violate the Constitutional rights of Constitutional-rights-bearing entities—a conclusion that reflects my belief that judges can make such decisions without exercising strong discretion since there are internally-right answers to all Constitutional-rights questions. Second, it calls into question the legitimacy of judges' "declaring unconstitutional" on personal-ultimate-value grounds government decisions that violate no one's rights—that is, declaring unconstitutional government decisions against claims that we are not morally committed to upholding, claims that are based on interests that are improperly called "unenumerated rights." The preceding sentence contained the expression "calls into question" instead of the expression "reveals to be illegitimate" because two types of objections can be made to the proposition that judges' exercising strong discretion when reviewing the Constitutionality of a government decision is inconsistent with the appropriate, equal respect and concern a liberal State owes all moral-rights holers for which it is responsible. The first of these objections implies the liberal legitimacy of the courts' exercising strong discretion across a wide variety of cases. It focuses on the possibility that an instruction to judges to exercise strong discretion when engaging in judicial review might actually increase the representativeness of our democracy because judges are selected more representatively than legislators or members of the executive branch, because judges are more responsive to the general population's views than members of the other branches or levels of government, or because judges are non-representative in either their selection and/or their responsiveness in ways that increase the representativeness of our government as a whole—that is, that distribute power more evenly among our citizens. Although the first two of the above three arguments seem clearly wrong empirically, there may be something to the third argument just delineated. Indeed, something like it underlies Ely's contention that the courts should intervene in the interest of our society's political underdogs.

The second objection to the claim that it is illegitimate for judges in a liberal State to exercise strong discretion when engaging in judicial review has implications only in those cases that deal with features of our governing processes that affect their representativeness. Assume that there is no internally-right way to resolve some disputes about the structure of our government institutions or processes if the resolution is to be judged by its impact on the equality of the political power of all (relevantly-competent) moral-rights-holding citizens. If this is so, any judicial intervention in such cases that went beyond striking down related government decisions that were wrong would have to involve the exercise of strong discretion. Nevertheless, an approach that authorized judges to pick the governmental process that they thought most consistent with their understanding of the equal-power criterion might promote such equality in an objective sense if judges were less likely to make wrong decisions on these issues than legislators and members of the executive branch and "transaction costs" would preclude courts from detecting and eliminating the errors of others. Something like this argument underlies Ely's conclusion that the courts should take a more active role in supervising the structuring of governmental decision-making.

I think that there is some force to both these objections to the claim that in a liberal, rights-based State it is always illegitimate for judges to exercise strong discretion when reviewing the Constitutionality of State decisions. However, pragmatic considerations lead me to conclude that even the limited permission these objections suggest judges might be given to exercise strong discretion when engaging in judicial review is likely in practice to reduce the extent to which we fulfill our Constitutional commitments. I would therefore conclude that in a liberal, rights-based State it would be improper for judges to exercise strong discretion when engaging in judicial review. Since I believe that the United States is a liberal, rights-based State, I agree with the first strict-constructionist position that our judges are not authorized to exercise strong discretion when engaging in judicial review, though the strict constructionists have themselves offered no justification for it.

B. The Claim That the Only Sources of Judicially-Cognizable Constitutional Meaning Are the Self-Declaring Meaning of Texts and Historical Evidence about "What Those Who Adopted a Text Understood It to Mean"

For both positive and negative reasons, I disagree strongly with this position. The positive reason is that there are internally-right ways to identify unenumerated rights and to interpret vague or open-textured enumerated rights. In particular, judges who pay attention to my distinction between "moral principles" and "personal ultimate values" will in theory be able to discover the internally-right responses to Constitutional-rights-and-obligations claims that cannot be resolved from the self-declaring meaning of the text and historical evidence about its ratifiers' specific expectations—will be able to resolve such claims without exercising strong discretion.

I also have two basic negative reasons for rejecting this strict-constructionist position (though strict constructionists may conclude that these reasons imply that there should be less rather than more judicial review than they currently advocate). My first negative reason is that no text has self-declaring meaning. Although mechanical, dictionary-based interpretations may sometimes turn out to be correct and although we may sometimes "intuit" that they clearly are correct, that "intuition" is the product of a non-mechanical though perhaps subconscious interpretive analysis.

My second negative reason is actually a set of reasons that relate to (1) the ambiguity of the phrase "what those who adopted it understood it to mean,"[165] (2) the weakness of the argument that strict constructionists make for their resolution of this ambiguity, (3) the fact that historical research suggests that those who drafted and ratified the Constitution had a different understanding of "what they understood it to mean" from the strict-constructionist understanding of that phrase, (4) the "fact" that the drafters' and ratifiers' understanding of the phrase is more consistent with general social practice in analogous situations, and, relatedly, (5) the fact that the drafters' and ratifiers' understanding of the phrase is more consistent than the strict constructionists' understanding of that phrase with the point of the enterprise in which the Constitution's drafters and ratifiers were engaged.

I will now address each of these points in turn. First, the phrase "what those who adopted it understood it to mean" is ambiguous. The relevant ambiguity relates to Dworkin's distinction between concepts and conceptions. If I tell someone to treat others fairly in a particular context, do I mean for him to (1) think through the concept of fairness to which we are committed in our society and treat the individuals in question as he concludes that concept requires or (2) discover what at the moment I made the relevant utterance I thought that concept would require in the relevant cases (to implement my contemporaneous-to-utterance conception of that concept or my application of that concept to the relevant cases)? Many strict constructionists simply assume that Instruction (2) captures the meaning of the phrase "what those who adopted it understood it to mean"—that is, they do not even advert to the possibility that Instruction (1) may capture the ratifiers' interpretive intent or should, in any case, be assumed by a Constitutional interpreter to do so.

Second, the only argument that those strict constructionists who seem to be aware of the relevant ambiguity have offered for their conclusion that judges are obligated to assume that they have been issued with the second set of instructions just delineated is the implicit argument that Instruction (1) would not be permissible because (A) there is no internally-right way to move from concepts to conceptions—in other words, Instruction (1) would be an instruction for judges to exercise strong discretion when engaging in judicial review—and (B) it is illegitimate in our polity for judges to exercise strong discretion when engaging in judicial review. Since my conclusion that there are internally-right answers to moral-rights questions is based on an argument that there are internally-right ways to define, concretize, and apply the vague concepts whose interpretation is at issue, I do not find this strict-constructionist argument for Instruction (2) persuasive.

Third, historical research indicates that the strict-constructionist conclusion on this issue is also inconsistent with the intentions of the Constitution's drafters and ratifiers to give its interpreters the first rather than the second set of instructions delineated above.[166]

Fourth, the strict-constructionist position on this issue is inconsistent as well with my armchair-empirical assumption that in our culture "instruction-givers" who issue vague or open-textured moral instructions designed to cover a wide variety of cases over a considerable period of time to inter-preters who are as skilled as the instructors at handling the relevant princi-ples generally intend those instructions to be interpreted in the first rather than the second way delineated above.

Fifth, the strict-constructionist position is disfavored by functional con-siderations—that is, by the fact that in both Constitutional and other settings in which the above conditions are fulfilled speakers who want moral princi-ples to be effectuated will find that this objective will be furthered if their communications are interpreted to instruct the instructees to effectuate the principles as the instructees understand them at the moment of decision rather than as the instructors understood them in the possibly-flawed, ap-plied sense on which strict constructionists focus.

C. The Claim That the Text of the Constitution Establishes Only a Few Individual Rights against the Central or State Governments

In part, this strict-constructionist position reflects their premise that, in Lino Graglia's words: "The purpose of the Constitution was to create a stronger central government, primarily for practical and mundane reasons of trade and defense. It was not adopted, as constitutional theorists seem to assume, to meet a felt need for additional protection of individual rights."[167]

In fact, though partially correct, this statement presents the issue in an ei-ther/or fashion that disregards the rights-consciousness of the Founding Fa-thers (which, as Graglia recognizes in the next sentence, had much to do with the system of checks and balances the Constitution establishes within the central government and which, in any case, was articulated in many con-temporaneousness discussions of the original Constitution and the Bill of Rights) and ignores the point of the post–Civil War amendments.[168] Pri-marily, however, the third strict-constructionist position follows from the second. If the Constitution protects only those concrete, specific rights that can be derived from the text either mechanically or historically by discover-ing what "rights" the text's ratifiers "meant" to protect (in the strict-con-structionist sense of "meant"), the Constitution might very well be con-cluded to protect only a very few rights of individuals against the central and state governments. However, to my mind, the fact that the third strict-con-structionist position follows from the second implies that it falls with the sec-ond.

D. The Pragmatic Claim That More Ambitious Attempts to Enforce the
Constitution through Judicial Review Will Be Self-Defeating

Many strict constructionists also seem to be making the pragmatic argument that any attempt to authorize our judges to seek meaning in the Constitution that is not self-declaring or historically-ascertainable in the way
they advocate will in practice disserve Constitutional principles even if (contrary to their belief) in a first-best world of ideal judicial institutions, ideal
judges, and ideal judicial efforts, it would further Constitutional principles. I
have three points to make in response to this claim.

(1) The Possible Illegitimacy of the Strict Constructionists' Pragmatic Argument

Strict constructionists assume that if imperfections in our judicial institutions and personnel create a situation in which our society will live
up to its commitments to a greater extent if its judges do not follow a
first-best decision-procedure when engaging in judicial review, it clearly
will be legitimate for our imperfect judges to adopt some different-from-
first-best (second-best or third-best) decision-procedure to enable society
to perform better in the relevant respect. It is important to remember,
however, that it may be morally impermissible for a rights-based society
to respond to such institutional and personnel imperfections by altering
its instructions to judges on how they should practice judicial review.
Since I have already discussed these issues in the course of analyzing the
illegitimacy of various prudential arguments in Chapter 1, I will say no
more about them here.

(2) The Possible Erroneousness of the Strict Constructionists' Short-Term
Pragmatic Prediction

The strict constructionists' conclusion that judges who exceed the strict
constructionists' preferred instructions will make things worse rather than
better from the appropriate Constitutional perspective is based on evidence
that is not always accurate and is sometimes less persuasive than they believe.
Strict constructionists either have made or could make at least nine different
points to support their pragmatic conclusion. I will now delineate and comment on each of these points in turn.

First, the strict constructionists could argue that judges would be likely to
do more harm than good from the perspective of our society's commitments

if they exceeded the strict constructionists' recommended instructions because judges are just lawyers and lawyers have not been trained to make the kind of moral and philosophical arguments that I think count in adjudicative settings and do not in fact make or consider such arguments in their normal professional lives. This point is really a generalized version of Learned Hand's second argument for opposing any attempt by courts to determine whether government decisions violate the Constitution's "fundamental fairness" clauses. My response to this point is the same as my response to Hand's argument: although I admit that legal education does not contain much (enough) explicit philosophical instruction, law professors teach philosophy all the time without admitting it or even realizing it, and although I agree that lawyers and judges usually make their arguments and explain their decisions in doctrinal terms that conceal the fact that they are really drawing on philosophical distinctions and making arguments of moral principle, they too do philosophy all the time. In fact, in practice, I think that skilled lawyers often do philosophy better than philosophers—that the lawyer's need to deal with a particular case or set of cases forces him to operationalize abstract notions that philosophers may not specify sufficiently.

The second pragmatic point that strict constructionists sometimes make focuses on the methods we actually use to pick the judges who will engage in judicial review. They argue that even if we could pick judges who would help our society live up to its moral commitments by exceeding the strict-constructionist judicial-review instructions, the people we actually pick to fill these roles will not do so. Our actual judges are less able than candidates we might have picked, less well-trained or experienced at doing philosophically-sensitive legal analysis than various superior available alternatives, and more political both in the primary sense of being active in politics and in the causally-related and more-relevant secondary sense of being inclined to base their decisions on their personal ultimate values. I agree with all these claims and would prefer a different judicial-recruitment system. However, I think that strict constructionists exaggerate the extent to which the existing system of recruitment reduces the efficacy of giving judges first-best instructions.

Third, some strict constructionists argue that our current system gives judges an incentive to impose not only personal ultimate values in general but liberal personal ultimate values in particular even when their doing so is not legitimate. The negative facts that strict constructionists cite in support of this conclusion are that federal judges are lifetime appointees, that their individual salaries are not merit-based, that the collective real salaries of the relevant judges are rarely altered significantly, and that the relevant judges' job description is in practice beyond Congressional or popular control. The positive facts that strict constructionists cite in support of this conclusion are that judges like to have good reputations and that the reputation of a judge is determined by academic and media commentators, who tend to be both liberal and oriented to (in my terms) personal ultimate values as opposed to moral principles. In any event, this incentive-argument leads some strict constructionists to conclude that giving judicial reviewers instructions that cannot be mechanically applied and enforced will result in their disserving the Constitution by imposing inappropriate liberal values. Although, again, I admit that there is something to this point, its significance will clearly be substantially reduced if the liberal norms that judges have a private incentive to implement are moral principles that our society is committed to effectuating in rights-and-obligations-claims-related contexts and not personal ultimate values.

Fourth, strict constructionists could claim that judges are likely to disserve the Constitution if my set of complicated instructions are substituted for their set of simple instructions because our federal judges in general and Supreme Court Justices in particular are overworked and do not have enough time to spend on individual cases or issues. I agree that our Constitutional-law judges are overworked. In fact, I would prefer to replace our general-federal-jurisdiction Supreme Court with a Supreme Constitutional-Law Court of the German type. I also agree that our current judges could do a better job of following my instructions if our judicial institutions were changed in this way. However, I still think that even given our extant judicial institutions, judicial-review decisions will help our society live up to our moral commitments more if the judges are given my instructions than if they are given the strict-constructionists' instructions.

Fifth, the strict constructionists point out that the ability of my instructions to produce the results I think we are committed to securing is substantially undercut by the fact that in practice there is almost no dialogue between (or among) members of the Supreme Court—that majority opinions and dissents are written independently, that the Justices do not really try to face up to each other's arguments. Although I agree that this "fact" is or could be undesirable and that it undermines the value of my instructions more than it undermines the value of the strict constructionists' instructions, I do not find this argument decisive.

Sixth, strict constructionists have also argued against the kind of instructions I am advocating by pointing out the low quality of the arguments the

Supreme Court has made to support its conclusions. I agree that most Constitutional-law doctrine is woefully inadequate. For example, I agree that (1) the due process clause is a procedural clause, (2) that "strict scrutiny," "intermediate scrutiny," and "ordinary scrutiny" are misnomers in that they imply that the carefulness of the scrutiny as opposed to the test under which the government decision under review is being scrutinized is varying, (3) that "strict scrutiny" and "intermediate scrutiny" are also misclassified as "tests of Constitutionality" to the extent that they really focus on factors that relate to the degree of deference the court owes the decisionmaker whose decision it is reviewing as opposed to the test it should use to determine the probability that the decisionmaker's decision was unconstitutional.[169] However, I find these facts less telling than do the strict constructionists: (1) I place more weight on the conclusions the judges reached than on the arguments they used to support those conclusions and (2) I trace much of our doctrinal fiasco to the fact that lawyers have been taught that law and morals are separate—an error that my instructions would correct. In my opinion, once judges realize that the separation of "law and morals" that is "correct" is the separation of adjudicatory analysis and personal-ultimate-value-oriented moral-ought analysis and not the separation of adjudicatory analysis and moral-principle-oriented moral-rights analysis, they will evolve doctrines that capture what is driving their decisions—namely, to a considerable extent, their perceptions of the moral principles to which we are committed.

Seventh, most contemporary strict constructionists would also justify their dire predictions about the actual consequences of judges' being given my instructions by citing the illegitimacy and undesirability of the conclusions that the Supreme Court has reached so far—that is, by citing the fact that the Supreme Court has reached conclusions that are inconsistent with both majority preferences and the strict constructionists' conclusions about the types of argument it is appropriate for judges to consider when engaging in judicial review. No doubt, some Supreme Court conclusions are incorrect—the decision in *Blaisdell* cited by Graglia comes readily to mind.[170] However, I agree with many of the Supreme Court rulings of unconstitutionality that strict constructionists regard as unfounded and illegitimate: although the doctrinal justifications the Court has offered for many of these decisions are unpersuasive, I suspect that courts that followed my instructions would reach and be able to justify many of the conclusions in question (though these conclusions could not be justified by a court that was restricted to the types of arguments the strict constructionists consider to be judicially cognizable in our moral, political, and legal culture). I am therefore less discouraged than the strict constructionists by the substantive conclusions that the Supreme Court has reached and expect that the Court would help our society to fulfill its commitments to an even greater extent if it operated with my instructions (on the basis of a sounder understanding of "the relationship between law and morals").

Eighth, some strict constructionists would also oppose my proposal on the ground that it would lead people to conclude that all government decisions that the Supreme Court held Constitutional were deemed socially and morally desirable by the courts. Although I do not deny that some might interpret such decisions in this way, my approach indicates that such an inference is unjustified. In particular, my strong distinction between moral principles and the rights-and-obligations conclusions to which they are relevant, on the one hand, and personal ultimate values and the evaluation of moral-ought statements to which they are relevant, on the other, should help people realize that the fact that the Court concluded that a decision it reviewed did not violate the State's Constitutional obligations implies virtually nothing about the decision's desirability from any personal-ultimate-value perspective. In short, the conclusions about "the relationship between law and morals" on which my instructions are based should—if publicized—reduce the likelihood that the public will assume that the Supreme Court is placing its personal-ultimate-value imprimatur on all State choices whose Constitutionality it upholds.

Ninth, strict constructionists could argue that the more extensive judicial review my instructions would engender will disserve Constitutional principles on balance because the extra protection to those principles they induce the courts to provide directly will be more than offset by the disservice to those principles they will cause by reducing the extent to which other government officials are themselves concerned with and guided by Constitutional principles. This fact is salient because many of the decisions of these other government officials will not be reviewed by the courts at all and those that are reviewed will be assessed only after substantial delay. Although Supreme Court review may cause non-judicial officials to ignore their duty to conform to the Constitution—to leave such concerns to the courts—it seems more likely to me that the prospect of a State official's being told by the Court that she has made a decision that was inconsistent with her Constitutional obligations would be more likely to encourage that official to take the Constitution seriously than to discourage her from doing so. However, even if I am wrong on this issue, this ninth point does not seem so weighty to me as some strict constructionists appear to believe.

In short, although some of the arguments and evidence that strict constructionists adduce in support of their pragmatic conclusion do carry some weight, I would not be persuaded that their pragmatic conclusion was correct even if I accepted its relevance to any conclusion about the types of arguments that judges in our polity are authorized to consider when engaging in judicial review.

(3) The Possible Long-Run Benefits of First-Best Judicial Decisionmaking

Even if the effective substitution of my instructions for judicial review for the strict-constructionists' instructions would reduce the extent to which our society lived up to its moral commitments in the short run, I suspect that it would increase the extent to which our society fulfilled its moral commitments in the long run. As the courts, their company, and the public at large became more sophisticated about the nature of Constitutional argument and its relationship to moral arguments of different kinds, law professors will become more self-conscious about the philosophical assumptions and arguments they are making, legal education will on that account improve, lawyers and judges will be more open about the moral basis of their arguments and decisions and will become better at executing legal-philosophical analyses because they will undertake such analyses both more frequently and more openly, a more appropriate subset of lawyers will become judges, judicial institutions and informal judicial decisionmaking procedures will be reformed in ways that increase their efficacy, and academic and media commentary will alter in a way that improves the incentives of judges to adjudicate Constitutional disputes properly. Admittedly, taken to the extreme, this last sentence is somewhat Pollyannish: as my mother used to say, "too much of anything is excessive." But I am confident that some improvements of each of the types just described would be generated by the open adoption of the instructions that I think our society is committed to giving its Constitutional adjudicators. To the extent that this is so, the pragmatic case for my instructions will be stronger overall in the long run than in the short run.

I have tried to play fair with the strict constructionists—to articulate their positions in the most defensible forms I could imagine and to make all the plausible arguments for their conclusions I could devise. Strict constructionism is not as silly as many (liberal or left-of-center) commentators would have us believe. However, if my analysis of adjudication is correct, three of the four basic strict-constructionists positions are insupportable.

11. Philip Bobbitt and the Claim That Legal Practice Is Self-Legitimating

As Chapter 1 indicates, although my jurisprudential position differs in various critical respects from Philip Bobbitt's,[171] I have borrowed significantly and profited substantially from his work. This section delineates the four basic parts of Bobbitt's analysis and explains my response to each.

A. The Four Basic Parts of Bobbitt's Analysis

(1) The Six "Modalities" of Legal Argument

Bobbitt claims that our legal culture uses six different types of legal argument: textual, historical, structural, doctrinal, prudential, and "ethical." Chapter 1 explored the first five. In Bobbitt's terminology, an "ethical" argument is one that relies on the overall "ethos" of limited government as centrally constituting American political culture.

(2) The Distinction between the "Legitimacy" of and "Justification" for Judicial Review and Each of the Modalities of Constitutional Argument

Bobbitt distinguishes between the "legitimacy" of and "justification" for judicial review and the various modes of legal argument. In his terminology, the legitimacy of judicial review is "maintained by adherence to rules within the practice of judicial review,"[172] and the legitimacy of each modality of Constitutional argument is established by its use as a modality of Constitutional argument.[173] By way of contrast, the "justification for judicial review [or an individual mode of legal argument] . . . must come from grounds external to its practice"[174]—that is, it is provided by the "ideology . . . that lies behind the jurisprudence of [judicial review or the relevant particular type of] argument."[175]

(3) The Equal Status of the Various Modalities and Single-Modality Variants of Constitutional Argument That Have Actually Been Used in Practice

Bobbitt does not believe that the various modalities and modality-variants of Constitutional-law argument that have been legitimated through use can be arranged hierarchically. Thus, he does not believe that any one mode of argument determines the legitimacy of the other modes.[176] Relatedly,

Bobbitt does not believe that any variant of a given mode of legal argument that has been used significantly in practice can be illegitimate. For example, since lawyers and judges have used both narrow-gauged and broad-gauged historical arguments, Bobbitt finds both these types of historical argument legitimate.

(4) The Claim That Although Many Answers to Constitutional-Law Questions Are Internally Wrong, More Than One Answer Will Frequently Not Be Wrong

For Bobbitt, "law's indeterminacy"—"the daily observation of ordinary legal practice"[177]—follows from his premise that none of the modalities of legitimate legal argument is dominant in the sense of determining the legitimacy or appropriate operationalization of the others. As Bobbitt states, this premise leads to the conclusion that there will be a unique, internally-right answer to a Constitutional-law question only if all the modalities and modality-variants of argument that are legitimate and relevant in the specific case lead to the same answer. In all other cases, although some answers may be internally wrong—that is, favored by no legitimate mode or mode-variant of argument—more than one answer will be "not internally wrong."[178]

B. My Response to Bobbitt's Positions

(1) The Six Modalities of Legal Argument

Bobbitt's descriptions of the six types of arguments that American courts use when engaged in judicial review, his account of various cases in which these types of arguments have been used, and his analysis of the reasons why the tendency of courts to concentrate on certain modalities of argument in one period will cause them and their successors to shift their focus to other types of argument in following periods (i.e., his analysis of the dynamics of the pattern of modality use) are not only accurate but highly creative and illuminating. My only problem with Bobbitt's "thick" description of the types of legal argument is that his comments on the category of argument he denominates "ethical argument" leaves me uncertain about the relationship between "ethical argument" in Bobbitt's sense and "arguments of moral principle" in my sense.

According to Bobbitt:

"Ethical argument" is a term of art, the meaning of which is less intuitively obvious than those of the other forms of argument. It denotes argument that relies on an appeal to those elements of the American cultural *ethos* as reflected in the Constitution. The fundamental American Constitutional ethos is the idea of limited government, the presumption of which assumes that all residual authority remains in the private sphere. Thus, ethical arguments are principally limit arguments: They usually arise as a consequence of the fundamental American constitutional arrangement by which rights are defined as those choices beyond the power of government to compel. Structural and ethical arguments share certain similarities. Like structural arguments, ethical arguments arise from certain textual commitments in the constitution, specifically the ninth and tenth amendments, and potentially the privileges and immunities clause of the fourteenth amendment. But, also like structural arguments, they do not depend on the construction of any particular piece of text, but rather on the necessary relationships that can be inferred from the overall arrangement captured by the text. The tenth amendment, we are often reminded, is a truism; but the same may also be said of the ninth, because it simply restates the fundamental understanding of the federal system of powers and rights. The privileges and immunities clause might also be characterized as superfluous to the extent that the fourteenth amendment has superimposed the federal system of human rights on the states (a goal we have relied upon the textualist strategy of incorporation to achieve). The principal error one can make regarding ethical argument is to assume that any statute or executive act is unconstitutional if it produces effects that are incompatible with the American ethos. This equates "ethical argument," a constitutional form, with moral argument generally, which has no special constitutional status.[179]

Unfortunately, this definition and series of comments on "ethical" arguments leave me uncertain about the relationship between such arguments and the type of argument I call "arguments of moral principle." If the "cultural *ethos*" of the American people to which the above statement indicates "ethical" arguments refer are our rights-and-obligations practices and if the category of argument that the above statement distinguishes from "ethical" argument and indicates has "no special constitutional status"—namely, "moral argument generally"—coincides with my category of moral-ought-statement arguments (or perhaps moral-ought-statement arguments based on consensus personal ultimate values or popular morality), Bobbitt's category "ethical argument" would coincide with my category "arguments of moral principle," though we might still disagree about whether our society's basic ethical or moral principle was determinate. Since there is a clear connection between limited government and the liberal commitment to valuing individuals' choosing their own values, Bobbitt's "ethical arguments" may be the same as my "arguments of moral principle." However, Bobbitt's failure to explore the moral point of our Constitutional commitment to limited government, which he thinks is the basis of "ethical argument" in his sense, leaves me unable to determine whether Bobbitt's concept of "ethical arguments" is in practice the same as my concept of "arguments of moral principle." In the end, I must admit that I do not know what Bobbitt means by "ethical arguments"—that is, by "limited government."

(2) Legitimacy versus Justification

Bobbitt's concept of legitimacy is "non-critical." Judicial review and the various modes of legal argument he identifies are "legitimate" simply because they are part of our legal practice, not because they are in any sense "justified." I draw no similar distinction. For me, the fact that judicial review has been practiced does not "legitimate" it: judicial review is legitimate if and only if it is consistent with or—better yet—is required by the moral commitments that define our State. Similarly, for me, the fact that courts have used a particular kind of argument does not render that modality or mode-variant "legitimate": if the relevant type of argument is "unjustified" in the sense that its use (in conjunction with the use of the other types of arguments the courts have employed) is inconsistent with the moral commitments that define our State, it is on that account illegitimate as well.

One consequence of my refusal to distinguish between "legitimacy" and "justification" is my conclusion that some types of argument the courts have accepted are illegitimate. Thus, the fact that American courts have accepted prudential arguments that focus on (1) the possible political risk to the courts of deciding a case in a particular way, (2) the possibility that a correct decision will not be enforced or obeyed, and (3) the possibility that a decision that is required by the principles to which we are committed will lead to more general lawlessness does not deter me from concluding that these arguments are "illegitimate" because their consideration is inconsistent with our rights-and-obligations commitments. Similarly, although the fact that a State choice is desirable from some personal-ultimate-value perspective is relevant to whether it violates the equal-protection clause, there are many other sorts of cases in which I would conclude that it was illegitimate to count arguments based on this type of prudential consideration.

(3) The Equal Status of the Various Modes of Legal Argument

I disagree with Bobbitt's conclusion that none of the modes of legal argument dominates the others. On my account, except for the fact that clear Constitutional text dominates moral principle when the two conflict, arguments of moral principle dominate the other types of legal argument by determining their legitimacy, by determining the way in which those arguments it reveals to be legitimate should be operationalized (which modality-variant is legitimate), and by determining the relationship between each type of legitimate legal argument and the right answer to the legal-rights questions to which it is relevant.

(4) The Existence of Internally-Right Answers to Legal-Rights Questions

Although I admit the possibility that there may be no unique internally-right answer to some moral-rights questions, I think that this outcome is rare and that even when it occurs there will be internally-right answers to legal-rights questions that are related to the moral-rights question whose answer is theoretically indeterminate. Just as Bobbitt's conclusion that there is no internally-right answer to many law questions reflects his belief that none of the modalities of legal argument dominates the others, my conclusion that there are internally-right answers to all legal questions reflects my belief that arguments of moral principle dominate all other types of legitimate legal argument other than contrary Constitutional-textual argument (as well as my belief that the legal system has conventions to deal with any cases of moral-rights indeterminacy).

12. Communitarianism

Communitarians propound a somewhat diffuse set of ideas and related critiques of liberalism that emphasize the importance of community to moral analysis.[180] Given the diffuseness of communitarian ideas, it is not surprising that proponents of virtually all the other positions this chapter has canvassed are in some respects communitarians. This section will state the six positions identified with communitarianism, list the various scholars or groups of scholars that subscribe to those positions, discuss whether and the respects in which moral-integrity-oriented liberalism agrees or disagrees with the positive positions communitarians take, and relatedly indicate whether the communitarian claims about such liberalism are correct.

A. Anti-atomism

All scholars other than libertarians and perhaps the John Rawls of *A Theory of Justice* agree with the communitarian claim that moral choices are choices made by individuals whose moral identities and value-choices reflect their social histories. Although liberalism originated as a response to the supposed right of isolated individuals for protection against each other, modern, moral-integrity-oriented liberalism shares the communitarian premise that our moral identities are socially embedded. Indeed, such liberalism acknowledges the important role that intimate relationships play in our discovering what we value by recognizing the duty of a liberal State to foster rather than hinder its subjects' entering into, nurturing, and maintaining intimate relationships.

Given this fact, the claim of many members of the CLS movement, many civic republicans, and many feminists that liberalism rests on an atomistic view of human nature[181] is nothing less than bewildering. My only account of this critique of liberalism is that the relevant critics must have confused moral-integrity-and-autonomy-oriented liberalism with libertarianism.

B. The Claim That Our Self-Conceptions Turn on Our Political and Community Roles

Communitarians also believe that all moral-rights holders' self-conceptions critically involve their roles as citizens and participants in a community life.[182] The type of liberalism to which I think our culture is committed is not based on such a "political man" premise. Moral-integrity-and-autonomy-oriented liberals recognize that some individuals define themselves substantially in terms of their political and community roles, but they also recognize that others do not.

C. The Related Claim That by Their Very Nature Humans Obtain the Most Fulfilling Kind of Satisfaction from Participating in a Virtuous Community

Communitarians believe not that the good will be discovered through rational deliberation by members of a virtuous community[183] but that the good consists of devoted participation in the affairs of a "virtuous" community. This belief underlies the "fair and equal opportunity" principle of Rawls's *A Theory of Justice*, the position of many political liberals, the preferences of most neo-republicans including those such as Mark Tushnet who have embraced republicanism as a useful response to CLS skepticism,[184] and the preferences of some strict constructionists, whose jurisprudential position reflects their desire to uphold community traditions that are illiberal in my sense in order to allow community members to fulfill their nature by participating in a peaceful, "virtuous" community. However, moral-integrity-oriented liberalism is not premised on the specially-rewarding character of the devoted and skillful performance of important social or political roles or any variant of this Rawlsian belief. Such liberalism does not deny that some individuals may support values and have preferences (dispositions and skills) that lead them to find such political and social activities especially rewarding, but it does not assume that such inclinations and capacities are part of human nature and acknowledges that many individuals do not find such activities particularly attractive or satisfying.

D. The Metaethical Claim That the Only Source of Binding Values Is Community

Meta-ethical communitarians do not believe that political values can be justified by their truth. Some hold this position because they do not believe that substantive values can be "true." Others subscribe to this position because they think that the political value of self-rule, which is connected to the value of individual freedom—of being the author of the legal constraints that bind you—renders it impermissible to base political decisions on values to which assent has not been given, regardless of whether they are "true."

There are at least three problems with this communitarian position. First, it appears to imply that any purported value-choice that is supported by a community consensus is binding on community members—that is, it does not seem to take a critical position on what counts as a "value" and does not distinguish moral principles from personal ultimate values. This feature of communitarianism is surprising, given the privileged position that at least the second justification for communitarianism seems to give to freedom or autonomy. Can one—consistent with the valuing of autonomy—conclude that a community consensus against autonomy is binding?

The second problem is related to the first. The communitarians have never specified the level of abstractness at which the binding values, traditions, and practices should be defined. This issue will be crucial when specific practices are arguably inconsistent with each other—that is, manifest a rejection of values to which other behaviors suggest the community is committed.

The third problem relates to the communitarian concept of "consent." How, according to communitarianism, can we justify requiring someone who does not support a particular value, social practice, or tradition to be bound by it? Admittedly, this problem will not arise in societies in which there is no disagreement on such matters, but in the real world that is not much of a concession.

In any event, many of the alternatives to my own jurisprudential position share the communitarian claim that communities are the only source of binding values. Thus, the Dworkin of *Taking Rights Seriously* argues that a community's rights-and-obligations practices and the moral principles on which they are grounded are binding on its members, the Rawls of *A Theory of Justice* assumes the binding character of the consensus social-justice views of the members of contemporary Western democracies, and the Robert Bork of *The Tempting of America* and the Patrick Devlin of *The Enforcement of Morals* assume that the specific moral views and social traditions that are favored by most or the overwhelming majority of a society's members are binding on all members of that society. Somewhat more selectively, the Dworkin of *Law's Empire* assumes that at least our kind of society is bound by the moral value-choices implicit in the legislative, administrative, executive, and political decisions of its government officials, and Bobbitt and Owen Fiss believe that a community's legal practices are self-legitimating.[185] Moreover, the apparent belief of political liberals such as Bruce Ackerman and neorepublicans such as Sunstein and Frank Michelman that the human good is a second-order phenomenon generated by participation in rational political dialogue in a proper community seems to imply that the decisions such communities reach through reasoned deliberation are binding upon us not by virtue of their substance but because of the "virtue" of the procedure that generated them.

In fact, with two important qualifications, the position I have taken also shares this communitarian premise. Admittedly, the qualifications are important. The first is that "community values" control only rights and obligations: community consensi on personal ultimate values are not binding. The second is that my position rejects the notion that a community's view that a particular standard, practice, or tradition is moral is self-legitimating. Purported moral values may not be moral values at all, and traditions and practices that are thought to be morally acceptable—indeed, morally desirable—may be immoral from any perspective that deserves to be called moral. Indeed, I fear that some of the traditions that conservative communitarians cherish and some of the decisions that would be generated by the kind of reasoned deliberation that political libertarians value may be not only illiberal in the sense that is relevant to our commitments but immoral from any value-perspective.

E. The Claim That Liberalism Has No Conception of the Good

This communitarian claim is wrong for two reasons. First, although liberalism has no conception of the first-order good (does not endorse any particular personal ultimate value or any particular way to instantiate a personal-ultimate-value choice), it does have a conception of the second-order good—in other words, liberals are committed to respecting lives of moral integrity, which can be led only by people who have exercised autonomy when choosing values and how to live their lives. Second, if this communitarian claim implies that liberalism has no theory of the "bad," it is wrong on this account as well. Life-choices that are unreflective or intentionally arbitrary, that preclude or substantially militate against others' exercising autonomy, and that preclude or substantially militate against the chooser's exercising autonomy in the future are all "bad" choices to a liberal who is committed to respecting and promoting autonomy and lives of moral integrity.

F. The Claim That Communities Have the Right to Promote and Enforce Their Value-Choices

In Stephen Gardbaum's words, communitarians believe that a "community has the right to express, promote, and preserve its social identity and to this end both law and public opinion are appropriate and legitimate instruments."[186] Contrary to the suppositions of many communitarians, moral-integrity-oriented liberals do not categorically deny the right of communities to express, promote, and preserve their value-choices. Indeed, liberalism stresses that a liberal State has a duty to promote the second-order value to which its society is committed. The fact that a liberal State may not endorse any conception of the first-order good is a corollary rather than a denial of the duty/right of a State to express, promote, and preserve its "official values."

★

A summary may be useful. Moral-integrity-oriented liberalism

(1) agrees with the communitarian premise that human beings are not unencumbered, though most moral-integrity-oriented liberals probably place greater weight on the possible importance of family and other intimate relationships than the communitarians tend to do (or probably assume that these latter relationships are more autonomous from the community than communitarians would suppose);

(2) disagrees with the communitarian claim that all humans' self-conceptions focus to an important extent on their role as citizens and social participants in a community life;

(3) disagrees with the related communitarian conclusion that human nature makes community participation and *a fortiori* the skillful and devoted performance of important social roles more satisfying or fulfilling than other types of activities;

(4) partially agrees with the communitarian claim that binding values are community-based—that is, it concludes that the moral norms from which our rights and obligations derive are community-based but disagrees with the communitarians' implicit assumption that any purported moral norm (any "norm" to which a community may consider itself to be committed) counts as a "moral" norm as well as with their assumption that personal ultimate values as well as moral principles are community-based (more precisely, disagrees with their implicit rejection of my distinction between "moral principles" and "personal ultimate values");

(5) does (contrary to what some communitarians claim) have a conception of the good, though it arguably is a conception of the second-order good since the value in question is moral integrity (which an individual can have only if in some meaningful sense he chooses what he considers to be the good and conforms his life to his choice) rather than a value that states a first-order good; and

(6) agrees with the communitarian conclusion that a State has the right to express, promote, and preserve its view of the good—in fact, it asserts that a liberal State has not only the right but also the duty to express, promote, and preserve the autonomy and integrity values to which liberalism is committed—though these second-order values imply the impermissibility of a liberal State's endorsing any conception of the first-order good, even if that conception is shared by the overwhelming majority of all community members.

Conclusion

This chapter states and analyzes the various major alternatives to the jurisprudential position taken in Chapter 1. Although I have learned much from the authors of all these positions and a great deal from Dworkin, Rawls, and Bobbitt in particular, they have not persuaded me that their analyses and conclusions are as convincing as my own.

3

The Duty of Appropriate, Equal Respect

Some Constitutional-Law Implications

This chapter analyzes various issues raised by a liberal State's duty of appropriate, equal respect. Chapter 4 focuses on its duty of appropriate, equal concern. Since the duty of appropriate, equal concern is a corollary of the duty of appropriate, equal respect, it is somewhat misleading to consider these two duties in separate chapters. I have done so despite this fact because the two duties raise significantly different analytical, empirical, and doctrinal issues.

Chapter 3 has seven sections. The first elaborates on the respect-related obligations of a liberal State. The second explains and illustrates the appropriate way for courts to resolve Constitutional-law claims based on the government's purported failure to treat relevant parties with appropriate, equal respect. Section 3 articulates and criticizes the formal doctrines the Supreme Court has developed to deal with the State's duty of appropriate, equal respect outside the affirmative-action context and criticizes various decision-rules that are not captured by the formal doctrine that some judges or commentators have advocated. Section 4 discusses some special doctrines the Supreme Court has developed and the decisions it has reached in various school-segregation cases. It is designed to point out the costs of prudentialism and illustrate the importance of focusing on the insulting character of "equal protection" violations. Section 5 analyzes the moral legitimacy of "affirmative action" programs in a liberal State, evaluates various objections that have been made to such programs, illustrates these analyses with a law-school-admissions example, and delineates and criticizes the Court's doctrinal approach to affirmative action. Section 6 comments on some aspects of the court's treatment of gender discrimination in both Constitutional-law and statutory cases. The final section examines the way in which both the courts and their company have misused language when dealing with the issues with which this chapter is concerned.

1. *The Duty of Appropriate, Equal Respect: An Insult Analysis*

Basically, the members of a liberal society and a liberal State itself violate their moral obligation to treat all relevant moral-rights holders with appropriate, equal respect whenever they *insult* someone in the relevant category. In this context, the concept of "insult" is objective. The fact that the target of an insult does not believe that he has been insulted—for example, responds by saying "You can't insult me" (i.e., you cannot damage me by lowering my self-esteem by insulting me)—does not demonstrate that no insult has occurred. In the other direction, the fact that someone mistakenly believes himself to have been insulted does not prove that the person he accused of insulting him actually did so (though, as we shall see, the fact that the alleged insultor's past wrongs against the individual who is accusing him or against some group to which that individual belongs caused his accuser or others to misinterpret his behavior may be relevant to the insulting character of his choice). An individual or the State can fail to show a relevant moral-rights holder the respect to which she is entitled through both malfeasance and non-feasance—both by committing inappropriate positive acts and by failing to act when the duty of appropriate, equal respect required the commission of a positive act. The remainder of this section analyzes seven of the more concrete duties that can be derived from the liberal duty of respect.[1]

A. The Duty Not to Impose a Loss on a Moral-Rights Holder for No Reason at All or for an Illegitimate Reason

With a possible quality-control qualification that Section B below explains, an individual member of a liberal society or a liberal State has a respect-related duty to reject any choice (to act or not act) that would impose a loss on a relevant moral-rights holder for no reason at all or to secure a goal that liberalism deems illegitimate. The link between this duty and the insulting character of each such choice that must be rejected has two significant implications. First, any analysis of this possibility should take into consideration whether the actor could have achieved the legitimate goal(s) he was pursuing to the same or greater extent by making an alternative choice that was less damaging to the supposed target of the purported insult. Hence, rather than comparing the choice in question solely with doing nothing to achieve the goal(s) it would be devised to further, the analyst should compare it as well with other choices that would have promoted the goal(s) in question at least to the same extent (should search for "less restrictive means" of achieving the relevant goal[s]).

Second, since the insult depends on the actor's state of mind at the time at which she made the choice, the fact that the choice was the least-restrictive means of furthering some legitimate goal to a relevant extent is not crucial if the chooser was not motivated by that goal when she made the choice—if, from the chooser's perspective, the choice was pointless or motivated by a desire to achieve an illegitimate goal. Of course, since actors often do not articulate their motivation for making choices prior or contemporaneous to making them, analysts will frequently have to base their goal-attributions on empirical studies of the actual consequences of the choice in question or on other evidence that goes to chooser-motivation. Many different types of evidence may give the analyst insight into the chooser's actual motivation: statements made by the chooser before, contemporaneous with, or subsequent to the choice in question; other choices the chooser made; statements made by the chooser's family, friends, or constituents before, contemporaneous with, or after his choice; and other choices made by these individuals. Admittedly, when actors have not articulated their motivations, it will often be extremely difficult to identify them. However, in some cases, a review of the actor's other decisions will enable one to infer enough about his (1) personal ultimate values and preferences and (2) assumptions about the relationship between various states of the world and the furthering of those values or satisfaction of those preferences to justify the conclusion that unless the relevant chooser has had a change of heart or mind he would not have made the choice he made unless it would have enabled him to indulge his prejudices or secure various other goals whose pursuit is illegitimate in a liberal society (see below). In any event, when the analyst actually does know the chooser's motive or has evidence that leads him to reach a more-probable-than-not conclusion about the chooser's motive, the motive the analyst believes the chooser had and not the possible motives the chooser could have had control.

The standard objection to this position is that a State that could have made a given choice for legitimate reasons but did so for illegitimate ones can respond to a conclusion of unconstitutionality by making the same choice again and claiming that it was properly motivated the second time around. I see no reason why a reviewing court should have to accept such a

State's claim. Indeed, even if the State were in good faith, its re-enactment of the policy in question might be rendered unconstitutional by the consequences of its motivation's being misunderstood by the policy's victims or by those who are prejudiced against them (Section E below).

The notion of "illegitimate goals" that the preceding analysis employs requires further consideration. I will focus on the goals that are illegitimate for government officials in a liberal State to pursue. Most obviously and least contestably, such officials may not justify a decision by citing any straightforward bribe they were paid to make it. Officials of liberal States may also not be able to justify a choice they made by citing the fact that it generated benefits that were more highly valued because they were received by their loved ones, family-members, friends, or members of their racial, ethnic, or religious cohorts (see Section C below). In addition, officials of a liberal State cannot justify a choice by citing any tendency it may have to promote a particular view of the good life as opposed to a more generic tendency to encourage people to live lives of moral integrity (which requires them to develop their own views of the good life as well as to take their moral obligations seriously). Finally, officials of a liberal State may not make choices to promote disrespect (e.g., racial hatred), to encourage the politics of racial, ethnic, religious, or gender hostility, to deter the choices' supposed beneficiaries from developing their own capacities, or to give the choices' supposed beneficiaries a feeling of inferiority.

Choices whose selection is critically affected by any of these motivations are insulting (violate the duty of appropriate, equal respect) because they fail to show the requisite concern for their victims' welfare, manifest their makers' disrespect for their victims directly, or are inconsistent with the right of moral-rights holders to make up their own minds about the (permissible) values they want their lives to instantiate. The preceding sentence's claim that the presence of an illegitimate motive converts an otherwise non-insulting choice into one that is insulting if and only if the motive was critical to the choice made implies that a choice is not insulting even when the chooser's illicit motive is a sufficient condition for his making the choice unless it is also a necessary condition of his doing so. Admittedly, a chooser who is partially but not critically motivated by illicit considerations (e.g., by prejudice) deserves to be condemned on that account, but that conclusion does not seem to me to imply that his choice violates his duty of respect.

Obviously, it will be very difficult to determine whether an illicit motive whose presence has been established played a critical role in an individual's and a fortiori in a group's decisionmaking—whether, for example, a city council's decision to impose a particular minimum-acreage zoning-requirement was critically influenced by a prejudice-related desire to exclude Blacks, Latinos, or the poor in general. However, this issue cannot be legitimately avoided when deciding whether in itself the presence of such an illicit motivation makes the council's choice unconstitutional. I say "in itself" because the presence of an illicit motive that would not otherwise render the relevant choice unconstitutional might do so if the choice in question is misperceived by bigots and/or its victims to be critically affected by prejudice in a straightforward way and various conditions specified in Section E below are fulfilled.

The respect-related duty on which this section has focused does not entail the more thoroughgoing duty not to harm any moral-rights holder by making a decision that is inconsistent with the past decisions one has made—for example, by rejecting a choice that would be more desirable than a previous choice if the chooser continued to subscribe to the values that led him to make his earlier choice. Individuals do not face such a consistency-constraint because they have a right to change their minds. Multi-member decisionmaking bodies do not face such a constraint because public-choice problems whose presence is no one's fault may cause such bodies to make sequences of decisions that are inconsistent from any conceivable value-perspective despite the fact that each chooser in the decisionmaking body has voted consistently.[2] Of course, as Section B argues, the fact that no such consistency-constraint is operative is consistent with the conclusion that a chooser's inconsistency may manifest his violating his duty of respect by failing to adopt appropriate quality-control procedures.

B. The Duty to Subject Decisions to Appropriate Quality-Control

The duty of respect requires the individual members of a liberal society and the liberal State itself to adopt decision-procedures to reduce to morally-acceptable levels the probability that choices will be made that injure someone either pointlessly or to secure an illicit goal. Even if it were possible to do so, I would not think that members of a liberal society or a liberal State were obligated to establish quality-control procedures that would eliminate the possibility of pointless or illicitly-motivated decisions' imposing losses on any moral-rights holder. The obligatory degree of care will depend on the cost of increasing quality-control to various additional extents.

This quality-control duty both increases and decreases the respect-related duties of a liberal individual or State. In the one direction, the quality-control obligation reduces such liberal duties since it raises at the least the possibility that a damaging choice that was pointless or made to secure illegitimate goals might not violate the duty of respect if it were made despite the fact that the relevant decisionmakers had instituted appropriate quality-control procedures. In the other direction, the quality-control obligation could expand the liberal duty of respect by implying that an individual member of a liberal society or a liberal State that never made a choice that violated the first respect-related duty described above might still have failed to have fulfilled its respect-related obligations because it failed to institute the requisite quality-control procedures. Of course, this last point would be "legally significant" only if individuals who have suffered no direct material harm could still sue to recover the loss the pure insult imposed on them.

Obviously, much could be written about the various procedures that a legislature, administrative agency, police department or other State decision-making body could adopt to reduce the weighted-average-expected or certainty-equivalent net "losses" it generates by making decisions that are disrespectful because they are either pointless or motivated by the desire to secure illegitimate goals. However, considerations of space preclude my doing so.

C. The Duty Not to Discriminate

In the sense that is relevant in the current context, one actor discriminates against another if the former disadvantages the latter when his reason for doing so is inconsistent with his liberal duty of respect and he knew or should have known this fact. Often, discriminators allege justifications for their conduct that fail to render their choices non-discriminatory.

Some discriminators' attempts to exculpate themselves fail because they are based on a "value" premise that is inconsistent with liberal convictions about the attributes of a creature that make it a moral-rights holder: claims that it is not discriminatory to disadvantage homosexual males because they are not real men (read, "real persons") and claims that it is not discriminatory to disadvantage Blacks because they are not fully human fail for this reason. To put the point more generally, in a liberal society it is always illegitimate for the State or an individual to disadvantage someone because (1) some attribute that does not affect the latter's status as a moral-rights holder or as a person leading a life of moral integrity, (2) some preference, religious belief, or personal-ultimate-value conviction the latter has, or (3) some act the latter has committed that he is entitled to commit makes the State decisionmaker conclude that the latter does not deserve to be treated with the respect that is due all moral-rights holders. This claim does not imply the illegitimacy of taking even immutable characteristics that are irrelevant for their possessor's moral-rights holder status into account for other consequentialist reasons—for example, of counting gender against female applicants for security-guard positions in maximum-security prisons for males many of whose prisoners have been convicted of violent sexual crimes. The preceding claim also does not imply that liberalism requires people to believe that other people's different religious beliefs, personal-ultimate-value convictions, or patterns of conduct are as "good" as theirs: to the contrary, it recognizes and does not condemn the fact that people will not think that. Still, liberalism does impose positive and negative duties on its adherents that relate to their treatment of those with whom they disagree. Positively, liberalism insists that each individual respect the right of others to disagree with him—indeed, respect other people who do disagree with him if they take such issues and their lives morally seriously. Negatively, liberalism forbids each individual from disadvantaging others inappropriately because of such disagreements (though I do not think that individuals are barred from taking into consideration their greater affection for those who share their values or their desire to promote their views and the conduct those views commend when deciding how to distribute their property and efforts).

Other discriminators' attempts to escape that characterization fail because they are based on an empirical premise that is either demonstrably wrong or dubious and inadequately supported. Thus, an employer cannot demonstrate that it is not discriminatory for him to reject Latino job-applicants by asserting that Latinos are untrustworthy unless he has completed the research into this issue that he should know would be in his conventional interest to undertake. This research would cover not the general trustworthiness of Latinos relative to that of other groups but (1) the general trustworthiness of the relevant Latino job-applicants relative to other classes of job-applicants, (2) the other abilities of the relevant Latino job-applicants relative to their competitors', and (3) the possible profitability of using more selective procedures to ascertain the trustworthiness and/or other relevant attributes of different classes of job-applicants. Obviously, the preceding statement implies that the relevant employer could not escape a charge of discrimination by citing even the accurate fact that most or nearly all non-Latinos believe that Latinos are more untrustworthy than others both because the relevant believers almost never have a reasonable basis for their belief and because that belief, even if justified, would not usually make the employer's behavior *ex ante* profitable.

Still other discriminators' attempts to exonerate themselves from charges of discrimination fail because their supposed justification is nothing more than their emotional reaction to the victim of their discrimination—an emotional reaction that is a manifestation of their prejudice. One cannot bootstrap oneself out of a discrimination charge by claiming that an emotional reaction that manifests the prejudice that underlies the discrimination makes what would otherwise be a discriminatory choice non-discriminatory. Thus, an employer could not demonstrate that he did not discriminate against Jews by citing the fact that they disgusted him (even if they did). Admittedly, however, in some situations, an individual may have a right to indulge his prejudices. For example, an anti-Semite who refused to consider a Jew as a possible marriage partner because Jews disgusted him would be entitled to make that choice even though it was based on prejudice—even though it was discriminatory and insulting.

The liberal duty of respect may be violated by discrimination *in favor of* particular individuals or groups as well as by discrimination *against* particular individuals or groups. Most of those State choices that are unconstitutional because they favor some individuals or groups are properly held to be discriminatory because they are insulting to those who are disfavored. Unfortunately, however, the analysis of this issue is far from straightforward since it cannot be resolved without determining whether it is legitimate for a liberal State or its citizens acting in their political capacities to favor individuals or groups for reasons that they are entitled to count when acting in their private capacities.

A clear distinction must be made between (1) the factors that an individual member of a liberal society can legitimately take into account in his private life when deciding how to distribute benefits and (2) the factors that such an individual can take into account in this context when acting in a political capacity or the factors that a liberal State can take into account when generating and distributing costs and benefits. More particularly, although liberalism would not condemn an individual's making his gift decisions depend on his personal loyalties to loved ones, friends, family members, and members of groups to which he belongs, his admiration for members of groups to which he does not belong or groups for which his membership is irrelevant to his desire (e.g., active proprietors of small family-farms), or his sympathy for particular classes of individuals (e.g., the handicapped), I do think that liberalism condemns both individual members of a liberal society acting in their political capacities and a liberal State from being influenced by such considerations.

Admittedly, the argument that has led me to this conclusion is not without difficulties. Both individual members of a liberal society acting in their private capacities and a liberal State have a duty to treat all moral-rights holders with appropriate, equal concern. However, for two reasons, the content of this duty is different for individuals acting in their private capacities than for the State or individuals acting in their political capacities. First and less importantly, liberalism permits individuals to favor certain others in their private lives because doing so supports the institution of private property and in practice this institution contributes to individuals' leading lives of moral integrity by providing them with a space within which they can experiment and the means to exercise autonomy. Second, and more importantly, certain types of favoritism do not violate liberal values because (1) the duty of respect is a corollary of our commitment to valuing creatures' living lives of moral integrity, (2) individuals cannot live such lives without discovering what they value and which acts or activities will be part of a life that instantiates these values, and (3) loves, friendships, family ties, and perhaps even religious, ethnic, and racial affiliations (the last because of the partially regrettable commonalities of experience shared by members of given races in our society) play an important role both in our discovering ourselves and in our participating in affective relationships through which we instantiate our values: in other words, liberalism also permits certain kinds of favoritism because it recognizes the fact that a generic love of mankind or even of our "fellow Americans" cannot or does not have the same significance for people's lives as the more specific relationships, ideals, and sympathies in question, none of which presupposes a view that those favored are more capable than others of living lives of moral integrity or are, in fact, living such lives.

However, when an individual acts in a political capacity, she is more constrained by liberal principles. In part, this conclusion reflects the fact that the benefits the State is in a position to distribute do not belong to its individual citizens—the fact that the private-property justification for individuals' engaging in favoritism when distributing their own property and efforts does not apply when individuals are acting in political capacities or when the State is acting. In part, it reflects the fact that a liberal State and derivatively its citizens acting in their political capacities have a duty to be equally concerned for each moral-rights holder for whom they are responsible—to act as if they were intrinsically indifferent to the personal identities or group affiliations of the various people whose interests their choices affect. And in part (though this point may be redundant), it reflects the fact that the political decisions of individuals and *a fortiori* the decisions of States have less to do with supporting or validating the kinds of personal relationships that liberals value than do the private decisions of individuals.

Admittedly, the preceding conclusion is highly contestable, and the arguments I developed to support it are open to serious challenge. If liberals should support relationships that contribute to self-discovery and instantiate important self-chosen values, why should it not be acceptable for a liberal State to support such relationships by favoring the loved ones, friends, relatives, co-religionists, and so on, of a majority of its citizens? One answer may be that (1) any attempt of a State to do so would inevitably disfavor those to whom the minority was attached and (2) such a policy would be inconsistent with a liberal State's duty to show equal concern for the "affections" of all.

Three possible or actual implications of this analysis require some elucidation. First, it does not imply that individual members of a liberal society acting in their political capacities or a liberal State may not support or adopt policies to effectuate various distributional values that do not make relevant the types of individual attachments, ideals, or sympathies on which the analysis focused. Second, for their pursuit to be permissible in a liberal State many of these values may have to be redefined to eliminate the effect they would otherwise give to attachments, ideals, and sympathies that a liberal State may not take into account. Thus, the version of utilitarianism that could legitimately be effectuated by a liberal State would have to exclude the utility that some citizens secured because a government choice increased the utility of other citizens to whom the former were attached (as well as the utility bigots experienced when the targets of their prejudice were injured or disadvantaged). The third is really just an extension of the second. The analysis also implies that a liberal State that is trying to effectuate "utilitarian-like" values may also have to ignore the utility its citizens experience when others (such as handicapped individuals) for whom they feel sympathy as opposed to attachment receive benefits. Of course, this conclusion does not imply that a liberal State may not try to effectuate distributional values that make an individual's being handicapped relevant (for reasons unrelated to such utility-interdependencies); for example, the fact that someone was handicapped could legitimately count in favor of his receiving some benefit in a liberal society whose State was attempting to effectuate appropriately-revised utilitarian, equal-utility egalitarian, or equal-opportunity egalitarian values if people who were handicapped obtained more utility from resources, had lower-than-average utility, or needed more resources to have certain valued opportunities on that account. Choices that favor a particular individual or group may also be unconstitutionally discriminatory because they are insulting to the favored individual or group. This paradoxical conclusion reflects the fact that the motivation for some such decisions may have been a desire to undermine the self-esteem of their beneficiaries (by implying that they are incapable of competing on a level playing-field), to induce their beneficiaries to develop a psychology of dependency (rather than to become self-reliant), to foster the politics of racial, ethnic, or religious hostility, or to encourage prejudice and bigotry in non-political contexts. If such motives critically affected a State choice, that fact would render it unconstitutional. Indeed, State choices whose selection was critically affected by an indifference to or an underweighting of these consequences or a failure to consider them appropriately might also be unconstitutional on that account. Hence, decisions to favor some individuals or groups may be unconstitutional because they are insulting to either the favored or the non-favored group.

Obviously, I have not discussed many difficult issues connected to the concept of discrimination. Thus, I have not analyzed whether a person should be said to be discriminating in a pejorative sense if he is not prejudiced himself but allows his choice (say, of what salesperson to hire) to be influenced by the fact that customers and other employees are prejudiced. Nor have I analyzed whether a buyer or seller can correctly be said to be discriminating in a pejorative sense if he practices "price discrimination" against an individual—if the actor pays the alleged target of his alleged moral discrimination a lower price than the actor pays others for a product or service the actor is buying or charges the "target" a higher price than he charges others for a product or service the actor is selling. My own conclusion is that actors in neither of these categories can properly be said to be discriminating in the pejorative sense, but certainly the answer to at least the former question is contestable.

D. The Duty to Combat Prejudice and the Commission of Impermissible Prejudiced Acts

Although the duty of individual members of a liberal society to combat prejudice and the commission of impermissible prejudiced acts may be contestable, the duty of a liberal State to engage in these activities is clear. Obviously, this claim reflects my conclusion that the misfeasance/non-feasance (action/inaction) distinction is not morally relevant—more specifically, my belief that a liberal State is just as obligated to combat prejudice and impermissible prejudiced acts as it is to avoid committing such acts itself. The possible moral distinction between misfeasance and non-feasance is examined in some detail in the course of Chapter 4's discussion of various abortion issues. For present purposes, I will simply assert that

(1) the claim that this distinction is morally critical in our society strikes me as empirically incorrect (indeed, even the law is increasingly rejecting it),

(2) the distinction is not morally persuasive in general,

(3) the purported moral point of the distinction (to protect a private actor's autonomy) does not apply when the actor in question is the State, and

(4) the conditions for the accepted exceptions to the "no general duty to rescue" position to which some people subscribe are fulfilled when the actor is the State and the action is the prevention of prejudice or the commission of impermissible prejudiced acts since in most of the relevant cases the State is responsible for the situation that needs correction (because it contributed to the relevant prejudice or because it cannot separate itself from its citizens) or since the State has a special status relationship (*parens patria*) to the individual(s) who would benefit from its intervention.

A liberal State can adopt a variety of policies to fulfill its duty to combat prejudice and impermissible prejudiced acts. Its officials can speak out against prejudice both in the abstract and in the context of particular social events. It can provide educational programs in the schools to combat prejudice. It can subsidize the creation, performance, and/or display of poems, novels, plays, movies, non-fictional studies, and various visual arts that combat prejudice by revealing its nature, consequences, or the erroneousness of the empirical beliefs that bigots claim justify what are in fact their prejudices. It can provide opportunities to members of groups that are targets of prejudice that enable them to perform in ways that contradict the prejudiced empirical claims of bigots and/or can publicize such performances when they occur. It can make prejudiced acts and utterances criminally or civilly actionable.[3] A liberal State may have a duty to adopt some of these individual policies, but, if it does, that duty is a corollary of its more general obligation to adopt an appropriate set of policies to combat prejudice and impermissible prejudiced acts.

A final comment is required. The word "impermissible" modifies the expression "prejudiced acts" both in the heading to this subsection and in the final sentence of the preceding paragraph because, as I have already indicated, there are contexts (e.g., when choosing a marriage partner or, in most such cases, when choosing a dinner-party guest) in which individuals are entitled to indulge their prejudices.

E. The Duty to Give Appropriate Weight to What Would Otherwise Be Misperceptions of the Discriminatory Character of a Choice

This possible duty arises in the following circumstances:

(1) a choice that would not be insulting if its character were not misperceived disadvantages an individual or group that has previously been the target of discrimination,

(2) the chooser is morally responsible for the previous acts of discrimination because he (or his agent or officer) was the discriminator, actively (and critically?) contributed to the prejudice that led to the discrimination, failed to fulfill his duty to deter or combat the prejudice, or is not entitled to separate himself from the discriminator (as the State may not be entitled to distinguish itself from its citizens), and either or both

(3a) the choice will be misperceived by bigots to reflect the view that their prejudices are not prejudices and/or

(3b) the choice will be misperceived as being discriminatory in a way that is not unreasonable by the victims of the previous discrimination or their successors.

When these conditions are fulfilled, the relevant chooser (regardless of whether it is an individual or the State) may have to give appropriate weight to the harm the relevant losers (and other victims of any induced prejudice) would suffer from what would be the mischaracterization of the choice in question if its existence would not make the choice insulting: the direct damage to their happiness and self-esteem, the consequential damages they would suffer because their related unhappiness or low self-esteem caused them to alter their behavior in ways that were not in their interest, and any losses they sustained because the choice affected the behavior of bigots or potential bigots by appearing to legitimate what are actually prejudices. Of course, this obligation does not imply that all such "misperceived" choices are violative of rights. Even when the above losses are given appropriate weight, the choice may be defensible from the chooser's actual, legitimate value-perspective.

F. The Duty Not to Be Critically Influenced by the "Fruit of a Poisonous Tree"

The "fruit of a poisonous tree" doctrine precludes the State from using evidence to which it was led either directly or indirectly by an illegal act such as an illegal search and seizure or an illegally-obtained confession.[4] In part, this doctrine has been adopted to deter the police from engaging in illegal (often unconstitutional) behavior. But in part, it also reflects the notion that even a wrongdoer has a right not to be disadvantaged because of a wrong committed against him. This latter moral notion would seem to me to apply *a fortiori* when the issue is the permissibility of holding against someone who is not a wrongdoer something about him that is a consequence of a rights-violation perpetrated against him or others on whom he was dependent.

This conclusion suggests to me a more general, respect-related moral: the State cannot justicize its disadvantaging an individual or group by citing what would otherwise be a legitimating empirical reality when that reality is a consequence of a prior wrong for which the State was responsible. Assume, *ad arguendo*, that, if the State were not morally responsible for any illiterate's inability to read, literacy-requirements for voting (1) would not violate anyone's moral (or Constitutional) right to vote and (2) would not violate equal-protection norms even if in practice the requirement disenfranchised a higher-than-average percentage of the otherwise-eligible members of a group whose treatment was suspect (say, Blacks). However, such a literacy requirement might nevertheless be unconstitutional on either of these grounds if the illiterate individual's inability to read or the greater incidence of a disadvantaged group's illiteracy reflected an independent wrong for which the State was responsible—for example, segregated and less-than-equal schooling for Blacks.[5] Put crudely, this conclusion reflects the view that it is insulting for someone or the State to rub another person's nose in the consequences of a rights-violation from which the latter suffered, at least if the person making the relevant choice or the State is morally responsible for that rights-violation.

G. The Duty to Redress the Consequences of Insulting or
   Discriminatory Behavior

Since the action/inaction distinction does not apply to a liberal State and since such a State cannot be separated from its citizens, a liberal State must make actionable all discriminatory acts in which an individual does not have the right to engage, insure that all victims of discrimination have the wherewithal to pursue their related legal rights, and create judicial remedies and other policies that adequately redress the emotional and material harms that discrimination inflicts on its direct and indirect victims. Obviously, to determine what remedies this principle requires or renders judicially appropriate, the harms the discrimination in question generated will have to be analyzed carefully. As we shall see, the courts' analysis of this harm-issue has not always been satisfactory: indeed, a substantial portion of the deficiencies in the doctrines the courts have developed and the conclusions they have reached in both the school-segregation cases and the affirmative-action cases reflect their failure to examine adequately the harms that segregation generated (and, in the latter cases, the senses in which government choices can be said to be "remedial" or "permissibly remedial").

2. *The Appropriate Approach for Courts in Our Liberal State to Take to Respect-Related Constitutional-Rights Claims*

Judges engaged in judicial review must answer three separate questions or sets of questions:

(1) What is the probability that the government choice under review violated a right the Constitution protects?

(2) In the case in question, what number must the judge assign to the probability that the relevant choice violated any Constitutional right it might have violated for the judge to be authorized to declare the relevant government-choice unconstitutional on the ground that it violated that right?[6] and

(3) If the judge declares the choice unconstitutional, what remedies is it legitimate for the court to award and which of these remedies would be optimal for the court to award?

I will use the expression "test or tests of Constitutionality" to refer to the standard(s) a judge (or anyone else) is obligated to use when deciding the probability that a government choice violated a particular Constitutional right. I will use the expression "test of deference" to refer to the standard(s) a judge is obligated to employ to determine how much deference to give the government decisionmaker whose choice he is reviewing— to what extent the number that he assigns to the probability that the choice is unconstitutional must exceed 50.01% for him to be authorized to declare that choice unconstitutional. No special term will be used to refer to the standards courts are obligated to employ when deciding what remedy to award.

The remainder of this section will specify (A) the tests of Constitutionality I think our courts are obligated to use when analyzing whether some governmental unit has violated its duty of respect, (B) the tests of deference that courts are obligated to employ whenever they exercise judicial review, and (C) various senses of the word "remedial" that need to be distinguished when analyzing the remedies that courts can legitimately and ought to award in cases in which a governmental unit has violated some Constitutional duty (such as its duty of appropriate, equal respect).

A. The Applicable Tests of Constitutionality

When the central government violates a moral-rights holder's right to appropriate, equal respect without violating an enumerated right, the relevant claim should be brought and adjudicated under the Ninth Amendment— that is, the right should be described as one of the unenumerated rights which that Amendment protects. When a state or local government violates its duty of respect in this way, the case should be brought under the "equal protection" or "privileges or immunities" clauses of Section 1 of the Fourteenth Amendment. In particular, when the respect-related complaint is that the government has discriminated against an individual or group of moral-rights holders by treating them differently[7] from others absent an adequate reason to do so or by treating them (in one sense) "the same" when they should have been treated differently, the proper textual base for the claim is the equal-protection clause. However, when the respect-related complaint is that the state or local government insulted all those its choice harmed by making a decision that was pointless, by making a decision that was designed to achieve illegitimate goals, or by using a decision-procedure that did not provide sufficient quality-control, the proper textual base for the claim is the "privileges or immunities" clause.[8]

In any event, my conclusions about the appropriate approach for courts to take to respect-related Constitutional-rights claims follow directly from my analysis of the relevant moral-rights issues:

(1) no distinction should be drawn between State non-feasance and State misfeasance—that is, between cases in which the State has failed to show appropriate and/or equal respect by failing to act (for example, by failing to protect individuals or members of some group from violation of their rights by bigoted private actors) and cases in which the State has violated its respect-related duties by committing insulting positive acts;

(2) the courts should focus on the actual motive of the State chooser in question[9] and should not automatically allow a governmental unit that has made a choice that was critically affected by an illicit motive to do the same thing or something similar when it repeats the choice and attempts to justify it in terms that would have legitimated the choice in question had it been the actual motive originally: in part, this conclusion reflects my skepticism about such changes in motives and in part my fear that, even if the change in motive is real, the repeated choice might be misperceived by bigots and its victims; and

(3) the State can violate its duty of respect in any of the same ways the preceding section of this chapter delineated.

Rather than restating these various possibilities in abstract terms, I will illustrate them by examining a hypothetical based on a landmark gender-discrimination case, *Reed v. Reed*.[10] Assume that a state legislature has passed a statute providing that when a male and female are otherwise equally qualified to be appointed the administrator of an estate, the male candidate must be preferred to the female. Assume as well that the legislature claims that this statute is justified because (1) estate-administration exclusively involves the performance of various accounting and paper-pushing administrative tasks and (2) across the whole population, men are better than women at performing such tasks. There are at least nine different categories of grounds on which a court could base a conclusion that the legislature had violated its Constitutional duty of appropriate, equal respect in passing this legislation.

First, a court might find the statute unconstitutional on the ground that—its claim to the contrary notwithstanding—the legislature was actually ill-motivated: that the passage of the legislation was critically affected by some legislators' beliefs that women are genetically inferior in the relevant respects and/or some legislators' desires to keep women "in their place."

Second, a court might overturn the statute on the ground that (1) the alleged correlation would not favor male-appointments over gender-neutral appointments and (perhaps) (2) the legislature knew or ought to have realized this fact. The alleged correlation might be irrelevant either because there was no correlation in the population as a whole or because there was no such correlation in the relevant populations—the males and females who were otherwise eligible to serve as estate administrators and who had applied for the position. The state might be at fault in relation to this error because it knew its factual allegations were false, could have discovered its errors at *ex ante* non-prohibitive cost by assessing existing data, or would have discovered its errors had it done *ex ante* "profitable" research into the empirical issues (because it would have been *ex ante* "profitable" for the state to "validate" its assumption by doing additional empirical research).

Third, the state may have acted unconstitutionally because (1) it misdescribed the job of "estate administrator"—ignored the importance of such administrators' preventing bad feelings from developing between or among the estate's actual or potential beneficiaries; (2) even if taken as a group the relevant female candidates were less adept than their male counterparts at the accounting and paper-pushing part of estate administration, they were sufficiently superior at the relevant interpersonal-relations tasks to render incorrect the conclusion that the policy of selecting the male applicant when both a male and a female applicant were qualified was superior to random selection; and (3) the state knew this fact or would have discovered it had it given *ex ante* "profitable" attention to this issue (where the "profits" in question are calculated on an equal-respect assumption).

Fourth, even if the male-preference policy were superior to a random-selection policy, the state's choice might be unconstitutional if (1) a more individuated procedure would have been superior to the male-preference policy and (2) the state knew or ought to have known this fact (would have discovered it had it done *ex ante* "profitable" research into the cost of individual assessments and the benefits that would be generated by the on-balance superior appointments to which they would have led).

Fifth, even if the execution of all *ex ante* "profitable" research would have validated the state's male-preference policy, the state may have behaved unconstitutionally in failing to carry out such research.

Sixth, the state's male-preference policy may have been unconstitutional because the statistical difference in predicted performance that otherwise would have justified it reflected discriminatory behavior (gender-based differences in socialization-patterns, education, and/or employment-opportunities that left women worse-off on balance or put women in an inferior position on balance) for which the state is responsible. The state could be held responsible for the illicit generation of such differences because (1) it made (say, education-policy) decisions that caused them, (2) it encouraged private parties (say, parents) to make decisions that caused them by explicitly or implicitly approving of differentiated gender-roles, (3) it failed to allocate sufficient resources to preventing private parties from making the relevant choices, or (4) it cannot in any case separate itself from the decisions of its citizens. In brief, this argument is based on the proposition that it is insulting for a State to add injury to insult-and-injury when it is responsible for the original insult-and-injury.

Seventh, even if the statistical generalization is accurate, individuated selections would not be cost-effective but for the consideration that this paragraph considers, and the state has appropriately validated its policy, the male-preference policy might be rendered unconstitutional by the losses females experience because they misperceive the state to be mistreating them. Particularly if the females' reaction reflects the fact that women have been mistreated in the past and especially if the state was either directly guilty of or morally responsible for such mistreatment for other reasons, the state might be obligated to take account of such losses. In one sense, this claim amounts to an argument that otherwise-non-insulting behavior may be rendered insulting by its "victims'" otherwise-incorrect but reasonable belief that it was otherwise-insulting when the perpetrator of the relevant act was responsible for previous insulting behavior that led to the victim-misperception in question. Admittedly, however, this consideration will not always be critical when it is relevant.

Eighth, even if the statistical generalization is accurate, individualized selections would not be cost-effective but for the consideration this paragraph considers, and the state has appropriately validated its policy, the male-preference policy might be rendered unconstitutional by the disutility females experience because males misperceive the state to have made a choice that proceeds from the assumption that females are inherently inferior or because the policy entrenches negative female stereotypes. Particularly if this male reaction can be partially attributed to previous bad acts by the state but (in my opinion) even if it cannot, the state's overall policy-evaluation must take account of such consequences. This observation does not imply that the presence of such male reactions automatically renders the choices that engendered them unconstitutional—just that these policy-consequences are relevant to whether the choice's overall effect is such that its adoption implies that an insultingly-low weight is being given to women's welfare.

Ninth and finally, even if the statistical generalization is accurate, individuated selections would not be cost-effective but for the consideration this paragraph discusses, and the state has validated its choice, the male-preference policy might be rendered unconstitutional by its tendency to reduce the incentives of individual women to develop the relevant capabilities since automatic male-preferences will preclude individual women from obtaining positions they should get on their individual merits (will cause women to be tyrannized by their small decisions). Once more, this argument will be far stronger if the relevant statistical generalization reflects rights violations for which the state is responsible. In essence, this argument reflects a conclusion that it is insulting for a State to ignore or give inadequate weight to this type of consequence of its choices.

Obviously, although I have used a gender-classification case to illustrate the above nine possible bases for holding a disadvantaging classification to be insulting and hence unconstitutional, the same possible arguments will also be relevant in any kind of group-classification case.

B. The Applicable Test of Legitimate Deference

This subsection delineates and discusses the factors to which a judge should give weight when deciding how much deference to give a government decisionmaker whose choice the judge is subjecting to judicial review. However, before proceeding to this issue, three background points need to be made about the "test of deference."

The first is an admission: it is certainly arguable that courts should never defer at all to the government decisionmakers whose choices they subject to judicial review—that in all cases a judge is obligated to hold unconstitutional any government choice that to her mind is more likely unconstitutional than not. I reject this conclusion for the following reasons:

(1) particularly when disagreements about the Constitutionality of a government choice are more likely to reflect non-conceptual disagreements about the empirical consequences of the choice under review rather than conceptual disagreements about the appropriate

characterization of the relevant moral principles but possibly in other situations as well, a judge may legitimately defer to the Constitutional-law conclusions of the government chooser in question because the judge believes that this party or institution has more expertise—is more likely to be right—than the judge himself and

(2) because the courts have neither the resources nor, in some cases, the skill to identify and redress all the Constitutional-rights violations that the government could potentially commit and because, usually, the courts can intervene only after some harm has resulted from the Constitutional-rights violations that have been committed, a judge may conclude that he can increase the extent to which Constitutional rights are protected by deferring to the Constitutional-law judgment of government decisionmakers whose choice is being reviewed, at least if the relevant chooser has the inclination and capacity to take Constitutional rights seriously and actually has done so in the case at hand—that such an approach will simultaneously remind such government choosers of their Constitutional duty and give them an incentive to consider seriously the Constitutionality of their choices.

The second background point is that although actual courts often do vary the deference they give to government decisionmakers whose choices they are subjecting to judicial review they usually do not explicitly distinguish their treatment of the deference issue from their discussion of the test of Constitutionality. Thus, as Section 3 of this chapter argues, both the "intermediate scrutiny" and the "strict scrutiny" approach that the courts have taken to different "equal protection" cases mix together test-of-Constitutionality and test-of-deference issues indiscriminately.

The third point that needs to be emphasized in this context is significant because it reveals the importance of distinguishing the two tests in question. That point is that the correct "standard of review" could combine a test of Constitutionality that it is relatively easy for the State to pass with no deference whatsoever or a test of Constitutionality that is difficult for the State to pass with great deference. Thus, at the one extreme, the easy-to-satisfy "minimum rationality" test of Constitutionality—according to which a government choice is Constitutional if, in comparison with doing nothing, it will further the achievement of a legitimate goal to even a minimal extent— could be combined with no deference at all so that the judge would hold the relevant choice unconstitutional if he concluded that the probability that it would not further a legitimate goal even minimally was 50.01% or higher.

At the other extreme, the difficult-to-satisfy "strict scrutiny" test of Constitutionality—according to which a government choice is unconstitutional unless it is "necessary" and "narrowly tailored" to achieve a "compelling" State goal—could be combined with extreme deference so that the judge would hold the relevant choice unconstitutional only if he concluded that the probability that it was not necessary and narrowly-tailored to achieve a compelling State goal was 99.99% or higher.

Now that these preliminary matters have been discussed, I can turn to the factors that a judge is obligated to consider when deciding how much deference to show to a government decision-maker who has made the choice being challenged in a particular case. At least six such factors need to be distinguished.

First, the judge should defer less to the maker of the choice in question the greater the likelihood that disagreements about the Constitutionality of the relevant choice depend on disagreements about the characterization of the events or values it implicates and the lower the probability that any such disagreements about Constitutionality reflect disagreements about facts that the government actor whose choice is under review is better-placed to ascertain (technical facts about national defense that the Department of Defense or the Congress can gather and assess more accurately, for example). Although some Constitutional commentators have doubted the special ability of judges to characterize "fundamental fairness" values,[11] I disagree. Lawyers and judges are trained in law schools to analyze issues of this kind and do so all the time: such analyses are the stuff of much common-law and statutory-law adjudication. In fact, not only the training and experience of judges but also the institutional structure within which they operate gives them a comparative advantage over legislators or executive officers in relation to fundamental-value characterization and weighting. The first deference-factor reflects this judgment.

Second, courts should defer less to a government actor's Constitutional judgment when his decision disadvantages a group, restricts a liberty, or disserves a value that he, government actors in his position, or perhaps government actors in other positions have historically unconstitutionally respectively disadvantaged, restricted, or disserved. Even if the government actor possesses the relevant skills, if he has behaved unconstitutionally in the past in relation to the values in question, the court should be less trustful of his decisions in the present.

Third, courts should defer less to government actors whose choices were made in haste, in a crisis situation, or in response to dubious political pressures than to government actors who have carefully deliberated the Constitutionality of their choices. Indeed, a court should also defer less to government actors who had no reason to act in haste if they proceeded on the basis of controversial factual assumptions that they did not actually investigate despite their capacity to do so. This principle reflects the fact that circumstance and inclination as well as inherent skills affect the quality of decisionmaking. Clearly, regardless of whether judicial deference is justified by the judge's conclusion that the decisionmaker in question has more relevant skills or information than the judge or by the courts' need to encourage government decisionmakers to take seriously their obligation to uphold the Constitution, the considerations just listed are highly relevant.

Fourth, courts should defer less to government actors when evidence suggests that there is some probability that the decision under review was illicitly motivated. Even if that probability is not high enough to justify a conclusion that the decision is unconstitutional because of its illicit motivation, the suspicion that such motivation may be present should reduce the extent of the deference the court shows.

Fifth, courts should defer less to government actors when the decision under review disadvantages a group that appears not to have enough political power to protect itself against State wrongdoing by participating in normal political arenas. Courts should consider different kinds of evidence when evaluating the political power of a group: (A) structural evidence that suggests that the group is unlikely to be able to muster much political influence—for example, the fact that the group is not "discrete" and not "insular" may suggest that it will have more difficulty in organizing itself politically, be less able in any case to elect one of its own, and be less likely to have substantial influence on those who are elected to represent the districts in which they reside (assuming that they do not constitute a critical swing-vote),[12] (B) "sociological" evidence about the prevalence of prejudice toward the group in question, and (C) historical evidence both about the extent to which the group was mistreated in the past (about whether it was protected by its own efforts or through *noblesse oblige*) and about changes in the "structural" and "sociological" situation that affect the predictive power of past outcomes.

Sixth, courts should show less deference to government actors who are not their coequals—for examples, less deference to policemen than to legislators, heads of the FBI, or Attorneys General. The traditional justification for this factor is the supposed obligation of judges to show respect for other government officials, respect that allegedly is supposed to increase with the status of the decisionmaker whose choice is under review. If this really were the only point of taking account of this factor, I would reject its consideration: clubbiness is inappropriate when Constitutional rights are at stake. However, I do think that other arguments can be made for considering the status of the decisionmaker under review. In part, status should be considered or would in any case be considered indirectly because it correlates with several of the other determinants of appropriate deference already delineated. Thus, the status of the government actor whose decision is under review will already have been considered when comparing his skills with the judges', when assessing his historic performance in this or analogous areas, and when examining the circumstances in which he made his decision, the procedure he followed when making it, and the political pressures that may have influenced him. In part, however, I think that the status of the decisionmaker whose choice is being reviewed is an appropriate determinant of the deference judges should show him for a somewhat different reason that relates back to the justification for such deference—namely, the higher the status of the decisionmaker in question, the greater the likelihood that he will be encouraged to consider the Constitutionality of his choices by a judicial decision to defer to his judgment if he does and the greater the gains such additional consideration is likely to generate (given the correlation between status and relevant skills and information).

C. The Appropriate Remedy

Once a court has declared a State act unconstitutional (because it has violated the State's duty of appropriate, equal respect or any other State Constitutional duty), it is obligated to award an appropriate remedy. Judicially-created "remedies" are supposed to compensate the plaintiffs for the harm they suffered from the legal wrongs the court found to have been committed, prevent further violations of the victim's or victims' legal rights, and prevent or offset the "consequential damages" generated by the initial wrong.

To be in a position to craft appropriate remedies, judges must first identify the immediate harm that has been done by the illegal act in question to the plaintiffs in the relevant case and the consequential damages they will or may suffer if nothing is done to prevent them. A State's violation of its duty of appropriate, equal respect may inflict a variety of harms on a variety of different categories of victims. Thus, a State's insulting behavior will harm the specific individuals who were the direct victims of its disrespectful choice by imposing material losses on them (when the State choice disadvantaged them materially), by imposing psychological losses on them by insulting them, and by inflicting consequential material and psychological losses on them to the extent that any related reduction in those direct victims' self-esteem leads them to alter their behavior in ways that are against their interest and/or the State's insulting behavior encourages prejudice and bigoted behavior directed at them. State violations of its duty of respect may also impose all but the first kind of material loss just listed on members of society who share the attributes that led the State to insult the direct victims of its disrespectful behavior. The State's choices may also inflict material and psychological losses on individuals who do not share its direct victims' attributes to the extent that the State's disrespectful behavior to one group induces its agents or others to treat members of other groups disrespectfully. Indeed, the State's failure to fulfill its duty of respect may also inflict psychological and related losses on individuals who fear that they may be treated disrespectfully to the extent that it increases the risk that they will be treated this way even if this risk does not materialize. In addition, the State's violation of its respect-duties will harm all those who are committed to the "appropriate, equal respect" principle to the extent that they suffer when their society fails to fulfill its duty of respect. Finally, when the State shows its disrespect for the members of some group, its violation will harm not only the targets of its prejudice but also those who wish to interact with them (when the relevant choice is segregative), those who suffer material consequential damages from the more general distorted behaviors that insulting behavior engenders, and those who have been implicitly told that they are superior.

Admittedly, for at least three reasons, some of these harms will not be judicially cognizable. First, judges are not authorized to provide remedies to individuals who were not plaintiffs in the underlying suit. However, although American legal doctrine does deny standing to individuals whose stake in the outcome of a suit cannot be differentiated from that of all citizens,[13] in many of the duty-of-respect cases that have been brought the plaintiffs could have included not only the direct victims of the State's insulting behavior but also the class of all others who shared the attribute that led the direct victims to be treated disrespectfully. Indeed, although the lawyers of the plaintiffs in these cases failed to make this point explicit, those who suffered the direct harm could also have represented the interests of the larger class of individuals who possessed the attribute that caused the State to insult its direct victims (of all those whom the State choice insulted), though their tangible loss may have made them a less-than-ideal representative of this broader class.

Second, judges may not be authorized to "remedy" some of the harms that a State's insulting choices generates because the relevant plaintiffs will not be able to prove them. Although the psychological damage to members of "the direct victims' group" seems to me to be sufficiently obvious to legitimate a court's finding it to have occurred and although judges may be able to accept the claim that a State's insulting behavior harmed its targets by leading them to behave in a way that was not in their interest, the tendency of State insults to cause damage by inducing bigotry or dissatisfaction with one's society's conduct will be difficult to prove.

Third, even if some of these more indirect harms could be established, courts might hold that the State's wrong was not a proximate (i.e., legally accountable) cause of these losses. I should add, however, that I have grave doubts about the moral legitimacy of the "proximate cause" doctrine, which seems to deny recovery to wronged individuals for utilitarian reasons[14] that are not justicizing in a liberal society in this context.

Still, I have no doubt that judges are authorized to award remedies in "disrespectful behavior by the State" cases that address a broader range of resulting harms than the courts actually have tried to remedy. Section 4 of this chapter analyzes this issue more concretely in the context of the school-segregation cases.

Although the preceding discussion of "legal remedies" has concluded that it is appropriate for courts to grant very broad and far-ranging remedies in duty-of-respect cases, I realize that courts are not authorized to order the full range of actions that can properly be called "remedial" in a non-adjudicatory sense. I repeat: to be legitimate, a judicially-ordered remedy must be a response to the consequences for a plaintiff in the relevant case of the legal wrong committed against him. Legislatures, other governmental units, and private individuals are not so limited. They may attempt to "remedy" undesirable situations for which they are not legally responsible, regardless of whether the condition to be corrected was anybody's fault or moral responsibility. Thus, it is perfectly legitimate (indeed, probably praiseworthy) for an individual or the State to try to remedy an undesirable situation that arose through nobody's fault and that is no private actor's moral responsibility (e.g., to remedy a disability from which someone suffers because of a genetic defect that due care would not have prevented). This last point may be obvious. I make it because, as Section 5 of this chapter discusses, the Supreme Court's doctrinal position on affirmative action fails to recognize it.

3. The Supreme Court's Doctrinal Approach to Non-Affirmative-Action "Appropriate, Equal Respect" Cases: A Critique

This section analyzes (A) the Supreme Court's approach to the non-feasance/misfeasance distinction in alleged State-disrespect cases—that is, the State Action doctrine; (B) the Court's three-tier-scrutiny formal doctrinal approach to these cases and some other tests that some judges and commentators have proposed—that is, the "tests of Constitutionality" the Court has employed or others have recommended; and (C) the "tests" the Court has implicitly used when deciding how much deference to give the allegedly-disrespectful State chooser in non-affirmative-action cases.

A. The State Action Doctrine

I have already argued that a liberal State's obligation to treat the moral-rights holders for which it is responsible with appropriate, equal respect requires it

(1) to secure for each such individual appropriate, equal influence on government decisionmaking (subject to any constraint on equality imposed by our nation's federal structure),

(2) to adopt appropriate government-choice quality-control procedures to control the amount of losses government inflicts on such individuals pointlessly or for an illegitimate reason,

(3) to adopt procedures for applying laws or individual regulations to individuals that provide the law's addressees with an appropriate opportunity to express their positions when the law is applied to them (when that opportunity is valued in itself and not just as a means to increase the accuracy of the law's implementation), perhaps

(4) to avoid imposing losses on such individuals pointlessly or to achieve illegitimate goals,

(5) to avoid endorsing any first-order view of the good life,

(6) to avoid discriminating against any moral-rights holder for which it is responsible,

(7) to combat the development of prejudices by private parties and the commission of prejudiced acts by private parties who do not have the right to indulge their prejudices in the relevant context,

(8) to allocate an appropriate amount of resources to protect all such individuals against non-discriminatory State or private wrongs (e.g., murders and robberies not motivated by prejudice), and

(9) to secure for all such individuals the general resources, formal education, and life-experiences that will significantly contribute to their exercising meaningful life choices—becoming and remaining persons of moral integrity (though this last obligation could arguably be said to be a corollary of the duty of appropriate, equal concern).

This list implies that a liberal State's duty of respect imposes positive obligations on it as well as constraining it to avoid misfeasance of various kinds.[15] This conclusion that our liberal State has positive obligations runs counter to a century-old[16] American Constitutional-law doctrine—the State Action doctrine. This doctrine declares that the Fourteenth Amendment imposes no positive duties on the states[17]—for example, (1) no duty on the states to combat private discrimatory acts in which the discriminators do not have the moral right to engage, (2) no duty on the states to prevent private, non-discriminatory, moral-rights violations, and (3) no duty on the states to secure for the moral-rights holders for whom they are individually responsible the resources and experiences that will contribute significantly to the moral-rights holders' becoming and remaining individuals of moral integrity.[18]

In fact, however, the State Action doctrine cannot be justified through legitimate legal argument. Traditionally, supporters of this doctrine have tried to justify it in textual terms—that is, by the fact that the Fourteenth Amendment provides that "No State shall make or enforce any law which shall abridge the privileges or immunities of citizens of the United States; nor shall any State deprive any person of life, liberty, or property, without due process of law; nor deny to any person within its jurisdiction the equal protection of the laws."[19] However, in fact, this text does not support the interpretation that advocates of the State Action doctrine have placed on it. Admittedly, the wording of the "privileges or immunities" clause—"No State shall make or enforce any law . . ."—does favor the State Action doctrine. However, this textual argument is undercut by the fact that the wording of neither the "due process" clause nor the "equal protection" clause favors the doctrine since linguistically the State can "deprive" a person of life, liberty, or property by failing to prevent a private individual from taking those things from him and can "deny" a person the equal protection of the laws by failing to act on his behalf. The overall textual argument for the State Action doctrine is also undercut by the fact that the Declaration of Independence declares that governments are instituted among men to secure their inalienable rights as well as by the fact that the Preamble to the Constitution indicates that that document and, presumably, the government it constituted were designed, *inter alia*, "to establish justice" and "secure the blessings of liberty."

Our relevant moral practices and history also cut against the State Action doctrine. Thus, advocates of the State Action doctrine can find no support in our Good Samaritan practices (which some think do sometimes distinguish between non-feasance and misfeasance) because (1) the justification for any such distinction that is made—our commitment to recognizing the autonomy of the individual—has no counterpart when the actor being evaluated is a State (i.e., a government) and (2) even if our Good Samaritan practices did suggest that most individuals usually have no positive duty to render assistance, the State is normally operating in circumstances that are analogous to the (allegedly) exceptional cases in which individuals would be held to have a positive duty to render aid (since each state and the central government has a special *parens patria* status-relationship to those for whom it is responsible and is frequently a culpable cause-in-fact of the relevant individuals' predicaments in that it encouraged the prejudices involved in the case in question).

I should note in addition that the assumption that in our culture individuals do not generally have Good Samaritan moral duties is dubious. Admittedly, the common law (in contrast with the civil law) has traditionally not imposed a general duty to rescue, but I believe that our law has been inconsistent with our moral commitments in this respect. This claim is supported by the fact that our law is increasingly imposing legal duties to "rescue" on parties who previously would not have been held to have them.[20]

The position of supporters of the State Action doctrine is also undercut by the relevant history. Two facts are salient in this connection. The first is that much of the harm to which the Fourteenth Amendment was a possible response was done by private acts (lynchings and social customs) that the states could prohibit without violating the relevant actors' rights. The second is that many of the individuals who drafted the Fourteenth Amendment believed that it would render "retrospectively Constitutional" a provision of the Civil Rights Act of 1866 (for which they also had voted) that prohibited private acts such as lynchings.

The only mode of legitimate legal argument that supports the State Action doctrine is precedential. But even this argument does not provide much support: the State cannot justify its continuing failure to fulfill its positive moral obligations by claiming that it did not have fair notice that its moral duty was also a legal duty and even if one would hesitate on this ground to hold a state responsible for past failures there could be no objection to a court's overruling the State Action doctrine prospectively (as opposed to repeating its error by continuing to apply it).

B. The "Tests of Constitutionality" in Non-Affirmative-Action Duty-of-Respect Cases

(1) The Supreme Court's Three-Tier-Scrutiny Doctrinal Approach

The Supreme Court has adopted a trichotomized approach to duty-of-respect, "equal protection" cases. If the government choice under review disadvantages a group whose treatment is "suspect," (i.e., most importantly, Blacks, Latinos, and presumably other racial or ethnic groups that have historically been the target of prejudice in the United States), it is subjected to "strict scrutiny"—held unconstitutional unless it is "necessary" and "precisely tailored" to the achievement of a "compelling" State goal; if the government-choice under review disadvantages a group whose treatment is quasi-suspect (women, those born outside of marriage [illegitimates], aliens), it is subjected to "intermediate scrutiny"—held unconstitutional unless it is "substantially related to" the achievement of an "important" State goal; and if the treatment of those whom the government choice under review disadvantages is not at all suspect, it is subjected to "ordinary scrutiny"—held constitutional unless it can be shown not to be even "rationally related" to the achievement of a "legitimate" State goal.

This formal doctrinal approach to "appropriate, equal respect" cases is inadequate for three reasons. First, the doctrines I have just articulated trichotomize several relevant variables that in fact vary continuously: (1) the treatment of different groups is more or less suspect, not "suspect," "quasi-suspect," or "not suspect"; (2) State goals are also more or less important, not "compelling," "important," or just "legitimate" but "not even important"; and (3) the government choice under review is more or less "substantially related to" the achievement of a particular goal—that is, it promotes that goal to a greater or lesser extent in comparison both with doing nothing to achieve the goal and with other less-restrictive or less-transaction-costly or more accurate procedures of furthering the goal in question, not "necessary for," "substantially related to," or just "rationally related to" the achievement of the goal in question. I realize, of course, that bright-line rules are sometimes justifiable even when their "costs" and "benefits" are measured in rights-protection terms—that the costs the errors their use generates are sometimes lower than the benefits their use generates by saving transaction-costs (for subsequent rights-securing uses) and increasing the predictability of legal outcomes. However, in my judgment, the various "scrutiny"-doctrine trichotomizations cannot be justified in this way: even if the general structure of the Supreme Courts' approach were justified, the costs that will be generated by the substantive errors caused by the use of such crude categories will exceed the transaction-cost-related and in-creased-predictability-of-legal-outcomes-related benefits they permit (benefits that are likely to be quite small, given the dullness of the purportedly bright lines in question and the outcome-importance of any classifications they are used to make).

Second, as formally stated, the various "scrutiny" tests ignore both the extent to which the choice under review disserved the group it disadvantaged and the extent to which it furthered the legitimate goal that supposedly justified it.

Third, and most basically, the scrutiny tests do not lead the courts to consider appropriately the various possible reasons why a State choice might be unconstitutionally disrespectful. Thus, the scrutiny tests do not do a good job of detecting or responding to the possibility that the State may not have instituted appropriate quality-control. The branch of the three-tier scrutiny approach that is most connected to this quality-control issue is the minimum-rationality test applied to choices that allegedly insult members of groups whose treatment is not at all suspect. However, this test does not require a judge to detect or respond appropriately to a State's failure to institute appropriate quality-control:

(1) it does not even directly advert to the adequacy of a State's quality-control procedures:

(2) a State's quality-control procedures may be insultingly ineffective even if in a given case the choice made is rationally connected to a legitimate State goal (a problem if one rejects the "no harm, no foul" principle in such cases on the ground that inappropriately-low quality-control is harmfully insulting in itself), and

(3) a choice that failed the minimum-rationality test may have slipped through an adequate quality-control procedure (a fact that is relevant if one concludes that it is not disrespectful of the State to have harmed someone pointlessly if it made appropriate efforts to prevent such errors).

Furthermore, in many cases, the minimum-rationality test the courts normally employ also does not require them to determine whether the choice made really was pointless: because in practice the test does not lead its judicial employers to compare the choice made with other choices the State could have made that would have furthered the relevant legitimate goal to the same extent or more, it does not reveal the pointlessness of those choices that had less-damaging, equally-effective alternatives. The three-tier-scrutiny approach (more particularly, its minimum-rationality tier) also does not do an acceptable job at detecting the fact that a government choice was designed to achieve venal goals or to impose an orthodox view of the first-order good life: since in practice courts using this approach tend to supply the legitimating rationale themselves, it does not lead them to reject choices whose selection was critically affected by the desire to achieve one of the above illicit goals when others could have made the same choices for legitimate reasons: indeed, this inadequacy of the minimum-rationality test would not be remedied by the courts' requiring the State to provide a legitimating rationale itself (on appeal, at trial, or at the time the choice was made) so long as the courts accepted the State's statement of purpose at face value. Moreover, although the scrutiny tests make relevant the relevant group's historic mistreatment, they do not by themselves lead the courts to investigate (1) whether the decisionmaker whose choice is being scrutinized or his constituents made statements or engaged in other conduct that suggest that prejudice influenced his decision by leading him to place a lower negative, zero, or positive value on the losses it imposed on its victims; (2) the probability that the members of the disadvantaged group would misperceive an otherwise-legitimate choice to be insulting in circumstances in which that misperception would critically influence the choice's Constitutionality because the State could be held responsible for it; (3) whether enough members of the public at large would misperceive an otherwise-legitimate choice to reflect the State's endorsement of what are in fact their prejudices to render the choice unconstitutional; (4) whether the choice disadvantaged some individuals because of empirical realities that are relevant but reflect historical rights-violations for which the State is responsible; (5) whether the choice reduced the likelihood that members of the disadvantaged group would improve their relevant capacities by utilizing presumptions that reflect current empirical realities that are traceable to rights-violations for which the State is responsible—particularly if the presumptions preclude individual members of the group who develop requisite skills from attaining the positions to which they are relevant; or (6) whether the choice was critically motivated by a desire to promote the politics of racial hostility.

Of course, nothing precludes the courts from supplementing a straightforward application of the relevant scrutiny test with analyses that consider these possibilities. Indeed, in some cases, the courts have done so. However, even in these cases, one must say that the courts have considered these possibilities *despite* the scrutiny test rather than *because* of it.

In short, viewed as pure "tests of Constitutionality," the various "scrutiny" tests do not pass muster. They ignore many of the possible bases for concluding that a government choice was unconstitutionally insulting; they ignore some of the factors that are relevant to those possibilities on which they do implicitly focus; and they trichotomize a number of relevant variables that in fact vary continuously. In my opinion, all these deficiencies of the current doctrinal approach are traceable to the failure of the courts to consider systematically the point of the Constitutional provisions that are relevant to the resolution of "appropriate, equal respect"–related cases.

(2) Four Supplementary or Alternative Tests of Constitutionality the Courts or Others Have Imposed

A number of other tests of Constitutionality have sometimes been announced by the courts or proposed by commentators for use in what I call "appropriate, equal respect" cases. Some of these tests can be combined with the three-tier-scrutiny tests; others are alternatives to them.

First, although the courts have never accepted this position, it has sometimes been argued that the Fourteenth Amendment protects only individuals of African descent (an admittedly problematic category, given the extent of racial mixing in the United States). The argument for this claim is the historical argument that the Fourteenth Amendment was a response to slavery, the Civil War, and the need to protect Black Americans.

The response to this argument is textual and moral. Unlike the texts of the Thirteenth and Fifteenth Amendments, the text of the Fourteenth Amendment does not limit its protections to specific categories of individuals—it does not refer, for example, to persons who had experienced "a previous condition of servitude." Although the Reconstruction Amendments' drafters and ratifiers clearly had persons of African descent primarily in mind when they wrote and voted on these amendments, they knew how to use language that focused on this group when they wanted to protect it exclusively (see the Civil Rights Act of 1866): the fact that they did not use such language in the Fourteenth Amendment, but rather "citizen" and "person," clearly implies that they intended its protections to extend to non-Blacks as well as Blacks.

This textual argument is reinforced by a moral argument. The set of individuals who are morally entitled to the rights the Fourteenth Amendment is designed to secure is all moral-rights holders for which the United States and its constituent states are responsible not just individuals of African descent. This moral argument is particularly forceful in the Constitutional context: as Chief Justice John Marshall put it, "We must remember that it is a constitution we are expounding."

Second, the Supreme Court has sometimes left the impression that any State choice that explicitly makes race a criterion for decision is unconstitutional on that account.[21] Although the courts would almost certainly not be misled by this pronouncement in many cases in which it would matter, it is important to emphasize that a State decisionmaker's use of an explicit racial criterion does not render his choice unconstitutional. For example, consider a statute that explicitly requires Blacks to have a blood-test to obtain a marriage license. Assume that the motive for this requirement is the desire to insure that prospective marriage-partners who might both have recessive sickle-cell-anemia genes learn whether they do. If no problems arose because of the conceptual and empirical difficulty of determining whether an individual was Black in this context, if questions were not raised by the State's failure to impose similar requirements on others similarly placed (for example, to require East European Jews to undergo similar testing for Tay-Sachs-disease-related genetic problems), and if it were not possible to improve the situation by imposing a more selective testing-requirement, this law would certainly not be unconstitutionally discriminatory (though one might argue [unblushingly?] that it placed an unconstitutionally severe burden on the exercise of the liberty to get married). Similarly, the fact that a checkerboard zoning-ordinance placed racial restrictions on who could buy particular houses would not render it unconstitutionally discriminatory if it were designed to promote integration by deterring White flight by assuring Whites that minority-residency in their block would not go beyond the so-called tipping-point (though it might be argued to constitute an unconstitutional taking or an unconstitutional restriction on the relevant buyers' and sellers' economic liberties). Finally, as Section 5 below analyzes, the fact that a so-called "affirmative action" program explicitly establishes race or ethnicity as a criterion of choice does not in itself render that program unconstitutional.

Indeed, if those who voted for such a program did so reasonably and in good faith to promote legitimate social goals, it would be Constitutional unless it were rendered unconstitutional by relevant misperceptions or fruit-of-the-poisonous-tree problems.

I should add, however, that in the "affirmative action" context, at least some Justices have asserted or supported a proposition that they seem to believe is inconsistent with this last claim. Thus, Justice Sandra Day O'Connor's opinion announcing the judgment of the Court in *City of Richmond v. J. A. Croson Co.* asserts, "The guarantee of equal protection cannot mean one thing when applied to one individual and some thing else when applied to a person of another color."[22] Although this claim is totally unobjectionable if it asserts nothing more than the proposition that the equal-protection clause guarantees the right of each individual not to be treated discriminatorily insultingly, it is wrong if it asserts that the equal-protection clause forbids the states from differentiating their choices by race since perfectly-legitimate goals may be furthered in unobjectionable ways by such differentiated treatment.

Third, the unconstitutionality of a statute or regulation cannot be established by showing that it has a disparate impact on different social groups. Indeed, even if in comparison with random selection, the statute or regulation in question disfavors members of a group that has traditionally been a target of prejudice, it will not be unconstitutional on that account. Relevant misperceptions, fruits of the poisonous tree, and independent illicit motivations aside, so long as the chosen decision-standard promotes a legitimate goal, its racially-disparate impact is Constitutionally irrelevant.

Fourth, one cannot establish the Constitutionality of a statute, regulation, or informal decision-standard by proving that it provides for formally-identical treatment of members of all races it affects. Thus, the fact that an anti-miscegenation statute "treats Whites and Blacks identically"—prohibits Whites' marrying Blacks just as it prohibits Blacks' marrying Whites and does not make the penalty that an individual will incur for participation in an inter-racial marriage depend on his or her race[23]—does not render the statute Constitutional since it does not remove the insulting character of the assumptions or values that underlie it. Nor does the fact that a segregated-school plan prohibits White schoolchildren from going to school with Black schoolchildren just as it prohibits Black schoolchildren from attending school with White schoolchildren (that it affects each race's ability to associate "equally" in one mechanical sense) render the plan Constitutional.[24]

C. The Court's Implicit "Tests of Appropriate Deference" in Disrespect Cases

The preceding subsection assumed that the various scrutiny tests were pure tests of Constitutionality. In fact, the scrutiny tests also function as tests of the appropriate degree of deference for judges to show government decisionmakers whose choices are alleged to be unconstitutionally disrespectful. This section analyzes whether the scrutiny tests do a satisfactory job at leading the courts to consider appropriately the various factors that determine the deference a court engaged in judicial review is obligated to show a government decisionmaker whose allegedly-unconstitutionally-insulting choice it is reviewing.

The first such factor is the likelihood that disagreements about Constitutionality reflect disagreements on issues courts are relatively more or relatively less skilled at resolving than is the actual decisionmaker. Although the various scrutiny tests make it more likely that a court will declare a government choice unconstitutional if it disadvantages a group whose treatment is suspect or quasi-suspect, it does not focus on the contestability of the characterization of the choice under review.

The scrutiny tests also do a mixed job at directing the courts' attention to the extent to which the relevant decisionmaker has mistreated the disadvantaged group in the past. Thus, although the scrutiny tests make it more likely that a court will hold a decision unconstitutional that disadvantages a group that has been mistreated in the past, they do not consider whether the mistreatment was at the hands of the decisionmaker in question (or by someone in his position, recruited in the same way he was, or subject to the same pressures and influences he was). In other words, the scrutiny tests in effect assume that the decisionmaker whose choice is under review should be tarred with the same brush that tarred the government historically. Obviously, in some cases this assumption will not be justified.

In addition, the scrutiny tests do not themselves advert to whether the decisionmaker whose choice is under review considered the Constitutionality of his choice or simply reacted to the political pressures generated by a crisis situation. Admittedly, however, courts have sometimes supplemented the scrutiny test they were employing by taking account of this factor directly.

Moreover, the scrutiny tests do not advert to the existence of direct, contemporaneous, non–circumstantial evidence suggesting that the choice under review may have reflected the decisionmaker's prejudice. Once more, of course, courts can take this possibility into account separately in cases in which it may matter—namely, when the evidence of improper motivation is not strong enough to justify the conclusion that the choice in question was more probably unconstitutional than not.

In addition, the scrutiny tests do a far-from-perfect job at directing the courts' attention to the ability of a disadvantaged group or the direct beneficiaries of the protection of a particular value or liberty to protect themselves politically. In particular, the scrutiny tests ignore the second political-power-of-"victim" issue entirely and address the first such issue satisfactorily only if (1) past mistreatment reflects the disadvantaged group's lack of political power and (2) no relevant change in the political position of the relevant group has reduced the predictive power of the past (in particular, has made it less likely that the group would be mistreated in the present). Although the first of these two conditions is probably fulfilled, the second (I am glad to say) is far more dubious.

Finally, the scrutiny tests also ignore the relative status of the decision-maker whose choice is under review. Again, however, courts can and do supplement the scrutiny tests by taking this factor into consideration separately.

In short, the scrutiny tests do make relevant both some factors that determine the appropriate degree of deference for judges to give decisionmakers whose choices they are subjecting to judicial review and other factors that are positively correlated with other relevant deference determinants. The scrutiny tests also do instruct judges to adjust their conclusions in the direction that the deference-analysis would deem appropriate. Nevertheless, the deference component of the scrutiny tests is far from perfect: the tests ignore several factors that are relevant to the determination of the appropriate degree of deference and focus on other factors that, though relevant, are imperfectly correlated with the actual determinants of the appropriate degree of deference.

This general critique of the Supreme Court's doctrinal approach to appropriate, equal respect cases has concluded that its distinction between State misfeasance and State non-feasance (the State Action doctrine) is legally unsound, that its tests of Constitutionality are deficient, and that its tests for deference are not only implicit but inadequate.

4. The School-Segregation Cases: A Selective Summary and Critique

This section presents a selective summary of the development of school-segregation law that focuses on the failure of the Supreme Court to address the immorality of school segregation and the consequent inadequacy of its Constitutional arguments and remedial awards.[25] Supreme Court school-segregation doctrine developed from *Plessy v. Ferguson*,[26] which upheld as a valid exercise of Louisiana's police power a statute that required railroads operating within the state to "provide equal but separate accommodations for the white and colored races." The opinion of the Court steadfastly refused to acknowledge the insulting character of such segregation:

> Laws permitting, and even requiring [the] separation [of the two races] in places where they are likely to be brought into contact do not necessarily imply the inferiority of either race to the other. . . .
>
> We consider the underlying fallacy of the plaintiff's argument to consist of the assumption that the enforced separation of the two races stamps the colored race with a badge of inferiority. If this be so, it is not by reason of any thing found in the act, but solely because the colored race chooses to put that construction upon it. The argument necessarily assumes that if, as has been more than once the case, and is not unlikely to be so again, the colored race should become the dominant power in the state legislature, and should enact a law in precisely similar terms, it would thereby relegate the white race to an inferior position. We imagine that the white race, at least, would not acquiesce in that assumption.[27]

Although the point of the first of these passages is logically correct, it is experientially obtuse: as Justice Oliver Wendell Holmes once said in an admittedly-different context, "the life of the law is experience not logic."[28] The second passage seems to assume that the Constitution does not forbid the states to engage in insulting behavior if the relevant conduct does not substantially reduce the status of the target of the insult (no material harm, no foul). It also seems to assume that behavior cannot be insulting if it does not substantially affect the self-esteem of the target of the insult. In my judgment, both these propositions are insupportable.

The *Plessy* court tried to justify its conclusion by arguing that "[l]egislation is powerless to eradicate racial instincts or to abolish distinctions based on physical differences, and the attempt to do so can only result in accentuating the difficulties of the present situation. . . . If one race be inferior to the other socially, the Constitution of the United States cannot put them on the same plane."[29] In addition to refusing to acknowledge that at least some of the "racial instincts" to which it refers might be characterized as prejudices, this passage assumes that the State is not responsible for its citizens' prejudices and has no duty to combat them, in part because its duties extend to civil and political equality but not to social equality.[30] Indeed, the opinion as a whole assumes that civil equality is not violated by State-required separation (segregation) so long as the facilities available to the races in question are otherwise equal. Finally, the opinion anticipates the arguments of conservative contemporary judges such as Antonin Scalia and Clarence Thomas that attempts by the State to do something about social inequalities will only exacerbate the situation—a prudential argument that is probably wrong empirically and not decisive in the relevant context in any event.

Although *Plessy* was not a schools case, the *Plessy* Court did try to support its conclusion by citing several state-court decisions upholding the Constitutionality of "separate schools for whites and colored children."[31] It is therefore not surprising that the *Plessy* statute's "equal but separate" standard was subsequently adopted by the Supreme Court as the standard for evaluating the Constitutionality of segregated schools. According to *Gong Lum v. Rice*,[32] decided in 1927, segregated schools were Constitutional if they were otherwise equal.

Between 1938 and 1950, the Supreme Court wrote four "segregated school" opinions (subsequently regarded as trial balloons) that held state segregated-school policies unconstitutional on the ground that they did not offer the relevant Black student(s) an equal education. In 1938, *Missouri ex rel Gaines v. Canada*[33] held that Missouri's policy of paying the tuition of Missouri Blacks who attended out-of-state law schools while excluding them from the state law school denied them equal protection. In 1948, *Sipuel v. University of Oklahoma Board of Regents*[34] held that the petitioner had a right to equal education that was violated by the state's policy of excluding her from the state law school solely because of her race.[35] In 1950, *Sweatt v. Painter*[36] held that the state of Texas had violated its equal-protection obligations by excluding Blacks who wanted to attend law school from consideration for admission to the University of Texas while offering them the alternative of a legal education in a hastily-established, segregated law school. According to the Court, this alternative law school was unacceptable not only because of the inferiority of its material resources but also both (1) because of its inferiority in terms of "qualities which are incapable of objective measurement" such as "reputation of the faculty, experience of the administration, position and influence of the alumni, standing in the community, traditions and prestige" and (2) because legal education "cannot be effective in

isolation from the individuals and institutions with which the law inter-
acts."[37] Finally, on the same day on which *Sweatt* was announced, *McLaurin
v. Oklahoma State Regents*[38] held unconstitutional an Oklahoma policy requiring a Black student admitted to the "White" state university to participate in a graduate program not offered at the state school for Blacks to sit in
separate, roped-off sections of the classroom, library, and cafeteria.[39] The
opinion of the unanimous Court was based on the premise that such segregation deprived the petitioner of an equal education by "impair[ing] and
hinder[ing] his ability to study, to engage in discussions and exchange views
with other students, and, in general, to learn his profession."[40]

Two points should be noted about these opinions. First, none of them referred to the immorality or insulting character of the relevant state school
policies. Second, and relatedly, the opinions did not discuss the harm that the
insult inflicted on all those who shared the attributes that incited the prejudice directed at the excluded (separated out) students.

Chief Justice Earl Warren's opinion for the unanimous court in *Brown v.
Board of Education*[41] did not correct these deficiencies, though it did build on
the *McLaurin* Court's claim that the separation of the plaintiff in that case
from his classmates "hindered the plaintiff's ability to study." The *Brown* opinion proceeded on the stipulated (counterfactual) premise that the buildings,
equipment, and teachers in the Black and White schools in the segregating
school districts in question were equal. Chief Justice Warren's opinion for a
unanimous court begins by arguing that, for two reasons, the fact that many
states had segregated schools at the time at which the Fourteenth Amendment was passed does not demonstrate that public-school segregation is
Constitutional under the Amendment: (1) we simply do not know what the
majority of the members of the Congress that proposed the Fourteenth
Amendment[42] and the majority of the members of the state legislatures that
ratified it thought it would or should be interpreted to imply for the Constitutionality of school segregation and (2) public education is far more important today than it was in 1868—indeed, "is perhaps the most important
function of state and local governments" and is vital both to success in life
and to the proper performance of the duties of citizenship.[43] The Court
failed to make the most telling argument about the relevance of the pro-
posers' and ratifiers' specific expectations (conceptions of what "equal protection" entailed in relation to school segregation): that since the Amendment is part of a Constitution and was couched in general moral terms, it
should be interpreted to promulgate the moral concept it articulated, not its
framers' and ratifiers' conception of that moral concept.

The opinion then builds on *Sweatt* and *McLaurin* and argues that even though the Black and White schools in question are assumed to be materially equal, the racial segregation they reflect makes them unequal. The inequality in "intangibles" that was decisive in the graduate-school contexts of *Sweatt* and *McLaurin* "apply with added force to grade and high schools":[44]

> separating children in grade and high schools . . . from others of similar age and qualifications solely because of their race generates a feeling of inferiority as to their status in the community that may affect their hearts and minds in a way unlikely ever to be undone.

Warren proceeds to support this conclusion in two ways. First, he cites a statement made by the Kansas Court in the same case:

> [T]he policy of separating the races (in public schools) is usually interpreted as denoting the inferiority of the negro group. A sense of inferiority affects the motivation of the child to learn. Segregation with the sanction of law, therefore, has a tendency to [retard] the educational and mental development of negro children and to deprive them of some of the benefits they would receive in a racial[ly] integrated school.[45]

Second, in footnote 11, he cites various (dubious) social-science studies that supposedly support his conclusion of damage.[46] On this basis, Warren concludes that "in the field of public education 'separate but equal' has no place."[47]

In fact, however, this argument contains a non sequitur. Even if in our society segregation by race does disserve the educational and mental development of the children who are the targets of prejudice, that fact does not preclude separate schools from being equal in the sense of being equally good at fostering the educational and mental development of the children who attend them. Segregating school districts could offset the effects of segregation on the progress of the "minority" children who are separated out by giving them more educational resources of other kinds than they give White schoolchildren. Even if materially-equal segregated schools are unequal, materially-unequal segregated schools may be equal if the Black schools receive enough additional resources. Segregated schools are unconstitutional not because they cannot be made equal in the sense of producing equal performance or equal enhancement of performance but because even if they are made equal in these outcome senses that fact will not alter their insulting character. The *Brown* Court's failure to see or acknowledge this point may have reflected its desire, in Warren's words, to write an opinion that was "unemotional and, above all, non-accusatory."[48] However, I find the fact that to this day no one else has made this objection to the *Brown* argument completely inexplicable.

The preceding discussion of the first *Brown* opinion focused on what it said. However, for my purposes, the more important attribute of *Brown I* is what it did not say. From virtually the beginning of his consideration of the school-segregation issue, Chief Justice Warren was convinced that "the separate but equal doctrine rests on [the] basic premise that the Negro race is inferior"[49] and that this premise is Constitutionally unacceptable in the kind of society that the United States represents. This perception should have led Warren to argue, correctly, that school segregation is unconstitutional because it manifests disrespect for Black Americans—because it amounts to discrimination against them, insults them by indulging its supporters' prejudice. For precedential and doctrinal support, Warren could have referred to *Strauder v. West Virginia*, which implicitly held unconstitutional a statute excluding Blacks from grand and petit juries in an opinion that explicitly held that "every citizen of the United States has a right to a trial of an indictment against him by a jury selected and impaneled without discrimination against his race or color."[50] According to *Strauder*, the Fourteenth Amendment's "aim was against discrimination because of race or color," and the West Virginia statute under review violated the Amendment because it was "practically a brand upon [the excluded Blacks], . . . an assertion of their inferiority, and a stimulant to . . . race prejudice"[51] (a statement that the *Plessy* Court probably had in mind when it articulated its contrary conclusion). But the Warren Court wanted to be "non-accusatory" and "tolerant"—even of prejudice. Their greatest concern was not protecting the rights of those they correctly perceived to have been wronged but protecting the authority of the Court—insuring that the Court's remedial order would be obeyed.[52] For this reason, the *Brown I* opinion did not accuse those that operated segregated school systems of prejudice or discrimination. The opinion was not just non-rhetorical, it was non-moral and non-condemnatory. It creates the impression that school segregation is unconstitutional for a combination of incorrect, arcane legal reasons (e.g., it is impermissible for the states to use any explicitly-racial criteria in its decisionmaking) and non-rights-related policy reasons (e.g., as modern psychology demonstrates, it is bad policy to stunt the development of some of the state's schoolchildren by running a segregated school system).[53]

The failure of the *Brown I* opinion to condemn segregation morally had four undesirable sets of consequences. First, because the *Brown I* opinion focused on the damage to the hearts, minds, and educational and mental development of schoolchildren and ignored the generally-insulting character of segregation, it created doubts about the Constitutionality of state segregation of facilities other than grade schools and high schools. Was *Brown* a segregation case, a school-segregation case, or a segregation-of-children case? The answer to this question turns on whether the crucial fact in *Brown* was the insult or the damage to the Black schoolchildren. Even if the uncertainty created by the *Brown* opinion generated certain types of prudential gains by mollifying some segregationists, it was not legitimate for the Court to create it since the segregation whose Constitutionality it left in doubt violated the moral and Constitutional rights of moral-rights holders for whom the United States is responsible.

Second, the Court's failure to focus on the moral issue vitiated its legal argument. I have already pointed out that, even if segregated schooling always would damage those it was designed to exclude, the Court's claim that separate schools could never be equal would be incorrect. In reality, the social-science research on which the Court relied would have been irrelevant even if it had been of high quality: (1) segregation would have been unconstitutional as insulting even if it did not damage the targets of the prejudice that underlay it and (2) if segregation were morally defensible because Blacks were an inferior species, the fact that it injured the inferior human beings at which it was directed would not render it unconstitutional—sometimes, the segregationists could point out, "the truth hurts." In any event, the Court's reliance on weak social-science research provided an easy target for segregationist anger. Moreover, by refusing to discuss the morality of segregation, the Court surrendered the best argument against the segregationists—the only argument to which they would have had trouble responding. I realize that persuasive argument does not always persuade, but in most situations one does not increase the probability of persuading others by choosing not to make the best argument for one's position on the merits.

Thirdly and relatedly, the *Brown I* opinion also was unfortunate in that, by obscuring the connection between their Constitutional conclusion and our society's moral commitments, the Justices lost an opportunity to remind us of our moral identity and encouraged us to think of ourselves as being ruled by arcane legal principles and non-rights-related policy concerns.

Fourth, the failure of the Court in *Brown I* to address the morality of segregation and its related failure to acknowledge the harm school segregation generated by insulting all Blacks certainly contributed to the inadequacy of some of the Court's remedial efforts, though some of the major actors in the cases that followed *Brown I* were aware of the unprincipled character of the

decisions they were recommending and making.[54] Because the relevant remedial decisions clearly reveal the importance of taking rights and the principles that underlie them seriously, I will discuss several of them in considerable detail.

Brown I restored the case to the docket for reargument on the relevant remedial issues—a morally dubious decision in itself since it guaranteed that
the plaintiffs' rights would continue to be violated for at least a year. When
the Court finally rendered its remedial judgment, its decision (in *Brown II*)[55]
was to remand the case to the District Courts with instructions that they
should make such orders and decrees that are necessary and proper to the
plaintiffs' being admitted "to public schools on a nondiscriminatory basis
with all deliberate speed."[56] More operationally, the Court specified that the
defendants must "make a prompt and reasonable start toward full compliance," but "[o]nce such a start has been made, the courts may find that additional time is necessary to carry out the ruling in an effective manner. The
burden is on the defendants to establish that such time is necessary in the
public interest and is consistent with good faith compliance at the earliest
practicable date."[57]

Three points need to be made about this order. The first is its substantive
modesty—timing aside. The order does no more than require segregating
school districts to stop discriminating. It does not even refer to the possibility that segregating school districts (or the states in which they are located)
might also be required to provide monetary or educational-resource compensation to the schoolchildren whom the Court found school-segregation
had damaged (either a specified amount of resources or whatever it takes to
raise the relevant children's performance on standardized tests to what it otherwise would have been or to some higher level such as the community's average). Moreover, *Brown II* does not consider the possibility that the segregating school districts (or their states) might be required to adopt policies to
compensate the more general victims of their insulting behavior or to eliminate or combat the more general prejudice that their school-segregation
policies fostered as well as manifested. Finally, *Brown II* seems to assume that
any remedies that are awarded would be awarded solely against the segregating school districts rather than against the states of which they are political
subdivisions.

Second, the *Brown II* opinion does not give the lower courts guidance
about how to respond to various problems they will encounter when trying
to achieve even the modest goal it instructs them to secure (ending intra-
school-district discrimination): (1) empirical problems that arise when try-

ing to assess the quality of teachers in different schools (as opposed to their salaries and seniority), the quality of school buildings and equipment (as opposed to their book value), or the importance of having the children of well-educated parents in a classroom—problems that might favor requiring formerly-segregating school districts to move to a system in which the racial compositions of all schools of a given grade-level were identical or very similar and tracking was forbidden; (2) empirical problems that relate to the determination of the extent to which the disparity in the racial composition of the relevant district's various schools of any level would have differed had segregation not been practiced (*inter alia*, how school segregation affected residential patterns and school-siting, school-closure, and school-size decisions) and conceptual problems that relate to the characterization of school policies that would not be discriminatory if their racial-composition consequences were not affected by past acts of discrimination; (3) empirical and conceptual moral problems related to tracking—(A) empirical problems relating to the determination of whether discrimination is being practiced in the admission procedures to the different tracks, whether different amounts of resources (taking quality into consideration) are being devoted to the average child in the different tracks, and whether (if the tracks' compositions are racially disparate) the desire to separate the races played a critical and hence impermissible role in the development of the program and (B) conceptual moral problems relating to the legitimacy of giving children with different current performance levels and potentials different amounts of educational resources; and (4) empirical and conceptual moral problems relating to White flight to other school districts, to private schools, or to reduced-time or reduced-quality public schools, all of which tend to decrease the material resources per child in the formerly-segregating school district and some of which will also deprive children from families with lower educational achievement of classmates from better-educated families—empirical problems in analyzing the extent to which this response was caused by the segregation and conceptual moral problems relating to the school district's responsibility for these responses.

Admittedly, considerations of judicial competence, separation of powers, and federalism may limit the range of remedies the lower courts could legitimately award. Indeed, some might think that even state legislatures could not Constitutionally respond to some of the consequences of segregation in ways that might otherwise be effective (e.g., that parental rights and religious rights would preclude even legislatures from preventing White flight of certain types by requiring all children of school age to attend public schools a certain minimum number of hours per day).[58] Moreover, most lawyers will react to this second criticism of *Brown II* by saying that higher courts should allow lower courts to discover and work out solutions to these sorts of problems. At least in this instance, I disagree. It would not have required any feat of clairvoyance for the Supreme Court to anticipate these difficulties, and there was every reason to believe that at least many of the district courts would refuse to recognize or address them satisfactorily. In my judgment, the Supreme Court's failure to address these issues was totally unprincipled—reflected nothing more than its illegitimate prudential concerns (its desire not to anger various White majorities), not its legitimate doubts about its capacities or knowledge.

Third and finally, *Brown II*'s temporal instructions to the lower courts were at least as unsatisfactory as its substantive instructions. If, as I suspect, the Court, in referring to the possibility that delay might be justified by "the public interest," defined that concept in a utilitarian or some other non-rights-related sense, the temporal part of its remedial order would be legally incorrect because it would be inconsistent with our moral commitments. A liberal State cannot justify delaying the securing of the rights of a moral-rights holder for which it is responsible by citing the utilitarian cost of more rapid action. In fact, I do not think that a liberal State can justify this type of delay even in overall-rights-securing terms when the rights that would be violated if no delay were allowed would be violated by the unlawful or moral-rights-violating responses of private citizens to a remedial order that required more immediate compliance: the obligation of a liberal State is to prevent such private rights-violations, not to cave in to the prospect of their occurring. Even if delay could be justicized by States that would have to forego expenditures that would secure other rights-related interests of greater weight to allocate resources to prevent the threatened rights-violations, this argument certainly was not available in *Brown II*: the relevant school districts' (and *a fortiori* the relevant states') budgetary positions would have allowed them to prevent the requisite amount of moral-rights violations without sacrificing rights-related interests that outweigh those that would be secured by immediate enforcement.

All this is obvious and deeply troubling to me, but at least anecdotal evidence suggests that it is not to others. For example, I am aware of classes on *Brown II* in introductory Procedure courses in two leading American law schools in which no one (neither the teacher nor any student) articulated the rights-objection to delay. In one of these classes, a heated discussion took place about the pragmatic need for delay—about the prudential issue that played such a large role in the *Brown* opinions, but no one mentioned even the possibility that *Brown II*'s temporal remedial instruction that delay could be justified for utilitarian or other non–rights-related reasons may have violated the Constitutional rights of the plaintiffs. Non-rights-based policy analysis rather than rights analysis is a regrettable but (I believe) typical story.

In any event, rather than "deliberate speed" America got a lot of deliberation and very little speed. Some previously-segregating school districts in the deep South closed their public schools, and nearly all dragged their feet. Moreover, when segregative states or districts did respond to *Brown II* in other ways, they often did so with plans that, though neutral on their face, failed in the relevant social situation to produce the school-composition patterns that would have resulted had there been no discrimination. Thus, some segregationist states passed pupil-placement acts that directed their school districts (1) to assign pupils initially on the basis of a series of criteria including home environment, the effect of admission on prevailing academic standards, and the possibility of friction, disorder, and ill-will within the community that virtually always assigned children initially to schools in which their race was in the majority and (2) to allow transfers only if an individual application satisfied the same criteria that were used to make the initial assignment. States that did not rely on such pupil-placement schemes produced similar results by using freedom-of-choice plans. These plans required each student or his parent to choose his school each year. However, despite the fact that such plans were non-discriminatory on their face and despite the fact that many of these plans were conjoined with programs that required districts to furnish free transportation to students who wished to transfer from a school in which their race was in the majority to one in which it was in the minority, social pressures and the threat of harassment or worse prevented these plans from altering the racial composition of schools to any significant extent—an outcome that could have been avoided in many if not most Southern communities simply by establishing neighborhood schools (since Black and White residences were often not geographically separated). Other districts used minority-to-majority-transfer plans to maintain separation. These plans allowed any Black or White student to transfer from a school in which his race was in the minority to one in which it was in the majority. Although also neutral on their face, these plans in practice caused Whites to leave Black schools and Blacks to leave White schools. For at least eight years, all these types of plans were upheld by the lower courts and, in one instance,[59] by the Supreme Court. The net effect of these maneuvers was that in 1964 only 1 percent of Black children in the deep South attended schools with any Whites.[60]

In 1963, the Supreme Court finally started to enforce its remedial order. In *Goss v. Knoxville Board of Education*, it unanimously held that minority-to-majority-transfer provisions were unconstitutional because they were "based solely on racial factors which . . . inevitably lead toward segregation of the students by race."[61] Finally, in 1968, in a case that held that freedom-of-choice programs were unconstitutional when their effect was to perpetuate long-standing segregation, the Supreme Court operationalized *Brown II* in a way that had some bite. According to *Green v. New Kent County School Board*,[62] *Brown II*'s requirement that formerly-segregative school districts end their discrimination implied that school districts (like New Kent County's) that had operated a "dual school system" must move immediately to a "unitary" school system (must "come forward with a plan that promises realistically to work [to create a unitary system], and promises to work realistically *now*"). Unfortunately, the Court was not very forthcoming about the definition of either a "dual" or a "unitary" school system.

Since there was no residential segregation in New Kent County, such definitions may have been unnecessary in *Green*. There can be no doubt that the Board had run a dual school system regardless how that expression was defined in that it had completely separated the races at the cost of busing some Black and some White children across the county to their racially-defined schools. And, regardless of the relationship between establishing a unitary school system and ending straightforward discrimination in general, in this case, putting an end to such discrimination would yield a unitary-school-system outcome even on that concept's most restrictive definition in that the disparity in the racial composition of schools of the same grade levels would be virtually eliminated by the most obvious non-discriminatory school-admissions program—geographic zoning (neighborhood schools).

However, in other circumstances, more operational definitions of "dual" and "unitary" school systems would be required. Would a school board be guilty of operating a dual school system in *Green*'s sense if the central board or one or more of its individual schools or school-zone authorities had made some segregative decisions that increased the disparity in the racial composition of the district's schools without completely or largely separating the races? In the general case, does the obligation to move to a unitary school system require more than ceasing to engage in straightforward discrimination? If so, does it require the relevant school district to secure the racial-composition-of-schools distribution that would have resulted had it made no segregative school-decisions, even if that entails sacrificing clearly legitimate and valuable educational goals? More drastically, does it require the relevant school districts to do whatever it takes to eliminate or virtually eliminate any disparity in the racial (or ethnic) compositions of the various schools of any level that it operated? And once a formerly dual school system has met one of these last two standards (if it is required to do so), must it continue to meet them if demographic changes create what would otherwise have been unacceptable disparities? *Green* answers none of these questions either directly or indirectly by giving an account of the basis of its order—that is, by relating its order to the harms the offending district's segregative policies generated and threatened to continue to generate (the harms the court was authorized to remedy or prevent).[63]

Swann v. Charlotte-Mecklenburg Board of Education[64] answered some of these questions. *Swann* makes explicit the fact that school districts that have run dual systems must do more than renounce straightforward discrimination—they may have to forego policies such as neighborhood schools that would otherwise be desirable. The opinion indicates that this conclusion reflects three considerations:

(1) the difficulty of enforcing a "no straightforward discrimination" rule if districts can adopt neighborhood-school policies—a difficulty linked to the trickiness of assessing school-construction and school-closure decisions;

(2) the need to eliminate what would otherwise be the continuing consequences of past school-location and school-size decisions; and

(3) the belief that something more than non-discrimination is required to "lessen the impact" on current students "of the state-imposed stigma of segregation"—a consideration that led the Court to deem majority-to-minority-transfer programs to be "an indispensable remedy."[65]

(Surely, this last assumption that the subsequent experiences of Blacks who shift to majority-White schools would lead them to feel less stigmatized by the state's past discrimination [or by the treatment they and their race receive in general] was unlikely to be accurate, given the prejudice and hostility the transferring students were likely to encounter in their new school.)

However, *Swann* also states that the obligation to move to a unitary system does not require the school district to secure identical racial compositions in each of its schools at any level. Indeed, according to the Court, "the existence of some small number of one-race, or virtually one-race, schools within a district is not in and of itself the mark of a system that still practices segregation by law . . . [though] the burden upon the school authorities will be to satisfy the court that [the relevant school's] racial composition is not the result of present or past discriminatory action on their part."[66]

Finally, *Swann* holds that once the school authorities establish a unitary school system, they will not be "constitutionally required to make year-by-year adjustments of the racial composition of student bodies."[67]

Four points need to be made about the unitary-school-system remedy *Green* announced. First, although the *Green* Court claimed that this remedy was implicit in *Brown II*'s command that the relevant districts cease racial discrimination, it clearly goes beyond that command. Even if one admits that it would be "discriminatory" for a school district to fail to redress the separation operated by its past discrimination or to make decisions that separate the races because of the effects of past discrimination, the order that districts that generated dual systems move to a unitary system would seem to require some actions that go beyond not discriminating in the extended sense just indicated—would seem to require them to forego choices that would otherwise be permissible to reduce racial-composition disparities more than even the extended no-discrimination order would require.

Second, the Court's opinions in the unitary-school-system cases do not do a better job than *Brown I* or *Brown II* of explaining either the harms that segregative school-policies of different sorts generated or the relationship between the proposed remedy and those harms. Why must a segregating school district that ran a dual system move to a unitary system when a school district that practiced a more limited type of segregation need not? Do the two categories of school segregation generate different sets of harms? Do the two types of remedial orders—move to a unitary school system and stop discriminating—yield different sets of benefits? If so, is there a match between the different sets of harms that the two types of school segregation generate and the different sets of preventative and compensatory benefits generated by moving to a district-wide unitary system on the one hand and eliminating discrimination by the offending individual schools or school zones on the other? If the point of the move to a unitary system is to obviate the courts' assessing the discriminatory character of the decisions of school districts that have been subjected to lesser constraints and to make a symbolic gesture acknowledging the equal moral worth of all races, why are these considerations critically less important after a school district has established a unitary school system than before? Will not the pragmatic problem be as troubling after the system meets the unitary standard? Will not maintaining the unitary character of a system in the face of change be as important a gesture as establishing a unitary system in the first place? Regardless of whether the point of the move to a unitary system is pragmatic or symbolic, why should not inter-district remedies be appropriate, particularly given the difficulty of assessing the segregative character of future school district line-drawing choices?[68]

Third, the unitary-school-system remedy imposes no obligation on the offending school districts to offer injured students compensatory educational resources (or other kinds of compensation), to admit its moral culpability, or to act to prevent prejudice or combat prejudiced behavior either inside or outside the schools.

Fourth, the unitary-school-system remedy does not directly address the quality-of-schooling issue.[69] So long as the disparity in the racial compositions of the individual schools of given grade-levels that a school district operated was reduced to the ill-defined required extent, the school district was in compliance. Perhaps the failure of the Court to address this issue explicitly reflected its conclusion that by guaranteeing that White and Black kids would get the same education the order that a school district move to a unitary system would guarantee that all children would get the same education, the education they would have received had the schools never been segregated, and an education of acceptable quality. In fact, for several reasons, this conclusion is unwarranted. Thus, in a world of tracking in which more resources are devoted to educating each child in the higher tracks and the proportion of White kids in the higher tracks exceeds their proportion in the overall student body, unitary school systems may still provide more resources to White than to Black kids taken as classes—indeed, may provide acceptable education to its White students and an unacceptable one to its Black students. Moreover, in a world in which parents can supplement the state education their children receive with private expenditures or services and parents of White schoolchildren as a class are financially more able to do so than parents of Black schoolchildren, the narrowly-defined interests of parents of White schoolchildren might not lead them to insure that public education in unitary school systems with a substantial percentage of Black students was adequate even if their children attended such schools and received the same education in them as did their Black classmates. And, of course, in a world in which the more affluent parents of White schoolchildren can withdraw them from the unitary school systems whose student populations contain a substantial portion of Black schoolchildren—by moving to other school districts or sending their children to private schools, one can certainly not rely on the interest such parents have in the education of their children to guarantee the adequacy of education in unitary public school systems.

The failure of the Court to address these issues may be explicable in a variety of ways. In part, it may have reflected the NAACP's refusal to focus on educational quality. In part, it may have reflected the Court's belief that the low quality of public education was not caused by the legal wrong (segregation) it was authorized to remedy. In part, it may have reflected an understandable fear that any attempt of lower courts to do something about the quality of the schooling in the formerly-segregating school districts would require them to make orders that have budgetary implications that would substantially alter the options available to the relevant cities and states, to get involved in the details of educational planning, and perhaps to make the kind of inter-school-district orders the Court had ruled out in *Milliken*. In part, it may have reflected the Court's unwillingness to investigate the Constitutionality of the tracking programs that are valued so highly by many parents of White (and Black) children. And in part, it may have reflected the Court's unwillingness to contemplate, much less to embrace, the view that, segregation aside, the states may have a positive obligation to provide a certain minimum level of education to all moral-rights holders for whom they are responsible (as well as the clearly-relevant fact that neither *Brown* nor any of the later school-segregation cases had been argued on this basis).

In any event, the Supreme Court has never addressed the school-quality issue directly. In 1995, in *Missouri v. Jenkins*,[70] the Court did address the appropriateness of a quality-related District Court order to a Kansas City, Missouri, school board that had operated a dual system. This order required the school district to make capital expenditures, to reduce the student-teacher ratio, to raise salaries to virtually all instructional and non-instructional employees, and to provide a variety of special or expanded programs (magnet programs, full-day kindergarten, expanded summer school, before-school and after-school tutoring, and an early-childhood-development program). The District Court had concluded that these steps were necessary to raise student-achievement-test scores to some unspecified level and to attract back into the Kansas City school system White children (and Black children) whose families had flown to various suburban school districts. The Supreme Court rejected the District Court plan on the ground that it was not devised "to remedy the violation"—that is, (in *Milliken*'s cited language) "to restore the victims of discriminatory conduct to the position they would have occupied in the absence of such conduct."[71] Thus, the Court apparently (correctly) believed that the District Court's (ill-specified) test-score goal was inappropriate because not all the deficiencies in the remaining Kansas City students' test-scores could be attributed to the school district's segregative acts. And it clearly believed that the District Court's goal of attracting non-minority students back to Kansas City schools was inappropriate because White flight resulted from desegregation, not *de jure* segregation[72]—a conclusion whose problematic character the dissenters (Justice David Souter, joined by Justices John Paul Stevens, Ruth Bader Ginsburg, and Stephen Breyer) hastened to point out. The Supreme Court also objected to the District Court order on the ground that it gave insufficient weight to state and local control[73]—to "federalism and the separation of powers," as Justice Thomas put it in his concurrence.[74] The Court did not address the possibility that at least some portions of the District Court order might be justified as a response to the more general harm the school board had inflicted on Blacks as a group by running a dual school system. It also did not address the possible appropriateness of school-quality orders that did respond to reasonable assessments of the continuing consequences of past segregation on the performance of Black schoolchildren. Nor did it consider whether its own move-to-a-unitary-system remedy or its refusal to make inter-district orders that involved districts that had not engaged in segregation were consistent with its duty "to restore the victims of discriminatory conduct to the position they would have occupied in the absence of such conduct."

I am not claiming that all deficiencies of school-segregation law were caused by the Court's concern with prudential issues and its related failure to address, much less explicate, the relevant issue of principle.[75] However, many of these deficiencies were certainly made more likely by the Court's pursuit of prudence over principle.

Fifth, the Court's failure to address the morality of segregation—to focus on its insulting character—prepared the way for the errors it has made more recently when assessing the Constitutionality of various affirmative-action programs that city councils and state legislatures have adopted. Had the Court correctly explained why segregation violated moral and Constitutional rights, it would have better understood the full range of harms segregation generated. Had it understood these harms, it would not have held various affirmative-action programs unconstitutional on the ground that they were not remedial in the adjudicatory sense (even if it had made the mistake of assuming that legislated affirmative-action programs cannot be Constitutional unless they compensate victims of legal wrongs, reduce the consequential damages those wrongs inflict, or prevent the State from repeating its legal violations). Moreover, had the Court focused on why segregation was morally and Constitutionally impermissible, it would have been less likely to have concluded that any state actor that uses a racial (or ethnic) criterion must bear the burden of demonstrating that its use passed the Court's (incorrect) test of Constitutionality—would have realized that what justifies showing no deference or perhaps imposing such a burden is not the actor's use of a racial or ethnic criterion but his history of insulting (discriminating against) the members of the group disfavored by the use of that criterion. Section 5 discusses these "affirmative action" issues in more detail.

My assessment of the *Brown I* and post–*Brown I* school-segregation case-law has been harsh. Obviously, one could easily argue that *Brown v. Board of Education* and its progeny were a triumph of principle: a Supreme Court that had rarely declared unconstitutional state decisions that had violated some relevant-moral-rights holders' right to appropriate, equal respect finally made some rights-protecting decisions. I have emphasized what was missing rather than what was present. The Court's opinions were not opinions of principle. They did not articulate or interpolate our commitments.

The premise of this section has been that courts in a rights-based State such as ours are obligated to be 100 percent principled 100 percent of the time—when they answer legal-rights questions, when they explain the rationales of their legal-rights conclusions, and when they answer and explain the timing and substantive remedial issues they must resolve. This obligation is a corollary of our duty to do justice. Even if a Court could promote some utilitarian or other non-rights-based goal by departing from principle, it would be obligated not to do so.

This section has attempted to delineate the principled answers to the various substantive and remedial Constitutional-law questions that school-segregation raises as well as the rationales for those answers. It has also criticized the Supreme Court for failing to give principled answers and explanations to these questions—indeed, for intentionally failing to give such answers.

Many experts will find this critique naive. Of course, they will say, the Supreme Court is a political institution that ought to be guided by non-rights-related, prudential considerations. The analysis of this section should give these experts pause—it should lead them to reconsider the intrinsic cost of even well-intentioned, "unprincipled" decisionmaking and the various rights-"costs" and goal-"costs" it tends to generate.

5. "Affirmative Action": A Moral and Doctrinal Analysis and Critique

"Affirmative action" or "racial (ethnic, gender) preference" policies are policies that favor members of the preferred group either (in effect) by giving them points because of their group membership in a point competition with other candidates or by reserving for them a specific number of favorable outcomes that exceeds the number they would have obtained had their group membership not been taken into consideration directly (quotas). Although such programs could relate to any type of "competitive" situation, in the United States, they have been most important in university-admissions, government-contract-award, and public-and-private-employment contexts. Section A analyzes the moral and Constitutional permissibility of affirmative-action programs for which the State is responsible (whether they violate anyone's moral or Constitutional rights); Section B illustrates the analysis by assessing the moral and Constitutional permissibility of law-school-admissions affirmative-action programs; and Section C criticizes various doctrinal positions the Supreme Court or various Supreme Court justices have taken on affirmative-action issues.

A. Moral and Constitutional Permissibility

The moral and Constitutional permissibility of State decisions to effectuate (or not prohibit private) affirmative-action programs should be analyzed in the same way as the moral and Constitutional permissibility of any other kind of State choice. Affirmative-action choices violate moral and Constitutional rights if they are insulting to those they disfavor or favor or if they violate some "independent" right (e.g., property or liberty right). Since affirmative-action choices that compensate individual victims of moral-rights or legal-rights violations, prevent future moral-rights or legal-rights violations, or secure various future-oriented personal ultimate values or ideals normally will not be insulting, a demonstration that an affirmative-action program will produce these effects or would not have been adopted but for its supporters' reasonable belief that it would produce these effects will normally establish its moral and Constitutional permissibility. Although supporters of affirmative action (both on the bench and off) tend to argue for particular affirmative-action programs in backward-looking, compensatory terms, such arguments rarely if ever are justified on the merits: (1) in a liberal society, group-compensation as opposed to individual-compensation is not a valid goal and (2) the match between the victims and perpetrators of past moral-rights or legal-rights violations and respectively the beneficiaries and victims of contemporaneous affirmative-action programs is far too imperfect for such programs to be justified on an individual-compensation basis. However, virtually all the affirmative-action programs that have actually been adopted clearly do further or could be reasonably predicted to further various future-oriented goals (and related personal ultimate values). The next subsection illustrates this claim in the law-school-admissions context. Although I would have opposed a number of the affirmative-action programs that have been proposed or adopted on non-rights-oriented grounds (because I thought the benefits predictions were too optimistic or the costs were prohibitive), I have no doubt that the overwhelming majority of such programs violated no moral right or related Constitutional right.

All claims to the contrary have been based on arguments that are either irrelevant or marred by conceptual or empirical errors. Thus, some have argued that State-run affirmative-action programs are unconstitutional because they use race (ethnicity, gender) as an explicit criterion of choice. As I have already explained and illustrated with a sickle-cell-anemia blood-testing example, since the use of such a criterion is not necessarily insulting, it does not automatically violate anyone's moral or Constitutional rights.

Others have argued that State-run affirmative-action programs are unconstitutional because they do not treat candidates as individuals, but rather rely on statistical generalizations made about members of groups. In fact, however, virtually all choices rely on such generalizations. For example, when graduate schools base their admissions decisions on grade-point averages, undergraduate-college attended, and graduate-admissions-test scores, they are also relying on statistical generalizations. In itself, the use of such "non-individualized" data is inoffensive—it simply reflects the cost-ineffectiveness of more individualized assessments.

Some opponents of State affirmative-action programs argue that these programs violate their rights and are unconstitutional because they "penalize" them for possessing an attribute that is beyond their control and rewards members of the favored group for possessing an attribute for which they deserve no credit. Even if one acquiesced in the highly-contestable assumption that the other criteria used in the relevant selection-processes do respond to candidates' deserts—that individuals deserve credit for their labor-productivity or their predicted raw scores on university exams, this argument would deserve no weight. We are not committed to making all decisions turn exclusively on factors for which the relevant candidates are morally responsible. The decisions that affirmative-action programs implicate are not designed to reward those who are entitled to or personally deserve to be rewarded: they are designed to achieve various forward-looking goals. Although some supporters of affirmative-action programs talk as if such programs' individual beneficiaries deserve the favorable treatment that such programs give them, the reality is that those favored are fortunate beneficiaries of policies whose rationales have nothing to do with the justness or inherent desirability of benefiting them. The fact that affirmative-action programs benefit individuals for possessing attributes for which they deserve no moral credit and disadvantage people for possessing attributes for which they deserve no blame does not justify the conclusion that such programs violate moral or Constitutional rights.

Still other opponents of State affirmative-action programs complain that such programs are insulting and unconstitutional because they use race as a surrogate for other characteristics when it would be more accurate or cost-effective to focus on those other characteristics directly. Two objections can be made to this argument. First, it is based on an incorrect empirical premise in that some affirmative-action programs value race (ethnicity, gender) in itself, not as a surrogate for something else. Thus, if the race of a Black candidate for medical-school admission is counted in her favor because the medical school believes that it is valuable (1) to provide role models and sources of hope for Black schoolchildren whom it thinks can "profit" more than others from the encouragement such role models can provide and/or (2) to provide examples of achievement to combat prejudiced stereotypes about the potential of Blacks, race is being valued in itself not as a surrogate for something else. Similarly, if the race of a Black candidate for admission to law school is counted in his favor because the law school believes that, *ceteris paribus*, it is more valuable to increase the legal services provided to Black potential clients and these individuals are more likely to go to a Black lawyer than to a non-Black lawyer because of the former's Blackness (as opposed to his actual sympathies, ability to speak their "language," or understanding of their situation), race is once more being valued in itself, not as a surrogate for something else.

Second, this complaint is unjustified because in many cases in which race is being used as a surrogate for something else its use is the most cost-effective way to secure the something else. Given the difficulty of assessing the truthfulness of law-school or medical-school applicants' claims that they intend to devote a substantial part of their professional lives to servicing "underserved" clients or patients (and the willingness of such candidates to establish histories that support this claim), professional schools that want to increase the amount of legal or medical services that underserved Blacks, Latinos, or poor people receive may find that using race or ethnicity (and/or, admittedly, family poverty) as a surrogate for interest in serving this population is the most cost-effective way to further their goal through their admissions processes.

Another allegedly-Constitutional argument that has been made against State affirmative-action programs is, basically, that they are undesirable for non-rights-related reasons. Those who make this argument sometimes focus on a variety of non-sensitive costs the program generates (the allegedly-lower productivity of employees hired because of affirmative action, the higher cost or lower quality of work done by affirmative-action contractors, the pedagogic costs of mixing students of different abilities or backgrounds in the same classroom). But, more often, these critics argue that affirmative-action programs generate a series of costs that are socially more awkward to discuss: insult their supposed beneficiaries by implying that they are incapable of competing on a level playing-field, induce their supposed beneficiaries to develop a psychology of dependency (deter them from becoming self-reliant), encourage prejudice by vitiating the power of examples of success to combat the view that members of the "favored" group are inherently incapable of good performance, promote race (ethnicity, gender) consciousness or hostility in non-political interactions, and foster the politics of racial (ethnic, gender) hostility. Two objections can be made to these arguments. First, most seem to be based on empirical predictions about the consequences of affirmative-action programs that are certainly contestable, probably exaggerated, and undoubtedly untested. Second, unless some of them are expanded in ways their supporters probably would reject, they are not Constitutionally decisive. Without more, these objections are ones that a legislature should consider but not ones that suggest that the programs in question violate anyone's moral or Constitutional rights. To be Constitutional-rights objections, it would be necessary to establish either (1) that these consequences preclude the relevant program from being desirable from any legitimate personal-ultimate-value perspective and its supporters knew or ought to have known this fact or (2) that the program's adoption was critically affected by some of its supporters' desire to insult its beneficiaries, deter them from becoming self-reliant, or encourage prejudice, interpersonal hostility, or the politics of group hostility. I doubt that the proponents of this argument believe either of these two propositions, neither of which strikes me as even remotely plausible.

Some critics of affirmative-action programs claim that they violate moral and Constitutional rights because the empirical premises on which they are based have been insufficiently validated. The argument is that even if the State believes that its explicit use of race, ethnicity, or gender as a criterion of choice will benefit our society on balance by furthering various legitimate goals and instantiating legitimate personal ultimate values it is insulting for the State to proceed on this belief unless it has subjected it to some unspecified amount of empirical testing (the amount necessary to raise the probability of desirability to x percent or the amount that would be *ex ante* desirable for the State to execute). Normally, considerations of appropriate deference would lead me to conclude that the courts should not hold all state decisions unconstitutional that have not been based on the amount and kind of empirical research that would have been *ex ante* efficient for the government to undertake. Admittedly, when a government choice disadvantages a group that has historically been treated with disrespect or disserves a value that the State has historically denigrated, deference is less appropriate and a requirement of validation more persuasive. However, even if it were legitimate for the Court to require government choosers to validate (to some specified extent) the empirical premises of those of their choices that injure groups (denigrate rights-related values) that have been targets of State or private discrimination (that the State has traditionally denigrated), that conclusion would not imply the legitimacy of such a validation-requirement for decisions that favor groups (further rights-related values) whose rights have been traditionally violated (values that have been traditionally denigrated). Basically, the proponents of this argument are guilty of wooden analysis. Their refusal to focus on the relevant moral issue has led them to suppose that a validation-requirement can legitimately be imposed whenever the State uses an explicitly racial, ethnic, or gender criterion rather than whenever the State's choice injures some group that has historically been a target of discrimination.

In short, none of these arguments for the unconstitutionality of affirmative-action programs is persuasive. Admittedly, however, an affirmative-action program may be unconstitutional for many of the reasons that the first section of this chapter indicated any choice may violate a liberal State's duty of appropriate, equal respect. Thus, an affirmative-action program may be unconstitutional because its adoption was critically affected by one or more of the following illicit motivations:

(1) by its supporters' receipt of a bribe;

(2) by their personal loyalties or sympathies for its beneficiaries;

(3) by their desire to insult its supposed beneficiaries by implying that they cannot compete on a level playing-field;

(4) by their desire to induce its supposed beneficiaries to develop a psychology of dependence (to deter them from becoming self-reliant);

(5) by their desire to reduce the extent to which the success of members of the supposed beneficiary-group reduces prejudice by disproving the claim that such persons are inherently incapable;

(6) by their desire to promote racial (ethnicity, gender) consciousness and hostility in non-political interactions;

(7) by their desire to foster the politics of racial (ethnic, gender) hostility; and

(8) by the insult it inflicts on (some or all of) its victims, given the insultingly-low weight its supporters must have put on the losses these victims experience to have concluded that the choice was desirable—an argument that is likely to be persuasive only when the victims are a subset of the disfavored majority, a subset against whom prejudice has also been directed (for example, when redistricting helps Blacks but injures Hassids).

Of course, even when there is reason to suspect that some of these illicit motivations played a role in the decisions of some of the supporters of an affirmative-action program, it will be hard to justify a conclusion that it or they played the *critical* role they must play to render the program unconstitutional on that account when the program does further legitimate goals—especially since it would be hard to justify requiring the State to demonstrate the non-criticality of such motivations even in cases in which their presence could be established.

Moreover, some affirmative-action programs could conceivably violate the property or liberty rights of some of their victims. In fact, however, I doubt that such a claim ever will be justified. Thus, the owner of a business clearly does not have a Constitutionally-protected property right that would be violated by an affirmative-action hiring-program whose application reduced his profits.

In addition, an affirmative-action program that used race, ethnicity, or gender as a surrogate for some other attribute might be unconstitutional if the use of some other surrogate or the attribute itself would have been more desirable from any legitimate personal-ultimate-value perspective. Although this possibility must be taken seriously, I doubt that a court will often be justified in second-guessing the State decisionmaker whose choice is under review on this issue. In fact, except when the program disadvantages a subset of the majority that has been the target of discrimination or (conceivably) has been accepted by decisionmakers whose choice may have been influenced by sympathies or loyalties to which they could not legitimately give rein, I also doubt that a court would be justified in imposing the burden on the State to validate its use of a racial, ethnic, or gender criterion—to demonstrate its cost-effectiveness.

Finally, an affirmative-action program could conceivably be unconstitutional because it was adopted through a process that did not provide sufficient protection against the adoption of programs that were pointless or ill-motivated. In practice, however, I doubt that this insufficient-quality-control argument will often be available.

This summary implies that few affirmative-action programs violate moral rights and that even fewer can legitimately be held unconstitutional by reviewing courts. There may be non-rights-related grounds for opposing some or many such policies, but there are moral-rights-related or Constitutional-rights-related grounds for opposing few of them.

B. A Law-School Admissions Example

The maximand of a State law school is an increasing function of the contribution it makes (1) to the "net social product" of the legal system (net of its opportunity costs), (2) to the "net social product" lawyers produce by being sources of information for members of their community and by performing various public roles, and (3) to the quality of the lives of law graduates (and others) by enriching them intellectually and providing them with the technical education and values that will help them gain satisfaction from their lawyering roles, their non-lawyering work, and their personal lives. I realize, of course, that none of these goals can be operationalized without employing moral principles or personal ultimate values. When issues of this kind are at stake, there is no neutral place to stand.

The preceding analysis implies that law schools will often not maximize their performance by selecting a student body to maximize its students' raw-point scores on exams and papers, though law schools with certain kinds of faculties may be more productive if their students are more able and substantial pedagogic benefits are generated by having student bodies that are homogeneous in ability-terms.

There are at least six categories of reasons for giving points to members of racial or ethnic minorities or to women in the law-school-admissions process—that is, six types of reasons why doing so may increase a law school's social product. (To shorten the exposition, I will assume henceforth that points are being given to African-Americans.) First, a clearly non-affirmative-action reason: if the law school concluded that its productivity would increase with its student body's abilities, one might give points to Black Americans to offset the fact that the standard "hard" predictors of ability underpredict the actual ability of Black American students (although one could describe this procedure in a non-point-awarding way) and/or to offset the tendency of members of the Admissions Committee to undervalue Black American performance in interviews and applications or to be prejudiced in their assessment of all data on Black Americans they consider.

Second, the law school might give points to Black American candidates because it has reason to believe that it can improve their raw-score-exam performance or (more importantly) their performance as lawyers in lawyering and other public roles and/or their lives more than it can improve the counterpart "performances" of non-minority candidates with higher predicted law-school raw-scores.

Third, the law school may give points to Black American candidates for admission because doing so will increase the total number of Black American lawyers nationwide and because, for four reasons, the relative social contribution that Black lawyers of given raw-score ability make through their lawyering activities will be higher than its counterpart for non-minority lawyers of the same raw-score-measured ability:

(1) Black American lawyers are more likely to work for minorities or do public-service work, and additional efforts of these kinds are more socially valuable than the other types of lawyering services that the point-award program in effect sacrifices;

(2) *ceteris paribus*, Black American graduates will be better able to serve at least some Black American clients than will their non-Black counterparts because the Black American lawyers have better relevant communication skills (are more able to speak some such clients' language [a point that applies more strongly to Hispanic lawyers] and more able to understand the factual background of the legal-claim-related stories these clients tell);

(3) inclination-to-serve and ability-to-serve considerations aside, Black American graduates are more likely to increase the quantity of legal

services obtained by Black Americans because Black Americans are more likely to seek needed legal help from a fellow Black American; and

(4) Black American graduates of given raw-score-measured ability are more likely to get lawyering work of social importance that does not relate to the traditional representation of poor minority-members in relation to traditional private actions or needs.

Fourth, a State law school may give points to Black American candidates for admission because it believes that they are more likely to have opportunities to perform non-lawyering public roles of social importance so that improving their ability to perform such roles to a given extent may be more socially valuable than improving the ability of non-minority members of equal raw-score-measured ability to perform such roles.

Fifth, a State law school may give points to Black Americans because it believes that their presence in the student body will improve the school's impact on its non-Black students—that Black American students will provide insights into the factual background of cases or the weight to be given to particular values in certain contexts that will increase the non-minority students' legal sophistication, will emphasize the importance of certain issues and problems and thereby incline non-minority students to alter their lawyering and other work activities in ways that increase their social product (will incline them to do more pro bono, public interest, or public-service work and to perform more non-lawyering public roles), and will improve the ability of non-minority students to communicate and build relations with minority members in their professional and personal lives. Obviously, to the extent that programs that award points to minority members increase the number of minority students in law schools that have substantial non-minority enrollments (as opposed to just increasing the quality of the law schools that minority students attend), the minority students will obtain similar benefits from their association with non-minority students.

Sixth, a State law school may decide to award points to minority admissions-candidates for a variety of symbolic reasons: (1) in the hope that minority graduates will provide positive role-models for members of their group, (2) in the hope that the success of the minority candidate in question will encourage other minority members to develop their capacities by combatting their perception that they would not be allowed to succeed in any case, and (3) in the hope that minority graduates will provide examples of success that increase the self-respect of other members of the group in question as well as the respect of non-minority members for the minority group concerned.

I do not mean to imply that all the empirical assumptions on which the preceding arguments are based are accurate or that there are no counteracting possibilities to consider when evaluating the overall desirability of a point-awarding system. For example, candidates who are given points for their race or ethnicity may in fact do worse than predicted on law-school exams (because they become discouraged when confronted with more-able, better-educated fellow students); the presence of less-able students may reduce the quality of the education other students receive by inducing professors to reduce the amount of demanding material they teach and by reducing non-minority-student school work incentives by insuring that a percentage of the students in each class (who, in practice, receive passing grades for performances that traditionally may have been given failing grades) will do worse than the non-minority students; the fact that minority members receive points may cause individual members of the group in question who would be capable of gaining admission without such points to slack off; the fact that some minority graduates were given a critical number of points for their race or ethnicity in the admissions process and received passing grades for dubious academic performances may cause non-minority members (and minority members) to underestimate the number of minority members whose raw-score-type performance merited admission, graduation, and good jobs; and, relatedly, the realization by minority members that they will tend to be viewed as having received preferential treatment regardless of whether they did or whether it mattered may also discourage some from performing as well as they could. In fact, I suspect that from my own personal-ultimate-value perspective some affirmative-action law-school-admissions programs did more harm than good. But clearly, many such programs were and are desirable from legitimate personal-ultimate-value perspectives, and most that I would vote against can be legitimately defended—that is, my evaluation reflects my contestable resolution of various empirical issues and my personal commitment to a set of values with which others can legitimately disagree.

Moreover, I see no reason to believe that any of these programs violated moral or Constitutional rights for any other reason. The law professors who voted for them had not been bribed, had no critical insulting motivations, were not negligent or careless, did not refuse to do empirical research whose execution would have been *ex ante* profitable for their institution, and so on.

There is simply no basis for declaring these programs unconstitutional, regardless of whether one finds them desirable.

One final thought: Recent public discussion of affirmative-action university-admissions programs leaves the impression that they are novel departures from a tradition of admission on an exclusive predicted-GPA-performance basis. In fact, there never has been such a tradition. Universities have always taken into account non-GPA-related considerations of the same kind that play a role in the modern affirmative action programs. In particular, universities have always tried to enrich their student bodies by increasing the diversity of their student bodies' geographical distribution, by admitting candidates who have special talents or interesting backgrounds that do not increase their likely GPAs, and by admitting the children of the rich and powerful (not only for the venal and dubious reason of obtaining alumni contributions but also because the greater opportunities available to such individuals make it more important to educate them well and the experience and contacts of such individuals make them likely to be greater contributors to the overall college experience of their classmates). Affirmative-action programs are business as usual at American universities. All that has changed is the label, the publicity, and the identity of the direct beneficiaries of the programs in question. To the extent that the labels "affirmative action" and "preferential admissions" give a different impression, they are misleading on this account.

C. Affirmative-Action Doctrine: A Critique

Rather than reviewing the various affirmative-action cases that the Supreme Court has considered, I will list and comment on these cases' seven most important doctrinal propositions. The first is that the test of Constitutionality that applies to the use of racial (ethnic, gender) classifications does not make relevant whether the State decision in question benefits or harms groups whose treatment is suspect.[76] I am not persuaded by the supposed justifications for this position. I do not believe that it is often difficult to distinguish benign from insulting uses of such classifications, and I also do not think that such classifications seldom provide a relevant basis for disparate treatment. In part, this latter disagreement reflects my conclusion that the disparate treatment of such groups can be legitimated by its tendency to further forward-looking goals as well as by any tendency it may have to achieve traditional adjudicatory remedial goals (see below).

The Court's second doctrinal pronouncement is that affirmative-action programs or any other State choice that draws racial or ethnic lines are to be subjected to strict scrutiny, while affirmative-action programs or any other State choice that draws gender lines are to be subjected to intermediate scrutiny. I reject the strict and intermediate scrutiny tests in the affirmative-action context for the same reasons that I reject them in all contexts. I see no reason why the use of racial or ethnic classifications should be Constitutional only if they are narrowly-tailored and necessary for the achievement of a compelling State goal. Nor do I see why the use of gender classifications should be Constitutional only if it is substantially related to the achievement of an important State goal.

The Supreme Court's third relevant doctrinal proposition is that State affirmative-action programs can be justified only if their goal is to compensate the victims of legal wrongs the State in question committed or to prevent the same wrong from being repeated or the original wrong from yielding consequential damages. There has been one exception to this proposition: the Court's acknowledgment in *Bakke* that the goal of achieving true diversity may justify affirmative-action educational-admissions programs.[77] With this exception, the Court has insisted that forward-looking goals and the goal of remedying societal discrimination cannot be considered legitimate, much less important or compelling[78] when applying its strict-scrutiny or intermediate-scrutiny test of Constitutionality. As already indicated, no sound moral or Constitutional justification can be offered for this proposition.

The Supreme Court's fourth affirmative-action doctrinal pronouncement is that—at least in the context of educational admissions—the use of minimum quotas is per se unconstitutional.[79] Since economies-of-scale considerations[80] often result in special-admissions programs' being desirable only after they have achieved some minimum scale, a minimum quota may be perfectly legitimate.[81]

The Supreme Court's fifth affirmative-action doctrinal proposition is that the facts that an affirmative-action program is of limited duration, seeks to establish but not to maintain a situation in which the percentage of workers in some racial, ethnic, or gender class in a given position equals the percentage that racial, ethnic, or gender class constitutes of the relevant labor pool, and leaves some new positions of the relevant type available to members of non-favored classes all favor its Constitutionality. Once one admits that the usual justification for affirmative-action programs is forward-looking, the fact that a particular program is of limited duration, seeks to establish rather than maintain "proportionality," and leaves some positions open to members of the disfavored group seems much less Constitutionally significant than the Court appears to suppose.

The Supreme Court's sixth affirmative-action doctrinal proposition is that the facts that an affirmative-action program upsets settled expectations or imposes a larger burden on an innocent victim both count against its Constitutionality. However, although the facts that an affirmative-action program upsets settled expectations that do not give rise to property rights and imposes a larger burden on its innocent victims may be relevant prudentially (may reduce its overall desirability both directly and by increasing the probability that it will generate an undesirable backlash), these facts are not Constitutionally relevant unless they cause the program to be so undesirable from any legitimate personal–ultimate–value perspective that its adoption must be considered to be unconstitutionally motivated or unconstitutionally careless. In my opinion, the members of the Court who have emphasized these considerations are playing an illegitimate prudentialist game—that is, they are operating as a super-legislature. This view is confirmed by the distinction the Court drew in *Wygant*[82] between affirmative-action hiring programs, whose effects on their victims are said to be diffused, and affirmative-action lay-off programs, whose effects on their victims are said to be concentrated. Of course, the fact is that *ex post* the effects of these two types of programs are equally concentrated: somebody who otherwise would have been hired is not, and somebody who otherwise would not have been laid off is. The difference in the two programs is not *ex post*, it is perceived *ex ante*: the individuals who are laid off or whose probability of being laid off is increased by an affirmative-action lay-off program may suffer a bigger perceived *ex ante* loss on this account than the (usually) larger number of individuals whose perceived probability of being hired is reduced by an affirmative-action hiring program. This fact may be relevant to the likelihood that the relevant victims will react hostilely and destructively to the programs, but it is not relevant to the magnitude of their actual *ex post* loss.[83]

The seventh and final affirmative-action doctrine I want to discuss is the doctrine that the State must bear the burden of coming forward and establishing the ability of its affirmative-action program to achieve the required justifying effects—allegedly, in racial affirmative-action cases, of establishing its classification's ability to achieve a compelling State goal. As I have already indicated, there is no justification for such a shift in the burden of proof when the classification in question does not disfavor a group whose treatment is suspect.

Current affirmative-action doctrine is intellectually embarrassing. The Court has lost sight of the relevant moral issues and has promulgated a series of incorrect legal doctrines that reflect little more than a majority of the Justices' non-rights-related political preferences. Justices who claim to be judicial conservatives are acting like judicial activists with politically-conservative agendas. The performance of the Court in this area has harmed us in two ways: directly by militating against our properly considering the personal-ultimate-value desirability of specific affirmative-action programs and indirectly by discouraging us from thinking of ourselves as a rights-based society whose Constitutional law is based on moral-rights considerations.

6. Gender Discrimination

In any liberal society, gender should not be destiny. In our liberal society, the victims of the overwhelming majority of gender-related violations of the duty of appropriate, equal respect are women. Negatively, a liberal State must show women the respect that is their due by making no positive choices that violate any of the "tests" section one of this chapter delineated and our discussion of *Reed v. Reed* illustrated. Positively, a liberal State has an obligation to combat prejudices against women and prejudiced acts that violate women's rights (e.g., unjustifiable, gender-based socialization patterns and role assignments). On this account, a liberal State may be obligated to educate people out of prejudice, to provide socialization experiences to schoolgirls that combat what they receive at home, to train men in various household-production skills, (conceivably) to provide parental services to offset the unwillingness of fathers to accept a fair share of parental responsibilities, and to forbid discrimination against women (and men) by private actors who do not have the right to indulge their prejudices in the relevant context.

Unfortunately, limitations of space preclude me from analyzing these and various other contestable moral-obligation and Constitutional-duty issues that relate to the right of women to appropriate, equal respect. In fact, I do not even have space to analyze in any detail the considerable body of recent case-law on gender classifications and gender discrimination. Instead of providing such a detailed account and critique, I list and briefly elaborate on six deficiencies of the opinions that have been written in this area. No citations are given to the relevant cases.

Under current Supreme Court doctrine, government choices that use gender criteria or have a disparate impact on the two genders are subjected to intermediate scrutiny—they are concluded to be unconstitutional unless they are substantially related to the achievement of an important State goal. My first set of objections to gender doctrine are the objections I have already made to the three-tier-scrutiny approach in general.

My second objection to gender doctrine is more salient in the context of affirmative-action cases. Current doctrine refuses to distinguish between affirmation-action programs that favor women and those that favor men (just as it refuses to distinguish between affirmative-action programs that favor Blacks and those that favor Whites). This position is indefensible because in our culture (1) power is still in the hands of men who are unlikely to make choices that insult their male "victims" and (2) a variety of legitimate goals may be achieved by policies that favor women that have no counterparts or are less valuable in relation to policies that favor men. (The list would not be that different from the list that Section 5B generated for Blacks.)

Third, many of the cases incorrectly analyze whether the policy choices being reviewed disadvantage women. Some of the cases misanalyze even the short-run effects of the policy in question by focusing exclusively on a subset of the women they affect (on the fact that they hurt female wage-earners and not on the fact that they help widows of male wage-earners). The analysis of this issue in other cases is deficient because it ignores certain long-run effects (the tendency of policies that benefit [harm] women in the short run to harm [benefit] women in the long run by deterring [encouraging] them from developing [to develop] their productive potentials).

Fourth, the cases do not deal adequately with the legitimacy of the State's using accurate statistical generalizations that relate to gender.[84] The Court waffles on the issue of whether the administrative cost-savings the use of such statistics generates can legitimate gender-based decisionmaking: sometimes, it states that such cost-savings cannot justicize the use of gender-oriented statistical generalizations, while in other cases it accepts decisions based on such generalizations that could be justified only by the "transaction-cost" savings that reliance on such data generates. Moreover, the Court sometimes ignores the possibility that policies that are based on accurate statistical generalizations may perpetuate current gender-related differences whose existence is undesirable. The Court's treatment of the use of statistical generalizations about gender is also deficient in that it fails to take account of whether the generalizations in question reflect something about the treatment of women that is or is not against their interest on balance. In addition, the Court's analyses of the use of gender-oriented statistics is also inadequate in that it does not focus on whether the generalization in question reflects moral-rights violations (discrimination) or on-balance harmful and undesirable socialization patterns for which the State is responsible (because it engaged in the violations itself, actively encouraged them [e.g., through its choice of school textbooks], failed to combat private attitudes that led to them, or cannot be separated from the private actors for whom it is responsible).

Fifth, in some cases the Court has ignored the possibility that the conduct it is reviewing may constitute price discrimination against women, among women, or among men. This possibility is relevant (in a Constitutional-law context) because saving money is a legitimate goal for the government to pursue (though its importance to the government is different from its importance to private companies)[85] and price discrimination is not inherently insulting to the parties against whom the discrimination is practiced.

The sixth and final deficiency of the recent gender-discrimination cases is implicit in some of its predecessors. The Court has not focused explicitly on the insult issue that should guide its Constitutional analyses. Had it done so, it would have realized that

(1) administrative-cost savings can justify the use of gender-oriented statistical generalizations because their presence will sometimes imply that the use of such data is not insulting;
(2) the fact that a statistical generalization reflects previous discrimination against women for which the State is responsible is also relevant to the Constitutionality of basing a decision on it;
(3) the fact that the use of a statistical generalization that reflects discrimination for which the State is responsible deters women from developing their capacities is relevant to its Constitutionality; and
(4) the fact that the use of a gender classification perpetuates a negative stereotype about women that disadvantages them is relevant to its Constitutionality.

The gender-discrimination case-law is deficient for the same reasons that the three-tier-scrutiny approach, the school-segregation cases, and the affirmative-action cases are deficient. All these bodies of law are inadequate because they manifest the Court's failure to focus on the moral-rights concepts and issues that the relevant cases implicate. When judges lose sight of the point of the law, outcomes become ad hoc and explanations, unconvincing.

7. Writing Like a Lawyer: Equal-Protection Analysis

Lawyers take pride not only in thinking clearly but also in writing clearly.[86] This chapter has already criticized many of the substantive arguments in the judicial opinions and academic analyses of the duty of appropriate, equal respect on which it has focused. Section 7 criticizes the language in which these arguments have been expressed.

Two sets of linguistic "errors" are distinguished. The first contains "innocent mistakes"—errors that may be misleading but were not made intentionally for some ulterior purpose. The second contains intentional errors—intentional misuses or stipulative definitions that were designed to bias the analysis in the direction their authors favored.

A. Innocent Errors

(1) "Ordinary Scrutiny," "Intermediate Scrutiny," and "Strict Scrutiny"

Section 3 of this chapter explained my substantive objections to the three-levels-of-scrutiny approach to equal-protection analysis. This section is concerned with the fact that the name of this approach is a misnomer. The phrases "ordinary scrutiny," "intermediate scrutiny," and "strict scrutiny" make it appear that the categorization of the cases in question reflects "the care with which the Court will scrutinize" the decisions it is reviewing rather than the test it will use to assess their Constitutionality and the degree of deference it owes the decisionmaker in question —that is, rather than the review-standard each judge will use to decide whether to declare the relevant decisions unconstitutional. I do not know whether this misnomer affects the care with which the courts execute judicial review in the cases in question: if it does, that result would be unfortunate, but even if it does not, the Court's terminology is unnecessarily misleading.

(2) "Suspect Group"

On many occasions, the Supreme Court has indicated that one of the factors that determine the kind of scrutiny it will give a State decision under review is the extent to which the "classification" the decision employs is "suspect." Linguistically, there is nothing wrong with this usage. On the other hand, on several occasions, members of the Court[87] and various Constitutional-law commentators have substituted the expression "suspect *groups*" for "suspect *classifications*." This usage is unfortunate in that it implies that the group rather than its treatment or disadvantagement (i.e., rather than the classification) is suspect. Even if one rejects the hypothesis that this error manifests the same prejudices that make the relevant groups' treatment suspect, the usage is incorrect and misleading.

B. Intentional Misuses and Stipulative Definitions

(1) "Discrimination" and Its Various Cognates

The word "discriminate" has two senses. First, we say that someone "discriminates" in the neutral or positive sense of the word when he discerns and responds appropriately to differences that are present and merit a differentiated response. In this sense, a gourmet or wine expert is said to have a "discriminating" palate. Second, we say that someone "discriminates" in a pejorative sense when he differentiates his evaluation or treatment of someone else inappropriately—for example, because he believes inappropriately that a victim of this discrimination deserves less respect and concern. In the context of Constitutional-law "equal protection" cases, the type of discrimination that is Constitutionally forbidden is discrimination in the pejorative sense. Despite this fact, many academic Constitutional-law experts, judges, and legislators use the word "discriminate" in this context in a bivalent sense that covers both pejorative and non-pejorative usages of the term. Thus, Dean Paul Brest of Stanford explicitly defines his "antidiscrimination principle" to "mean the general principle disfavoring classifications and other decisions and practices that depend on the race (or ethnic origin) of the parties affected,"[88] and Brest and Sanford Levinson continue the usage in question in their superb textbook by adopting the standard practice of characterizing affirmative-action programs as involving "reverse discrimination."[89] Similarly, the Supreme Court uses the terms "discriminate," "discrimination," and "discriminatory" in this bivalent sense (so that in "equal protection" cases the justices occasionally write of "discrimination" that is "not invidious"[90] and often add the word "invidious" to indicate that the discrimination to which they are referring involves unjustified, insulting differentiation[91]—that is, the Court finds it necessary to use an adjective that should be redundant). And again, when drafting legislation, Congress sometimes explicitly uses the words "discrimination" and "discriminate" in the bivalent sense[92] and sometimes in a way that leaves its denotation and connotation uncertain.[93]

Brest and Levinson attempt to justify this non-conventional, bivalent usage of the word "discrimination" and its cognates in two ways: (1) by arguing that in our culture "race-dependent decisions that are rational and purport to be based solely on legitimate considerations are likely in fact to rest on assumptions of differential worth of social groups or on the related phenomenon of socially selective sympathy and indifference"[94]—Constitutionally-critical realities (they seem implicitly to be suggesting) that are hard to verify in individual cases—and (2) by arguing that prohibitions of non-prejudiced race-dependent decisions that disfavor a racial, ethnic, or gender group make good policy sense because of the tendency of such decisions (like the tendency of the automatic-male-preference policy in *Reed v. Reed*) to discourage members of the disfavored group from improving their skills.[95]

I do not think that either of these arguments justifies the bivalent use of the word "discriminate." The first argument is relevant but, in the end, unpersuasive. Although legislatures often promulgate overinclusive prohibitions and courts sometimes interpret statutes overinclusively when they think that the transaction-cost and error-prevention benefits of doing so outweigh the error-causing costs of proceeding in this way, it is not appropriate for courts to employ an overinclusive Constitutional doctrine for such reasons. In effect, the use of the bivalent antidiscrimination principle attributes improper motives to government actors on the basis of not-implausible but still armchair-empirical assumptions about the way in which our society has dealt with and will continue to deal with minorities. Such an attribution is inconsistent not only with the Supreme Court's normal approach to motive-analysis in "judicial review" cases but also with its general practice in relation to (and my analysis of) the appropriate degree of deference for it to show government decisionmakers whose choices it is subjecting to judicial review.

Although Brest and Levinson's second argument for their usage of the word "discriminate" seems more than plausible to me and might provide a sound (personal-ultimate-value-related) policy-reason for prohibiting private employers from making non-prejudice-based race-dependent decisions disfavoring a racial minority, it does not justify a conclusion that a state violates "equal protection" when it makes such a race-dependent decision or, if one accepts my argument against the State Action doctrine, when it fails to prohibit private actors from making such decisions.

In any event, even if I were persuaded by Brest and Levinson's arguments, they would justify using a bivalent anti-racial-*classification* principle, not an anti-*discrimination* principle: even though the anti-racial-classification principle is designed to prevent racial discrimination properly so called, it would be less misleading to give it a clearly bivalent label rather than a label that makes it appear to condemn choices all of which are illegitimate. At a minimum, such labeling would avoid the confusion generated by the following kind of sentence:

> The distinction between race-dependent decisions or de jure discrimination on the one hand and de facto discrimination or disproportionate impact on the other is a conventional one and provides a common terminology for discussing constitutional doctrines involving race.[96]

(2) "Segregation"

Properly used, "segregation" is a pejorative term that refers to separation or isolation of a race, ethnic group, or similar class for discriminatory reasons. However, the courts and their company have used the term in a bivalent sense to refer to any "separation" of races, ethnic groups, or similar classes. Since segregation properly so called can result from purposive, discriminatory acts by private parties as well as from State acts, the expression "*de jure* segregation" is not redundant and the expression "*de facto* segregation" is not an oxymoron. However, the distinction between the two types of segregation the preceding sentence distinguished is not the linguistic distinction between "segregation" and "separation" the courts seem to have in mind when differentiating *de jure* and *de facto* "segregation": "The differentiating factor between de jure segregation and so-called de facto segregation . . . is purpose or intent to segregate."[97] If this were the relevant distinction, "*de jure* segregation" would contain a redundancy and "*de facto* segregation" would be an oxymoron. Admittedly, the preceding quotation could be redeemed if its author intended the word "State" to appear before "purpose or intent." Of course, my conclusions that in our culture the State (1) has almost always been complicitous in the private, discriminatory acts that caused segregation, (2) is obligated to combat private discrimination in which the private actor has no right to engage, and (3) cannot usually separate itself from its citizens in any event when the issue is the State's responsibility for their behaviors imply that such a reconstructed distinction should play no role in Constitutional analysis.[98] In sum, the failure of the courts[99] and various Constitutional commentators[100] to distinguish the term "segregation" from the expression "mere separation" does seem to me to have caused unnecessary confusion and, once more, to have biased discussions about the Constitutionality of State choices that lead to separation in favor of the conclusion that those choices are unconstitutional.[101]

(3) "Racially Motivated"

A number of academics with whom I have discussed race-treatment-related "equal protection" issues as well as Brest and Levinson have used the phrase "racially motivated" to describe both those race-conscious choices that are discriminatorily insulting and those that are not.[102] It seems to me that the expression "racially motivated" should not be used in such a neutral or bivalent sense—that in normal use it implies that the motive in question is discriminatory, just as the expression "influenced by racial considerations"[103] implies such discriminatory motivation. In general, the expression "race-conscious" should be used whenever the speaker wants to express no opinion about the legitimacy of the choice in question. I should note that the Supreme Court's usage of these expressions has been far more careful and far less confusing. Thus, the Court seems always to use the terms "race-conscious" or "racial classification" when it does not want to imply that discrimination properly so called has taken place[104] while using such expressions as "racially discriminatory motivation,"[105] "racially discriminatory purpose,"[106] and "invidious discriminatory purpose"[107] in conjunction with choices it believes are discriminatory.

(4) "(Racially) Disproportionate Impact" and "(Racial) Imbalance"

The Court[108] and virtually all commentators[109] use the expression "disproportionate impact" in a neutral or bivalent sense to indicate that a choice (say, the use of an employment criterion or test) has disadvantaged a group whose treatment is suspect relative to its impact on others, regardless of whether the disparate impact in question was discriminatory (properly so called) or legitimate. Similarly, the Court and virtually all commentators use the word "imbalance"[110] or the expression "racial imbalance" to indicate that the percentage of the members of a purportedly or functionally non-racial group (residents of a neighborhood, members of a student body, workers for a particular employer or in a particular type of job) that belongs to the group whose treatment is suspect is lower than the percentage of the latter group in the pool of people from which the former group was drawn (residents in a larger geographical area, residents in a school district, members of a sloppily-defined relevant labor pool), regardless of whether differences in (say) the racial composition of the purportedly non-racial groups reflected discrimination or the operation of other factors whose presence was not delegitimating (differences in wealth [which can have disparate effects on the racial composition of neighborhoods], the combination of a "neighborhood school" policy and neighborhoods with disparate racial compositions that reflect legitimate inter-racial wealth-differences, or inter-racial [inter-ethnic or inter-gender] differences in "bona fide occupational qualifications"). The now-standard judicial and academic use of the words "disproportionate" in "equal protection" contexts is inaccurate, confusing, and misleading because the word "disproportionate" has a pejorative connotation. I also think that the use of the word "imbalance" is misleading for the same reason, though one might argue that the use of the word "imbalance" in this context accurately expresses the fact that the differences in question are regrettable even if they do not reflect any culpable behavior.

Like the other usages discussed above, these usages bias the analyses in which they are employed—they set things up in a way that implies the illegitimacy of the conditions to which they refer (imply that these conditions reflect discrimination toward the "under-represented" groups). As the Court and its company are perfectly aware, these biases could be avoided if the expression "disparate impact"[111] or the expression "racially disparate or differentiated impact"[112] were substituted for the expression "disproportionate impact." The substitution of the expression "racially differentiated pattern" for "racial imbalance" would yield the same benefits.

This section has suggested that, at least in the equal-protection area, legal writing has sometimes been sloppy and often been duplicitous. The lawyers' misuse of language has made it more difficult to execute proper moral and legal analyses of the issues that have confronted the Court. There is a real chance that the efforts of the lawyers to secure correct liberal legal outcomes by initiating or supporting these misuses may have backfired. By confusing the moral discussions, they have made it easier for those not so committed to liberal principles to reach incorrect conclusions about various moral issues (e.g., about the morality and Constitutionality of affirmative action). If this is true, lawyers' writing is not only duplicitous and confusing but too clever by half.

Conclusion

This chapter has analyzed a liberal State's duty of appropriate, equal respect, the conclusions the courts have reached in many duty-of-respect cases, and the opinions they have written in those cases. The correct legal analysis of all duty-of-respect issues is inseparable from the correct moral–rights analysis of these issues. Legal analyses of duty-of-respect issues that ignore their moral point are illegitimate and generate wrong conclusions and unpersuasive arguments. Courts that are influenced by prudential considerations and lawyers who misuse language in the hope of securing rights or furthering legitimate personal ultimate values do our society a great disservice. Illegitimate judicial decisionmaking is costly in itself and generally does not yield the benefits that those who engage in it or encourage it hope to secure.

4

The Duty of Appropriate, Equal Concern

Some Constitutional-Law Implications

A liberal State is obligated to show appropriate, equal concern for all moral-rights holders for whom it is responsible—most importantly, to show such concern for their actualizing their potential to become and remain individuals of moral integrity. This obligation has two basic implications. First, a liberal State has a duty to take all appropriate steps to enable such moral-rights holders to make meaningful choices about whether to fulfill their obligations, which personal ultimate values to support, and how—given their obligations, rights, values, tastes, talents, and opportunities—to lead their lives. Second, a liberal State has a duty to allow these moral-rights holders to commit those acts and engage in those activities that contribute substantially to their self-realization either (1) by helping them to discover what they value and/or how they can best effectuate their values or (2) by effectuating the values they have chosen.

It is important to emphasize at the outset that the rights that are corollaries of these duties are qualified in important ways. A liberal State does not have to allow those moral-rights holders for whom it is responsible to commit acts that sacrifice weightier rights-related interests of others. Nor does it have to give a value-neutral account of illiberal values or to allow individuals to make choices that do not violate the rights of others but do significantly militate against the chooser's being able to exercise autonomy in the future. In addition, a liberal society's commitment to the second-order goal of meaningful choice may also obligate it to prohibit people from (autonomously?) choosing to surrender their autonomy.[1]

This chapter contains seven sections. The first discusses a variety of concrete implications of a liberal State's duty to put all moral-rights holders for whom it is responsible into a position to lead lives of moral integrity. The second focuses on the liberty rights of the moral-rights holders for whom a liberal State is responsible: in particular, it analyzes the correct standard in a liberal society for determining whether a moral-rights holder has a liberty interest in committing particular acts or engaging in particular activities and comments on the legitimacy of various alleged justifications for a liberal State's restricting liberty properly so called. Section 3 describes and criticizes our current doctrinal approach to the duty of our liberal State to put those moral-rights holders for whom it is responsible in a position to become individuals of moral integrity. Section 4 describes the general doctrinal approach the Supreme Court has taken to liberty issues and outlines and criticizes the arguments it has used and the conclusions it has reached on the Constitutionality of government-imposed restrictions on four sets of concrete liberties: sexual liberty; the right to marry, divorce, and live together; the right to create children and the right to parent children one has created or adopted; and the liberty to make some choices that endanger or surrender the chooser's autonomy. Next, Section 5 analyzes the right to accelerate one's death and comments on various aspects of both Ronald Dworkin's[2] and the Supreme Court's analyses of this issue. Section 6 criticizes Judith Jarvis Thomson's analysis of the moral right of a woman to abort her pregnancy; delineates the liberal analysis of a variety of abortion-related issues;[3] analyzes the abortion-related Constitutional-law arguments of two lawyer-philosophers, Donald Regan[4] and Ronald Dworkin;[5] and examines and criticizes the Supreme Court's analysis of various abortion-related Constitutional rights. Finally, Section 7 returns to my "writing like a lawyer" theme and delineates some examples in which the Supreme Court, particular Supreme Court Justices, or a variety of other judges have "persuasively defined" concepts that are highly relevant to the analysis of various privacy and liberty issues—that is, they have given these concepts non-standard, implicit definitions in the hope of persuading their audience to accept their conclusions.

Two introductory tasks remain. First, a warning must be given—one that is designed to protect the author as much as his readers. Although Section 5's analysis of abortion is detailed, many of this chapter's other concrete-moral-right analyses are far less thorough. The point of these sketchy analyses is to suggest the basic implications of liberalism for the proper approach to take to the issues in question, not to analyze them totally, much less to resolve them definitively.

Second, two admissions and demurrers must be made. Admittedly, the approach that I think our liberal commitments require us to take to particular liberty issues will often generate contestable conclusions, and, in many of the cases in which the conclusion liberalism requires is not contestable, it is also not surprising. I demur to these two admissions. Since the liberal answer to a large number of moral-rights questions turns on difficult, debatable issues, and since the arguments that are relevant to the resolution of many moral-rights questions from a liberal perspective are almost in equipoise, an account of our liberal commitments that suggests that clear right answers to all moral-rights questions can be easily generated is unlikely to be correct. The persuasiveness of my account of our society's moral commitments is also not undermined by its generating unsurprising answers to many moral-rights questions, answers that are consistent with our society's consensus views on these issues: after all, my claim that our society is a liberal, rights-based society is partly based on a criterion of fit.

The preceding two admissions also do not suggest that my account of our rights practices will not help us deal with specific cases. Although this account will not yield clear or radically-different conclusions to many moral-rights and Constitutional-rights questions, it will sometimes yield surprising results (since, like any society, ours sometimes fails to live up to its commitments) and at other times will generate alternative, illuminating, and persuasive justifications for rights-conclusions that we have already reached but could not satisfactorily explain.

1. A Liberal State's Duty to Put Moral-Rights Holders in a Position to Exercise Autonomous Choice and Lead Lives of Moral Integrity

Liberal States have a duty to put the moral-rights holders for whom they are responsible in a position to become and remain individuals of moral integrity. This obligation implies that a liberal State must supply the mothers of all foetuses who have the prerequisites to become moral-rights holders with the prenatal care, nutritional and other advice, and resources that will protect the development of their foetuses and must enact and enforce criminal and civil laws to deter pregnant women and others from endangering the development of such foetuses.[6]

A liberal State also has a duty to provide the material support to children that will enable them to develop into individuals of moral integrity. In part, this support is conventionally economic, and in part, it is educational. Children must be taught to think critically and must be given the information they need to make meaningful choices. *inter alia*, to help children become individuals of moral integrity, the State must provide them with information about (1) liberal norms and our society's commitment to them, (2) alternative personal ultimate values, and (3) various secular and religious ways of trying to instantiate a good life. A liberal State is also obligated to give its children a variety of personal and vicarious experiences (*inter alia*, an opportunity to "observe" real or fictional people who are committed to different kinds of values and/or are living different sorts of lives).

Perhaps hardest of all, a liberal State must try to instill in its children the independence of mind that will help them make up their own minds about what they value and how they want to lead their lives. This duty will be more important and more difficult to execute satisfactorily when the children's parents are not liberal, especially when the children's parents belong to an illiberal sub-community.

The amount of resources that must be devoted to all these tasks will vary from child to child. More resources will have to be allocated for this purpose to educating children who are mentally handicapped, blind, deaf, and so forth, but who still have the neurological prerequisites to become individuals of moral integrity.

I realize how unpalatable many people will find these conclusions. Some will be opposed to its curricular implications—for example, to its implications for the way in which a liberal State must teach the "gender is destiny" issue, discuss alternative religions and religious ways of life, and analyze such morally- and religiously-controversial issues as homosexuality. Many will be even more opposed to its implications that a liberal State may be obligated to require children to attend State schools for a certain number of hours per day as opposed to attending no school at all (studying at home) or studying exclusively at a private (religious or secular) school that restricts their horizons in various ways. I do not think that in a liberal society such policies would violate the religious freedom of the children or the liberty-rights of their parents. In a liberal society, religious freedom does not entail a right to avoid the information and experiences that are necessary for making meaningful religious choices, and the religious and parental rights of parents do not include the right to control the religious choices of their children by precluding them from having the information, experiences, and intellectual and psychological capacities that will enable them to make meaningful religious choices.

Of course, when dealing with sensitive issues of this kind, a liberal State must take into consideration the possibility that what would otherwise be a correct conclusion would end up disserving the rights-related interests of the children who are its supposed beneficiaries because (1) children are most likely to develop into individuals of moral integrity in a nuclear family in which the parents have the authority that comes with their children's respect and (2) State instruction in and for liberalism may undermine the authority of parents who do not try to foster the autonomy of their children in certain important areas of decisionmaking by undermining the respect in which such parents are held by their children.

A liberal State must also provide its adult moral-rights holders with at least the opportunity to have the absolute and relative amount of material resources that contributes significantly (in our materialistic culture) to their developing self-respect and that are a prerequisite to their having an opportunity to make meaningful choices about how they want to live their lives. This duty has implications not only for the material support of healthy adults but also for the medical resources that must be made available to those who are at risk of dying or deteriorating to the point that they lose their moral-rights-holder status. (Obviously, the arguments of this paragraph will be strengthened to the extent that a liberal State is also obligated to be concerned for the utilitarian welfare of the moral-rights holders for which it is responsible—that is, *ceteris paribus,* to place the same weight on each unit of utility each such creature obtains for reasons that liberalism can countenance.)

In addition, a liberal State's duty to put the moral-rights holders for which it is responsible in a position to become individuals of moral integrity implies that it may not violate such individuals' privacy. Privacy has three elements: secrecy, anonymity, and solitude.[7] Privacy is highly valued in a liberal society because, in a number of ways, it enables individuals to discover who they are morally (what they value) and facilitates their deciding what kind of life will enable them to instantiate their values. Thus, secrecy promotes integrity because it reduces the cost to people of experimenting with alternative values and alternative ways of living their lives. Secrecy also contributes to individuals' leading lives of moral integrity because by enabling us to be trustworthy and to reveal ourselves selectively to others it facilitates our entering into the kinds of intimate relationships that foster integrity by increasing their participants' self-respect and enabling them to discover themselves. Anonymity promotes integrity both by enabling people to discover their moral identities by behaving in a less self-conscious way and by preserving secrecy. And solitude promotes integrity by facilitating the relevant individual's contemplating how he wants to live his life. In any event, for these reasons, a liberal State's duty to put people in a position to become individuals of moral integrity obligates it not to violate their privacy.[8]

A liberal State also has a *prima facie* integrity-related duty not to prohibit or work against individuals' forming the kinds of intimate relationships that help people live lives of moral integrity by contributing to their self-respect and self-discovery. Given the link between sexual and other types of intimacy—it is not by chance that the Bible speaks of a man's "knowing" a woman and vice versa—this duty has implications for the permissibility of a liberal State's criminalizing homosexual sex, non-married sexual intercourse, and various types of sodomy both inside and outside marriage.

The preceding analyses imply that a liberal State has a related duty to enact and enforce criminal and civil laws to prevent private actors from invading the privacy, hindering the intimate relations, undermining the autonomy, or endangering the life or mental functioning (moral-rights-holder status) of the moral-rights holders for whom it is responsible. In some cases, this duty may also obligate a liberal State to override parental wishes for and control of their children.

In addition, liberal States may have obligations to prohibit acts, activities, or relationships that preclude or militate against individuals' continuing to exercise autonomy. This possibility raises the paradoxical question of whether one can be said to be fostering autonomy by precluding individuals from autonomously choosing to surrender their autonomy or to engage in activities or enter into relationships that endanger their autonomy—for example, by committing suicide, taking addictive drugs, joining authoritarian religious or secular cults (that engage in so-called "brain-washing" or "thought control"), or entering into other types of relationships that tend to endanger autonomy (the relationship between prostitutes and their pimps or the very different relationship between the participants in an abusive marriage). I do not deny the contestability of all these issues even from a liberal perspective. In part, that contestability reflects the availability to the State of arguably-less-restrictive means of protecting autonomy (e.g., distributing addictive drugs for free). In part, it reflects the difficulty of anyone's, much less the State's, accurately resolving various salient "empirical" or "characterization" issues: Are polygamous marriages more authoritarian than the alternative relationships in which polygamous-marriage partners would otherwise participate? Do the practices of a particular secular or religious cult amount to "brain-washing" or "thought-control" (do such cults overbear the will of their members)? In part, it also reflects the difficulty of other sorts of relevant conceptual issues: Can an individual's choice to commit suicide enhance the integrity of her life. My goal is not to resolve these issues but to indicate how their analysis should be structured in a liberal society.

Finally, a liberal society may be obligated to prohibit certain types of activities that militate against some non-participating moral-rights holders' taking their lives morally seriously by encouraging private acts and attitudes that endanger these parties' autonomy. It has been argued that a liberal State may be obligated to prohibit certain types of pornography on this account. However, this proposal is disfavored not only by the difficulty of defining and identifying the relevant types of pornography but also by the fact that reading or viewing pornography may provide a safety-valve for some that deters them from engaging in rights-violating behavior (though it may have the opposite effect on others) and/or enables them to participate in the kind of intimate relationships that liberals value (because they help their participants both to discover what they value and to instantiate their value-choices).

Obviously, the conclusions this section has reached on many specific issues do not fit our State's and culture's actual practices in relation to these issues. This fact does not surprise me. Societies whose general conduct manifests their commitment to particular principles often fail to follow these principles in particular classes of situations. Although our society has increasingly fulfilled its liberal commitments over time, it has a long way to go. From my scholarly perspective, this reality has the advantage of making my conclusions about moral-rights analysis far less conservative than they otherwise would be.

2. *Liberty Rights in a Liberal Society*

This section analyzes two general questions: (A) How should "liberty" be defined for use in moral-rights discourse in a liberal State? and (B) What kinds of justifications must a liberal State offer to legitimate its restricting liberty properly so called?

A. Defining "Liberty" for Use in Liberal Moral-Rights Discourse

To be useful in moral-rights discourse, the concept of liberty must be defined to make liberty rights or liberty-rights-related interests function in the same way that other types of rights and rights-related interests function in our moral discourse. In other words, liberty must be defined so that restrictions in liberty cannot be justicized by their furthering some personal-ultimate-value-related goal or social ideal (so that restrictions in liberty can be justicized only if they secure weightier rights-related interests). In my opinion, one does not have to stipulate a definition of liberty to achieve this outcome. Indeed, the fact that "liberty" is used in this way in ordinary language confirms my hypothesis that our society is rights-based.

Unfortunately, many academic commentators have implicitly defined "liberty" in ways that neither correspond to the way in which the concept is employed in ordinary language nor yield a concept of liberty that can perform a significant role in rights discourse. Thus, some scholars have defined liberty-rights in a utilitarian fashion.[9] In this usage, a policy impermissibly restricts liberty if it reduces total utility; it restricts liberty permissibly if the restriction increases total utility (presumably in comparison with the alternative that is next best from a utilitarian perspective). Obviously, since this usage implies that a restriction of liberty that liberals would find problematic would be justicized by its furthering the utilitarian goal, its use is inconsistent with our liberal commitments or, indeed, with our being a rights-based society in my sense.

Many economists define liberty even more expansively. In this "economic" usage, an individual is said to have a liberty interest in making any choice for any reason. Correlatively, any restriction in the "opportunity set" available to any individual is said to be a restriction in her liberty.[10] This "billiard ball" concept of liberty is both illiberal and inconsistent with ordinary usage. To see why it is illiberal, note that it leads to the conclusion that someone can have a liberty interest in sticking a knife into another human being who was not threatening the attacker. To see why this usage is non-standard, note that we would not say that a law prohibiting someone from making this kind of attack restricted his liberty. Nor (for that matter) would we say that an individual has a liberty interest in driving north on a street that is one-way southbound. Clearly, if the concept of liberty is defined in this "restriction of opportunity set" way, it cannot play an important role in moral-rights discourse because the government needs no special justification for restricting individuals' liberty in this billiard-ball sense—for prohibiting people from committing many acts or engaging in many activities that would be said to restrict their liberty in the billiard-ball sense of that term.

Other analysts define the concept of liberty more restrictively by stipulating that acts or activities involve liberty interests if and only if they are important for the "mental health" of the relevant actors—contribute to their becoming or remaining "psychologically whole." Although this usage comes closer to our linguistic practice, it wrongly presupposes a value-free notion of "mental health" and "psychological wholeness."

John Stuart Mill's definition of liberty comes closest[11] to capturing the way in which our liberal society defines this concept in use. Mill distinguishes between "self-regarding" and "other-regarding" behavior and argues that we have liberty-rights in engaging in self-regarding conduct. Although Mill's distinction is often assumed to turn on whether the conduct in question produces external effects on others, I believe that it actually relates to the extent to which the conduct in question expresses or establishes the actor's personality. According to Mill, then, individuals have liberty interests in engaging in those kinds of conduct and activities that express or contribute to the formation of their personal identities.

In my judgment, the correct definition of "liberty" in a liberal society is a refinement or clarification of Mill's definition, a refinement that clarifies the sense in which "personality" or "personal identity" (my terms, not Mill's) are used in the preceding paragraph. In liberal societies, moral-rights holders should be said to have liberty interests in engaging in those acts or activities that contribute significantly to their discovering what they value and/or leading a life that instantiates a value choice that they have made that is consistent with liberal tenets. In this usage, an individual would usually not have a liberty interest in driving north on a one-way southbound street because this act would not contribute to his discovering or actualizing his moral identity. Nor would a person have a liberty interest in sticking a knife into a non-threatening moral-rights holder since such an act would not contribute to his making or instantiating a value-choice that is consistent with liberalism.

B. Justicizing Liberty Restrictions in a Liberal State

For a liberal State's restriction of liberty to be justicized, the rights-related interests it secures must be weightier than the rights-related interests it sacrifices. Unfortunately, this reiteration of the balance-of-rights-related-interests standard does not clarify the justificatory relevance of various gains that restrictions of liberty can generate—it does not help us determine whether members of a liberal society are entitled to have these benefits count as (legitimate) interests secured. The remainder of this section will comment on the justificatory status of twelve types of benefits whose relevance is contestable.

First, in some cases, attempts have been made to justicize restrictions of liberty (say, the criminalization of homosexuality) by arguing that they are necessary to preserve values or institutions (say, heterosexual marriage and conventional families) that enjoy consensus approval. Indeed, supporters of this argument often (1) claim that their society has defined itself in terms of these values and institutions, (2) analogize behavior that is inconsistent with such values to treason, and (3) analogize the right of a society to prohibit such conduct to the right of a society to prohibit treason.[12] This argument is not acceptable in liberal societies, which define themselves in terms of their not having an official position on first-order (personal ultimate) values. In liberal societies, people do not have an obligation to support particular personal ultimate values or related social institutions. All values and institutions may be criticized and rejected. Indeed, even the moral attractiveness of being a rights-based society or a liberal rights-based society may be questioned, though a liberal State is obligated to prohibit moral-rights violations, *ceteris paribus.*

Second, and relatedly, in a liberal society, the State may not justicize restricting someone's liberty by arguing that doing so will promote the survival of particular personal ultimate values, religions or religious beliefs, or communities. Even though the survival of such values, beliefs, and communities may benefit their adherents or members as well as others who enjoy living in a diverse society and even though it may on this account be permissible for a liberal State to subsidize such beliefs or communities monetarily and in other ways, such a State may not promote their survival by restricting the information or experiences available to minor or adult members of such communities and must prohibit others (such as the minors' parents) from doing so as well. It may be that you cannot keep them down on the farm after they've seen Paris, but the State may not itself prohibit such people's travels or allow others to do so on this account.

Third, a liberal State may not restrict an individual's liberty because others regard the behavior in which the actor wants to engage as sinful so long as the behavior does not violate anyone's moral rights. The duty of respect that each member of a liberal society owes fellow members precludes us from forcing others to act in the way that our religious beliefs or personal ultimate values command so long as their behavior does not violate anyone's moral rights. The disutility or disgust some will experience if they observe behavior that is sinful or immoral from their personal perspective or know that someone is behaving in such a manner cannot justicize prohibiting the conduct in question. Such bootstrap arguments fail in a liberal society because, so long as I am not violating anyone's rights, my conduct is "none of your business" and "no concern of yours" in the entitlement sense of those expressions.

The fourth supposed justification for restricting liberty that requires some comment is the need to prevent the "harm" or "offense" the conduct in question might cause others. Attempts have sometimes been made to distinguish between harm and offense in this context: the prevention of harm but not the prevention of offense is said to justicize restricting liberty.[13] I have never found this distinction helpful. It seems to me that the crucial issue in many of the cases in which this distinction has been employed is not the severity of the loss but its etiology. Assume that neighbors of a synagogue want to restrict the blowing of the shofar on the Jewish New Year, supposedly because the sound hurts their ears, or that neighbors of a Catholic church or a Hindu temple want to restrict the use of incense because they claim they find the smell noisome. Even if the interest of such neighbors would otherwise suffice to warrant restricting the religious practices in question (perhaps by requiring sound insulation or closed windows), that conclusion would be undermined if the neighbors' reactions to the sounds or smells were not straightforwardly physical but reflected their distaste for Judaism and Jews, Catholicism and Catholics, and Hinduism and Hindus. Of course, in practice, it will be difficult to tell whether prejudice played a critical role in these reactions, but in some instances it may be possible to prove that the neighbors' reactions reflected their lack of proper respect for those they want to restrain.

Fifth, in some circumstances, individuals have asserted that their privacy interests justify restricting the liberty of others. This position may be justified when the behavior in question generates noise or smells that seriously undermine one or more moral-rights holders' solitude (prevent "quiet enjoyment"). However, there are other circumstances in which the justificatory power of the asserted privacy interests are more questionable. For example, some people would like to restrict the ability of others to wear revealing clothing or no clothing at all *inter alia* because if they observe such scantily-clad or unclad individuals their interest or reaction will reveal things about themselves to others that they wish to keep private. I do not think that in a liberal society people have a right to control others for this reason.

Sixth, it is sometimes claimed that our State can legitimately restrict the behavior of particular individuals to prevent others from being characterized in ways that are costly to them. For example, some people may want to prohibit nude bathing or the wearing of revealing clothing because they do not want to be characterized as prudes for not engaging in such conduct. The liberal duty of respect seems to me to be inconsistent with this desire's being given any justificatory role.

Seventh, some people assert that a liberal State is entitled to restrict the liberty of some to protect others from competition. In the economic sphere, workers who do not want to work long hours may support maximum-hour legislation to protect themselves against competition from others (in the *Lochner* era, greenhorns) who are willing to work longer hours. In the personal sphere, men or women who do not want to participate in sexual activities as early in a relationship as others are pleased to do may support prohibitions of non-marital sexual intercourse to prevent themselves from being placed at a competitive disadvantage. Once more, I do not think that restrictions of liberty can be justified with this type of anti-competitive argument in a liberal society.

Eighth, restrictions on liberty are sometimes said to be justicized by their tendency to create a social milieu that helps someone live the life he wishes to lead. For example, those who want to live a life of the mind as opposed to the senses may wish to restrict the dress and deportment of others, the showing of titillating films, or the publication of titillating literature to protect themselves from temptation. In my judgment, a decision to give this argument any weight would violate a liberal State's duty of respect by treating those whose liberty was restricted as means rather than as ends.

The same conclusion is warranted in relation to a ninth argument, which is a variant of its predecessor—the argument of a parent who wishes to constrain the behavior of another to create a social milieu that would increase her ability to educate her child to lead the kind of life the parent most values. In this case, the parent's position might also be weakened by her child's rights-related interest in learning about personal ultimate values and ways of living that the child's parents consider to be inferior.

This ninth contestable, asserted justification for restricting liberty is related to a tenth—the argument that a parent has a right to restrict his child's liberty and to enlist the State's efforts in doing so to increase the probability that the child will end up subscribing to the parent's values and leading the kind of life of which the parent approves. This argument is also unacceptable in a liberal society. Parents have no more right than the State or anyone else to treat their children as means rather than as ends. Although the parents who make this tenth argument would contest this characterization, in a liberal society in which meaningful choice is valued more than what is chosen, the desire of parents to control their children's choices is inconsistent with the duty they (like everyone else) have to respect their children.

The eleventh set of arguments that require discussion relates to restrictions of liberty imposed through criminal-justice sentences. Such restrictions of liberty are usually said to be justicized by their ability to generate general deterrence (to deter everyone from committing crimes), to provide specific deterrence (to deter the convicted criminal by removing him from the community), to further retributive goals, and (if this is different) to right the moral order. Which of these supposed justifications for restricting the liberty of convicted criminals is compatible with liberalism? To the extent that retributive and "right the moral order" justifications reflect the principle that a criminal should pay for the wrong he committed, they are consistent with liberalism in that they treat the criminal with respect by holding him responsible for his actions. I also find the specific-deterrent rationale for restricting the liberty of convicted criminals consistent with liberal norms (though, from a liberal perspective, the way in which we treat criminals when they are incarcerated is highly problematic). On the other hand, I doubt that one can justicize increasing the unpleasantness or length of a criminal's sentence by citing the general-deterrence advantages of doing so: incarcerating someone for general-deterrence purposes seems to me to be treating him as a means, not as an end, and I do not think that such treatment can be justicized by arguing that the State has informed people in advance that they may be treated in this way if they are convicted of a criminal offense.

The twelfth and final ground for restricting liberty that requires some consideration is paternalism—the view that the State knows what is in an individual's interest better than the individual does herself (perhaps because her will is being overborne). Three different kinds of choices must be distinguished in this context: choices that affect the capacity of an individual to lead a life of moral integrity (choices to take addictive drugs, to join illiberal cults or religions that try to curtail her autonomy, or [at least in some cases] to commit suicide), choices about the personal ultimate values the individual wants her life to instantiate, and choices about the best way to instantiate a particular personal-ultimate-value choice. Regardless of whether a government decision to prevent someone from precluding herself from leading a life of moral integrity can properly be described as being paternalistic, a liberal State has a duty to prevent people from incapacitating themselves in this respect. By way of contrast, a liberal State may not override an individual's personal-ultimate-value choice so long as the "value" she chooses is not incompatible with liberalism. The debatable issue is whether or when it is legitimate for a liberal State to override an individual's means-end choice about the best way for her to instantiate the value-choices she has made. The case for such State interventions is disfavored not only by the possibility of State misuse of any such power and the general advantage of placing decisionmaking power in the hands of those with better access to the relevant information but also by the fact that our society is committed to valuing an individual's attempting to instantiate her values as much as (or perhaps rather than) her succeeding in instantiating her values.

3. The Duty to Put Moral-Rights Holders in a Position to Lead Lives of Moral Integrity: Constitutional-Law Doctrine

A. The General Position

Current Constitutional-law doctrine rejects the claim that our State has positive obligations to put the moral-rights holders for whom it is responsible into a position to live lives of moral integrity. The basic position is that the Constitution "generally confer[s] no right to governmental aid, even where such aid may be necessary to secure life, liberty, or property interests of which the government itself may not deprive the individual."[14] "As a general matter, a State is under no constitutional duty to provide substantive services for those within its borders."[15] This conclusion is a generalization of the State Action doctrine, which has already been discussed—a doctrine that rests on the dubious distinction between action and inaction (misfeasance and non-feasance), assumes incorrectly that our society does not impose "Good Samaritan" moral duties on its moral-rights holders, and ignores the fact that in many situations the State's position would lead many who claim that there is no general duty to rescue to conclude that the State did have a duty to provide aid.

This basic doctrinal position does have one qualification, whose content is somewhat contested. The majority of the Supreme Court in *Deshaney v. Winnebago County Department of Social Services* expressed this qualification in the following terms: "when the State by the affirmative exercise of its power so restrains an individual's liberty that it renders him unable to care for himself," it incurs a duty "to provide for his basic human needs—*e.g.*, food, clothing, shelter, medical care, and reasonable safety."[16] According to the dissent in *Deshaney*, the relevant qualification is that the State has an obligation to render someone assistance whenever its preceding conduct "separated him from other sources of aid."[17] Both these statements of the relevant qualification capture elements of standard duty-to-rescue analysis—the conclusions that even if there is no general duty to rescue, a duty to rescue does exist both for individuals who have put others at risk (whether culpably or not) and for individuals who have initiated a rescue attempt (in part because in so doing they have discouraged others from providing assistance).

Clearly, however, even if this qualification is given the most expansive interpretation possible, it would not yield as general a duty to aid as I believe a liberal State bears. Moreover, even when the qualification does create a duty of the State to aid, it does not relate that duty to any responsibility to put moral-rights holders in a position to lead lives of moral integrity.

I have already explained why the State Action doctrine is indefensible and why liberal States have positive (as well as negative) duties to put their moral-rights holders into a position to lead lives of moral integrity. The Supreme Court's discussion of these issues has assumed that the relevant textual provisions of the Constitution are the "due process" clauses of the Fifth and Fourteenth Amendments. I would give the correlative rights of the relevant moral-rights holders a different set of textual homes—the Ninth Amendment's reference to "[un]enumerated rights" when the government in question is the central government and the Fourteenth Amendment's "privileges or immunities" clause when the relevant government is a state.

B. Two Related Concrete Rights: Privacy and Educational Rights

(1) Privacy

This section will not attempt to survey those of our Constitutional-law doctrines that relate to privacy—the doctrines that constrain the government's invasion of privacy by quartering troops in people's homes, executing searches and seizures, extracting confessions, using evidence illegally seized by private actors, or (to a minor extent—see Section 6) forbidding women to have abortions. Nor will it attempt to provide a survey of the extent to which our private law adequately protects the privacy interests of the moral-rights holders for whom our State is responsible. Instead, it will focus on one issue that is relevant to two of this book's themes—the doctrine of privilege. According to this doctrine, even if the defendant has made a public disclosure of private facts that would be highly offensive and objectionable to a reasonable person of ordinary sensibilities, the plaintiff will not be entitled to recovery if the public has "a legitimate interest in having the information made available."[18] In particular, this section will show that this doctrine has been operationalized in a way that is impermissible in a liberal State and that the mistake the courts made may have reflected a kind of linguistic confusion that this book has frequently pointed out. In particular, this section argues that the doctrine of privilege has been misapplied to yield the conclusion that a disclosure that sacrifices someone's privacy interests can be justified by the non-rights-related "interest" of the public and that the courts may have made this error because they have conflated the various senses of the words "interest," "concern," and "public." (I say "may have" because there is no way to exclude the possibility that the judges who made the relevant decisions believed that in our society rights can be trumped by the pursuit of personal-ultimate-value-related goals and intentionally conflated the meanings of the relevant words to conceal the premise on which they were operating.)

I first discuss the various meanings of "interest," "concern," and "public" and then analyze the way in which these terms should be used and have actually been used by the courts when applying the doctrine of privilege. For my purposes, three senses[19] of the word "interest" need to be distinguished: a psychological sense, a welfare sense, and an entitlement sense. In its psychological sense, "interest" denotes a desire to pay attention to something. Psychological interest is something we "have," "show," "take," or "feel."

The second sense of the word "interest" is a welfare sense. Something is "in" or "to" my interest (or against my interests) if it is of some advantage (disadvantage) to me. "Interest" in this sense relates to events, processes, activities, or states of affairs that can affect someone's welfare. Thus, although books are not in my interest, reading may be. The difference between the psychological and welfare senses of the word "interest" is manifested by the fact that it can be either in or against one's welfare interest to take a psychological interest in someone or something.

"Interest" also has an entitlement sense—that is, the word "interest" is sometimes used to refer to the fact that its possessor is entitled to make a rights-claim in relation to the referent of the interest. Thus, we speak of controlling interests, possessory interests, and so on. It is important to note that the fact that something affects my interests (*a fortiori* the fact that something interests me in the psychological sense of the word) does not necessarily give me an interest in it in the entitlement sense. Thus, despite the fact that X may be in my interest and consequently may be of psychological interest to me, I may still not have an interest in—that is, a claim as of right in relation to— X. An example may clarify this point. Assume that individual A obtains buyer surplus by purchasing a particular product X produced by firm B. Obviously, the fact that B's decision to discontinue the production of X affects A's (welfare) interests and consequently interests him psychologically as well does not ipso facto give him an entitlement interest in relation to that decision.

In short, the existence of either or both a psychological interest and a welfare interest is not a sufficient condition for the existence of an entitlement interest. Unfortunately, this fact is obscured by ordinary language, for the expression "I have an interest in X" can mean either "I am disposed to take an interest (psychological) in X" or "I possess an interest (entitlement) in X."[20]

The word "concern" suffers from the same ambiguities as the word "interest." Like "interest," "concern" has a psychological, a welfare, and an entitlement sense.

To say that a person is concerned in the psychological sense is to say that he wants to pay attention to someone or something because he is (say) anxious about it. (The psychological sense of "concern" thus denotes both a disposition and the reason for its existence. The word "interest" does not seem to do both jobs at once.) Psychological concern is something we "feel" or "show."

The second sense of the word "concern" is its welfare sense. To say that an event or policy concerns X in the welfare sense means that it (relates to or) affects X's welfare. This sense seems to be a subtype of a more general relational sense of the word as, for example, in the expression "the book is concerned with. . . ."

The third sense of the word "concern" is the entitlement sense. It indicates that the actor who has the interest is entitled to make claims as of right in relation to the referent. Thus, when I say "X is my concern" I mean that "I am entitled to make rights-claims concerning or in relation to X."

These three senses of the word "concern" are distinct. We can be concerned (psychological) about something that does not concern us (does not relate to our welfare) and/or which is none of our concern (entitlement). For instance, imagine the following dialogue. A says to B: "I am concerned about you." B responds: "Don't be, what happens to me is none of your concern." Indeed, something that concerns us (in both the psychological and the welfare senses) can still be none of our concern. To return to our old example, if B decides to discontinue the production of X, A will very likely be concerned (psychological) about his decision, which will, in fact, concern him (relate to his welfare) directly. Still, B's choice will be "none of C's concern." In short, the fact that an act concerns an individual (in both the psychological and the welfare senses) is not a sufficient condition for its being one of that individual's concerns—it does not entitle him to make any claims in relation to that act.

The description of the doctrine of privilege that I took from *Prosser and Keeton on Torts* contained one more expression that requires elucidation—

"legitimate interest." This expression (and its cognate "legitimate concern") is particularly confusing. Although it appears to indicate that the individual in question has an entitlement interest or concern in relation to the referent, it actually means only that he has good reason to be psychologically concerned about it—in other words, that his concern is appropriate and decent, not improper or indecent. Thus, legitimate concerns should be contrasted with indecent interests and not—as it appears—equated with entitlement interests in the subject in question.

The adjective "public" is also ambiguous. It has a non-political distributive, a political-collective, and a political-conjunctive sense. In its non-political distributive sense, the adjective "public" indicates that the noun it modifies relates to all members of the community in their private capacities without distinction—that is, it relates to the whole public and not just to some segment of the public. Thus, public inns, public theaters, public houses, and public accommodations are open to all the individual members of the public without distinction. Similarly, when books are published, they are made available to any person who might be interested in purchasing them. In the same way, a man's public life is exposed to the view of each member of the public, and items of public interest (e.g., public-interest stories) are those that are likely to interest the public in general.

In its political-collective sense, the adjective "public" modifies its noun so that the expression relates to the members of a politically-organized society taken together—that is, to the "community at large" acting as a political entity. Thus, we speak of public affairs, public officials, public issues, public expenditures, public finance, public ownership, public housing, public offices, and public law. The distinction between the non-political distributive and political-collective senses of the adjective "public" would seem to be clear. Thus, for example, it makes perfectly good sense to say that a man performed his public duty in private or that a public figure was not a public official. In the same way, the meaning of the word "public" in the expression "*X* is entering into public (i.e., political) life" differs from its meaning in the phrase "*X*'s public (i.e., not private) life." However, the two senses are frequently confused, in part, no doubt, because both are often contrasted with the word "private." Thus, we contrast "public" in its distributive sense with "private" in such expressions as a man's private life, private theaters, and so on, and we contrast "private" with "public" in its political-collective sense in such phrases as private ownership and private law.

On some occasions in which we use the word "public" to refer to some aspect of a politically-organized society, the adjective has a political-conjunctive and not a political-collective meaning. Thus, although X can be publicly owned despite the fact that no individual member of the public owns any of it, the public cannot be concerned about (or interested in) X unless some individual members of the public are concerned.

Now that the various meanings of the above terms have been distinguished, it should be possible to state the version of the doctrine of privilege that would be consistent with our liberal commitments and to assess the version the courts actually have applied. In a liberal society, the public's interest in information can justify the sacrifice of someone's privacy interests by the public disclosure of private information if and only if the public in the political-collective sense has an entitlement interest in the information concerned and that interest is weightier than the privacy interest that was sacrificed by the relevant disclosure. In practice, the courts have not defined the doctrine in this way; rather, they have applied it decisively in cases in which the non-political distributive public had no more than a psychological interest in the information in question. Although the courts often say that the doctrine applies only to matters of "legitimate" public interest or concern, they hold the interest to be "legitimate" whenever the public's psychological interest does not "offend ordinary sensibilities"[21] or "violate ordinary notions of decency."[22] Within that constraint, defendants can successfully invoke the doctrine of privilege whenever the publication has that "indefinable quality that attracts public attention"—that is, when it is of psychological interest to the non-political distributive public. Indeed, even those who unwillingly attract public attention[23] through no fault of their own "are subject to the privilege which publishers have to satisfy the curiosity of the public."[24] "News for the purpose . . . [of the doctrine of privilege] comprehends no more than relatively current events such as in common experience are likely to be of public [psychological] interest. . . . [N]o distinction should be made between news for information and news for entertainment in determining whether the publication is privileged."[25] Thus, news "is privileged whenever it is . . . of general public interest." This result is often traced to a famous article by Charles Warren and Louis Brandeis, but their comments do not support the current rule. Although Louis Brandeis and Charles Warren do state that "the right to privacy does not prohibit any publication of matter which is of public or general [psychological?] interest,"[26] their examples—public officials and candidates for public office—clearly show that they intended the limitation to be restricted to matters about which the public had a right to know.[27]

I do not know whether this incorrect definition of the doctrine of priv-ilege was caused by the judges' confusing the various senses of the words "in-terest" and "concern" on the one hand and "public" on the other. The judges may have preferred to reach a conclusion that was inconsistent with liberal-ism and tried to conceal this reality by explaining their conclusion in words that would make it consistent with liberalism if (contrary to fact) certain meanings could be attributed to some of the words in question in the rele-vant context.[28]

(2) The Right to the Educational Prerequisites for Leading a Life of Moral Integrity

James Dwyer and David A. J. Richards have described the point and con-stituent elements of the kind of education for moral integrity to which I think all moral-rights holders in a liberal society are entitled. According to Dwyer, all children in a liberal society are entitled to "an education that de-velops in them independence of thought, keeps open for them a substantial range of alternative careers, lifestyles, and conceptions of the good, and is sensitive to their developing individual inclinations as they gain maturity."[29] According to Richards, in a liberal society,

> the purpose of education is not merely to prepare the child for the specialized skills the industrial society demands. Education also plays a critical role in fos-tering the values of autonomy that are fundamental to those liberal principles of justice that require that persons be treated as equals. Accordingly, such ed-ucation should eschew indoctrination in rigid sectarian ideology. Instead, it should seek to develop the general capacities that any person would want in order to determine his or her vision of the good life. Thus, schools should cul-tivate self-critical capacities such as precise expression, logic, various forms of analysis, sensitivity to evidence and rational weighing of it, and an open cu-riosity and readiness to take the risk of an experimental attitude toward prob-lems and life.[30]

Unfortunately, far from requiring the State to provide such an educa-tion, current Constitutional-law doctrine (1) seems not to require any American government to provide its moral-rights holders with any educa-tion at all and (2) recognizes a right of parents of moral-rights-holding children to reject the education the State does offer them in favor of no formal schooling at all (at least in some cases) and largely-unsupervised pri-vate schooling (which may have a substantial sectarian component). This subsection elaborates on these claims and explains and criticizes the premises that underlie them.

The Supreme Court realizes that "[p]roviding public schools ranks at the very apex of the function of a State."[31] It accepts that "some degree of education is necessary to prepare citizens to participate effectively and intelligently in our open political system if we are to protect freedom and independence . . . [and that] education prepares individuals to be self-reliant and self-sufficient participants in society."[32] However, both these propositions focus on what children can end up doing for the State (or obviate the State's having to do for them—supporting them financially). The Court has never acknowledged that the State may have positive educational obligations to its children—namely, to provide them with the education that will enable them to make meaningful choices about what they value and how they want to lead their lives. This omission undoubtedly reflects (1) the Court's general belief that our State has few if any positive obligations toward the moral-rights holders for whom it is responsible and (2) the Court's inability to distinguish education "from the specific personal interests in the basics of decent food and shelter,"[33] which it is certain our State has no obligation to secure. For these reasons, the Court has concluded that "[e]ducation, of course, is not among the rights afforded explicit protection under our Federal Constitution. Nor do we find any basis for saying it is implicitly so protected."[34] Obviously, I disagree both with the premises that led the Court to reach this conclusion and with the conclusion itself.

The courts have also decided that parents' liberty interests in parenting (supposedly protected by the "due process" clause) and in practicing their religion (protected by the "free exercise" clause of the First Amendment, which has been incorporated into the Fourteenth Amendment) gives them legitimate interests and frequently the right to control their children's education in general—to place them into private schools (which may be illiberally sectarian and whose teaching is usually not significantly inspected)[35] rather than public schools[36] and (at least in some cases) to withdraw them from school altogether[37]—even if there would be sound grounds for concluding that the parents' choices were disserving the temporal interests of the children. Moreover, although the courts have never recognized a right of parents to engage in home schooling and have rejected a claim that a state's authorizing private schooling without authorizing home schooling violates the "equal protection" clause,[38] as of 1986, thirty states and the District of Columbia had authorized home schooling (half of which did so for the first time between 1982 and 1986) subject to only minimal supervision.[39]

Indeed, the school-case opinions on and legislative discussions of private schooling and home schooling pay virtually no attention to the rights-related interests of the children concerned. Rather, they focus exclusively on the supposed rights of the parents, the purported rights of teachers and owners of private schools, and the interest of the State in having citizens who can support themselves and perform their citizenship obligations adequately. *Wisconsin v. Yoder* is typical in this regard. *Yoder* held that Amish parents had the right to withdraw their fourteen- and fifteen-year-old children from state-prescribed formal education (indeed, from formal education of any kind) after eighth grade to prevent them from being exposed to "worldly influences" that would lead them to value "intellectual and scientific accomplishments, self-distinction, competitiveness, worldly success, and social life with other students,"[40] all of which would disfavor their remaining in the Amish community. Positively, the Court justified this conclusion by citing (1) the "traditional interests of parents with respect to the religious upbringing of their children,"[41] (2) the risk that compulsory school attendance to age sixteen might "undermine the Amish community and religious practice,"[42] (3) the possibility that requiring the children to attend state schools "would gravely endanger if not destroy the free exercise of the parents' religious beliefs,"[43] and (4) the belief that Amish informal education prepares Amish children for life in an Amish community.[44] Negatively, the Court justified this conclusion by citing the fact the Amish community has traditionally been self-supporting and dismissing as "speculative"[45] the risk that the children will choose to leave the Amish community and will be ill-equipped for life outside it. The interest of the children in escaping indoctrination—in being put in a position to make meaningful life-choices—was never considered. Although the Court did not have to determine whether parents have the right to override the expressed wishes of their children to attend state or non-sectarian schools (since none of the children in the case in question had expressed such a wish), it did express the view that recognizing a right of minor children to attend high school if they express a desire to do so "would, of course, call into question traditional concepts of parental control over the religious upbringing and education of their minor children recognized in this Court's past decisions. It is clear that such an intrusion by a State into family decisions in the area of religious training would give rise to grave questions of religious freedom."[46]

In fact, none of these arguments is persuasive. The tradition of parental control is not decisive for two reasons: (1) it is anomalous and, relatedly, (2) no sound moral reason can be given for the conclusion it allegedly favors. These points will now be discussed in turn.

The tradition of parental rights to control the education (medical treatment, etc.—see Section 4 below) of their children conflicts with virtually all our other moral-rights and legal-rights practices.[47] It conflicts with our conclusion that children are moral-rights holders, a conclusion that is manifest in such Supreme Court decisions as *In re Gault*[48] (minors have a Constitutional right to counsel in juvenile-court proceedings even though such proceedings are technically not criminal prosecutions) and *Tinker v. Des Moines School District*[49] (public school students had a Constitutional right to wear black armbands to protest the United States' waging of the Vietnam War so long as their conduct was not disruptive). It conflicts with the rule that no one is entitled to treat a moral-rights holder as a means rather than as an end (in that it implies that parents are entitled to sacrifice both the autonomy and various other temporal interests of their children to get them to conform to the parents' religious beliefs or view of the good life). Although slavery and the nineteenth-century law of married women violated this rule (rationalizing the result by viewing slaves as property rather than as human and by arguing that women had consented to be treated this way by choosing to get married), both these exceptions have long been removed from the law. The best analogy in current law relates to the rights of parents to control the treatment of their mentally-retarded adult children (who may or may not be rights-bearing): although both legislation and judicial opinions have given parents the opportunity to communicate their views to the relevant decisionmaker, parents have not been given the right to make such decisions. Instead, courts have used a substituted-judgment procedure—have attempted to make the decision that the incompetent would have made had he been competent.[50] Thus, one reason why we are not bound by our narrowly-defined tradition of giving parents the right to control their children's education is that the tradition is a non-fit—it is inconsistent with our more general, related moral and legal practices.

The narrow tradition of parental control over their children's schooling and religious education is also not decisive because no moral argument can justicize it. Thus, giving parents the right to control the education of their children even in ways that liberals would conclude were against the children's interests cannot be said to be in the best interest of the child since limiting the control of parents will protect children against their parents' using them as means to further the parents' life-plans when the choices that the parents make for this purpose are against the children's temporal interests—for example, when such choices sacrifice the children's health or reduce their ability to exercise autonomy. Moreover, decreasing the control of parents is at least as likely to improve the quality of parenting by convincing actual parents that they are obligated to treat their children as ends (*inter alia*, by preparing them to make meaningful life-choices) and by deterring individuals who would want to use their children as means from raising as many children as they would otherwise choose to raise as it is to reduce the quality of parenting by reducing the attachment of parents to their children by reducing their ability to control their children. In a liberal society, one also cannot justicize giving parents the right to control their children's education by arguing that parents are entitled to such control: in a liberal society, no one ever has a right to use another person as a means to achieve his own goals unless the latter consented to such treatment. And finally, parental control can also not be justicized by its securing various social goals. In part, this reflects the fact that, in a rights-based society, rights trump over the pursuit of non–rights–related goals. And in part, it reflects the fact that less restrictive means will always be available to the State even if its reason for granting parents control is the protection of rights.

None of the other arguments the Court made in *Yoder* to support its conclusion can bear scrutiny. Thus, the desirability of preserving the Amish community and religion does not justify the Court's ruling that Amish parents can withdraw their (consenting) children from school after the eighth grade before they reach the age of sixteen (Wisconsin's age for compulsory school attendance). Regardless of how socially desirable cultural diversity is and how severe the loss current Amish will experience if their communities dwindle, a liberal State may not help the Amish preserve their communities by sacrificing the moral right of Amish children to be put in a position to make a meaningful choice about their personal ultimate values, religious beliefs, and more concrete life-choices. Even if it would be legitimate for a liberal State to subsidize the survival of the Amish way of life, it would have to do it through a less restrictive means. Granting Amish parents control over their children's education to help preserve Amish society violates the liberal principle that moral-rights holders must be treated as ends not as means.

Yoder also cannot be justicized by arguing that the opposite decision would have violated the "free exercise" rights of the relevant Amish parents. In a liberal society, free exercise relates to *self*-determination: it does not encompass the right to control the religious beliefs and associated behaviors of others (regardless of whether they are the children of the person asserting the right).

The attempt by the *Yoder* majority to justify its decision by citing the fact that the Amish community's informal education prepares its children to function well within it is also besides the point—even assuming, *ad arguendo*, that the children will choose to stay in the Amish community. As David Richards argues, in a liberal society, the point of a liberal education is not just to make the student economically and socially viable: it is also to enable him or her to live an autonomous life (in my terms, a life of moral integrity). Even if Amish education enables Amish children to function well economically and socially in their society, it militates against their being able to make meaningful choices about how to live their lives. Indeed, the Amish explicitly admitted that they wanted to remove their children from the Wisconsin schools to exercise control over their children's thoughts and choices.[51] Even if the Amish expert witness were correct in claiming that attending public high school would inflict "great psychological harm" on Amish children "because of the conflicts it would produce,"[52] that fact would not justicize the parents' removing them from the Wisconsin schools: there are costs to exercising meaningful choice. Liberalism opts for meaningful choice despite such costs. If Amish parents raise their children in a way that causes exposure to contrary values and beliefs in their adolescent years to be damaging, the proper response of a liberal State would be to intervene earlier in the upbringing of the children in question to prevent the situation's arising rather than to adjust to this illiberal reality after the children's rights have been violated by their parents and communities.[53]

It would be a mistake to assume that the *Yoder* example is not socially important. The Amish and Menonnites may be small communities, but the problem of illiberal childrearing practices is far more widespread. Some conservative Catholics, Hassidim, conventional orthodox Jews, Hindus, Moslems, fundamentalist Christians, and secular ideologues also try to limit the information coming to their children in ways that undermine these young people's ability to make meaningful life-choices. In addition, some parents who belong to these (and other) groups also try to educate their children to accept gender-role and other restrictions that are illiberal. The extent of the problem is suggested by Mark Murphy's estimate that in 1992 a million families in the United States educated a child at home.[54] The failure of the courts to recognize the obligation of a liberal State to provide its moral-rights holders with the educational wherewithal to lead lives of moral integrity is highly regrettable. As the next section points out, the belief in parental rights that lies behind this failure has had other unfortunate consequences as well.

4. *Liberty Rights: Constitutional-Law Doctrine*

A. The General Position

Current Constitutional-law doctrine takes a "three-tier scrutiny" approach to liberty issues. Government choices that disserve values (restrict "liberties") that are "not particularly important" are said to be Constitutional if they are at least "rationally related" to the achievement of a "legitimate" State goal; government choices that disserve values (restrict "liberties") that are "important" are said to be Constitutional if they are at least "substantially related" to the achievement of a State goal that is at least "important"; and government choices that disserve values (restrict "liberties") that are "fundamental" are said to be Constitutional if and only if they are "necessary and narrowly tailored" to the achievement of a "compelling" State goal. All the various criticisms I make of this three-tier-scrutiny approach in the context of Chapter 3's analysis of the duty of appropriate, equal respect (*inter alia*, "equal protection" issues) apply *mutatis mutandis* in the current context. For example, just as the three-tier-scrutiny approach inaccurately trichotomizes the suspectness of a classification, it inaccurately trichotomizes the importance of values or liberties. Furthermore, just as the formal statement of the three-tier-scrutiny approach ignores the extent of the loss suffered by the disadvantaged group, it ignores the extent to which the value (liberty) in question is disserved (restricted) by the government choice under review. Moreover, to the extent that the three-tier-scrutiny approach promulgates tests that are a mixture of "appropriate degree of deference" tests and "tests of Constitutionality," the importance of the value or liberty in question may not be much correlated with the appropriate degree of deference—that is, with the likelihood that differences in the Constitutionality conclusions reached by the Court and the decisionmaker whose choice it is reviewing reflect differences in the way that they characterize or evaluate the importance of the value or liberty in question. Most basically, the three-tier-scrutiny approach is deficient in that it does not make the Constitutionality of the liberty-restrictions it is used to assess depend on whether they secure or sacrifice rights-related interests on balance.

One further general issue needs to be addressed: the method the Courts have used to determine whether an individual has a Constitutionally-relevant liberty interest in committing a particular act, engaging in a particular activity, or participating in a particular relationship.[55] Some relevant liberties were enumerated in the Bill of Rights. The Court has determined whether various unenumerated liberties were Constitutionally protected by asking whether their protection was "implicit in the concept of ordered liberty"[56] or "so rooted in the traditions and conscience of our people as to be ranked as fundamental."[57] However, when trying to answer these questions, the Court has not adopted the kind of approach I have taken— it has not surveyed all our moral-rights-relevant practices to identify the principle that underlies the acts, activities, and relationships in relation to which people have entitlement interests and then derived the implications of that principle for the importance of the relevant actor's interest in doing what he or she wants to do. Rather than taking this broad-gauged approach, it has focused narrowly (and sometimes inaccurately—see below) on the society's attitude toward and treatment of the particular liberty interest in question. For example, when analyzing the Constitutionality of restrictions on homosexual sex or abortion, the Court focused on the way that our society regarded and treated homosexuality or abortion rather than on the principle that we are committed to instantiating in our moral-rights decisions in general and its implications for the Constitutionality of the restrictions under review. Obviously, I think that courts in a liberal society are obligated to execute the more broad-gauged analysis—to execute a broad-gauged search for "first principles" and analyze the implications of the principles that have been identified for particular issues. The more narrow-gauged analysis creates the risk of basing decisions on non-fits—on social practices that are inconsistent with the commitments of our society.

B. Four Sets of Concrete Liberties

(1) Sexual Liberty

Liberalism does not denigrate the sheer pleasure of sexual activity. From a variety of personal-ultimate-value perspectives that are perfectly consistent with liberalism, the experiencing and giving of sexual pleasure is a decidedly good thing. However, for the liberal, sexual liberty is important primarily because sexual intimacy can lead to or cement a more comprehensive intimacy between (or among) the sexual partners. This more comprehensive intimacy is valued by liberals because it tends to lead to self-discovery and plays an important role in an individual's instantiating the values he has chosen. Since not only non-sodomous marital sex but also homosexual sex, heterosexual sodomy, non-marital sex, and polygamous sex can contribute to the establishment and maintenance of the type of intimacy liberals value, a liberal State would have to have strong rights-related reasons for restricting the ability of an individual to engage in any of these kinds of sex in circumstances in which they might contribute to the establishment or maintenance of comprehensive intimacy.

The current Constitutional-law doctrine on sexual activities is decidedly illiberal. In *Bowers v. Hardwick*,[58] the Court upheld the Constitutionality of a Georgia sodomy statute that prohibited heterosexual as well as homosexual sodomy. The Court attempted to justify its conclusion in two ways: by pointing out that (1) proscriptions of homosexual consensual sodomy "have ancient roots" and that "[s]odomy was a criminal offense at common law and was forbidden by the laws of the original thirteen states when they ratified the Bill of Rights"[59] and (2) "it would be difficult, except by fiat, to limit the claimed right to homosexual conduct while leaving exposed to prosecution adultery, incest, and other sexual crimes even though they are committed in the home."[60] In fact, neither of these arguments is persuasive. The history of American criminalization of homosexual sex is both different from and more complicated than the Court indicates,[61] and, even if it were not, the Court would be obligated to consider whether the persistent condemnation and criminalization of homosexuality it posits was inconsistent with the moral principle that we are committed to using in moral-rights discourse. Moreover, from the perspective of liberalism, it may not be that difficult to make principled distinctions among the various kinds of sexual activities the Court claimed could be distinguished only on an *ad hoc* basis. Thus, if from the perspective of liberalism sexual activity is protected primarily because of its positive link to the establishment and maintenance of comprehensively-intimate relationships that contribute to self-discovery and the instantiation of an individual's legitimate value and life choices,

(1) adultery may merit less protection than non-adulterous sex (because it is more likely to endanger existing comprehensive intimacy and is also more likely to violate contractual promises),

(2) incest may also merit less protection (because it often involves a young partner who cannot give meaningful consent and may damage both that partner and a variety of intra-familial relationships in ways that militate against their promoting self-discovery and the instantiation of value-choices that are consistent with liberalism), and

(3) casual sex and prostitution may also merit less protection both because they are less likely to promote comprehensive intimacy (though some participants may find that such sex is a useful safety-valve that enables them to conduct themselves in other relationships

in ways that enhance their chances of establishing comprehensive intimacy) and because they involve greater medical and other sorts of risks.

The Supreme Court decisions upholding both the Mann Act (which prohibits the transportation across state lines of "any woman or girl for the purposes of prostitution or debauchery, or for any other immoral purpose") in general[62] and its application to polygamous married couples in particular[63] are also difficult to reconcile with the liberal evaluation of sexual activities that can help to establish or maintain comprehensive intimacy.

On the other hand, the conclusions of the Court in *Griswold v. Connecticut*[64] and *Eisenstadt v. Baird*[65] are consistent with liberalism's evaluation of sex, though the Court's justifications for these decisions do not focus on this issue. *Griswold* held unconstitutional as an impermissible invasion of "privacy" the application to married couples of a Connecticut statute prohibiting anyone (including married couples) from using "any drug, medicinal article or instrument for the purpose of preventing conception" and prohibiting anyone from assisting another person to prevent conception. *Eisenstadt v. Baird* held unconstitutional a statute prohibiting the distribution of contraceptives as applied to both unmarried and married couples. The Court concluded (spuriously) that the relevant statute failed the minimum rationality test and also argued that it violated its targets' Constitutional right of "privacy," which entailed a right "to be free from unwarranted governmental intrusion into matters so fundamentally affecting a person as the decision on whether to bear or beget a child."[66] Although the Court's privacy rationales are not convincing, these cases' outcomes could be justified by citing the relationship between the availability of contraceptives and the incidence of sexual intimacy, the relationship between sexual intercourse and comprehensive intimacy, and the importance of comprehensive intimacy for its participants' discovering and instantiating their values.

(2) The Right to Marry, Divorce, and Live Together

Liberalism recognizes a right to marriage because marriage

(1) promotes the kind of intimacy that leads to self-discovery,
(2) enables many of its participants to lead the lives they value by putting them in a position to help their spouses lead the lives the spouses wish to lead and to be helped by their spouses in turn to do the same, and

(3) creates a structure for the raising of children that favors their becoming individuals of moral integrity.

Liberalism recognizes a right to divorce because some marriages do not fulfill those functions despite the fact that their participants could enter into relationships with others that would help both parties to discover and instantiate their values and raise children to become individuals of moral integrity. However, these facts do not imply that a liberal State is obligated to permit its moral-rights holders to divorce at will. Even if one ignores the need to make appropriate financial arrangements (which might reflect the relative faults of the parties)[67] a liberal State would be obligated to consider that

(1) easy divorces may reduce the care with which individuals choose their marriage partners and the timing of their marriage both by making exits from marriage less costly and by leaving the impression that the State (society) does not take marriage and marital obligations that seriously,

(2) individuals may choose to seek a divorce if doing so is easy when they would serve their own interests better by working on their marriage (a paternalistic argument that might justify a waiting period), and

(3) divorce may injure the children of the marriage by reducing the likelihood of their becoming individuals of moral integrity as well as their prospects for material success and happiness.[68]

Liberalism also recognizes the rights-related interests that individuals have in living together (whether or not they have a sexual relationship) since living with someone can promote the kind of intimacy that can lead to self-discovery and enable friends (and lovers) to instantiate their values. This interest in living together is not restricted to members of traditional families, though permitting family-members to live together may be more likely to promote the kinds of relationships that liberalism particularly values and on which their participants can rely.

From the perspective of liberalism, the case law on this set of liberty issues is mixed. Not surprisingly, given the fact that all American states have always established a marriage regime, no case has ever addressed the possible duty of our states to do so. *Griswold v. Connecticut* describes the importance of marriage in terms that are very similar to those I used to describe the liberal account of marriage: "Marriage is a coming together for better or worse,

302 | *The Duty of Appropriate, Equal Concern*

hopefully enduring, and intimate to the degree of being sacred. It is an association that promotes a way of life, not causes; a harmony in living, not political factors; a bilateral loyalty, not commercial or social projects. Yet it is an association for as noble a purpose as any involved in our prior decisions."[69] This proclamation certainly establishes a basis for the conclusion that a liberal State is obligated to establish a legal category of marriage (though one might argue that, in its absence, individuals could still enter into a similar relationship without the legal form simply by pledging their troths).

The Supreme Court has never held that our states have a Constitutional obligation to establish a legal category of marriage, though two cases have addressed related issues. The first is *Loving v. Virginia*,[70] which invalidated Virginia's anti-miscegenation law on equal-protection grounds. If one accepts my earlier argument that any tradition we have of condemning homosexuality cannot justify a liberal State's distinguishing between homosexual and heterosexual intimate relationships, *Loving* would provide a precedent for the conclusion that a state must provide for homosexual marriages if it creates a legal form for heterosexual marriages unless it can come up with some other argument to justicize its distinguishing the two.[71] The second case is *Zablocki v. Redhail*,[72] which invalidated a law forbidding people to marry who have not met their child-support obligations. Admittedly, however, neither of these cases is precisely on point.

I can imagine certain states of the world that might justicize a liberal State's distinguishing between heterosexual and homosexual marriages if the facts in question did not reflect the effects of prejudice for which the State was responsible and/or if the State's drawing such a distinction would not encourage or perpetuate such prejudices. Thus, a liberal State *might* otherwise be able to justicize not allowing homosexual couples to enter into legal marriages despite the fact that it allowed heterosexual couples to do so if

(1) homosexual marriages promoted their participants' self-discovery and self-chosen-value instantiation to a lesser extent than did heterosexual marriages even while they lasted,

(2) homosexual marriages were far less enduring than heterosexual marriages,

(3) homosexual divorces were more traumatic and raised more financial complications (which would have been avoided had the parties not married) than heterosexual marriages, or

(4) a decision to enable homosexuals to enter into legal marriages would induce people who could be either homosexual or heterosexual to become homosexual and that decision would not be in the relevant individuals' interests on balance (regardless of whether homosexuality was in the interest of other homosexuals).

However, I

(1) suspect that none of these propositions is true,
(2) know that the State has not validated them to the extent it must for its reliance on them to be legitimate,
(3) doubt that some of them would legitimate a liberal State's making the relevant distinction even if they were true and did not reflect prejudices for which the State was responsible and even if a State decision not to provide for homosexual marriages would not legitimate and perpetuate such prejudices, and
(4) fear that some of these propositions if true would reflect prejudice for which the State is responsible.

Thus, I fear that if homosexual marriages would be less enduring than heterosexual marriages, that fact might well critically reflect the operation of prejudices against the homosexual partners in question. Similarly, I fear that if the choices of persons who could be either homosexual or heterosexual to become homosexuals were against their interests, that fact might well critically reflect prejudices directed against them. Moreover, I have no doubt that the State would be responsible for these prejudices—both because it fostered them through its criminalization of homosexual sex and its related endorsement of the condemnation of homosexuality[73] and because it cannot separate itself from its citizens' prejudices in any case.[74] The State's responsibility for current prejudice against homosexuals also implies that the tendencies of a State decision not to provide for homosexual marriages while permitting heterosexuals to enter into legal marriages (1) to cause homosexuals to feel that they have been targeted for discrimination and (2) others to conclude that the State believes in the legitimacy of what in fact are prejudices against homosexuals count against the moral permissibility and Constitutionality of its doing so. Finally, even if the legitimating force of some of the possible arguments for restricting marriage to heterosexual couples did survive this critique, those arguments would be at best somewhat offset by the probable fact that the legal recognition of homosexual marriages would do more than the legal recognition of heterosexual marriages to prevent the spread of AIDS and various other venereal diseases by encouraging homosexuals to enter into enduring relationships.

Everything considered, then, it seems to me that a liberal State has a duty (in the United States, under the Ninth Amendment or privileges or immunities clause of the Fourteenth Amendment) to provide for the legal recognition of both homosexual and heterosexual marriage and that any decision to grant such recognition to heterosexual marriages and not to homosexual marriages would be a violation of "equal protection" notions (under the Ninth Amendment or the Fourteenth Amendment).

This analysis of the right to enter into a homosexual marriage also applies to the right to participate in a polygamous marriage.[75] As in the case of homosexual marriage, I can imagine various grounds that might justify a ban on polygamous marriages. Thus, a liberal State might be able to justicize its refusal to recognize such marriages, its criminalization of such marriages, or its levying civil fines on those who participate in such marriages if

(1) one or more of their participants was usually unable to give meaningful consent to them,
(2) they tend to be associated with hierarchical relationships that cost one or more of their participants her (or his) autonomy,
(3) most of them are against the interests of their participants for other reasons, or
(4) they disserve the interest of their offspring.

However, I doubt that these propositions are true, know that they have not been sufficiently validated, and fear that the non-recognition or prohibition of polygamy will foster prejudice against polygamists and perpetuate prejudice against them for which the State is partially responsible. Hence, even if one ignores any special issues raised by the possible religious duty of polygamists to engage in this practice, I doubt the permissibility of a liberal State's refusing to recognize polygamous marriage or subjecting polygamists to civil fines or criminal penalties.

The case-law on this issue is all to the contrary. The Constitutionality of applying a federal anti-bigamy statute to a polygamist was upheld in 1878.[76] The Court's opinion offered two justifications for its conclusion. First, our narrowly-defined practices in relation to polygamy: "Polygamy has always been odious among the northern and western nations of Europe. . . . [F]rom the earliest history of England polygamy has been treated as an offence against society. . . . [T]here never has been a time in any State of the Union when polygamy has not been an offence against society, cognizable by the civil courts and punishable with more or less severity."[77] The same argument that led me to conclude that our alleged historical position on homosexuality is not decisive applies with equal force to this argument from tradition against polygamy.

The Court's moral justification for its conclusion was that"polygamy leads to the patriarchial principle, . . . which, when applied to large communities, fetters the people in stationary despotism, while that principle cannot long exist in connection with monogamy."[78] The Court's subsequent comments make it clear that its concern is not with the autonomy interests of the female partners in polygamous marriages but with the risk to the republic. Even if this risk were substantial, there would almost certainly be less restrictive ways of countering it.

The Supreme Court has never addressed the issue of whether the states have a Constitutional obligation to allow married people to obtain divorces. As I have already suggested, it seems to me that a liberal State could legitimately require parties who want to divorce to satisfy certain conditions—for example, to endure a waiting period or to receive counseling about the importance of their continuing to parent any offspring of their dissolved marriage—but the Supreme Court has never pronounced on these issues or the more basic issue of whether the Constitution requires American states to permit divorce at all.

In *Boddie v. Connecticut*,[79] the Supreme Court held that if a state permits divorce it cannot condition married people's access to the courts on their paying even modest filing fees and service-of-process charges (forty-five dollars and fifteen dollars, respectively, in 1971) if these charges effectively deny them an opportunity to get divorced (because of their poverty). However, neither the majority opinion nor the concurrences suggest their authors' belief that moral-rights holders have a moral and Constitutional right to obtain divorces. Although the majority opinion indicates that the "Court on more than one occasion has recognized [that] marriage involves interests of basic importance to society" and refers to the connection between divorce and remarriage,[80] there is no indication that it endorses the liberal conception of the importance of marriage I previously articulated. Moreover, its grounds for declaring the Connecticut statute in question unconstitutional—that "persons forced to settle their claims of right and duty through the judicial process must be given a meaningful opportunity to be heard"[81]—does not assume that individuals have a moral and Constitutional right to dissolve their untenable marriages. The concurrences by Justices William Douglas and William Brennan are no different in this respect: they would have held the Connecticut statute unconstitutional on the ground that it constituted an invidious discrimination based on poverty.

On the other hand, the fact that in *United States v. Kras*[82] the Court subsequently refused to declare unconstitutional the central government's refusal to waive a fifty-dollar fee for an indigent petitioner in bankruptcy does suggest that *Boddie* may reflect the Justices' belief that we do have a moral and Constitutional right to divorce. Thus, although the *Kras* Court did distinguish *Boddie* on the ground that "the [central] government's control over the establishment, enforcement, or dissolution of debts [is not] nearly so exclusive as Connecticut's control over the marriage relationship," it also emphasized that "[g]aining or not gaining a discharge will effect no change with respect to basic necessities. We see no fundamental interest that is gained or lost depending on the availability of a discharge in bankruptcy."[83]

The final issue I want to address under this heading is the right of individuals to live together. The Court's doctrinal approach to this issue is based on the proposition that "the Constitution protects the sanctity of the family precisely because the institution of the family is deeply valued in this Nation's history and tradition," a tradition that includes extended families composed of "uncles, aunts, cousins, and especially grandparents sharing a household along with parents and children."[84] This narrow focus on a specific set of social practices led the Court in *Village of Belle Terre v. Boraas*[85] to uphold a local ordinance restricting land-use to one-family dwellings and defining "family" so as to exclude more than two unrelated people living together. It also led the Court in *Moore v. City of East Cleveland*[86] to invalidate an ordinance limiting occupancy of a dwelling unit to members of a single nuclear as opposed to extended family.

The Court's mistake in these cases was to focus on the narrow practice of respecting families rather than on the reason that families are respected in our liberal society. If the Court had acknowledged that the reason that individuals have a right to live with particular others is the contribution such living arrangements can make to the establishment of intimacy and thereby to the discovery and actuation of personal ultimate values, it would have required the village of Belle Terre to offer a stronger justification for its zoning ordinance.

(3) The Right to Create Children and the Right to Parent Children One Has Created or Adopted

(A) THE RIGHT TO CREATE CHILDREN

From a liberal perspective, creating children is not normally highly valued in itself.[87] There are exceptions, such as when someone becomes a gestational surrogate for the foetus of a loved one. But liberalism does not value the desire to be a Johnny or Joanie Appleseed (assuming that the latter would be feasible). On the other hand, liberalism does recognize the importance to individuals of parenting children. Parenting can help an individual discover what he values, can enable him to understand himself and his own conduct better, and can provide the means through which he can instantiate the values he has chosen.[88] It can also provide substantial pleasure and satisfaction to those who engage in the activity. To the extent that creating children increases the opportunities for people to parent children, or to the extent that parenting one's biologic child is more rewarding than parenting someone else's biologic child,[89] moral-rights holders in liberal societies may have rights-related interests in creating a child.

These rights-related interests are relevant to the assessment of the moral permissibility of the following actual or possible State choices: (1) compulsory sterilization of the mentally defective; (2) compulsory sterilization of habitual criminals; (3) compulsory sterilization for men or women who may pass on various handicaps to their children, compulsory abortions for women whose offspring will be handicapped in various ways, or the imposition of civil fines or criminal penalties on such individuals' begetting a child or carrying a foetus beyond a specified stage of development; (4) compulsory sterilization of individuals who have neglected or abused their own children with a frequency that makes recidivism seem likely or the imposition of civil fines or criminal penalties on them if they create another child; (5) the imposition of civil fines or criminal penalties on unmarried moral-rights holders or gays who create a child they intend to parent; (6) prohibitions of the use of various methods of reproduction—tubal reconstruction, vasectomy reversals, fertility drugs, artificial insemination, in vitro fertilization, collaborative reproduction, gestational surrogates, and so on; (7) decisions to deny financial support for individuals who cannot otherwise afford to create (and parent) a child; and (8) prohibitions of any individual's creating more than some specified maximum number of children for herself to parent. I will now analyze the moral-rights issues these possibilities raise and comment on the current doctrine that relates to them.

Before proceeding, another warning. Many of the questions I have just posed are highly unpleasant. Unfortunately, unpleasant questions sometimes beget unpleasant answers. The fact that some of the answers that my understanding of liberalism requires make me feel uncomfortable is not irrelevant to the accuracy of that understanding, the persuasiveness of my claim that ours is a liberal, rights-based society, or the correctness of my analysis of the concrete-rights implications of that claim. But it also does not demonstrate that my conclusions are erroneous. Sometimes, principles to which we are committed have implications that we dislike.

From the perspective of the liberal position to which I believe our society is committed, the permissibility of compulsory sterilization of the mentally defective depends in part on the extent of the relevant party's handicap. If he does not have the neurological prerequisites for becoming an individual of moral integrity, such sterilization would not violate his rights because he would not be a moral-rights holder. Moreover, if he does not have the capacity to engage in meaningful parenting, such sterilization will not violate his right to create a child to parent on that account.

Admittedly, however, many mentally-handicapped individuals are moral-rights holders and could engage in and profit from satisfactory parenting (perhaps with some help from the State—see below). Furthermore, since the offspring of many such people would not be likely to have a wrongful life or impose a financial burden on the State, compulsory sterilization could not be justiced on either of these bases.

Moreover, at least three other considerations favor the conclusion that such sterilization is morally impermissible. First, the sterilization operation itself may be impermissibly costly to the individual sterilized—though the relevant comparison must take into consideration the cost to the relevant individual of the alternatives to sterilization (of being given contraceptives, of closer supervision and tighter restraint, of abortions, or of giving birth). Second, even if sterilization would not violate the rights of the handicapped because she was not a moral-rights holder, it might violate the rights of those who liked or loved her (particularly if they were related). Third, compulsory sterilization might be rendered impermissible because the probability that the State might make a mistake or might misuse its authority to execute such procedures (e.g., to punish political opponents by acting on them or their spouses, children, more distant relatives, or friends) is unacceptably high.

The issue strikes me as a close one. It might be permissible for a liberal State to sterilize at least some of the mentally-handicapped if it set up procedures that afford sufficient protection against error or intentional misuse—

for example, if it required approval by judges using a substituted-judgment approach (in which they try to decide what the "person" in question would have chosen had she been competent to make the choice).

There is not a great deal of law on this issue. The only Supreme Court case to deal directly with the issue (*Buck v. Bell*) upheld the Constitutionality of a state program that authorized the sterilization of mental defectives when, after a procedure the Court viewed as fair,[90] the superintendent of a covered institution concludes that sterilization is for the best interest of the patient and society. In Justice Oliver Wendell Holmes's words: "Three generations of imbeciles are enough."[91] The other Supreme Court case that comes closest to being on point is *Skinner v. Oklahoma*,[92] which held unconstitutional as a violation of the equal-protection clause an Oklahoma statute requiring sterilization of a criminal offender convicted three times for felonies "involving moral turpitude" but exempting certain felonies, including embezzlement, from the "moral turpitude" category. Although Justice Douglas's opinion for the Court did state that sterilization forever deprives the person sterilized of a basic liberty, it did not decide the case on that basis alone but rather held that that fact required the state's classification scheme to be subjected to "strict scrutiny" (in a usage that pre-dated the development of the three-tier-scrutiny approach), which Oklahoma's scheme could not survive (since it distinguished among people who committed "intrinsically the same quality of offense").[93] Although I have not researched this issue systematically, various state court cases have upheld the kind of sterilization program reviewed in *Buck v. Bell* if and only if (1) the case for sterilization is heard by a judge; (2) the "person" to be sterilized is deemed incompetent only if he does not understand the nature of the judicial proceeding, the nature of the sterilization procedure, or the consequences of sterilization (not if the judge regards the individual's expressed preferences as unwise); (3) the decision for those deemed incompetent to make their own choice is to be based on a "substituted judgment" standard (which focuses exclusively on the relevant individual's interests and ignores the interest of society except to the extent that the individual would have chosen to consider them); (4) the judge considers the evidence for sterilization with "utmost care"; and (5) the person at risk of being sterilized is represented by a guardian *ad litem*.[94]

Compulsory sterilization of habitual criminals[95] seems far harder to justicize than compulsory sterilization of mental defectives. There is, to my knowledge, no sound theoretical or empirical basis for concluding that criminal behavior has any genetic basis at all, much less a sufficient genetic basis to justicize sterilization on something like general-deterrence grounds.

Moreover, as I indicated before, the legitimacy of allowing sentencing to be influenced by general-deterrence goals is doubtful. Nor can sterilization be justicized on the ground that the offspring whose existence it would prevent would have had wrongful lives (would have been "better off" had they never been born). Finally, I do not think that sterilization can be justicized as straightforward punishment: viewed as punishment, it is an act of degradation that fails to show the respect that is still due the criminal. To my knowledge, the only case-law on this issue is *Skinner v. Oklahoma*. As already indicated, although the *Skinner* Court struck down Oklahoma's statute on compulsory sterilization of habitual criminals on equal-protection grounds, the opinion does contain language that suggests that the Court would have invalidated it on "substantive due process" grounds (what should be "privileges or immunities" grounds related to the notion of "cruel and unusual punishment") had the equal-protection argument not been available.

Although liberal States probably cannot justicize the compulsory sterilization of criminals, I do not think that liberal States are morally precluded from deterring individuals from creating wrongful lives by sterilizing people with severe incurable diseases that will be passed on to their foetuses (e.g., AIDS or advanced syphilis) as well perhaps as people who have curable diseases or addictions that they have knowingly passed on to their offspring. In this latter group are heroin or crack addicts, venereal-disease sufferers, and phenylketonuric (PKU) mothers who have become pregnant without altering their diet for the period necessary to protect their offspring from neurological damage and have failed to have an early abortion. Short of sterilization, a liberal State may also try to deter the creation of wrongful lives by criminalizing such individuals' becoming pregnant or continuing their pregnancy beyond some specified point or by imposing civil fines on individuals who violate such rules.

I realize that both these policies will raise religious problems for people who are religiously forbidden to accept medical treatment or to have abortions. However, I do not think that a liberal State may allow people to fulfill their religious obligations by committing acts that violate the rights of others, and I do think that in this context it is proper to consider the rights of non-existent creatures not to be created.

No case deals directly with the possible Constitutional right of individuals who would create wrongful lives not to be restricted in the ways I think liberal rights-considerations require. However, several cases that do not implicate the interest of moral-rights holders in creating children do conclude that the State may prohibit religiously-motivated acts that expose the actors' children to particularly-grave dangers. These cases are highly relevant to the issue under consideration because, as I have previously argued, the interest that people have in creating children derives from their interest in parenting children, and that interest is at best attenuated when the child in question would lead a wrongful life. Admittedly, the cases that are on point are not really consistent with liberal principles in that they do not focus on the rights of children (approach the issue through a test that balances the parents' supposed rights-related interests with the State's interest and assume, therefore, that the parents' free-exercise rights are not restricted to their self-determination but extend to their control of those others who are their children).[96]

The three leading Supreme Court cases are *Prince v. Massachusetts,*[97] *Jehovah's Witnesses v. King County Hospital,*[98] and *Wisconsin v. Yoder.*[99] *Prince* affirmed the conviction of a Jehovah's Witness for violating a statute that sought to keep children out of dangerous situations by prohibiting parents and guardians from directing or permitting their children to sell publications (in this case, religious literature) in public places. The Court held: "The right to practice religion freely does not include the liberty to expose the community or the child to communicable disease or the latter to ill-health or death."[100] *King County Hospital* affirmed a District Court ruling[101] declaring a child of Jehovah's Witnesses a ward of the State for the purpose of authorizing an emergency blood-transfusion to which its parents would not consent. The opinion distinguished sharply between the parents' free-exercise right to control the religious indoctrination of their children and their right to control other aspects of their children's lives. Both the Supreme Court opinion in *Prince* and the District Court opinion in *King County Hospital* indicated that parents' free-exercise interests will entitle them to sacrifice their children's temporal interests to some extent. As we have seen, *Yoder* held that parents' free-exercise right to control the religious indoctrination of their child entitled them to withdraw the children from public school after the eighth grade, to isolate the children from outside influences for the purpose of inducing the children to subscribe to the parents' religious beliefs. However, this decision is not really applicable to the policy on which we are currently focusing since *Yoder* is an indoctrination case and the parents' acts neither exposed children to grievous bodily harm nor created a risk to "public safety, peace, order or welfare."[102]

A liberal State may also be able to justicize sterilizing individuals whose persistent mistreatment of their children creates a substantial probability of their neglecting or abusing any additional offspring they produce. The legitimate interest of such potential parents in parenting additional offspring is highly attenuated at best and even if the additional children they would produce would not have wrongful lives, these non-existent creatures do not have a right to be created that would be violated by their potential parents' sterilization or by a law that imposed civil fines or criminal penalties on their potential parents if they created an additional child.

The State may also seek to prohibit unmarried persons and gays from creating and parenting their own child. I can see no way in which a liberal State could justicize such a policy. Single people and gays can profit just as much from their relationship with their child as can heterosexual married couples, and gays who have a partner can profit just as much from the effect of parenting on their relationship with their partner as can heterosexual married couples. Moreover, I am unaware of any persuasive evidence suggesting that the children of such parents are sufficiently likely to be sufficiently harmed by the parenting they receive or by the reaction of other people in their society to them because of their parents for a liberal State to be able to justicize such a policy on this basis.

State policies that restrict the ability of individuals to create children by prohibiting or increasing the difficulty or cost to them of using various procedures or drugs to enhance their ability to create children are also morally problematic. Assume that moral-rights holders do have rights-related interests in creating children as opposed to parenting a child who is not their biologic offspring—interests that relate to the probability that parenting one's own biologic offspring might lead to more intimacy, value-discovery, self-insight, and satisfaction as well as the possibility that creating children together can contribute to the parents' relationship. On this assumption, a liberal State could not justify its prohibiting potential parents from undergoing tubal-reconstruction or vasectomy-reversal surgery, taking fertility drugs, attempting to have children through artificial insemination, in vitro fertilization, or by obtaining the services of a gestational surrogate unless it can establish that doing so would protect weightier rights-related interests than it sacrificed.

Legal restrictions of some reproduction procedures might be justified if the procedures were sufficiently likely to yield children that had biologic defects that made their lives wrongful or if parents who used these procedures were sufficiently likely to be bad parents to create a substantial risk that their offspring would lead wrongful lives on this account.[103] This latter possibility could reflect the characteristics of the prospective parents who choose to use these procedures (though one might want to distinguish between situations in which the choice reflected physical disabilities and those in which the prospective mother did not want to undergo a pregnancy for career or social reasons) or their missing the bonding experience of the woman's pregnancy (though the performance of adoptive parents makes this argument unpersuasive). A liberal State might also want to prohibit parents who could create children in the conventional coital way from using a non-coital approach if there were good reason to believe that the child produced coitally would have a better genetic endowment or receive better parenting than the child the same parents would create through a non-coital procedure. However, even if this concern were realistic, the permissibility of such a prohibition would be problematic—in part because the argument for doing so involves a comparison of the interests of two non-existent creatures.

A liberal State may also be able to justicize some restrictions on the use of gestational surrogates. Some women who might otherwise be well-qualified to perform this function (e.g., young healthy adults who have never been pregnant) may be unable to assess the cost to them of the pregnancy itself, the dietary and behavioral restrictions the surrogacy contract imposes on them, and the subsequent surrender of the child. However, although this possibility might justicize restricting who can become a gestational surrogate and prohibiting even otherwise-qualified candidates for the "job" from undertaking it until they have participated in an appropriate educational and counseling program, it would not justicize a universal ban on such surrogacy. I realize that other non-paternalistic arguments have been made for the moral permissibility of prohibiting surrogate-motherhood contracts, but I do not find any of them convincing. Thus, I do not think that one can justicize prohibiting gestational surrogacy to protect the autonomy of the surrogate mother (see below). I also do not think that the goal of avoiding the transaction cost of settling the disputes that surrogate-motherhood contracts may generate can justicize a liberal State's prohibiting such contracts outright—though I do not deny that many such disputes may arise (when the surrogate mother is not behaving in the way the contract requires, wants to terminate the pregnancy, or wants to keep the baby). The risk that babies born through surrogate-motherhood contracts will have wrongful lives because they are biologically deficient or because their social parents have not bonded to them during the course of the prospective social mother's pregnancy is certainly not sufficiently high to justicize State proscriptions of surrogate-motherhood contracts. In any event, the evaluation of any restrictions on gestational-surrogacy contracts would have to take into consideration not only the interests of the potential creator/parents but also the interests of the potential surrogates (which may be both financial and non-financial).

To my knowledge, no Constitutional-law case has ever dealt with any of these issues explicitly. The common-law courts' disinclination to enforce personal-service contracts (supposedly justified by a concern for the autonomy of the person who has contracted to supply the personal service) may support the claim that common-law judges believe that it would be morally impermissible to require gestational surrogates to render specific performance (not to abort or to surrender the baby when they want to keep it). However, I consider these personal-service-contract cases to be mistaken: at least when the service-provider was competent to enter into the contract in question, the decision that supports her autonomy is the decision that enforces the contract she entered.

If parenting one's biologic offspring really were a significantly more valuable experience from a liberal perspective than parenting someone else's biologic child and/or if contributing to the creation of a biologic child with one's partner did contribute substantially to the partners' relationship, I would conclude that a liberal State had an obligation to provide its moral-rights holders with the financial wherewithal to have some number of such experiences—including, when necessary, the ability to pay the extra cost of the more complicated reproduction procedures just discussed. Such support would be part of the minimum real income to which all of a liberal State's moral-rights holders are entitled. I leave to another day the discussion of the number of such experiences to which moral-rights holders are entitled in varying circumstances.

Although this issue has never been explicitly addressed by any court, the reluctance of our courts to conclude that the State has any positive obligations to its moral-rights holders makes it extraordinarily unlikely that they would conclude that individuals have a positive Constitutional right to financial support for using any of these more expensive reproductive procedures. However, courts might find that legal prohibitions of the use of these techniques or legal rules that make their use more expensive or difficult do violate the relevant moral-rights holders' right to create a child.

Finally, is it morally permissible for a liberal State to limit the number of children its individual moral-rights holders can create (for the purpose of parenting their offspring themselves)? Such a State policy could be enforced by the sterilization of people who had reached the limit or by imposing civil or criminal sanctions on individuals who exceed the limit.[104] The first question that any liberal analysis of this question would have to address is the strength of the rights-related interest that moral-rights holders have in creating and parenting successive children. Since the presence of additional children reduces the emotional and time investment one can make with one's older children and with other friends and family members (to an extent that depends in part on the financial position of the family and the age-distribution of the children), beyond some point having additional children may not promote—indeed, may disserve—some of the purposes that make liberals value parenting. However, I will assume that most adults do have rights–related interests in parenting a fifth, sixth, seventh, or eighth child—though one that diminishes with each successive child in question (unless, perhaps, the individual in question wants to parent the additional child with a new partner). Of course, this assumption does not imply that moral–rights holders have a rights–related interest in parenting an *n*th child of their own biologic creation: unless one concludes that parenting an *n*th child that one has created with one's partner is more valuable to the parent in liberal terms than parenting a child one has adopted or agreed to foster, a moral–rights holder would have no rights–related interest in *creating and parenting* an *n*th child. Even if one grants *ad arguendo* that parenting some number of children you have biologically created with your partner (or that one of you has biologically created) is more rewarding in the relevant ways than parenting someone else's biologic creation, it seems unlikely to me that the comparative advantages in question would continue *ad infinitum*.

The second question that a liberal analysis would have to answer is: What kinds of justification can a liberal State give for restricting the number of children a person can create and parent? If the restriction in question will sacrifice the rights–related interests of those it constrains, it would be justified only if it protected more weighty rights–related interests. Since our society is wealthy enough to fulfill its obligations even at current population-growth rates, the fact that increases in population raise the extent to which it fails to do so cannot justicize restricting the number of children its individual members may create. On the other hand, beyond a certain point (partly determined by the financial position of the family), increases in the number of children in given nuclear families clearly disserve the rights–related interests of the older children they contain. A liberal State is entitled to take this consideration into account. A liberal State is also entitled to prohibit people from having children whose upbringing and adult lives are predicted to impose net costs on others. Once each moral–rights holder has been permitted to have the number of children to which any moral–rights holder is entitled, she can be required to pay the cost of any additional children she creates or can be prohibited from creating children whose existence would be predicted to impose costs on others. The opposite conclusion would imply that non-paying parents have a right to use others as means to securing benefits to which the non-paying parents are not entitled.

The third question that a liberal approach would ask is: Assuming that a liberal State is entitled to adopt policies that reduce the number of children some of its moral-rights holders can create and parent, is sterilization or the imposition of criminal penalties the least restrictive means of securing the results that allegedly justicize this policy? In many situations, I suspect that less restrictive means will be available, such as civil fines, the reduction of tax benefits, the imposition of tax "penalties" (policies that, in effect, require prospective parents to pay for the privilege of having additional children). Admittedly, however, such approaches will not be satisfactory if the creation of the additional child in question would disserve the rights-related interests of its siblings by more than it served the rights-related interests of its beneficiaries. In these instances, a liberal State might be obligated to take steps that are more likely to secure the relevant older siblings' rights and to manifest the fact that liberalism disapproves of the choice the relevant parents are seeking to make.

Since no policy of this kind has ever been enacted, no Constitutional-law case has ever dealt with this issue explicitly. The case that is closest to being relevant is *Dandridge v. Williams*.[105] *Dandridge* upheld a provision of Maryland's Aid to Families with Dependent Children statute that established a maximum of $250 for the monthly grant to any given family, regardless of the number of children it contained or the state's computation of its financial needs. This decision (which I find Constitutionally dubious) suggests that the Court might be willing to uphold restrictions on the number of children individuals can create since it implies that individuals do not have the right to State support of the children they have created.

The discussion in this section has given only scant attention to two arguments that Chapter 3 indicated are sometimes morally and Constitutionally critical. The first such argument assumes that (1) a particular policy disadvantages members of some group whose treatment is suspect to a greater extent than it disadvantages the members of the other groups that contain some victims and (2) this difference reflects consequences of discrimination for which the State is responsible. I have argued that in some circumstances policies for which these two conditions are fulfilled may be unconstitutional on this account. In my judgment, this argument will rarely be critical in the current context. Even if the above two conditions are fulfilled, the rights-related interests that their fulfillment implies the policies would sacrifice would have to be set off against the net gain in rights-related interests that would otherwise justicize the policies in question.

The second argument I have in mind has three premises:

(1) the government policy in question does disadvantage the members of some group relative to the members of other groups,

(2) the policy will be perceived by the members of the relatively-disadvantaged group and/or by others to manifest the government's disrespect for the victims' group, and

(3) although this perception would be unjustified but for the government's responsibility to take it into account, it would be a reasonable misperception, given the fact that the government was responsible for previous discrimination against members of the group in question.

Once more, although this argument might be critical in the current context, it is less likely to be so here than elsewhere since the rights-related interests a decision against the policy would generate on this account would have to be set off against the net gain in rights-related interests the policy would otherwise generate.

(B) PARENTING RIGHTS

Two moral-rights issues need to be discussed under this heading: (1) Who has parenting rights both in general and in relation to particular children? and (2) What do parental rights entitle their possessor to do?

I have already indicated my conclusion that in a liberal society unmarried individuals and gays cannot in general be barred from parenting their biologic offspring or adopting the children of others. This conclusion is compatible with adoption agencies' taking into consideration the advantages of a child's being raised in two-parent households. It also is compatible with such agencies' taking into consideration any net disadvantages a child will suffer from being raised by gays (though I am unaware of any reliable evidence supporting the claim that there are such net disadvantages). The claim that it is legitimate for a liberal State to be influenced by the disadvantages a child may suffer as a result of being raised by gays (relative to the alternative situation that could be found for the child) is contestable when the disadvantage reflects prejudices directed at gays or their children. In my judgment, if the children were to be harmed by these prejudices, a liberal State would be obligated to take that fact into account, though it would also have to consider the extent to which its doing so would be perceived by gays as being discriminatory and by bigots as confirming the legitimacy of their prejudices (given that our governments both contributed to the relevant prejudices and would be responsible for their citizens' prejudices in any case). Somewhat relatedly, although I do not think that it is morally permissible for a liberal State to require the adoptive parents of a child to share the religious affiliation of its biologic parents, such a State may take into consideration any negative consequences that a child put up for adoption would suffer because one or both of the adoptive parents did not share its race: once more, although these consequences clearly reflect prejudices, I do not think that a liberal State may sacrifice important, rights-related interests of a child to make a symbolic point. As I have also indicated, it would be morally permissible for a liberal State to deny parenting rights to individuals who have repeatedly abused and neglected children they were parenting or had been convicted of sexual abuse of children when these individuals' past conduct makes the risk of recidivism unacceptably high. In addition, if one concludes that it is morally permissible for a liberal State to limit the number of children its individual members may create, it would also be morally permissible for such a State to deny individuals who have exceeded that limit the right to parent their "over the limit" offspring. A difficult issue that falls into this category is whether a biologic father of a child who has provided the child with substantial parenting services can be denied all parenting or visiting rights if the child is the issue of an adulterous relationship and its mother continues to be married to the man who was her husband at the time of the adulterous impregnation. In my judgment, in a situation in which the biologic father has engaged in considerable parenting of the child, the combination of his interest and the child's interest in continuing an important relationship outweighs the contestable interest of the biologic mother and her husband in keeping the adultery secret and in separating themselves from the biologic father and any more diffuse interest of the State in supporting existing marriages by denying putative fathers who claim to have begot the child in an adulterous relationship the opportunity to establish their paternity.

To my knowledge, only two Constitutional-law cases deal with any of these issues. Unfortunately, both seem to me to have been wrongly decided. In *Palmore v. Sidoti*,[106] the Supreme Court unanimously invalidated "a judgment of a state court divesting a natural mother of the custody of her infant child because of her marriage to a person of a different race."[107] Custody had been reassigned to the biologic father of the White child because the mother's perfectly respectable second husband was Black. According to Chief Justice Warren Burger, "[t]he question . . . is whether the reality of private biases and the possible injury they might inflict are permissible considerations for the removal of an infant child from the custody of its natural mother. We have little difficulty concluding that they are not. The Constitution cannot control such prejudices but neither can it tolerate them. Private biases may be outside the reaches of the law, but the law cannot, directly or indirectly, give them effect."[108] Moral-rights and Constitutional-rights analyses cannot be blind to realities. For three reasons, the Court cannot justicize shutting its eyes by arguing that "[w]hatever problems racially-mixed households may pose for children in 1984 can no more support a denial of constitutional rights than could the stresses that residential integration was thought to entail in 1917."[109] First, this statement incorrectly assumes that the definition of Constitutional rights does not turn on the relevant realities. Second, it ignores the fact that the child involved in *Palmore v. Sidoti* was innocent of any wrongdoing, whereas those who opposed residential integration were the beneficiaries if not instigators of wrongdoing. And third, it seems to assume that the "stresses of residential integration" in 1917 were as great as the "pressures and stresses" that a White child would face in 1984 in Florida—"peer pressures" and "social stigmatization that is sure to come"[110]—once it became known that the child's stepfather was Black. I am not in a position to make that comparative assessment, nor were the Justices of the Supreme Court. Their apparent conclusion that any such comparison is irrelevant is appalling.

The second case that is relevant in the current context is *Michael H. v. Gerald D.*[111] In this case, the Supreme Court upheld a California decision to deny paternity status (through a conclusive presumption that the husband is the father of a child conceived during his marriage to his wife) and visitation rights to a biologic father who had provided important parenting services to the child he had conceived in an open, adulterous relationship. The Court argued that in order to succeed in his claim Michael needed to demonstrate that "our society has traditionally ... [accorded] a natural father in his circumstances ... parental rights, or at least has not traditionally denied them."[112] According to the Court, the decisive fact was that "quite to the contrary, our traditions have protected the marital family ... against the sort of claim Michael asserts"[113] (both to avoid having children declared illegitimate and to promote the "peace and tranquility of States and families"). The Court went on to declaim that "whatever the merits of the guardian ad litem's belief that ... [establishing Michael as the child's legal father] can be of great psychological advantage to a child, the claim that a State must recognize multiple fatherhood has no support in the history or traditions of this country."[114] This argument is wrong for two reasons. First, once more, it focuses exclusively on the social practices that relate most closely to the claim under consideration rather than to the general principles to which we are committed. And, second, it ignores the possible rights-related interests of the child and considers only the possible parental interest and the supposed State interest. Unfortunately, these two failings are common and, as in the case of Michael D., are often critical.

I have already addressed the second parental-rights-related issue—what parental rights entail—in the course of discussing the rights of children to an education that will put them in a position to make meaningful life-choices. I have no doubt that individuals who are recognized as parents of children have the moral and Constitutional right to control their children's upbringing in a large variety of ways: the State may not supplant them because it believes it can do as good a job or because those in control of the State disagree with the parents' personal ultimate values, have different "life-style" preferences, or (*a fortiori*) subscribe to different religious beliefs from those of the child's natural parents. This conclusion reflects both the rights-related interests of the parents and those of the child. However, in a liberal society, parents do not have the right to disserve the temporal interests of their children in order to indoctrinate them into subscribing to the parents' own religious beliefs or personal ultimate values or in order to induce them to make choices that the parents' religious beliefs require. Parents do not have the right to isolate their children to prevent them from obtaining the informational base, personal experiences, analytic skills, and frame of mind that are prerequisites for the exercise of autonomy. Parents also do not have the right to deny their children medical treatment that is in the children's temporal interests.

Unfortunately, the case-law at both the Supreme Court and the state-court level is almost entirely to the contrary. In "parental-rights" cases, the courts virtually never recognize that children have rights-related interests that must be taken into account. Instead, they balance the parents' supposed rights-related interests in controlling their children (including denying them autonomy) against various "State interests" that the parental choices disserve. In general, parents win unless their choice will inflict grievous physical harm on their child or create a substantial risk that their child will become a financial burden on the State.[115] As I have already said, this body of law cannot be defended in liberal terms and is completely anomolous in our contemporary legal system: no other body of law allows a legal agent to use another who has not consented to such treatment as a means to further his own ends.

(4) Liberties That Endanger or Surrender Autonomy

The basic duty of a liberal State is to protect and promote the efforts of the moral-rights holders for whom it is responsible to exercise autonomy and lead lives of moral integrity. What does this duty imply for the obligations of a liberal State when those for whom it is responsible want to make choices that endanger or surrender their autonomy? This section comments briefly on a liberal State's duty in relation to a variety of moral-rights-holder choices that clearly raise this question and analyzes in somewhat more detail a liberal State's duty when a moral-rights holder chooses to die.

Moral-rights holders may endanger their autonomy in a number of ways, including consuming addictive drugs that take over their lives, entering into personal relationships that involve their surrendering their autonomy, and joining religious or secular cults or organizations that demand that they follow someone else's moral instructions. Liberal States not only may but are obligated to condemn such choices. Liberals do not have to take a neutral position in relation to illiberal choices, even if (contrary to fact) they affect only the chooser. I also have no doubt that a liberal State would be obligated to adopt other more concrete policies that militate against moral-rights holders' making these sorts of choices if (1) choices that endanger or surrender autonomy could be identified with certainty and (2) the State could be trusted to analyze choices that might fall into this category in good faith. Unfortunately, at least in relation to some choices of these kinds, one or both of the above conditions are not fulfilled. Moreover, even when they are, it will be very difficult to determine the best pro-autonomy policies (the policies that will secure the weightiest set of rights-related interests).

At the abstract level, the least problematic set of issues in this category are those raised by a moral-rights holder's choosing to consume addictive drugs. Although a State could conceivably misuse its authority to criminalize the use of narcotics by forcibly injecting and then arresting political opponents or their family-members or friends, I doubt that this option significantly increases the likelihood that an evil State would combat opposition in this sort of way. The difficult issue posed by narcotics addiction is the concrete issue:

put crudely, whether, everything considered, the best approach (in terms of rights-related interests) is the American approach (universal prohibition and criminalization) or the Swiss approach (prohibition and criminalization combined with State administration of drugs to registered addicts in a facility that educates and counsels them and encourages and helps them to kick their habit). The American approach probably deters more people from becoming addicts, but the Swiss approach reduces the amount of crime those who are addicted commit and may increase the percentage of addicts who escape their addictions.

A variety of different categories of personal relationships may endanger one or more of their participants' autonomy. Most autonomy-threatening relationships involve physical and psychological abuse. Some relationships (e.g., the relationship between a prostitute and her pimp) may be sufficiently likely to be abusive to justicize their prohibition. But others (marriage) that sometimes do involve abuse clearly are not.

State attempts to prevent moral-rights holders from entering into personal relationships that endanger their autonomy or to free them from such relationships that have cost them their autonomy are somewhat problematic because they often involve significant invasions of their supposed beneficiaries' privacy and may be unacceptably paternalistic in practice. At a minimum, a liberal State is obligated to educate its people to appreciate the importance of autonomy, to help them detect the characteristics of others that suggest that they may be autonomy-threatening, to provide the legal means (e.g., divorce) for people to escape from autonomy-threatening relationships, to provide shelter and psychological and economic help (including training) to people who have been abused, and to criminalize certain types of abusive behavior. In some circumstances, a liberal State might also be obligated to take more intrusive steps: to condition the issuance of marriage licenses to people in general or to members of some groups in which the incidence of abuse has been shown to be sufficiently high on their participating in abuse-education and abuse-counseling sessions.

Moral-rights holders also sometimes choose to join religious or secular groups that require their members to surrender their moral autonomy. At the extreme, some religious groups have been accused of engaging in brainwashing. But some much more conventional religions also require their members to follow the moral dictates of their leaders. Although, admittedly, most of us defer to others to some extent on some moral issues, there comes a point at which the deference that a group can require of its members and indoctrinate them to give really entails an assault on their autonomy. In some situations—for example, at some times in relation to some choices in battle-field situations in the armed forces—policies that restrict autonomy may be legitimate, even from a liberal perspective. However, the restrictions of autonomy that the religious and secular groups I have in mind seek to impose on their members clearly are unacceptable from the perspective of liberalism.

Nevertheless, a liberal State's duties in relation to these types of organizations are not clear. The sticking-point is not the liberal commitment to freedom of religion: religions do not have to be illiberal, and liberals do not have to respect illiberal religions. It is rather the privacy cost of State interventions, the risk that attempts to control or prohibit illiberal organizations of this sort will simply drive them underground, the reality that the people who join such organizations may have personalities that will lead them to surrender their autonomy in some other way if these organizations are eliminated or curtailed, and the very real danger that an evil State may misuse the authority to combat such illiberal organizations to attack religious and secular groups that oppose the governments in question.

These considerations all favor a liberal State's taking a cautious approach to this issue. Obviously, a liberal State is entitled to (if not obligated to) educate its moral-rights holders in ways that will discourage them from surrendering their moral autonomy to such groups, to comment on the illiberal character of such groups, and to prosecute the members of such groups for any kidnaping or other generic offense that they commit. However, from the perspective of liberalism, direct prohibitions of such groups may not be advisable, much less obligatory.

I have already indicated that a liberal State may be obligated to take steps to prevent its moral-rights holders from consuming addictive drugs whose use will threaten their autonomy. Does a liberal State have a similar obligation in relation to choices that would threaten their maker's autonomy by tending to shorten their lives—choices to smoke cigarettes, eat foods with high fat content, lead sedentary lives, and so on? In my judgment, no. Although no objection could be made to a liberal State's educating its moral-rights holders about the consequences of such choices and helping them to break any such bad habits they want to break, such choices are too likely to reflect personal-ultimate-value conclusions that are compatible with liberalism for stronger intervention to be legitimate.

5. *The Right to Determine When and How to Die*

A. Liberalism and the Right to Die

This section analyzes the moral and Constitutional rights of members of a liberal, rights-based culture to choose when and how to die; Section B comments on various aspects of Ronald Dworkin's analysis of these issues; and Section C discusses the Supreme Court's analysis of these issues.

What are the obligations of a liberal state

(1) when a moral-rights holder for whom it is responsible chooses to die by killing himself through a positive act, with no one's assistance, by killing himself with the assistance of a physician or someone else, or by refusing life-maintaining medical treatment or nutrition?

(2) when someone who is a competent moral-rights holder signs either a living will that instructs others to kill the incompetent creature he may become or to allow that creature to die in specified circumstances or a medical-proxy document that authorizes someone else to give such an instruction?

(3) when someone who is not competent to choose between life and death at a particular time but may become so in the future has not signed a living will or medical-proxy document?

(4) when someone who will never again be competent to choose between life and death has not signed a living will or medical-proxy document?

I address each of these questions in turn. Unfortunately, not only the questions but also some of the answers that my understanding of a liberal society's commitments implies are disturbing.

The first issue that must be addressed in relation to a competent person's choosing when and how to die while he is still competent is whether he has a liberty interest in making that choice. I have argued that in a liberal society, a moral-rights holder has a liberty interest in making and effectuating a particular choice if and to the extent that the relevant choice enables him to discover or instantiate his values. Even if deciding when and how to die does contribute substantially to moral self-discovery,[116] that fact would not provide much support for a related liberty claim because

(1) from the perspective of liberalism, this type of self-understanding is important to the extent that it enables the person who knows what he values to lead a life of moral integrity and

(2) the metric for the extent to which a choice enables someone to lead a life of moral integrity has a substantial longitudinal component.

However, in many instances, an individual's choice to die sooner than he must or in one way rather than another may help him effectuate the values to which he subscribed—in Dworkin's words, "may keep faith with the way [he] want[s] to live."[117] Thus, an individual who enjoys physical activity, being productive, and providing financial and emotional benefits to her friends and loved ones may increase the integrity of her life as a whole by foreshortening the period in which she is inactive, unproductive, and a psychological and financial burden on her loved ones. If such a person enjoys the esteem and love of those she loves, she may also value preventing her "family's happy recollections [of her] being replaced by horrific ones."[118] Less dramatically, she may value highly her loved ones' remembering her living the life she chose to live rather than the diminished life she led at the end. I do not deny that individuals may misjudge the effects on their loved ones of their living versus those of their choosing to accelerate their death. The point is not to deny that it may be legitimate for a liberal State to prohibit or make it more difficult for someone to choose death for paternalistic reasons related to this possibility. It is to establish the paradoxical claim that a moral-rights holder may have a strong autonomy interest in ending her ability to choose by choosing to die—may be able to increase the moral integrity of her life by accelerating her death—and therefore may have a strong liberty interest in choosing to die.

The next issue posed by a competent person's choosing to die while he is still competent is: What arguments can a liberal State use to justicize its restricting such a person's liberty to die? At least eleven such justifications have been proposed.

The first is "paternalistic"—that is, it is based on the State's belief that the chooser's choice is not in his best interests as he would define them if properly informed even though his error does not reflect anyone else's coercing him or overbearing his will. The paternalistic case for a State's overriding a moral-rights holder's choice to die will be strongest if the physical pain he is enduring, his emotional state (say, the depression brought on by his rejection by or the death of a loved one), or various imperfections in the information available to him are likely to have led him to reach a decision not in his own interest (given his values and preferences). In some circumstances, paternalism can justicize a liberal State's overriding a moral-rights holder's choice to die or, less restrictively, imposing a waiting period on him (sacrificing his autonomy interest in making the choice in question in order to further his own best interests). In the "right to die" context, this conclusion is supported by the fact that many individuals who ask for help in committing suicide change their minds when given pain-killers, advice on their medical condition and prospects, and counseling.

The second possible justification for even a liberal State's not allowing someone to hasten his death is duress. The State may fear that the will of the person who has chosen to die was overborne by, for example, family members (who do not like to see him suffer, who want to escape from the duty of visiting or looking after him, and/or who do not want his estate to be diminished by medical expenses) or doctors (who prefer dealing with patients they can cure, feel compassion for his suffering, and may be in the employ of hospitals or insurance companies that will sustain losses if his life is prolonged).

A third legitimating ground for a liberal State's restricting a moral-rights holder's liberty to choose to die is the fear that allowing individuals to agree to accelerate their deaths in some circumstances may result in some of the relevant individuals' being killed despite the absence of even their nominal consent—that doctors or family members may take it upon themselves to substitute their judgment for that of the person whose death was accelerated.[119] Of course, this alleged justification would not be available if there were a less restrictive means of preventing this kind of abuse and might be rejected in any case on the ground that it uses those whose choices to die would be uncoerced and in their own interest as a means rather than as an end.

A fourth argument that may legitimate a liberal State's restricting a moral-rights holder's liberty to choose when and how to die assumes that doctors or some other authoritative figure play an important role in the relevant decisions. The State may fear that in practice these decisionmakers may let their prejudices influence their choices. In other words, they may let their decisions be influenced by their beliefs that the lives of the aged, the poor, the handicapped, members of various racial and ethnic minorities that have been the targets of prejudice in the relevant society, and so on, have relatively less value.

A fifth possible justification for prohibiting a competent moral-rights holder's choosing to die is the bandwagon effect (Werther syndrome)—that one person's justifiable choice to die may lead others to make the same choice despite the fact that it is against their interests to do so. Even if this hypothesis is empirically correct, it is far from clear that it can justicize restricting the autonomy of someone who can exercise it in his own interest. Would not doing so amount to using this person as a means rather than as an end?

A sixth argument assumes that doctors are involved in a formal procedure that someone must follow to be permitted to accelerate his death, presumably because the protection their participation provides against mistakes and overbearing relatives exceeds the risk of their abusing their authority. In particular, some claim that even if a liberal State would otherwise be obligated to permit competent individuals to choose to die after receiving the advice of a physician, it does not have to do so, given that the doctors' participation will corrupt them and reduce the quality of the services they provide in general. This argument is based on the empirical premise that doctors, who allegedly would otherwise be exclusively concerned with improving health and saving lives, would start to take other considerations into account if they become involved with authorizing death. There are four objections to this claim. The first is empirical: since doctors appear to play a major role in decisions to die now, often without the authority to do so, their authorized participation in the making of these choices is unlikely to significantly alter their general professional conduct. Second, the State should have to validate its fears on this issue through an experimental program before basing its decision on them. Third, this argument may be illegitimate because it treats the moral-rights holder who would increase the integrity of his life and serve his own interests by accelerating his death as a means rather than as an end. And fourth, even if this argument were empirically sound, sufficiently researched, and otherwise morally permissible, there would almost certainly be less restrictive means of deterring the feared consequences.

A seventh possible justification for a liberal State's restricting a competent moral-rights holder's liberty to control his death also assumes that doctors would have to be involved in any procedure to authorize such choices. The argument is that doctors' participation in such a procedure will reduce the quality of the services they can provide by destroying the trust that patients have for their physicians. At least two objections can be made to this argument. The first is that it incorrectly assumes that doctors do not now play a major role in these sorts of decisions—for example, in deciding whether to treat a patient's pain with medication that will accelerate death. The second is that it reflects a misunderstanding of the doctor-patient relationship, fails to take account of the fact that "the good physician is not just a mechanic of the human body whose services have no bearing on a person's moral choices, but one who does more than treat symptoms, one who ministers to the patient."[120] To the extent that this is the case, a doctor's giving responsible and sympathetic help to a patient contemplating accelerating his death should increase rather than decrease the trust between them and between doctors and patients in general.

The eighth through tenth alleged justifications for overriding a moral-rights holder's choice for death are the desirability of preventing harm to her relatives and friends, the costs that some people who may or may not have a personal connection with her would incur because they disapprove of her choice or find it sinful, and the cost to the State of losing her productivity. These arguments fail because (with some conceivable exceptions)[121] the persons who suffer these losses have no entitlement interests in relation to the chooser's choice.

Eleventh and finally, it has been argued that our State is entitled to prohibit individuals from choosing death when doing so would be in their interest, to protect the "sacred" character of life—the notion that life is "inviolate." This argument fails for two reasons. First, in a liberal culture, human life is valued because humans have the capacity to lead lives of moral integrity and, *ex hypothesis*, allowing the relevant individuals to choose to accelerate their deaths is consistent with life's being sacred on that account both because it respects the chooser's autonomy and because it enables him to make a choice that increases the integrity of his life as a whole. Second, and relatedly, this argument also fails because it treats the individual who wants to accelerate his death as a means rather than an end.

Unfortunately, the preceding analysis does not yield a straightforward conclusion—in part because it may be difficult in practice for a supervisory authority to control the circumstances in which deaths are accelerated and in part because we lack a lot of information that is highly relevant to the right answer to various "right to die" questions. It probably would be impermissible for a liberal State simply to prohibit anyone under any circumstances from purposefully accelerating his death. However, a liberal State also may be obligated to protect individuals who are not being coerced but who are in pain, are in stressful situations, or are depressed from making irreversible, life-and-death decisions that are against their interests, to prevent those for whom it is responsible from having their will overborne, and to stop doctors or others from ending the life of a moral-rights holder without obtaining even his nominal consent.

I certainly cannot identify the regime that best accommodates these concerns in this country at this time. The optimal regime might take into consideration whether the chooser was in substantial physical pain that would not be permanent, had recently suffered a substantial loss, was clinically depressed, or would die if life-saving services were withdrawn. It might also take into account the probability that the individual in question might totally recover or experience an improvement in her condition. Possibly, the optimal regime would honor only those requests to die that had been persistently repeated over a significant period of time after the chooser had received medical, psychological, and ethical counseling not only from individuals of her own choice but from independents trained in the field. Even after all the empirically or morally dubious arguments are dismissed, a great deal must be learned to determine the concrete implications of liberalism for the rights of competent moral-rights holders to choose to die while they are still competent. However, our ignorance does not imply that a liberal State may simply leave this area to democratic decisionmaking. As I will argue when discussing the Supreme Court's decisions in this area, a liberal State may be obligated to do research on some of the relevant empirical issues—perhaps by establishing a series of experimental programs.

I, too, feel uncomfortable with the implications of my conclusions for the proper resolution of the second set of "right to choose death" cases previously distinguished: What are the obligations of a liberal State when a "living will" signed by a competent moral-rights holder instructs others not to use certain medical procedures to keep him alive in specified circumstances or to kill any incompetent creature he may become in specified circumstances (or when a "health-care proxy" document authorizes someone to decide whether to end its signer's life in specified circumstances and the proxy chooses to do so)? All but one of the arguments that were deemed relevant when the "death target" was unambiguously the person who gave the "death instruction" are relevant in this context as well. The exception is the possibility that a physician or someone else might decide for death without obtaining its target's even nominal consent.

However, this case raises four special issues. First, assuming *ad arguendo* that the incompetent "death target" is a moral-rights holder, is he the same person as the competent signer of the living will or medical-proxy document—in other words, is the signer of the living will morally entitled to decide the fate of the incompetent creature he has become because the competent person is entitled to decide his own fate? My inclination is to give a negative answer to these two (equivalent?) questions.

Second, is the incompetent "death target" a moral-rights holder? My general conclusion is that in a liberal society a creature is a moral-rights holder if and only if she has the neurological prerequisites to become and remain an individual of moral integrity. I assume that some "individuals" who are not competent to choose between life and death may be able to lead lives of moral integrity, and some may not. If the creature to whom the living will's death-instruction (medical-proxy document) applies is a moral-rights holder, one will have to decide whether she is the same person as the signer of the living will or medical-proxy document. If she is, a court using a substituted-judgment approach could cite the living will or medical-proxy document to justify a conclusion that the incompetent would have chosen to die had she been competent. If, on the other hand, the incompetent moral-rights holder is a different person from the signer of the living will, enforcing its terms would in effect permit one person to cause another person to be put to death or allowed to die. Obviously, a liberal State would have to come up with an extraordinary argument to justicize its permitting a living will's death-instruction to be carried out in these circumstances. The execution of the living will's (or medical proxy's) instruction would further several moral-rights-related interests (despite the fact that, on this account, its signer is dead): (1) the "posthumous" interest of its signer (all others who will share her fate) in not having her (their) loved ones' and friends' memory of her (them) contaminated by the latter's experience with the creature she has become (those similarly situated will become), (2) the signer's "posthumous" autonomy interest in having her instructions followed, and (3) the interests that those similarly situated have in not being induced to kill themselves when they are still competent to avoid becoming an incompetent whose death they cannot control. Although I think these interests are substantial, they would not justicize permitting the relevant incompetents to be put to death or to be allowed to die: in our culture, moral-rights holders are allowed to kill innocent others (for example, the temporarily insane) who threaten them with death or serious bodily harm only when there is no opportunity of safe withdrawal, and this condition is not fulfilled in the situations under consideration.

However, I suspect that, in most instances of this second case, the incompetents to whom the living will or medial-proxy document apply will not be moral-rights holders—they will have permanently lost the neurological prerequisites for leading lives of moral integrity. If so, the execution of the living will's or medical proxy's death-instructions will not violate their moral rights because they have no moral rights. Nor, for reasons discussed in relation to the first case, do the relatives and friends of the living will's or medical-proxy document's signer or anyone else for that matter have rights-related interests in frustrating the execution of his living will or the instructions of the medical proxy. Hence, given the strength of the signer's "posthumous" interests and those of others who are or will be similarly situated, a liberal State would be obligated to allow his instructions to be carried out.

The third case focuses on incompetents who may become competent in the future for whom there is no living will or medical-proxy document. I will assume that the fact that such "creatures" may become competent to make a life-death choice in the future implies that they still have the neurological prerequisites to lead lives of moral integrity—that they are still moral-rights holders. What are a liberal State's obligations in relation to the continuance of such an individual's life? Is a liberal State obligated to keep him alive? Is it obligated on its own motion to execute a substituted-judgment procedure and kill him or allow him to die if it concludes that he would have preferred this outcome in the circumstances in question? Is it obligated to keep him alive in the hope that he will recover sufficiently to be able to give instructions about the acceleration of his death? It seems to me that unless a liberal State can reach a conclusion about such an individual's preference about which it has no substantial doubts, it is obligated to keep him alive in the hope that he will be able to make an autonomous choice about the last stages of his life.

The fourth case focuses on a liberal State's obligation to a "creature" who is not and will never again be competent to choose between life and death and has not signed a living will or medical-proxy document. I assume that most if not all such creatures no longer have the neurological prerequisites for leading a life of moral integrity. The few who do are moral-rights holders to whom a liberal State owes a duty of respect. That duty may require their being put to death or allowed to die if the State concludes that such a choice would have been their preference (perhaps because it would have increased the integrity of their lives). It is a mistake to assume (as Justice William Rehnquist did in *Cruzan*)[122] that little in the way of rights-related interests is sacrificed if someone who would have chosen to die is kept alive: not only has that person suffered a loss (to the integrity of her life and by the degradation of the way in which she is remembered) but others similarly placed have suffered similar losses as well.

In the vast majority of situations covered by this fourth case, the creature whose fate is to be decided is not a moral-rights holder. From a liberal perspective, the person whose body is now the creature's has already died. At one extreme, the creature whose fate is at stake will be in a persistent vegetative state. However, that fact does not imply that a liberal State has no obligations in relation to the survival of such a body. Even if those who loved the person now in this condition are not thought to have entitlement interests in this matter, the "dead" moral-rights holder to whom the body in question belonged has a posthumous interest in her body's treatment, as do other moral-rights holders who may suffer her fate. I cannot fathom what opposing interests would justicize a liberal State's refusing to allow such a body to die. True, a liberal State does have an interest in supporting the sanctity and inviolability of human life (to the extent that doing so deters rights-violations and perhaps to the extent that it encourages people to lead lives of moral integrity). However, since vegetating "human" bodies no longer house a moral-rights holder, whose capacity to lead a life of moral integrity made her life sacred, and since (if you do not grant this conclusion) the prolongation of a vegetative life would decrease the integrity of the life led by the person to whom that body belongs (in my judgment used to belong), keeping such bodies alive desecrates human life rather than celebrating its sacred character.

Admittedly, not all cases in this category involve "people" who are in a vegetative state. Some who are permanently incompetent to make choices for death and will never again be able to lead lives of moral integrity will nevertheless be capable of experiencing real pleasure and perhaps even of interacting in some meaningful way with others. The competent moral-rights holder to whom their bodies used to belong may have subscribed to values that would not be disserved by keeping this new creature alive. In such cases, one could not say that keeping such creatures alive would reduce the integrity of their "predecessors'" lives. Assuming that these creatures are not moral-rights holders, could a liberal State be obligated to keep them alive? Would it be morally permissible for a liberal State to kill such a person or to allow him to die to save the cost of sustaining him or to respond to the expressed preferences of his relatives? Does the moral-rights holder to whom such a person's body used to belong (and others who may one day be in a similar position) have rights-related interests in his being allowed to live so long as his living would not reduce the integrity of his predecessor's life? If his continuing to live would reduce the integrity of his predecessor's life and this fact is the best information available about how his predecessor would have preferred to have been treated in these circumstances, is a liberal State obligated to help him die or allow him to die? To what extent is the proper resolution of this issue affected by the risk that the State may intentionally misuse any authority it has to cause death to punish political opponents and deter political opposition? If one simply cannot tell how a person who is no longer competent to choose death would have wanted to be treated in the actual circumstances, do those who love him have a right to have their preferences determine how he is treated? Recall that, although a liberal State's duty of appropriate, equal concern primarily focuses on a moral-rights holder's actualizing his potential to lead a life of moral integrity, a liberal State must also be concerned with the pleasure and satisfaction such creatures obtain from their lives.

Although this section has focused on the various moral-rights issues raised by the possibility of accelerating an individual's death, I do not think that there is any difference between these moral-rights issues and their Constitutional-rights counterparts. In substantial part, this conclusion reflects my rejection of the State Action doctrine, or, more generally, my rejection of the premise that our State has no obligation to take positive steps to secure the moral rights of the moral-rights holders for whom it is responsible. In any event, since the primary duties and constraints with which this section is concerned would relate to the states, the textual home for the analysis I think is relevant is the privileges or immunities clause of the Fourteenth Amendment. To the extent that the central government is implicated (say, in the need to collect additional information), the relevant text is the Ninth Amendment.

The issues this section has addressed are empirically extremely important. They are also growing more important every day as medial-care advances enable increasing numbers of people to live to ages in which they are very likely to suffer substantial diminutions of their capabilities. I have tried to suggest the way in which the version of liberalism to which I believe our culture is committed would structure the analysis of the right to determine how and when to die. Although some of the conclusions I have reached are conventional, others are not only surprising but no doubt disturbing, at least to some (sometimes even to me). I suspect that most of the conclusions that cause dismay primarily reflect my "boundary-condition" conclusion that in a liberal, rights-based society a "creature" who no longer has the neurological prerequisites to lead a life of moral integrity is not a moral-rights holder and the related conclusion that in such a society, for moral-rights-analysis purposes, such a creature should not be considered to be the same person as the moral-rights holder to whom its body used to belong.

B. Ronald Dworkin's Analysis: A Comparison

Dworkin's analysis of the right to die emphasizes our commitment to al-lowing persons to define for themselves what is sacred about life.[123] His analysis differs from mine in five basic respects. First, he does not seem to distinguish between what I call moral-ought analysis and moral-rights analysis.

Second, and partly relatedly, Dworkin does not always take account of the fact that our society distinguishes between two types of values: the second-order value of autonomy (which is closely connected to our rights-commit-ments) and the first-order values to which individual moral-rights holders choose to subscribe (which underlie their non-rights-based moral-ought conclusions). I say "not always" because at critical places in his analysis he does pay attention to this distinction. For example, it underlies his claim that three issues must be considered when deciding whether to allow someone's death to be accelerated: the individual's autonomy interest (the second-order value), his best interests (which relate to the first-order values he has chosen), and the effect of the State choice on the sanctity of human life (which I think relates to the second-order value of autonomy—see below) (*LD* 188–96). It is also implicit in his statement that "it is a terrible form of tyranny, destruc-tive of moral responsibility, for the community to impose tenets of spiritual faith or conviction on individuals" (*LD* 15). And, it may be implicit in the distinction he draws between States that aim to have their citizens take moral issues seriously and those that aim to have their citizens conform their views to those of the majority (*LD* 150).

On the other hand, at various times Dworkin seems to lose sight of this distinction and of our related societal commitment to the second-order value of autonomy. For example, Dworkin states that in our society "[i]t is obvious enough that the abstract idea of life's intrinsic value is open to dif-ferent interpretations" (*LD* 70). Admittedly, this passage may mean nothing more than that people who share the same abstract understanding of "life's intrinsic value" may reach different conclusions about whether particular acts violate that value; they may apply their shared abstract understanding differently (an interpretation favored by the examples that appear next in *Life's Dominion*). However, I suspect that this passage reflects Dworkin's be-lief that we are not committed to the view that human life is valuable be-cause humans have the capacity to lead lives of moral integrity—a view that implies that the second-order value of autonomy has a higher status than the various first-order values to which people are entitled to subscribe. This second account is favored by many other passages in *Life's Dominion*. Thus, Dworkin says that "[t]he sanctity of life is a highly controversial, *contestable* value" (*LD* 151). He refers to"two sometimes competing traditions, both of which are part of America's political heritage. The first is the tradition of personal freedom. The second assigns government responsibility for guarding the public moral space in which all citizens live" (*LD* 150). If the relevant moral space is liberal and the government's responsibility to guard it is the responsibility to protect its moral-rights holders' autonomy, the traditions of personal freedom and government responsibility for guarding our public moral space are not competing. Again, contrary to what Dworkin states or implicitly assumes, if we are socially committed to the liberal second-order norm I have articulated and that norm has the boundary-condition implications I have ascribed to it, the moral-rights-bearing status of foetuses at different stages of development and of creatures in a persistent, permanent vegetative state would not be a matter of individual conviction but of social commitment. And finally, if Dworkin recognized the link between autonomy and our moral-rights commitments, he would not regard liberal convictions about the value of human life as just one among many such convictions extant in the society and would be much more forthcoming about the meaning of his concept of "frustration of life" (*LD* 90).

Third, relatedly and somewhat repetitively, I believe that Dworkin's moral analysis leaves far more to individual choice than does our society. To Dworkin, what makes life sacred, what creatures deserve protection, and what choices desecrate the sacred all seem to be a matter of personal conviction. I think not. Similarly, Dworkin assumes that our moral-rights practices can provide no right answer to such critical questions as when a foetus becomes a moral-rights holder, whether someone in a permanent vegetative state is a moral-rights holder, and whether a "human" in a vegetative state or someone less damaged but also not capable of leading a life of moral integrity is the same person as his moral-rights-holder predecessor. I think that there are internally-right answers to all these questions. Dworkin appears to disagree.

Fourth and, I suspect, partly because Dworkin does not think that there are internally-right answers to many questions to which I think such answers can be given, he is willing to accept the fact that individuals take inconsistent positions on issues related to some questions (e.g., on whether the foetus is a moral-rights holder at various stages of its development or on what counts as sacred [*LD* 80]) as evidence for their being no right answer to the relevant questions. I think that these inconsistencies simply manifest the relevant individuals' confusion about the right answer to these difficult questions.

Fifth, and again partly relatedly, Dworkin assumes that longstanding legal practice is self-legitimating—that, for example, the fact that "American law had never in the past treated foetuses as constitutional persons" implies the correctness of the decision that a foetus is not a Constitutional person (*LD* 110). If one recognizes that ours is a rights-based society that distinguishes moral-rights analysis and moral-ought analysis and that to be morally legitimate the legal system of a rights-based society must make arguments based on the moral norm on which it is committed to grounding its moral-rights discourse the dominant form of legal argument, longstanding legal practices and conclusions that are inconsistent with those norms will be respectively illegitimate and incorrect (unless those norms justicize following a precedent that was wrong when it was first announced).

I have learned a great deal by reading Dworkin's analysis of "living and dying." The differences in our analyses reflect the basic disagreements I have just articulated, which were previously discussed in an abstract way in Section 1 of Chapter 2.

C. Constitutional Doctrine

One could review a variety of Constitutional-law doctrines that relate in some fashion to the right to choose death and see what they imply for the consistent positivist resolution of the issue in question.[124] Thus, one could see whether, under current law, an individual's liberty interest in choosing death should be considered fundamental, important, not important, or non-existent—a characterization that would determine the type of scrutiny the Court would give to any government choice that restricted the "liberty" to accelerate death. Unfortunately, the cases fail to clarify what attributes of a choice qualify it to involve a liberty interest at all or determine the strength of an individual's liberty interest in making it. One could also try to resolve this issue historically in terms of the traditions of our people. Although this task would be simple and would yield a clear conclusion if the relevant history were narrowly gauged (since suicide and assisted suicide have virtually always been prohibited in this country), the Court sometimes does broad-gauged historical analysis and has never indicated what determines the appropriate breadth for any legal analysis of tradition. I could go on, but I do not think that much would be learned by doing so.

Instead, I will focus on the opinion of the Court and the various concurrences and dissents written in three cases the Supreme Court has decided that deal explicitly with the right of an individual to have her death "accelerated." The first such case is *Cruzan v. Director, Missouri Department of Health*.[125]

The question posed by *Cruzan* was whether it was Constitutional for the state of Missouri "to require a now-incompetent patient in an irreversible persistent vegetative state to remain on life-support absent rigorously clear and convincing evidence . . . of specific statements of treatment choice made by the patient when competent."[126] The majority of the Court concluded that this policy was Constitutional.

The opinion of the Court by Chief Justice Rehnquist seems to accept that the Constitution does obligate the states to enforce the instructions or effectuate the explicitly-stated preferences of a competent person that life-saving sustenance not be provided in this sort of case.[127] Typically, the Court's justification for this conclusion is not an argument from first principles but a narrow-gauged historical argument that "[a]t common law, even the touching of one person by another without consent and without legal justification was a battery" and that the related "notion of bodily integrity" led to the "entrench[ment] . . . in American tort law" of the "informed consent doctrine" that a patient generally has a right to refuse medical treatment.[128] However, it holds that a state may Constitutionally require both that those instructions be given or preferences be stated explicitly by the competent person and that the evidence establishing this fact be "clear and convincing." According to the Court, in the absence of such evidence, a state has no Constitutional duty to carry out the wishes of even the most-highly-qualified, best-motivated family members of the creature whose fate is being decided.

The majority opinion contains at least three dubious assumptions and makes at least two dubious arguments. The first dubious assumption is implicit—namely, that the person Nancy Cruzan is still alive. From a liberal perspective, the person Nancy Cruzan died on the night of the tragic automobile accident that left her in an irreversible, persistent, vegetative state. Admittedly, however, this mistake may not be critical: one may be able to generate the same conclusions by focusing on the posthumous interests of Nancy Cruzan and the current interests of those who may find themselves in her position in the future.

The majority opinion's second dubious assumption is that the state of Missouri has a legitimate "interest in the protection and preservation of human life"[129] that can be furthered by a decision to reject the choice of someone to accelerate her death even when that choice is in the relevant person's interest because it will increase the integrity of her life. This claim that a state in a liberal society has "an unqualified interest in the preservation of human life" is straightforwardly mistaken. Although individual members of a liberal society are perfectly entitled to base their own decisions about death and evaluate the decisions of others on the conviction that human life is valuable (perhaps *inter alia*) because it is a gift of God (not just because of the way in which humans can live their lives), neither such individuals nor a liberal State can justicize restricting the liberty of others on this sort of ground.

I have already mentioned the third erroneous assumption of the *Cruzan* majority—that little is lost by a decision to continue to provide someone like Cruzan with life-sustaining hydration and nutrients. As Justice Brennan argues in dissent: "An erroneous decision not to terminate life support . . . robs the patient of the very qualities protected by the right to avoid unwanted medical treatment; his own degraded existence is perpetuated; his family's suffering is protracted; the memory he leaves behind becomes more and more distorted."[130] Moreover, as I have already indicated, such a decision also imposes costs on moral-rights holders who are concerned about the prospect of being treated similarly in similar situations.

The first dubious argument that the majority makes is that our tradition of "treating homicide as a serious crime" and "of imposing criminal penalties on one who assists another to commit suicide" imply not only that a state is not "required to remain neutral in the face of an informed and voluntary decision by a physically able adult to starve to death" but also that the states have "an unqualified interest in the preservation of human life."[131] This argument ignores both the possibility that specific traditions of this kind may be non-fits that deserve no weight as well as the possibility that the traditions in question may be consistent with the liberal analysis of those issues—an analysis that does take "quality of life" considerations into account in the process of determining whether the acceleration of death would increase or decrease the integrity of the relevant individual's life.

The majority's second unconvincing argument is that Missouri's requirement that the relevant individual's preference be established by clear and convincing evidence of explicit statements that individual made on the relevant issue "is justified because it is more important not to terminate life support for someone who would wish it continued than to honor the wishes of someone who would not."[132] As Brennan and Stevens point out in dissent, this argument underestimates the cost to the relevant individual of not having his preferences followed, disregards the effects of such a decision on third parties (family and friends and others who fear they may suffer the same fate as the individual in question), and ignores the possibility that as much protection against inaccurate findings of preferences can be secured less restrictively by adopting such alternative procedures as the appointment of a neutral guardian *ad litem*.[133]

I also want to comment briefly on the jurisprudential assumptions of the separate concurrences written by Justices Sandra Day O'Connor and Antonin Scalia. Justice O'Connor's opinion appears to be based on the premise that a decision restricting a state's authority in the right-to-die area can be justified only if it is supported by a national consensus.[134] Absent such a consensus, she seems to think, the Court's proper role is to turn the "challenging task" over to the states, which can act as laboratories for "crafting appropriate procedures for safeguarding incompetents' liberty interests" in this area.[135] Implicitly, she seems to be arguing that if as a result of the states' efforts or otherwise a national consensus does develop, the Court would be justified in Constitutionalizing that consensus—for example, in holding that "the Constitution requires the States to implement the decisions of a patient's duly appointed surrogate."[136]

Obviously, since I believe that the principles to which we are committed can obligate us to respond in particular ways to given situations even if there is no consensus in our society on the specific obligation in question, I disagree with Justice O'Connor's apparent assumption that such a specific consensus is either a necessary or a sufficient condition for the states' being constrained in this area (or for the legitimacy of the Court's declaring that the states are so constrained).

Five assumptions Justice Scalia adopted in his concurring opinion deserve mention.[137] First, Scalia assumes that Constitutional rights must be based either on Constitutional text or on specific traditions. I explained why I reject this premise when analyzing "strict constructionism" in Chapter 2.

Second, and relatedly, Scalia assumes that specific traditions are self-legitimating. As I have argued, since rights-based societies may not always fulfill their commitments in specific behavior areas, I do not think that specific traditions are self-legitimating in a rights-based society such as ours.

Third, Scalia assumes that the person Nancy Cruzan is still alive. From the perspective of liberalism, although her body lingered on, the person Nancy Cruzan died at the time of her accident.

Fourth and relatedly, Scalia assumes that our traditional handling of suicide is relevant to the resolution of the *Cruzan* case—indeed, that it renders "the power of the state to prohibit suicide ... unquestionable."[138] From a liberal perspective, even if that tradition were self-legitimating or consistent with our moral principles, it would be irrelevant to *Cruzan* since Nancy Cruzan was already dead when her parents requested that she be disconnected from the machines providing her with hydration and nutrition.

Fifth, Scalia assumes that for Constitutional purposes, there is no right answer to the question of why human life is valuable, sacred, or inviolate. For that reason, he concludes that "even when it is demonstrated by clear and convincing evidence that a patient no longer wishes certain measures to be taken to preserve her life, it is up to the citizens of Missouri to decide, through their elected representatives, whether that wish will be honored."[139] Obviously, I disagree both with this premise and with this conclusion.

I have already made reference to the dissenting opinions by Justices Brennan and Stevens. Both are exceedingly eloquent, highly perceptive, and completely consistent with the approach I have argued our liberal commitments demand our State take to the issues posed by the *Cruzan* case. Stevens's opinion is particularly notable in this respect. In addition to the points already mentioned, it recognizes that

(1) "death is not life's simple opposite, or its necessary terminus, but rather its completion";[140]

(2) "for patients like Nancy Cruzan, who have no consciousness and no chance of recovery, there is a serious question as to whether the mere persistence of their bodies is 'life' as that word is commonly understood, or as it is used in both the Constitution and the Declaration of Independence";[141]

(3) "Missouri's protection of life in a form abstracted from the living is not commonplace; it is aberrant";[142]

(4) "[i]t is not within the province of secular government to circumscribe the liberties of the people by regulations designed wholly for the purpose of establishing a sectarian definition of life."[143]

I could not have said it better.

In June 1997, the Supreme Court handed down two additional "right-to-die" cases. *Washington v. Glucksberg*[144] rejects a facial "due process" (i.e., "privileges or immunities") attack on a Washington statute prohibiting any person (including a physician) from "knowingly caus[ing] or aid[ing] another person to commit suicide" in an overall legislative scheme in which (1) "withholding or withdrawal of life-sustaining treatment" at a patient's direction "shall not, for any purpose, constitute a suicide"[145] and (2) "a patient who is experiencing great pain has no legal barriers to obtaining medication, from qualified physicians, to alleviate that suffering, even to the point of causing unconsciousness and hastening death."[146] *Vacco v. Quill*[147] rejects an "equal protection" attack on a New York legislative scheme that permits "those in the final stages of terminal illness who are on life-support systems ... to hasten their deaths by directing the removal of such systems" but prohibits them "to hasten death by self-administered drugs"[148] as part of an overall regime that also permits palliatives to be given that may hasten death.

Unfortunately, once one moves beyond these somewhat facile statements, it is difficult to determine what these cases stand for. Admittedly, they do manifest the existence of a clear majority supporting some positions that I think are either inconsistent with liberalism or questionable from a liberal perspective: contrary to the view of the majority of the Justices, liberal States do not have an "unqualified interest in the preservation of human life,"[149] and it is questionable whether it is legitimate for liberal States to prohibit some individuals from controlling the timing and manner of their deaths who would otherwise have the right to do so to prevent other individuals from making uncoerced but mistaken life or death decisions, from being coerced into choosing death, or from being put to death without even their nominal consents.

However, there is every reason to believe that there is no majority on the Court for the basic doctrinal conclusions Chief Justice Rehnquist's supposed "opinions of the Court" articulate. Rehnquist's majority opinions are (in the words of my colleague Sandy Levinson) "honorary majority opinions"— opinions that are honored more in the breach than in the observance. Almost certainly, five of the Justices disagree with Rehnquist's apparent conclusion in *Glucksberg* that the liberty interests that moral-rights holders have in determining the time and manner of their deaths are never fundamental or even important (so that, to be Constitutional, State restrictions in the exercise of this liberty need be only rationally related to the achievement of a legitimate State goal).[150] Rehnquist argues that to be "fundamental" in Constitutional parlance, an interest must be "carefully described" and "deeply rooted" in our nation's narrow-gauged history and tradition. (These two conditions are connected since there is more likely to be a consensus on the way to articulate a right to the extent that it is deeply rooted in practice.) Neither of these requirements is met for the interest at stake in *Glucksberg*. Thus, at various times, the Ninth Circuit (whose judgment the Court was reviewing), the respondents in the case at hand, and other analysts like me have referred to "the right to die," "the liberty to choose how and when to die," "the right to die with dignity," "the right to choose a death that increases the integrity of one's life," and so on. However, I demur to this accusation— each such articulation captures part of a complex set of interests I think all moral-rights holders in a liberal society have. I see no reason why this variation in the relevant interests' articulation should matter. Admittedly as well, the right of terminally-ill, mentally-competent adults to commit suicide is not part of our narrow-gauged tradition (though I think that under some conditions it is implied by our broader-gauged practices and is also consistent with rules allowing life-support to be withdrawn and palliatives that will hasten death to be administered). But again, so what? The narrow-gauged tradition may be a non-fit.

Rehnquist justifies this two-pronged test by arguing that it "tends to rein in the subjective elements that are necessarily present in due-process judicial review."[151] I reject the claim that "subjective elements" are logically necessarily present in fundamental-rights analyses as well as the claim that Rehnquist's approach confines subjectivism. In this connection, Rehnquist's failure to specify how under his approach one determines the level of abstraction at which a fundamental interest should be articulated or the breadth of the relevant historical inquiry is highly noteworthy. If the analyst has strong discretion when making these choices, in what sense does the approach rein in the subjective elements in the relevant analysis? In any event, since five Justices seem to reject Rehnquist's conclusion that the individual interest involved in *Glucksberg* is never fundamental, they must reject his approach to assessing the character of an interest as well.

I simply do not know whether the majority of the Court (in particular, the authors of the four concurrences) accepts Rehnquist's contention that the distinction under attack in *Vacco*—between taking positive steps to help someone hasten his death and withdrawing life-sustaining treatment—is "important," "logical," and "rational"[152] and in any case legally valid. In part, Rehnquist's argument for this distinction is that it has traditionally been drawn both by the law and by the medical profession.[153] But primarily his argument is that "[t]he distinction comports with fundamental legal principles of causation and intent."[154] The causation argument is mystical, and the interest argument is wrong.

According to Rehnquist, "when a patient refuses life-sustaining medical treatment, he dies from an underlying fatal disease or pathology, but if a patient ingests lethal medication prescribed by a physician, he is killed by that medication."[155] These statements may reflect standard legal usage, but clearly they reflect nothing more. Scientifically, the death of the patient who has accelerated his demise by refusing life-sustaining medical treatment or sustenance was "caused" by this refusal as well as by his disease or pathology—*ex hypothesis*, both were necessary causes of his dying when he did. Similarly, scientifically, the death of a patient who ingests lethal medication was also caused by his disease or pathology (which was an "anterior" cause of his consuming the medicine and dying). There is nothing intrinsically important, logical, or rational about the legal usage. Rehnquist's suggestion to the contrary is nothing more than an attempt to use tradition as a bootstrap.

Rehnquist's "intent" argument is equally dubious. According to the Chief Justice:

> a physician who withdraws, or honors a patient's refusal to begin, life-sustaining medical treatment purposefully intends, or may so intend, only to respect his patient's wishes and "to cease doing useless and futile or degrading things to the patient when [the patient] no longer stands to benefit from them." Assisted Suicide in the United States, Hearing Before the Subcommittee on the Constitution of the House Committee on the Judiciary, 104th Cong., 2d Sess., 368 (1996)(testimony of Dr. Leon R. Kass). The same is true when a doctor provides aggressive palliative care; in some cases, painkilling drugs may hasten a patient's death, but the physician's purpose and intent is, or may be, only to ease his patient's pain. A doctor who assists a suicide, however, "must, necessarily and indubitably, intend primarily that the patient be made dead." *Id.* at 367. Similarly, a patient who commits suicide with a doctor's aid necessarily has the specific intent to end his or her own life while a patient who refuses or discontinues treatment might not. See, *e.g., Matter of Conroy* [98 *N.J.* 321] at 351, 486 *A.2d* [1209] at 1224 (patients who refuse life-sustaining treatment "may not harbor a specific intent to die" and may instead "fervently wish to live, but to do so free of unwanted medical technology, surgery, or drugs"); *Superintendent of Belchertown State School v. Saikewicz*, 373 *Mass.* 728, 743, n. 11, 370 *N.E.2d* 417, 426, n. 11 (1977) ("[I]n refusing treatment the patient may not have the specific intent to die.")[156]

In fact, however, these ascriptions of "intent" all confuse "intent" with "desire" and ascribe desire inconsistently and uselessly. A patient who commits suicide with a doctor's aid may desire only to escape pain and degradation; she may not desire to die even though she knows that taking the lethal medicine in question will kill her. Such a patient's desires may be no different from those of a physician who administers palliatives wishing to reduce pain but knowing that he will be simultaneously hastening death. One can of course stipulate that an agent "intends" the natural consequences of his act, regardless of whether he desires them, but not much is accomplished by so doing or by defining "suicide" to include only those acts that have death as a natural consequence. The issue is not linguistic; it is moral. I do not question the relevance of the moral distinctions on which the law focuses. My objection to Rehnquist is that his attempts to detach our legal practice from its moral moorings have caused him to confuse the relevant moral distinctions. Neither the law nor Rehnquist can escape facing up to the relevant moral issues.

I want to close my discussion of these two cases by commenting on the significance of two facts on whose implications a majority of the Court seems to agree. The first is that the right-to-die issues on which we are now focusing are currently being discussed seriously in democratic fora in circumstances that suggest that their resolution is not likely to disadvantage any group that does not have a fair amount of political power (which may not be the case in this area—c.f., the fear that physicians might let their prejudices affect their choices if empowered to determine whether certain individuals can choose to die or [in practice] can be put to death). A majority of the Justices seems to think that these facts imply that the Court should not intervene on these issues. Although I think that these facts justify the Court's giving more deference to the relevant legislature's decision, they do not justify its altering its test of Constitutionality or willingness to assess the choice that was made. Serious deliberation in politically-fair institutions can still produce decisions that violate the rights of some of those they affect.

The second fact is that the proper resolution of many of the issues we have been discussing is difficult to identify, in part because we do not know many of the facts that determine the correct conclusion. The Court seems to think that this fact implies that our governments have no obligations in this area. I think they imply something quite different: given the strength of the liberty interests at stake, the central government is obligated to investigate the operation of existing programs (such as the Netherlands' scheme) and to provide the states with the wherewithal to run and study experimental programs to learn what we would have to know to discover the right answers to the relevant rights questions.

6. Abortion-Related Rights

I now turn from the end of life to its beginning. My comments on abortion-related rights are divided into four sections. Section A delineates and criticizes Judith Jarvis Thomson's[157] famous analysis of the moral right of a human to abort her pregnancy. Section B presents my own analysis of various abortion-related moral rights and Constitutional rights in a liberal, rights-based society. Section C describes and criticizes the Supreme Court's two most important abortion decisions—*Roe v. Wade*[158] and *Casey*.[159] And Section D briefly considers Donald Regan's[160] and Ronald Dworkin's[161] analyses of the Constitutional-rights issues raised by a woman's desire to abort her pregnancy.

A. Thomson and the Right of a Pregnant Woman to Abort Her Pregnancy

In a well-known article, Judith Jarvis Thomson at least purports to argue that , even if the foetus is assumed *ad* arguendo to have a right to life, it would not by virtue of this "fact" have the right to require its mother to carry it to term (or even to the point at which it could safely be removed through a caesarean section).[162] This conclusion is unexceptionable—at least in so far as it relates to cases in which the pregnant woman would have to incur a significant risk of serious bodily harm or death to provide the required gestational services. However, like many lawyers, I read Thomson actually to be making a far stronger claim that, even if the foetus does have a right to life, it would never have a moral right to the gestational services of its mother. I reject both the abstract argument that I think Thomson made to support this strong conclusion and the most important example she used to illustrate this less-modest argument.[163]

Thomson's abstract argument focuses on our alleged general Good-Samaritan-duty practices. The argument begins by analogizing the request that a pregnant woman carry a foetus to term to a request that a Good-Samaritan provide rescue services to someone who requires them. On my reading, it then asserts that in our culture individuals do not have a Good-Samaritan moral duty to rescue a moral-rights holder who will otherwise die, even when the potential rescuer would not have to face any significant risk of serious bodily harm or death to effectuate the rescue. These two premises lead to the conclusion that a pregnant woman would not have a moral duty to carry her foetus to term (or to the point at which it would not be significantly harmed by being removed through a caesarean section) even if it were a moral-rights holder at the time of choice.

I have six objections to the abstract argument I believe Thomson made. First, even though, historically, the common law rarely imposed Good-

Samaritan duties, this legal practice seems to me to be inconsistent with the moral-duties beliefs of most members of our society. Second, if Thomson is correct about our specific moral practices in relation to Good-Samaritan duties, they would seem to me to be inconsistent with the moral principle to which our moral practices as a whole commit us. Third, as I indicate in Chapter 3,[164] more recent case-law and legislation has substantially expanded the legal duty to render assistance—a fact that confirms my claim that in the past our law was inconsistent with our moral-rights beliefs and commitments. Fourth, even if, in most situations, the conclusion that people do not have Good-Samaritan moral duties could be reconciled with the value of autonomy on which we are committed to basing our moral-rights discourse, the autonomy case for a no–duty-to-rescue rule is far weaker in the abortion context. Fifth, in standard Good-Samaritan-duty analysis, a woman's refusal to provide rescue services to her foetus would be considered a positive disengagement or a refusal to complete a service once begun (neither of which is covered by the alleged no–duty-to-rescue practice) rather than a failure to provide rescue services. And sixth, a pregnant woman's status-relationship to her foetus, her "cause in fact" connection to her foetus's predicament, and sometimes her culpability for its predicament may place her in one of the supposedly-exceptional situations in which even supporters of the no–duty-to-rescue rule recognize a duty to render aid (at least if the fact that the pregnant woman is a cause of the foetus's existence and not just of its being at risk is not critical).

Rather than addressing each of these objections in the abstract, I will do so in the context of the example Thomson uses to illustrate her argument. However, before doing so, I want to elaborate on my claim that a no–duty-to-rescue rule is inconsistent with the moral principle that we are committed to instantiating in our moral-rights discourse and practice.

The main evidence to support the claim that members of our culture are not in general morally obligated to be Good Samaritans is the fact that historically the common law rarely imposed such legal duties. However, three "legal" facts do or may undercut this evidence. I have already mentioned the first: our law has recently substantially increased the range of situations in which it imposes Good-Samaritan legal duties. The second is that the modern law of other Western European countries (civil-law as opposed to common-law countries) whose moral commitments are probably not that different from our own (France, for example) has always imposed much more extensive Good-Samaritan legal duties. The third is that an argument can be made[165] for the legitimacy of a liberal State's refusing to make the moral right to rescue services legally enforceable—namely, that particularly when there are multiple potential rescuers a State might misuse the authority to impose Good-Samaritan legal duties by imposing such duties selectively on its political opponents and their friends and families.

I have no systematic evidence about the moral beliefs and practices of members of our culture in relation to Good-Samaritan duties. However, casual empiricism suggests that we do believe that people have a moral duty to render positive assistance to those in significant peril when providing such help would not subject us to a substantial risk of significant bodily harm or death. Such a commitment would in any case be more consistent with our liberal commitment to autonomy, which implies not only that each moral-rights holder's ability to lead a life of moral integrity be respected by the State but also that each moral-rights holder show appropriate, equal respect for each other moral-rights holder in the relevant society and appropriate, equal concern for each such person's actualizing his potential to lead a life of moral integrity. Indeed, in various circumstances, the State's imposing a legal duty to rescue could actually further the interest of moral-rights holders in exercising autonomy and leading lives of moral integrity. For example, a State's enforcing someone's promise would further his autonomy both in holding him to his presumptively-autonomous decision and by enabling him to further his own purposes by committing himself to perform various acts if particular conditions are fulfilled. In fact, it might also be consonant with some notions of autonomy for the government to attach duties to render aid to certain (voluntary) status-relationships since the presence of officially-recognized status-relationships may very well broaden the options available to each individual: this conclusion reflects not only the fact that it is time-consuming to craft relationships out of whole cloth but also the fact that such individualized relationships are different on that account from socially-recognized or institutionalized relationships. Indeed, autonomy may also be furthered by imposing a legal duty to render assistance on any moral-rights holder who culpably created the potential rescuee's need for assistance since individual responsibility is the flip side of individual autonomy and we generally have a duty to mitigate any losses we have culpably caused.

I now turn to Thomson's example. To illustrate her analysis, Thomson conjures up the image of a concert violinist with a rare blood-type who is dying of kidney malfunction. She asks us to assume that fans of the violinist kidnap a woman with the same blood-type and attach her to a blood-transfer machine that enables her kidneys to cleanse the violinist's poisoned blood. Thomson assumes that this process involves no unusual discomfort or long-term risk to the woman and that after nine months the violinist's kidneys will have healed sufficiently to enable him to function satisfactorily without her. Thomson then asks whether the violinist, who obviously is a moral-rights holder and therefore does in some abstract sense have a right to life, is entitled to this woman's continued help. Thomson argues that our Good-Samaritan moral-duty practices imply that the violinist has no such entitlement and concludes that this result implies that even if the foetus does have a right to life in some sense (is a moral-rights holder in my terminology) it is not entitled to life support from its mother.[166]

On my reading, Thomson's argument can be expressed in the following way: (1) the kidnaped woman's decision to unplug herself from a blood-transfer machine is a decision not to render aid (to make a harmful omission rather than to commit a harmful act); (2) the kidnaped woman has no positive duty to aid the violinist; therefore (3) the kidnaped woman is entitled to unplug herself from the blood-transfer machine; (4) a decision to have an abortion is analogous to a decision to unplug oneself from a blood-transfer machine: both are harmful omissions rather than harmful acts; (5) the pregnant woman's position is the same as the kidnaped woman's: neither has a duty to render positive assistance; therefore (6) the pregnant woman is entitled to have an abortion even if the foetus is a moral-rights holder from the moment of conception (does in some abstract sense have a right to life).

I argue that, even if one grants the first three premises of the argument I read Thomson to be making,[167] premises four and five are incorrect, so that her argument cannot justify her conclusion. In other words, I will argue that the analogy I think Thomson is drawing is inapposite and that it therefore fails to establish the strong conclusion I am attributing to her (or, indeed, even the more modest conclusion for which she purports to be arguing).

Thomson's violinist example is supposed to present a case of a person who must choose between rendering aid and failing to render aid. Although one might question Thomson's assumption that unplugging oneself from the machine is not a positive act from the perspective of the act-omission distinction,[168] let's assume that Thomson is correct in her characterization of this event. However, Thomson's fourth premise—that a woman who has decided to have an abortion has merely refused to render aid—is clearly incorrect for many types of abortions and is arguably incorrect for all types of abortions. Thus, several abortion methods such as curettage, vacuum aspiration (suction), and the administration of a saline solution do involve direct acts against the foetus—that is, they injure the foetus directly and not just indirectly by disconnecting it from the pregnant woman's supplies. Moreover, although the remaining abortion methods (hysterotomy and the administration of prostoglandins) do not directly injure the foetus,[169] courts would almost certainly characterize them as positive acts of disengagement[170] that are equivalent to positive harmful acts: once the pregnant woman has taken the foetus into her lifeboat, the attempt to push it back into the water is unlikely to be considered a refusal to render aid. Unlike the abortion case, Thomson's example does not involve a positive harmful act or an act of affirmative disengagement, and therefore, (1) it is not analogous to the abortion case and (2) one's conclusions about Thomson's case (premise three) do not have any bearing on the abortion situation.

Thomson's analysis also assumes that, like the kidnaped woman in her own example, a pregnant woman has no positive duty to aid the violinist. In fact, this premise is unjustified. Even those who believe that our society is committed to a no-general-duty-to-rescue rule recognize that under some conditions individuals do have a positive duty to render assistance to others—namely, when they have promised to do so, when they have a significant status-relationship to the person in need of help, when they were the culpable cause of the person's need for help, and when they were a non-culpable cause in fact of the potential rescuee's need for assistance. (Indeed, although this last possible source of a positive duty to aid seems to me not to be justifiable or justicizable in general, since in a world of imperfect information making such rescuers strictly liable is as likely to decrease allocative efficiency by deterring allocatively-efficient avoidance by the rescuer as it is to increase allocative efficiency by inducing the potential rescuer to engage in allocatively-efficient assistance, it may be justifiable in the context of abortion in which strict liability will not deter the potential rescuee from engaging in avoidance.) None of these conditions is fulfilled for the woman in Thomson's violinist example.

Thomson's woman made no relevant promise, has no relevant status-relationship to the violinist, and is in no way responsible for the position in which the violinist finds himself. By way of contrast, a pregnant woman may have made a relevant promise, does have a status-relationship with her foetus, was a cause in fact of its predicament, and may have been a culpable cause in fact of its predicament. At this point, I do not want to argue that these differences clearly establish that every pregnant woman would have a duty to render assistance to her foetus if it were a moral-rights holder and she could do so without incurring a substantial risk of serious bodily harm or death. Many pregnant women have made no relevant promise; the status-relationship between a pregnant woman and her foetus may be *sui generis*; some pregnant women are not culpable causes in fact of their foetus's predicament; and those who are, are culpable causes in fact of their foetus's existence as well as of its being at risk (a fact that may be critical even if non-culpable causation does justicize imposing a duty to aid).

Again, my current point is not that the strong conclusion I am attributing to Thomson is wrong; it is that the analysis of her violinist example does not reveal much about the obligations of a pregnant woman because none of the possible grounds for concluding that a pregnant woman does have a duty to provide gestational services to her foetus is present in her example. In short, the argument I believe that Thomson uses to demonstrate that pregnant women do not have a positive duty to render gestational services to their foetuses is questionable, and her example is inapposite.

B. A Liberal Analysis of Abortion-Related Rights

(1) The Right to Terminate a Pregnancy If One Can Pay for the Abortion

(A) WHEN THE FOETUS IS A MORAL-RIGHTS HOLDER

In Chapter 1 I argued that (1) a foetus becomes a moral-rights holder when it has developed the neurological prerequisites for leading a life of moral integrity and (2) a foetus will not have reached that stage of development until the thirtieth week of the pregnancy.[171] Less than 1 percent of actual abortions performed take place after the pregnancy has advanced this far, but if foetuses are moral-rights holders after their thirtieth week, it is still important to explain why abortions performed at or beyond that stage would rarely be morally permissible in a liberal State.

Assume that a general no-duty-to-aid rule were consistent with or required by a commitment to liberal values. Even on this contestable assumption, there would be six possible grounds for concluding that, beyond the thirtieth week (when the foetus was a moral-rights holder), a pregnant woman would normally have a duty to her foetus either to carry it to term or to delay its removal or delivery until it would not significantly harm the foetus. First, within Good-Samaritan-duty practice, the abortion of a foetus would be considered to be a positive disengagement, which is outside the no-duty rule, rather than a refusal to render aid.

Second and relatedly, the abortion of a foetus after the thirtieth week might be considered to be the breaking-off of a rescue-attempt that one initiated (which is not covered by the no-duty rule) rather than a refusal to render aid. Admittedly, however, the two most persuasive justifications for the breaking-off-of-a-rescue-attempt "exception" to the no-duty-to-rescue rule do not apply in the pregnancy context: the initiation of the rescue attempt (the failure to terminate the pregnancy) will not have deterred others from attempting a rescue and will not have made things worse for the potential rescuee by raising and then crushing its hopes.[172] However, if the abortion is delayed until sentience, the delay may have produced a morally-equivalent effect by increasing the pain the foetus experiences.

The next four possible grounds would apply even if the refusal of a pregnant woman to provide gestational services would be categorized as a refusal to render aid. The third possible ground is by far the least important empirically. In a few cases, a pregnant woman may have an obligation to provide gestational services to her foetus because she has promised to do so. I do not think that a promise to this effect can be found to be implicit in a woman's decision to get married.[173] However, in rare instances, a pregnant woman may be bound because she has explicitly promised to complete her pregnancy in exchange for her husband's or lover's agreement to obtain a vasectomy. In this case, the foetus would be a third-party beneficiary of the relevant contract. Of course, such a contract may not be valid or specifically enforceable. At least if the parties to such a contract are married, I doubt that it would be held *contra bones mores*. And although the general belief is that personal-service contracts are rarely if ever specifically enforceable, the reality is to the contrary, particularly when (as in this situation) the service-supplier is unique.[174]

Fourth, a pregnant woman may also have an obligation to supply gestational services to her moral-rights-holding foetus because of her status-relationship to this creature. Liberal societies may be obligated to impose moral and legal duties on participants in certain types of relationships—especially those that involve the kind of intimacy liberals value. Of course, this conclusion does not imply that a liberal society may or is obligated to force an obligation-generating relationship on someone by requiring her to carry her foetus to term or safety, even if the State's motivation is to confirm the importance of the relationship between mother and child. However, the fact that the pregnant woman did not assume her status voluntarily (by intentionally conceiving the foetus) or negligently (by failing to take reasonable precautions to reduce the risk of pregnancy) is not dispositive: children may have obligations to support their parents (or parents their children) despite the fact that they did not voluntarily or negligently enter into that status relationship. Nor can we distinguish the case of the child's duty to its parents from that of a pregnant woman to her foetus by pointing to the fact that the child has received benefits from the parents. At least, the irrelevance of this consideration is suggested by the fact that a woman living at a time in which abortion was unlawful had an obligation to protect and nurture her newborn infant (even if the child was conceived through rape). Admittedly, if the status-relationship of a pregnant woman to her foetus is *sui generis*, it may not be possible to determine whether it imposes a duty on her to render her foetus gestational services.

Fifth, a pregnant woman may also have a duty to provide gestational services to her foetus because she is a culpable cause in fact of the foetus's requiring aid. Thus, a pregnant woman may be "at fault" because she engaged in voluntary sexual intercourse without taking any birth-control precautions with or without the intention of becoming pregnant (that is, because she became pregnant willfully or advertently)[175] or because she was raped while walking alone across Central Park in the middle of the night ignorantly or unthinkingly (that is, because she became pregnant negligently though inadvertently). In this latter connection, it is important to note that negligent behavior that leads to the damage of a third party cannot always be excused on the ground that the risk that made the behavior negligent arises from the possible moral-rights-violating (and illegal) behavior of another. Thus, one may be held liable for injuries caused by joyriders if one leaves one's keys in the car in a dangerous neighborhood. Perhaps more persuasively, since we are now concerned with abortions after the thirtieth week of pregnancy, the pregnant woman may be at fault for not having the abortion earlier, when the foetus was not sentient or moral-rights-bearing. Admittedly, there will be cases in which changes in the pregnant woman's circumstances make her late decision to abort non-culpable (or, at least, would do so if the foetus she is carrying were not a moral-rights holder). Of course, as already indicated, the preceding discussion ignores what may be a critical point—namely, if the pregnant woman is "at fault," she is at fault for the foetus's existence and not just for its being at risk. Once more, I do not know what to make of this complication.

Sixth and finally, a pregnant woman may incur an obligation to render the foetus assistance simply because she was a cause in fact of its predicament. Admittedly, however, the only way I can reconcile this conclusion with liberalism is to assume that it is a response to our inability to determine fault in a situation in which the creature requiring rescue clearly could not have been at fault. Once again, of course, the fact that the pregnant woman was a cause in fact of the foetus's existence and not just of its need for aid would have to be taken into account.

I admit that each of the last three arguments is problematic. None matches its standard counterpart perfectly. Moreover, although the promissory argument does work, it is not important empirically. Still, given my doubts about whether we really have adopted a no-duty-to-rescue rule, my suspicion that such a rule violates liberal tenets, and my conclusion that an abortion would be categorized as a positive disengagement or the breaking-off of a rescue rather than as a mere refusal to render assistance, I am confident that pregnant women would normally have a moral duty not to kill or endanger their foetus once it becomes a moral-rights holder unless (1) the active killing of the foetus were a justifiable homicide (for example, a killing in self-defense), (2) carrying a foetus to term were too burdensome a task to be required of someone whose duty was simply to provide reasonable aid (which is the only duty that is ever imposed), (3) requiring someone to carry a foetus from the thirtieth week to term or at least to safety would (in Thirteenth Amendment terms) amount to imposing "involuntary servitude" on them, or perhaps (4) the foetus would have a wrongful life. Each of these possibilities will now be addressed in turn.

The following example suggests that a pregnant woman's killing her foetus cannot be regarded as a justifiable homicide. Assume that a woman who is still lactating is caught in an early blizzard while hiking in Alaska. She finds refuge in a cabin that is not her own, which is also inhabited by another trespassing woman and her newborn infant. The cabin is well-stocked with enough food and other supplies to get the two adults through the long winter ahead. But there is no baby food, and it is clear that the infant will die if the lactating woman does not nurse it. The infant's mother (who is not lactating) tells the woman who is lactating that she will force her to nurse and help care for the infant. Assume that the mother is sufficiently strong to carry out this threat. If the woman who is lactating does not agree to nurse the baby, the mother will tie her up at feeding times without causing her any significant harm or pain. Would the woman who is lactating be justified in killing or inflicting serious bodily harm on the mother in such a case?[176] Would any attempt by her to do so be criminally punishable? My criminal-law colleagues tell me that the woman who is lactating would be criminally liable for killing or seriously injuring the mother in this case despite the fact that, unlike the foetus in the pregnancy case, the mother in this case has threatened to criminally assault the defendant: since the woman who is lactating was under no threat of serious bodily harm or death, she could not justify seriously harming or killing another to free herself from the inconvenience and physical and psychological cost of nursing and caring for the infant.

Of course, the relevance of this hypothetical turns on the relationship between the costs the lactating woman is being forced to bear and the cost to the pregnant woman of continuing her pregnancy from the thirtieth week either to term or to some earlier date in which a caesarean section or an induced birth would not significantly endanger the foetus and having the foetus removed or delivered through a procedure that does not endanger it inappropriately. One should not underestimate the cost to the lactating woman of nursing the other woman's baby. These costs include

(1) the loss of physical freedom associated with being restrained and forced to nurse the baby;
(2) the physiological consequences of continuing to lactate and nurse;
(3) the inconvenience and discomfort of nursing; and
(4) the cost of eventually severing the relationship with the baby to whom she will become attached through nursing (though these costs will be offset by the cost of knowing that her refusal to nurse the baby has caused its death).

Moreover, the hypothetical is consistent with the lactating woman's having to nurse the baby for longer than the time the pregnant women on whom we are currently focusing would have to continue their pregnancies. Still, these "costs" to the lactating woman may well be significantly smaller than the "costs" to a pregnant woman of continuing her pregnancy the necessary time beyond the thirtieth week and having the foetus safely removed or delivered.

A pregnant woman has a variety of legitimate interests in terminating her pregnancy even after the thirtieth week:

(1) an interest in physical health and well-being—to the extent that the last weeks of pregnancy are costly in this regard and the physical cost of a termination-procedure at this stage that would protect the foetus is higher than the physical cost the pregnant woman would otherwise have to incur;
(2) an interest in avoiding the discomfort, pain, and inconvenience of any additional weeks of pregnancy as well as any additional inconvenience incurred to protect the foetus;
(3) an interest in being able to control her own body;

(4) an interest in avoiding any additional financial cost of giving birth as opposed to having a late abortion and the substantial financial cost of raising the baby if she decides to keep it (though this interest is attenuated by her ability to give the baby up for adoption);

(5) an interest in not having to sacrifice her educational and career goals to parent the child;

(6) an interest in not having to reduce the quality of her parenting to her other children to take care of an additional child;

(7) an interest in not having her relationships with her spouse, parents, siblings, other family members, and friends suffer as a result of the time she spends parenting this child (though any such costs must be compared with the counterpart "costs" that she would generate by having an abortion);

(8) a related interest in not having these others suffer from the reduction in the quantity and quality of the time she can give them;

(9) an interest in not having to forego bearing and raising another child at a subsequent time when she could parent it more effectively and at less cost to her other relationships and goals; and

(10) an interest in avoiding the privacy cost of having the child—most importantly, the loss of anonymity during her last weeks of pregnancy, the loss of solitude she will incur if she raises the child, the privacy (and other) cost of having to stay in contact with the child's biologic father, and the loss of solitude and secrecy she will suffer if she gives the child up but it contacts her in the future (a more likely result now that many states have given such children the legal right to information on the identity of their birth-mothers).[177]

Admittedly, a pregnant woman's legitimate interest in terminating her pregnancy after the thirtieth week in a way that does not protect the foetus versus going to term or accelerating the removal or delivery of the foetus in some way that protects it may well be weightier than the legitimate interest of the lactating woman in not nursing. However, except when the protection of the foetus would create a significant increase in the probability that the pregnant woman would suffer serious bodily harm or death, any extra differences would probably not be critical. Remember that the pregnant women on whom we are now focusing would not have to carry the foetus much or perhaps at all longer: at most, what is involved is a couple of extra weeks of pregnancy and the use of a delivery or removal procedure that is safe for the foetus. If the position of the pregnant woman is not critically different from that of the lactating woman, the late-term abortion could not be considered to be a justifiable homicide.

I also do not think that a pregnant woman could justify terminating a normal pregnancy after the thirtieth week in a way that would kill the foetus by arguing that going to term or protecting the foetus in some other way would be too burdensome to be permissible or would entail her being subjected to involuntary servitude. In fact, I think that any argument to the contrary is morally equivalent to the "justifiable homicide" argument I just rejected.

Admittedly, if there were strong grounds for believing that the pregnant woman's foetus would have a wrongful life (though he would be able to lead a life of moral integrity), that fact would (I think) justicize her aborting her pregnancy. Indeed, I think a strong argument can be made for the pregnant woman's having a duty to abort such a pregnancy even if she has religious objections to doing so. Although the following principle may not apply to the current situation, in general a person's religious beliefs do not entitle him to control the conduct of someone else.

I therefore think that women who have not aborted their pregnancy before the thirtieth week would normally have a duty to protect their foetus by carrying it to term or accelerating its removal or delivery through some procedure that does not endanger it inappropriately. I use the word "normally" for two reasons. First, pregnant women would not have this duty if fulfilling it created a significant additional risk of their suffering serious bodily harm or death. Second, a pregnant woman would also be entitled to abort her pregnancy if the thirty-week-plus foetus were handicapped in a way that deprived it of its moral-rights-bearing status.

I hasten to add that these qualifications do not legitimate a variety of the more concrete exceptions to a pregnant woman's duty not to abort her pregnancy that have been proposed and sometimes adopted both in the United States and elsewhere.[178] For example, the late-term abortion of a foetus that is already a moral-rights holder cannot be justified by the discovery that it will suffer from a handicap (whether genetic or not—for example, from blindness [which can be either congenital or caused by the mother's contracting rubella]) that does not deprive it of its moral-rights-bearing status and will not cause its life to be wrongful. Nor can such an abortion be justified on the ground that raising the child will be unusually difficult for the mother (*inter alia* because the State has provided her with the option of giving it up and any preference she may have to kill it rather than give it up does not deserve respect because it does not show appropriate respect for the moral-rights-holding foetus). Similarly, the foetus's being a product of incest or rape will not justify terminating the pregnancy in a way that kills or endangers it unless these facts create a sufficient probability that the foetus would have genetic defects that would make its life wrongful or increase to a prohibitive level the psychological burden to the woman of continuing the pregnancy until the foetus can be removed or delivered safely. The genetic condition is unlikely to be fulfilled. Although the psychological-cost condition might be fulfilled earlier on in the pregnancy (when to my mind it will almost always be otiose), it is unlikely to be fulfilled for pregnancies that have already reached the thirtieth week: even if the woman discovered that her pregnancy was the product of rape or incest that late, the cost to her of having the foetus removed in a way that would not kill or injure it (or, indeed, of carrying it for a week or two longer to improve its chances) are unlikely to be prohibitive.

(B) WHEN THE FOETUS IS NOT A MORAL-RIGHTS HOLDER

The relevant analysis is different in several respects when the foetus is not a moral-rights holder. Most obviously and importantly, in this case, the woman can abort her pregnancy without disserving the rights-related interests of the foetus she kills because it has no rights-related interests (though unsuccessful abortion attempts that damage a foetus that develops into a moral-rights holder do disserve the rights-related interests of that future moral-rights holder). In addition, if the foetus is not a moral-rights holder because the pregnancy is not advanced, a number of the pregnant woman's legitimate interests in aborting will be much stronger. Early on, the abortion will generate larger health-cost, financial-cost, and psychological-cost savings. It will also save the pregnant woman more pain, discomfort, and inconvenience. Moreover, an abortion in the initial stage of a pregnancy will protect the pregnant woman's privacy to a greater extent by enabling her to avoid being an object of attention and by preserving her secrecy—by enabling her to conceal the fact that she was sexually active, had become pregnant, and chose to have an abortion. Admittedly, in a liberal society, some of her desires for such secrecy may not be legitimate—they may reflect her wish to "defraud" (1) her husband or friend by keeping him from discovering that she had killed his foetus or that she had been sexually involved with someone else or (2) her parents or others to secure more financial and personal benefits from them. However, although some of those with whom the pregnant woman is involved (for example, her husband or her parents if she wants to obtain financial support from them that they are not obligated to provide) may have the right to be informed of her choice and some (again, the impregnating husband and perhaps the parents of a minor child) may even be entitled to have their say about what the pregnant woman ought to decide so long as there is no significant risk that they will attempt to coerce or assault her, no one else has, with one possible exception, a rights-related interest in the woman's continuing her pregnancy that justicizes requiring her to do so. I have already mentioned the exception: a lover (or, better yet, a husband) who wants to parent and has been induced to have a vasectomy by the pregnant woman's promise to carry his foetus to term or to safety or, perhaps, a husband who wants to parent who has become incapable of fathering additional children since impregnating his wife with the foetus in question.

Moreover, I do not see that the State has any independent rights-related-type interests that could justicize its requiring a woman to continue to provide gestational services to a foetus that is not a moral-rights holder. Certainly, the State could not justicize such an order by citing the goal of increasing population or the desirability of having a person born who would produce more than he would consume. There are less restrictive means of achieving these goals. I also do not think that a liberal State can justicize the prohibition of early abortions on the ground that doing so protects the sacred or inviolate character of human life. A liberal society is committed to the position that human life is valuable because it can be lived with integrity. Preventing a woman from aborting a foetus that has not yet developed the neurological prerequisites to live such a life does not protect the sanctity of human life. The creature that is preserved is not the kind of physical entity that can lead such a life, and the prohibition prevents a moral-rights holder from making a choice that is consonant with her values. People who oppose abortion because they subscribe to the religious position that human life is valuable because it is a gift of God are entitled to that view and to make their own choices conform to it, but neither the members of a liberal State nor a liberal State itself may force others to conform to this view. Nor can a liberal State justicize prohibiting a woman from having an abortion by citing the fact that doing so would prevent the losses that would otherwise be incurred by those who find the relevant abortions sinful or morally undesirable. Such people may have a psychological and even a welfare interest in the abortion choices others make, but in a liberal society they have no entitlement interest in these choices: these choices are none of their (entitlement) concern or business.

I should probably stop now, but at the risk of appearing or being inconsistent, I will raise one other issue to which I cannot find a satisfactory response. I have no doubt that in a liberal society a pregnant woman has the right not just to abort an early pregnancy but to have enough time to consider what she wants to do in a thorough and responsible manner. Unless the woman discovers her pregnancy unusually late or is financially or physically trapped in a location in which she cannot secure a safe abortion, those rights would clearly be respected by a rule permitting a woman to abort her pregnancy in the first trimester. My doubts relate to abortions between that period and the point of the pregnancy at which the foetus becomes a moral-rights holder—most importantly when the foetus is viable but not a moral-rights holder or is close to being viable but not a moral-rights holder. I am uncomfortable with the conclusion that a liberal State may not prohibit abortions of normal pregnancies at such times even though I do not think that a prohibition of such abortions could be justicized in terms of the foetus's rights. In a few of these cases, such a prohibition might be justicized by the fact that the husband's or impregnator's rights-related interest in having the child outweighed the pregnant woman's legitimate interest in ending the pregnancy somewhat sooner or in having the baby delivered or removed in a way that happened to kill it as opposed to protecting it: as I have already indicated, this argument would be strongest if the husband had undergone a bargained-for vasectomy or had lost the capacity to father children biologically since the pregnancy began. But my reaction that it would be proper for a liberal State to constrain a woman's choice during this intermediate period is not confined to these sorts of cases.

In other "second-trimester pregnancy" cases, the State could cite only goals to justicize its prohibiting a woman from aborting. My position has always been that one cannot justicize restricting someone's rights-related interests by citing the ability of the restriction to further a legitimate goal. I see two ways out of this difficulty, but neither is satisfactory. The first is the notion of constructive waiver. If the State warns women that it will prohibit abortions after or shortly before the foetus is viable, a woman who delays her abortion to that point might be said in most cases to have waived her right to abort. Unfortunately, the concept of this type of "constructive waiver" strikes me as oxymoronic. The second way out is to argue that in most cases pregnant women do not have a right to abort their pregnancy in the twenty-fourth week as opposed to having a C-section in the twenty-seventh week, when the baby could survive, or to have a twenty-seven- to thirty-week-old foetus removed or delivered through a procedure that would be likely to damage or kill it as opposed to a method that would not injure it directly. This latter argument has more appeal—particularly in light of my conclusion about the illegitimacy of some of the desires that would lead women to want to abort just before or after viability or to kill the foetus as opposed to having it removed or delivered safely. However, I would be less than honest if I did not confess to the difficulty I have in establishing a reflective equilibrium between my conclusions about the internally-right answer to this question and my account of the principles to which our society is committed.

(2) Some Subsidiary Abortion-Related Rights Issues

As some of my previous remarks imply, I have no doubt about the legitimacy of a liberal State's controlling the procedures and institutions through which a pregnant woman obtains an abortion both to protect her health and to prevent unsuccessful abortion-attempts from damaging a foetus who is or becomes a moral-rights holder. Of course, government choices that further these ends may be impermissible if they unduly burden the choice to have an abortion by increasing its cost more than can be justified by the benefits they generate.

I have also already commented on the legitimacy of a liberal State's requiring a wife to inform her husband of her pregnancy and intent to abort, an adult child to inform her parents of these facts if she intends to obtain financial support from them to which she has no moral or legal right, and a minor child to inform her parents of these facts. It seems to me that these potential informees have a right to know this information—that a liberal State is obligated not to be complicitous in their being defrauded. However, since these individuals have no right to control the pregnant woman's choice, she should be relieved of this duty to inform them of her situation and intentions if there is a significant risk that they will try to coerce her into making the choice they prefer. A liberal State that imposes a duty to disclose (say, by conditioning the right to obtain an abortion on making the relevant disclosure) must establish a procedure (say, an immediate *ex parte* hearing before a judge) to enable a woman to obtain an exemption by establishing a significant risk that the potential informee would react coercively (or violently).

Since a liberal society values people's taking their moral choices seriously, it would seem perfectly appropriate for a liberal State to condition a pregnant woman's legal right to pay for and obtain an abortion to which she is otherwise morally entitled on her becoming informed about various issues related to her choice—the financial, career, and emotional costs and benefits of raising a child with a partner or on one's own; the emotional cost to women of having an abortion; the availability of adoption or fostering alternatives; the life-prospects of children who are raised by single mothers, adopted, or fostered out; various religious and secular ethical positions taken on abortion, and so on. It may also be appropriate for a liberal State to require women who want to have an abortion to go through some psychological counseling (though the privacy cost of participating in such a process may be too high for such a requirement to be legitimate). Of course, this discussion ignores the risk that any such educational or counseling program would not be neutral in the sense that liberalism requires—a risk that is difficult to combat, given that it is as likely to be caused by the way in which the relevant material is conveyed as by the substance of the material itself. A court should hesitate to uphold such an educational or counseling requirement unless the State has instituted an effective review procedure to prevent any such program from being perverted by administrators, teachers, or counselors.

A liberal State's commitment to valuing responsible moral choosing also favors the legitimacy of a waiting period— a requirement that women who want to have an abortion to which they are otherwise entitled register their intention and then wait a certain number of days before actually obtaining it. The point of such a requirement is to encourage the women in question to think through their choices. Although some would maintain that waiting periods are insulting to women in that they assume that a substantial percentage of the women who apply for abortions would not otherwise take this decision morally seriously, I am not persuaded by this argument (though I certainly think it plausible). But there are other problems with waiting periods. Such a requirement may impose critical secrecy, financial, and safety costs on women who live in small towns, villages, or in the country where there are no abortion clinics and who must therefore travel to the city both to register their intention to abort their pregnancy and to secure the abortion. Such individuals may be able to afford and conceal one trip but not two. Requiring them to return also forces them to run the gauntlet of right-to-life supporters, who often congregate outside abortion clinics, on two separate occasions. States that want to impose such a waiting period may be obligated to reduce some of these costs by paying the cost that poor women must incur to make a second trip or stay over. However, even if a State does stand ready to foot the financial bill, the waiting period may impose undue burdens on some women who want to have an abortion.

Finally, does a liberal State have a duty to pay for an abortion for which a pregnant woman would be entitled to pay? My basic answer is "yes." Given the importance of the interest a pregnant woman may have in not having to bear a child at a particular time, she is entitled to have some abortions paid for. However, I do not think that this right has no bounds. Even though the woman's privacy interests make me hesitate to allow the State to make its payments depend on whether a woman's pregnancy was willful, negligent, or just unlucky, there comes a point at which even a poor woman would be taking unfair advantage of her fellow citizens by repeatedly becoming pregnant and having publicly-financed abortions. Of course, even if one concludes that such a woman has no right to the relevant subsidy, it might be more desirable for the State to pay for the abortion than to have an unwanted child born.

C. The Supreme Court's Two Major Decisions on the Right to Abort

(1) Roe v. Wade

Roe v. Wade[179] held unconstitutional as a violation of the "due process" clause of the Fourteenth Amendment a Texas statute that made it a crime to "procure an abortion" or to attempt one except on "medical advice for the purpose of saving the life of the mother."[180] After commenting on three aspects of the majority opinion, I will quote and assess from a liberal perspective the abortion regime it promulgates.

The first point to note about the majority opinion is the way in which it approaches the issue of whether the foetus is a Constitutional person—that is, whether it has Constitutional rights. The Court tries to resolve this issue not by reference to first principles—that is, by looking to the relevant moral practices of our culture—but by examining Constitutional language and legal practice. It concludes that the foetus is never a legal-rights-bearing entity for two reasons: (1) in nearly all the instances in which the word "person" is used in the Constitution, "the use of the word is such that it has application only postnatally. None indicates, with any assurance, that it has any possible prenatal application";[181] and (2) "[t]he unborn have never been recognized in the law as persons in the whole sense." As I have already indicated, Dworkin finds this argument indisputable.[182] I do not. Even if the above conclusions were definitive, legal practice is not self-legitimating. Our society's relevant moral practices include but do not consist entirely or even primarily of our legal practices. If the best construction of our moral practices is that at some stage of its development a foetus is a moral-rights bearer, that fact would justify the conclusion that the relevant foetuses are Constitutional-rights bearers as well, legal practice to the contrary not withstanding.

The second remarkable feature of the majority opinion is the fact that it bases its conclusion that the Texas statute under review is unconstitutional on the woman's right to privacy, which it finds implicit in a number of Constitutional provisions and a variety of Supreme Court opinions.[183] I agree that privacy is an extremely weighty rights-related interest in a liberal culture such as ours and that our interest in privacy is Constitutionally protected. I also agree that a pregnant woman's choice to have an abortion can further her privacy interests in a variety of ways.[184] However, privacy properly so called is certainly not the primary interest furthered by a rule allowing pregnant women to have abortions. A woman's right to have an abortion primarily reflects her interest in autonomy, non-subordination, health, physical well-being, and freedom from physical invasion, not her interest in privacy.

I have two explanations for the Court's focus on privacy. The first is positive. The Court tried to justify its conclusion in privacy terms even at the cost of having to use the word in a non-standard way because it realized that privacy is a fundamental value in our liberal society and hoped that its implicit persuasive definition of the concept would persuade its audience of the correctness of its conclusion. The second explanation is negative. I suspect that the Court did not want to base its decision on the woman's right to autonomy because, even more than privacy, the value of autonomy has implications for the Constitutionality of laws prohibiting homosexual sex, heterosexual sodomy, adultery, and (non-married) fornication that the Court was unwilling to accept.

The third feature of the majority opinion that is noteworthy is its failure to make any explicit reference to the three-tier-scrutiny approach the Court had decided to follow in liberty cases. Although Justices in subsequent cases have implied that *Roe v. Wade* used the strict-scrutiny "test of Constitutionality,"[185] the majority opinion never makes explicit reference to that or any other test.

The majority opinion concludes by summarizing its Constitutional regime for abortion regulation:

(a) For the stage prior to approximately the end of the first trimester, the abortion decision and its effectuation must be left to the medical judgment of the pregnant woman's attending physician.

(b) For the stage subsequent to approximately the end of the first trimester, the State, in promoting its interest in the health of the mother, may, if it chooses, regulate the abortion procedure in ways that are reasonably related to maternal health.

(c) For the stage subsequent to viability, the State in promoting its interest in the potentiality of human life may, if it chooses, regulate, and even proscribe, abortion except where it is necessary, in appropriate medical judgment, for the preservation of the life or health of the mother.[186]

I have four sets of observations about this regime. First, the statement that first-term abortions must be left to the "medical judgment of the pregnant woman's attending physician" is extraordinarily puzzling. The necessary judgment will usually not be primarily or critically "medical," and there is certainly no reason why the choice should be left to the pregnant woman's physician rather than to her (although, in practice, cost-considerations aside, pregnant women would be free to search for a physician who was willing to provide the abortion they wanted).

Second, the protocol's statement that the states could regulate the abortion procedure in the interest of maternal health in the second but not the first trimester is obviously indefensible. The supposed justification for this conclusion—"that until the end of the first trimester mortality in abortion may be less than mortality in normal childbirth"[187]—is no justification at all: this fact presupposes that safe abortion procedures are used in the first trimester, which is precisely what the states would be trying to accomplish by regulating first-trimester abortion procedures.

Third, since the Court's rejection of the possibility that a foetus might at any stage be a Constitutional-rights-bearer precludes it from concluding that a state's "interest in the potentiality of human life" is derivative from the foetus's rights, it needs to specify the state's interest in the potentiality of human life, to explain why that interest arises only after viability, and to justify its own conclusion that post-viability (in the third trimester) this state interest trumps the pregnant woman's various interests in having an abortion (can justicize a prohibition of third-trimester abortions).

The *Roe v. Wade* opinion never does specify the states' interest in the potentiality of human life. As I have already indicated, at least one of those supposed interests—protecting the sanctity of human life—would probably not be furthered by the prohibition of post-viability or third-trimester abortions if (as the Court assumes) the foetuses in question are not moral-rights holders. Moreover, I doubt that in our liberal society the states' interest in protecting the sanctity of human life or any other interest one might imagine the states having (increasing total human utility by securing the birth of a human whose own positive utility would exceed any diminution in the utility of others his existence generated, increasing the utility of other humans, preventing the losses that people who disapprove of late-term abortions would otherwise sustain) could legitimate restricting a pregnant woman's right to have such an abortion. In any event, if I am wrong on this account, few or none of the interests just listed would be critically affected by whether the foetus was viable (whether the abortion took place in the third trimester). All this is highly unsatisfactory.

Yet, the regime the Court promulgated is not that much different from the regime that I think a liberal society is obligated to create. The Court would allow the states to prohibit abortions not necessary to protect the pregnant woman against a significant risk of serious bodily harm or death after viability or in the third trimester. I think a liberal society is obligated to prohibit abortions that are not needed to protect the woman against such risks (or to protect the foetus against a wrongful life) after the thirtieth week of the pregnancy. The difference between these two positions reflects the fact that, unlike the Court, I think that our states have a positive obligation to secure our rights. Like the Court, I also think that the State may not prohibit abortions in the first trimester. Admittedly, I am reluctant to conclude that our states may not prohibit abortions late in the second trimester just before the foetus is viable, but I am uncertain about the implications of liberalism for the proper resolution of this issue. By and large, a Court that has made something of a hash of the relevant abstract issues has come up with a regime that does not differ substantially from what I think liberalism requires.

Perhaps this result is surprising, but, actually, I think it is typical. Judges often reach right results for wrong reasons. In my judgment, the results are right because case-outcomes are controlled by the judges' feel for what is right. The reasoning is wrong because the judges have been taught that legal reasoning is an arcane process in which the moral-rights considerations (which lie behind the "feel" that actually guides their decisions) are irrelevant.

(2) *Planned Parenthood of Southeastern Pennsylvania v. Casey*

I will not attempt to address all the issues on which *Planned Parenthood of Southeastern Pennsylvania v. Casey* focuses.[188] Instead, I will limit myself to commenting on its revision of the basic abortion regime *Roe v. Wade* established and the novel "test of constitutionality" Justice O'Connor proposed in one of the portions of her opinion that served as the opinion of the Court.

Although *Casey* claimed to have adopted *Roe v. Wade*'s basic regime, it altered it in two significant respects. First, it replaced the trimester approach with a before-and-after-viability approach. This revision was a perfectly sensible response to changes in medical technology that moved viability forward to a point before the onset of the third trimester. Second, it corrected the *Roe* Court's error by acknowledging that the states' interest in maternal health is present in the first as well as the second trimester—that is, that this interest legitimates state regulation of abortion procedures in the first as well as the second trimester.

More interestingly, *Casey* substitutes a "no undue burden" test,[189] operationalized through a rule prohibiting the states from imposing any "substantial obstacle" to abortion prior to viability[190] for *Roe v. Wade*'s unarticulated, arguably implicitly assumed, "strict scrutiny" test. I think that the "no undue burden" test is the right test, at least if it is interpreted to make the conclusion turn on a balancing of the relevant moral-rights holders' rights-related interests. Admittedly, however, in practice the *Casey* Court did not operationalize or apply its "no undue burden" test in the way in which the preceding interpretation would require. Thus, in the one direction, like the *Roe v. Wade* Court, the *Casey* Court did not hold that the states had an obligation to prohibit all "medically-unnecessary" abortions of foetuses who would not have wrongful lives and were at least thirty weeks old. And, in the other direction, the *Casey* Court's holding would allow states to impose less-than-substantial obstacles to abortions in circumstances in which a balancing of the relevant rights-related interests would suggest that such burdens on abortion were impermissible. Still, O'Connor's "undue burden" language may prove useful if it enables advocates to persuade the Court that the appropriate test of Constitutionality in liberty cases is a balancing test in which the weights in the balance are rights-related interests.[191]

D. The Constitutional-Rights Arguments of Donald Regan and Ronald Dworkin

(1) Donald Regan

In a highly-respected article,[192] the lawyer-philosopher Donald Regan made an equal-protection argument for the conclusion that it is Constitutionally impermissible for an American legislature to prohibit a woman from having an abortion in the first two trimesters of her pregnancy.[193] Limitations of space preclude me from doing justice to Regan's rich and subtle moral and legal arguments. I will confine myself to stating his legal argument in admittedly-crude terms and explaining why I disagree with it.

Regan begins by arguing that any requirement that a woman provide gestational services to her foetus imposes a Good-Samaritan duty on her that "touches on the constitutional values of non-subordination and freedom from physical invasion."[194] He then argues that our law imposes no similar Good-Samaritan duty on any other individual. He acknowledges that the military draft (whose Constitutionality, he says, no one doubts) involves similar physical invasions and restrictions on "the specially sensitive area of sexual intimacy."[195] However, he rejects the contention that the draft is a counterexample to his claim: "The [pregnant] woman is being required to aid a specific other individual (the foetus); the draftee is not. Rightly or wrongly, our tradition distinguishes between obligations to aid particular individuals and obligations to promote a more broadly based public interest."[196] According to Regan, the fact that the physical invasion, subordination, and sacrifice of sexual intimacy that would be imposed on pregnant women by a rule prohibiting them from terminating their pregnancies in the first two trimesters would be unique in our law renders the prohibition unconstitutional as a violation of the equal-protection clause.

I disagree with Regan's argument for six reasons. First, I do not think that prohibitions of abortions impose Good-Samaritan duties on pregnant women since all abortions qualify as positive disengagements and most later abortions qualify as terminations of voluntarily-initiated aid. Second, I believe that even if abortions did constitute refusals to render aid, pregnant women would fall into one of the exceptions in which a duty to aid is recognized. Third, I do not think that the members of our culture believe in a no-duty-to-aid rule, and I also do not think that our culture is committed to such a rule. Fourth, I believe that increasingly the legal system is adjusting to that reality. Fifth, I do not think that the draft analogy is inapposite because (apparently like Regan—"[r]ightly or wrongly, our tradition") I do not find the distinction between aiding "a specific other individual" and promoting "a more broadly based public interest" morally defensible. And sixth, if I did think that the imposition of a moral-rights-related legal obligation on one group would be defensible if similar moral-rights-related legal obligations were imposed on others, I would conclude that a liberal society that legalized the first moral obligation but not the second (set of such obligations) would be obligated to correct this inequality by legally enforcing the second set of obligations rather than by eliminating the legal duty to fulfill the first obligation. One wrong may be worse than no wrongs, but two wrongs are worse than one wrong.

I want to close this discussion of Regan's equal-protection argument by emphasizing a basic jurisprudential disagreement that underlies two of my objections to Regan's analysis. Regan assumes that longstanding legal practice is self-legitimating. This assumption underlies his failure to question the moral persuasiveness of our alleged Good-Samaritan law. It also underlies his willingness to accept for the purpose of legal analysis the distinction between aiding individuals and serving the public interest. In addition, it lies behind the distinction he draws between Constitutional-law analysis and moral philosophy.[197] In this respect, as in many others, Regan is in good company. Both Philip Bobbitt and Ronald Dworkin agree with Regan on this issue. I do not. Although I agree that there are often substantial differences between the analysis of legal rights and moral rights even when the alleged legal right is moral-rights-related, I do not think that legal practice is self-legitimating. Traditional legal distinctions that cannot bear moral scrutiny deserve no weight unless our notion of fair notice requires that precedent be given some weight even when it was wrong when originally announced.

(2) Ronald Dworkin

I begin by summarizing Dworkin's analysis of a woman's Constitutional right to abort her pregnancy:

(1) The state has two different types of interests in protecting foetal life: (A) derivative interests—that is, interests that are derived from the moral rights of the foetus—and (B) detached interests—interests that are not so derived—most importantly, an interest in protecting the intrinsic value or sanctity of human life.

(2) Although many claim to believe that the foetus is a moral-rights holder, a closer examination of their views reveals that they believe no such thing. The fact that they do not believe that the foetus is a moral-rights holder can be inferred from their endorsement of specific conclusions such as the permissibility of a woman's aborting any pregnancy produced by rape or incest or any pregnancy that involves a foetus that is significantly handicapped (even if it would still be capable of leading a life of moral integrity) that are inconsistent with the belief that the foetus is a moral-rights holder. Virtually no one believes

that the foetus is a moral-rights holder. The foetus is therefore not a moral-rights holder.

(3) Regardless of whether the foetus is a moral-rights holder, it is not a Constitutional-rights holder—a "person" for Constitutional purposes. This conclusion reflects (A) the way in which the term "person" is used in the Constitution, (B) the fact that our private law does not treat the foetus as a moral-rights holder, and (C) the facts that (i) "[i]f the foetus is a constitutional person, then states not only *may* forbid abortion, but at least in some circumstances, *must* do so" and (ii) "[n]o justice or prominent politician has ever advanced this claim."[198]

(4) "[T]he debate about abortion should be understood as essentially about the following philosophical detached-State-interest issue: is the frustration of a biological life, which wastes human life, nevertheless sometimes justified in order to avoid frustrating a human contribution to that life or to other people's lives, which would be a different kind of waste?" (*LD* 94).

(5) The "conviction" of liberals is that "in some cases, at least, a choice for premature death minimizes the frustration of life and is therefore not a compromise of the principle that life is sacred but, on the contrary, best respects that principle" (*LD* 90).

(6) However, the liberal position has no special status in our culture. The belief of people who are conservative about abortion that abortion is always wrong (for example, because it destroys a life whose value reflects the fact that it is God's creation) has the same moral status in our culture as the liberal conviction just articulated.

(7) Our culture is committed to the position that the State should not endorse or enforce any particular view about what makes life sacred or inviolate. More positively, our State is committed to the view that choices of this kind must be left to the individual.

(8) Since the moral assessment of abortion turns on such views, the abortion decision must be left to the pregnant woman.

I will now discuss each of these propositions. I agree with Dworkin's distinction between derivative and detached interests. However, in my judgment, Dworkin ignores most of the detached interests that actually have motivated our states to prohibit abortions and, for reasons related both to the last two propositions just delineated and to my conclusion that some foetuses are moral-rights holders, I doubt the legitimacy of our states' pursuing most of these so-called detached interests by either allowing abortions (in most cases) after the thirtieth week of pregnancy or by prohibiting them in at least the first fourteen weeks of pregnancy.

I also agree that many people make inconsistent claims in relation to abortion. This fact reflects their failure to analyze the relevant rights-issues consistently (to reach a reflective equilibrium on their personal convictions about what pregnant women or our State ought to do on this issue [if its resolution were not controlled by rights]). However, I do not think that this fact demonstrates that there is no right answer to the relevant rights questions. I suspect that Dworkin's conclusion to the contrary reflects his current view that moral-rights analysis (and legal-rights analysis for that matter) must be narrowly focused—that there is no more general web of moral practices (even I would not say that the actual web is seamless) from which one can infer the required internally-right answers. Obviously, I disagree.

Relatedly, I also disagree with Dworkin's conclusion that foetuses can never be Constitutional-rights bearers (that is, Constitutional persons). I have already discussed the *Roe v. Wade* Court's argument from Constitutional language and more general legal practices. Dworkin's own argument about Justices and prominent politicians seems to reflect his view that for a society to have integrity its official decisions must be consistent. I disagree with this view and with the critical role that Dworkin assigns to the decisions of leading officials in general. Although the behavior of such individuals clearly must be considered when analyzing a society's moral commitments, more attention must be paid to the conduct of ordinary people and to the possibility that some conduct of prominent officials may be non-fits. In the abortion context, this latter possibility is very real. A number of explanations can be given for the relevant official "non-fits": (1) the abortion issue is intellectually and psychologically difficult and, like everyone else, public officials are personally confused and conflicted about it; (2) public officials' official conduct in this area is also affected by their desire to avoid offending any significant constituency; and (3) public officials are also confused and hamstrung by the State Action doctrine, which declares that the State "must" do nothing to protect the rights of the moral-rights holders for whom it is responsible so long as it "does nothing" in a non-discriminatory manner.

Dworkin's articulation of the "philosophical issue" on which he claims the abortion controversy rests is typically deft. However, he fails to indicate or emphasize that this philosophical issue is the crux of the issue confronting the individual who wants to evaluate an abortion choice from a personal-ultimate-value or religious perspective when the foetus is not a moral-rights holder. It is not the crux of the issues of whether the foetus is a moral-rights holder or of whether an abortion would violate anyone's moral rights. Moreover, as Dworkin himself later suggests, the crux of the State-obligation issue when the foetus is not a moral-rights holder is not his philosophical question itself but the fact that this question lies at the heart of the abortion controversy in such cases.

Dworkin's account of the liberal "ought" issue is also lucid and convincing. However, his discussion of the status of this liberal position in our society is at least misleading and possibly wrong. Dworkin is right in indicating that pregnant women are almost always[199] entitled to make the abortion decision that best instantiates their own views about the good life (be they liberal or conservative) when their foetus is not a moral-rights bearer. However, that fact does not imply that liberal and conservative views on "what makes life sacred" have the same role to play in the overall analysis of abortion-related rights. Liberal views determine when the foetus is a moral-rights holder. And, as Dworkin himself implicitly argues, they also determine the State's duties in relation to abortion. It seems to me that, like the political liberals, Dworkin has incorrectly assumed that the fact that our State may not endorse or enforce any particular view of the first-order good implies that our society is not committed to any view of "what makes life sacred"—the premise that drives Dworkin's conclusion that the abortion decision must be left to the pregnant woman. In reality, however, the fact that our society has no view of the first-order good (indeed is morally obligated to eschew such a view) is a corollary of our society's more general liberal commitment to the view that what makes human life sacred is the capacity of humans to exercise autonomy and lead lives of moral integrity. For purposes of rights analysis in our culture, the conservative view that human life is "sacred" because it is a creation of God does not have the same status as the liberal view that human life is valuable because it can be lived with moral integrity. This fact is relevant to the resolution of the abortion controversy not only because it clarifies the detached interest of the State in the way in which pregnancies are treated (namely, that pregnant women take their abortion-choices seriously) but primarily because it informs or controls the resolution of the "boundary condition" issue, which in turn implies that once the pregnancy has reached a certain stage the foetus will normally be a moral-rights-bearing entity whose life the State has a derivative interest in protecting.

As the first section of Chapter 2 stressed, my moral-philosophical and jurisprudential positions are closely related to (indeed, are derivative of) Dworkin's. From his perspective, I have traveled down the road not taken or, perhaps, abandoned. The difference between our abortion-rights analysis manifest two basic disagreements:

(1) Dworkin's rejection of my claim that one can infer the internally-right answer to moral-rights questions that many individuals answer inconsistently and on whose answer there is no social consensus by examining the general web of moral practices in which members of our culture engage and

(2) Dworkin's related belief that both moral and Constitutional-law analyses must be narrowly-gauged in the sense of focusing on practices that relate specifically to the conduct whose treatment by government is being subjected to judicial review.

7. Writing Like a Lawyer: Liberty Analysis

Just as various judges and commentators intentionally misuse ordinary language in the "equal protection" cases to induce their audience to accept their conclusions, persuasive definitions also abound in liberty-rights cases and commentary. I have already pointed out several examples of persuasive definitions of ordinary-language concepts in liberty-rights opinions: Justice Harry Blackmun's conclusion in *Roe v. Wade* that the Texas criminal abortion-law under review was unconstitutional because it violated "privacy" and Justice Scalia's claim in his concurring opinion in *Cruzan* that the case turned on the Constitutionality of a state's prohibiting a "person" who had a "desire" to "commit suicide" from doing so come readily to mind. Sometimes, judges commit similar offenses with technical language: Justice Owen Roberts's claim in *Nebbia* that, as a matter of logic, all industries are "affected with a public interest" because all "affect the public interest" exemplifies this possibility.[200] Many other examples of persuasive definitions could be cited. Thus, Justice Brennan's claim in *Maher v. Roe* that the "disparity in funding by the State [of abortions and live births] clearly operates to *coerce* indigent pregnant women to have children they would not otherwise choose to have"[201] (emphasis added) also fits this description: although, like Justice Brennan and unlike the majority in that case, I think that a woman has a right to have the State pay for the termination of at least a certain number of unwanted pregnancies, budget constraints or government-provided financial incentives to give birth cannot properly be said to "coerce."

As the preceding examples suggest, no ideological group has a monopoly on the practice of persuasive definition. Regardless of whether those who misuse language in this way belong to the Left or the Right, their conduct is reprehensible, harmful, and often self-defeating.

Chapter 4 has analyzed the obligations of a liberal State to show appropriate, equal concern for its moral-rights holders' actualizing their potential to lead lives of moral integrity. It has also reviewed and criticized the positions that the Supreme Court, various judges and Justices, and a number of philosophers, legal philosophers, and economists have taken on the abstract and concrete liberty issues to which this duty relates. I have tried to establish the relationship between the moral-rights and Constitutional-rights analyses of the relevant liberty issues. When the Constitutional-law analysis of liberty becomes arcane and is detached from its moral-rights-analysis moorings, Constitutional-law arguments are likely to be unpersuasive, and Constitutional-law conclusions will often be wrong and will sometimes be absurd.

Conclusion

The moral identity of the United States is defined by its standard *for* living, not by its standard of living.

More specifically,

(1) our society is a liberal, rights-based society, which is morally committed to basing its moral-rights discourse on the moral principle that all moral-rights holders are entitled to appropriate, equal respect and appropriate, equal concern for their actualizing their morally-defining potential to become and remain individuals of moral integrity;

(2) our society is also morally committed to making arguments derived from this principle the dominant type of legal argument;

(3) such arguments of moral principle are supposed to operate not only directly but also indirectly by controlling both the legitimacy of the other general modes of legal argument used in our culture and the identity of the variants of those modes that are legitimate;

(4) legitimate legal argument can generate internally-right answers to all legal-rights questions; and

(5) legitimate legal argument yields the conclusion that our State is morally and Constitutionally obligated to secure the moral rights of all moral-rights holders for whom it is responsible whenever it can do so without sacrificing the rights-related interests of all relevant moral-rights holders on balance.

Like all societies, the United States has often failed to fulfill its moral commitments, though over time progress has been made. In part, the failures of our society to fulfill its moral commitments reflects a simple venality: the rights-violating political and personal choices we have made served the interests of those with the power to control them. Regrettably, one should not be surprised when the "haves" come out ahead. However, these failures have also sometimes reflected intellectual errors about the moral principles to which we are committed, their implications for the resolution of concrete moral-rights issues, and the general legal or Constitutional-law relevance of both arguments of moral principle and the moral-rights conclusions to which they lead.

Bad moral and legal theory make bad law. Lawyers, judges, and other State decisionmakers who do not understand that we are a rights-based society, who fail to see that there are or may be internally-right answers to all moral-rights questions in our culture, who misperceive the moral principle on which we are committed to basing our moral-rights discourse, and/or who do not grasp the connection between the moral legitimacy of a legal argument in a rights-based culture and its consistency with that culture's rights-commitments will make bad legal arguments, ignore good legal arguments, and reach wrong legal conclusions.

The Supreme Court's approach to and conclusions about the various "equal protection," autonomy, and liberty issues currently being debated have been far from satisfactory. With a few significant exceptions, its recent performance has frustrated the hopes generated by the Court's attempts to secure moral-rights-related Constitutional rights in the 1950s, 1960s and early 1970s. The efforts of the overwhelming majority of the Court's company have been equally disappointing. Legal philosophers, Constitutional-law scholars, and social critics of both the Left and the Right have failed to take moral rights or legal argument seriously. Non-rights-related policy analysis and illegitimate, morally-disconnected, arcane "legal analysis" have been substituted for morally-connected, legitimate legal argument. Our society's moral identity—our commitment to rights—is endangered both by those who reject the claim that there can be objectively-right answers to moral-rights and legal-rights questions in our society and by those who think that the internally-right answer to any legal-rights question in our culture can be ascertained by executing an arcane, morally-disconnected legal argument.

I have written this book to help us preserve our society's moral identity and to encourage us to fulfill our moral commitments—to combat the academic forces that are tending to convert us into a goal-based society and the judicial forces that are tending to convert us into a morally-unreflective and unreflected-upon democracy. I hope to have convinced you that my central argument is correct. But even if I have not, I will have achieved my goals to some extent if the book persuaded you to take legal argument seriously and to consider the possibility that in our culture legitimate legal argument may be able to yield internally-right, morally-responsible answers to all legal-rights questions.

Notes

NOTES TO THE INTRODUCTION

1. For a detailed discussion of this distinction, see Chapter 1 starting at the text that contains the reference to note 2.

2. For an explanation of the protocol for ascertaining the basic moral principle of a rights-based society, see the text of Chapter 1 following the reference to note 5. For an analysis of "becoming and remaining an individual of moral integrity," see Section 1B(2)(A)(ii) of Chapter 1.

3. For a discussion of such arguments, see the text of Chapter 1 following the reference to note 29.

4. For a discussion of the ways in which arguments of moral principle are supposed to be dominant, see the text of Chapter 1 starting in the paragraph following the reference to note 35.

5. See Chapter 1.

6. See Chapter 2.

7. See Chapter 3.

8. See Chapter 4.

9. For a detailed discussion of these various modes of legal argument, see Chapter 1 starting in the paragraph preceding the reference to note 31.

10. The judges in question are also reacting to the related attack made on the Supreme Court when it struck down various pieces of New Deal legislation on the ground that they violated a particular moral-rights-related value instantiated by the Constitution. To my mind, the Court's general approach in the cases that provoked the attack was correct (it interpreted the Constitution as a moral document), but its conclusions were incorrect (in that it mistakenly found that the Constitution instantiates libertarian as opposed to liberal values).

11. For a detailed discussion of this distinction, see Richard Markovits, The Relevance of Economic-Efficiency Conclusions for Moral-Ought, Moral-Rights, and Legal Analysis (unpublished manuscript available from the author, 1996).

NOTES TO CHAPTER 1

1. To forestall misunderstanding, I should state that the principle articulated in the text is a "consequentialist" as opposed to a deontological principle—in particu-

lar, that it is instantiated by choices that on balance further the rights-related interests they affect.

2. See Ronald Dworkin, *Taking Rights Seriously* (hereinafter *Taking Rights Seriously*) (Harvard University Press, 1977).

3. The relevance of all these issues can be traced to our commitment to the liberal moral principle delineated in the Introduction. In particular, liberalism recognizes promissory obligations because in fulfilling promises the promisor shows respect for the promisee. Similarly, liberalism recognizes that any individual who was a culpable cause-in-fact of another's predicament has a special duty to render assistance to his victim because the liberal duty of respect imposes both a duty not to wrong others and a duty to mitigate in any reasonable available way the consequences of any wrong one has done.

Liberalism also can explain the role that status relationships play in the relevant analyses. In particular, liberalism recognizes that status relationships can impose duties because non-voluntary status relationships can promote intimacy, voluntary status relationships often involve intimacy, intimate relationships enable individuals to discover what they value (who they are), and this kind of self-discovery is an important part of the process of becoming and remaining the kind of moral agent (a person of moral integrity) that liberalism values.

Admittedly, however, liberalism cannot justicize a conclusion that Jill would be obligated to me if she were merely a non-culpable cause-in-fact of my predicament—a conclusion that I therefore doubt would be justified. The opposite conclusion would have to rest on the almost-certainly-mistaken notion that we wrong someone when we do not compensate him for a loss we imposed on him by pursuing our own interests even when our action was not wrong in itself (even when its profitability was not critically affected by our not having to compensate him for his loss). This notion is almost certainly mistaken because it ignores the fact that, just as a non-negligent injurer would for his own benefit be imposing losses on his victim if compensation were not required, the non-contributorily-negligent victim would for his own benefit be imposing losses on the injurer if compensation were required. This argument from symmetry will fail only when it clearly would be morally impermissible to require the victim to make the avoidance-moves he would have to make to prevent the losses for which his strictly-liable potential injurers would otherwise be liable. Thus, if the victim is a moral-rights-bearing foetus that can free its "gestator" from liability for injuring it only by doing away with itself, we would be unwilling to conclude that its responsibility for harming its gestator in a regime that would require the gestator to compensate the foetus for any harm she inflicted on it was equivalent to the gestator's responsibility for harming the foetus if the gestator did not have to compensate the foetus for any harm the gestator caused it. The same argument would presumably apply to non-foetal potential victims who could reduce the certainty-equivalent losses others should be held to impose on them only by doing away with themselves. In my judgment, strict liability can be morally justified only as a response to imperfect information—that is, only by arguing that (1) courts are often unable to assess the negligence of injurers and victims and (2) strict liability will allocate losses according to fault in cases in which negligence has not been proved better than either a no-liability or a negligence regime.

4. Admittedly, any statute authorizing the Court to review such exercises of emergency powers as a matter of original jurisdiction would violate one of the holdings of *Marbury v. Madison*, 5 *U.S.* (1 *Cranch*) 137 (1803)—namely, that Congress may not increase the original jurisdiction of the Supreme Court by moving cases from its appellate to its original jurisdiction.

Justice John Marshall's opinion in *Marbury* argues that this holding is required by the text of Article III, Section 2, Clause 2. The first sentence of Clause 2 declares that the Supreme Court should have original jurisdiction "[i]n all cases affecting Ambassadors, other public Ministers and Consuls, and those in which a State shall be a Party." The second sentence of the clause declares that in all the other cases to which (according to Section 2, Clause 1) the judicial power of the United States "shall extend," the Supreme Court "shall have appellate jurisdiction, both as to law and fact, with such exceptions, and under such regulations as the Congress shall make." According to Marshall, the "plain import" of the text of these two sentences is that some classes of cases are assigned to the original jurisdiction of the Supreme Court while others are assigned to its appellate jurisdiction and that Congress may not switch cases from the former category to the latter or vice versa. Indeed, in Marshall's view, the argument for this interpretation is strengthened by the fact that it "cannot be presumed that any clause in the Constitution is intended to be without effect," since the only alternative interpretation he can imagine—an interpretation under which "Congress remains at liberty to give this court appellate jurisdiction, when the Constitution declares their jurisdiction shall be original; and original when the Constitution has declared it shall be appellate"—would render "the distribution of jurisdiction, made in the Constitution, form without substance."

I will now assess Marshall's argument not only or even primarily to demonstrate that my proposal for expedited judicial review does not violate the Constitution but also to illustrate the model of legitimate legal argument this chapter develops. Even if no other type of legal argument were relevant, Marshall's textual argument would not be persuasive. The interpretation of Clause 2 that Marshall implies is the only alternative to his own is not the only interpretation that is compatible with this text. In particular, this text could equally well be read to authorize Congress to move cases from the Supreme Court's appellate jurisdiction to its original jurisdiction but not vice versa. In fact, this alternative to Marshall's interpretation not only makes as much linguistic sense as Marshall's if Clause 2 is read in isolation, it is strongly favored by both structural and historical considerations.

The structural argument relates to the implications of Marshall's interpretation of the second sentence of Clause 2 for the meaning of its "exception expression." On Marshall's reading, the relevant exceptions could consist solely of restrictions of review to questions of law (and not of fact) or, less plausibly (given the fact that "[i]t is emphatically the province and duty of the judicial department to say what the law is"), to questions of fact (and not of law). In practice, however, Marshall's reading has always been assumed to imply that the relevant "exceptions" include as well outright withdrawals of cases from the Supreme Court's appellate jurisdiction (as opposed to shifts of cases from its appellate to its original jurisdiction). This implication is structurally unsound because it leaves the most vulnerable branch of the central government (a branch that controls neither the sword nor the purse) extremely vulnerable to Congressional attack. If Congress can remove virtually all challenges to the Constitutionality of its decisions from Supreme Court jurisdiction, the ability of the federal judiciary to check Congressional decisionmaking will obviously be severely compromised. In my judgment, this structural argument defeats Marshall's interpretation of Clause 2, Section 2 of Article III.

My reading also is favored by a historical argument—namely, by the fact that many members of the Congress that passed the Judiciary Act of 1789 that Marshall claimed improperly increased the original jurisdiction of the Supreme Court participated both in the Constitutional Convention that drafted Article III and in the ratifying process in their respective states. *Ceteris paribus*, the argument goes, one should presume that such individuals knew what the Constitution meant and would not violate its terms in the blatant way Marshall claims they did. Admittedly, this argument does not deserve a great deal of weight. The counter-argument is not that the Founding Fathers may not have understood the full implications of a moral principle they instantiated (since no moral principle is directly involved here) but that the Federalists who passed the relevant statute had crass incentives to increase the jurisdiction of the Supreme Court even when it was unconstitutional for them to do so—namely, the desire to increase the power of an institution they thought they could control even after they were voted out of legislative and executive office.

Still, when these structural and historical arguments are taken into account, the case for overruling this part of *Marbury v. Madison*'s holding becomes overwhelming, particularly given the fact that the precedential argument to the contrary is very weak (since no private party can say he was unfairly disadvantaged by his reasonable reliance on this part of *Marbury v. Madison*'s holding). Therefore, my proposal that Congress authorize the Supreme Court to give expedited review via the exercise of original jurisdiction over any other branch's exercise of emergency powers would not violate the Constitution, even though it would contravene part of the holding of *Marbury v. Madison*. For a more thorough discussion of textual, historical, structural, and doctrinal argument, see the text of this chapter starting at the reference to note 31.

5. The fundamental distinction between moral principles and personal ultimate values relates to (1) differences in the kinds of moral discourse to which the two sets of moral norms are relevant and (2) differences in their lexical ordering when they conflict rather than to (3) differences in the strength of the social consensus for the

norms in question. A moral norm may have even the conscious articulated support of the vast majority of a society's members and still be a personal ultimate value because it is used in moral-ought statements and not in moral-rights-claim arguments. And a moral norm may be a more or less concrete moral principle to which a society is committed even if it or its relevance to a particular fact-situation which implicates it would be rejected on first thought or even after some consideration by the overwhelming majority of a society's members. (Cf. the attitudes of a substantial percentage or majority of our country's citizens in 1800 about the appropriate treatment of women and individuals of African descent.) Conscious allegiance to or grudging acknowledgment of the force of a particular moral norm by the majority of a society's members is not a necessary condition for its being either the society's basic moral principle or a more concrete corollary of that basic moral principle. Indeed, although (as I will argue below) a necessary condition for a moral norm's being a society's basic moral principle is that the behavior of the society's members substantially conform to that principle, this "fit" requirement does not imply that the behavior of a majority of a society's members substantially conforms to each more concrete corollary or proper application of the basic moral principle to which it and they are committed. Hence, a society may be committed to a concrete moral principle in my sense of that expression even if the majority of its members would reject the claim that they are committed to it and/or behave inconsistently with it in various important ways. Indeed, much of the value of moral and political philosophy reflects the fact that individuals and societies sometimes fail to live up to their commitments because they fail to understand the principles to which they are committed or the implications of those principles—failures that political philosophy may help us correct.

6. William Shakespeare, *Henry IV*, Part I, Act III, Scene I, lines 53–55.

7. I realize, of course, that there are a number of possibly-overlapping and certainly-combinable ways of demonstrating that the liberal principle just articulated is the best conceivable moral norm: (1) by deriving the liberal principle's more concrete corollaries, examining what their instantiation would secure, and comparing the world that their effectuation would yield with the worlds that would be created by the application of other moral norms; (2) by giving a convincing account of human flourishing and demonstrating that the effectuation of the liberal principle is essential to the promotion of such flourishing (for example, by demonstrating that individuals can flourish in the most valuable way only in political communities and that appropriate reflection reveals that even if an individual's personal ultimate values or comprehensive philosophies are right they cannot, from the standpoint of politics, be seen as special); and/or (3) by giving a convincing account of human freedom or rational autonomy (for example, that an individual can be free only if he/she is the author of his/her own life and the origin of the laws that govern his/her actions) and demonstrating that a commitment to the liberal principle articulated above is the only commitment that is consistent with true freedom. However, be-

cause I believe I can analyze legitimate legal argument in our culture without showing our moral-rights practices to be optimal, I will say no more about this issue in the text that follows. My son, Daniel S. Markovits, deserves credit for anything of merit in this footnote. I take full responsibility for all sins of omission and commission.

I should add that although an individual can have moral integrity only if his/her conduct is consistent with his/her personal-value commitments, a society's moral integrity depends on its fulfilling its rights-commitments, not on the consistency of its decisions with an official ultimate-value position. My position on social integrity differs from Dworkin's. See Ronald Dworkin, *Law's Empire* (hereinafter *Law's Empire*) at 166, 176–86, 189–90 (Harvard University Press, 1986). See also Ronald Dworkin, *Freedom's Law: The Moral Reading of the Constitution* at 83 (Harvard University Press, 1996). See Section 1B(7) of Chapter 2 for a detailed discussion of this issue.

8. These closeness-of-fit and explicability-of-non-fit criteria are adapted from Dworkin's *Taking Rights Seriously*, *supra* note 2. Dworkin employs a third, so-called "best light" criterion that I reject on the ground that it collapses the distinction between moral principles and personal ultimate values—a distinction that I find critical to both moral-rights and legal-rights analysis.

9. *Id.* at 22.

10. In fact, this claim is even inconsistent with Dworkin's position in *Law's Empire*. Although Dworkin does focus primarily on official behaviors in *Law's Empire*, I am sure that he would agree that his determination of the official ultimate-value choices of a given society's executive and legislative officials would be substantially influenced by data on the consensus ultimate-value preferences of members of the relevant society (on what be calls "popular morality"). See *Law's Empire* at 97. Clearly, Dworkin would also insist that his identification of the moral principles that were part of the law would be affected not only by extant judicial decisions and opinions but also by the assertion and assessment of moral-rights-and-obligations claims in non-legal settings by members of the relevant community.

11. *Lochner v. New York*, 198 *U.S.* 45 (1905).

12. My objection to *Lochner* is not that the Supreme Court engaged in an inapposite enterprise when it tried to determine the moral principles the Constitution endorsed but that it reached the wrong conclusion about the content of those principles.

13. These mistakes continue to this day. See, e.g., Learned Hand, *The Bill of Rights* (Harvard University Press, 1958) and *The Spirit of Liberty* (Knopf, 1952); John Hart Ely, *Democracy and Distrust: A Theory of Judicial Review* (Harvard University Press, 1980); and the writings of virtually all scholars who identify themselves as "strict constructionists" or members of the Critical Legal Studies movement.

14. I have chosen thirty weeks as a cautious estimate (from the perspective of those concerned about protecting foetal rights) of the stage of foetal development at

which the foetus is likely to possess the physical equipment that is a prerequisite to its learning to take its life morally seriously. Thus, according to Harold J. Morowitz and James S. Trefil,

> [F]or humans . . . there is a period between twenty-five and thirty-two weeks when the cortex is coming into existence as a functional entity. During the last few weeks of this period (roughly from twenty-eight or thirty-three weeks in the pregnancy), there is a spurt of growth of spines on the dendrites, which greatly increases the area on which synapses may form.
>
> A similar picture emerges when we look at the process of adding myelin to nerve axons in the brain. Although there is some myelination during the second trimester, the rate at which it is added begins to increase rapidly during the third trimester, starting earliest in the brain stem (where significant myelination can be seen starting at twenty-four weeks) and moving up to the cerebral cortex (where many parts do not show significant myelination even at birth).

See Harold J. Morowitz and James S. Trefil, *The Facts of Life: Science and the Abortion Controversy* at 119 (Oxford University Press, 1992). Morowitz and Trefil add that the available research on electrical activity in the brain is consistent with their argument about the development of the cortex. *Id.* at 121–25. Admittedly, for purposes of legal or policy analysis, the real concern that pregnant women may (intentionally or unintentionally) misreport the date of conception may justify moving the critical date up one menstrual period (say, to twenty-six weeks)—that is, proceeding on the assumption that foetuses become moral-rights holders twenty-six weeks after the credibly-reported date of conception).

15. The claim that our State has positive obligations runs counter to a particular American Constitutional-law doctrine (the State Action doctrine), which distinguishes between state non-feasance (which on extreme views can never be unconstitutional) and state misfeasance. For an explanation of why this doctrine is incorrect, see Sections 1D and 3A of Chapter 3.

16. For a discussion of this issue, see Sections 1D and 3A of Chapter 3.

17. I do not think that this position converts my moral-integrity-oriented conception of a successful life into a "self-selected mixed bag of goals"–oriented version of this concept. See the text of this chapter following the reference to note 24. In essence, I am suggesting that some level of material welfare is a prerequisite to becoming a person of moral integrity.

18. These beliefs were clearly held by the Radical Republicans after the Civil War. In their view, all citizens had an equal right not only to contract and own property but also to receive subsidized education and training. See Forbath, Race, Class, and Equal Citizenship at 41 (unpublished manuscript, 1996) (hereinafter Forbath). In fact, some Radical Republicans believed that property was so "essential for both individual and collective self-governance" that "every citizen should have some." See Akhil Amar, Forty Acres and a Mule: A Republican Theory of Minimum Entitle-

ments, 13 *Harv. J. L. & Pub. Policy* 37 (1990). The Radical Republicans were eventually defeated by the Democrats and the Klan, aided by the Northern weariness with Reconstruction, which enabled the Democrats to regain control of Congress. See Forbath at 37. The Radical Republicans' view on the positive rights of citizens to property was arguably shared by at least some of the Founding Fathers. Thus, Jefferson's Draft Constitution for Virginia guarantees every adult fifty acres of land. See Thomas Jefferson, Draft Constitution for Virginia, Sec. 4 (June 1776) in *The Portable Thomas Jefferson* at 244, 248 (Viking Press, 1975). Jefferson also believed that each citizen should be given a free public education. See Robert Shalhope, *The Roots of Democracy: American Thought and Culture, 1760–1800* at 115 (Twayne Publishers, 1990).

Late-nineteenth-century populists also claimed that the Constitution gave citizens positive rights to resources and opportunities: "Imbedded in our Constitution ... [is the] principle of securing the widest distribution of wealth and education by maintaining equality in the opportunities to gain them." See Harry Tracy, Corporations: Their Uses and Abuses, and Their Effect on Republican Institutions and Productive Industries, 2 *I. Nat'l Economist* at 187, 188 (1890). See also James B. Weaver, *A Call to Action* at 34 (Iowa Printing Co., 1892). Both these citations are taken from Forbath at 39.

In a similar vein, according to Forbath, "Gilded Age labor and agrarian spokespeople rejected the prevailing view that institutional liberties were only 'negative.' Theirs was a 'positive' Constitutional order, although they envisioned not welfare entitlements, but a 'Reconstructed' political economy, as the vehicle for securing the constitutional norms of decent livelihoods, independence, responsibility, and remunerative work." See Forbath at 43–44.

Admittedly, although early-twentieth-century progressives such as Herbert Croly, Louis Brandeis, and John Dewey believed that in a Constitutional democracy citizens must be given positive rights and sometimes asserted that "the Law promised property to all" (see Herbert Croley, *Progressive Democracy* at 209–11 [Macmillan, 1914]), they seemed to assume that the United States Constitution did not guarantee the rights in question. See Forbath at 45–52.

Finally, Franklin Delano Roosevelt's arguments for his New Deal—for his "four freedoms" and his "second, economic Bill of Rights"—were clearly cast in Constitutional rhetoric. Thus, Roosevelt argued that his proposals reflected new understandings of "liberty" and "equality" which implied that government has an "inescapable obligation" to "protect the citizen in his right to work and his right to live" no less than "in his right to vote." See Franklin Delano Roosevelt, Acceptance of the Recommendation of the Presidency (June 27, 1936) in *The Public Papers and Addresses of Franklin Delano Roosevelt*, vol. 5 at 232–34 (Russell and Russell, 1969). Roosevelt seems to have thought that the existing Constitution guaranteed the rights he wanted to be Constitutional. Thus, he asked his radio audience to re-read the Constitution in the belief that if they did they would legitimately conclude that his programs were consistent with it if not required by it. See Franklin Delano Roosevelt, A "Fireside Chat" Discussing a Plan for Reorganization of the Judiciary (March 9, 1937), *id.*, vol. 6 at 124. Of course, Roosevelt also believed that an amendment to the Constitution would be necessary to convince the sitting Supreme Court to conclude that his programs were Constitutional. See Forbath at 66–70. (According to Forbath, the New Deal attempt to secure economic rights for all citizens was defeated by a combination of laissez-faire Republicans and racist Dixiecrats. *Id.* at 77–86.)

19. See Lawrence M. Friedman, *Total Justice* (Russell Sage Foundation, 1985).

20. What constitutes "a good life, . . . what makes one life successful or meaningful or enviable and another impoverished or wasted or pointless." See Ronald Dworkin, *Life's Dominion* at 199 (Knopf, 1993).

21. The two quoted expressions come from *id.* at 202.

22. Dworkin recognizes that these "goals" (my term, not his) are highly diverse. Thus, in *Life's Dominion*, he includes in the relevant category (1) "pleasurable or exciting . . . experiences" (*id.* at 201)—which relate to the satisfaction of preferences—and (2) achievements that relate to value-convictions (establishing close friendships, having good relationships with one's children, "manag[ing] some success in [one's] work," and securing an intellectual grasp of how the world works) (*id.* at 202), developing certain virtues (*id.* at 206), and being faithful to one's origins ("to [one's] Jewish roots, for example") (*id.*). I doubt that some of these achievements (which Dworkin says relate to an individual's "critical" as opposed to "experiential" interests, *id.* at 201) really should be placed in a value-oriented as opposed to a preference-oriented category: being faithful to one's Jewish roots seems to me to reflect a preference unless it is conceived to involve the fulfillment of some status obligation or duty derived from the avoidable acceptance of the benefits generated by a joint enterprise. I also would not classify "secur[ing] some grasp, even if only desperately minimal, of the state of advanced science of my era" (*id.* at 202) into the value-oriented, "critical-interest-related" category. "Manag[ing] some success in [one's] work" is also critically ambiguous in this respect. Is success defined in terms of monetary reward, the esteem of others, the intrinsic pleasure or satisfaction of doing the work in question, the objective quality of one's performance—independent of its social consequences, or the social contribution of the relevant work? Surely, whether this goal is experiential or value-conviction-oriented in some non-hedonistic sense will depend on the answer given to the preceding question.

23. Dworkin's formulation of the metric for a life's success seems to focus on the extent to which the individual in question achieves the diverse self-selected "goals" discussed in the preceding note rather than the extent to which he becomes and remains an individual of moral integrity, as I have defined that expression. This feature of Dworkin's analysis is puzzling, given the importance he places on individual integrity (see, e.g., *id.* at 205–6, 210, 212, 213, 216), though his definition of "individual integrity" may differ from mine in a way that explains his use of an "achieving a mixed bag of self-selected goals"–oriented metric of a life's success. Admittedly, I

cannot be sure about this, for Dworkin does not really analyze the concept of individual integrity, but rather contents himself with linking it to dignity, not "acting out of character" (in some unspecified sense of "character"), and self-respect (*id.* at 205) as well as with autonomy and the right to self-creation in some unspecified sense of "self" (*id.* at 224). These associations are inadequate because, although Dworkin points out that "[a]utonomy encourages and protects people's capacity to lead their lives out of a distinctive use of *their own character*, a sense of *what is important to and for them*" (*id.* at 224; emphasis added), this formulation leaves open whether the italicized expressions refer to preferences, activities, non-moral personality-traits, or moral seriousness and personal-ultimate-value convictions. See Ronald Dworkin, What Is Equality? Part 1: Equality of Welfare, 10 *Phil. & Pub. Affairs* 185–246 (1981) and What Is Equality? Part 2: Equality of Resources, 10 *Phil. & Pub. Affairs* 283–345 (1981). The word "seems" is used both in the text and in the first sentence of this note because Dworkin's position on this issue is unclear. Dworkin's contention that resources (broadly defined) should be distributed in the way that would be optimal if one placed the same value on each human life's going well—on each right-holder's having a successful life—is neutral on the relevant metric issue. (Dworkin took this position in a paper presented at a conference on Liberal Justice and Liberal Ethics held on John Rawls's work at Santa Clara University in October 1995.) However, the fact that Dworkin is attracted to the "equal resources" version of egalitarianism because, as he said at Santa Clara, resources enable persons to achieve their goals and ambitions (are useful "in making something valuable of one's life") implies that he thinks that the relevant metric of a life's success is achievement-of-self-selected-goals-oriented as opposed to moral-integrity-oriented. On the other hand, the fact that Dworkin recognizes that a policy of indulging the expensive tastes or ambitions of an individual is inegalitarian in that it would subjugate the welfare of all others to such preferences (see *id.* at 300) implies that his view of success or at least the kind of success to which individuals are entitled or that ought to be secured for them cannot be a pure achievement-of-self-selected-goals view.

At the Santa Clara conference, Bernard Williams asked Dworkin a question that may have related to the distinction between the moral-integrity-oriented metric of success to which I think we are committed and the kind of "achievement of a self-selected mixed bag of goals"–oriented metric that Dworkin may find superior or more apposite. In particular, after noting that much of the disagreement in contemporary politics is not about whether we must act as if all successful lives were equally valuable but rather about whether the success that counts is the success individuals secure through their own efforts as opposed to through government help, Williams asked Dworkin to clarify what he meant by an equally-valued successful life in light of this distinction. Although this interpretation is clearly contestable, other statements Williams made lead me to suspect that Williams's category "the success individuals secure through their own efforts" coincides with my category "becoming and remaining an individual of moral integrity" and Williams's category "success individuals achieve through government help" coincides with Dworkin's category of "securing a mixed bag of self-selected goals." Dworkin responded to Williams by agreeing that additional thought had to be given both to the formulation of Williams's question and to its answer. I heartily agree.

24. Dworkin might even agree with and demur to this argument since his articles on equality are designed to articulate the most attractive conception of egalitarianism he can devise, not to discover the principle that underlies our society's rights-practices.

25. The modern, average-utility utilitarian principle may yield different conclusions from those that would be generated by its classical, total-utility counterpart in cases in which the relevant decision will affect the number of entities whose utility counts—for example, by affecting the number of creatures that develop the neurological prerequisites for becoming and remaining individuals of moral integrity.

26. This fact creates a real problem for the utilitarian resolution of the boundary issue—at least if utilitarianism claims to be not just the most attractive personal ultimate value but the value that best accounts for the moral actions of members of our society. (Most utilitarians would reject my claim that members of our culture distinguish between moral-rights discourse and moral-ought discourse.) In particular, if I am correct in concluding that utilitarians assume that the ability to experience utility is the defining moral characteristic of an entity for the purpose of identifying the consequences of an action or choice that are relevant to its assessment, consistency would seem to require the utilitarian to draw his boundary to include all entities that can experience utility—that is, to include non-human animals as well as humans. Although many utilitarians would readily acknowledge and accept this implication of their approach, it clearly makes it more difficult for them to claim that our culture is committed to utilitarianism (since most people in our culture would either give no weight to the utility of non-humans or less weight to the utility of non-humans than to the utility of humans).

I should add that the claim that members of our culture accept utilitarianism is also called into question by the fact that utilitarianism would not give as much importance to an actor's state of mind as members of our culture typically do. Utilitarianism can also be criticized on the ground that it assumes that ecstasy, fulfillment, satisfaction, pleasure, displeasure, dissatisfaction, depression, terror, and so on, can all be mapped into a common metric (units of utility or utils). I admit that some modern utilitarian work has addressed this problem.

27. Although supporters of the equality-of-resources norm do not explicitly take into account the quality of the parenting or neighborhood-environment moral-rights holders experience (the quantity of some difficult-to-define standardized unit of "good-parenting" and "supportive-neighborhood" resources different individuals receive), the norm almost certainly should be interpreted to include such resources in its calculus.

28. Community tastes are important in this connection for two reasons. First,

such tastes are important because many (other-directed) individuals measure their success *inter alia* according to the regard others have for them: the individual who strives to be respected and a poet (or, worse yet, respected as a poet) will find it difficult to succeed in achieving his goals in a community almost all of whose respected members believe poetry to be a waste of time. Second, community tastes are important because the tastes of other members of an individual's community will affect the market value of the various types of labor he can perform and hence the market value of what he produces.

29. See Robert Nozick, *Anarchy, State, and Utopia* (Basic Books, 1974).

30. To see the relevance of the distinction between marginal and average allocative product, note that although the allocative product of the last (equally-skilled, equally-industrious) doctor is undoubtedly higher than the allocative product of the last (equally-skilled, equally-industrious) sanitation worker, the average allocative product of doctors is probably lower than the average allocative product of sanitation workers. Put crudely, this conclusion reflects my assumption that even after society had adjusted to the absence of sanitation workers the illnesses that would result from the withdrawal of the labor of the average sanitation worker would exceed the illnesses the average doctor prevents or cures.

This distinction between average and marginal is highly relevant for the policy implications of libertarianism. Many libertarians support the following argument against the government's redistributing income:

(1) for non-instrumental reasons (i.e., economic-efficiency considerations aside), people ought to be paid what they produce;

(2) a free market will pay people what they produce; therefore

(3) the government ought not redistribute income.

This argument can be attacked on two grounds that do not relate to the marginal-average distinction:

(1) to the extent that "what an individual produces" is affected by factors over which she has no control, there would appear to be no purely-distributive appeal to paying people what they produce and

(2) our actual economy is not "free" in the relevant sense—that is, free of any Pareto imperfections—so that our actual economy does not pay people "what they produce" in any sense of that phrase.

However, for present purposes, the more relevant objection to this argument does turn on the marginal-average distinction:

(3A) even in a Pareto-perfect economy, workers would be paid "what they produce" only in the "marginal allocative product" and not in the "average allocative product" sense of that expression and

(3B) most of those who believe that people ought to be paid according to what they produce believe that rewards should reflect average not marginal allocative product (though they would find it difficult to accept the implication of this principle that on purely-distributive grounds doctors should be paid less than sanitation workers).

31. Actually, I would qualify this moral premise in a way that is, fortunately, currently irrelevant in the United States: textual argument that is inconsistent with the relevant society's moral commitments is legitimate if the text is a Constitutional text whose meaning was understood by its ratifiers but is inconsistent with the society's moral commitments.

32. The following list is based on Philip Bobbitt's analysis of the modes of legal argument in *Constitutional Fate* (Oxford University Press, 1982) and *Constitutional Interpretation* (Blackwell, 1992). My list substitutes "arguments of moral principle" for his "ethical arguments" and provides additional subtypes of the modes both our lists contain. Bobbitt's "ethical arguments" "appeal to those elements of the American cultural ethos that are reflected in the Constitution," most importantly, the idea of limited government. See *Constitutional Fate* at 20. See also *id.* at 135–38. For a comparison of Bobbitt's and my jurisprudential positions, see Section 11 of Chapter 2.

33. 505 *U.S.* 833 (1992).

34. *McCullough v. Maryland*, 17 *U.S.* (4 *Wheat.*) 316 (1819).

35. James Madison, Speech to the House of Representatives (1791) as reported in 2 Gales & Seaton's *Debates and Proceedings of the Congress of the United States*, 1944 (1834). For the relevant passages, see also Paul Brest and Sanford Levinson, *Processes of Constitutional Decisionsmaking* at 11–12 (3rd ed., Little, Brown, 1992).

36. See, e.g., Justice Clarence Thomas' argument in his concurrence in *United States v. Lopez*, 115 *S. Ct.* 1624 at 1644 (1995) that the majority's conclusion that Article I's "interstate commerce" clause and "necessary and proper" clause authorize Congress to regulate any activity that has "substantial effects" on interstate commerce cannot be correct because it renders "wholly superfluous" many of Congress's other enumerated powers under Article I, Section 8 (citing in particular the power to enact bankruptcy laws, to coin money, to fix the standard of weights and measures, to punish counterfeiters of U. S. coin and security, or to regulate trade with foreign countries and Indians).

I should add that this type of textual argument is not always compelling since an author who fears that his text may be misinterpreted may decide to preclude such a misinterpretation by writing a supplementary text that explicitly resolves an issue in the way that a correct interpretation would have resolved it. Thus, the fact that the Fifteenth Amendment explicitly guarantees equal protection in voting does not prove that the Fourteenth Amendment was not intended to secure equal protection in the exercise of political rights (which include voting and such other opportunities as serving on juries).

37. Admittedly, since structural arguments focus on various provisions of the Constitution's text, various features of our Constitutional history, and various aspects of our culture's moral practices—in particular, those that illuminate the basic struc-

ture of our Constitutional arrangement, they do not in one sense constitute a separate mode of argument. However, like Bobbitt, I have decided to place structural arguments into a separate category of argument because of their importance in our Constitutional system.

38. Andrew Jackson's supposed response to Chief Justice John Marshall's majority opinion in *Worcester v. Georgia*, 31 *U.S.* (6 *Pet.*) 515 (1832), is relevant in this context: "John Marshall has made his decision; now let him enforce it." See Leonard Baker, *John Marshall: A Life in the Law* at 745 (Macmillan, 1974).

39. Admittedly, I would qualify this "dominance claim" in one respect. In my judgment, Constitutional text that had a contemporaneous ordinary meaning that was understood by its ratifiers and that is inconsistent with the relevant society's rights-commitments dominates arguments of moral principle even when the ratifiers did not realize that the provision they were adopting was inconsistent with their rights-commitments. The only provisions of the United States Constitution that fit this description are those that manifest the Founding Fathers' agreement to allow (at least) the original slave-states to preserve the institution of slavery within their borders: (1) Article I, Section 2, Clause 3, which discusses the way in which "Representatives and direct taxes shall be apportioned among the several States which may be included within this Union" and which contains references to "free persons" and "other persons"; (2) Article I, Section 9, Clause 1 (the Importation of Slaves clause), which prohibits Congress prior to 1808 from (A) prohibiting the "Migration or Importation of such Persons as any of the States now existing shall think proper to admit" or (B) placing a tax exceeding ten dollars on the "Migration or Importation" of each "such Person," and (3) Article IV, Section 2, Clause 3 (the Fugitive Slave clause), which establishes the right of those who lawfully "hold" a "Person" to "Service or Labour" in one state to repossess that Person should he escape into another state. (Note that none of these provisions uses the word "slave": despite the fact that the Founding Fathers who opposed slavery were willing to compromise on the slavery issue, they were unwilling to contaminate the Constitution by including any explicit reference to "slaves" or "slavery" in its text.) I could try to rationalize the conclusion that arguments based on these texts dominated arguments of moral principle prior to 1865 (the year in which the Thirteenth Amendment was ratified) by (1) analogizing the position of the anti-slavery Founding Fathers to that of a nation's leaders in times of a national emergency that threatened the continued existence of a rights-based State and (2) arguing that the anti-slavery Founding Fathers (A) got the best slavery-deal they could secure, (B) honestly believed that the institution of slavery would not survive the prohibition of the importation of slaves they authorized Congress to promulgate and anticipated Congress would promulgate in 1808, and (C) secured an arrangement that was therefore less inconsistent with liberal principles than the situation that would have prevailed had the slave states not joined the Union. However, I do not really think that I would reach a different conclusion if these conditions were not fulfilled. At base, I just think that, although legal practice

is not in general self-legitimating, those who do law in a basically rights-based State are controlled (*inter alia*) by any text of the relevant State's Constitution whose meaning was understood by its ratifiers even when the relevant provision is in the straightforward sense inconsistent with the State's moral commitments. Obviously, and fortunately, this conclusion has no contemporary relevance in the United States.

40. Alexander Bickel's brilliant book *The Least Dangerous Branch* (Bobbs-Merrill, 1962) argued that the Supreme Court uses a variety of doctrines to avoid having to pronounce on the merits of cases whose internal-to-law correct resolution would not be accepted by the public. Bickel argued that it was wise for the Court to proceed in this way, that avoiding a decision on the merits was preferable both to announcing a correct decision that would not be accepted and to announcing and thereby legitimating an internal-to-law incorrect decision. In a review of Bickel's book, Gerald Gunther characterized Bickel's position with a witticism that exactly captures my assessment of Bickel's recommendation. In Gunther's words, Bickel's position amounted to "the 100% insistence on principle, 20% of the time." See Gerald Gunther, The Subtle Vices of the Passive Virtues, 64 *Col. L. Rev.* 1 at 3 (1964).

41. The text has focused on the practice of giving weight to prudential arguments directly when deciding the issue on the merits. As Bickel suggests, *op. cit. supra* note 40, courts have also given weight to prudential arguments when deciding whether to reach the merits of a case. And as I will show later in this section, courts have taken prudential considerations into account as well when deciding how much weight to give to precedents.

42. H. Jefferson Powell, The Original Understanding of Original Intent, 98 *Harv. L. Rev.* 885 (1985).

43. I refer to the national government as the "central" government rather than as the "federal" government to avoid the implication that the national government is the flag-bearer of federalism. It seems to me that John Marshall and others use the expression "federal government" as a rhetorical device to persuade their audience that when state "interests" and central-government "interests" conflict, federalism requires authority to be assigned to the central government. Marshall also tries to justify allocating power to the central government by arguing that the fact that the Constitution "and the laws of the United States which shall be made in pursuance thereof" are "the supreme law of the land" implies that the central government is the supreme government in the land. See *McCullough v. Maryland*, 17 *U.S.* (4 *Wheat.*) 316 at 405–6 (1819). Of course, since the Constitution creates a federal regime in which those powers not assigned to the central government are reserved to the states (or to the People), this argument from the Supremacy Clause is a non-sequitur.

44. Although the Preamble to the Constitution states that it was created by "the People of the United States," the fact that it was supposed to be and was in fact ratified by the People of the several states and that no state was bound unless its People ratified it implies that the several states rather than the People are the source of the

central government's power. Marshall often claimed that the central government's power came from the People rather than the states to weaken the state-sovereignty argument for allocating specific powers to the states. See, e.g., *id.* at 403–5.

45. The historical antecedent of the "interstate commerce" clause was the fact that under the Articles of Confederation the various states passed protectionist trade-legislation (tariffs and embargoes) that may have been in their individual interest (given their inability to control the choices of their fellow-states) but were not in their joint interest. Indeed, each state may have been better off had all the states forgone the relevant protectionist legislation. In my judgment, for interpretive purposes, the critical feature of this history is that the incentives of the individual states to pass protectionist legislation was critically distorted from the perspective of the collectivity by the external character of some of the losses their individual decisions generated. Externalities can critically distort individual-state incentives in many different contexts—not only (1) when the state is considering protectionist trade-legislation; but also (2) when it is considering cartelizing its own producers; (3) when it is considering pollution legislation or pollution-related options for state-owned enterprises; (4) when it is considering industrial, regulatory, or infrastructure choices in contexts in which there is a need for uniformity (when choosing the width of rail-road-track gauges, establishing safety-equipment requirements for trucks [such as mudguard-specifications], or selecting the width or load-bearing capacities of highways); and (5) when making regulatory or welfare choices that will affect other states by causing capital, labor, or potential welfare-recipients to change their locations (when establishing child-labor standards since lax standards may induce capital to locate in the jurisdiction that has them or when determining welfare benefits since the availability of generous benefits may induce their potential recipients to move to the jurisdiction that offers them).

It seems to me that *ceteris paribus* an appropriately-interpreted "interstate commerce" clause would authorize the Congress to intervene when the externalities that would be generated by state choices in any of these situations seem likely to distort critically the state decisions in question. Of course, as the text suggests, the relevant *ceteris* are not always *paribus*. The "interstate commerce" clause should also be held to make relevant (1) the comparative-efficiency advantages the states have because they are better-informed about local physical facts that may critically affect the consequences of alternative policies and about local preferences that may critically affect the desirability of alternative policies, (2) historic states-rights considerations that favor allocating authority to the states even when on balance state decisionmaking is likely to be less efficient collectively than central-government decisionmaking, and (3) moral-rights concerns that also favor assigning the relevant authority to the states, *ceteris paribus*.

Several of the examples cited in the fourth and fifth categories in the preceding list were involved in Supreme Court "commerce clause" cases. Thus, in the fourth category, *Southern Pacific Co. v. Arizona*, 325 *U.S.* 761 (1945), focused on a deviant rail-road-safety law passed by Arizona that prohibited the operation of trains with more than fourteen passenger cars or seventy freight cars within the state; *Bibb v. Navajo Freight Line, Inc.*, 359 *U.S.* 520 (1959), focused on a deviant Illinois requirement that all trucks on state highways use contoured mudguards; and *South Carolina State Highway Dept. v. Barnwell, Brothers*, 303 *U.S.* 177 (1938), focused on a deviant South Carolina law prohibiting trucks wider than ninety inches or heavier than twenty thousand pounds from operating on the state's highways. In the fifth category, *Hammer v. Dagenhart*, 247 *U.S.* 251 (1918), focused on a Congressional law "intended" to "prevent interstate commerce in the products of child labor," and *Shapiro v. Thompson*, 394 *U.S.* 618 (1969), focused on the attempt of various states and the District of Columbia to prevent their welfare policies from generating external benefits to others (external benefits to individuals who were not originally residents and, arguably, to the states in which these individuals originally resided) and related internal costs to them by establishing a waiting-period for eligibility for welfare. I have already indicated my view that the "interstate commerce" clause authorizes Congress to preempt the states only if (but not always if) state incentives would be critically distorted by the externalities the states' choices would generate as well as my view that the Constitution should be interpreted to authorize the Congress to preempt the states on this ground only if (*inter alia*) Congress has made an appropriate effort to help the states to eliminate such externalities by taking collective action. However, I do not think it desirable (indeed, it may not even be Constitutional) for the central government to return to the states decisionmaking authority over issues such as welfare in circumstances in which they will be tyrannized by their small decisions. The current all-Party consensus in Washington in favor of returning welfare policies and all family policies back to the states ignores this "externality" problem, and those who support this consensus have made no proposals for the central government's taking steps to help the states overcome this tyranny in the welfare and family-policy context.

46. See, e.g., *Champion v. Ames*, 188 *U.S.* 321 (1903).

47. See, e.g., *Caminetti v. United States*, 242 *U.S.* 470 (1917).

48. See, e.g., *Katzenbach v. McClung*, 379 *U.S.* 294 (1964). I hasten to add that, in my judgment, such legislation is clearly Constitutional—it can be justified as an exercise of Congress's authority to enforce the Fourteenth Amendment. Admittedly, this conclusion contradicts the State Action doctrine—first articulated in the *Civil Rights Cases*, 109 *U.S.* 3 (1883)—which holds that the Fourteenth Amendment does not require the states to take positive steps to prevent private acts of discrimination in which the discriminator is not entitled to engage. For a critique of that doctrine, see Section 3A of Chapter 3.

49. The current doctrine is very different from the approach the text articulates. At present, although the states will usually be allowed to exercise their police powers even when their choices have a substantial effect on interstate commerce if Congress has not chosen to preempt the field, Congress can always choose to preempt the field if the state's choice has a substantial effect on interstate commerce

or if the regulated activity is an activity in interstate commerce. This conclusion that the central government wins out over the state government in these cases is made more important by the way in which (with an important recent exception) the courts have implicitly defined "affects interstate commerce." According to the courts, a state decision or local activity affects interstate commerce whenever it alters the magnitude or composition of activities or transactions in interstate commerce. Obviously, this definition would permit Congress virtually to supplant state governments: for example, to take over education policy (since education affects the productivity of the educated, the ways in which they use their capacities, and the tastes of the students, it will affect the magnitude and composition of interstate commerce), family law (since divorce substantially affects the life-opportunities of the wife and children of the divorcing couple, it will affect the magnitude and composition of interstate commerce), and criminal law (for analogous reason). It seems to me that this fact demonstrates the incorrectness of this definition of "affecting interstate commerce." Recently, the Supreme Court, per Chief Justice William Rehnquist, recognized this deficiency of the current doctrine in a decision that held unconstitutional the "federal" Gun-Free School Zones Act of 1990 (which prohibited the knowing possession of a firearm within a distance of one thousand feet of a school) on the ground that Congress's choice was not authorized by the "interstate commerce" clause (or any other Constitutional provision). See *United States v. Lopez*, 115 *S.Ct.* 1624 (1995).

I should perhaps add that many other central-government policies strike me as Constitutionally dubious on federalism grounds. I am less concerned in this connection with the federal regulations of the maximum hours and minimum wages of state-government employees that the Court first declared unconstitutional in *National League of Cities v. Usery*, 426 *U.S.* 833 (1976) and then upheld in *Garcia v. San Antonio Metropolitan Transit Authority*, 469 *U.S.* 528 (1985). Admittedly, this Congressional legislation did significantly restrict the states' ability to exercise their reserved powers by (1) making it more difficult for the states to encourage the sense of community that voluntary-labor systems may foster; (2) making it less advantageous for the states to use mechanically-applicable decision-standards, which can be implemented by less-able and less-experienced personnel, as opposed to more open-textured decision-standards, whose proper application requires skill and experience; (3) making it advantageous for the states to abandon the programs that would otherwise have been implemented by volunteer or low-paid workers by making these programs' administration more expensive; and (4) making it necessary for the states to abandon programs by reducing the number of programs they could finance out of a given budget. However, these restrictions in the ability of the states to use their reserved powers seem small to me in comparison with those the central government imposes through its high level of taxation, its practice of conditioning monetary grants to a state on the state's adopting particular policies that the central government realizes it could not Constitutionally adopt itself, and its practice of making choices that are the states' business under the guise of exercising its power to regulate inter-state commerce.

The high level of federal taxation limits the states because it lowers the ratio of revenue-yield to misallocation-caused for state taxes *inter alia* by increasing the amount of allocative inefficiency state taxation causes by inducing the relevant tax-payers to substitute leisure, do-it-yourself labor, less-arduous labor, more pleasant working conditions, and untaxable fringe benefits of other sorts for taxable-income-generating labor: even if (contrary to my belief) a 10 percent state income-tax would have the same revenue-yield if it were added to a 30 percent federal income-tax as to a 15 percent federal income-tax, the higher federal tax would reduce the above ratio because a tax increase from 30 percent to 40 percent will induce more alloca-tive inefficiency in the above ways than a tax increase from 15 percent to 25 percent (because the taxable-income-generating labor that would be deterred by a tax hike from 30 percent to 40 percent would have been more allocatively efficient than the taxable-income-generating labor that would be deterred by a tax hike from 15 per-cent to 25 percent). If the current level of federal taxation is unconstitutional for fed-eralism reasons, the central government could respond either by reducing its levels of taxation or by giving a certain percentage of its revenues unconditionally to the states (as the German central government is constitutionally required to do).

Far from alleviating the states' position, the current central-government practice of conditioning grants to the states on their adopting policies the central government prefers but could not adopt itself exacerbates the states' situation. The Supreme Court has not found such conditional grants Constitutionally problematic. See, e.g., *South Dakota v. Dole*, 483 *U.S.* 203 (1987); *Oklahoma v. United States Air Service Commission*, 330 *U.S.* 127 (1947); and *Steward Machine Co. v. Davis*, 301 *U.S.* 548 (1937).

The text has already listed some examples in which the central government has (to my mind) usurped the states' legitimate decisionmaking authority on the pretext that it is exercising its power to regulate interstate commerce and pointed out that under current doctrine whenever an externality-of-decentralized-decisionmaking argument favors central-government decisionmaking the central government is held to be authorized to preempt the relevant field.

50. Admittedly, the case for centralized decisionmaking has probably increased through time with the mobility of capital, labor, and potential welfare-recipients. In my judgment, this increase in mobility (and the race to the bottom to which it may lead) make it more important for the courts to hold that Congress can preempt state-decisionmaking in collective-choice-problem situations only after attempting to help the states to overcome the tyranny of their small decisions (to make collective decisions, to formulate and enforce plans that bind them to act in their collective in-terest). See the text that follows.

51. A rare attempt by Congress to help the states overcome their collective-ac-tion problem was held unconstitutional by the Supreme Court. See *New York v. United States*, 505 *U.S.* 144 (1992).

52. Sanford Levinson, The Embarrassing Second Amendment, 99 *Yale L. J.* 637 at 646–51 (1989).

53. This adjective was first used in the Constitutional-law context by Vincent Blasi in his excellent article The Checking Value in First Amendment Theory, 1977 *Am. Bar. Found. Research J.* 521 (1977).

54. Levinson's illuminating article argues that Bobbitt's analytic framework leads to the conclusion that no internally-right answer can be given to Second-Amendment-interpretation questions since the various modes of argument Bobbitt considers to be legitimate favor different conclusions. Levinson fails to consider the type of argument Bobbitt denominates "ethical argument." Although this omission is not critical for Levinson's conclusion since Bobbitt does not believe that "ethical arguments" dominate the other forms of argument he distinguishes, it is critical from my perspective since I believe that my "ethical-argument" counterpart—arguments of moral principle—do dominate the other modes of argument in a way that enables legitimate legal analysis to yield internally-right answers to all Second-Amendment-rights questions. See Section 11 of Chapter 2.

55. 505 *U.S.* 833 (1992). The practice of precedent was discussed in a joint opinion announcing the judgment of the Court written by Justice Sandra Day O'Connor and joined by Justices Anthony Kennedy and David Souter and in partially-concurring and partially-dissenting opinions written by Chief Justice Rehnquist and Justice Antonin Scalia. The textual discussion ignores the differences in these various opinions' descriptions of our practice of judicial precedent—it lists all factors that any of these opinions claims influence the weight judges give precedent in our legal system.

56. Justice Scalia emphasized this factor. I should point out that the notion of "how wrong" a decision was is highly ambiguous. Thus, the relevant metric for measuring the wrongness of a decision could be

(1) the seriousness of the intellectual error(s) that underlies (underlie) the mistakes;

(2) the difference between the number of points that would be assigned to the losing and winning party if each side were awarded points for the strength of its arguments such that the points awarded to both sides together totaled 100,

(3) the net "badness" of the social consequences that were generated by the decision in the case in which it was announced, evaluated by the appropriate moral principles;

(4) the number of cases or the number of types of cases that would be resolved incorrectly if the decision in question were followed (note that the concept of a "type of case" is itself highly contestable);

(5) the "badness" of the social consequences that would result if the decision in question were followed in all cases to which it would be relevant (a set of cases that would depend on the level of generality of the holding attributed

to the wrongly-described case in question or wrongly-resolved issue in question); or

(6) some combination of the above possibilities.

I should note that this ambiguity of the notion of the wrongness of a decision is highly relevant to would-be as well as actual practicing lawyers. The Multi-State Bar Exam consists of a series of multiple-choice questions and instructs the examinees to pick the answer that is "least wrong." The ambiguity (I am tempted to write "incoherence") of this instruction is usually critical since (in my experience) all the answers the exam provides to many if not most of its individual questions are "wrong."

57. The word "perhaps" is included because of my uncertainty about the meaning of the word "unworkable." If a precedent is unworkable because it renders critical factual determinations that the courts cannot make with an acceptable degree of accuracy at any cost, the practice of taking this factor into account is clearly consistent with our moral commitments. However, if the precedent is "unworkable" because it is "prohibitively expensive" for the courts to reach acceptably-accurate conclusions on the factual issues it renders critical, the moral permissibility of taking this factor into account is problematic, given the dubiousness of the transaction-cost justification for not making moral rights legally enforceable.

58. The same prudential concern led the West Germans not to publish dissenting judicial opinions after World War II. The authorities appear to have believed that the West German people's commitment to the rule of law was too fragile to withstand evidence that judges could disagree about the correct resolution of legal questions. Dissenting judicial opinions were not published in West Germany until 1970.

59. See Article I, Section 10, Clause 1.

60. See Michael McConnell, The Importance of Humility in Judicial Review: A Comment on Ronald Dworkin's "Moral Reading" of the Constitution, 65 *Fordham L. Rev.* 1269 at 1280 and note 57 (1997).

61. See *Taking Rights Seriously* at 279–90.

62. See Roberto Unger, *Law in Modern Society* (Free Press, 1976) and *Knowledge and Politics* (Free Press, 1975).

63. See Martin Shapiro, *Freedom of Speech: The Supreme Court and Judicial Review* at 32 (Prentice-Hall, 1966): "If we are off on a democratic quest [and take a realistic view of governmental institutions] the dragon [the Supreme Court] begins to look better and better and St. George [Congress and the Executive] worse and worse."

64. Jesse Choper, *Judicial Review and the National Political Process* at 58 (University of Chicago Press, 1980).

65. This kind of argument might be used (indeed, has been used by the Court and some of its company) to justify judicial review in a more limited set of cases—namely, those that involve government decisions that disadvantage individuals or groups who do not have a fair share of political power—who are unable to protect themselves by participating in normal political processes. See *United States v. Carolene*

Products Co., 304 *U.S.* 144 at note 4 (1938); and John Hart Ely, *Democracy and Distrust: A Theory of Judicial Review* (Harvard University Press, 1980). However, as Bruce Ackerman has shown, the Supreme Court's assumption that "discrete and insular minorities" are unable to protect themselves in normal political processes is incorrect—indeed, "discreteness" and "insularity" actually enhance the political power of the groups that possess these attributes. See Bruce Ackerman, Beyond *Carolene Products,* 98 *Harv. L. Rev.* 713 (1985). As I have admitted when discussing the gaps in my protocol for determining a moral-rights-based society's basic moral principle, in practice, it will be very difficult to assess the political power of any group—in part, because that power may vary substantially from issue to issue.

66. I do not deny the existence of other kinds of justifications for democracy. In a utilitarian society, democracy might be justified on the ground that it promotes utility.

NOTES TO CHAPTER 2

1. Ronald Dworkin, *Taking Rights Seriously* (hereinafter *Taking Rights Seriously*) (Harvard University Press, 1977). All subsequent citations to *Taking Rights Seriously* are indicated in the text by *TRS* and the page number.

2. Ronald Dworkin, *Law's Empire* (hereinafter *Law's Empire*) (Cambridge University Press, 1986). All subsequent citations to *Law's Empire* are indicated in the text by *LE* and the page number.

3. Take, for example, the language of Article II, Section 1, Clause 5 of the Constitution specifying that "no person . . . shall be eligible to the Office of President [of the United States] who shall not have attained to the age of thirty five years" before the date on which he is supposed to assume that office. It might be obvious that the proper interpretation of the relevant language should be mechanical, but such an interpretation is not inevitable. One could propose a functional argument that the relevant language should be construed to require a President to have lived long enough to have achieved the breadth and depth of experience that a thirty-five-year-old would have achieved in 1788. If one believed that individuals achieved the desirable breadth and depth of experience at a younger age in 1788 than today, one might conclude, for example, that today one has to be forty-five years old to become President—that the term "thirty five" should be interpreted to mean "forty-five" today. A decision to reject such a functional interpretation in this context would be based *inter alia* on the recognition that (1) the drafters of the Constitution sometimes used vague or open-textured language and sometimes used specific language, (2) the drafters provided for the passage of Amendments to respond to changes that rendered the Constitution's specific provisions undesirable, and (3) a holding that this particular language be interpreted functionally would place the courts in a position of having to resolve a highly-politically-charged issue by operationalizing a highly-contestable concept without employing their own

personal ultimate values—indeed, even if they did employ their own personal values. In other words, the conclusion that "thirty five" should be interpreted mechanically in this context was easy to reach because subconsciously the interpreter knew that *inter alia* the preceding arguments generated an overwhelming case for mechanical and against functional interpretation *in this instance*. In other analogous instances, the validity of a similar conclusion might be much more in doubt. For example, it is not at all clear that the language of Article I, Section 6, Clause 2 of the Constitution providing that "no Senator or Representative shall during the time for which he was elected, be appointed to any civil office under the Authority of the United States, . . . the Emoluments whereof should have been increased during such time" should be interpreted to refer to increases in nominal-income as opposed to real-income emoluments. Since the point of this provision is to prevent at least one kind of self-dealing by members of Congress and since a real-income interpretation of the relevant language could be operationalized in a way that permitted it to be applied mechanically, the critical question would be whether a real-income interpretation would offer enough of the sought-for protection against self-dealing to make it superior, given the desirability of cost-of-living increases and the undesirability of the constraint in the set of individuals eligible for such offices that the clause would otherwise impose.

4. See *Taking Rights Seriously* at 134–36. See also, more recently, Ronald Dworkin, Bork's Jurisprudence, 57 *U. Chic. L. Rev.* 657 at 664–74 (1990). For a historical analysis that reinforces Dworkin's conclusion by suggesting that the framers almost certainly did not view the Constitution as embodying their conceptions, see H. Jefferson Powell, The Original Understanding of Original Intent, 98 *Harv. L. Rev.* 885 (1985).

5. According to Dworkin, the term "discretion" has two weak senses and one strong sense. Someone has discretion in one of the two weak senses if (1) the decision he has to make cannot be made mechanically (e.g., requires judgment or insight) or (2) the decision he makes is final in the sense of not being subject to reversal on review. Someone has discretion in the strong sense if he is authorized to use his personal ultimate values to make the decision in question (though he may be constrained in some ways—e.g., prohibited from basing his decision on his prejudices). A critical jurisprudential question is whether judges have discretion in this strong sense. I believe that they do not in most adjudicatory situations. Although this conclusion clearly is contestable, it is also clear that one cannot demonstrate that judges have discretion in this strong sense by proving that they have discretion in either or both of the two weak senses delineated above. See *Taking Rights Seriously* at 31–39.

6. See Ronald Dworkin, Unenumerated Rights: Whether and How *Roe* Should Be Overruled (hereinafter Unenumerated Rights), *U. Chic. L. Rev.* 381 at 390 (1992).

7. See *Law's Empire* at 266, 354. Dworkin uses the expression "hard cases" to refer to cases that are close and that pose intellectual difficulties. This usage differs from the traditional usage in such aphorisms as "hard cases make bad law," in which "hard

cases" are cases whose proper resolution has consequences that seem undesirable from a variety of value-perspectives—e.g., result in the eviction of a poor widow with seventeen children.

8. See Unenumerated Rights at 390–91. See also Rawls's concept of reflective equilibrium, discussed in Section 2A of this chapter.

9. Admittedly, in a recent article, Dworkin seems to reject this interpretation of his "best light" criterion: "the model of interpretation that . . . I favor is frequently criticized by those who charge that interpretation should aim at showing its objects as they really are, not in their best light. It is important to be able to answer, to this charge, that there is no difference." See Ronald Dworkin, Reflections on Fidelity, 65 *Fordham L. Rev.* 1799 at 1800 (1997). I cannot reconcile this claim either with Dworkin's listing the "best light" criterion as a separate criterion or with the following statement he made in another contribution to the same volume: "We argue for our constitutional interpretations by offering the best and most honest case we can for their superiority to rival interpretations, knowing that others will inevitably reject our arguments and that we cannot appeal to shared principles of either political morality or constitutional method to demonstrate that we are right." See Ronald Dworkin, The Arduous Virtue of Fidelity: Originalism, Scalia, Tribe, and Nerve, 65 *Fordham L. Rev.* 1249 at 1258–59 (1997).

10. Although *Taking Rights Seriously* does contain a chapter that is concerned with both "justice" and "fairness"—a chapter entitled "Justice and Rights" on John Rawls's *A Theory of Justice*—Dworkin does not offer his own definitions of these concepts in this chapter but simply uses the terms in question in Rawls's senses to refer to Rawls's principles of justice and the moral norms of fairness that his recommended procedure manifests. See *Taking Rights Seriously* at 150–83.

11. Dworkin does delineate his own explicit definitions of "justice" and "fairness" in *Law's Empire*. Thus, he says that "justice" is concerned with the decisions that the standing political institutions, whether or not they have been chosen fairly, ought to make "to distribute material resources and protect civil liberties so as to secure a morally defensible outcome." *Id.* at 165. On the other hand, "fairness in politics is a matter of finding political procedures . . . that give all citizens more or less equal influence in the decisions that govern them." *Id.* at 164–65. However, these formal definitions do not themselves reveal whether they have been applied in a way that makes them compatible with my usage, in which "justice" and "fairness" are both related to the satisfaction of the requirements of a society's "basic moral principle" in my sense.

12. See Section 1B(7) of this chapter.

13. See Section 1B(1) of this chapter.

14. See Chapter 4.

15. Dworkin's later work seems to manifest his preference for a "product" version of egalitarianism over a "process" version. See the text following the reference to note 20 in Chapter 1. However, it is not clear that he thinks that our society is

committed to such a product principle, though his belief that a "best light" criterion should be used to evaluate the principle to which we are committed supports that conclusion.

16. See Chapter 4 at 344–72 and 324–44, respectively.

17. Unenumerated Rights at 424.

18. I should note that I am surprised by the apparent strength of Dworkin's felt need to find a textual home for his analysis. His analysis is an example of the kind of "loose clause-bound" interpretation of the "privileges or immunities" clause that Douglas Laycock recommends (see Section 6 of this chapter) that I would have predicted Dworkin would reject on the ground that it places too much importance on textual arguments (on the distinction between enumerated and unenumerated rights). I agree, however, that the "free exercise" and "freedom of religion" clauses of the First Amendment are religious counterparts to the concrete moral principle my analysis would invoke. I also agree that the "data" supplied by the text of the Bill of Rights or the Constitution as a whole is relevant for the determination of the basic moral principle our society is committed to using when asserting and assessing rights-and-obligations claims.

19. See Section 1B(2) of this chapter.

20. *Law's Empire* at 166. See also Ronald Dworkin, *Freedom's Law: The Moral Reading of the Constitution* at 83 (Harvard University Press, 1996). All subsequent citations to *Freedom's Law* are indicated in the text by *FL* followed by the page number.

21. *Law's Empire* at 189–90. In Dworkin's words:

If people understood formal legislation as only a matter of negotiated solutions to discrete problems, with no underlying commitment to any more fundamental public conception of justice, they would draw a sharp distinction between two kinds of encounters with fellow citizens: those that fall within and those that fall outside the scope of some past political decisions. Integrity, in contrast, insists that each citizen must accept demands on him, and may make demands on others, that share and extend the moral dimension of any explicit political decisions. Integrity therefore fuses citizens' moral and political lives: it asks the good citizen deciding how to treat his neighbor when their interests conflict, to interpret the common scheme of justice to which they are both committed just in virtue of citizenship.

22. At least to academic lawyers, Dworkin's term "checkerboard" laws may be misleading. The cause of the relevant confusion is the fact that a famous article by Boris Bittker coined the term "checkerboard ordinance" to refer to a zoning law which (in order to prevent the separation of the races that is caused by White flight) required properties to be occupied (if at all) in a Black-White checkerboard pattern in a given neighborhood. Bittker's point was that this kind of ordinance would not be unconstitutional even though it did use an explicit racial criterion. See Bittker, The Case of the Checker-Board Ordinance: An Experiment in Race Relations, 71 *Yale L. J.* 1387 (1962). Given Bittker's usage, Dworkin would probably have been bet-

ter advised to use such terms as "compromise laws," "log-rolled" laws, or pork-barrel legislation instead of his expression "checkerboard laws."

23. *Id.* at 185 (emphasis added). When Dworkin returns to this issue toward the end of the book, he once more illustrates his analysis with an example that raises a matter of moral principle in my sense—the correct way to define "official, state-imposed racial discrimination." *Law's Empire* at 382.

24. *Id.* Dworkin goes on to indicate parenthetically that his standard "is at least part of what constitutional lawyers call, somewhat misleadingly, the 'rationality' requirement." I disagree. Constitutional doctrine contains many different kinds of "rationality" tests, but none of them comes close to requiring the kind of consistency that Dworkin's integrity-constraint demands. The most prominent "rationality" test is the version of the so-called "minimum rationality" test under which a State decision is unconstitutional only if it has no prospect of making any contribution to the furtherance of any legitimate goal the court can imagine. In my judgment, decisions that fail this test usually will be unconstitutional (1) because they fail to show the respect due to the victims the test reveals they injured pointlessly (though a full analysis of this issue would have to consider the cost of the additional quality-control necessary to reduce the incidence of such decisions), (2) because they fail to show the respect due to victims they injured to provide elicit gains to the relevant government decisionmakers, and/or (3) because they were motivated by a desire to achieve a Constitutionally-illegitimate goal—a goal whose pursuit violates our basic moral principle.

25. See Ronald Dworkin, Reflections on Fidelity, 65 *Fordham L. Rev.* 1799 at 1804 (1997).

26. *Id.*, citing Ronlad Dworkin, The Arduous Virtue of Fidelity: Originalism, Scalia, Tribe, and Nerve, 65 *Fordham L. Rev.* 1249 at 1259–62 (discussing Tribe) (1997); and Ronald Dworkin, Objectivity and Truth: You'd Better Believe It, 25 *Phil. & Pub. Aff.* 87 (1996). In other contexts, Dworkin seems to admit that judges at least sometimes have to use what I would call their personal ultimate values. For example, in *A Matter of Principle*, after explaining why judges cannot rely on either "institutional" or "psychological" intent when deciding whether the 1964 Civil Rights Act should be interpreted to prohibit voluntary affirmative-action programs adopted by private corporations, Dworkin argues that to decide this issue "judges must decide which of . . . two competing justifications [he previously articulated] is superior as a matter of political morality, and apply the statute so as to further that justification." According to Dworkin,

> It is no use protesting that this procedure allows judges to substitute their own political judgment for the judgment of elected representatives of the people. That protest is doubly misleading. It suggests, first, that the legislators have in fact made a judgment. . . . Second, the protest suggests that judges have some way to decide such a case that does not require them to make a political judg-

ment. But there is no such procedure, except a method that leaves the decision to chance, like flipping a coin.

See Ronald Dworkin, *A Matter of Principle* (Harvard University Press, 1985) at
329.

Unfortunately for my purposes, even this pronouncement is somewhat ambiguous because the two purported justifications in question are (within my framework)
alternative operationalizations of the concrete corollaries of the basic moral principle on which we are committed to basing our moral-rights discourse.

Life's Dominion is equally unclear on this issue. Thus, at one point, Dworkin argues:

Any interpretation of the Constitution must be connected on two large and
connected dimensions. . . . The second is the dimension of justice. If two different views about the best interpretation of some constitutional provision
both pass the test of fit—if each can claim an adequate grounding in past practice—we should prefer the one whose principles seem to us best to reflect
people's moral rights and duties, because the Constitution is a statement of abstract moral ideals that each generation must reinterpret for itself.

Ronald Dworkin, *Life's Dominion* at 111 (Knopf, 1993). This statement is unclear
because Dworkin has not indicated whether he currently believes that there are
internally-right answers to all moral-rights questions. The fact that "each generation must interpret" the relevant moral ideals for itself is perfectly consistent
with there being such right answers, but (if anything) it suggests that there might
not be.

Later in the same book, Dworkin says of three proferred Constitutional arguments: "If any of these three arguments is persuasive, it is so because the substantive
moral theory it assumes is an attractive one." *Id.* at 131. If anything, this claim suggests that Dworkin does not believe that there are internally-right answers to the relevant legal-rights questions since the word "attractive" certainly seems different from
"internally correct." Admittedly, however, Dworkin could mean that the relevant
theory is "attractive" because it is "internally correct."

27. John Rawls, *A Theory of Justice* (hereinafter *A Theory of Justice*) (Harvard University Press, 1971). All subsequent citations to *A Theory of Justice* will be indicated
in the text by *TJ* # and the page number.

28. *Id.* at 303. According to Rawls's initial statement of the difference principle,
it requires that "social and economic inequalities are to be arranged so that they are
. . . to the greatest benefit of the least advantaged group." *Id.* at 83.

29. According to Rawls, "the principles of social justice . . . provide a way of
assigning rights and duties in the basic institutions of society and they define the
appropriate distribution of the benefits and burdens of social cooperations." See *id.*
at 4.

30. In *A Theory of Justice*, "[e]veryone is presumed to act justly and to do his

part in upholding just institutions." In Rawls's terms, *A Theory of Justice*e "consider[s] primarily . . . strict compliance as opposed to partial compliance theory." See *id*. at 8.

31. See *id*. at 31–32, 396. For Rawls's "thin theory of the good," see *id*. at 395–99. For his "full theory of the good," see *id*. at 433–39. For his comparison of his theory of the good with his concept of right, see *id*. at 446–91. Rawls's analysis also resembles mine in that he relates the primacy of the right over the good to the notion of "respecting persons." In his words, "[t]o respect persons is to recognize that they possess an inviolability founded on justice that even the welfare of society as a whole cannot override." *Id*. at 586.

32. Admittedly, in Rawls's terminology, an individual's beliefs about what constitutes "the good" will contain not only his personal ultimate values (in my terminology) but also his specific conclusions about how he ought to live his life, given those values (which will also reflect his talents, personality-traits, and preferences).

33. See also *id*. at 198–99, 357.

34. Rawls admits that the content of the principle of impartiality to which we are committed is contestable. See *id*. at 189.

35. Admittedly, this "mistake" argument is less forceful today than it would have been in periods in which greater support was given to subjective theories of contract.

36. Relatedly, but irrelevantly in the current context, agreements are also not binding when they were obtained by physical coercion.

37. This argument is based on Ronlad Dworkin, The Original Position at 17–19 in *Reading Rawls* (ed. Norman Daniels) (Basic Books, 1975).

38. *Id*. at 137.

39. *Id*. at 62, 92, 93.

40. *Id*. at 426.

41. *Id*. at 84.

42. *Id*. at 143.

43. In Rawls's words, the Founding Fathers "are conceived as not taking an interest in one another's interests." See *A Theory of* Justice at 13. See also *id*. at 127.

44. This view may also be shared by the civic republicans. See Section 9 of this chapter.

45. See *A Theory of* Justice at 205–16. I have focused on liberty of conscience because Rawls repeatedly makes reference to this liberty. See, e.g., *id*. at 583.

46. Thus, he admits that his initial "remarks about liberty are unhappily abstract." See *id*. at 205.

47. Thus, he states: "If the basis of [legal] claims are [*sic*] unsure, so are the boundaries of men's liberties." *Id*. at 235.

48. This omission might reflect Rawls's belief that "[t]he fundamental liberties are always equal." *Id*. at 93. However, I suspect that Rawls does not subscribe to this

belief—that the quoted statement misstated his premise that in the relevant situation the distribution of the fundamental liberties was equal.

49. See *Wisconsin v. Yoder*, 406 *U.S.* 306 (1972).

50. John Rawls, *Political Liberalism* (hereinafter *Political Liberalism*) (Columbia University Press, 1993).

51. See Bruce Ackerman, *Social Justice in the Liberal State* (Yale University Press, 1980).

52. See Thomas Nagel, Moral Conflict and Political Legitimacy, 16 *Phil. & Pub. Aff.* 215 (1987).

53. Stephen Gardbaum, Liberalism, Autonomy and Moral Conflict, 48 *Stan. L. Rev.* 385 at 389–90 (footnote numbers omitted) (1996). I should point out that political liberalism is based on the same principle of appropriate disinterestedness on which Rawls based his argument for justice as fairness.

54. *Id.* at 391–409.

55. See the text of Chapter 1 immediately preceding and following the reference to note 17.

56. See Learned Hand, *The Bill of Rights* (Harvard University Press, 1958), and *The Spirit of Liberty* (Knopf, 1952).

57. 347 *U.S.* 483 (1954).

58. See John Hart Ely, *Democracy and Distrust: A Theory of Judicial Review* (Harvard University Press, 1980).

59. *Id.* at 35–37.

60. *Id.* at 22–41, 118–119.

61. *Id.* at 88, 101–102.

62. *Id.* at 87.

63. *Id.* at 88, 102–4.

64. Historical research confirms that the framers of the Ninth Amendment intended it to protect unenumerated rights. See H. Jefferson Powell, The Original Understanding of Original Intent, 98 *Harv. L. Rev.* 885 (1985).

65. This qualifying word is included both because in practice appointed judges or the judiciary as a whole may be no less "representative" than elected officials as a whole and because the "non-representativeness" of the judiciary may offset the non-representativeness of the legislative and executive branches and improve the "representativeness" of the government as a whole. On the former possibility, see Martin Shapiro, *Freedom of Speech: The Supreme Court and Judicial Review* at 32 (Prentice-Hall, 1966): "If we are off on a democratic quest [and take a realistic view of governmental institutions] the dragon [the Supreme Court] begins to look better and better and St. George [Congress and the Executive] worse and worse." But see Jesse Choper, *Judicial Review and the National Political Process* at 58 (University of Chicago Press, 1980): "The Supreme Court is not as democratic as the Congress or President, and the institution of judicial review is not as majoritarian as the lawmaking process."

66. Douglas Laycock, Taking Constitutions Seriously: A Theory of Judicial Re-

view, 59 *Tex. L. Rev.* 343 at 358 (1981), citing Ely, *op. cit. supra* note 58 at (88 and 101–2) and 11–12.

67. See Ely, *op. cit. supra* note 58 at 99.

68. See Laycock, *op. cit. supra* note 66.

69. *Id.* at 368.

70. *Id.* at 370.

71. Douglas Laycock, Constitutional Theory Matters, 65 *Tex. L. Rev.* 767 at 773 (1987).

72. Laycock, *op. cit. supra* note 66 at 371.

73. *Id.* According to Laycock, "By 'individualism' I mean the idea that every individual is valuable for his own sake, imbued with an irreducible minimum of human dignity and entitled to stand equal before the law and to be treated on his own merits. By 'personal autonomy' I mean the idea that each individual is entitled to control his own affairs and to be left alone by government insofar as feasible."

74. A short bibliography of Legalist Realist literature would include: Felix Cohen, Transcendental Nonsense and the Functional Approach, 35 *Cal. L. Rev.* 809 (1935); Jerome Frank, *Law and the Modern Mind* (Brentano's, 1930), Are Judges Human, Part I, 80 *University Pa. L. Rev.* 17 (1931), and Are Judges Human, Part II, 80 *University Pa. L. Rev.* 233 (1931); Leon Green, *The Judicial Process in Tort Cases* (West Pub. Co., 1931); Oliver Wendell Holmes, The Path of Law, 10 *Harv. L. Rev.* 457 (1897); Joseph Hutcheson Jr., The Judgment Intuitive: The Function of "Hunch" in Judicial Decisions, 14 *Cornell L. Q.* 274 (1929); Karl Llewellyn, *The Bramble Bush* (Oceana, 1930), Some Realism about Realism—Responding to Dean Pound, 44 *Harv. L. Rev.* 1222 (1931), Remarks on the Theory of Appellate Decisions and the Rules and Canons about How Statutes Are to Be Construed, 3 *Vanderbilt L. Rev.* 395 (1950), and *The Common Law Tradition: Deciding Appeals* (Little, Brown, 1960); Underhill Moore, Rational Basis of Legal Institutions, 3 *Cal. L. Rev.* 609 (1923); Moore and Charles Callahan, Law and Learning Theory: A Study in Legal Control, 53 *Yale L. J.* 1 (1943); Herman Oliphant, A Return to *Stare Decisis*, 14 *A.B.A.J.* 71 (1928); Max Radin, The Theory of Judicial Decision: Or How Judges Think, 11 *A.B.A.J.* 357 (1925), and Statutory Interpretation, 43 *Harv. L. Rev.* 863 (1930). Both this bibliography and my discussion of Legal Realism have been substantially improved by my reading of two manuscripts written by my colleague Brian Leiter. See Leiter, Legal Realism in *A Companion to the Philosophy of Law and Legal Theory* at 261, ed. Dennis Patterson (Blackwell, 1996) and Leiter, Rethinking Legal Realism: Toward a Naturalized Jurisprudence, 76 *Tex L. Rev.* 267 (1997).

75. Legal realists who agree that legitimate legal argument does not cause judicial decisions to be what they are also disagree about what does cause judges to render the decisions they make: personal psychological forces, social forces, and so on.

76. As we shall see in Section 11 of this chapter, this position is analogous to Philip Bobbitt's conclusion that whenever different types of arguments that lawyers have made (different modes of arguments or different variants of one of his modes

of argument) favor different legal conclusions, there is no internally-right answer to the relevant question.

77. See, e.g., Llewellyn, *The Bramble Bush, op. cit. supra* note 74 at 72–76.

78. See, e.g., Llewellyn, Remarks on the Theory of Appellate Decisions and the Rules and Canons about How Statutes Are to Be Construed, *op. cit. supra* note 74 at 399–406.

79. See Leiter, Legal Realism, *op. cit. supra* note 74 at 8. See also Leiter, Why Quine Is Not a Postmodernist, 50 *S.M.U. L. Rev.* 1739 (1997).

80. See Frank, Are Judges Human, Part I, *op. cit. supra* note 74 at 47.

81. See Neil MacCormick and Zipporah Wiseman, Llewellyn Revisisted, 70 *Tex. L. Rev.* 771 at 775–76 (1992).

82. CLS scholars went on to claim that the traditional argument to the contrary functioned to conceal the reality of law, which was the imposition of the will of the politically more powerful.

83. See Clare Dalton, An Essay in the Deconstruction of Contract Doctrine, 94 *Yale L. J.* 997 (1985); Mark Tushnet, Following the Rules Laid Down: A Critique of Interpretivism and Neutral Principles, 96 *Harv. L. Rev.* 781 (1983); and Duncan Kennedy, Form and Substance in Private Law Adjudication, 89 *Harv. L. Rev.* 1685 (1976).

84. See Roberto Unger, *Law in Modern Society* (Free Press, 1976) and *Knowledge and Politics* (Free Press, 1975).

85. See, e.g., Mark Tushnet, Does Constitutional Theory Matter? A Comment, 65 *Tex L. Rev.* 777 at 782 (1987).

86. Martin Flaherty, History "Lite" in Modern American Constitutionalism, 95 *Col. L. Rev.* 523 at 527 n. 16.

87. *Id.* at 524.

88. For example, Thomas Paine, Common Sense, reprinted in *The Essential Thomas Paine* at 24–26, 36–47, ed. Sidney Hook (New American Library, 1969), and *The Federalist* (Random House, 1937).

89. Louis Hartz, *The Liberal Tradition in America: An Interpretation of American Political Thought since the Revolution* (Harcourt, Brace, 1955); Bernard Bailyn, *The Ideological Origins of the American Revolution* (Harvard University Press, 1967); Gordon Wood, *The Creation of the American Republic, 1776–1787* (University of North Carolina Press, 1969); J. G. A. Pocock, *The Machiavellian Moment: Florentine Political Thought and the Atlantic Republican Tradition* (Princeton University Press, 1975); Thomas Grey, Origins of the Unwritten Constitution: Fundamental Law in American Revolutionary Thought, 30 *Stan. L. Rev.* 843 (1978); Joyce Appleby, *Capitalism and a New Social Order: The Republican Vision of the 1790s* (New York University Press, 1984); and John Phillip Reid, *The Concept of Liberty in the Age of the American Revolution* (University of Chicago Press, 1988) and *The Concept of Representation in the Age of the American Revolution* (University of Chicago Press, 1989).

90. Robert Shalhope, Republicanism and Early American Historiography, 39

Wm. and Mary Q. 334 (1982), and *The Roots of Democracy: American Thought and Culture, 1760–1800* (Twayne Publishers, 1990).

91. See Richard Epstein, On the Optimal Mix of Private and Common Property, 11 *Soc. Phil. & Pol'y* 17 (1994), The Federalist Papers: From Practical Politics to High Principle, 16 *Harv. J. L. & Pub. Pol'y* 13 (1993), Exit Rights under Federalism, 55 *J. L. & Contemp. Probs.* 147 (1992), A Common Lawyer Looks at Constitutional Interpretation, *B. U. L. Rev.* 699 (1992), The Path to *The T. J. Hooper:* The Theory and History of Custom in the Law of Tort, 21 *J. Legal Stud.* 1 (1992), *International News Service v. Associated Press:* Custom and Law as Sources of Property Rights in News, 78 *Va. L. Rev.* 85 (1992), The Utilitarian Foundations of Natural Law, 12 *Harv. J. L. & Pub. Pol'y* 724 (1989), The Classical Legal Tradition, 73 *Cornell L. Rev.* 292 (1988), Modern Republicanism—Or the Flight from Substance, 97 *Yale L. J.* 1633 (1988), Luck, 6 *Soc. Phil. & Pol'y* 17 (1988), The Mistakes of 1937, 11 *Geo. Mason U. L. Rev.* 5 (1988), The Proper Scope of the Commerce Power, 73 *Va. L. Rev.* 1387 (1987), Self-Interest and the Constitution, 37 *J. Legal Educ.* 153 (1987), Taxation in a Lockean World, 4 *Soc. Phil. & Pol'y* 49 (1986), and Possession as the Root of Title, 13 *Ga. L. Rev.* 1221 (1979). See also Cass Sunstein, *The Partial Constitution* (Harvard University Press, 1993), and Free Speech Now, 59 *U. Chi. L. Rev.* 255 (1992). See also Frank Michelman, Foreword: Traces of Self-Government, 100 *Harv. L. Rev.* 4 (1986), and Bruce Ackerman, *We The People: Foundations* (Harvard University Press, 1991).

92. Kathryn Abrams, Law's Republicanism, 97 *Yale L. J.* 1591 (1988); Richard Fallon, What Is Republicanism and Is It Worth Saving? 102 *Harv. L. Rev.* 1695 (1989); Daniel Rodgers, Republicanism: The Career of a Concept, 79 *J. Am. Hist.* 11 (1992); and Flaherty, *op. cit. supra* note 86.

93. Richard Epstein, History Lean: The Reconciliation of Private Property and Representative Government, 95 *Col. L. Rev.* 591 (1995), and Cass Sunstein, The Idea of a Useable Past, 95 *Col. L. Rev.* 601 (1995).

94. In addition to the sources cited in notes 157 and 159 *infra,* see Cass Sunstein, Neutrality in Constitutional Law (with Special Reference to Pornography, Abortion and Surrogacy), 92 *Col. L. Rev.* 1 (1992), Lochner's Legacy, 87 *Col. L. Rev.* 873 (1987), and Naked Preferences and the Constitution, 894 *Col. L. Rev.* 1689 (1984).

95. See the sources cited in note 91 *supra* and the first source cited in note 93 *supra.*

96. I say "most likely" because there might still be internally-right answers to legal-rights questions if the law were said to incorporate consensus personal ultimate values. Indeed, if this were the case, the associated account of legitimate legal argument might not be structurally very different from the account I have given for a liberal, rights-based society.

97. See Ackerman, *op. cit. supra* note 91. Indeed, even if I were persuaded about Ackerman's general claim, the change in our culture's character from whatever it was in the latter part of the eighteenth century to the liberal, rights-based society I claim

it is now almost certainly could not be said to reflect a new cultural consensus generated during a Constitution moment in a period of national crisis.

98. See Flaherty, *op. cit. supra* note 86, citing Bailyn, *op. cit. supra* note 89. Thus, Wood indicated that the "Federalist achievement" was "to make intelligible and consistent the tangles and confusions of previous American ideas," which he also describes as "diffuse and often rudimentary lines of thought." See Wood, *op. cit. supra* note 89 at 564, quoted by Flaherty, *op. cit. supra* note 86 at 548 n. 108.

99. Appleby, *op. cit. supra* note 89 at 14.

100. *Id.* at 14–15. Of course, according to Adam Smith, the invisible hand of the market would convert the private benefits such "private virtues" generated into social benefit. *Id.* at 32.

101. *Id.* at 16–17. Although Appleby is not clear on this point, she may believe that this type of liberty is the referent of social theorists such as Hobbes, whose most startling idea (at least to his contemporaries) "was his insistence that men were naturally equal." *Id.* at 20. See also Shalhope, Republicanism and Early American Historiography, *op. cit. supra* note 90 at 48.

102. See C. B. MacPherson, *The Political Theory of Possessive Individualism* (Clarendon Press, 1962).

103. See Flaherty, *op. cit. supra* note 86 at 570–71.

104. See Appleby, *op. cit. supra* note 89 at 99–100. Even later, when problems did appear, "[p]artly because of their Revolutionary heritage Americans could not really face the possibility that their liberty—their freedom to compete—was undermining their equality." See Ronald Bertholf and John Murrin, Feudalism, Communalism, and the Yeoman Freeholder, in Stephen G. Kurtz and James H. Hutson, eds., *Essays on the American Revolution* at 283 (University of North Carolina Press, 1973).

105. Shalhope, Republicanism and Early American Historiography, *op. cit. supra* note 90 at 341, citing Gary Nash, Radicalism and the American Revolution, I *Reviews in Am. Hist.* 75 (1973).

106. See Appleby, *op. cit. supra* note 89.

107. See note 98 *supra*.

108. Flaherty, *op. cit. supra* note 86 at 529. See also Shalhope, Republicanism and Early American Historiography, *op. cit. supra* note 90 at 346.

109. *Id.* at 584.

110. See Appleby, *op. cit. supra* note 89 at 81–82. See also Shalhope, *The Roots of Democracy: American Thought and Culture, 1760–1800, op. cit. supra* note 90 at 145. Admittedly, by the 1790s, many civic republicans (Federalists) had reached the conclusion that one could not even rely on the propertied classes to manifest the relevant political virtue of appropriate disinterestedness. However, these pessimists (or should I say realists) may not have attributed these failings to human nature. See notes 151 and 147 of this chapter and the texts with which they are associated.

111. Shalhope, *The Roots of Democracy: American Thought and Culture, 1760–1800,* *op. cit. supra* note 90 at 92 and 99.

112. See Flaherty, *op. cit. supra* note 86 at 544.

113. *Id.* at 543–45 and Grey *op. cit. supra* note 89 at 850–59.

114. Grey, *op. cit. supra* note 89 at 853.

115. Shalhope, *The Roots of Democracy: American Thought and Culture, 1760–1800,* *op. cit. supra* note 90 at 853.

116. For my purposes, then, Reid's claim that American Constitutional discourse was overwhelmingly framed in terms of the customary rights of Englishmen rather than in terms of Natural Law or Lockean liberty is quite irrelevant. See, generally, John Phillip Reid, *Constitutional History of the American Revolution,* vols. 1–4 (University of Wisconsin Press, 1986–93).

117. Grey, *op. cit. supra* note 89 at 863, citing Thomas Rutherford, *Institutes of Natural Law,* 2d American ed. (W. and J. Neal, 1832).

118. Grey, *op. cit. supra* note 89 at 869, citing *The Works of John Adams* vol. 2 at 521 (Little, Brown, 1850).

119. See Grey, *op. cit. supra* note 89 at 874, citing New York Petition to the House of Commons (Oct. 18, 1764), reprinted in *The Stamp Act Crisis; Prologue to Revolution: Sources and Documents on the Stamp Act Crisis, 1764–1766* (hereinafter *Prologue*) at 9–10 (University of North Carolina Press, 1959).

120. See Grey, *op. cit. supra* note 89 at 879, citing *Prologue* at 124.

121. See Grey, *op. cit. supra* note 89 at 884, citing *The Writings of Samuel Adams* vol. 1 at 185, ed. Harry A. Cushing (G. P. Putnam & Sons, 1904).

122. See Grey, *op. cit. supra* note 89 at 888, citing *Journals of the American Continental Congress* vol. 1 at 67, ed. Worthington C. Ford (Government Printing Office, 1904).

123. See Grey, *op. cit. supra* note 89 at 890, citing *The Essential Thomas Paine* at 24–26 and 36–47, ed. Sidney Hook (New American Library, 1969).

124. See the Declaration of Independence para. 1 (U.S. 1776): "We hold these truths to be self-evident, that all men are created equal, that they are endowed by their Creator with certain unalienable Rights, that among these are Life, Liberty and the pursuit of Happiness."

125. See *The Rights Retained by the People* at 351 (Appendix A), ed. Randy Barnett (George Mason University Press, 1989). According to Article 2 of this 1789 draft: "The people have certain natural rights which are retained by them when they enter into Society. Such are the rights of Conscience in matters of religion, of acquiring property and pursuing happiness & Safety; of Speaking, Writing and publishing their Sentiments with decency and freedom; of peaceably assembling to consult their common goal, and of applying to Government by petition or remonstrance for redress of grievances. Of these rights therefore they shall not be deprived by the Government of the United States."

126. John Adams, *A Defence of the Constitutions of Government of the United States*

of America vol. 1 at i–ii (printed by Budd and Bartram [et al.] for William Cobbett, 1797).

127. 3 *U.S.* (3 Dall.) 383 at 387–88 (1798).

128. William Blackstone, *Commentaries on the Laws of England* (A Facsimile of the First Edition of 1765) vol. 1 at 41 (University of Chicago Press, 1979).

129. Clinton Rossiter, *Seedtime of the Republic* at 356, 367–68 (Harcourt, Brace, 1953).

130. See Appleby, *op. cit. supra* note 89 at 20.

131. See Shalhope, *The Roots of Democracy: American Thought and Culture, 1760–1800, op. cit. supra* note 90 at 123.

132. See Reid, *op. cit. supra* note 89 at 189.

133. See Grey, *op. cit. supra* note 89 at 857. See also *id.* at 858.

134. *Id.* at 871, citing James Otis, The Rights of the British Colonies Asserted and Proud, in *Pamphlets of the American Revolution* vol. 1 at 409, ed. Bernard Bailyn (Harvard University Press, 1965).

135. Grey, *op. cit. supra* note 89 at 874, referring to the New York Petition of the House of Commons, *op. cit. supra* note 154 at 9–10.

136 Grey, *op cit. supra* note 89 at 874, 877, 878, citing respectively the Virginia Petitions to the King and Parliament (Dec. 18, 1764), reprinted in Bailyn, *op. cit. supra* note 89 at 17; Declaration of the Stamp Act Congress, *id.* at 63; and various Resolutions of the Sons of Liberty, reprinted in *id.* at 114, 115, 117, 118.

137. *Journals of the American Continental Congress* vol. 1 at 67, ed. Worthington C. Ford (Government Printing Office, 1904).

138. See Forrest McDonald, *Novus Ordo Seclorum: The Intellectual Origins of the Constitution* at 7 (University Press of Kansas, 1985): "The contract and natural-rights theories of John Locke were repeatedly iterated without reference to their source."

139. See the text immediately before and after the reference to note 26 of Chapter 1.

140. Indeed, I think that Epstein has the better of his argument with Flaherty on the relevance of Blackstone and the proper interpretation of the "obligation of contracts" and "just compensation" clauses of the Constitution. See Epstein, *op. cit. supra* note 93 at 595–600 (1965).

141. Shalhope, *The Roots of Democracy: American Thought and Culture, 1760–1800, op. cit. supra* note 90 at 158.

142. See Appleby, *op. cit. supra* note 89 at 99–100.

143. See Shalhope, *The Roots of Democracy: American Thought and Culture, 1760–1800, op. cit. supra* note 90 at 123.

144. See the writings of these historians cited in note 89 *supra*.

145. Indeed, one scholar concludes that civic republicanism offered Americans "a universe of discourse." See Shalhope, Republicanism and Early American Historiography, *op. cit. supra* note 90 at 342, citing Robert Kelley, Ideological and Political Culture from Jefferson to Nixon, 82 *Am. Hist. Rev.* 531 (1977).

146. See Shalhope, Republicanism and Early American Historiography, *op. cit. supra* note 90 at 338–42, citing the works of Foner, Hoerder, and Nash.

147. The quotation is from Tunis Wortman, *An Oration on the Influence of Social Institution upon Human Morals and Happiness* at 4–7 (C. C.Van Alen, 1796), as cited by Appleby, *op. cit. supra* note 89 at 82.

148. See the quotation in the text preceding the reference to note 131 in this chapter.

149. See Appleby, *op. cit. supra* note 89 at 49, 92.

150. See *id.* at 75, citing the 1796 argument of an anonymous critic in Newark's *Centinel of Freedom*, rejecting John Adams's claim that inequality was rooted in human nature.

151. See Cass Sunstein, Beyond the Republican Revival, 97 *Yale L. J.* 1539 at 1558.

152. As I have already indicated, many of these features could also be said to have been included to protect substantive rights.

153. For example, the United States Constitution did not incorporate a number of features of the Pennsylvania state constitution that Flaherty labels "classical republican devices." See Flaherty, *op. cit. supra* note 86 at 261. To be honest, the civic-republican character of some of these devices (a powerful unicameral legislature, a weak multiple executive, a dependent judiciary, annual elections, rotation in office) seems dubious to me. On the other hand, the Pennsylvania constitutional requirement that pending bills be posted on the statehouse door to facilitate public discussion does seem to be clearly promotive of the civic-republican goal of fostering rational deliberation. See Pennsylvania Constitution of 1776, Sections 2, 9, 11, 19, and 23. See also Wood, *op. cit. supra* note 89 at 132–42 for a discussion of the state constitutions passed in the Critical Period.

154. See Sunstein, *op. cit. supra* note 151 at 1561.

155. The quotation is from Wood, *op. cit. supra* note 89 at 615. It is also cited by Flaherty, *op. cit. supra* note 86 at 585 n. 295. Flaherty also quotes Wood's conclusion that eighteenth-century American ideological thought culminated in a new "American [s]cience of politics." See Wood, *op. cit. supra* note 89 at 593–615.

156. See Appleby, *op. cit. supra* note 89 at 54.

157. Thus, although the need for a self-governing people to be well-educated was acknowledged in the last decades of the eighteenth century (a need whose fulfillment could be justified by either liberalism or the version of civic republicanism that rejected the claim that virtue had a genetic origin), attempts by men like Jefferson and Webster to provide public education financed by property taxes in their respective states consistently failed. "Jefferson, for example, offered his plan of 1779 to the Virginia legislature in the 1790s, and again in 1817, only to meet repeated failure." See Shalhope, *The Roots of Democracy: American Thought and Culture, 1760–1700, op. cit. supra* note 90 at 115.

158. I cannot resist quoting Jack Balkin's inimitable words: "Sunstein's 'Madison-

ian' theory of the First Amendment is about as Madisonian as Madison, Wisconsin." See Jack Balkin, Populism and Progressivism as Constitutional Categories, 104 *Yale L. J.* 1935 at 1955 (1995).

159. Both Robert Bork and Lino Graglia believe that the "specific intent" of the ratifiers as opposed to that of the drafters of a Constitutional provision determines its meaning. Thus, Graglia argues: "Because the Constitution derived its legal authority only when it was ratified at state conventions, judges should take it to mean what it was understood to mean by the ratifiers or, more generally, the people they represented." See Lino Graglia, "Interpreting" the Constitution: Posner on Bork (hereinafter "Interpreting"), 44 *Stan. L. Rev.* 201 at 205 (1992). See also Robert H. Bork, *The Tempting of America: The Political Seduction of the Law* (Macmillan, 1990) and Graglia, "Constitutional Theory": The Attempted Justification of the Supreme Court's Liberal Political Program, 65 *Tex L. Rev.* 789 (1987). Neither Graglia nor Bork addresses the issue of how the Constitution should be interpreted if its self-declaring meaning conflicts with what its ratifiers supposed it to mean in the strict-constructionist sense of the latter phrase.

160. Although this account of "strict constructionism" is partially based on Dworkin's analysis in *Taking Rights Seriously* at 133, it differs from Dworkin's account in several respects.

161. I should admit that, although many strict constructionists subscribe to all four of the above positions, some do not: for example, Bork is sometimes willing to allow courts to depart from the ratifiers' specific intent when he finds that intent unacceptable. See Bork, *op. cit. supra* note 159 at 81–83 and, relatedly, at 107–9, 149.

162. See the Constitution of the United States, Articles I and II *passim* and Amendments XIV, XVII, XX, XXI, and XXV.

163. *Id.* at Article IV, Section 4: "The United States shall guarantee to every State in this Union a Republican Form of Government."

164. See *id.* at Amendment X: "The powers not delegated to the United States by the Constitution, nor prohibited by it to the States, are reserved to the States respectively, or to the people."

165. See Graglia, "Interpreting" at 1019 (1992); and Bork, *op. cit. supra* note 159 at 145.

166. See Powell, *op. cit. supra* note 64.

167. Graglia, "Constitutional Theory": The Attempted Justification of the Supreme Court's Liberal Political Program, 65 *Tex L. Rev.* 789 at 792 (1987).

168. See Amar, The Bill of Rights and the Fourteenth Amendment, 101 *Yale L. J.* 1 (1992), and The Bill of Rights as a Constitution, 100 *Yale L. J.* 1131 (1991).

169. For an elaboration of these and several related points, see Chapter 4.

170. See Graglia, "Interpreting" at 1031. *Home Bldg. & Loan v. Blaisdell*, 290 U.S. 398 (1934) upheld Depression-era state debtor-relief legislation that clearly violated the "obligation of contracts" clause of the Constitution: "No State shall . . . pass any . . . Law impairing the Obligation of Contracts." Article I, Section 10, Clause 1. Not

only the text itself but the history that led to the section's inclusion supports the conclusion that it was designed to prohibit precisely the type of debt-moratorium legislation held Constitutional in *Blaisdell*. I should add that the "obligation of contracts" provision is not inconsistent with liberal principles: even if preventing foreclosure seems desirable on personal-ultimate-value grounds or prevents the relevant debtors and their families from being placed in a material position that prevents them from developing into creatures that can function as moral agents or from turning their thoughts to any subject other than survival, it is not morally defensible to finance such debtor-relief programs by imposing its costs on debt-holders. (I am not convinced by the response that once debt-moratorium statutes are known to be Constitutional, the relevant creditors will pass on the risks in question in higher interest-rates or more-selective loan-practices.)

171. See Philip Bobbitt, *Constitutional Interpretation* (Blackwell, 1992), and *Constitutional Fate* (Oxford University Press, 1982).

172. Although Bobbitt usually refers to the "legitimacy" only of judicial review, he does sometimes write about the legitimacy of particular types of arguments (such as structural arguments). See Philip Bobbitt, Is Law Politics? 41 *Stan. L. Rev.* 1233 at 1255, 1266 (1979).

173. *Id.* at 162.

174. This view underlies Bobbitt's opposition to "unitary theories" (see *id.* at 1206) and his description of his own thesis as being "pluralist" and "anti-foundational" (*Id.* at 1308).

175. *Id.* at 1307.

176. *Id.* at 1299 n. 255.

177. *Id.* at 1284.

178. Bobbitt makes his conclusion on the internally-right answer issue clear by offering as "an illuminating metaphor of the process of constitutional decision" the following story "told by the great physicist John Wheeler about the game 'Twenty Questions'":

"You recall how it goes—one of the after-dinner party [is] sent out of the living room, the others agreeing on a word, the one fated to be questioner returning and starting his questions. 'Is it a living object?' 'No.' 'Is it here on earth?' 'Yes.' So the questions go from respondent round the room until at length the word emerges: victory if in twenty tries or less; otherwise, defeat.

Then comes the moment when I am . . . sent from the room. [I am] locked out unbelievably long. On finally being readmitted, [I] find a smile on everyone's face, sign of a joke or a plot. [I] innocently start [my] questions. At first the answers come quickly. Then each question begins to take longer in the answer—strange, when the answer itself is only a simple 'yes' or 'no.' At length, feeling hot on the trail, [I] ask, 'Is the word "cloud"?' 'Yes,' comes the reply, and everyone bursts out laughing. When [I was] out of the room, they explain, they had agreed not to agree in advance on any word at all. Each one around the circle could respond 'yes' or 'no' as he pleased to whatever question [I] put to him. But however he replied he had to have a word in mind compatible with his own reply—and with all the replies that went before."

After quoting the story (which describes an enterprise that is highly analogous to Dworkin's chain novel [see Chapter 2, Section 1B(9), and *LE* 228–38]), Bobbitt comments:

Note that if Wheeler had chosen to ask a different question, he would have ended up with a different word. But, by the same token, whatever power he had in bringing a particular word—"cloud"—into being was only partial. The very questions he chose arose from and were limited by the answers given previously.

See Bobbitt, Is Law Politics? 41 *Stan. L. Rev.* 1233 at 1299 n. 255.

179. *Id.* at 1284.

180. This account of communitarianism borrows heavily from (though it also differs significantly from) Stephen Gardbaum's excellent article Law, Politics, and the Claims of Community, 90 *Mich. L. Rev.* 685 (1992).

181. See, e.g., Roberto Unger, *Knowledge and Politics* at 211 (Free Press, 1975). See also Mark Tushnet, Following the Rules Laid Down, 96 *Harv. L. Rev.* 781 at 783 (1983).

182. Michael Sandel, Introduction in *Liberalism and Its Critics*, ed. Michael Sandel (New York University Press, 1984).

183. In Gardbaum's words, according to civic-republican or neo-republican communitarians, "the content of the human good is active citizenship in a virtuous political community." Gardbaum, *op. cit. supra* note 180 at 725. Admittedly, not all communitarians may subscribe to this view. Conservative communitarians do not explicitly relate their conclusion that communities have a right to enforce their consensus moral conclusions (whatever they may be and however they were arrived at) to any explicit claim that the human good is best obtained by participation in a suitable community and the only types of communities that are suitable are those that are based on a strong consensus on the first-order moral good.

184. Thus, Tushnet and other CLS members seem to believe that participation in a non-hierarchical community will enable people to overcome the painful separations of self from others and self from society (the alienation) that marks contemporary hierarchical, capitalist society.

185. At least this seems to me to be an implication of the use to which Fiss puts the concept of an interpretive community. See Owen Fiss, Objectivity and Interpretation, 34 *Stan. L. Rev.* 739 (1982).

186. See Gardbaum, *op. cit. supra* note 180 at 720. According to Gardbaum, this position has been most forcefully expressed by James Fitzjames Stephens in *Liberty, Equality, and Fraternity*, ed. R. J. White (Cambridge University Press, 1967); and Patrick Devlin, *The Enforcement of Morals* (Oxford University Press, 1959). Stephens's book was a response to John Stuart Mills, *On Liberty* (John W. Parker & Son, 1859).

Devlin's position was opposed by H. L. A. Hart, in *Law, Liberty, and Morality* (Stanford University Press, 1963).

NOTES TO CHAPTER 3

1. The text ignores the fact that a liberal State's duty of respect also requires it to give all moral-rights holders for which it is responsible appropriate roles in all governmental processes. In addition to having the right to participate in appropriate ways in adjudicatory proceedings in which they are parties, citizens of liberal States have a right to appropriate, equal influence in all legislative and executive decisions and the right to participate in appropriate ways in any administrative proceeding that applies laws or regulations to them. Although limitations of space preclude me from analyzing these participation-rights in any detail, I do want to comment briefly on the non-adjudicative participation-rights just listed.

Age and intellectual-competence qualifications aside, all citizens of a liberal State have the right to have appropriate, equal influence on the laws and enforcement-practices to which they are subject (metaphorically, to be the authors of the laws that govern them). Admittedly, it is difficult to determine what this right entails in concrete terms. The difficulty is partly conceptual and partly empirical. The conceptual problem relates to the definition of the influence of any relevant individual on his government's decisionmaking—an idea that is hard to operationalize when individuals rarely if ever critically affect their government's choices. The empirical difficulty relates to the fact that an individual's political influence (however defined) reflects not only his voting power but his ability to provide financial support and other types of services for the causes and candidates he favors (an ability that in turn reflects his organizational and oratorical skills, his personal attractiveness to others, and his access to media or useful venues). Although I do not have space to discuss in any detail the case-law that deals with these issues, what I have said implies that I doubt the correctness of the Supreme Court's "one man, one vote rule." See *Baker v. Carr*, 396 *U.S.* 186 (1962). See also *Shaw v. Reno*, 509 *U.S.* 630 (1993); and *Miller v. Johnson*, 515 *U.S.* 900 (1995). For an illuminating social-science discussion of the issue, see Mica Altman, What Are Judicially Manageable Standards for Redistricting? Evidence from History, *Cal. Tech. Soc. Sci. Working Paper* 976 (1996). For a useful discussion of the notion of "political equality," see Jonathan Still, Political Equality and Election Systems, 9 *Ethics* 375 (1981). For an illuminating analysis of and proposed index for "voting power," see John Bahnzof III, Weighted Voting Doesn't Work: A Mathematical Analysis, 19 *Rutgers L. Rev.* 317 (1965).

I also believe that moral-rights holders have the right to participate in a meaningful way in administrative decisions that apply laws or regulations to them. In part, these participation-rights derive from the right of each moral-rights holder to have any government decision that affects her welfare be made through procedures that reduce to acceptable levels the net weighted-average-expected or certainty-equivalent amount of harm the government generates through erroneous decisions of the relevant kind. The level of accuracy that is acceptable increases with the importance of the benefit to its potential recipients. However, I do not think that in a liberal State the only point of such participation-rights is quality-control: to liberals, the exercise of voice in such proceedings is valuable in itself. Again, limitations of space preclude me from addressing this issue in any more detail. However, I do want to point out that my position on this issue is different from the positions other leading scholars have taken. Thus, my argument provides an alternative to Tom Grey's explanation of the cases that appear to recognize a right of individuals to participate in various ways in administrative proceedings that relate to their eligibility for benefits—that is, to Grey's claim that such cases reflect the judges' subscription to two positions: (1) that the party in question has a Constitutional right to the benefits in question and (2) that considerations of institutional competence and authority make it improper for the courts to announce and enforce that right. See Thomas Grey, Procedural Fairness and Substantive Rights, 18 *Nomos* 182 (1977).

I also reject the law-and-economics contention that in our society parties to administrative proceedings have those and only those "procedural due process" rights that it is "economically efficient" to grant them—that is, those rights whose recognition would give its beneficiaries equivalent-dollar gains that exceed the equivalent-dollar losses it would impose on its victims. For two useful discussions of the values implicated by the "procedural due process" issue, see Jerry Mashaw, Administrative Due Process: The Quest for a Dignitary Theory, 61 *B.U. L. Rev.* 885 (1981), and The Supreme Court's Due Process Calculation for Administrative Adjudication in *Mathews v. Eldridge*: Three Factors in Search of a Theory of Value, 44 *U. Chic. L. Rev.* 28 (1976).

2. See Section 1B(7) of Chapter 2.

3. I do not think that group-libel laws can properly be said to violate free-speech rights.

4. Admittedly, there is an "attenuation" doctrine that allows the State to introduce evidence that would not have been discovered but for an illegal act if the connection between the illegal act and the discovery is sufficiently "remote."

5. For a literacy voting-requirement case that turns on precisely this point, see *Gaston County v. United States*, 395 *U.S.* 235 (1969).

6. I assume that the deference a judge owes the decisionmaker whose choice is under review relates to the quantity rather than the quality of the judge's doubts about the accuracy of his conclusion that the relevant choice was unconstitutional.

7. In most such cases, the government act that gave rise to the claim will have disadvantaged the claimant in some material way; however, in some cases of this kind, a government choice that places an individual or group at an advantage may violate the government's duty of respect by manifesting an insulting assumption that the individual or group is inherently incapable of competing on a level playing-field.

8. For a detailed discussion of why many rights currently protected through the

"equal protection" and "due process" clauses should actually be held to be protected by the "privileges or immunities" clause, see Michael Kent Curtis, *No State Shall Abridge* (Duke University Press, 1986). See also Chester James Antieau, *The Original Understanding of the Fourteenth Amendment* 28–43 (Mid-America Press, 1981); William Nelson, *The Fourteenth Amendment* (Harvard University Press, 1988); and William Wiecek, *Equal Justice under Law* at 435 (Harper & Row, 1982). Although the text of the Fourteenth Amendment prohibits any state from making or enforcing a law that abridges "the privileges or immunities of citizens of the United States," that language does not imply that only such citizens are protected by it. Indeed, I suspect that non-citizens would often be entitled to bring an equal-protection claim against their being denied particular privileges or immunities to which citizens were entitled. I acknowledge that the "privileges or immunities" clause of the Fourteenth Amendment has played only a minor role in Supreme Court case-analysis since *The Slaughterhouse Cases*, 83 *U.S.* (16 *Wall.*) 36 (1873).

9. Although some Supreme Court opinions have at a minimum given the impression that the Court would not look to actual motive—see *Palmer v. Thompson*, 403 *U.S.* 217 (1971)—more recent cases have indicated the Court's conviction that it should consider the presence of insulting intent in discrimination cases or respect-related cases in general. See *Batson v. Kentucky*, 476 *U.S.* 79 (1986); *Village of Arlington Heights v. Metropolitan Housing Development Corp.*, 429 *U.S.* 252 (1977); and *Washington v. Davis*, 426 U.S. 229 (1976). In fact, in *Hunter v. Underwood*, 471 *U.S.* 222 (1985), Justice William Rehnquist wrote an opinion for a unanimous Court stating that in cases in which a State decision had a more negative impact on Blacks than on others the crucial issue is discriminatory purpose and that "[o]nce racial discrimination is shown to have been a 'substantial' or 'motivating' factor behind enactment of the law, the burden shifts to the law's defenders to demonstrate that the law would have been enacted without this factor." *Id.* at 228.

10. 404 *U.S.* 71 (1971). In this case, the Supreme Court declared unconstitutional as a violation of the "equal protection" clause the Idaho statute discussed in the text that follows.

11. See, e.g., Lino Graglia, "Interpreting" the Constitution: Posner on Bork, 44 *Stan. L. Rev.* 201 (1982); Robert Bork, *The Tempting of America: The Political Seduction of the Law* (Macmillan, 1990); and Learned Hand, *The Bill of Rights* (Harvard University Press, 1958).

12. This analysis obviously rejects the assumptions of the famous footnote 4 of *United States v. Carolene Products Co.*, 304 *U.S.* 144, 152 n. 4 (1938). For a superb analysis of this issue, see Bruce Ackerman, *Beyond Carolene Products*, 98 *Harv. L. Rev.* 713 (1985).

13. Indeed, in *Allen v. Wright*, 468 *U.S.* 737 (1984), the Supreme Court held that only Blacks who had applied to a segregated private academy (not all Black schoolchildren in the relevant community) had Constitutional standing to attack the IRS's policy of giving tax-exempt status to racially-discriminatory private schools. Ac-

cording to the Supreme Court, the stigmatizing injury often caused by racial discrimination accords a basis for standing only to those persons who are personally denied equal treatment by the challenged discriminatory conduct. *Id.* at 753–56. Although I do not agree with this conclusion, it certainly suggests that as a practical matter public-interest organizations that want judges to award remedies that respond to the more general stigmatic injury a state's disrespectful behavior generates should either use plaintiffs who suffered tangible harms directly to assert this more general interest or cite the generally-recognized authority of courts to take the public interest into account when fashioning at least certain types of remedies (such as injunctions). (I should add that the legitimacy of this generally-recognized authority is at best problematic.)

14. For an economic analysis of this doctrine, see Richard Markovits, The Allocative Efficiency of Shifting from a "Negligence" System to a "Strict-Liability Regime: A Partial and Preliminary Third-Best-Allocative-Efficiency Analysis, 73 *Chic.-Kent L. Rev.* 11 at 112–23 (1998).

15. Admittedly, the distinction between misfeasance and non-feasance is problematic even at a conceptual level. For example, does the passage of a harmful, pointless piece of legislation through a process that does not involve any quality-control represent misfeasance or non-feasance? It represents misfeasance if one focuses on the act of passing the legislation, but non-feasance if one focuses instead on the failure to introduce appropriate quality-control procedures.

16. See *The Civil Rights Cases*, 109 *U.S.* 3 (1883). Admittedly, the courts have developed other doctrines that declare some private actions in some circumstances to involve state action. For example, state action is often found when the private actor is performing a so-called public function, when the state is sufficiently involved with the private actor as a lessor or perhaps as a licensor or inspector for the state to be seen to be endorsing the behavior of the private actor, or when the state is enforcing the supposed legal right of the private actor to discriminate (though in this case the state enforcement is said to constitute the "discriminatory" state action). Some extensions of these "exceptions" to the State Action doctrine in the late 1960s—see *Amalgamated Food Employees Union v. Logan Valley Plaza*, 391 *U.S.* 308 (1968)—raised my hopes that the Court was in effect abandoning the misfeasance/non-feasance distinction that the State Action doctrine operationalized by adopting a decision-rule according to which (1) state action would always be found when the private party that was committing an act had no moral right to do so—when the state could Constitutionally prohibit the private actor's act—and (2) state action would never be found when the private actor had a moral right to do what he did—when the State could not Constitutionally prohibit him from committing the act in question. This hope was nurtured by two 1972 cases in which the Supreme Court refused to find state action in circumstances that were consistent with my hypothesis. See *Moose Lodge No. 107 v. Irvis*, 407 *U.S.* 163 (1972), in which the Supreme Court held that a state's licensing of a bar in a private club did not convert into state action a decision

by the club not to serve the African-American guest of a member in an opinion that emphasized the interests of club-members in privacy and association; and *Lloyd Corp. v. Tanner*, 407 *U.S.* 551 (1972), in which the Supreme Court held that the decision of the owner of a large, enclosed shopping center to prohibit respondents from distributing anti-war leaflets in its interior mall was not state action in an opinion that emphasized petitioner's right to control its private property.

17. Judges and their company also assume that the Consitution imposes no positive duties on the central government to do the various things listed next in the text.

18. I believe that the central government also has these duties of respect—that they are the corollaries to an unenumerated right to respect covered by the Ninth Amendment.

19. The Fourteenth Amendment capitalizes the word "State" when the word refers to a state government as opposed to the central government: I use the word "State" to refer to any government and the word "state" to refer to the individual states in a political union.

20. See, e.g., Special Project, Texas Tort Law, 57 *Tex. L. Rev.* 381 at 411–21 (1979); *Wood v. Camp*, 284 *So.2d* 691 (Fla. 1973); *Szabo v. Pennsylvania R.R.*, 132 *N.J.* 331, 40 *A.2d* 562 (1945); *L. S. Ayres & Co. v. Hicks*, 220 *Ind.* 86, 40, *N.E.2d* 374 (1942); and *Carlisle v. J. Weingarten, Inc.*, 137 *Tex.* 220, 152 *S.W.2d* 1073 (1941).

21. Constitutional-law discussions in which this position is asserted often trace it (incorrectly, I believe) to the first Justice John Marshall Harlan's comment in dissent in *Plessy* that "[o]ur Constitution is color-blind." See *Plessy v. Ferguson*, 163 *U.S.* 537 at 559 (1896) (Harlan, J., dissenting). As the rest of Harlan's statement indicates, his point was that the Constitution "neither knows nor tolerates classes among citizens." *Id.* As Section 4 of this chapter relates, this conclusion was one of the premises of Chief Justice Earl Warren's argument against the Constitutionality of school segregation.

22. 488 *U.S.* 469 at 494 (1989).

23. See *Loving v. Virginia*, 388 *U.S.* 1 (1967).

24. Although the argument the text criticizes seems silly, it was made by a leading professor of Constitutional law at the time of *Brown v. Board of Education*, 347 *U.S.* 483 (1954), in an article that is the most cited law article in history. See Herbert Wechsler, Toward Neutral Principles of Constitutional Law, 73 *Harv. L. Rev.* 1 at 33–34 (1959).

25. Many of the historical references in this section have been taken from Lucas A. (Scot) Powe, The Warren Court and American Politics (forthcoming from Harvard University Press, 1999).

26. 163 *U.S.* 537 (1896). The Court's doctrinal analysis of the Constitutionality of segregation antedated its development of the three-tier-scrutiny approach to equal-protection analysis. The text therefore does not relate its discussion of the substantive doctrine to its preceding comments on the three-tier approach.

27. *Id.* at 550–51.

28. Oliver Wendell Holmes, *The Common Law* 1 (Little, Brown, 1881).

29. *Plessy v. Ferguson*, 163 *U.S.* 537 at 551–52 (1896).

30. *Plessy* did not invent this purported Constitutional distinction between civil and political equality on the one hand and social equality on the other. Many discussions of the equal-protection clause made reference to it, and many Northern states that did attempt to secure civil equality (equality before the law) for Americans of African descent did not attempt to secure their social and in some instances political equality. I do not find this distinction persuasive. It is not defensible morally, and, even if the drafters and ratifiers of the Fourteenth Amendment had in mind a conception of equality that entailed it, Constitutional interpreters would be bound not by their conception of equality but by the concept of equality to which our society's general moral practices commit us. For similar reasons, the existence of the Fifteenth Amendment does not persuade me that the Fourteenth Amendment does not itself protect the political rights the Fifteenth Amendment explicitly guarantees. Indeed, this conclusion reflects not only the possibility that its drafters and ratifiers may have misconceived the rights that the Fourteenth Amendment protected but also the possibility that they supported the Fifteenth Amendment to protect against other Constitutional interpreters' (e.g., legislators' and judges') misinterpreting the Fourteenth Amendment.

31. See *Plessy v. Ferguson*, 163 *U.S.* 537 at 544 (1896).

32. 275 *U.S.* 78 (1927).

33. 305 *U.S.* 337 (1938).

34. 339 *U.S.* 631 (1948).

35. 339 *U.S.* 629 (1950). Admittedly, when on remand the trial court gave the state the option of establishing a separate Black law school in the state, the Court refused to hold this segregation unconstitutional. See *Fisher v. Hurst*, 333 *U.S.* 147 (1948).

36. 339 *U.S.* 629 (1950).

37. *Id.* at 634.

38. 339 *U.S.* 637 (1950).

39. This policy was apparently adopted at the recommendation of the president of the university, who proposed it as a compromise to induce the Board of Regents to allow Black students to attend the university at all.

40. *McLaurin v. Oklahoma State Regents*, 339 *U.S.* 637 at 638 (1950).

41. 347 *U.S.* 483 (1954).

42. Recently, Michael McConnell has argued that the combination of the facts that (1) "between 1870 and 1875, both houses of Congress voted repeatedly, by large margins, in favor of legislation premised on the theory that de jure segregation of the public schools is unconstitutional" and (2) many members of these Congresses were also members of the Congress of 1866, which proposed the Fourteenth Amendment, provide "strong support" for the view that at least those who proposed the Four-

teenth Amendment thought that it rendered school segregation unconstitutional. See Michael McConnell, Originalism and the Desegregation Decisions, 81 *Va. L. Rev.* 947 at 1140 (1995).

43. 347 *U.S.* 483 at 493 (1954). Although these and various related realizations should have led the Court to conclude that each moral-rights-holding child has a Constitutional right to some minimum level of education, they have not yet done so.

44. *Id.* at 494.

45. *Id.*

46. Of the six such studies cited, the most prominent was the "doll test" study done by an NAACP consultant, Professor Kenneth Clark. This study drew inferences of harm from Black children's responses to questions about a Black doll and a White doll they were given. In particular, Clark asked six- to nine-year-old Blacks in both the North and South which of these dolls was nice and which was like them. The study was dubious because (1) it had no control group, (2) it was insufficiently replicated, and (3) its inference that any tendency of Black children to respond that the White doll was nice manifested the damage that segregation had caused them (as opposed to the socio-economic superiority of White families or the denigration that Blacks suffered from Whites in general) was unjustified. In any event, the study did not support the Court's conclusion since a higher proportion of the Black children in Northern non-segregated schools than of the Black children in Southern segregated schools said that the White doll was nicer.

47. 347 *U.S.* 483 at 495 (1954).

48. The quotation is from Richard Kluger, *Simple Justice* 711 (Knopf, 1976).

49. See Michael Klarman, Civil Rights Law: Who Made It and How Much Did It Matter? 83 *Georgetown L. Rev.* 433 at 444 (1994), citing Justice William Douglas's notes on the first Supreme Court conference held after *Brown* was reargued in December 1953.

50. *Strauder v. West Virginia*, 100 *U.S.* 303 at 305 (1880).

51. *Id.* at 308.

52. Admittedly, one might argue that the Court's failure to condemn the segregationists and its decision to accept delays in enforcement were motivated by a desire to secure the relevant victims' rights by reducing the extent to which its orders would be disobeyed. However, even if this were true, it would not legitimate the Court's conduct: courts in liberal societies may not eschew principle to prevent citizens from violating other citizens' rights.

53. Admittedly, the Warren Court's opinions in the District of Columbia (central government) companion-case to *Brown*—*Bolling v. Sharpe*, 347 *U.S.* 497 (1954)—and in *Brown's* remedial sequel—*Brown v. Board of Education*, 394 *U.S.* 294 (1955)—contained somewhat more moral language and argument. Thus, in *Bolling v. Sharpe*, Chief Justice Warren's opinion for the Court argued that central-government school segregation violated "our American ideal of fairness" and was uncon-

stitutional because it was "not reasonably related to any proper governmental objective." See 347 *U.S.* 497 at 500 (1954). Although the opinion could have explicitly addressed the standard Southern arguments for school segregation—that it promotes everyone's learning and reduces racial hostility—this dismissal of them is far more to the point than anything the *Brown I* opinion contained. Similarly, *Brown II*'s command that segregating school districts cease "racial discrimination" is also more condemnatory than anything the Court said in *Brown I*. However, neither *Bolling* nor *Brown II* made up for *Brown I*. *Brown II* was issued a year later, and *Bolling* received less attention because it did not directly relate to the states. Moreover, the power of *Brown II*'s reference to "discrimination" was vitiated by the fact that the Court and its company often used that term in a morally-neutral sense (see Section 7 of this chapter). (I should note that the Court's choice to base its *Bolling v. Sharpe* decision on the "due process" clause was basically unwarranted: the correct textual home of "equal protection" values as they apply to central-government decisions is the Ninth Amendment, with its reference to rights that are not enumerated.)

54. Thus, the author of the United States remedial position on school segregation—declare segregation unconstitutional and delay doing anything about it—openly admitted that it was "totally unprincipled." Philip Elman, The Solicitor General's Office, Justice Frankfurter, and Civil Rights Litigation, 1946–1960: An Oral History, 100 *Harv. L. Rev.* 817 at 827 (1987).

55. 349 *U.S.* 294 (1955).

56. *Id*. at 301.

57. *Id*. at 300.

58. Section 1 of Chapter 4 discusses these issues in more detail.

59. See *Shuttlesworth v. Birmingham Bd. of Educ.*, 358 *U.S.* 101, aff'g, 162 *F.Supp.* 372 (N.D. Ala., 1958), upholding a pupil-placement plan on its face.

60. Paul Brest and Sanford Levinson, *Processes of Constitutional Decisionmaking: Cases and Materials* 615 (Little, Brown, 1992). Much of the raw material on which this section is based has been taken from Chapter 6 of this excellent textbook.

61. 373 *U.S.* 683 (1983).

62. 391 *U.S.* 430 (1968).

63. In *Keyes v. School District No. 1, Denver, Colorado*, 413 *U.S.* 189 (1973), *Dayton Board of Education v. Brinkman* (*Brinkman I*), 473 *U.S.* 406 (1979), and *Dayton Board of Education v. Brinkman* (*Brinkman II*), 443 *U.S.* 526 (1979), the Court addressed the issue of whether a school system some of whose parts had committed some segregating acts could be required to move to a unitary system as opposed to being required to eliminate contemporary discrimination and the effects of past school-district discrimination. In *Keyes*, the Court held that "a finding of intentionally segregative school board actions in a meaningful portion of a school system . . . creates a presumption that other segregated schooling [i.e., racial-composition differences] within the system is not adventitious." See 413 *U.S.* 189 at 208 (1973). The Court went on to cite *Green* as support for its conclusion that "[i]f the District Court de-

termines that the Denver school system is a dual school system, respondent School Board has the affirmative duty to desegregate the entire system 'root and branch.'" *Id.* at 213. In *Brinkman I*, the Court held that even if some of the policies of the Dayton School Board (its high-school optional-attendance zones) were found to be designed with segregative intent, that finding would not justify a remedy extending to other schools—that is, it would not justify a finding that Dayton had run a dual school system that required it to move to a unitary system. In *Brinkman II*, the Court held that the fact that Dayton had been found to have intentionally segregated its schools in 1954 placed it under a continuing obligation to eliminate the effects of its discrimination, that the finding of past system-wide segregation provides *prima facie* proof that contemporary separation is at least partially attributable to past discrimination, and that the Board has "a heavy burden of showing that actions that increased or continued the effects of the dual system serve important and legitimate ends." 443 *U.S.* 526 at 538 (1979).

64. 402 *U.S.* 1 (1971).

65. *Id.* at 26.

66. *Id.*

67. *Id.* at 31.

68. In *Milliken v. Bradley*, 418 *U.S.* 717 (1974), the Supreme Court ruled out imposing remedies on any district that had not engaged in segregation, citing our tradition of local control of schools. In light of the substantial control that the states have always exercised over public education and the fact that school districts (as state subdivisions) could have been controlled by the state, it would seem to be appropriate to view the state as the defendant. If the real defendant in segregated-school cases is the state, inter-district remedies would be unproblematic even if some of the districts that are subjected to remedial orders had not engaged in segregation.

69. In fact, the Supreme Court continues to reject the notion that the State has a positive obligation to supply all moral-rights holders for whom it is responsible with at least some minimum level of education. Thus, although the Court recognizes that education is necessary to exercise effective speech, to perform citizenship duties, and to develop as an individual, it still has concluded that the Constitution does not guarantee a right to an adequate education. See *San Antonio Independent School District v. Rodriguez*, 411 *U.S.* at 35 (1973 [B&L 1283]). See also *Plyer v. Doe*, 457 *U.S.* 202 (1982), which (at 221) cites *Rodriguez* for the proposition "public education is not a 'right' granted to individuals by the Constitution."

70. 515 *U.S.* 70 (1995).

71. *Id.* at 79. The Court seemed unaware of the possible discrepancy between this standard and its later claim that "[t]he proper response to an intradistrict violation is an intradistrict remedy that serves to eliminate the racial identity of the schools within the affected school district by eliminating, as far as practicable, the vestiges of the de jure segregation in all facets of their operation." See *id.* at 81.

72. *Id.* at 84.

73. *Id.* at 83.

74. *Id.* at 97.

75. Among the important remedial deficiencies that probably do not reflect the Court's failure to discuss matters of principle are:

(1) its failure to consider ordering monetary or in-kind compensation for the segregated schoolchildren who had been targets of the discrimination;

(2) its failure to hold the states in addition to the school districts responsible for the wrongs that were committed;

(3) (relatedly) its refusal to allow orders that imposed duties on school districts that had not segregated their schools (its placing too much weight on our [empirically contestable] alleged tradition of local control of schools);

(4) its failure to address the possibility that some of the "integrated" school systems may not have provided some or all of their students with a minimally-acceptable education; and

(5) its failure to analyze the relationship between its own remedial orders and its own specification of the harms that school segregation had generated.

76. See *Adarand Constructors v. Pena*, 515 *U.S.* 200 (1995).

77. *Regents of the University of California v. Bakke*, 438 *U.S.* 265 at 314 (1978).

78. This proposition was first asserted in relation to affirmative-action programs adopted by a state or one of its subdivisions. See *Wygant v. Jackson Board of Education*, 476 *U.S.* 267 (1976). After *Adarand*—which correctly rejected the proposition that different standards govern the Constitutionality of state and central-government racial classifications (see 515 *U.S.* 200 at 224 [1995])—it must also apply to all central-government racial classifications.

79. See *Regents of the University of California v. Bakke*, 438 *U.S.* 265 at 289 (1978).

80. Some of these economies have to do with the cost-effectiveness of introductory or special-training sessions provided for the direct beneficiaries of affirmative action. Other economies relate to the fact that members of the favored group who are admitted to the program in question may function better if they have a support group of their "fellows" of a minimum size as well as to the related fact that the quality of the entrants into such programs may improve with the scale of the program up to a certain point.

81. See *United States Steelworkers v. Weber*, 495 *U.S.* 193 (1979). Although *Weber* is a Title VII case, the Court's handling of similar issues in *Wygant* leads me to believe that it would support the *Weber* proposition listed in the text in a Constitutional-rights context as well.

82. *Wygant v. Jackson Board of Education*, 476 *U.S.* 267 (1976).

83. In *Wygant*, the Court also seems to assume that it is worse to be laid off than not to be hired. Although *ceteris paribus* it may be worse to lose something than never to have had it, the *ceteris* are really not *paribus*: the person laid off may have savings and may be in a position in which he will receive compensation through his union;

the person not hired may be unemployed. Across all cases, I would not be surprised if not being hired is worse than being laid off.

84. Some of that case-law deals with Title VII issues that are not really relevant to this book—issues caused by the fact that the relevant provisions of Title VII prohibit employers not only from "discriminating against" or "segregat[ing]" individuals on the basis of "sex"(words that have a pejorative connotation) but also prohibit them from "limit[ing]" or "classify[ing]" individuals based on their "sex" (words that have no pejorative connotation). See also note 93 *infra* for an analysis of the interpretive problems this inconsistent language caused.

85. The government's interest is in the size of the real pie and the justness and desirability of the distribution of income, not in monetary savings themselves. Budgetary savings are important to the government because it must reduce the size of the pie to finance its operations (all taxes or money-printing decisions will be misallocative at the margin in a State that is run efficiently).

86. Law students are told that they are being taught to "think like a lawyer," though almost no instructional time is devoted to giving an account of what that process entails.

87. See the reference in the dissenting opinion of Justices Thurgood Marshall, Harry Blackmun, and William Brennan in *City of Richmond v. J. A. Croson Co.*, 488 *U.S.* 469 at 553 (1989) to "mak[ing] a racial group 'suspect.'"

88. Paul Brest, Foreword: In Defense of the Antidiscrimination Principle, 90 *Harv. L. Rev.* 1 at 6 (1976).

89. See Paul Brest and Sanford Levinson, *Processes of Constitutional Decisionmaking* 709 (Little, Brown, 1992) (3d Ed.).

90. Thus, in his concurring opinion in *Califano v. Goldfarb*, Justice John Stevens refers to "discrimination . . . that . . . was not invidious." See 430 *U.S.* 199 at 218 (1977). And in his majority opinion on the liability issue in another Title VII case, *Arizona Governing Committee for Tax Deferred Annuity and Deferred Compensation Plans v. Norris*, Justice Brennan characterizes as "discriminatory" a lifetime annuity contract that offers women a lower payment per month than it offers men who pay the same premium (because women have greater longevity). See 463 *U.S.* 1073 at 1075 (1983). Relatedly, in his dissent in *Metro Broadcasting, Inc. v. Federal Communications Commission*, Justice Anthony Kennedy refers to "'benign' discrimination." See 497 *U.S.* 547 at 615 (1990).

91. For example, in his opinion in *Parham v. Hughes*, 441 *U.S.* 347 (1979), Justice Potter Stewart uses the phrase "invidiously discriminate" (at 335); in his opinion for the Court in *Village of Arlington Heights v. Metropolitan Housing Development Corp.*, 429 *U.S.* 252 (1977), Justice Lewis Powell refers to "invidious racial discrimination" and "invidious discriminatory purpose" (at 264, 266); in his opinion for the Court in *Nashville Gas Co. v. Satty*, 434 *U.S.* 136 (1977) (admittedly a Title VII case), Justice Rehnquist refers to "invidious discrimination" (at 144); in his opinion for the Court in *Washington v. Davis*, 426 *U.S.* 229 (1976) (again, a non-Constitutional [statutory,

though not Title VII] case), Justice Byron White refers to "invidious racial discrimination" (at 238); in his opinion for the Court in *Geduldig v. Aiello*, 417 *U.S.* 484 (1974), Justice Stewart refers to "invidious discrimination" (at 494); in his opinion for the Court in *Griggs v. Duke Power Co.*, 401 *U.S.* 424 (1971) (another Title VII case), Chief Justice Warren Burger uses the phrase "invidiously to discriminate" (at 431); and in his opinion for the court in *McLaughlin v. Florida*, 379 *U.S.* 184 (1964), Justice White refers to "invidious official discrimination" (at 196).

92. Thus, the 1990 Americans with Disabilities Act provides that "no covered entity shall discriminate against a qualified individual with disability . . . in regard to. . . terms, conditions, and privileges of employment" where the term "discriminate" includes any failure to make an accommodation to a disabled employee's or applicant's needs that would not impose "undue hardship" (that would not require "significant difficulty or expense" "in light" of *inter alia* the "overall financial resources of the covered entity"). Similarly, the Pregnancy Discrimination Act of 1978 explicitly provides that, for purposes of Title VII, "discrimination" on the basis of sex includes discrimination "because of or on the basis of pregnancy, childbirth, or related medical conditions," presumably even if the disparate treatment that is forbidden contributes to the employer's profits for reasons that are unrelated to anyone's prejudices. The Supreme Court's conclusion that "discrimination" is used in a bivalent sense in Title VII is evident in the Court's statement that "[t]he statute . . . limits the situations in which discrimination is permissible to 'certain instances' where sex discrimination is 'reasonably necessary' to the 'normal operation' of the 'particular' business." See *UAW v. Johnson Controls, Inc.*, 499 *U.S.* 187 (1991) at 201.

93. Despite the Supreme Court's assumption in *Johnson Controls*, the language of Title VII leaves the denotation and connotation of "discriminate" unclear. What, for example, is to be made of the fact that although Section 703(a)(1) uses the term "discriminate"—namely, declares it "unlawful . . . for an employer to discriminate against any individual . . . because of such individual's race, color, religion, sex, or national origin"—Section 703(a)(2) uses the non-pejorative terms "limit" and "classify" as well as the pejorative term "segregate." There is some reason to believe that the original Congressional supporters of Title VII "intended" it to combat "affirmative action" programs designed to benefit disadvantaged minorities but tried to draft the statute in terms that would transfer to the courts the apparent responsibility for establishing that position. In my judgment, the courts should have responded to this attempt by referring the issue back to the Congress by holding the statute unconstitutional on the ground of "inconsistency"—a ground that is analogous to the traditional "void for vagueness" argument for unconstitutionality.

If the original Congressional intent is considered to be binding, cases such as *Griggs v. Duke Power* that interpreted Title VII to require some "affirmative action"— namely, to require companies to validate employment criteria that had a disparate, disadvantaging impact on minorities even if such validation would not be *ex ante* profitable for them—would have been incorrect when decided. However, since

Congress was aware of *Griggs v. Duke Power* and similar decisions when it amended the relevant statute and did nothing to overturn these cases, it is arguable that later versions of the statute should have been or should be interpreted to require rather than to forbid "discrimination" in the bivalent sense.

94. See Brest and Levinson, *op. cit. supra* note 89 at 643.

95. *Id.* at 645.

96. *Id.* at 687.

97. *Keyes v. School District No. 1, Denver, Colorado*, 413 *U.S.* 189 at 208 (1973), as quoted in *Washington v. Davis*, 426 *U.S.* 229 at 240 (1976).

98. For a similar conclusion based on the first of the three arguments delineated in the text, see Justice Powell's opinion in *Keyes v. School District No. 1, Denver, Colorado*, 413 *U.S.* 189 at 216 (1973) (concurring in part and dissenting in part).

99. In addition to the passage quoted in the text at the reference to note 88, see Justice White's opinion for the Court in *Dayton Board of Education v. Brinkman*, 443 *U.S.* 526 (1979), referring (redundantly if "segregated" were defined properly) to "intentionally segregated schools" (at 537); Justice Powell's opinion for the Court in *Village of Arlington Heights v. Metropolitan Housing Development Corp.*, 429 *U.S.* 252 (1977), describing a situation of racial separation that he assumed did not reflect discrimination as "exhibit[ing] a high degree of residential segregation" (at 260); and Justice Brennan's opinion for the Court in *Keyes v. School District No. 1, Denver, Colorado*, 413 *U.S.* 189 (1973), characterizing as "segregation" a condition of separation he was assuming *ad arguendo* was "the result of a racially neutral 'neighborhood school policy'" and describing (redundantly if "segregation" is used properly) as "deliberate" a situation of "racial segregation" (at 206).

100. Thus, Brest and Levinson consciously mimic the Court's usage by describing as "segregated" the Denver school system involved in *Keyes* when that judgment is based on the fact of separation of a group that has suffered economic and cultural deprivation and discrimination (which may not have caused the separation in question) (*op. cit. supra* note 89 at 628); use the term "racial segregation" to refer to the separation of races in a prison intentionally achieved for non-discriminatory reasons by prison authorities who acted in good faith in response to racial tensions to maintain security, discipline, and good order (*id.* at 650); and ask the reader to consider a case that involves a district that is "residentially segregated—through no unconstitutional action on anyone's part" (*id.* at 687).

101. In my judgment, the courts and their company have made a similar linguistic error by failing to distinguish "integration" from "desegregation." To "integrate" in the relevant sense is to make a conscious choice to reduce or end "separation"— whether or not the separation was caused by discriminatory choices (could properly be described as "segregation"). To "desegregate" is to end separation that is properly called "segregation." Thus, in their introduction to the Court's opinion in *Washington v. Seattle School District No. 1*, 458 *U.S.* 457 (1982), Brest and Levinson describe local-

school-district plans to integrate school systems that were not segregated as "deseg-regation plans." Brest and Levinson, *op. cit. supra* note 89 at 703. In his opinion for the Court, Justice Blackmun properly described the relevant local plans as "busing for in-tegration" (at 457).

102. Brest and Levinson point out the ambiguity of the expression "racially mo-tivate." *Id.* at 658–59. However, to my mind, they create similar confusion by using the adjective "race-motivated" to cover both non-insulting and illicit motivations. Although their explicit articulation of this usage (*id.* at 659) reduces the confusion it causes, it does not eliminate that confusion. Personally, I also find their neutral defi-nition of the expression "race-dependent" misleading (*id.* at 655, 659).

103. This phrase was used in a pejorative sense by Justice Brennan in his dissent-ing opinion (joined by Justices Marshall, Blackmun, and Stevens) in *McCleskey v. Kemp*, 481 *U.S.* 279 at 328 (1987).

104. See Justice Kennedy's use of the expression "race-conscious measures" in his dissent (joined by Justice Antonin Scalia) in *Metro Broadcasting, Inc. v. Federal Commu-nications Commission*, 497 *U.S.* 547 at 606 (1990); Justice Sandra Day O'Connor's use of the same phrase in her dissent in *Metro Broadcasting* (joined by Chief Justice Rehn-quist and Justices Scalia and Kennedy); Justice Marshall's contrasting of "race-con-scious measures" with "racist" actions in his dissent (joined by Justices Blackmun and Brennan) in *City of Richmond v. J. A. Croson Co.*, 488 *U.S.* 469 at 551 (1989); and Jus-tice Stevens's reference to "race-conscious decision" in his dissent in *Wygant v. Jack-son Board of Education*, 476 *U.S.* 267 at 317 (1986).

105. See Justice Rehnquist's use of this phrase in his opinion for the Court in *Hunter v. Underwood*, 471 *U.S.* 222 at 225 (1985).

106. See Justice White's use of this phrase in his opinion for the Court in *Wash-ington v. Davis*, 426 *U.S.* 229 at 239 (1979).

107. See Justice Powell's use of the phrase in his opinion for the Court in *Village of Arlington Heights v. Metropolitan Housing Development Corp.*, 429 *U.S.* 252 at 266 (1977).

108. Thus, although the Court was not misled by its misuse of the expression "disproportionate impact" in this instance, Justice White's opinion for the Court in *Washington v. Davis* did repeatedly misuse the word "disproportionate." *Washington v. Davis*, 426 *U.S.* 229 at 237 (1976). See also Justice Stevens's concurrence in this case (at 252). Justice O'Connor also misuses "disproportionate" in the same way in a dif-ferent context in her opinion for the Court in *City of Richmond v. J. A. Croson Co.*, 488 *U.S.* 469 at 507 (1989), when she states that Minority Business Enterprises "dis-proportionately lack capital."

109. See Brest and Levinson's use of the expression "disproportionate impact" to refer to the disparate impact on student-body populations of a "neighborhood school" policy in a district in which neighborhoods are racially non-homogeneous when the impact of the policy in question "reflects no unconstitutional action on

anyone's part." Brest and Levinson, *op. cit. supra* note 89 at 687. See also Charles Lawrence, The Id, the Ego, and Equal Protection: Reckoning with Unconscious Racism, 39 *Stan. L. Rev.* 317 (1987).

110. For a dubious use of the word "imbalance," see *Johnson v. Transportation Agency*, 480 *U.S.* 616 at 626 (1987).

111. See Justice White's proper use of the expression "disparate" in his majority opinion in *Wards Cove Packing Co. v. Atonio*, 490 *U.S.* 642 at 645 (1989); and Justice Powell's proper use of the expression "disparate impact" in his opinion for the Court in *Regents of the University of California v. Bakke*, 438 *U.S.* 265 at 309 (1978).

112. See Justice Powell's correct use of "disparate racial impact" in his opinion for the Court in *Regents of the University of California v. Bakke*, 438 *U.S.* 265 at 309 (1978); and Justice White's proper use of the expression "racially differential impact" in his opinion for the Court in *Washington v. Davis*, 426 *U.S.* 229 at 238 (1976).

NOTES TO CHAPTER 4

1. This qualification reflects my judgment that in some situations individuals do have the right to choose to die even if their condition would not preclude them from living a life of moral integrity for a significant period of time.

2. Ronald Dworkin, *Life's Dominion* at 179–241 (Knopf, 1993).

3. Judith Jarvis Thomson, A Defense of Abortion, 1 *Phil. & Pub. Aff.* 47 (1971).

4. Donald Regan, Rewriting *Roe v. Wade*, 77 *Mich. L. Rev.* 1569 (1979).

5. Ronald Dworkin, *op. cit. supra* note 2 at 3–178.

6. I realize, of course, that some attempts to protect foetuses may be self-defeating. For example, a rule making pregnant women liable for damaging or killing their foetuses by violating a doctor's instructions (to abstain from sex or from consuming drugs or alcohol) may do more harm by deterring pregnant women who might endanger their foetuses from going to doctors than good by deterring the endangering behavior of women who have been warned by doctors. I realize as well that it would be inconsistent with our rights–notions to obligate a pregnant woman to incur a significant risk of substantial bodily harm or death to reduce a significant relevant risk to her foetus.

7. The text borrows heavily from a superb article on privacy by Ruth Gavison. See Gavison, Privacy and the Limits of Law, 89 *Yale L. J.* 421 (1980).

8. This view of privacy differs from the reductionist position taken by Judith Jarvis Thomson that the concept of privacy is otiose because in any case in which privacy interests might otherwise be decisive there will be other rights–related interests (such as property rights) that would be decisive in any event. See Thomson, The Right to Privacy, 4 *Phil. & Pub. Aff.* 295 (1975).

This reductionist argument is incorrect for two reasons. First, in some cases privacy notions are essential to the rights-conclusion. Assume, for example, that an individual who is trespassing in another's house hides some pornographic material or other private documents he has stolen in a safe on the premises. If someone trains an X-ray eye on the safe and reads the material, he has violated the trespasser-thief's privacy rights but not his property rights. Second, even in cases in which the notion of privacy is not essential to the conclusion that a right has been violated, it is not irrelevant because the fact that the victim has suffered a loss of privacy as well as a violation of (say) his property rights will affect the extent of the damages to which he is entitled.

The liberal analysis of privacy also differs from the economic analysis of this concept offered by Richard Posner. According to Posner, non-commercial privacy should not be protected because the reason that people want to keep things secret is to defraud those with whom they interact, fraud is economically inefficient, and the proper criterion for evaluating any choice is economic efficiency. By way of contrast, Posner would protect commercial privacy because, in his judgment, it is economically efficient to enable people to profit by keeping things they have discovered secret. See Posner, The Right of Privacy, 12 *Ga. L. Rev.* 393 (1978).

Both Posner's secrecy-motivation hypothesis and his economic-efficiency analysis are dubious. For example, it is not at all clear that the amount by which protecting commercial privacy increases economic efficiency by inducing the execution of economically-efficient research and deterring expensive efforts to conceal one's own discoveries and discover someone else's discoveries exceeds the amount by which it reduces economic efficiency by inducing too many resources to be devoted to research from the perspective of economic efficiency. See Richard Markovits, Monopoly and the Allocative Efficiency of First-Best-Allocatively-Efficient Tort Law, 46 *Case West. Res. L. Rev.* 313 at 349–63 (1996), and Markovits, First-Best, Second-Best, and Third-Best Allocative-Efficiency Analysis: A Marine-Salvage Example (unpublished manuscript, 1991).

I should add that the high value that our society places on privacy is consistent with my conclusion that ours is a liberal, rights-based society, though it may be equally consistent with the claim that ours is a libertarian, rights-based society. See Richard Epstein, Privacy, Property Rights and Misrepresentation, 12 *Ga. L. Rev.* 455 (1978).

9. For an illuminating critique of utilitarianism, see J. C. C. Smart and Bernard Williams, Utilitarianism: For and Against (Cambridge University Press, 1963).

10. Some economists who mistakenly believe that they are adopting a utilitarian definition of liberty in fact define it so that a choice is said to increase liberty if it increases economic efficiency—if it gives its beneficiaries equivalent-dollar gains that exceed the equivalent-dollar losses it imposes on its "victims." This economic-efficiency definition is different from the utilitarian definition because in general the marginal utility of money to a choice's beneficiaries will not equal the marginal utility of money to its "victims." See Milton Friedman, *Capitalism and Freedom* (University of Chicago Press, 1962).

11. John Stuart Mill, *On Liberty* (Parker, 1859).

12. See Patrick Devlin, *The Enforcement of Morals* (Oxford University Press, 1965).

13. Joel Feinberg, *The Moral Limits of the Criminal Law* (Oxford University Press, 1984–88).

14. *Deshaney v. Winnebago County Department of Social Services*, 489 *U.S.* 189 at 196 (1989).

15. *Youngsberg v. Romeo*, 457 *U.S.* 307 at 317 (1982). See also *Dandridge v. Williams*, 397 *U.S.* 471 (1970), upholding Maryland's decision to place a maximum limit of $250 per month on AFDC awards; and *Lindsey v. Normet*, 405 *U.S.* 56 (1972), rejecting the claim that the "need for decent shelter" was a fundamental interest whose presence triggered the "strict scrutiny" "test of constitutionality."

16. *Deshaney v. Winnebago County Department of Social Services*, 489 *U.S.* 189 at 200 (1989).

17. *Id.* at 206 (Brennan, joined by Marshall and Blackmun, dissenting).

18. W. Page Keeton, Dan B. Dobbs, Robert E. Keeton, and David G. Owen, *Prosser and Keeton on Torts* 857 (Western Pub. Co., 1984) (5th ed.). See also Second Restatement of Torts, comment d of § 652D (American Law Institute, 1977).

19. A fourth, economic sense of the word—as in "rate of interest"—is not relevant here.

20. This distinction seems to have eluded the courts on several occasions. In *Nebbia v. New York*, 291 *U.S.* 502 (1934), for example, Justice Owen Roberts argued that the expression "affected with a public interest" was equivalent to the expression "affects the public interest." Clearly, however, although it may be true that the public has an (entitlement) interest in anything that affects the public (welfare) interest, this statement is not analytic: the fact that X is a sufficient condition for Y does not imply the fact that X means Y. Thus, in Lord Hale's time, the fact that a business affected the public interest was not a sufficient condition for its being "affected with a public interest." Of course, it may be that Roberts's "mistake" was intentional—that is, that it was made in the hope of obscuring the change that had taken place in the denotation of the expression "affected with a public interest."

21. *Wagner v. Fawcett Publications*, 251 *F.2d* 447 at 451 (*7th Cir.*, 1962).

22. *Barbieri v. New Journal Co.*, 56 *Del.* 67, 189 *A.2d* 773 at 774 (1963).

23. See also *Sweenek v. Pathe News*, 16 *F. Supp.* 746 at 747 (E.D.N.Y., 1936), which refers to "that indefinable quality of information which arouses public attention," and *Metter v. Los Angeles Examiner* 35 *Cal. App. 2d* 304 at 312, 95 *P.2d* 491 at 496 (1932), quoting *Associated Press v. International News Service*, 245 *Fed.* 244 (1917), *aff'd* 248 *U.S.* 215 (1918).

24. Second Restatement of Torts, § 652(D), comment f (American Law Institute, 1977).

25. *Jenkins v. Dell Pub. Co.*, 251 *F.2d* 447 (*3d Cir.*, 1958).

26. Charles Warren and Louis Brandeis, The Right to Privacy, 4 *Harv. L. Rev.* 193 at 214 (1890).

27. *Id*. at 215–16.

28. The courts have made a similar mistake when defining and applying another doctrine that can relieve defendants of liability in "public disclosure of private facts" privacy cases—the doctrine of waiver. The doctrine of waiver (a misnomer) holds that so-called "public figures" cannot recover for invasions of privacy through public disclosure of private information in circumstances in which others could. In Prosser and Keeton's words, *op. cit. supra* note 18 at 859–60: "A public figure has been defined as a person who, by his accomplishments, fame, or mode of living, or by adopting a profession or calling that gives the public a legitimate interest in his doings, his affairs, and his character, has become a 'public personality.' He is, in other words, a celebrity." The "public figure" waiver doctrine would be consistent with liberalism (though it would be unnecessary, given the doctrine of privilege) if and only if all individuals who were classified as public figures were people about whom the public had a right to know. In practice, however, plaintiffs who have not sought publicity and have become figures of psychological interest to the public through no fault of their own (victims of sexual assaults, wives of men murdered before their eyes, etc.) have been classified as public figures and lost their right of redress, even though they could not be said to have waived their rights, did not titillate interest in themselves, and did not occupy any position that gave the public a right to be informed about them.

29. James Dwyer, Parents' Religion and Children's Welfare: Debunking the Doctrine of Parents' Rights, 82 *Cal. L. Rev.* 1371 (1974). Although I had reached Dwyer's major conclusions before reading this superb article, Dwyer vastly increased both my understanding of the relevant moral issues and my knowledge of the relevant caselaw. The availability of Dwyer's article has led me to shorten my own discussion of these subjects.

30. David A. J. Richards, The Individual, the Family, and the Constitution: A Jurisprudential Perspective, 55 *N.Y.U. L. Rev.* 1 at 22 (1980).

31. *Wisconsin v. Yoder*, 406 *U.S.* 205 at 213 (1972).

32. *Id*. at 221.

33. *San Antonio Independent School District v. Rodriguez*, 411 *U.S.* 1 at 37 (1972).

34. *Id*.

35. See Dwyer, *op. cit. supra* note 29 at 1393.

36. See *Pierce v. Society of Sisters*, 268 *U.S.* 510 (1925).

37. *Wisconsin v. Yoder*, 406 *U.S.* 205 (1972).

38. *Scoma v. Chicago Board of Educ.*, 391 F. *Supp.* 452 at 461–62 (N.D. Fl. 1974) and *New Mexico v. Edgington*, 663 P.2d 374 at 378 (N.M. Ct. App.), *cert. denied*, 662 P.2d 65 (N.M.), *cert. denied*, 464 *U.S.* 940 (1983).

39. See Dwyer, *op. cit. supra* note 29 at 1391–92.

40. *Wisconsin v. Yoder*, 406 *U.S.* 205 at 211.

41. *Id*. at 213–14.

42. *Id*. at 218.

43. *Id.* at 219.

44. *Id.* at 222.

45. *Id.* at 224.

46. *Id.* at 231.

47. The discussion that follows borrows heavily from Dwyer, *op. cit. supra* note 29.

48. 387 *U.S.* 1 (1967).

49. 393 *U.S.* 503 (1969).

50. See Dwyer, *op. cit. supra* note 29 at 1420.

51. *Id.* at 212.

52. *Id.*

53. Admittedly, if we confronted an actual case in which a child's continuing attendance in the public schools would be damaging to her, it might be necessary to permit her to withdraw, though any such decision should probably be combined with counseling to help the child gain some autonomy.

54. Mark Murphy, Note: A Constitutional Analysis of Compulsory School Attendance Laws in the Southeast: Do They Unlawfully Interfere with Alternatives to Public Education, 8 *Ga. St. U. L. Rev.* 457 at 457 (1992).

55. For this purpose, I am ignoring the relationship between the Court's answer to this question and the identity of the restricting government in question (whether it was the central government or a state government). Doctrinally, the central government was said to be bound to give appropriate protection to the various liberties covered by the Bill of Rights (including some unenumerated liberties whose real textual home should have been said to be the Ninth Amendment). The state governments were then prohibited from illegitimately restricting those liberty interests "incorporated" into the "due process" clause of the Fourteenth Amendment. Over time, the difference between these two sets of liberties has substantially diminished. In my judgment, since the Bill of Rights creates some Constitutional rights that are not based on moral rights, the states may not be constrained as much as the central government in this area of conduct.

56. *Palko v. Connecticut*, 302 *U.S.* 319 at 324 (1937).

57. *Snyder v. Massachusetts*, 291 *U.S.* 97 at 105 (1934).

58. 478 *U.S.* 186 (1986).

59. *Id.* at 192.

60. *Id.* at 190. In dicta, the Supreme Court has stated that the Constitution does not forbid the prohibition of non-marital sexual intercourse or adultery. See *Eisenstadt v. Baird*, 405 *U.S.* 438 at 448 (1972). See also *Griswold v. Connecticut*, 381 *U.S.* 479 at 498–99 (1965) (Goldberg, concurring).

61. Anne Goldstein, History, Homosexuality, and Political Values: Searching for the Hidden Determinants of *Bowers v. Hardwick*, 97 *Yale L. J.* 1073 (1988).

62. *Caminetti v. United States*, 242 *U.S.* 470 (1917).

63. *Cleveland v. United States*, 329 *U.S.* 14 (1946).

64. 381 *U.S.* 479 (1965).

65. 405 *U.S.* 438 (1972).

66. *Id.* at 453.

67. As I indicated in Chapter 1 (see the text two paragraphs after the reference to note 4), a liberal State may not be obligated to enforce the moral right to compensation of the spouse that was comparatively less at fault since doing so might reduce the probability that the divorced spouses would function satisfactorily as parents to their children—would reduce the probability that their children would become individuals of moral integrity and/or lead happy and satisfying lives.

68. The financial consequences of divorce for the children of the divorced marriage are often severe. The psychological damage is harder to assess since the alternative to divorce may be life with parents who are unhappy in their marriage. However, it is clear that the life-opportunities and success of the children of a man's divorced first marriage are far worse than those of his subsequent marriage.

69. 381 *U.S.* 479 at 486 (1965).

70. 388 *U.S.* 1 (1967).

71. Similarly, on the same premise, my argument for the duty of a liberal State to provide a legal-marriage regime would apply, *ceteris paribus*, to homosexual marriages just as it applies to heterosexual marriages.

72. 434 *U.S.* 374 (1978).

73. See the text of this chapter following the reference to note 58, discussing the Supreme Court's opinion in *Bowers v. Hardwick*, 478 *U.S.* 186 (1986).

74. I suspect that even the views of most of those who condemn homosexuality as sinful for religious reasons deserve to be characterized as prejudices: at least this conclusion would be warranted if they did not interpret the rest of the Bible in the manner that led them to draw this inference from the passage that they claim justifies their position or if they tried to justify their conclusion as well by making allegedly-factual assertions that are not in fact "empirical," that were not properly validated, and/or that are not just wrong but implausible.

75. A similar analysis would apply to the right to engage in bigamous marriages. I am focusing on polygamous marriages because all parties to such marriages are aware of the others' participation in them, and (I will assume) the first wives were aware at the time of their marriage of the possibility that their husband would marry additional women later on. To the extent that some participants in bigamous marriages are unaware that their spouses are participating in bigamy, that fact would justicize a liberal State's refusing to recognize the bigamous marriages in question and subjecting knowing participants in them to civil fines or criminal penalties.

76. *Reynolds v. United States*, 98 *U.S.* 145 (1878). Subsequent cases upheld an act of Congress excluding polygamists and bigamists from voting or holding office—*Murphy v. Ramsey*, 114 *U.S.* 15 (1885)—and a law of the Territory of Idaho condi-

tioning the right to vote on the otherwise-eligible voter's swearing that he was not a practicing polygamist, did not support the practice, and did not belong to any group that advocated polygamy—*Davis v. Benson*, 133 *U.S.* 333 (1890).

77. *Reynolds v. United States*, 98 *U.S.* 145 at 164 (1878).

78. *Id.* at 165.

79. 401 *U.S.* 371 (1971).

80. *Id.* at 376.

81. *Id.* at 377.

82. *United States v. Kras*, 409 *U.S.* 434 (1973).

83. *Id.* at 445.

84. *Moore v. City of East Cleveland*, 431 *U.S.* 494 at 504 (1977).

85. 416 *U.S.* 1 (1974).

86. 431 *U.S.* 494 (1977).

87. Section 6 of this chapter addresses the related right of women not to bear children—to have an abortion.

88. Parenting achieves these results both through the parent's relationship with the child she is parenting and by intensifying her relationship with her parenting partner.

89. It is not clear whether the activity of parenting a child is more rewarding in the above respects when the social parent is also the biologic parent of the child in question. Parenting one's biologic child may be more likely to improve the parent's understanding of his own personality and behavior to the extent that the child resembles his parents for genetic reasons. Parenting one's biologic child may also be more satisfying to the extent that (1) the personalities, abilities, and motivations of people are genetically determined and (2) adults are better able to parent children who resemble them in these respects. Finally, parenting one's partner's biologic child may be more satisfying to the extent that one's love for one's partner is more likely to carry over to a child who resembles the partner. Of course, the opposite may be true as well—people may learn more from becoming intimate with others who are different from them and may be better able to help those who are different from them as well (may be better able to cope with problems that differ from their own than with the same problems they have or had).

90. *Buck v. Bell*, 274 *U.S.* 200 (1926) described and evaluated the procedure in the following way (at 206–7):

> The superintendent first presents a petition to the special board of directors of his hospital or colony, stating the facts and the grounds for his opinion, verified by affidavit. Notice of the petition and of the time and place of the hearing in the institution is to be served upon the inmate, and also upon his guardian, and if there is no guardian the superintendent is to apply to the Circuit Court of the County to appoint one. If the inmate is a minor, notice also is to be given to his parents if any with a copy of the petition. The board is to see to it that the inmate may attend the hearings if desired by him or his

guardian. The evidence is all to be reduced to writing, and after the board has made its order for or against the operation, the superintendent, or the inmate, or his guardian, may appeal to the Circuit Court of the County. The Circuit Court may consider the record of the board and the evidence before it and such other admissible evidence as may be offered, and may affirm, revise, or reverse the order of the board and enter such order as it deems just. Finally any party may apply to the Supreme Court of Appeals, which, if it grants the appeal, is to hear the case upon the record of the trial in the Circuit Court and may enter such order as it thinks the Circuit Court should have entered. There can be no doubt that so far as procedure is concerned the rights of the patient are most carefully considered, and as every step in this case was taken in scrupulous compliance with the statute and after months of observation, there is no doubt that in that respect the plaintiff in error has had due process of law.

Justice William Douglas's confidence in the fairness of the relevant procedure may have been somewhat shaken had he realized how inadequate the evidence was supporting the conclusion that Carrie Buck and her mother and baby were imbeciles, had he known that (at least when interviewed many years later) Carrie "was a woman of obviously normal intelligence," had he realized that Carrie had been institutionalized because she had become pregnant outside of wedlock (as a result of rape) and because her mother had had many illegitimate children, and had he been in a position to assess the intelligence of the child Carrie was carrying at the time the case was brought (a daughter Vivian who died at the age of eight of a poverty-related disease after having been "a perfectly normal, quite average student" at her elementary school). See Stephen Jay Gould, Carrie Buck's Daughter, 2 *Con. Comm.* 331 at 336–38 (1985).

91. *Id.* at 207.

92. 316 *U.S.* 535 (1942).

93. *Id.* at 541. In fact, the statute seems to have been designed to exempt white-collar criminals from a severe sanction it imposed on others.

94. See *In the Matter of Mary Moe*, 385 *Mass.* 555, 432 *N.E.2d* 712 (1982); and *In the Matter of Lavista Earline Romero*, 790 *P.2d* 819 (1990).

95. Compulsory sterilization of certain classes of criminals needs to be distinguished from programs in which the State conditions the parole of convicted rapists or pedophiles on their agreeing to be castrated. Although one might argue that such policies are morally impermissible because the position of the criminals in question precludes them from giving meaningful consent and/or because the State increases its sentences unjustly to increase the leverage it has over such criminals in relation to this option, the specific-deterrence advantage of this proposal cannot be denied—particularly because the recidivism rate for the crimes in question is high.

96. My discussion of these cases borrows heavily from Dwyer, *op. cit. supra* note 29 at 1380–1405.

97. 321 *U.S.* 158 (1944).

98. 390 *U.S.* 598 (1968)(mem.).

99. 406 *U.S.* 205 (1972).

100. 321 *U.S.* 158 at 166–67 (1944).

101. 278 *F. Supp.* 488 (W.D. Wash., 1967).

102. 406 *U.S.* 205 at 230. Subsequent lower-court decisions based on *Yoder* held that societal interests can trump parents' free-exercise "interests" in controlling their child, though the courts do continue to view children as a means to parental fulfillment rather than as rights-holders who must be treated as ends in themselves. See Dwyer, *op. cit. supra* note 29 at 1389, 1389–1405.

103. According to John Robertson, as of 1986, in vitro fertilization had shown "no higher rate of congenital deformity than occurs with coital reproduction." See John A. Robertson, Embryos, Families, and Procreative Liberty: The Legal Structure of the New Reproduction, 59 *S. Cal. L. Rev.* 942 at 991 (1986), citing Clifford Grobsteib, Michael Flower and John Mendeloff, External Human Fertilization: An Evaluation of Policy, 222 *Sci.* 127 at 128 (1983). No studies of psychological effects have yet been done. However, Robertson does proceed to sound a note of caution: "[T]he question of physical risk with IVF variations, such as freezing and thawing of sperm, eggs, and embryos, embryo biopsy, and other manipulations cannot yet be ruled out. Although the natural inefficiency of human reproduction suggests that those embryos hardy enough to survive manipulation and implant and go to term will not be handicapped, the possibility remains until more experience establishes a low risk of teratogenic effects." Robertson, *op. cit.* at 992. I have relied heavily on Robertson's discussion of State restrictions of the use of reproductive procedures of all sorts, which is scientifically knowledgeable and morally and legally sophisticated.

104. I ignore the complications that would ensue if a male who has already reached the limit and has no desire to exceed it impregnates a female who has not reached her limit and does not want to abort the pregnancy in question or vice versa.

105. 397 *U.S.* 471 (1970).

106. 466 *U.S.* 429 (1984).

107. *Id.* at 429.

108. *Id.* at 433.

109. *Id.* at 434.

110. *Id.* at 431.

111. 491 *U.S.* 110 (1989).

112. *Id.* at 126.

113. *Id.* at 124.

114. *Id.* at 130. The Court did not attempt to reconcile this specific conclusion with its own recognition that the interest of parents in not having their parental rights terminated is "fundamental." See *Santosky v. Kramer*, 455 *U.S.* 745 (1982).

115. See Dwyer, *op. cit. supra* note 29 at 1379–1405.

116. I am reminded of Dr. Johnson's famous remark that nothing so concentrates the mind as the prospect of being hanged in the morning.

117. Dworkin, *op. cit. supra* note 2 at 199.

118. *Id.* at 208.

119. Cass Sunstein's review of the relevant literature leads him to conclude that "there is at least a significant possibility of [physician] abuse" of this kind. See Sunstein, The Right to Die, 106 *Yale L. J.*, 1123 at 1145 (1997). Sunstein (at 1144–45) cites two authors who have concluded that the Dutch experience with euthanasia suggests that "physicians terminate lives partly or mostly on the basis of their own judgments rather than those of their patients": Herbert Hendin, *Seduced by Death* 76 (Norton, 1997), and John Keown, Euthanasia in the Netherlands: Sliding down the Slippery Slope? in *Euthanasia Examined* 261 at 277 (ed. John Keown) (Cambridge University Press, 1995). Sunstein (at 1145) also cites two authors who argue that significant abuse has not been demonstrated: Richard Epstein, *Mortal Peril* (Addison Wesley, 1997); and Richard Posner, *Aging and Old Age* 242 and n. 23 (University of Chicago Press, 1995).

120. *Washington v. Glucksberg*, 65 *LW* 4669 at 4691 (1997) (Souter, concurring).

121. I can imagine circumstances in which someone's spouse or children could claim that he was obligated to give them financial and emotional support so long as he could manage to do so even if dying would be in his best interest.

122. Sunstein, *op. cit. supra* note 119 at 1126 n. 11 cites Keown, *op. cit. supra* note 119, for the safeguards the Dutch system has incorporated: "The request must come from the patient and be free and voluntary; the request must be well-considered, durable, and persistent; the patient must be intolerably suffering, with no hope of improvement; euthanasia must be the last resort; euthanasia must be performed by the physician; the physician must consult with another physician trained in the field; and the death record must not indicate death of 'natural causes'." According to Sunstein, "it is not clear that these safeguards are respected in practice."

123. See *op. cit. supra* note 2 at 179–241. Subsequent citations to *Life's Dominion* are indicated in the text by *LD* and the page number.

124. For a well-executed analysis of this type, see Sunstein, *op. cit. supra* note 119 at 1131–41.

125. 497 *U.S.* 261 (1990).

126. *Id.* at 303, 316 (Brennan, joined by Marshall and Blackmun, dissenting).

127. See *Id.* at 279. Thus, the opinion states: "we do not think the Due Process Clause requires the State to repose judgment on these matters with anyone but the patient herself." *Id.* at 286. Admittedly, this sentence is consistent with the conclusion that the Constitution does not even require the State to permit the provisions of such a living will to be carried out or to insure that those instructions are carried out. (Of course, in my judgment, the proper textual basis for any such obligation is the "privileges or immunities" clause of the Fourteenth Amendment rather than that amendment's "due process" clause.)

128. Rehnquist conveniently ignores the possibly-relevant facts that states have been allowed to require vaccinations (see *Jacobson v. Massachusetts*, 197 *U.S.* 11 [1905])

and to pump the stomachs of attempted suicides over the relevant individuals' objections.

129. 497 *U.S.* 261 at 280.

130. *Id.* at 320 (Brennan, dissenting).

131. *Id.* at 280 (Rehnquist, opinion of the Court).

132. This account is from Brennan's dissent. *Id.* at 320.

133. *Id.* at 282.

134. *Id.* at 292 (O'Connor, concurring).

135. *Id.*

136. *Id.*

137. *Id.* at 287 (Scalia, concurring).

138. *Id.* at 300.

139. *Id.* at 293.

140. *Id.* at 343 (Stevens, dissenting).

141. *Id.* at 345.

142. *Id.* at 347.

143. *Id.* at 350. Stevens endorses one other proposition that I find contestable: although a state may properly "foster respect for the sanctity of life, . . . [it] may not pursue . . . [this goal] by infringing constitutionally protected interests for 'symbolic' effect." *Id.* To the extent that the "symbolic effect" prevents rights from being violated (and perhaps to the extent that it encourages people to lead lives of moral integrity), I would disagree with this conclusion unless there were less restrictive means of generating the symbolic effect in question.

144. 65 *LW* 4669 (1997).

145. See *id.* at 4670, citing Wash. Rev. Code § 70.122.070(1).

146. *Id.* at 4679 (O'Connor, concurring), citing Wash. Rev. Code § 70.122.010 (1994).

147. 65 *LW* 4695 (1997).

148. *Id.* at 4696.

149. *Id.* at 4676.

150. *Id.*

151. *Id.* at 4674.

152. *Vacco v. Quill*, 65 *LW* 4695 at 4697.

153. *Id.* Why the medical profession's practice is relevant is not made clear. Doctors are certainly not moral experts. The same sort of reference to medical practice occurs in *Roe v. Wade*, where its relevance is equally problematic.

154. *Id.*

155. *Id.*

156. *Id.*

157. Thomson, *op. cit. supra* note 3.

158. 410 *U.S.* 113 (1973).

159. *Planned Parenthood of Southeastern Pennsylvania v. Casey*, 505 *U.S.* 833 (1992).

160. Regan, *op. cit. supra* note 4.

161. Ronald Dworkin, *op. cit. supra* note 2 at 3–178.

162. See Thomson, *op. cit. supra* note 3. Thomson's actual conclusion is hard to pin down. On the one hand, Thomson claims that she is "arguing only that having a right to life does not guarantee having either a right to be given the use of or a right to be allowed continued use of another person's body." *Id.* at 56. In fact, she in essence reiterates this claim in a postscript written in response to John Finnis's critique of her original article. In this postscript, Thomson describes her claim as follows: "I had said that the right to life was not unproblematic—that man's having a right to life does not guarantee either that he has a right to be given the use of whatever he needs for life or that he has a right to continued use of whatever he is currently using, and needs for life." See Thomson, Rights and Deaths in *The Rights and Wrongs of Abortion* 114 at 114 (Princeton University Press, 1972), responding to Finnis, The Rights and Wrongs of Abortion in *id.* at 85.

163. My belief that Thomson's original article really makes the stronger claim just articulated has three sources. First, throughout the text, she appears to be willing to admit to no more than the possibility that there "might be" *some* cases in which the unborn person has a right to the use of its mother's body" (Thomson, *op. cit. supra* note 159 at 59)—that is, it has the "right to demand" such use. *Id.* at 61. Second, although she asserts that "we must not fall below" a standard of minimum decency and admits that a woman who requests a seventh-month abortion to avoid the nuisance of postponing a trip abroad is "positively indecent" (*id.* at 65–66), she elsewhere makes clear that individuals may have no obligation to behave decently (that those who would benefit from minimally decent behavior do not have a right to such treatment). Thus, she argues (*id.* at 59–60) that although it would be morally indecent not to save someone's life by spending a riskless hour attached to a machine that allowed your kidneys to cleanse his blood, he would have no right to demand your helping him in this way. Third, my suspicion that she really is making a stronger claim than she admits is also favored by the obviousness (even in 1971) of the claim she says she is trying to establish—namely, that the right to life does not guarantee the right to use someone's body to sustain life. Surely, one can establish this modest claim simply by citing our Good Samaritan practices (including the fact that no one is ever obligated to incur a significant risk of substantial bodily harm or death to render assistance to another) and the principles that underlie them. For this purpose, Thomson's various examples are totally unnecessary. Taken as a whole, then, I do think that the text of Thomson's article and the context in which she wrote it support the conclusion that it really argues that the foetus would never have a moral right to its mother's gestational services even if it had a moral right to life.

164. See Chapter 3 at note 20 and the accompanying text. Much of the analysis that follows is taken from Richard Markovits, Legal Analysis and the Economic Analysis of Allocative Efficiency, 8 *Hofstra L. Rev.* 811 at 892–903 (Appendix: The Foetus's Right to Life and the Abortion Cases) (1980).

165. Admittedly, I do not find this argument persuasive for the same reason that I find morally unacceptable the prudential argument that judges should take account of the tendency of the choices available to them to induce members of the public to engage in moral-rights violations.

166. Thomson, *op. cit. supra* note 3 at 55–56.

167. Thomson is unforthcoming about the procedure that the kidnaped woman would have to follow to separate herself from the blood-transfer machine or the violinist. Without information on this procedure, it is not possible to tell whether the woman's refusal to provide the service would qualify as a mere refusal to render aid.

168. Thomson, *op. cit. supra* note 3 at 49.

169. "Hysterotomy" is a surgical procedure in which an incision is made into the abdomen and the foetus is removed manually. Prostaglandins are drugs that induce labor without directly harming the foetus.

170. For example, although one would have no general duty to drag someone into a lifeboat, one would be liable for unreasonably tossing him or her back into the water.

171. See Chapter 1's discussion of the liberal "boundary condition" at the text accompanying and following the reference to note 14.

172. See William Powers, Book Review of Marshall Shapo, *The Duty to Act: Tort Law, Power, and Public Policy* (University of Texas Press, 1977), 57 *Tex. L. Rev.* 523 (1979).

173. The case might be closer if the husband wanted to parent and had lost the capacity to impregnate a woman after his wife became pregnant by him.

174. See Douglas Laycock, *The Death of the Irreparable Injury Rule* (Oxford University Press, 1991).

175. If pressed for an analogy to the woman who has become pregnant willfully or advertently by consciously ignoring a substantial risk, I would choose the position of a host who has invited someone to visit on a remote property (or in the case of the advertent but not willful pregnancy, a host who has invited someone knowing and accepting the fact that the invitee might bring along another guest). It seems clear to me that, unless special circumstances arise, such a host could not disinvite her guest (or his friend) if she knew that he could not survive once he was abandoned outside her property. Alternatively, one might analogize the pregnant woman to a hiker who invites an unskilled, ignorant companion to go on a hike or who allows such a person to follow her on a hike without commenting on the riskiness of the venture or her intolerance of inept laggards. Once more, it seems clear that the hiker who has invited her companion is not entitled to abandon him in a position in which he cannot survive. In fact, I believe that the hiker who acquiesces in such a person's accompanying her without verbally committing herself in any way would have a moral and legal obligation to secure her companion's safety even at the cost of considerable inconvenience to herself.

176. I ignore a question that is somewhat troubling to me: Would not the lactating woman have a moral duty to nurse the baby in these circumstances?

177. I have not listed three other desires that an abortion might serve because none of them strikes me as legitimate in a liberal society:
(1) a desire to avoid the psychological cost of giving up the baby (relative to the psychological cost of a late-term abortion);
(2) a desire to prevent the life of a partial genetic replica who would not be in her control at all (if she gave the baby up); and
(3) a desire to avoid having to choose whether to keep the baby.

178. See, in the case of (West) Germany, BGB1 I 1050–57 (1995) and BGB1 I 1213–15 (1976). For a useful account of Germany's legislative and Constitutional abortion controversy, see Christina Schlegel, Landmark in German Abortion Law: The German 1995 Compromise Compared with English Law, 11 *Int. J. Law, Policy, and the Family* 36 (1997).

179. 410 *U.S.* 113 (1973).

180. *Id.* at 117–18.

181. *Id.* at 157.

182. See the text of this chapter two paragraphs before Section 5C, citing *Life's Dominion* at 110.

183. *Roe v. Wade*, 410 *U.S.* 113 at 152 (1975).

184. See the text of this chapter at the list preceding the reference to note 179.

185. See *Planned Parenthood of Southeastern Pennsylvania v. Casey*, 505 *U.S.* 833 at 953 (1992) (Rehnquist, dissenting)

186. *Roe v. Wade*, 410 *U.S.* 113 at 164–65 (1973).

187. *Id.* at 163.

188. 505 *U.S.* 833 (1992). Chapter 1 made reference to the analysis of various judges in *Casey* of the determinants of the weight that should be attached to precedent. See Chapter 1, notes 55–57 and accompanying text. I will also ignore the *Casey* Court's analysis of the various subsidiary, abortion-related issues that Section 6B(2) of this chapter analyzed.

189. *Planned Parenthood of Southeastern Pennsylvania v. Casey*, 505 *U.S.* 833 at 953 (1992).

190. *Id.* at 846.

191. I do not want to close this discussion of *Casey* without at least noting that Chief Justice Rehnquist and Justices White, Scalia, and Thomas would have overruled *Roe v. Wade* and subjected abortion legislation to ordinary scrutiny—that is, would hold such legislation unconstitutional only if it were not rationally related to the achievement of any legitimate goal.

192. Regan, *op. cit. supra* note 4.

193. In fact, Regan's basic argument applies equally well to third-trimester abortions. Regan thinks that the *Roe v. Wade* Court's line between the second and third

trimester can be justified by the argument that the pregnant woman who has not aborted by the end of the second trimester has waived her right to do so. *Id.* at 1643. I have already explained why I do not find this "constructive waiver" argument persuasive. Regan does not try to justify this line by saying that a third-trimester foetus is a person while younger foetuses are not. In fact, he appears to believe that foetuses are never persons (*id.* at 1646) but argues (like Thomson) that even if the foetus is a person, it would have no right to its mother's gestational services, given (his understanding of) our Good-Samaritan practices. *Id.* at 1641.

194. *Id.* at 1630.

195. *Id.* at 1605.

196. *Id.* at 1606.

197. *Id.* at 1645–46.

198. Ronald Dworkin, Unenumerated Rights: Whether and How *Roe* Should Be Overruled, 59 *U. Chic. L. Rev.* 381 at 398–99 (1992).

199. There are two possible exceptions. First, in a few cases (for example, in the bargained-for vasectomy case), the pregnant woman may have a duty to carry their child to term or to safety. Second, and more important empirically, the pregnant woman may have a duty to abort her pregnancy if the foetus she is carrying would have a wrongful life even if it would be a moral-rights holder (regardless of whether it was currently a moral-rights holder). Dworkin ignores the first possibility, appears to believe that the woman in the second situation has no moral duty to abort, and clearly believes that the State could not constitutionally require a woman to abort in the second situation. Dworkin, *op. cit. supra* note 2 at 195.

200. See *Nebbia v. New York*, 291 *U.S.* 502 (1934). I have not included the courts' conflation of the various meanings of "interest," "concern," and "public" in this list because I suspect that these errors reflected honest intellectual mistakes, not the intentional use of "persuasive definitions."

201. 432 *U.S.* 464 at 483 (1977) (Brennan, dissenting).

Author Index

Case Index

Subject Index

Abortion-related rights, 344–72

Action/inaction (misfeasance, non-feasance) distinction, 196, 206, 221–24, 285–86, 419nn. 15–16. *See also* State Action doctrine

Affirmative action, 229, 249–62; case-law, 259–62; law-school admissions, 255–59; moral and Constitutional permissibility, 249–55

Autonomy (individual), 39–41, 136–37, 145, 148, 186, 192, 272, 381–82n. 7, 406n. 73; autonomy and the liberal conception of the second-order good, 192; autonomy-threatening relationships, 322; autonomy-threatening religious and secular groups, 322; communitarianism and autonomy, 190, 192; Constitutional-law doctrine, 285–96; education for autonomy, 291–96, 322, 323, 424n. 69; Dworkin's analysis of relationship between autonomy and abortion-rights and right to die, 334–35; enforcement of personal-service contracts (*e.g.*, surrogate-motherhood contracts) and autonomy, 314; Good-Samaritan duties and autonomy, 347; liberal State's duty to promote autonomy, 274–78; liberty whose exercise surrenders or endangers autonomy, 321–23; parental rights and children's autonomy, 283; paternalism and autonomy, 284–85; private property and autonomy, 203; right to die and autonomy, 324–25; State Action doctrine and autonomy, 223

Autonomy (of law), 12

Balancing tests of Constitutionality. *See* Constitutionality (tests of)

Best-light criterion, 94–95, 400n. 9

Boundary condition in a liberal society, 22, 35–39, 333, 335, 371; Rawls's boundary condition, 112–13; utilitarian boundary condition, 48–49

Choice (meaningful), 40–41, 43; children's choice and parental rights, 283; education and meaningful choice, 291–96; prerequisites for meaningful choice, 276

Civic-republican history and Constitutional interpretation, 156–57, 166–68

Closeness-of-fit criterion, 23, 24–27

Cohabitation. *See* Marriage, divorce, and cohabitation

Communitarianism, 188–93; compared with liberalism, 193

Concepts (versus conceptions), 92, 176, 399n. 4

Concern (duty of appropriate, equal concern), 4–5, 42–43, 272, 373

Conscience (freedom of), 119, 120–22. *See also* Liberty (of conscience); Parental rights (to control the religious and secular moral beliefs of others); Religion (right to free exercise)

Constitutionality (tests of), 210 (generic definition); balancing (of utility or rights-related interests), 54–55; intermediate scrutiny, 224, 297; ordinary scrutiny (minimum rationality), 215, 224, 225–27, 297, 402n. 25; strict scrutiny, 216, 224, 297; three-tier-scrutiny-approach critique, 224–27; three-tier-scrutiny approach and deference, 230–31, 265, 297; undue burden test, 54–55, 366

Counter-majoritarian objection to judicial review, 84–85, 144

Critical Legal Studies, 81–82, 153–55

About the Author

Richard S. Markovits is the Lloyd M. Bentsen Jr. Centennial Professor of Law at the University of Texas Law School. He has been a Visiting Professor at several Law Schools and Economics Departments in Germany and the United States. From 1981 to 1983, while serving as Co-Director of the Centre for Socio-Legal Studies at Oxford, he was a member of the Law Faculty of Oxford University and a Governing Board Fellow of Wolfson College. In 1985–86 he was a Fellow of the Institute for Advanced Studies, Berlin, and in 1988–89, a Guggenheim Fellow. Professor Markovits has a Ph.D. in economics (from the London School of Economics) as well as a law degree (from Yale). He has published numerous articles on micro-economic theory and welfare economics and is particularly interested in the relevance of economic-efficiency conclusions to moral and legal analyses of all sorts.

Professor Markovits has always enjoyed playing sports, though he is not the man he never was. He and his wife, Inga (who is also a Professor of Law at Texas), have five children—Daniel, Stefanie, Benjamin, Julia, and Rebecca—who are their friends as well as their children.